ENTRE NOSOTROS

Communicating with the Hispanic Client

BARBARA A. LOTITO

University of Connecticut—Hartford

NEWBURY HOUSE PUBLISHERS
A division of Harper & Row, Publishers, Inc.
New York, Philadelphia, San Francisco, Washington, D.C.
London, Mexico City, São Paulo, Singapore, Sydney

Project Coordination: Total Concept Associates
Text Design: Diana Designs
Text Design Adaptation: Judy Ashkenaz
Cover Design: Gabriel Molano
Compositor: Pine Tree Composition
Printer and Binder: The Murray Printing Company

Entre nosotros: Communicating with the Hispanic Client

Photo and art credits appear on page 536.

Library of Congress Cataloging in Publication Data

Lotito, Barbara Ann.
    Entre nosotros.

    English and Spanish.
    Bibliography: p.
    Includes index.
    1. Spanish language—Conversation and phrase books (for professionals) 2. Spanish language—Text-books for foreign speakers—English.   I. Title.
    PC4120.P76L68   1988   468.3′421   85-5136
    ISBN 0-88377-296-5

    87 88 89 90 9 8 7 6 5 4 3 2 1

NEWBURY HOUSE PUBLISHERS
A division of Harper & Row, Publishers, Inc.

Language Science
Language Teaching
Language Learning

TO MY PARENTS, ONOFRIO AND CATHERINE LOTITO

who taught me that the only cultural barriers
that exist are those we find within ourselves

THE FOLLOWING WORDS ARE INSCRIBED ON A PLAQUE THAT GREETS VISITORS TO THE MUSEUM OF THE STATUTE OF LIBERTY

"America . . .
has always declared herself
for equality of nationalities
as well as for equality of individuals . . .

America
has believed
that we must not only give
to the immigrant
the best that we have,

but
must preserve for America
the best
that is in the immigrant.

America
has believed
that in differentiation,
not in uniformity,
lies the path of progress.

—Louis D. Brandeis

Contents

Preface

Entre nosotros: Communicating with the Hispanic Client is intended for highly motivated adult professionals or college students who are or will be working in careers where they provide services to Hispanic clients. Its objective is to develop linguistic and cultural proficiency relevant to the communication needs of those in the fields of health care delivery, legal and social services, education, and business.

The text consists of twelve lessons, each of which focuses on a specific topic concerning clients' personal histories. Topics presented were chosen for their relevance to a wide range of professional interactions. Each lesson integrates the study of specific vocabulary and grammatical structures with appropriate cultural material that expands on its basic theme. The cultural focus is reinforced through a wealth of photos, illustrations, and authentic documents. The text also offers six **Evaluación del progreso** sections, which measure students' comprehension of the cultural material presented, as well as their progress in speaking and understanding spoken Spanish.

Entre nosotros is more than a textbook. It might more appropriately be termed a comprehensive cross-cultural training kit. It reflects the total communication reality faced by professionals who interact with Hispanic clients on a daily basis. The cultural readings in each lesson and their corresponding experiential activities encourage students to be introspective. Students learn to understand, analyze, and — when necessary — modify their reactions to the different culturally determined behaviors their Hispanic client may exhibit. The dialogues, examples, and exercises used to apply the study of Spanish to the real world are contextualized. Thus, communicative and listening activities parallel those that students encounter in their professional endeavors. *Entre nosotros* trains students not only to use and interpret the Spanish language but also to understand those attitudes, values, and beliefs that native Spanish speakers express nonverbally and that experts agree account for the greatest portion of the communication process.

Although the text presupposes no prior study of Spanish, its comprehensive functional approach to grammar usage provides a thorough review for students with some prior knowledge of the language. In addition, its professionally relevant vocabulary and vocationally oriented speaking and listening activities expand on the basic language contexts common to elementary texts. A third feature of the text that reflects its adaptability to the needs of intermediate students is its thematically arranged format, which integrates relevant cultural readings in English and literary selections in Spanish into the specialized language focus of each lesson.

Entre nosotros allows students to learn a great deal of vocabulary and structures outside of class. Clear explanations of vocabulary usage and grammatical structures are followed by self-correctional practice exercises of basic concepts presented in each lesson. A set of cassette tapes increases the adaptability of the text to self-instructional usage. Also available is an instructor's manual containing specific guidelines for teaching the various segments of the book as well as the scripts for the various listening comprehension exercises presented in each lesson and the six **Evaluación del progreso** sections.

The unique format for this text is a direct result of the author's twelve years of teaching and developing curricula for courses at the Schools of Medicine, Law, and Social Work at the University of Connecticut. It reflects the process of personal and professional growth she experienced in working closely with both Anglo professionals and their Hispanic clients in order to understand the needs of both and the obstacles that commonly prevent authentic cross-cultural communication. The book's personalized tone encourages students and teachers to explore such potentially explosive topics as racism, prejudice, anger, and hostility in a nonthreatening, constructive manner. *Entre nosotros,* then, offers a guided tour through the sometimes confusing but potentially rewarding and exciting world of cross-cultural communication between Hispanic clients and the non-Hispanic professionals who provide services to them.

COURSE DESIGN

The text is designed for a two-semester beginning (or intermediate) course that meets three days per week, or for approximately 90 hours of classroom instruction. Since it offers a variety of cultural and linguistic exercises, the instructor may wish to emphasize some more than others, depending on the needs of the students, their prior knowledge of Spanish, and the logistical limitations of class meetings. Although it is feasible to work with all the material presented in the text within the 90-hour time frame, choices can be made as to the content to be dealt with in class.

TEXT DESIGN

Each lesson in *Entre nosotros* has three main sections: **Raising Awareness, Comunicándose en español,** and **Combinándolo todo. Raising Awareness** is a unique feature of the text. Written in English, it consists of three subdivisions: (1) "Overview," which focuses on understanding yourself and your Hispanic clients within the process of cross-cultural communication; (2) "Historical Perspective," which traces the present-day reality of U.S. Hispanics back to its roots in the historical development of the Western Hemisphere; and (3) "Nonverbal Communication," which describes those aspects of the communication process *not* expressed by words, which experts theorize account for 65 percent of the messages we send and receive.

Comunicándose en español focuses on basic words and structures in Spanish needed to perform specific professional activities. It begins with "Pronunciación," which includes practice in saying and hearing the sounds emphasized in the lesson, and continues with "Diálogo introductorio." Presented in cartoon format with English translation given on the facing page, "Diálogo introductorio" provides a bridge between the cultural material in **Raising Awareness** and the vocabulary and structures in the rest of the lesson. The vocabulary and structures presented here are intended primarily for building comprehension and not for active mastery.

Comunicándose en español continues with "Estructuras básicas" I and II, which form the core material to be learned in each lesson. They are presented in bilingual format and divided in two parts. Each is followed by "¿Sabe usted?," which offers brief explanations of selected words, dialectal variations, and general rules of usage, and by "Notas lingüísticas," which provide grammar analyses designed for students to read at home. The sequence of grammar presentation is geared to proficiency goals relevant to students' professional needs. Discussion of grammar points in class should be limited to those with which students demonstrate difficulty.

"Práctica preliminar" is a self-instructional set of exercises to be done outside of class. Answers appear at the bottom of the page so that students have access to instant correction. The range of exercises is designed to reinforce vocabulary and structures presented in the "Estructuras básicas" and explained in "¿Sabe usted?" and "Notas lingüísticas." Doing these exercises in class is not recommended, since that would detract from class time available for the contextual communication activities in the next section of the chapter.

Combinándolo todo integrates the cultural material presented in **Raising Awareness** and the vocabulary and structures introduced in **Comunicándose en español**. In addition, it introduces related vocabulary through contextual exercises. The mixture of familiar words and structures with new ones is deliberate in order to train students to develop language analogies and become better prepared for the real world in which their Spanish-speaking clients will often use words with which they are unfamiliar.

This section introduces a challenging variety of exercises. The first part, "Práctica comunicativa," contains eight types of exercises:

- "Conversacion parcial," consists of short dialogues with missing words indicated by a slash.

- "Pregunte Ud." focuses on the one activity professionals do most—asking questions.

- "Dígalo" provides guided dialogues stimulated by oral cues given by the instructor.

- "Escuche bien" practices listening comprehension in short segments, focusing on both lexical items and grammatical concepts.

- "Diálogos cortos" reintegrate previously learned vocabulary and structures in new contexts. In later lessons, the client's portion of the dialogue is given in its entirety to exemplify native colloquial speech in a variety of contexts.

- "Ayude al cliente" offers writing practice to complement the text's main goal of developing listening comprehension and speaking ability.

- "¿Comprende Ud.?" gives more advanced listening comprehension practice, with students listening to longer segments of speech in order to perform specific tasks based on what they hear.

- "Piénselo," another oral guided dialogue, zeroes in on more conceptual questions designed to integrate all the material previously presented in the lesson.

The second part of **Combinándolo todo**, "Situaciones de la vida real," uses realia to stimulate conversation. "Imagínese" has pictures, segments from short, unabridged written announcements, brochures, and other aspects of real life that reflect topics Hispanic clients might discuss. "Haciendo el papel" gives written cues to role-play situations emphasizing cultural sensitivity as well as linguistic ability.

These are written in English in Lessons 1 to 6 and in Spanish in Lessons 7 to 12 to increase the student's ability to work exclusively in Spanish.

The third part of **Combinándolo todo**, "Reflejos de la cultura," consists of songs, poems, essays, short stories, segments of novels, theater scenes, and a portion of a movie script, all chosen for their relevance to the cultural and linguistic content of each lesson. They are presented bilingually to avoid abridging and distorting the beauty of the language as written by and for proficient speakers of Spanish.

SUPPLEMENTARY MATERIALS

The student's text of *Entre nosotros* is supplemented by a detailed instructor's manual. Included in this manual are sample lesson plans, instructions for working with each segment of the student's text described here, and suggestions for presenting each lesson in class. It also contains the script for those activities in each lesson to which students have no written access. These consist of the "Dictado" in the "Pronunciación" section, and "Dígalo," "Escuche bien," "¿Comprende Ud.?" and "Piénselo" in the "Práctica comunicativa" section. Also included are the comprehension activities in the six **Evaluación del progreso** segments, namely, "Pronunciación," "Discriminación auditiva" (**Comunicándose en español**), and "Comprensión oral" (**Combinándolo todo**).

A set of cassette tapes is also available. The lesson cassettes contain the following for each lesson: "Pronunciación" ("Práctica" and "Dictado"), "Diálogo introductorio," "Estructuras básicas" I and II, "Escuche bien," and "¿Comprende Ud.?" The comprehension activities in the six **Evaluación del progreso** segments are also recorded.

TO THE STUDENT: Guidelines for self-instructional practice

The design of this text presupposes that students desiring to learn Spanish and to become aware of Hispanic cultures for professional ends are highly motivated, self-disciplined individuals. Consequently, the **Comunicándose en español** section is meant primarily for self-instructional use so that class time can focus on communication activities from the **Raising Awareness** and **Combinándolo todo** sections. The following suggestions will make your home study more effective:

1. Study aloud as much as possible. Learning to speak and understand a new language requires practice involving your mouth and your ears. Your eyes alone cannot learn to speak!

2. Study in small, concentrated, active sessions, especially when learning new material. Three 20-minute segments are more efficient in learning a new language than a 1-hour nonstop session.

3. Repeat words and phrases often, in as many different ways as possible (writing, reading, speaking, hearing). Constantly review words and structures from former lessons while you are learning new material.

4. Carefully read through the explanations of Pronunciación, "¿Sabe usted?" and "Notas lingüísticas." Mark any explanations you do not understand so that

you can ask questions in the next class. Use the tape in working through the "Práctica" given in each "Pronunciación" section. Again, mark any sound you have trouble hearing or producing.

5. Use the tapes in learning the "Estructuras básicas," first repeating each sentence as accurately as possible while looking at the text. As soon as you can, practice repeating the "Estructuras básicas" *without* the written script. When you have mastered them, listen to the question segments of the "Estructuras básicas" on the tape and then answer them in as many different ways as you can. Throughout your practice sessions, force yourself to rely on oral cues rather than the written text.

6. Work through "Práctica preliminar" in each lesson *orally.* Since answers are given at the bottom of the page, you can check your accuracy immediately after each practice item. Cover the answers before you begin each exercise. Reveal the answer to each item after you have responded to it. Mark any items that presented particular problems to discuss in class.

FURTHER COMMENTS

The following key explains graphics and abbreviations appearing in the student text:

[cassette icon]	available on cassette.
(M)	commonly used in Mexican dialects.
(MA)	commonly used in Mexican American dialects.
(PR)	commonly used in Puerto Rican dialects.
(C)	commonly used in Cuban dialects.
(O)	commonly used in other Latin American dialects.

The word *Anglo* has been used in this text for lack of a better term to refer to non-Hispanic residents of the United States. Although it may be offensive to some, it seems to be the only accurate term in current use. Similarly, *Hispanic* (and, at times, *Latino*) has been used, again for lack of a better term to refer to Spanish speakers from Latin America.

It is impossible to discuss culture without generalizing. Although specific sections offer general guidelines regarding traditional cultural conditioning, the message that gives unity to the text is: *See each Hispanic client as the individual he or she is.*

Acknowledgments

Special thanks to Pierre Casse, whose work, *Training for the Cross-Cultural Mind: A Handbook for Cross-Cultural Trainers and Consultants* (Washington: D.C.: Society for Intercultural Education Training and Research, 1980), has been adapted in the writing of the "Overview" sections of this book. Special acknowledgment goes also to Carmen Judith Nine Curt whose work, *Nonverbal Communication in Puerto Rico* (Cambridge, Mass.: National Assessment and Dissemination Center for Bilingual Education, 1975), has been adapted in the "Nonverbal Communication" sections.

No single person ever writes a book. It takes many people contributing inspiration, ideas, moral support, research, advice, and hard physical labor to produce a book like *Entre nosotros: Communicating with the Hispanic Client*. To name them all here is impossible. Yet to omit the names of some key people would give the false impression that everything in this book is mine and mine alone. Those mentioned here have been instrumental in one way or another during the last ten years of my involvement in curriculum development in Spanish for Professionals, which has culminated in the writing of this text.

Research support has come from the U.S. Department of Education, through a grant awarded to the Center for International Community Health Studies at the University of Connecticut Health Center. The University of Connecticut Research Foundation, the University of Connecticut School of Social Work, and Title XX also contributed financial support.

The following current (and former) faculty members and administrators at the University of Connecticut encouraged my teaching at the various professional schools, without which this text could not have been written. Special thanks to Julius Elias, Russell Farnen, Bill Wadleigh, Steve Schensul, James Walker, Robert Green, Peter Lane, Julio Morales, Cathy Havens, Wendy Winters, James Walker, Richard Kinkade, Maria Shevtsova, José Luis Coy, and Lourdes Morales-Gudmundsson.

Support from the Hispanic community in Hartford as well as the various professional agencies in the state with which I have worked has provided much insight into the needs of members of these diverse cultures. I am particularly grateful to María Gonzales Borrero and Roberto García of the Hispanic Health Council; the Visiting Nurses Association; the Department of Children and Youth Services; St. Francis Hospital; the Connecticut Bar Association; and the Hartford Public Schools.

Students in the courses I have taught at the various professional schools have freely contributed valuable insights from their personal experiences in becoming more fluent in Spanish and more aware of cultural differences that affect their work. I would like to thank them all, and in particular Brad Paley, Brunella Ibarrola, Tom Odinak, Robert Redden, Mary Croce Fish, Patricia Maldonado, Charlotte Calhoun, Jean Malloy, David Levine, Curtissa Cofield, Nance Castillo, and Betsy Rubenstein.

In pulling together the various aspects of this text, I interviewed many people regarding their personal experiences as either Hispanic clients, or Anglo professionals. Betty Ann Schober, Carlos Carrion, John Stacek, and David Pilkenton were instrumental in facilitating these interviews in many parts of the United States.

A very special thank you goes to Vincent G. Smith who contributed greatly to the writing and refining of portions of the text, the instructor's manual, and the cassette tape program, and to Elizabeth Lantz, whose confidence in this project was instrumental in having it published.

The actual writing of the text involved the hard work of many individuals. Those who contributed their creative talents include Dalila Soto, Nylsa Ubarri-Young, and Lourdes Morales-Gudmundsson. Without the assistance of Claudia Anastasio, Jaime Ibarrola, and Robert Mayott, the manuscript would never have made its way through the word processor. My thanks also to Alvino Fantini, Migdalia Reyes, Marilyn Eddington, and Fernando González-Reigosa for their valuable time in reading and critiquing the first-draft manuscript.

The long hours of the many months needed to write a text of this size were made much more bearable with the loving support of such colleagues, friends, and family as Kathy Porcello; Lois Sigman-Young; Ruth Solomkin; Amy B. Robinson; Peter Kelman; Sandy Edmonds; Brad Paley; Héctor Soto; Robert Mayott; Robert Vitale; Robert Roxby; Juan and Becky Brito; Marge Paquette; Anita Udell; Lourdes Morales-Gudmundsson; Anthony, Mary, Tony, and Jim Trupiano; Manny, Sue, Crystal, Beth, Heidi, Joe, Jim, Diane, David, and Michael Lotito.

Finally, without the encouragement, suggestions, and careful editing of Leslie Berriman and the Newbury House–Harper and Row staff, this text might never have been written.

ENTRE NOSOTROS

LECCIÓN 1

El primer encuentro

LOS OBJETIVOS

Raising awareness

1. To realize the importance of cultural conditioning in defining the individual
2. To understand how names are used in Hispanic cultures
3. To compare and practice Hispanic and Anglo ways of greeting

Comunicándose en español

1. To learn the Spanish alphabet to be able to spell and understand spellings of Spanish words and names
2. To use appropriate expressions to greet and say good-bye to clients, to assess and describe linguistic abilities in Spanish and English, to inquire about names, health, and other problems in the first encounter
3. To employ the present tense of regular verbs in Spanish

Combinándolo todo

1. To integrate all material from previous sections by applying the knowledge in work-related communication activities
2. To become increasingly independent of the printed word in speaking and understanding Spanish
3. To appreciate the advantages of bilingualism and biculturalism as well as the difficulties of learning a second language

Raising awareness

OVERVIEW: What is culture?

Every day an individual performs thousands of actions and perceives thousands of stimuli without conscious thought. They are evidence of learned behaviors taught us by our parents and others in the environment in which we were raised.

We could not survive as individuals if we did not operate for so much of the time from this subconscious set of learned behaviors and assumptions, values and beliefs. If, for example, you had to think *consciously* about how to tie your shoelace or how you are expected to behave in a movie theater, you would have very little psychic energy left to learn new things, to solve new problems, to share thoughts with others, to remember good times, or to create new artistic forms. These learned behaviors make our lives easier and more enriching by freeing our mental energy for more exciting activities.

Just as each individual has learned to perceive and act on the world outside from this subconsciously learned behavioral state for much of the waking time, so, too, the society in which one lives has learned to operate from a similar set of values, beliefs, behaviors, norms, and assumptions shared by the majority of those members living in that society. *Culture,* then, can be defined as those values, beliefs, behaviors, norms, and assumptions that members of a given community hold in common.

Just as the individual could not survive if he or she had to consciously control each action, from the simple act of breathing to the complex behavior of driving a car, so, too, would society cease to survive if its members did not perform many of their social interactions from this subconsciously shared set of what we can call *cultural patterns.* For example, if all members of a given society did not agree that a red light means *stop,* traffic pandemonium would result.

Many of these culturally determined values and beliefs that are valid and operable in one society or culture may be inappropriate in another. This explains why at times one may feel ill at ease when traveling to another country or meeting someone from a cultural background different from one's own. What we have learned and accepted subconsciously in our own culture to help us to define the external reality and predict the behavioral responses of others is no longer a reliable guide.

So often we concentrate only on trying to learn a foreign language system, leaving aside all other culturally determined behaviors and thought patterns. We tend to do this because we both take them for granted and know so little

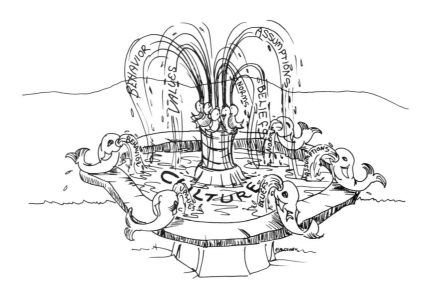

about them *at a conscious level.* Yet they are still working their subconscious magic on us (as well as on the "foreigner") as we try to communicate across cultural boundaries. Although we may adequately bridge the language barrier, we may still find that we are not communicating satisfactorily, which may leave us with a vague feeling of not really understanding each other.

Whether or not you learn to speak Spanish, your interaction with Hispanic clients will be affected by your personal cultural background which has conditioned you to think, act, and react in specific ways. In this text you will raise your awareness of how these subconscious patterns can impede true communication across cultural boundaries.

Applications

Indicate by checking the appropriate column after each statement whether you believe it is true for all human beings (*Universal*) or descriptive only of U.S. cultural patterns (*United States*). Check the *Undecided* column if you are not sure.

	Universal	*United States*	*Undecided*
1. One must always tell the truth even when it hurts.	1. _____	_____	_____
2. A dinner guest is expected to offer to help the host or hostess with the dishes.	2. _____	_____	_____
3. Parents have a responsibility to become involved with their child's school system.	3. _____	_____	_____
4. Hard work is the key to success.	4. _____	_____	_____
5. Women should have all the rights and privileges afforded to men.	5. _____	_____	_____
6. Clothes make the person.	6. _____	_____	_____
7. One should eat three well-balanced meals a day.	7. _____	_____	_____
8. Young children should be treated as individuals with a right to express their opinion.	8. _____	_____	_____
9. One should strive to arrive on time for all appointments.	9. _____	_____	_____
10. One should maintain strong eye contact when speaking to someone in authority.	10. _____	_____	_____

Reflections

A. Which items were easier to respond to and which required more thought? Why?

B. If you were to compare your responses with those of friends or members of your family, do you think they would agree with you? Why or why not?

C. Do cultures change? If so, do any of the above items reflect changes that have occurred in the United States in the last thirty years? If so, which ones?

D. Do you know if any of the above beliefs are very different from those in a specific Hispanic culture? Which one(s)?

HISTORICAL PERSPECTIVE: What's in a name?

Spanish, spoken by over 251 million people, is the fourth most widely spoken language in the world (after Mandarin Chinese, English, and Russian). There is no single name that can be used to refer accurately to all of these 251 million people, although *Spanish-speaking* (*los de habla española* or *hispanohablantes*) comes the closest.

Even the name *Latin America* is somewhat of a misnomer. Latin is not spoken there, although that language was the basis for the various Romance Languages of the Spanish, Portuguese, and French colonizers of the area. It does not give any clue to the indigenous identity that still prevails in much of the region. *Hispanoamérica* and *Iberoamérica* likewise offer an incomplete reflection of the various indigenous groups living there.

People living in the United States face a similar problem. While the name of the country is certainly reflective of the geographical and political reality, there is no one adjective that adequately refers to citizens of the United States. Although *American* is widely used, it is not restrictive enough, since South and Central Americans feel that they, too, are *Americans*. *North American* eliminates that confusion but adds another, since it also identifies Mexicans and Canadians. Although a more correct term would be *United Stater*, it would be an uphill struggle to establish it in lieu of the less specific (and technically inaccurate) term *American*, which is in common use.

1. How are the terms Latin America, Hispanoamérica, *and* Iberoamérica *inadequate in describing the reality of that region?*

2. How accurate is the term American *in describing people from the United States?*

Often, when meeting Spanish speakers, Americans ask, "Are you Spanish?" ("*¿Es Ud. español?*"), without realizing that this term denotes only those from Spain. It is comparable to someone from the United States being asked "Are you English?" because the individual *speaks* English. Asking "Are you Hispanic?" or "Are you Latin?" ("*¿Es Ud. hispano?*" or "*¿Es Ud. latino?*") also reflects an undifferentiated view of Spanish speakers since the terms *hispano* and *latino* do not distinguish between regional and national differences. This uninformed approach may alienate Hispanics, who tend to view their national identity from the perspective of their own country of origin and *not* from that of the shared heritage derived from the colonization of the New World by Spain in the sixteenth century.

One of the legacies that Spanish-speaking nations of Latin America inherited from their colonizers is a fierce sense of national and, especially, regional pride. In Spain, linguistic and cultural regionalism abounds. Many dialects (including *aragonés, andaluz,* and *gallego*) are spoken there, as well as at least two separate languages, *catalán* and *vascuence*. Spaniards are more likely to identify themselves as, for example *madrileño(a)s, catalanes,* or *valenciano(a)s,* than as *españoles*.

In the same way, most Latin Americans tend to define themselves by their regional background. Thus, you may hear "*Soy veracruzano*" ("I'm from Veracruz," an east coast state of Mexico), rather than "*Soy mexicano,*" or "*Soy de Santiago*" (the second largest city in Cuba) rather than "*Soy cubano.*" While the Anglo world may view all Spanish speakers as *Hispanics* or *Latins,* individual Spanish speakers almost never identify themselves by saying "*Soy hispano(a)*" or "*Soy latino(a),*" except when the response "I'm Hispanic" is expected according to the uninformed usage of many Americans.

---

3. *What problems may arise when using the following terms:* español, hispano, latino?
4. *How does nationalism affect the terms Hispanics may use to identify themselves?*

Similar historical traditions are evidenced in the selection of proper names and the origin of surnames in Spanish-speaking countries. It is not uncommon for Hispanics to be named not only after saints recognized by the Catholic Church but also after Christ. Thus, males might be named *Jesús*, females *Jesusa* or *María de Jesús*. It is not uncommon for a man to be named *José María*, after Joseph and Mary, parents of Jesus. Females are often named after special venerations to the Virgin Mary — for example, *Concepción* (the Immaculate Conception), *Asunción* (the Assumption into Heaven). Nor is it unusual for females to bear the names of virtues — for example, *Mercedes* (Mercy or Grace), *Esperanza* (Hope), *Consuelo* (Consolation), or *Piedad* (Piety).

In recent years a common tendency in the Hispanic world has been to christen children with English-sounding names that may be written with either the English spelling or phonetically in Spanish. The pronunciation, however, tends to reflect phonetic patterns in Spanish. Common examples are *Nelson*, *Eddy*, and *Mary*.

In addition, Hispanics are fond of nicknames (*apodos*), which often refer to physical characteristics. While calling someone Fats or Blondie in English may sound crude, in Spanish it is quite common to use such nicknames among close friends and family to express affection. Examples include *Gordo* (Fat One, male), *Negrita* (Dark One, female), *Rubio* (Blond One, male). The terms *mamita* y *papito* (*mommy* and *daddy*) are commonly used by married couples to address each other and even their children, in anticipation of their future roles. Mexican Americans often use the nicknames *jefecito*, *jefecita* (boss man, boss lady) to refer to parents, and *viejo*, *vieja* (old man, old lady) to refer to their spouses.

Surnames in Spanish often end in *-ez* (or, less commonly, *-oz* or even *-iz* or *-uz*), a suffix that was originally added to the father's first name to denote *son of*. Thus, just as *Johnson* in England originally meant *son of John*, *López* originally meant *son of Lope*, *Hernández*, *son of Hernando*, *Martínez*, *son of Martín*, etc.

---

5. *What criteria can affect the selection of first names in the Hispanic world?*
6. *Why do so many Hispanic surnames end in* -ez?

JOSEFINA ÁLVAREZ
DE GONZÁLEZ

ESTEBAN
GONZÁLEZ

ANTONIO
GONZÁLEZ
ÁLVAREZ

When a Hispanic woman marries, she does not lose her surname and adopt that of her husband as has been the custom (although changing of late) in the United States. For example, when *Margaret King* marries *Sam Addison* in the U.S. system, she becomes *Mrs. Sam Addison*, although she is known informally as *Margaret Addison*. Under the Spanish system, which is also used in Latin America, when *Josefina Álvarez* marries *Esteban González,* she now becomes known as *Josefina Álvarez (de) González.* She would never be known by her husband's first name, as in the U.S. system.

Children of Josefina and Esteban will retain *both* parents' surnames, that of the father, considered the primary last name, preceding that of the mother. Hence their son Antonio would write his full name as *Antonio González Álvarez* (commonly abbreviated to *Antonio González A.*), although the mother's surname (*Álvarez*) may not be used all the time.

---

7. *If* Margarita Santos *marries* Juan Moreno, *what is her new name? What is the full name of their son* Manuel?
8. *What problems might Manuel experience in the United States if he uses his full Hispanic name in some instances and not in others, especially when filling out forms that are filed by Anglos unfamiliar with the Hispanic surname system?*

NONVERBAL COMMUNICATION: Greetings

Each day we greet the people we know in much the same manner as we did the day before. For English-speaking Americans — Anglos — this means smiling, saying "Hi," "Hello," or "How ya' doin'?" to friends, and perhaps in more formal situations offering to shake hands. Embracing in public when greeting someone you know is rarely done except when someone is returning from a trip or between members of the same family or very close friends, especially when they greet each other at the beginning of a visit to the home.

Hispanics, however, tend to greet each other with much more physical involvement. When friends or even acquaintances of the same sex greet each other, they may kiss and hug each other, usually making contact between the upper parts of their bodies. More specifically, men usually greet each other with a firm hug, a strong handshake, and several pats on the back or upper arm. Women usually hug each other (less energetically than the men do) and kiss each other's cheek (or, at least, graze the other's cheek with the lips or the side of the face).

It should be noted, however, that in Hispanic cultures it has been, until quite recently, rare for members of the opposite sex to touch (except for perhaps a very weak handshake) when greeting each other unless they are married, engaged, members of the same family, or close friends. Although hugging and kissing each other's cheek has become acceptable in some *Latino* circles in the United States among members of the opposite sex, it is reserved for those who share some common bond.

When a male and a female are introduced, the handshake should not be either too tight a grasp, held too long, or too energetic, especially on the part of the woman. This same type of handshake serves to greet *all* the people in a room when one enters as well as when one leaves, especially in social situations.

In meeting someone for the first time, Hispanics use a polite handshake with less animation than accompanies the greeting of one's friends. In English the expression *to shake hands* contrasts with the Spanish *to give one's hand (dar la mano)*, the latter describing the offering of one's hand minus the strong grasping and shaking of the other's hand common in the United States.

Putting it into practice

1. Without using any words, greet a classmate of the same sex whom you know well, first in the Anglo tradition, then in the Hispanic. Repeat the process with a classmate of the opposite sex.

2. Without using any words, greet in the Hispanic way a client of the same sex whom you are meeting for the first time. Now do the same with a member of the opposite sex. What differences do you observe from the way you would greet clients in the Anglo tradition?

3. Without using any words, greet each person in the room in the Hispanic way as you enter. Do the same as you exit.

4. Discuss how it felt using the Anglo customs and the Hispanic ones in the above exercises.

Comunicándose en español

PRONUNCIACIÓN: El alfabeto 🔲

It is important for you to know the Spanish alphabet for two reasons:

1. By knowing the names of the letters you can ask Spanish clients to spell out words, names, etc., which you may not understand.

2. By knowing the order of the letters in the Spanish alphabet, you can make better use of a dictionary or glossary in looking up the words you need to know.

a	a	**h**	hache	**ñ**	eñe	**u**	u
b	be[1]	**i**	i	**o**	o	**v**	uve[6]
c	ce	**j**	jota[4]	**p**	pe	**w**	doble u[7]
ch[2]	che	**k**[5]	ca	**q**	cu	**x**	equis
d	de	**l**	ele	**r**	ere	**y**	i griega[8]
e	e	**ll**[2]	elle	**rr**[2]	erre	**z**	zeta
f	efe	**m**	eme	**s**	ese		
g	ge[3]	**n**	ene	**t**	te		

Práctica 🔲

A. Pronounce the names of the letters in Spanish, using the descriptions that follow as a guide:

1. The names of the five vowels are the same as the sound they represent. They are pronounced similar to the indicated English vowels, but shorter and crisper:

   a—f*a*ther   **e**—*e*gg   **i**—f*ee*t   **o**—st*o*ne   **u**—t*u*ne

2. The following consonants have one-syllable names, with the vowel sound similar to *e* in the English word *egg*, but pronounced more quickly and crisply.

   b   c   ch   d   g   p   t

---

[1]**B** is also known as *be larga, be grande,* or *be de burro.*

[2]**Ch, ll,** and **rr** are called digraphs—that is, two letters represented by one sound. You may also hear them called *ce hache* (**ch**), *doble ele* (**ll**), and *doble ere* (**rr**), respectively.

[3]The name of the consonant **g** sounds like English *hay* with a shorter, crisper vowel sound.

[4]The first syllable of *jota* sounds like English *hoe* with a shorter, crisper vowel sound.

[5]**K** is found only in words of foreign origin (e.g., *kilo*).

[6]**V** is also known as *be corta, be chica,* or *be de vaca.*

[7]**W** is also known as *doble be* or *doble uve;* found only in words of foreign origin.

[8]*I griega* literally translates as *Greek i.*

3. The following consonants have two-syllable names which nearly rhyme with the English word *essay,* but with shorter, crisper vowel sounds.

   f   l   ll   m   n   ñ   r   rr   s

4. The names of the following consonants do not follow any particular pronunciation pattern and must be learned individually:

   h   j   k   q   v   w   x   y   z

B. Spell the following names and surnames in Spanish:
   1. **Felipe Navarro**
   2. **Héctor Hernández**
   3. **Jesusita Delgado**
   4. **Eliseo García**
   5. **Eugenia Bonilla**
   6. **Isabel Fonseca**
   7. **Alba Vargas**
   8. **Adela Solís**
   9. **Carlos Ríos**

Dictado

Write the letters of the names your instructor spells in Spanish:

1. _____   4. _____

2. _____   5. _____

3. _____   6. _____

¿Ha entendido bien?

You are able to understand more than you think. Using the visual cues and language in the cartoon, answer the following questions.

1. ¿Cómo se llama el cliente?
2. ¿Cómo se llama la recepcionista?
3. ¿Cómo se escribe el apellido del cliente?
4. ¿Cómo se escribe el apellido de la recepcionista?
5. ¿Cuál (*what*) es el nombre completo del cliente?
6. Sánchez es el apellido de la mamá de Ricardo, ¿verdad?
7. La mamá de Ricardo se llama Amalia. ¿Cuál es el nombre completo de ella?
8. ¿Cómo se escribe el apellido de usted?
9. En el sistema hispano, ¿cuál es el nombre completo de usted?
10. En el sistema hispano, ¿cuál es el nombre completo de la mamá de usted?

INTRODUCTORY DIALOGUE: Your full name, please

The client: Good morning, ma'am.

The receptionist: Good morning, sir.

R: What is your name?

C: My name is Ricardo Hinojosa.

R: How do you spell your last name?

C: It's spelled H-i-n-o-j-o-s-a.

R: Your name is spelled R-i-c-a-r-d-o, isn't it?

C: Yes, ma'am, that's the way it's spelled.

R: Then, Ricardo Hinojosa is your complete name?

C: It's Ricardo Hinojosa Sánchez, but here in the United States I only use **Hinojosa**.

R: I see, Mr. Hinojosa. I'm Mrs. Pierson. I'm pleased to meet you.

C: The pleasure is mine, ma'am.

BASIC STRUCTURES I: Greetings and farewells

The employee (m.)

Good morning, miss.
Good afternoon, ma'am.
Good evening, ma'am.

Hi, friend,
- what's up?
- how's it going?
- how are you?

How are you?

How are you feeling today?

What's wrong?
(Literally, What do you have?)

What's wrong?
(Literally, What's happening to you?)

Good-bye. See you tomorrow.
See you soon, ma'am.

Say hello
- to the family.
- to your husband.

The client (f.)

Good morning, sir.
Good afternoon, sir.
Good evening, sir.

Okay. And you (familiar)?
So-so.
Same as always.

I'm very well, thank you.
Pretty well. And you (formal)?

I'm feeling
- bad.
- fine.
- better.
- worse.

I have
- a headache.
- a cold.
- a bad cold.

I have problems
- at home.
- at work.
- at school.

If God wills (it).
Yes, we'll see each other then.

Thank you. The same to you.

¿Sabe usted?

1. **Buenos días** is used until noon, **buenas tardes** until the sun goes down (it varies with the season), and **buenas noches** from sundown until the end of the evening, as well as to say good-bye at night.

2. The **hola, amigo/a** greetings are informal ones and should be reserved for use with clients whom you know well.

3. **¿Qué tiene Ud.?** usually inquires about physical health and appearance. **¿Qué le pasa?** usually refers more to emotional or situational conditions.

4. **Si Dios quiere** is commonly used as a response to a statement about the future and reflects the strong religious faith of many Hispanics. In some Hispanic homes, children ask parents for a blessing when arriving and leaving (**la bendición**), which is given by saying **Dios te bendiga, hijo/a.**

5. **Saludos a la esposa** sends greetings to someone's wife. It is common for Hispanics to ask about or send greetings to each other's families, even when speaking in a professional context.

6. You may hear these dialectal variations:
   Tengo la monga. (PR)*   I have a severe flu.

ESTRUCTURAS BÁSICAS I: Saludos y despedidas

El empleado	*La cliente*
Buenos días, señorita.	Buenos días, señor.
Buenas tardes, señora.	Buenas tardes, señor.
Buenas noches, señora.	Buenas noches, señor.

Hola, amiga.	¿Qué tal? ¿Qué hay? ¿Cómo estás?	Regular. ¿Y tú? Así así. Igual que siempre.	

¿Cómo está usted?	Estoy muy bien, gracias. Bastante bien. ¿Y Ud.?

¿Cómo se siente hoy?	Me siento	mal. bien. mejor. peor.

¿Qué tiene usted?	Tengo	dolor de cabeza. un resfriado. la gripe.

¿Qué le pasa?	Tengo problemas en	casa. el trabajo. la escuela.

Adiós. Hasta mañana. Hasta luego, señora.	Si Dios quiere. Sí, nos vemos entonces.

Saludos	a la familia. al esposo.	Gracias. Igualmente.

Estoy de lo más bien. (PR)*	I'm feeling great.
Tengo resfrío. (MA)*	I have a cold.
Tengo la gripa. (O)*	I have a cold.

Notas lingüísticas I

A. There are two ways of addressing someone in Spanish. The **tú** form is used when addressing someone with whom you are on a first-name basis—friends, family, children, and some acquaintances. **Usted** (often abbreviated **Ud.**) is more formal and is used with someone whom you address by a title + surname, e.g., **Sr. Torres, Dra. Vargas.** It is best to use the **usted** form with clients, at least until you know them better. You may wish to use **Don** or **Doña** + first name with the **usted** form to refer to clients who are much older than you. This expresses both respect and close rapport.

B. Verb endings in Spanish reflect the subject of the sentence much more than they do in English. It is important to focus on the end of the verb in Spanish in order to understand the sentence, since the subject pronoun is often eliminated (e.g., ¿Cómo se sient*e* hoy? Est*oy* muy bien, gracias.)

---

*PR = Puerto Rican; MA = Mexican American; O = other.

BASIC STRUCTURES II: Courtesy and communication

The employee (m.)	*The client (f.)*
Thank you very much, ma'am. Thanks a million (thousand), ma'am. I appreciate it very much.	You're welcome. At your service. Don't mention it.
May I come in? Excuse me. Pardon me.	Yes, come in (forward). Yes, of course. Don't worry (about it).
Don't bother (trouble yourself). I'm very sorry, miss.	It's no bother at all. Thank you. (You're) very kind.
What's your name?	My name is Elena Gómez.
Do you understand?	Yes, sir, I understand.
Do you understand { Spanish? English?	Yes, I understand it well. No, I don't understand it.
Do you speak { Spanish? English?	Yes, I speak it rather well. Well, I speak it very little.
Please repeat.	Yes, with (much) pleasure.
Please speak { slower. louder. softer.	Yes, of course.
How do you say *woman* in Spanish? How do you spell *Julio*? What does *hijo* mean?	You say *mujer.* You spell (it) *J-u-l-i-o.* It means *son.*

¿Sabe usted?

1. **Con permiso** is used to ask permission *before* an action that may inconvenience someone (e.g., interrupting someone who's talking, passing in front of someone, etc.); **perdón** is used to excuse oneself *after* doing something that might have hurt or offended someone (e.g., accidentally bumping into a person).

2. **Comprender** usually refers to understanding an idea or a concept; **entender** refers to understanding linguistically and/or conceptually.

3. *Yes–no* questions in Spanish begin with the verb. Your voice goes up to signal the end of the question (e.g., **¿Entiende Ud. español?**). Information questions begin with an interrogative word (**cómo, qué,** etc.) followed by the verb. Your voice goes down at the end of an information question (e.g., **¿Cómo se dice *woman* en español?**)

14

El empleado

Muchas gracias, señora. ⎤
Mil gracias, señora. ⎬
Se lo agradezco mucho. ⎦

¿Se puede?
Con permiso.
Perdón.

No se moleste Ud.
Lo siento mucho, señorita.

¿Cómo se llama Ud.?

¿Comprende Ud.?

¿Entiende Ud. ⎰ español?
⎱ inglés?

¿Habla Ud. ⎰ español?
⎱ inglés?

Repita Ud., por favor.

Hable Ud. más ⎰ despacio, ⎱
⎱ alto, ⎰ por favor.
bajo,

¿Cómo se dice *woman* en español?
¿Cómo se escribe *Julio*?
¿Qué quiere decir *hijo*?

La cliente

⎡ De nada.
⎨ A la orden.
⎣ No hay de qué.

Sí, adelante.
Sí, cómo no.
No se preocupe.

No es ninguna molestia.
Gracias. Muy amable.

Me llamo Elena Gómez.

Sí, señor, comprendo.

⎰ Sí, lo entiendo bien.
⎱ No, no lo entiendo.

Sí, lo hablo bastante bien.
Pues, lo hablo muy poco.

Sí, con mucho gusto.

Sí, cómo no.

Se dice *mujer*.
Se escribe *J-u-l-i-o*.
Quiere decir *son*.

Notas lingüísticas II

A.

Subject pronouns			
I	yo	we (masc.)	nosotros
		we (fem.)	nosotras
you (s.)	tú (familiar)	you (pl.)	ustedes
	usted (formal)		
he	él	they (masc.)	ellos
she	ella	they (fem.)	ellas

1. When speaking to someone, care must be taken to choose the appropriate form of *you* (**tú, usted,** or **ustedes**).

2. When speaking as one of a group of all males or a group of males and females, the masculine form **nosotros** is used. **Nosotras** refers to an all-female group. The same distinction applies to **ellos** and **ellas**.

3. There is no equivalent for the subject pronoun *it;* the verb form is used alone: **Está bien,** *It's fine.*

4. Subject pronouns are usually eliminated in Spanish when the subject is clearly understood in context.

Buenos días, señor Díaz.   Good morning, Mr. Díaz.
¿Cómo se siente (Ud.) hoy?   How are you feeling today?

They are used, however, to clarify or emphasize:

Ella tiene dolor de cabeza   She has a headache,
y él tiene un resfriado.   and he has a cold.

B. Verbs in Spanish are listed in dictionaries in the infinitive form (e.g., **hablar**), the equivalent of the *to + verb* in English (e.g., *to speak*). All Spanish verbs are classified as belonging to one of the three verb conjugations, according to the ending of the infinitive: **-ar, -er,** or **-ir.** The present-tense forms of regular verbs of these three conjugations are as follows:

	I -AR hablar (to speak)	II -ER comprender (to understand)	III -IR escribir (to write)
yo	habl*o*	comprend*o*	escrib*o*
tú	habl*as*	comprend*es*	escrib*es*
Ud., él, ella	habl*a*	comprend*e*	escrib*e*
nosotros/as	habl*amos*	comprend*emos*	escrib*imos*
Uds., ellos/as	habl*an*	comprend*en*	escrib*en*

1. Notice that the present-tense endings are added to the stem of the infinitive (the infinitive form minus **-ar, -er,** or **-ir**). The **-o** ending indicates the **yo** form of the present tense, while **-mos** indicates the plural **nosotros/as** form of the verb.

2. The endings **-as** and **-es** indicate the **tú** form.

3. **Usted, él,** and **ella** share the same endings: **-a** for **-ar** verbs and **-e** for **-er** and **-ir** verbs. **Ustedes, ellos,** and **ellas** also share the same endings, either **-an** (**-ar** verbs) or **-en** (**-er** and **-ir** verbs).

4. The conjugations of regular **-er** and **-ir** verbs are identical *except* for the **nosotros/as** form (*-e*mos versus *-i*mos).

C. Languages change over time, and those elements used most often tend to evolve the most irregularities. The most commonly used verbs are often irregular in form. In Spanish, these irregularities include: (1) irregular **yo** forms; (2) changes in the vowel of the stem of the infinitive in all forms *but* **nosotros/as;** and (3) completely irregular conjugations. The following common verbs introduced in "Estructuras básicas" have irregular conjugations:

1. irregular **yo** forms:

tener	*tengo*	decir	*digo*	estar	*estoy*
agradecer	*agradezco*	conocer	*conozco*	ver	*veo*

2. Changes in the vowel of the stem in all forms *except* **nosotros/as**, from **e** to **ie, o** to **ue** (all three conjugations) or **e** to **i** (-**ir** *verbs* only).*

	entender (e-ie)	poder (o-ue)	decir (e-i)	repetir (e-i)
yo	ent*ie*ndo	p*ue*do	d*i*go	rep*i*to
tú	ent*ie*ndes	p*ue*des	d*i*ces	rep*i*tes
Ud., él, ella	ent*ie*nde	p*ue*de	d*i*ce	rep*i*te
nosotros/as	ent*e*ndemos	p*o*demos	d*e*cimos	rep*e*timos
Uds., ellos/as	ent*ie*nden	p*ue*den	d*i*cen	rep*i*ten

3. completely irregular conjugation:

   estar: est*oy*, est*amos*, est*ás*, est*á*, est*án*

D. Some of the verb forms introduced in "Estructuras Básicas" are **usted** (or formal) command forms. For now, just notice how the ending differs from the **usted** form of the regular present-tense conjugation. You will learn to form commands in subsequent lessons:

Present-tense **Ud.** *form:*

hablar	¿Habl*a* Ud. español?	Do you speak Spanish?
molestar	Usted me molest*a*.	You are bothering me.
preocupar	Usted se preocup*a* mucho.	You worry a lot.
repetir	Usted lo rep*i*t*e*.	You repeat it.

Ud. *command form:*

hablar	Habl*e* más bajo, por favor.	Please speak more softly.
molestar	No me molest*e* (Ud.).	Don't bother me.
preocupar	No se preocup*e*.	Don't worry.
repetir	Rep*i*t*a* (Ud.), por favor.	Please repeat.

E. Some verbs are used with a reflexive pronoun, which indicates that the subject of the verb and the object are the same. Often the English equivalent does not directly translate this reflexive usage. Study carefully the following examples from the "Estructuras básicas":

¿Cómo se llama Ud.?	What's your name? (How do you call yourself)?
(Yo) me llamo Elena Gómez.	My name is (I call myself) Elena Gómez.
¿Cómo se siente Ud.?	How do you feel (yourself to be)?
(Yo) me siento mejor.	I feel (myself to be) better.

F. Other verbs are used reflexively in an impersonal sense, where the Spanish subject is the equivalent of *it, one,* or the universal *you* in English:

¿Cómo se dice *woman*?	How do you say (does one say) *woman?*
Se dice *mujer*.	You say (One says) *mujer.*
¿Cómo se escribe *Julio*?	How is *Julio* spelled (written)?
Se escribe *J-u-l-i-o*.	It is spelled (written) *J-u-l-i-o.*

---

*A more detailed description of these *stem-changing* verbs is given in the Appendix.

G. When introducing yourself to a client, you usually give your full name as you extend your hand (**dar la mano**). You may follow your name with **a la orden** or **a sus órdenes** (*at your service*). The person to whom you are introduced will respond with one of the following equivalents of *Pleased to meet you* (the words in parentheses may be omitted):

Mucho gusto (en conocerlo).   (when introduced to a male)
Mucho gusto (en conocerla).   (when introduced to a female)
Encantado (de conocerlo).   (spoken by one male to another)
Encantado (de conocerla).   (spoken by a male to a female)
Encantada (de conocerlo).   (spoken by a female to a male)
Encantada (de conocerla).   (spoken by one female to another)

You would then respond with either:

El gusto es mío.   (The pleasure is mine.)
Encantado.   (if you are a male)
Encantada.   (if you are a female)

PRÁCTICA PRELIMINAR

Follow the guidelines for self-instructional practice given in the Preface.

A. Repeat the question in Spanish ¿**Cómo se escribe** . . . ? with each of the following names. Then answer the question by spelling the name in Spanish. Consult "Pronunciación" section of this lesson if you experience difficulties.

Ejemplo: Arturo.
¿**Cómo se escribe Arturo?**
Se escribe A-r-t-u-r-o (A-ere-te-u-ere-o).

1. Fernández
2. Manuel
3. Echeverría
4. Constanza
5. Felipe
6. Candales
7. Jorge
8. Humberto
9. Javier
10. Quinella

B. Practice reading the following questions with the proper intonation, rising if it is a *yes–no* question, and falling if it is an *information* question.

Ejemplo: ¿Entiende Ud. inglés?
voice rises (yes–no question)

1. ¿Cómo estás?
2. ¿Qué tiene Ud.?
3. ¿Habla Ud. español?
4. ¿Cómo se llama Ud.?
5. ¿Qué quiere decir *despacio?*
6. ¿Se siente Ud. bien hoy?
7. ¿Qué te pasa?

B 1. voice falls 2. voice falls 3. voice rises 4. voice falls 5. voice falls 6. voice rises 7. voice falls 8. voice falls 9. voice rises 10. voice rises

8. ¿Cómo se escribe *Milagros?*

9. ¿Comprenden Uds.?

10. ¿Habla Ud. inglés?

C. Conjugate the verb in each of the following expressions according to the instructions given. Remember that subject pronouns are optional in Spanish, but are commonly omitted.

Ejemplo: Using the **yo** form of the verb, tell the client that you:
comprender el problema
(Yo) comprendo el problema.

1. Using the **yo** form of each verb, tell the client that you

   (a) estar bien

   (b) tener un dolor de cabeza

   (c) agradecer (selo) mucho

2. Using the **nosotros** form of each verb, tell the client that you and the doctor:

   (a) hablar inglés bien

   (b) comprender el problema

   (c) escribir mal en inglés

3. Using the **tú** form of each verb, ask the client if he or she:

   (a) entender inglés

   (b) tener un resfriado

   (c) hablar español

4. Using the **Ud.** form of each verb, ask the client if he or she:

   (a) sentir(se) mejor hoy

   (b) estar bien

   (c) comprender(lo) bien

5. Using the **Ud.** *command* form of each verb, tell the client to:

   (a) hablar más despacio

   (b) no molestar(se)

   (c) no preocupar(se)

6. Using the **Uds.** form of each verb, ask the client and his wife if they:

   (a) entender inglés

   (b) estar bien hoy

   (c) tener problemas en casa

7. Using the **él** form of each verb, ask the client if her husband:

   (a) sentir(se) mejor hoy

   (b) llamar(se) Carlos

   (c) entender español

C 1. **a.** (Yo) estoy bien. **b.** (Yo) tengo un dolor de cabeza. **c.** (Yo) se lo agradezco mucho. 2. **a.** (Nosotros) hablamos inglés bien. **b.** (Nosotros) comprendemos el problema. **c.** (Nosotros) escribimos mal en inglés. 3. **a.** ¿Entiendes (tú) inglés? **b.** ¿Tienes (tú) un resfriado? **c.** ¿Hablas (tú) español? 4. **a.** ¿Se siente (Ud.) mejor hoy? **b.** ¿Está (Ud.) bien? **c.** ¿Lo comprende (Ud.) bien? 5. **a.** Hable (Ud.) más despacio. **b.** No se moleste (Ud.). **c.** No se preocupe (Ud.). 6. **a.** ¿Entienden

8. Using the **ellos** form of each verb, ask the client if his children:
   (a) hablar inglés
   (b) entender español
   (c) escribir bien

9. Using the *it* form of each verb, ask the client:
   (a) qué querer decir *hijo*
   (b) cómo escribir(se) *Lidia*
   (c) cómo decir(se) *wife*

D. Give the verb form that is missing in the following questions, using the answer provided as your cue.

Ejemplo: ¿Cómo se _____ Ud.?
              Me *llamo* Mercedes Colón.

1. ¿Qué _____ Ud.? *Tengo* un resfriado.

2. ¿ _____ (tú) español? Lo *hablo* un poco.

3. ¿Se _____ bien hoy? Me *siento* peor hoy.

4. ¿Cómo se _____ *Elena?* Se *escribe* E-l-e-n-a.

5. ¿Ellos _____ inglés? Sí, *entienden* inglés.

6. ¿Cómo se _____ *sir* en español? Se *dice señor.*

7. ¿Cómo _____ Ud.? *Estoy* bien, gracias.

8. ¿Cómo se _____ su esposa? Se *llama* Concepción.

9. ¿ _____ Uds.? Sí, *comprendemos.*

10. Adiós, amiga. Nos _____ mañana. Sí, nos *vemos* entonces.

(Uds.) inglés? **b.** ¿Están (Uds.) bien hoy? **c.** ¿Tienen (Uds.) problemas en casa? **7. a.** ¿Se siente (él) mejor hoy? **b.** ¿Se llama (él) Carlos? **c.** ¿Entiende (él) español? **8. a.** ¿Hablan (ellos) inglés? **b.** ¿Entienden (ellos) español? **c.** ¿Escriben (ellos) bien? **9. a.** ¿Qué quiere decir *hijo?* **b.** ¿Cómo se escribe *Lidia?* **c.** ¿Cómo se dice *wife?*

D 1. tiene **2.** Hablas **3.** siente **4.** escribe **5.** entienden **6.** dice **7.** está **8.** llama **9.** Comprenden **10.** vemos

E. For each of the following situations, give the most appropriate response from the "Estructuras básicas" presented in this lesson.

Ejemplo: You need to interrupt Mrs. Álvarez while she is speaking to someone else.
Con permiso, señora Álvarez.

1. You have just been introduced to Mr. Gómez.
2. You greet an older woman who has just come into your office this afternoon.
3. You ask Miss Ríos how she feels today.
4. You ask the young man what is wrong.
5. You send greetings to your client's family.
6. You tell your supervisor, Mr. Ortiz, that you have problems at work.
7. You tell Mr. Suárez that you are grateful for everything.
8. You want the client to repeat (it) more slowly.
9. You say good-bye to Mr. Vargas, tell him you'll see him tomorrow. Then send regards to his wife.

F. Formulate questions addressed to the person named, conjugating the verb used in the phrase that follows each name. Be careful to choose the verb form that is the most appropriate equivalent of *you* (**tú, Ud.,** or **Uds.**) *without* using the subject pronoun.

Ejemplo: Señora Chávez/tener problemas en casa
Señora Chávez, ¿tiene problemas en casa?

1. Miguel/hablar inglés
2. Sra. Vidal/sentir(se) mejor
3. Sr. Rodríguez/cómo estar
4. Marisol/tener dolor de cabeza
5. Francisco y Carmen/entender inglés
6. Señor/cómo llamar(se)
7. Felipe/comprender el problema
8. Srta. Valencia/escribir inglés
9. Señor y señora/hablar español
10. Ramón/entender inglés

E 1. Mucho gusto (en conocerlo), señor Gómez. Encantado/a (de conocerlo), señor Gómez. 2. Buenas tardes, señora. 3. ¿Cómo se siente hoy, señorita Ríos? 4. ¿Qué le pasa, señor? 5. Saludos a la familia. 6. Señor Ortiz, tengo problemas en el trabajo. 7. Señor Suárez, se lo agradezco todo. 8. Repita(lo) Ud. más despacio. 9. Adiós, señor Vargas, hasta mañana. (Nos vemos mañana.) Saludos a la esposa.
F 1. Miguel, ¿hablas inglés? 2. Sra. Vidal, ¿se siente mejor? 3. Sr. Rodríguez, ¿cómo está? 4. Marisol, ¿tienes dolor de cabeza? 5. Francisco y Carmen, ¿entienden inglés? 6. Señor, ¿cómo se llama? 7. Felipe, ¿comprendes el problema? 8. Srta. Valencia, ¿escribe inglés? 9. Señor y señora, ¿hablan español? 10. Ramón, ¿entiendes inglés?

Combinándolo todo

PRÁCTICA COMUNICATIVA: El primer encuentro

Conversación parcial

Practique Ud. oralmente la siguiente conversación. Cada raya (/) implica que falta una palabra. Es necesario conjugar cada verbo *en bastardillas*.

Ejemplo: ¿Cómo / *sentir* / , señor?   Me *sentir* / , gracias.
       ¿Cómo se siente Ud., señor?   **Me siento bien, gracias.**

El empleado	*La cliente*
1. ¿ / se *llamar* / , señora?	/ *llamar* Alicia López.
2. Mucho / en / , señora López.	/ , señor.
3. ¿ / *estar*, señora?	*Estar* / bien, señor. ¿Y / ?
4. / más alto, / favor. No / bien el español.	Sí, señor, / mucho / .
5. ¿ / se / hoy? ¿Mejor?	Sí, me *sentir* mucho / .
6. Lo / mucho, pero no / *comprender. Repetir* Ud., por / , y hable / alto.	Muy / . ¿*Estar* mejor?
7. Sí. ¿Qué / pasa, señora? ¿ / problemas / casa?	Sí, mi hijo / *sentir* muy / hoy.
8. ¿Qué / *decir hijo* / inglés?	*Querer* decir / .

Pregunte Ud.

Dé Ud. oralmente las preguntas correspondientes en la siguiente entrevista con Enrique Alarcón, un paciente de la doctora Sánchez, que está de vacaciones hoy.

Ejemplo: Me siento un poco mejor hoy, gracias.
       ¿Cómo se siente hoy?

1. Me llamo Enrique Alarcón.

2. Se escribe *A-l-a-r-c-ó-n.*

3. Lo hablo un poco, pero no lo entiendo muy bien.

4. No me siento muy bien hoy.

5. Tengo un dolor de espalda.

6. Quiere decir *back* en inglés.

7. Sí, me siento mejor ahora (*now*).

8. Sí, nos vemos mañana. Saludos a la doctora Sánchez.

Dígalo

Pregunte a un/a compañero/a de clase lo que le diga su profesor/a sobre los temas de saludos, nombres completos, habilidades lingüísticas, salud, problemas y despedidas.

Escuche bien

A. Ud. oirá seis nombres de clientes y cómo se escribe el apellido completo de cada uno. Escriba el apellido completo en el espacio.

1. Carlos _____   4. Rafael _____

2. Rosa _____   5. Sonia _____

3. Julio _____   6. Antonio _____

B. Ud. oirá a seis clientes que describen sus habilidades de hablar y entender el inglés. Escriba Ud. **muy bien, regular, o mal** en la columna apropiada, según lo que dicen.

	hablar	entender
1. Raúl		
2. La señorita Salinas		
3. Miguel, el hijo de Carmen		
4. Los señores Pérez		
5. Pedro Martínez		
6. Isabel Dávila		

Diálogos cortos

Haga Ud. el papel del empleado en los diálogos cortos.

I. *El empleado*

Buenos _____ , señora.

¿Ud. se _____ María Pérez?

Mucho _____ en

_____ , señora Pérez.

La cliente

Buenos días, señor.

Sí, me llamo María Pérez.

Igualmente, gracias.

El empleado

_____ Pérez, ¿ _____
Ud. inglés?

Sí, un _____ . Si yo

_____ inglés, ¿Ud. lo entiende?

La cliente

Lo entiendo pero no lo hablo. ¿Habla Ud.
español?

Sí, lo entiendo bastante bien.

II. *La doctora Strauss*

_____ noches, señor.

¿Cómo _____ Ud.?

Bien, _____ . ¿ _____

se _____ Ud.?

Yo _____ la doctora
Strauss.

_____ gusto en _____ .

¿Vargas _____ escribe

_____ B o V?

¿ _____ tiene, señor?

_____ Ud. despacio, por

_____ .

¿El _____ de Paquito es
Vargas?

¿Paquito _____ inglés?

_____ permiso, señor.

El señor Vargas

Estoy muy bien. ¿Y Ud.?

Me llamo Francisco Vargas.

Igualmente, doctora.

Se escribe con V. V-a-r-g-a-s.

Es mi hijo, Paquito. No se siente bien.
Creo que tiene la gripe.

Sí, como no. Creo que Paquito tiene la
gripe.

Sí, así es.

Sí, entiende bastante. Lo estudia en la
escuela.

Sí, como no.

Ayude al cliente

Write a short letter to Mr. Morales, who reads only Spanish. Mr. Morales has been ill and unable to attend the teacher conference he was to have with you today about his son David, a high school junior. You need to write to him in Spanish about David's progress in learning English. Begin the letter with *Muy estimado señor Morales*.

1. Then tell him what your name is, that you speak Spanish a little and you write it poorly. Ask him how he is today and tell him that David says he is not well and that you are very sorry.

2. In a new paragraph, tell him that David understands English very well but he speaks it only a little. Add that David speaks very softly and very slowly. Then state that David writes very well in Spanish but he has problems in school because (*porque*) he doesn't write well in English. Tell Mr. Morales that David is very intelligent (*es muy inteligente*) and he wants (*quiere*) to speak English very much.

3. Close the letter by saying that you'll see each other soon (*pronto*). Send greetings to his wife and close with *Yours truly* (*Muy atentamente*) and sign your name.

¿Comprende Ud.?

Escuche bien el diálogo siguiente entre un empleado del "Youth Services Bureau" y una cliente y las oraciones basadas en el diálogo. Después escriba Ud. "V" si la oración dice la verdad y "F" si es falsa según lo que pasa en el diálogo.

1. _____ 4. _____ 7. _____

2. _____ 5. _____ 8. _____

3. _____ 6. _____ 9. _____

Piénselo

Prepárese para poder hablar con el/la profesor/a o con otros estudiantes sobre los temas siguientes, contestando las preguntas que le sugiere el/la profesor/a:

1. Los saludos y la comunicación sin palabras
2. Los problemas que Ud. tiene con el español
3. Los problemas que los clientes tienen con el inglés
4. Problemas físicos que tienen los clientes
5. Problemas que tienen los clientes en casa, en la escuela, o en el trabajo

Imagínese

Describa Ud. a cada una de las personas en las fotos, contestando las preguntas siguientes:

1. ¿Cómo se llama? (su nombre completo)
2. ¿Cómo se siente hoy?
3. ¿Qué problemas tiene?
4. ¿Entiende inglés?
5. ¿Habla inglés?
6. ¿Entiende español?
7. ¿Habla español?
8. ¿Habla bajo o alto?
9. ¿Tiene esposo/a?

Haciendo el papel

Haga Ud. el papel del empleado/de la empleada en las situaciones siguientes mientras otro/a estudiante hace el papel del (de la) cliente. Use la communicación sin palabras cuando sea apropiada.

1. You are speaking on the phone with Juan Cintrón Guerrero. Verify that this is his complete name, that *Cintrón* is his father's surname and *Guerrero* his mother's. Then verify the spelling of his full name. Ask him if he understands English and if he speaks it. Tell him that you do not understand Spanish very well and that you speak it only a little. He tells you not to worry, that you speak Spanish fine. Thank him for his kindness.

2. A woman enters the office in the evening. Greet her and ask her name. She asks you yours and you respond. Shake hands and tell her you are pleased to meet her. At the end of the interview, thank her for everything, say good-bye, and tell her again that it's been a pleasure to meet her.

3. You greet a young female client you know very well, Leonor Serrano de Rivera. Ask her how she feels today and how her husband is. She tells you that she doesn't feel too well and that her husband is worse. Respond appropriately and ask her what's going on. She says there are problems at home. Tell her you don't understand and ask her to repeat more slowly and more loudly.

4. Introduce yourself to a classmate in Spanish before interviewing him or her in order to fill out the following form. Be sure to use appropriate nonverbal communication while making the necessary introductions.

	Client	Spouse
Last name _____ First name _____		
Spouse's full name _____		
Ability to understand English _____		
Ability to speak English _____		
Ability to understand Spanish _____		
Ability to speak Spanish _____		
General physical state _____		

REFLEJOS DE LA CULTURA: "México-americano"*

The following lyrics illustrate the sense of "double" identity typical of many Hispanics living in the United States, in this case, Mexican Americans. The advantages of speaking and understanding two languages, of feeling comfortable in two cultures, of seeing one's "homeland" encompassing two countries are stressed. The music is typical of the U.S. border region shared with Mexico. You should be able to understand most of the words. Consult the English translation only if you are having problems understanding.

Por mi madre yo soy mexicano.	On my mother's side I am Mexican.
Por destino soy americano.	Because of fate I am American.
Yo soy de la Raza de Oro.	I am of the golden race.
Yo soy méxico-americano.	I am Mexican American.
Yo te comprendo el inglés.	I understand your English.
También te hablo en castellano.	I also speak to you in Spanish.
Yo soy de la Raza Noble.	I am of the noble race.
Yo soy méxico-americano.	I am Mexican American.
Zacatecas a Minnesota,	Zacatecas [a state in northern Mexico] to Minnesota,
De Tijuana a Nueva York.	From Tijuana [a border town south of San Diego] to New York.
Dos países son mi tierra.	Two countries are my homeland.
Los defiendo con mi honor.	I defend them with my honor.
Dos idiomas y dos países.	Two languages and two countries.
Dos culturas tengo yo.	Two cultures have I.
En mi suerte tengo orgullo.	I am proud of my luck.
Porque así lo manda Dios.	Because that's how God wills it.

*"MÉXICO-AMERICANO" words and music by Rumel Fuentes © by Tradition Music Co. (BMI) used with permission. Performed by Los Pingüinos Del Norte from the Arhoolie LP 3005 "CHULAS FRONTERAS"—the sound-track recording of the documentary film by the same title. For a complete catalog of historic Mexican-American recordings send $1 to ARHOOLIE RECORDS, 10341 San Pablo Ave., El Cerrito, CA 94530.

LECCIÓN 2

¿Quiénes somos?

LOS OBJETIVOS

Raising awareness

1. To understand how cultural conditioning interacts with personal experiences to form the uniqueness of each human being
2. To become familiar with the ethnic, social, historical, political, and economic differences among Hispanic groups living in the United States
3. To learn and practice Hispanic hand gestures

Comunicándose en español

1. To spell, recognize, and pronounce Spanish vowel sounds
2. To use appropriate expressions to discuss a client's national origin, citizenship, profession, and working papers
3. To use basic commands common to the work setting and to form direct formal commands and softened requests
4. To learn gender, number, and agreement of nouns and adjectives
5. To use the present tense of **ser** with identity and origin

Combinándolo todo

1. To integrate all material from previous sections by applying the knowledge in work-related communication activities
2. To hear and use gender and number references and agreement with nouns, adjectives, and verbs
3. To understand the sense of nationalism common to each Hispanic country through the appreciation of "La Borinqueña," the national anthem of Puerto Rico

Raising awareness

OVERVIEW: The relationship between individuals and their culture

Each of us is a unique human being. There will never be another you. For example, although it may be hard to conceive, no two sets of human fingerprints are exactly alike. Even our voice patterns can never be exactly duplicated. As the Spanish proverb states, *"Cada cabeza es un mundo"* ("Each head is a world"). Each person we meet offers a unique personality, unlike any other. It is this variety that makes life interesting and fascinating, especially for those of us who work in a field in which we are in constant contact with other human beings.

Yet, despite these differences, we all share a basic quality that might be termed *humanness.* This may be defined as a three-dimensional form consisting of mind, body, and emotions. Each of these components has its own set of needs, universal needs shared by all men and women. For example, the mind needs stimulation, in the form of input from external and internal sources. The body needs food and water, sleep and rest, air and exercise. It also needs to reproduce itself, the source of our sexual desires.

Emotional needs seem more complicated. The basic emotions may be reduced to four: *glad, sad, mad,* and *scared.* All four need to be expressed. Their repression can result in stress-induced physical and mental illness. In addition, human beings need to feel loved and appreciated and to find meaning in their lives. On the spiritual plane, there is a need to transcend the physical limits of this world and somehow make contact with an inner reality, the source of truth within.

With all these human needs and individual differences we can be compared to trees in a forest. Each is alike in its need for the basic elements of life and its dependence on the greater force of nature. Yet each is different, not only because of the species to which it belongs but also because of its specific circumstances—where it grows, the amount of light it receives, and other environmental factors.

E. M. CLARK

Somewhere between the concrete specific set of individual circumstances and the cosmic concept of *human being* lies the cultural imprinting each of us receives. The individual is born to a given set of parents, each of whom has, of course, come through a similar process. He or she then lives in a certain home, in a given location, in a particular country. This environment of birth and upbringing can be further defined in terms of geography, geology, topography, climate, all of which have some bearing on the type of life experiences the individual will encounter.

For the most part the individual's family shapes those early experiences that play a key role in the formation of the personality. Although the parental influence is usually considered the most important, the influence of siblings, extended family members, and friends can be significant. The educational background and religious beliefs of parents and other relatives also contribute greatly to the development of the individual's value system and behavior.

Besides the physical realities of place and people surrounding one's childhood, other sociological factors are also instrumental in shaping that individual's life patterns. One of the most in-fluential is social class and the economic condition of the family. The experience of being born and raised in Spanish Harlem in New York City, for example, will be quite different from that of growing up in Beverly Hills, California.

Into this sociological plane enters the concept of *cultural formation*. *Culture* evolves through the process of association among human beings. Indeed, there is a culture of being female as well as a culture of being male, a culture of poverty as well as a culture of the privileged. Nevertheless, we usually use the term *culture* to refer to a nationality—for example, American, Italian, Spanish, Mexican. Members of each of these groups share beliefs, norms, values, and behaviors agreed on through human association within the boundaries of a country.

Consequently, each of us is a complex individual, a combination of innate qualities, cultural conditioning, and personal experiences. Once we accept this vision of ourselves, we have found the secret to communicating across cultures—*see each person as the unique individual he or she is.*

Often, as we work with people on a day-to-day basis and concentrate on carrying out our work efficiently, we may lose sight of this uniqueness. The result is undoubtedly a loss on both sides of the communication process. It may take only a minute to refocus our gaze on the person in front of us in order to see the unique individual there rather than simply to stereotype him as the "Mexican undocumented worker" or her as the "pregnant Cuban female" or the teenager as the "Puerto Rican boy with a broken leg."

Despite the fact that all individuals are unique, there are behavior patterns and belief systems that are predictably determined by the *political* culture—that is, the country of origin. In working with Hispanic clients, it is helpful to have guidelines on some of the more predictable ways of behaving and thinking common in the various countries in Latin America.

In discussing "Hispanic" culture, we run into the same problem as in talking about the individual: the Spanish language unites many different political cultures such as those of Puerto Rico, Mexico, Cuba, Argentina, Spain, El Salvador, Chile, and Peru. These countries do share, to varying degrees, other similarities besides language, because of the heritage that Spain imparted to the New World through the colonization process. But it is erroneous to think of the cultures of all Hispanic countries as identical. Each has its own culture stemming from its historical development and the resultant present-day reality.

In this text those cultural factors that seem to be universally demonstrated in most Hispanic areas of the world are presented. There are no absolutes—a Mexican American third-generation Californian may be as different from a recently arrived Cuban refugee as a palm tree from a pine. Even among members of the same ethnic group, it is difficult to generalize owing to the impact of certain subcultural realities—social class, rural versus urban, male versus female, length of time in the United States—that exist *in addition to* the individual's own personal history and set of experiences.

As you learn some of the more common culturally determined behaviors and beliefs of the various Hispanic groups, you are reminded that these may not all apply to every Hispanic person you meet. Just as the language you hear may vary from the patterns presented in this text, so, too, may the effects of acculturation and assimilation vary—each person does not internalize all aspects of his or her native culture in the same way. In addition, the experience of living in a new culture will affect people in different ways, producing, at times, unexpected behaviors—hybrids due to the mix of culture + individual + new experiences. Do rely on Hispanic colleagues and on the clients themselves to help you unravel some of the complexities of cross-cultural living and working. Above all, if you remember to focus on the uniqueness of each Hispanic client you meet, your experiences in communicating across cultural boundaries will be more rewarding and enriching.

Applications

The following are generalizations often made about the mainstream cultural patterns in the United States. Decide whether or not each generalization accurately describes your own personal value and belief systems.

1. In informal situations in U.S. homes, people tend to be very casual about how they sit. They may sit on the floor, slouch in chairs, and/or put their feet on the furniture when they relax.

2. Frankness is valued in all aspects of communication in the United States. One is expected to "tell it like it is" rather than to tell white lies in order to please someone.

3. Although U.S. citizens may be proud of their country's achievements, they are also quick to criticize its failures and shortcomings, although they do not usually appreciate a nonnative doing the same.

4. A fast, efficient pace is kept in most circles of life in the United States. The general feeling is that the more that is accomplished in one day, the better.

5. Most U.S. citizens feel that every individual is in charge of his or her own destiny and that with motivation, determination, and hard work anyone can achieve his or her own dreams.

6. There is a preoccupation with youth in the United States, coupled with a lack of reverence for the aged.

7. Teenagers in the United States may date as young as age thirteen or fourteen, but definitely by age sixteen or eighteen. Dates are not chaperoned and young people may date many different people before getting married. Premarital sex has become more accepted, and birth control is easily available.

8. The nuclear family is the norm; that is, grandparents usually live elsewhere, and children are encouraged to move out to be on their own as soon as they are financially able.

9. Personal freedom is highly valued in the United States. Many people operate on the principle that "if it feels good, do it."

10. Americans tend to eat a relatively heavy breakfast of eggs, toast, or pancakes, juice and coffee, a light lunch of a salad, sandwich, or fast-food item, and the main meal of the day, usually a leisurely event in the early evening, consisting of meat, vegetables, and salad.

Reflections

A. How does your personal culture vary with regard to those statements you feel do not describe your values and beliefs? What accounts for the difference(s)?

B. Did your parents' ethnic background influence your responses? In what way(s)?

C. Did any of the above generalizations personally offend you? Which one(s)? Why?

D. Would you like to change or modify any of the cultural descriptions that apply to you? Which ones? Which would be the most difficult for you to modify, and why?

E. List below three statements similar to those listed in "Applications" that you feel describe Hispanic cultures:

1. _____

2. _____

3. _____

HISTORICAL PERSPECTIVE: A Mexican is not a Cuban is not a Puerto Rican is not a Guatemalan

The world the Spaniards "discovered" in 1492 was a mosaic of different indigenous groups. Some had achieved very sophisticated social organization and scientific knowledge (the Incas of Peru, Ecuador, and parts of Colombia and Bolivia; the Aztecs of Central Mexico; the Mayas of Central America). Others (e.g., the Chibchas in Colombia, the Araucanos in Chile, and the Taínos in Puerto Rico) were less extensive, more regionally developed groups. A third type of indigenous peoples included the more nomadic, less evolved tribes inhabiting Venezuela, Paraguay, Argentina, and other regions of the eastern coast of South America.

The nature of the contact with the colonizing Spaniards differed for each group, depending on when it occurred, the extensiveness and development of the indigenous culture, and the needs and objectives of the Spaniards. For example, in the Caribbean islands, the site of the first Spanish settlements in the New World, the indigenous populations died out quite rapidly, succumbing to smallpox and other diseases introduced by the Europeans and to the unaccustomed rigors of the hard labor to which they were subjected. The latter involved building forts and churches out of stone, common in Europe but an anathema to the native architectural style and climatic conditions of the tropics. Later, when the economic worth of the cultivation of sugarcane and tobacco on these same islands was recognized, Africans were brought in as slaves to replace the defunct indigenous population. Thus, the basic racial mixture in these islands was first Spanish and Indian and later Spanish, Indian, and African, even though few traces now remain of the indigenous populations.

In those areas of the east coast of South America where most of the Indian tribes were more nomadic and less evolved, the few that survived were insufficient to produce much of a racial mix. Although some Africans were brought to these areas for slave labor (predominantly by the Portuguese in Brazil), most of the settlers were Spaniards. Except for Brazil, the east coast is mostly Caucasian in origin, with little of the racial mixture common to the Caribbean or to the rest of Latin America.

In areas of highly developed indigenous populations — the Andean countries of Colombia, Ecuador, Peru, and Bolivia, as well as the central plateau regions of Mexico and much of Central America, which were colonized some twenty to fifty years later than the Caribbean — there was more resistance to the diseases and hard labor introduced by the Spaniards. This was due partly to the more structured lifestyle of the Indians, which the colonizers put to use in mining and construction work, and partly to the cooler temperatures of the mountains as opposed to the more difficult climate of the tropics. Although some Africans were also brought in to work in these areas, the basic mixture of races that resulted from the colonial period is that of Indian and Spaniard. Thus one sees three basic types of cultural interaction: that of the *mestizo* (Indian + Spaniard), common to Mexico, Central America, and western (or Andean) South America, that of the European or primarily Caucasian population of eastern and central (non-Andean) South America (excluding Brazil), which has been increased by large immigrations from western Europe in this century, and the third of the Caribbean *mulato* (Indian + Spaniard + African, or in the case of Brazil, African + Portuguese), often referred to as *criollo* within the Spanish-speaking Caribbean Islands.

---

1. *Define the three types of indigenous groups the Spaniards met, indicating the areas where each lived.*
2. *Describe the three basic racial mixtures found in Latin America and tell where each predominates and why.*

It is not just skin color or facial or bodily features that illustrate the different heritages of these three groups of people. The mixture of cultural elements, including religion, values, foods, patterns of male–female interaction, as well as the inevitable linguistic blending due to the mutual contact between coexisting languages, add to the colorful mosaic of the Spanish-speaking world known as Latin America.

In addition, each country that has evolved in one of these three geographic/cultural regions has had a different history and in this century faces its own realities: the discovery of oil in Venezuela and Mexico, the socialist economic system of Cuba, the current status of Puerto Rico as a commonwealth of the United States, the extensive Mexican heritage, which continues to be an integral part of the continental United States, and the political struggles of El Salvador, Nicaragua, and Guatemala in Central America.

Any attempt to understand Hispanics in the United States must take into account the realities of their native countries as well as the facts of life regarding immigration. The latter include the newcomers' conflict regarding acculturation to the dominant society and the maintenance of their cultural and linguistic identity. The melting-pot myth of cultural assimilation does not hold water in a discussion of the situation of Hispanics in the United States. Since most Latin American Hispanics show evidence of mixed races, they have a harder time blending in than do Caucasian western European immigrants. Many encounter racism in their personal and professional lives. Those who have decided to assimilate and have been able to do so may feel they have betrayed their roots and their own cultural identity in joining the mainstream culture.

The total number of Hispanics living in the United States is estimated at nearly 17 million people, roughly 8 percent of the total population, according to 1985 census figures. Many Hispanic groups feel these numbers are grossly underestimated, because of both the large numbers of un-documented workers who evade being counted and certain inadequacies of the census forms and methods used. Their calculations indicate that between 9 and 12 percent of the population is Hispanic. Trends extrapolated from the census data indicate that, at current immigration levels, the Hispanic population will double by the year 2000. Since Hispanic Americans have a lower median age and produce more children per couple than white non-Hispanics, it is predicted that within the next century the numbers of Latinos in the United States will virtually equal that of white non-Hispanics, each accounting for approximately one-third of the population (with Asians and blacks making up the remaining third).

---

3. *List several cultural factors that may vary among Hispanic groups and explain what accounts for the variance.*
4. *Describe what the current census figures indicate regarding the present and future Hispanic population of the United States.*

Although official figures regarding the various ethnic groups counted under the term *Hispanic* are incomplete, it is agreed that Mexican Americans[1] make up the largest group of U.S.

---

1. *Chicano* is another term used by choice by many, but not all, Mexican Americans, in order to emphasize the relevance of their cultural heritage to their personal identity. The term *La Raza* or *La Causa* is used to refer to their cultural unity and the struggle for its preservation. *Atzlán* is used to refer to what was once Mexican territory in the U.S.

Hispanics. Nearly 80 percent of Mexican Americans live in the southwestern United States, especially in California, Arizona, New Mexico, Colorado, and Texas, in what was once Mexican territory, originally settled by Spanish and mestizo settlers as early as the sixteenth century. Many Mexican Americans also live in northern cities, including Chicago, Detroit, and Toledo, and in rural communities as far north as Vancouver and Toronto, Canada, the terminal points of the various migrant-farm-worker routes.

As a result of the Mexican–American War (1846-1848), a response to the continued western expansionist movement of the United States government, the Treaty of Guadalupe Hidalgo of 1848 granted U.S. citizenship to Mexicans who chose to remain in the conquered territories. They were also guaranteed full religious, civil, and political rights, including the right to equal protection and treatment under the U.S. Constitution, as well as the freedom to maintain their property, culture, and language.

Although religious freedom for Mexican Americans has been maintained, their other rights have been violated often as they have been the object of racial discrimination in what was once their own homeland. Many Anglos who have migrated to those areas have looked upon their Mexican American neighbors as a source of cheap labor, rejecting them as equals because of their different culture, language, and ethnic identity. Although many Mexican American citizens have been integrated and assimilated into the American mainstream, many others have maintained their cultural ties to Mexico. Unlike immigrants from Europe, there is no ocean separating the old country from the new. The shared border with Mexico has seen the continued immigration of both documented and undocumented workers lured by the promise of better economic gain (although they are often underpaid and mistreated by large farm owners and factory owners who are not obligated to pay the required wages and benefits "legal" workers protected by the Constitution would earn). The long-established influence of Mexican culture in the Southwest, especially in architecture, food, and religion, has kept Mexican Americans in constant contact with their homeland.

The Puerto Rican story is different. Unlike most of its Latin American neighbors, Puerto Rico has never truly controlled its own destiny, although it spent most of the second half of the nineteenth century trying to liberate itself from Spanish domination. At the same time, Cuba was also involved in its fight for independence. In 1898, the mysterious explosion of the battleship *Maine* in the Havana harbor brought the United States into the war with Spain. Both Cuba and Puerto Rico did succeed in gaining their independence, the latter very briefly. Nevertheless, the United States continued to war with Spain. The Treaty of Paris in 1899 ended the war, declaring Puerto Rico to be a possession of the U.S. government, despite the protests of the island inhabitants. Thus, the island of Puerto Rico merely changed hands from one owner to another, while Cuba retained its newly won freedom.

The influence of North American culture has triggered vast changes in the culture of Puerto Rico. The Puerto Ricans[2] themselves often have had very little choice in the matter. Earlier in this century, there was an abortive attempt to replace Spanish with English as the official language of education. American holidays were instituted and an American governor, appointed by the U.S. government, ruled over the island. In 1917 the Congress of the United States voted limited U.S. citizenship for the Puerto Rican people, requiring mandatory U.S. military service for eligible males.

Puerto Ricans are exempt from U.S. income tax, paying rather high island income taxes instead. Island residents are not allowed to vote in U.S. presidential elections, although Puerto Ricans who meet state residency requirements on the mainland can do so. Puerto Rico has no elected representatives in the U.S. House or Senate, although there is one nonvoting representative in the House who serves mostly as a liaison between the mainland government and the island.

The American presence and influence have also brought about economic changes on the island, transforming it from a basically agricultural economy to an industrial one, which now must import over half of its food supplies. In turn, the rural lifestyle of the island has changed to an

---

2. *Borinqueño* and *boricua*, terms derived from *Boriquén*, the original indigenous name for the island, are also used by choice by many Puerto Ricans to refer to themselves and their cultural heritage.

urban one. U.S. business firms have been offered economic incentives to locate industries in Puerto Rico. While the increasing industrialization has given rise to a larger middle class, salaries at all professional levels are lower in Puerto Rico than on the mainland. At the same time, the cost of living in San Juan is now higher than that in most mainland cities. High unemployment and extensive reliance on government assistance have become the norm for many in recent years.

As U.S. citizens, Puerto Ricans may migrate to the mainland without visas or migration quotas and have been encouraged to do so at various times through the combined efforts of the United States government and the private sector, especially after 1940. Manhattan became the first settlement point for these early migrants. Currently, large communities of Puerto Rican citizens can be found in cities in many eastern states, including Connecticut, New Jersey, Pennsylvania, and Massachusetts. Chicago, which has the greatest mix of the various Hispanic groups of any U.S. city, also has a large Puerto Rican community, as do other southeastern and midwestern states.

There has been constant migration, with families (or family members) coming and going between the mainland and the island. Some Puerto Ricans born on the mainland, often referred to as *Nuyoricans* ("New York Ricans"), have sought to reestablish their roots and those of their children by returning to the island. In addition, Puerto Rico, already a very densely populated island, has attracted immigrants from other Caribbean islands, especially from Cuba and the Dominican Republic.

The question of alternatives for the status of Puerto Rico dominates the island political scene and, occasionally, the mainland political agenda. The three prevalent political views regarding the status of the island are: (1) a continuation of the commonwealth (in Spanish, *Estado Libre Asociado*) as is or with greater autonomy and diversity in economic relations, (2) Puerto Rican statehood, and (3) independence. Any change in the status of Puerto Rico would create problems as well as solve them with regard to citizenship, residency, language, and the island's economy.

The Cuban population forms the third largest group of Hispanics in the United States. In the second half of the nineteenth century significant numbers of Cubans established colonies in Florida, primarily in Tampa and Key West (still called by many *Cayo Hueso*). These were refugees from the war with Spain. Their descendants still make up a large segment of the population of these two cities. The next large influx from this independent island came in 1959 as a result of the Cuban Revolution's overthrow of the Batista re-

gime, a dictatorship that had ruled the island from the mid-1930s. The United States had maintained friendly relations with Batista and had strong economic ties with the island because of the large sugarcane industry and the tourist attractions of Havana, for years the tropical playground for many wealthy North Americans.

Castro's takeover, which began as a social revolution to distribute more equitably the riches of a virtual two-class society, led to the exodus of many from the wealthy and professional class to Miami and Puerto Rico. They brought with them their well-developed professional and entrepreneurial skills, skills that are often lacking in the rural migrants from Mexico and Puerto Rico who come with only a rudimentary formal education. These twentieth-century Cuban immigrants were soon able to reestablish themselves economically in Dade County, Florida. Today Miami is often considered the Spanish-speaking capital of the United States in terms of services, businesses, schools, and medical facilities which meet the needs of many of the wealthy members of the upper classes from other Latin American countries as well. Much to the chagrin of many Anglo Miamians, Miami has become a bilingual city.

Many semiskilled and unskilled workers, often disenchanted with the lack of goods and freedom in Castro's socialist state, began to immigrate to the United States in the late 1960s and 1970s. They were attracted by the jobs offered in factories and industries owned and operated by Cubans whose strong sense of ethnic ties encourages "the taking care of one's own." The most recent emigration from Cuba was that of the famous *Marielitos* in 1980. It brought not only many unskilled and semiskilled workers but also former mental hospital patients and prisoners (although it must be remembered that in a totalitarian state, people can be imprisoned or committed to mental institutions for so-called crimes against the state—that is, opposition to the regime). Many of these later immigrants have settled in other areas along the southeastern coast of the United States; farther north in New Jersey, New York, and Chicago; and in other large urban areas, including Los Angeles. In some areas, especially in Miami and Los Angeles, an increase in crime has been attributed to some of the *Marielitos.*

Cuban Americans, on the average, enjoy the highest per capita income of any of the three larg-

"Portrait of Farabundo Marti"
Batik © 1982 by Lisa Kokin

est U.S. Hispanic groups. Like their other U.S. Hispanic counterparts, however, they have not attained a proportionate level of political power. This has been attributed to the desire of many older Cubans to reestablish their life in Cuba by working to overthrow Fidel Castro's regime.

The most recent immigration of Hispanics to the United States has been a political exodus from Central America. These include members of the *Contra* forces, supporters of the former right-wing Somoza regime in Nicaragua who actively support the overthrow of the current Sandinista government in their homeland. In addition, members of the rebel forces in El Salvador have come seeking asylum from the political repression from the United States–backed government currently in power. Guatemalan refugees also seek to escape the political upheavals in their own land related to the internal conflicts of their Central American neighbors. The largest majority of Central American immigrants live in the Southwest, primarily in Los Angeles and Texas, although there exist long-standing Salvadoran communities in Washington, D.C., and San Francisco.

Although the U.S. government rarely offers political asylum to Salvadorans and Guatemalans, an increasing number of churches and communities throughout the United States have elected to offer sanctuary to those fleeing political repression in these countries. The legality of this form of political asylum is currently being tested in the U.S. court system.

---

5. *Name the four largest groups of Hispanics residing in the United States and the areas in which they live.*
6. *Describe the historical factors that account for the presence of these Hispanic groups in the United States.*

Political disenfranchisement is one characteristic common to all Hispanic groups living in the United States. Mexican Americans, for example, for years have been excluded by Anglo politicians who control the various state political power machines in the southwest. In addition, the political heritage of Mexico, which has been in the hands of a single political party for over fifty years, the PRI (Partido Revolucionario Institucional), has not given the recent Mexican immigrant ample experience in working within a more democratically run election system. Puerto Ricans, while very active in their political parties on the island, where they now elect their own governor, have not been as active in mainland politics. This may be due to the confusing differences in political rights for mainland and island residents as well as the continued back-and-forth migration pattern and the demands of the struggle to survive in a new environment. Cuban Americans have only recently begun to focus more on U.S. politics and less on those of their homeland.

Those Hispanics who do participate actively in U.S. politics tend to vote along class and ideological lines. Mexicans and Puerto Ricans, who are mostly in the working class, usually vote Democratic. Cubans, who are mostly middle class, tend to vote Republican. For the most part, they support President Reagan's foreign policy in Latin America, while the other Hispanic groups do not.

There are some signs of united political action among U.S. Hispanics (for example, LULAC—the League of United Latin American Citizens) to achieve political representation at all levels commensurate with their total population. Attempts to consolidate efforts and pull together politically are often thwarted by the fierce sense of nationalism that is still a part of the Hispanic tradition. Often U.S. Hispanic groups focus more on the cultural differences which separate them as each struggles to preserve its ethnic identity while acculturating to the U.S. economic and political mainstream. Ironically, the mainstream is often oblivious to these differences, viewing Hispanics as a single group with a single set of problems. The mosaic made up of U.S. Hispanics continues to be colorful and complex.

---

7. *What accounts for the disproportionate level of political power among U.S. Hispanic groups?*
8. *How do the histories of Mexico, Puerto Rico, and Cuba affect U.S. residents from those countries with regard to their participation in mainland politics?*

NONVERBAL COMMUNICATION: Hand gestures

Although we primarily use words to convey our thoughts and feelings, we also communicate *nonverbally* by using our bodies to give messages. Our fingers and hands, arms and legs, heads and eyes, noses and mouths, even our posture enhance the communication process by sending out signals. At times, our body language communicates for us when we are completely silent. We may not remember learning any of these gestures or postures overtly, but we did subconsciously incorporate them into our own communication repertoire by imitating the people around us.

People from different cultures learn different ways of communicating with their bodies. When trying to communicate across cultural boundaries, it is very easy to misread the other's body language if we are not aware of the differences. Unless one learns to use and interpret *both* the verbal and nonverbal means of sending messages, it is impossible to communicate fully with someone raised in the culture where another language is spoken. Often nonverbal messages convey more of the truth than the words spoken, giving us a clearer insight into what an individual is really thinking.

In general, Hispanics tend to use more nonverbal gestures than do Anglos, and often communicate effectively without speaking a word. You will need to retrain your eye as well as your ear, "looking for" language as well as listening for it. Training yourself to become more sensitive to nonverbal language in the cross-cultural communication context can also aid your communication skills in your native language. Awareness is the key to effective communication in any language.

The following finger and hand gestures are commonly used, with slight variation, throughout the Hispanic world. Variations are indicated by either (PR) (Puerto Rican), (M) (Mexican), and (C) (Cuban). As with all linguistic and cultural information presented in this text, the following are guidelines regarding *behaviors that may or may not be used by an individual Hispanic client.* Rely on the native speakers with whom you work as ultimate authorities.

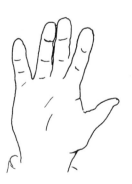

Gesture: Elbow bent at waist level, right hand up, palm out, fingers spread apart.

Meaning: Espere un momento. (Wait a moment.)

Gesture: Thumb and/or index finger held parallel, separated about an inch.

Meaning: Pequeño (PR) (talking about something small); *Momentito* (M) (Just a moment.)

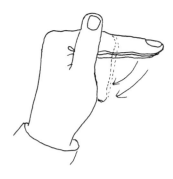

Gesture: Hand held above head, palm out, fingers snapping open and closed several times. (This gesture is often confused with the American "goodbye" gesture.)

Meaning: Ven acá (Come here). Used to call someone at a distance after calling his or her name.

Gesture: Index finger moved from side to side (may be accompanied by clicking sound of tongue against upper palate).

Meaning: ¡No! (usually in response to a question or invitation).

Gesture: Elbow bent at waist level, hand held comfortably in front, palm up, thumb rubbed against index finger several times.

Meaning: Dinero (money).

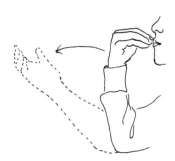

Gesture: Elbow bent at chest level, bunched fingers and thumb touch lips, then suddenly open as they recede.

Meaning: ¡Estupendo!; ¡Fantástico! (Great!)

Gesture: Elbow bent at waist level, bunched fingers and thumb move back and forth at wrist toward mouth.

Meaning: Comer (to eat).

Gesture: Elbow bent loosely at chest level, thumb and pinky finger, or thumb alone (C) extended with middle fingers touching palm, thumb lowered and raised several times near mouth.

Meaning: Tomar (to drink).

Gesture: Right elbow bent at chest level, then hit several times with closed left fist (PR, C); *left* elbow bent at chest level, then hit several times by open right palm (M).

Meaning: Tacaño (miserly).

Gesture: Arm stretched above head, palm out, fingers loosely open, hand waved side to side (PR, C). Arm stretched above head, palm facing in, with four fingers of hand opened and closed several times (M). (This looks like the American "come here" gesture.)

Meaning: Adiós, hasta luego. (Good-bye.)

Putting it into practice

1. Can you recall an instance where someone's body language communicated something different from what was said? Describe it.

2. Are there any hand or finger gestures which you are aware of using regularly? What are they and what do they mean? How did you learn them?

3. Using the Hispanic cultural variation most appropriate to the area in which you live, "say" the following in Spanish *without* words:

   a. He's a miser.
   b. It's a question of money.
   c. Juan, come here. (You may shout, "*¡Juan! ¡Ven acá!*")
   d. That's the best thing I've heard in a long time.
   e. Absolutely not!
   f. I'm going out drinking.
   g. Wait, hold on a minute.
   h. Hey, I want to eat!
   i. See you later.
   j. It was so tiny.

Comunicándose en español

PRONUNCIACIÓN: Las vocales

There are five vowels in Spanish: **a, e, i, o, u.** *All* are pronounced as short, crisp sounds, even when they do not receive the main emphasis in a word or phrase. This contrasts with English, which tends to diphthongize, that is, to draw out vowels, while reducing others to an *uh* sound (called a *schwa*), like the *e* in *the* and the *i* in *possible*.

Práctica

Following the model of the instructor or the tape, pronounce these pairs of similar words in English and Spanish. Note that the final vowel is not diphthongized in the Spanish words.

English	Spanish	English	Spanish
may	**me**	low	**lo**
say	**se**	no	**no**
see	**si**	two	**tú**
tea	**ti**	Sue	**su**

Now say these words, taking care to pronounce each vowel clearly and crisply.

a—Spanish **a** is similar to the English *ah* sound as in *father*, only shorter.

la	nada	habla	mañana
más	pasa	llama	trabaja

e—Spanish **e** is similar to the English vowel sound in *egg*, only shorter. You may hear slight variations in the pronunciation of this vowel, depending on the region from which the Spanish speaker comes.

de	tres	hable	Elena
se	que	pase	bastante

i—Spanish **i** is similar to the English *ee* sound in *feet*, only shorter. **Y** alone, meaning *and*, has the same sound.

y	mil	dice	repita
mi	así	escribe	Felipe

o—Spanish **o** is similar to the English *o* sound in *open*, only shorter.

yo	como	doctor	permiso
con	poco	dolor	entonces

u—Spanish **u** is similar to the English *oo* sound in *moon*, only shorter.

su	Cuba	saludos	preocupe
tú	mucho	ninguna	Jesusita

Pronounce these sentences in Spanish, paying special attention to the vowel sounds.

1. Mucho gusto en conocerlo, señor Fernández.
2. No tengo problemas en el trabajo.
3. Hasta mañana, señorita Solís.
4. ¿Cómo se llama su marido, señora?

Dictado 📼

Now write the words and sentences your instructor will pronounce.

1. _____   4. _____   7. _____

2. _____   5. _____   8. _____

3. _____   6. _____   9. _____

10. _____

11. _____

12. _____

¿Ha entendido bien?

1. ¿Cómo se llama el cliente?
2. ¿Es puertorriqueño o cubano el cliente?
3. La empleada es cubana, ¿verdad?
4. ¿Cómo se dice *empleo* en Cuba?
5. En Puerto Rico, ¿cómo se dice?
6. En México, ¿cómo se dice?
7. ¿Qué quiere decir *pega* en Puerto Rico?
8. ¿Cómo se dice *goma de pegar* en México?
9. ¿Tiene la señora un empleo para el señor Aguirre?
10. ¿Qué quiere decir el verbo *pegar* en la frase: *Aquí tengo una pega que "pega"*?

INTRODUCTORY DIALOGUE: How do you say . . . ?

The employee: What can I do for you, Mr. Aguirre?

The client: I need a *pega*, ma'am.

E: I'm very sorry. I don't understand. What does *pega* mean?

C: In Cuba it's a job. You are not Cuban, are you?

E: No, I'm Mexican. In Mexico, they say *chamba*.

C: Also in Puerto Rico. There *pega* means *glue*.

E: *Goma de pegar?* Ah, now I understand. They say *pegadura* in Mexico. Well, Mr. Aguirre, I have here a "job" that "sticks" (also "hits the mark").

C: Great!

BASIC STRUCTURES I: At the employment office

The employee (f.)	*The client (m.)*
	May I (come in)?
Yes. Come in.	Good afternoon, ma'am.
Good afternoon sir. What can I do for you?	Are you Mrs. Carmen Molina?
Yes, I am. And you, sir, what's your name?	My name is Enrique González. Are you (a) Puerto Rican?
No, I'm (a) Cuban. I'm from Santiago. What nationality are you?	I'm (a) Mexican.
Are you a citizen of the United States?	I'm not, but my wife is. She's Puerto Rican.
Then you need a green card in order to work, don't you?	Yes, Mrs. Molina.

¿Sabe usted?

1. Since Puerto Ricans are U.S. citizens, marriage to a Puerto Rican confers immediate permanent residence in the United States or its possessions to someone from another country. The spouse can apply for citizenship after three years, instead of the normal five-year waiting period.

2. A *green card* is a work permit granted to legal residents of the United States. A *white card* (**tarjeta blanca**) allows residents of another country to work in the United States (common in border areas).

3. In Spanish, one does not use the indefinite article (**un** or **una**) when identifying someone as belonging to a given ethnic group, religion, profession, political party, etc. **Soy cubana** is the equivalent of both *I'm Cuban* and *I'm a Cuban*. The names of such groups are not capitalized in Spanish.

4. The definite article (**el, la, los, las**) is used when using a title + last name to refer to someone: **¿Es Ud. la señora Molina?** When addressing someone by that title, the article is omitted: **Sí, señora Molina.**

5. **Soy yo** is the correct way to identify oneself (equivalent of *That's me, It is I, I am*). The pronoun **yo** must be used in this context.

6. **EE.UU.** is the abbreviated form of **Estados Unidos.**

7. **¿Verdad?** is added to the end of a statement in order to verify its contents and is the equivalent of *Do you?, Aren't you?, Isn't it?*, etc., in English.

ESTRUCTURAS BÁSICAS I: En la oficina de empleo 🔘

La empleada	*El cliente*
	¿Se puede?
Sí. Pase Ud.	Buenas tardes, señora.
Buenas tardes, señor. ¿En qué puedo servirle?	¿Es Ud. la señora Carmen Molina?
Sí, soy yo. Y Ud., señor, ¿cómo se llama?	Me llamo Enrique González. ¿Es usted puertorriqueña?
No, soy cubana. Soy de Santiago. ¿De qué nacionalidad es Ud.?	Yo soy mexicano.
¿Es Ud. ciudadano de los Estados Unidos?	Yo, no, pero mi esposa, sí. Ella es puertorriqueña.
Entonces, Ud. necesita una tarjeta verde para trabajar, ¿verdad?	Sí, señora Molina.

Notas lingüísticas I

A. There are several verbs in Spanish that are the equivalents of *to be* in English. For now, it is best simply to remember the contexts in which each is used. In this lesson, **ser** is used to identify name, profession, religious or political affiliation, and other characteristics that define a person or thing.

ser + noun, pronoun or adjective that identifies:

Soy yo.　　　　¿*Es* usted la señora Carmen Molina?
Soy cubana.　　¿*Es* usted puertorriqueña?
¿*Es* usted ciudadano de los Estados Unidos?

It is also used to identify place of origin:

ser + **de** + place of origin

Yo *soy* **de Santiago.**　¿*Es* usted de aquí?

B. The verb **ser** is irregular. These are its forms in the present tense.

yo **soy**	nosotros/as **somos**
tú **eres**	
Ud., él, ella **es**	Uds., ellos/as **son**

BASIC STRUCTURES II: At the employment office

	The employee (f.)		*The client (m.)*	

What line of work are you in?
(In what do you work?)

I'm a
- dentist.
- lawyer.
- doctor.
- social worker.
- businessman.
- language teacher.

Does your wife work, too?

She's a(n)
- psychologist.
- nurse.
- elementary school teacher.
- secretary.
- accountant.
- housewife.

You have to fill out several
- documents.
- forms.
- papers.

Yes, I understand.

Please
- sit down over there.
- come here.
- wait a moment.
- follow me.
- take them.
- call this telephone number.
- write to this address.
- come back later.
- speak with the receptionist.
- go to that office.

Yes, of course.

¿Sabe usted?

1. The following anglicisms are commonly heard (the standard Spanish expression is given in parentheses):

Trabajo en una *factoría* (fábrica).	I work in a factory.
Necesito una *aplicación* (solicitud).	I need an application.
Mi esposa es *norsa* (PR—enfermera).	My wife is a nurse.
No puede *venir para atrás* (volver).	He can't come back.
No quiero *ir para atrás* (volver).	I don't want to go back.

2. Both **psicóloga** and **sicóloga** are accepted spellings.

3. **Tener + que + infinitive** is used to express an obligation. (**Tengo que volver.** = I have to return.)

4. *Yes-no* questions in Spanish begin with the verb form, followed by the subject (if expressed) and the rest of the sentence:

Statement	*Yes-no question*
Ud. es médico.	**¿Es Ud. médico?**

ESTRUCTURAS BÁSICAS II: En la oficina de empleo 📼

La empleada		El cliente	
¿En qué trabaja Ud.?		Yo soy	dentista. abogado. médico. trabajador social. hombre de negocios. profesor de lenguas.
¿También trabaja su esposa?		Ella es	(p)sicóloga. enfermera. maestra de primaria. secretaria. contadora. ama de casa.
Ud. tiene que llenar ciertos	documentos. formularios. papeles.	Sí, comprendo.	
Siéntese allí, Venga aquí, Espere un momento, Sígame, Tómelos, Llame a este teléfono, Escriba a esta dirección, Vuelva Ud. más tarde, Hable con la recepcionista, Vaya a esa oficina,	por favor.	Sí, cómo no.	

---

5. Negative sentences in Spanish are formed by placing **no** *before* the verb (and *after* the subject, if it is expressed):

    Affirmative   *Negative*
    (Yo) soy dentista.   **(Yo)** *no* **soy dentista.**

6. Negative answers to yes–no questions begin with a **no** to respond negatively; a second **no** is placed before the verb to make the rest of the sentence negative:

    ¿Es Ud. colombiana?   *No, no* **soy colombiana.**

7. **Maestro/a** is normally used for elementary teachers, **profesor/a** for high school and college teachers.

8. A noun used to describe another noun follows this rule: noun + **de** + noun:

    maestra de primaria   elementary school teacher
    profesor de lenguas   language teacher

9. **De** is used to express possession in Spanish:

    la esposa de Rafael   Rafael's wife
    la solicitud de la cliente   the client's application

10.   There are only two contractions in Spanish:

del = de + el   **al = a + el**

Vaya Ud. *al* Departamento de Empleo.
Vaya Ud. a la oficina *del* doctor Franco.

Notas lingüísticas II

A.   As you may have noticed, you must be careful when talking about males and females in Spanish, since terms that refer to each must have the appropriate ending. You must also consider whether you are talking about one or more than one, since terms describing people reflect both number and gender. Just as people have gender (male or female) and number (singular or plural), *all* nouns in Spanish are classified as *masculine* or *feminine, singular,* or *plural*. The gender classification has little to do with reality; for example, men wear **corbatas** (*neckties*), a feminine noun, and women wear **vestidos** (*dresses*), a masculine noun.

1.   The ending of a noun is a fairly reliable clue to its gender, although there are some exceptions. It is important to learn the gender of each noun you add to your vocabulary.

a.   Most nouns ending in **-a, -d, -ión,** and **-sis** are feminine.

b.   Most nouns ending in **-o, -l, -n, -s,** and **-r** are masculine.

c.   Exceptions are noted as such in most dictionaries. Two nouns in *Lección 1* are irregular in that they end in **-a** but are masculine: **el día** and **el problema.**

2.   To form the plural of nouns, add **-s** to those ending in **-o, -a,** or **-e** and **-es** to those ending in a consonant.

Example: **el hij*o***   **los hijo*s***
                 la tard*e*   **las tarde*s***
                 el pape*l*   **los pape*les***

3.   The definite article (equivalent to *the* in English) has four forms to agree with the gender and number of the noun it refers to:

	Singular	*Plural*
Masculine	**el**	**los**
Feminine	**la**	**las**

4.   The indefinite article (equivalent to *a* or *an* in English) is used mostly in the singular, although its plural form exists and is the equivalent of *some* in English:

	Singular	*Plural*
Masculine	**un**	**unos**
Feminine	**una**	**unas**

5. Study the following list of professions, focusing on the differences for gender and number and on the agreement of the definite article. Notice that nouns referring to professions that end in a consonant have *four* forms (e.g., **profesor, profesora, profesores, profesoras**).

Female		Male	
Singular	*Plural*	*Singular*	*Plural*
el abogado	los abogados	la abogada	las abogadas
el médico	los médicos	la médica	las médicas
el psicólogo	los psicólogos	la psicóloga	las psicólogas
el secretario	los secretarios	la secretaria	las secretarias
el enfermero	los enfermeros	la enfermera	las enfermeras
el maestro	los maestros	la maestra	las maestras
el doctor	los doctores	la doctora	las doctoras
el profesor	los profesores	la profesora	las profesoras
el contador	los contadores	la contadora	las contadoras
el trabajador social	los trabajadores sociales	la trabajadora social	las trabajadoras sociales

a. Professions ending in **-a** usually have one form for both masculine and feminine:

el dentista	los dentistas	la dentista	las dentistas
el artista	los artistas	la artista	las artistas

b. Only recently have Hispanic women in the United States and Latin America entered into traditionally male professions. Thus, some of the above feminine forms are not officially listed in the dictionary, and their usage varies.

B. Words that describe nouns are adjectives. They must agree in gender and number with the nouns they describe.

L*a* **clien***te* **es puertorriqueñ***a*.
Manuel y Rafael son cuban*os*.
No es ningun*a* **molesti***a*.
Usted necesita ciert*as* **solicitud***es*.
Tengo ciert*os* **document***os*.

1. Adjectives that end in **-o** have four forms (masculine, feminine, singular, and plural). Those adjectives ending in **-e** or a *consonant* have only two, singular and plural. To form the plural, add **-s** to adjectives ending in a vowel and **-es** to those ending in a consonant.

	Singular	*Plural*
Masculine	**cuban***o*	**cuban***os*
Feminine	**cuban***a*	**cuban***as*
Masculine/Feminine	**verd***e*	**verd***es*
	liber*al*	**liber***ales*

2. Study the following list of Latin American countries and the corresponding adjectives of nationality. Those with similar endings have been grouped together as a study aid. Notice that adjectives of nationality are not capitalized in Spanish.

Cuba	cubano	El Salvador	salvadoreño
México	mexicano	Panamá	panameño
(El) Perú	peruano	(El) Brasil	brasileño
La República Dominicana	dominicano	Honduras	hondureño
Venezuela	venezolano	Puerto Rico	puertorriqueño
Colombia	colombiano	(El) Paraguay	paraguayo
(El) Ecuador	ecuatoriano	(El) Uruguay	uruguayo
Bolivia	boliviano		
Nicaragua	nicaragüense	Chile	chileno
Costa Rica	costarricense		
Guatemala	guatemalteco	(La) Argentina	argentino

C. Command forms are used to tell someone to do something. The following command forms were introduced in Lessons 1 and 2. Practice them until you can use them without difficulty. Make sure that you know the meaning of each. Check "Estructuras básicas" for any you are not sure of.

Repita Ud.	**Hable Ud. más despacio.**
Pase Ud.	**Espere un momento.**
Siéntese.	**Vuelva Ud. más tarde.**
Sígame.	**Llame a este número.**
Tómelos.	**Escriba a esta dirección.**
Vaya a esta oficina.	**Hable con la recepcionista.**

1. The use of **Ud.** with the command forms is optional.

2. Object pronouns (e.g., **me, los, se** = *me, them, yourself*) are attached to the affirmative commands. The forms for these pronouns will be discussed in subsequent chapters.

3. **Por favor** may precede or follow the command and is used to soften the effect of giving a direct order.

4. When giving a direct command to two or more people, simply add **-n** to the **usted** command form:

Singular
Espere Ud. un momentito.
Sígame, por favor.

Plural
Esperen Uds. un momentito.
Síganme, por favor.

D. To form an **usted** command, drop the **-o** of the **yo** form of the present tense and add **-e** if the infinitive ends in **-ar** and **-a** if the infinitive ends in **-er** or **-ir**.

-ar   esperar: ──→ **esper**ø ──→ **esper-** ──→ **esper***e*
-er   comer: ──→ **com**ø ──→ **com-** ──→ **com***a*
-ir   escribir: ──→ **escrib**ø ──→ **escrib-** ──→ **escrib***a*

The following list includes the infinitive of some of the regular verbs presented in this lesson, the present tense forms for **yo** and **usted, él, ella,** and the command forms. Study it carefully. Practice these **usted** commands and others that you use frequently in order to feel comfortable with them.

| Infinitive | Present tense | | Ud. command | English command |
	yo	Ud., él, ella		
pasar	paso	pasa	pase	enter
llamar	llamo	llama	llame	call
tomar	tomo	toma	tome	take
trabajar	trabajo	trabaja	trabaje	work
comprender	comprendo	comprende	comprenda	understand
describir	describo	describe	describa	describe

1. Since the **yo** form of the present tense is used to form commands, verbs with an irregularity in the **yo** form will have that same irregularity in the command forms, including all stem-changing verbs. There are three types of stem-changing verbs (see *Lección 1,* "Notas Lingüísticas II," C. 2):

   e to ie   All three conjugations   sentar(se), sentir(se), etc.
   o to ue   All three conjugations   volver, poder, etc.
   e to i   -ir conjugation only   repetir, seguir, etc.

Infinitive	yo	Ud., él, ella	Ud. command	English command
sentar(se)	me siento	se sienta	siéntese	sit
volver	vuelvo	vuelve	vuelva	return
repetir	repito	repite	repita	repeat
seguir	sigo	sigue	siga	follow

   (**Seguir** and **sigue** have a silent **u** before **i** and **e** to maintain the hard **g** sound. See *Lección 10* for more details.)

2. **Decir** (e-i) and **tener** and **venir** (e-ie): these stem-changing verbs have an irregular **yo** form in the present tense.

Infinitive	yo	Ud., él, ella	Ud. command	English command
tener	tengo	tien	tenga	have
venir	vengo	viene	venga	come

3. **Ir** and **ser.** Both these irregular verbs have irregular command forms.

Infinitive	yo	Ud., él, ella	Ud. command	English command
ser	soy	es	sea	be
ir	voy	va	vaya	go

   The remaining present-tense forms of **ir** are:

   (tú) vas   **(nosotros/as) vamos**   **(Uds., ellos/as) van**

E. There also are three easy ways to make any verb into a command:
   Favor de + infinitive:

   Favor de venir aquí.   Please come here.

   Quisiera (*would you like to*) or **podría** (**pudiera**) (*would you be able to*) + infinitive in a question:

   ¿Quisiera Ud. esperar aquí?   Would you like to wait here?
   ¿Podría Ud. venir hoy?   Could you come today?

   These are often called *softened command forms.* They are more appropriate when a direct command would sound harsh or impolite.

PRÁCTICA PRELIMINAR

Follow the guidelines for self-instructional practice given in the Preface.

A. Construct a complete question for each set of cues, using the appropriate form of **ser**. Then answer the question in the negative. Pay special attention to the agreement between nouns and adjectives.

Ejemplo: ¿Ud.? ¿Cubano?
   ¿Es Ud. cubano? No, no soy cubano.

1. ¿Panameña? ¿Su esposa?
2. ¿Uds.? ¿Salvadoreños/as?
3. ¿Dominicano? ¿Su esposo?
4. ¿Peruanas? ¿Las clientes?
5. ¿Ud.? ¿Profesor/a aquí?
6. ¿Dentista? ¿Manuel López?
7. ¿Tú? ¿De México?
8. ¿Uds.? ¿Puertorriqueños/as?
9. ¿Tú? ¿Hijo/a de Pedro?
10. ¿San Juan? ¿La capital de Cuba?

B. Ask the person whose name is given where he or she is from, using the place given as a cue. Use the **tú** form when only a first name is given, the **Ud.** form if the last name is given, and the **Uds.** form for two people or more.

Ejemplo: El señor Soto, Puerto Rico.
   Señor Soto, ¿es Ud. de Puerto Rico?

1. Manolo, Colombia.
2. La señora Ríos, México.
3. Ana y Felipe, Cuba.
4. El señor Espinosa, La República Dominicana.
5. Matilde, Puerto Rico.
6. La señorita Iriarte, Nicaragua.
7. Esteban, Bolivia.
8. La doctora Ramos, Ecuador.
9. Los señores Echeverría, Guatemala.
10. El profesor Hernández, El Salvador.

A 1. ¿Es panameña su esposa? No, no es panameña. 2. ¿Son Uds. salvadoreños/as? No, no somos salvadoreños/as. 3. ¿Es dominicano su esposo? No, no es dominicano. 4. ¿Son peruanas las clientes? No, no son peruanas. 5. ¿Es Ud. profesor/a aquí? No, no soy profesor/a aquí. 6. ¿Es dentista Manuel López? No, no es dentista. 7. ¿Eres tú de México? No, no soy de México. 8. ¿Son Uds. puertorriqueños/as? No, no somos puertorriqueños/as. 9. ¿Eres tú hijo/a de Pedro? No, no soy hijo/a de Pedro. 10. ¿Es San Juan la capital de Cuba? No, no es la capital de Cuba.

B 1. Manolo, ¿eres tú de Colombia? 2. Señora Ríos, ¿es Ud. de México? 3. Ana y Felipe, ¿son Uds. de Cuba? 4. Señor Espinosa, ¿es Ud. de la República Dominicana? 5. Matilde, ¿eres tú de Puerto Rico? 6. Señorita Iriarte, ¿es Ud. de Nicaragua? 7. Esteban, ¿eres tú de Bolivia? 8. Doctora Ramos, ¿es Ud. de Ecuador? 9. Señores Echeverría, ¿son Uds. de Guatemala? 10. Profesor Hernández, ¿es Ud. de El Salvador?

C. Now repeat Exercise B, substituting the adjective of nationality for the place. Pay special attention to the gender and number agreement of the adjective of nationality.

Ejemplo: El señor Soto, Puerto Rico.
Señor Soto, ¿es Ud. puertorriqueño?

D. Change all pronouns, nouns, adjectives, and verbs in the following questions and commands from singular to plural.

Ejemplo: ¿Tiene Ud. el documento necesario?
¿Tiene*n* Uds. *los* documentos necesarios*?*

1. ¿Es Ud. peruano?
2. ¿Necesita Ud. la tarjeta verde?
3. ¿Tengo yo que llenar la solicitud?
4. ¿Tiene Ud. un papel?
5. ¿Es costarricense la cliente?
6. Tome Ud. esta dirección.
7. ¿Podría Ud. escribir el número aquí?
8. ¿Quisiera Ud. hablar con el doctor?
9. ¿Cómo se llama Ud.?
10. Repita Ud. el número.

E. Give the direct command that is the equivalent of each of the following polite requests. Pay special attention to singular and plural forms.

Ejemplo: ¿Quisiera seguirme, por favor?
Sígame, por favor.

1. ¿Quisiera esperar aquí un momento?
2. ¿Quisieran pasar a la oficina?
3. ¿Quisiera sentarse allí, por favor?
4. ¿Podría llamar a este teléfono?
5. ¿Podrían tomarlos, por favor?
6. ¿Podría hablar con el contador?
7. Favor de escribir a esta dirección, señores.
8. Favor de ir a la oficina del director, señora.
9. Favor de repetirlo, señor.

C 1. Manolo, ¿eres tú colombiano? 2. Señora Ríos, ¿es Ud. mexicana? 3. Ana y Felipe, ¿son Uds. cubanos? 4. Señor Espinosa, ¿es Ud. dominicano? 5. Matilde, ¿eres tú puertorriqueña? 6. Señorita Iriarte, ¿es Ud. nicaragüense? 7. Esteban, ¿eres tú boliviano? 8. Doctora Ramos, ¿es Ud. ecuatoriana? 9. Señores Echeverría, ¿son Uds. guatemaltecos? 10. Profesor Hernández, ¿es Ud. salvadoreño?

D 1. ¿Son Uds. peruanos? 2. ¿Necesitan Uds. las tarjetas verdes? 3. ¿Tenemos nosotros que llenar las solicitudes? 4. ¿Tienen Uds. (unos) papeles? 5. ¿Son costarricenses las clientes? 6. Tomen Uds. estas direcciones. 7. ¿Podrían Uds. escribir los números aquí? 8. ¿Quisieran Uds. hablar con los doctores? 9. ¿Cómo se llaman Uds.? 10. Repitan Uds. los números.

E 1. Espere aquí un momento. 2. Pasen a la oficina. 3. Siéntese allí, por favor. 4. Llame a este teléfono. 5. Tómenlos, por favor. 6. Hable con el contador. 7. Escriban a esta dirección, señores. 8. Vaya a la oficina del director, señora. 9. Repítalo, señor.

F. Give the polite request for each direct command, using the form given in parentheses. Be careful to maintain the same person, singular or plural, given in the direct command.

Ejemplo: Pase Ud. a la oficina. (quisiera)
   ¿Quisiera Ud. pasar a la oficina?

1. Venga mañana. (podría)
2. Vuelvan más tarde. (quisieran)
3. Hable más bajo. (favor)
4. Siéntese, por favor. (quisiera)
5. Sígame, por favor. (favor)
6. Espérenme aquí. (podrían)
7. Escríbalo, por favor. (quisiera)
8. Vayan a esta oficina. (favor)
9. Repítalo, por favor. (podría)

G. Now give the English translations for both the direct and polite commands given in Exercise F. Indicate if the command is given to one (**s** = singular) or more than one (**p** = plural).

H. Form a complete sentence for each verb form given by choosing the appropriate subject from column A to begin the sentence and the most logical expression from column B to end the sentence.

Column A   *Column B*
Felipe   de contador
Yo   español
Tú   los documentos
Mi esposo y yo   mexicanos
Ustedes   más tarde

1. _____ vuelvo _____.

2. _____ somos _____.

F 1. ¿Podría venir mañana? **2.** ¿Quisieran volver más tarde? **3.** Favor de hablar más bajo. **4.** ¿Quisiera sentarse, por favor? **5.** Favor de seguirme. **6.** ¿Podrían esperarme aquí? **7.** ¿Quisiera escribirlo? **8.** Favor de ir a esta oficina. **9.** ¿Podría repetirlo, por favor?

G *Direct Commands:* **1.** Come tomorrow. (s) **2.** Come back later. (p) **3.** Speak more softly. (s) **4.** Sit down, please. (s) **5.** Follow me, please. (s) **6.** Wait for me here. (p) **7.** Write it, please. (s) **8.** Go to this office. (p) **9.** Repeat it, please (s) *Polite Commands:* **1.** Could you come tomorrow? (s) **2.** Would you come back later? (p) **3.** Please speak more softly. (s) **4.** Would you like to sit down, please? (p) **5.** Please follow me. (s) **6.** Could you wait here for me? **7.** Would you like to write it? (s) **8.** Please go to this office. (p) **9.** Could you repeat it, please? (s)

H 1. Yo vuelvo más tarde. **2.** Mi esposo y yo somos mexicanos.

3. _____ tienen _____ .

4. _____ trabaja _____ .

5. _____ hablas _____ .

I. Choose the correct form of each article or adjective in the following sentences. **X** indicates no article needed.

Ejemplo: No tengo ((los) las) documentos.

1. (Buenos Buenas) tardes, señora.
2. No tengo (el los las) papeles aquí.
3. ¿Tiene Ud. (el la las) dirección?
4. Es (un una) día muy (bueno buena).
5. Repita Ud. (el la) número, por favor.
6. Mi esposa es (un una X) maestra.
7. (Los Las) tarjetas (verde verdes) son (necesario necesarias necesarios).
8. La cliente es (un una X) (peruano peruana).
9. (El La X) señora Sánchez es (hondureño hondureña).
10. No tengo (mucho muchas muchos) problemas.

Combinándolo todo

PRÁCTICA COMUNICATIVA: Preparación para el trabajo

Conversación parcial

Practique Ud. oralmente la conversación siguiente. Cada raya (/) implica que falta una palabra. Es necesario conjugar cada verbo *en bastardillas*.

Ejemplo: ¿Cómo/*llamar* Ud.?
    ¿Cómo se llama Ud.?

La empleada	El cliente
1. Me / Ramona Ramos ¿ / se *llamar* / ?	Yo *ser* Felipe Vargas.
2. ¿En / *poder* / , señor Vargas?	*Necesitar* empleo.
3. ¿En / *trabajar* Ud.?	*Ser* mecánico.
4. ¿*Ser* ciudadano / los / Unidos?	No, pero *ser* residente.
5. ¿ / qué / *ser* Ud.?	*Ser* nicaragüense.
6. ¿*Tener* / tarjeta / ?	No, señora. Yo la *necesitar*.
7. Ud. / que llenar / formularios.	Sí, cómo / .
8. Por / , *sentarse*. Yo *volver* en / momentito.	Gracias, / .

Pregunte Ud.

Usted tiene una entrevista con Matilde Ramos. Ella busca empleo. Dé Ud. oralmente las preguntas necesarias en la siguiente conversación que tiene con ella.

Ejemplo: Me llamo Matilde Ramos.
    ¿Cómo se llama Ud.?

1. Estoy muy bien, gracias. ¿Y usted?
2. Pues, busco trabajo.
3. Soy secretaria bilingüe.
4. Sí, yo hablo muy bien el inglés y el español.
5. Sí, también escribo bien en inglés y en español.
6. No, no soy ciudadana de los Estados Unidos.
7. Soy guatemalteca.
8. Sí, tengo una tarjeta verde.
9. No, no tengo experiencia de trabajar en los Estados Unidos.
10. Sí, puedo trabajar mañana.

Dígalo

Pregunte a un/a compañero/a lo que le diga su profesor/a sobre los temas de cortesía en la oficina, la nacionalidad, preparación para el trabajo, y los documentos necesarios. Después, dé a un/a compañero/a los mandatos que le indique su profesor/a.

Escuche bien

A. Ud. oirá una serie de oraciones que describen a varias personas. Decida si cada oración describe a un hombre, a una mujer, a dos hombres, o a dos mujeres y escriba una X en la columna apropiada.

	un hombre	una mujer	dos hombres	dos mujeres
1.				
2.				
3.				
4.				
5.				
6.				

B. Ud. escuchará a una cliente que habla con un empleado. Para cada oración escriba:

A– si la cliente se refiere *al empleado (to the employee).*
B– si la cliente se refiere *a sí misma (to herself).*
C– si la cliente se refiere *a sus hijos (to her children).*
D– si la cliente se refiere *a su esposo y a sí misma (to her husband and herself).*

1. _____ 5. _____ 8. _____

2. _____ 6. _____ 9. _____

3. _____ 7. _____ 10. _____

4. _____

Diálogos cortos

I. *La empleada*   *El cliente*

_____ días, señor.   Buenos días. Me llamo Juan López.

¿ _____ se llama _____ ?

¿En qué _____ servirle?   Busco a mi esposa, Socorro. Ella es tra-
                                      bajadora social.

¿ _____ qué _____   Trabaja en el departamento de seguro
trabaja ella?   social.

No entiendo. _____ Ud.   Sí, cómo no. (*Habla más alto*) En el de-
                                      partamento de seguro social.
_____ alto, _____ favor.

¿ _____ su teléfono?   No, no lo tengo.

Favor _____ ir a la   Muchas gracias, señor.

_____ de la recepcionista.

Ella _____ la lista

_____ números de teléfono

_____ empleados.

II. *El empleado*   *La cliente*

Ud. _____ Rosa Aguirre,   Sí, soy yo.
¿verdad?

Siéntese. _____ qué   Gracias. Necesito un empleo.

_____ servirle?

¿ _____ ciudadana _____ ?   No, todavía no.

¿De qué _____ es Ud.?   Soy de Cuba.

¿ _____ qué _____   En Cuba yo trabajé de costurera.
Ud.?

_____ entiendo. ¿Qué   En inglés quiere decir *seamstress*.

_____ decir *costurera*?

¿Trabaja _____ esposo?   El es contador, pero ya no puede traba-
                                      jar.

¿ _____ Ud. _____   No, no tengo, pero mi esposo sí tiene.
verde?

Ud. tiene _____   Sí, cómo no.

llenar este _____.

Ayude al cliente

You have been the employer of Carlos Gómez and his wife Gilda for the last two years. They have decided to go to Puerto Rico to work and they need a letter in Spanish confirming their work history with your company.

Begin the letter with *Estimado señor Meléndez*. In the letter state that:

1. Mr. Gómez is an accountant and that he works for _____ (make up a name for your company). Mention that he is very intelligent and an excellent employee (*un empleado excelente*). Then say that his wife Gilda also works for (*para*) the company as (*de*) a social worker. Mention that she, too, is an excellent employee.

2. Mr. Gómez is from Venezuela but now he is a citizen of the United States. Also mention that his wife is Dominican and is not a citizen, but she has a green card.

3. Say that, if it is necessary, you can fill out the documents that (*que*) they need to verify this information (*para verificar esta información*).

4. End the letter with *Attentively* (*Atentamente*), and sign your name.

¿Comprende Ud.?

Escuche bien lo que le dice Marta Rodríguez, de la Oficina de Empleo de Trenton. Después, escriba Ud. **V** si la oración *en inglés* dice la verdad, y **F** si es falsa, según lo que dice la señorita Rodríguez.

1. _____   4. _____   7. _____

2. _____   5. _____   8. _____

3. _____   6. _____   9. _____

Piénselo

Prepárese para poder hablar con el/la profesor/a o con otros estudiantes sobre los siguientes temas, contestando las preguntas que le sugiere el/la profesor/a:

1. Los requisitos (*requirements*) para trabajar en los EE.UU.

2. Los problemas que pueden tener los clientes hispanos con el trabajo

3. La comunicación sin palabras

4. Las nacionalidades latinoamericanas

SITUACIONES DE LA VIDA REAL

Imagínese

Estudie bien las fotos y conteste las siguientes preguntas:

1. ¿Cómo se llama la señora?
2. ¿Es ingeniera (*engineer*) o ama de casa?
3. ¿Habla español o inglés?
4. ¿De qué nacionalidad es?
5. ¿Necesita una tarjeta verde?
6. ¿Tiene esposo? ¿Cómo se llama?
7. ¿De qué país es ella? ¿Su esposo?
8. ¿Tiene ella problemas en el empleo?
9. ¿Tiene ella problemas en casa?
10. ¿Busca ella un empleo? ¿Por qué (no)?

(a)   (b)   (c)   (d)   (e)   (f)   (g)

1. ¿Cómo se llama cada uno de estos señores?
2. ¿De qué nacionalidad es cada uno de ellos?

3. ¿En qué trabaja cada uno de ellos?
4. ¿Hablan alto o bajo?
5. ¿Hablan inglés o español?
6. ¿En qué oficina están ellos?
7. ¿Qué documentos tiene el señor F?
8. ¿Qué tarjeta tiene el señor G?
9. ¿Tienen ellos problemas en el trabajo?

Haciendo el papel

Haga Ud. el papel de la persona indicada en las siguientes situaciones mientras otro/a estudiante hace el papel del/de la cliente. Use la comunicación sin palabras cuando sea apropiada.

1. You are the director of the employment office. Victor Guerrero and his wife (Ana Torres de Guerrero) need work. Ask them how they spell their names and where they're from. Ask them what kind of work they do. They respond that he is a dentist and she is an elementary school teacher. Ask them to wait a moment (use hand gesture) and tell them that you'll be back soon.

2. You are a social worker. Use a hand gesture and the names to call Manuel Berríos Matos and his son Jorge (would Jorge's full surname be the same as his father's?), who are Mexican, to come into the office. Tell them to sit down and then ask them what you can do for them. Ask them if they speak and understand English. You don't understand what Jorge says, so you ask him to repeat it more slowly. You find out that they both need green cards in order to work. Tell them where they have to go in order to get the application forms they need to fill out.

3. You are a nurse working at the employee clinic in a large factory. A Puerto Rican employee comes in saying he doesn't feel well. Tell him to sit down and ask him his name. Then tell him you speak Spanish only a little (use hand gesture) and ask him to speak up a little. He asks you if you are a doctor. You say no (use hand gesture), that you are a nurse. You ask him what's wrong. He responds with a hand gesture to signal "drinking" and holds his stomach. Tell him he has to speak with Dr. Sánchez. Tell him he has to fill out a form and go to the receptionist's office.

4. Interview a classmate in order to fill out the following form. Be certain to get the full names of both the person interviewed and his or her spouse.

Last name _____	First name _____
Nationality _____	Citizen of U.S. _____
Line of work _____	Work permit _____
Spouse's full name _____	
Nationality _____	Citizen of U.S. _____
Line of work _____	Work permit _____

REFLEJOS DE LA CULTURA: "La Borinqueña"

La Borinqueña, the national anthem of Puerto Rico, is an old melody whose composer and date of composition are uncertain. It is known and beloved in many countries throughout the Western Hemisphere, danced to and sung in Peru, Chile, Haiti, Brazil, Cuba, and Puerto Rico. Several sets of lyrics have been written to accompany this popular melody.

The first version printed below was written in 1868 by a poet from San Germán, Puerto Rico, Doña Lola Rodrígez de Tió, whose words instilled such patriotic feeling when sung to the familiar melody that the new combination was acclaimed as the national anthem. It has been recorded by Danny Rivera, a popular Puerto Rican vocalist, in an album entitled *Danzas para mi pueblo* (the *danza* is a folkloric dance of the island).

Version I

¡Despierta, borinqueño,	Wake up, people of Borinquen
que han dado la señal!	They've given the signal!
¡Despierta de ese sueño,	Wake up from that dream,
que es hora de luchar!	It's time to fight!
A ese llamar patriótico	To that patriotic call
¿no arde tu corazón?	Does not your heart burn?
Ven, nos será simpático	Come, the noise of the cannon
el ruido del cañón.	Will be music to our ears.
Vámonos, borinqueños,	Let's go, people of Borinquen,
vámonos ya;	Let's go now;
que nos espera ansiosa,	since waiting for us anxiously,
ansiosa, la libertad.	anxiously (is) freedom.
Nosotros queremos la libertad,	We want freedom,
y nuestro machete nos la	And our machetes will give it
dará.	to us.

These lyrics were replaced by a second version written by Manuel Fernández Juncos at the turn of the century, coinciding with the change of sovereignty of the island from Spain to the United States. These words have remained as the current national anthem of Puerto Rico.

Version II

La tierra de Borinquen	The land of Borinquen
donde he nacido yo	where I have been born
es un jardín florido	is a flowering garden
de mágico primor.	of magical beauty.
Un cielo siempre nítido	An ever clear sky
le sirve de dosel	serves as your backdrop,
y dan arrullos plácidos	and the waves send gentle
las olas a sus pies.	lullabies to your feet (shore).
Cuando a sus playas llegó Colón	When Columbus first arrived at your beaches,
exclamó lleno de admiración:	filled with admiration he exclaimed:
¡Oh! ¡Oh! ¡Oh!	Oh! Oh! Oh!
Esta es la linda tierra que busco yo;	This is the beautiful land that I seek;
Es Borinquen la hija,	Borinquen is the daughter,
la hija del mar y el sol,	the daughter of the sea and
del mar y el sol.	the sun, of the sea and the sun.

Evaluación del progreso—Lecciones 1~2

RAISING AWARENESS

A. Now that you have experienced entry into a foreign language that organizes reality from a different perspective, how would you define *culture?*

B. What factors regarding the uniqueness of the individual are evident in the statement, "A Mexican American third-generation Californian may be as different from a recently arrived Cuban refugee as a palm tree from a pine"?

C. Rosa Varela Echeverría is married to Fernando Sabio Lizaur. What is Rosa's full name on her *tarjeta verde?* What full name appears on their son Enrique's driver's license?

D. Discuss three important historical factors that account for the largest Hispanic population's residency in your area.

E. Decide how the following pairs of individuals would greet each other according to the norms for Hispanic greetings.

	Handshake	*Kiss on cheek*	*Pat on back*
1. Rafael and his good friend Lola	_____	_____	_____
2. Pedro (age 27) and his favorite neighbor, Marta	_____	_____	_____
3. Mrs. Sánchez and her new male client	_____	_____	_____
4. Alberto and Ricardo, two business partners	_____	_____	_____

F. Write the message communicated by each of the four pictures:

a. _____

b. _____

c. _____

d. _____

COMUNICÁNDOSE EN ESPAÑOL

A. Pronunciación

1. Write the full names that your instructor spells:

a. _____

b. _____

c. _____

2. Fill in the blanks with the appropriate vowel in each of the following new words that your teacher will pronounce.

a. d __ m __

b. __ t __ l __ d __ d

c. d __ s __ sp __ r __ d __

d. __ c __ __ n __

e. s __ s __ rr __

B. Discriminación auditiva   Circle the letter of the most appropriate response to each oral question or statement you hear.

1. **a b c**   5. **a b c**   8. **a b c**

2. **a b c**   6. **a b c**   9. **a b c**

3. **a b c**   7. **a b c**   10. **a b c**

4. **a b c**

COMBINÁNDOLO TODO

A. **Comprensión oral** Write in English the problem stated by each of the clients you hear.

1. _____

2. _____

3. _____

4. _____

5. _____

B. **La entrevista** Give the questions and/or responses needed in the following dialogue, which takes place at the employment office.

El empleado	*La cliente*
	Con permiso, ¿es Ud. el señor Báez?
1. Sí, ¿_____?	Pues, busco un empleo.
2. ¿_____?	Me llamo Elena López.
3. ¿_____?	No, no soy ciudadana.
4. ¿_____?	Soy peruana.
5. ¿_____?	Sí, señor, la tengo.
6. ¡Qué bien! Entonces, ¿_____ _____?	Soy secretaria bilingüe.

C. **En acción** Choose one of the following situations and act it out with your instructor or another classmate.

1. Meeting a client for the first time, exchanging names, verifying spelling, and finding out what the client needs

2. Interviewing a client for a job, finding out relevant information

3. Seeing a new patient in the hospital, finding out language ability, country of origin, and name of family physician

4. Clarifying a client's citizenship and residency status

5. Giving a client specific instructions needed in a common situation in your place of employment

LECCIÓN 3

¿En qué puedo servirle?

LOS OBJETIVOS

Raising awareness

1. To understand how cultural conditioning and personal experiences influence the individual's personal version of reality
2. To be aware of present socioeconomic realities of Latin American cultures and their impact on (im)migration to the United States
3. To interpret how Hispanics use nonverbal communication to show respect for authority

Comunicándose en español

1. To pronounce and spell words containing diphthongs
2. To initiate an intake interview in Spanish by establishing rapport with the client
3. To ascertain the reason for clients' visits, their prior contact with the agency, their source of referral, and other relevant data

Combinándolo todo

1. To integrate vocabulary and structures presented in Lessons 1 to 3 in order to ask questions, understand, and give appropriate responses with a fair degree of accuracy
2. To interpret and adapt to cultural patterns of behavior that may be encountered in the initial intake interview
3. To gain insight into the oppression of the lower socioeconomic classes in Latin America and its effect on cross-cultural differences between Anglos and Hispanics

71

Raising awareness

OVERVIEW: Creating our own realities

Our uniqueness as individuals creates for each of us a personal version of reality. In our day-to-day actions and interactions, we perceive reality by means of the "camera" or mind's eye that each of us has evolved in the lifetime process of learning and growing. As infants, we learned not only to perceive and understand the world around us but also to express what we were experiencing in our native language. In turn, the language(s) learned as children shaped our view of reality. The link between language and culture is a strong one.

Consider the word *family* in English. The equivalent word in Spanish is *familia*. They look alike because they are cognates; that is, both are based on the same Latin root. However, there is a difference in the connotation of each word that is determined by the culture in which the language is spoken. In the English-speaking world, *family* most often refers to the nuclear family, composed of mother, father, and children. In the Spanish-speaking world, *familia* usually refers to the extended family, including grandparents, aunts, uncles, and cousins. It can even be extended to nonblood ties such as those of the *compadrazgo* (godparent) system. A further example is seen in the word *tío* in Spanish, the dictionary equivalent of *uncle,* which may also refer to a parent's first cousin in addition to his or her brother.

Each person learns the meaning of the concept termed *family* in his or her own home environment. If you grew up in a family where a grandparent lived in the household, your concept of family lies somewhere between the norms for Anglo and Hispanic cultures. A Hispanic whose nuclear family left the extended family back in Puerto Rico or Mexico in order to come to the U.S. mainland to live and work might have evolved a different concept of *familia* based on this experience.

One's personal reality, then, is a combination of cultural norms and personal experience. The following illustration may help you to see just how we select from what is happening around us in order to construct our own personal reality. It also shows how we further select from what we perceive when we verbalize it.

Our perception of reality is not limited to our sense of vision. It includes the other physical senses of hearing, tasting, touching, and smelling. It also includes our intuitive or sixth sense, which relies on imagination to determine what's happening. It is that inner voice that somehow tells us more information than what is perceived by the five physical senses.

What we perceive from the external world is then filtered through our personal reality interpreter; that is, it derives its meaning according to our inner rules of interpretation. These rules are nothing more than the accumulated knowledge we have gained from both our cultural conditioning and our personal experiences.

We never *consciously* perceive the total reality to which we are exposed, although it is believed that it is all registered somewhere in the subconscious. Our conscious mind would be overloaded and most likely collapse under the strain of trying to process the totality of our daily experiences. So we select from the wide range of stimuli presented to us each day what we wish to process into our awareness.

Just as we cannot *consciously* perceive all that we sense, we cannot verbally relay to another person all that we *do* perceive consciously. For example, try to describe completely the environment in which you are currently situated. Include the physical details of the space, the color,

72

weight, and volume of each object you see, the odors in the air, what you are touching (including the contact between your body and whatever you're sitting on), all the noises you hear, everything that is going on inside your body and mind, and so on. By the time you are able to finish the description, the reality will have changed! Just as you select *what* to process consciously, you must select *which* of those perceptions you wish to communicate to someone else.

In using a given language to communicate, the words we choose to describe our perceptions are subject to the individual interpretation of the person with whom we are communicating. For example, the word *snow* may have a very different meaning for an Eskimo than for a tropical islander who has never experienced it. This is especially true for more abstract words such as *loyalty, democracy, sexuality,* and *spirituality.* Even two people who were born into the same culture, have been raised within the same general environment, and speak the same native language may not fully understand each other at times because of the different connotations of the words used.

When you consider that each of us is walking around with a very personal view of reality, you may wonder how we manage to communicate anything to anybody. That we are still able to communicate with others and get along with them is no small feat. What is even more remarkable is that we are able to communicate not only with those from a similar linguistic and cultural background but also with those whose native language and personal perception of reality are different from our own.

True communication across cultural boundaries requires skill, practice, and knowledge. Most important, it requires a flexible mental attitude. Only if you are willing to experience a perception of reality that may be completely at odds with your own can you hope to understand someone from another culture.

Applications

1. Study the following drawing. What do you see? Compare your perceptions with those of other members of the class.

2. Look at the following photograph. Describe what you see. Now describe what you perceive using your sixth sense or imagination. Compare your results with those of other members of the class.

3. List three words that you associate with each of the following terms. Compare your lists with other members of the class.

    a. home   _____

    b. cat   _____

    c. divorce   _____

    d. politics   _____

    e. computers   _____

4. Compare the following English–Spanish "equivalents" by defining each and listing any culturally determined differences you may be aware of:

    a. house   _____

        casa   _____

    b. lawyer   _____

        abogado   _____

    c. Miss   _____

        señorita   _____

    d. coffee   _____

        café   _____

e. respect _____

respeto _____

Reflections

1. How long did it take you to see both images in the drawing in the first item under "Applications"? Do you have more trouble "seeing" one image than the other?

2. How do your perceptions of what is happening in the photograph in item 2 of "Applications" differ from those of other members of the class? What accounts for the difference?

3. How do your associated words differ from those of other members of the class. What do these differences show?

4. How do the English–Spanish equivalents differ in meaning and usage? What role does culture have in determining these differences?

HISTORICAL PERSPECTIVE: Social classes in the Hispanic world

In speaking of our cultural background, we refer not only to our ethnic origins and the country in which we have been raised but also to other social determinants, such as sex, social class, and rural, urban, or suburban residence, that affect who we are, what we believe and value, and how we act.

One of the most crucial factors affecting the cultural conditioning of an individual raised in a Spanish-speaking country is that of social class. In fact, there may be more similarities between a member of the upper class from Mexico and one from the Dominican Republic than between an upper-class and a lower-class Mexican, even though the latter may live in the same household, one as owner, the other as servant! This phenomenon of social-class differentiation may be difficult to understand for those who have been raised in the United States, where the majority of the population belongs to the middle class, which is not the case for most Latin American countries.

The following diagrams give an idea of the differences in social-class strata and interclass mobility between the United States and a Latin American country such as Mexico, which is still locked into a third world pattern of economic development.

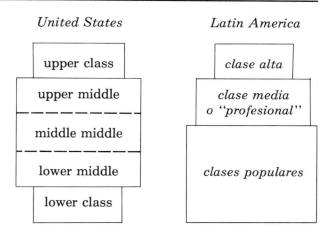

The rigidity of class mobility coupled with a bottom-heavy class structure explain many of the political tensions facing much of Latin America today. Extreme poverty and high unemployment among members of the *clases populares* account for the increased exodus to the United States in search of a better economic life. The different class systems operating in the United States and much of Latin America are the result of historical developments and need to be examined from that perspective in order to understand the present-day reality of Hispanics residing in the United States.

A comparison of the colonization of the United States with that of Latin America highlights two basic factors. First, the early colonizers of the original thirteen states, who began arriving in 1606, more than a hundred years after the first Spanish settlement in the Caribbean, came primarily to establish a new way of life. Freedom from religious and economic persecution was their goal, and equality among all settlers an accepted fact.

The Spanish colonizers, however, came to Latin America in the early 1500s, at a time when Spain was at the apex as a world power and was involved in expansionist wars throughout Europe. They sought primarily personal wealth and adventure. Whereas many of the early settlers of the United States came as families seeking to establish roots in the new land, most of the Spanish colonizers came alone as adventurers, seeking to exploit the gold, silver, and other minerals that abounded in Mexico, Central America, and South America. Their interests also focused on Latin America's rich agricultural resources, such as spices, chocolate, tobacco, coffee, and sugar. They exported the bulk of these resources to Spain, where they were used to finance the wars in which she was involved in Europe. So, whereas the focus in the northern colonies was one of settling into the new land and establishing roots, that of the colonies to the south was primarily to extract riches in order to maintain status in European society, which Spain ruled at that time.

The second main difference in the colonization patterns was the treatment of the original inhabitants of the newly colonized lands. The U.S. colonists either attempted to coexist peacefully with these populations or warred with them in order to establish their own territories. The colonizers of Latin America, however, subjugated the indigenous population (and, later, imported Africans as slaves) in order to have a large work force to build the forts, settlements, and other buildings needed to survive in the New World, as well as to extract the minerals and work the farm lands. These lands were distributed in large parcels to the new Spanish immigrants, and to this day land ownership accounts for most of the wealth in Latin America. This inequitable distribution of land is one of the greatest obstacles to social change.

1. *How does the social class system of the United States differ from that of most Latin American countries?*
2. *What two factors account for the different colonization patterns of the United States and Latin America?*

Thus the origins of the different social-class systems date back at least as far as the early colonization period of both areas. In addition, the highly developed indigenous civilizations of Mexico, Central America, and the Andean regions operated on a pyramid-type division of labor. Their political orientation and the distribution of land and wealth, however, reflected a communal social system, with the lower classes treated equitably. In these areas the Spanish *conquistadores* (conquerors) were able to simply replace the *jefe* or *cacique* (leader) with one of their own in order to exploit the existing social structure to serve their ends. The small middle classes in these areas arose because of the need for intermediaries — Indians who could serve as translators, traders, tax collectors, and supervisors of the large labor force. These were mostly priests, merchants, and nobles who had enjoyed a higher social rank in the old order. In those areas where the indigenous population died out soon after the original contact with the Spaniards, Africans filled the ranks of the exploited class who served the needs of the colonizers.

Although there has been much debate regarding the treatment of the Indians by the Spaniards, it is not our purpose here to judge Spain's role but, rather, to understand the effects of the historical events on present-day realities. For the lower-class populations of Latin America, there has been no reality other than that of colonizer and exploited class. The concept of social mobility has never been typical of most of Latin America. Even in those countries that have become more industrialized, there are still large segments of the society that live marginally in a cultural limbo, where survival is the primary goal. The subsistence level of these people is so low, their awareness of the possibility of change so limited, that the concept of social mobility has little or no meaning for them. After having lived for nearly five hundred years as a colonized people, most Latin Americans cannot easily conceive of a way of life not based on a two-class system. The privileged classes, whose own five-century history has been based on the continued economic exploitation of the many in exchange for the comforts and well being of a few, are, for the most part, not eager for social change.

Why haven't these exploited members of society united to seek a more equitable distribution of land and wealth? Such changes very rarely begin in the lower strata of society. When one's principal focus is feeding and clothing one's family, trying to survive at a basic subsistence level, there is little time or energy to devote to reform. In addition, the educational level of most lower-class members is often very low; in many countries, the illiteracy rate reaches 50 percent and higher.

This century has, however, seen growing movement toward change in the established social order in Latin America. The first truly social revolution was the Mexican Revolution (1910–1917), which rid the country of the dictatorship of Porfirio Díaz and established a more democratic form of government. Some improvements were made in the distribution of the land. Nonetheless, the ever-growing Mexican lower class is still trapped in poverty.

Puerto Rico has also experienced some degree of socioeconomic change since the turn of the century. The U.S. presence there has shifted the economy from a predominantly agricultural base to an industrial one. Although as a result Puerto Rico has the highest per capita income of any Latin American country, Puerto Ricans' earnings are still substantially lower than those of their counterparts on the U.S. mainland. Prices for food and manufactured goods are extremely high,

while unemployment rates are rarely below 25 percent. The relatively rapid and dramatic changes in the socioeconomic system also account for the need for government assistance programs, predominantly food stamps, for a large portion of island residents as well as for the increased migration of Puerto Ricans to the mainland.

The Castro-led revolution of 1959 in Cuba drastically altered the social-class structure, cutting sharply into the property and wealth of the "haves," who constituted the first wave of Cuban immigrants to the United States. Many of the primary needs of the population are met by the socialist government. Literacy has increased greatly, but the economic status of the island continues to be shaky, so that there is a limited supply of all goods and rationing is often the norm.

The recent Sandinista upheaval in Nicaragua, which ousted the wealthy and powerful Anastasio Somoza in 1979, marked the beginning of social revolution. The largest number of emigrés from Nicaragua have been from the ranks of *la gente acomodada* (the wealthy class). Many have reorganized in exile as the *contras* (epithet for *counterrevolutionaries*) and, with the backing of U.S. military aid, continue attempts to thwart the efforts of the socialist Sandinista regime to restructure the social order.

In El Salvador, Nicaragua's northern neighbor, the U.S.-backed Duarte regime, which favors a status quo in the social order, is under constant attack from guerrilla rebel forces seeking social change. Honduras, the land bridge between Nicaragua and El Salvador, has become involved in the insurrections by default: the Sandinistas support the Salvadoran guerrillas' struggle, whereas the *contras* and the Duarte regime have politically more in common. Neighboring Costa Rica, the only country in the Western Hemisphere without a regular army, and Guatemala, where repression of efforts for social change is common, are also affected by the political unrest in the area.

3. *What factors explain the scarcity of true social revolutions in Latin America?*
4. *Which Latin American countries have succeeded in altering the social structure in this century?*

The social-class system in Latin America, as well as the internal struggles for control of the social order, greatly affect immigration to the United States. Although there has been some immigration of *gente acomodada* to the United States, most often to study, to gain work experience, or to escape from the effects of social revolution in their native lands, relatively few members of the wealthy classes of Latin America have sought permanent residence in the United States. Most have little desire to leave the comfortable existence they lead at home in exchange for a life in what is often seen as the "young, uncultured" country to the north. Recently, a large number of professionals from Puerto Rico have come to the mainland because of the greater earning power available. Many of the Mexican Americans whose families have lived in the United States for many years have attained a high professional level, although educational opportunities in some of the regions with high Mexican American populations have only recently improved. The early Cuban immigrants in the 1950s, principally from the upper and middle classes, have reestablished themselves in the economic mainstream of the United States. Many of the older generation, however, still dream of overthrowing Castro and returning to their homeland.

Yet most immigrants from Hispanic countries have been from the *clases populares*. They have come for one of two reasons: (1) to earn a better living for themselves and their families, or (2) to escape political oppression, as is the case in the recent large influx of politically active Salvadoran and Guatemalan refugees. Social mobility is rarely the basic motivation. Survival, either economic or political, is the primary goal.

Although many immigrants are lured to the U.S. mainland by images of economic prosperity, at the same time they view Horatio Alger rags-to-riches tales as virtually impossible for them. Professionals providing services to such clients may feel frustrated at what, in the Anglo culture, may be viewed as a lack of ambition or laziness. In reality, it is the cumulative effect of five centuries of social-class immobility. Although it is not impossible for some Latinos to open themselves to the possibilities that their new environment may offer them, it will not happen quickly. Immediate economic needs must be met before far-reaching changes can begin. Economic survival in the present often outweighs the promise of social mobility in the future.

In addition to the economic condition common to members of the lower strata of Latin American society, their cultural conditioning is different from that of the middle and upper classes. Often, it is in the higher social classes that new ideas take hold and that the influence of international culture (music, dress, etc.) is first felt. When one has the means to travel, to read, to attend concerts, plays, and movies, one's cultural world is broadened. Many of the traditional values of a society survive longer in the lower classes than in the upper and middle classes, which are exposed to more variations via a broader range of personal experiences.

---

5. *What effects does the social-class system of most of Latin America have on the influx of Hispanics to the United States?*
6. *What factors may account for the seeming lack of ambition of many lower-class Hispanics living in the United States?*

NONVERBAL COMMUNICATION: Attitudes toward authority

One of the earliest types of nonverbal communication that we learn is how to behave in the presence of authority figures. The way we are expected to behave when dealing with superiors is predominantly dictated by the culture in which we are raised. In the Hispanic world, with its sharp social-class distinctions, these lessons are important for survival. Hispanic children, like children everywhere, learn how to deal with superiors both by direct instruction from their parents and by observing adult members of the family interacting with authority figures outside the home. Hispanic children soon learn their "place" in society, a status assigned as much by sex as by the socioeconomic class into which they are born.

The Spanish language reflects this cultural distinction in its varied forms for the pronoun *you.* The speaker must choose between *tú* (and in some countries, *vos*) and *usted,* according to the relative status of the people who are communicating. *Tú* is reserved for either those with whom the speaker is on fairly intimate terms — namely, close friends and relatives — *or* those who are younger or of a lower social status. In countries where *vos* is an option, it reflects an even closer relationship than *tú. Usted* is used for those who must be addressed with a title + surname — namely, strangers or acquaintances or those who are older or of a higher social status. Even in the close family unit, *usted* is used in many Latin American countries when children address parents.

Respect is shown by the use of *usted,* which should be chosen when one is in doubt about the proper mode of address. Using *tú,* even in an attempt to make a client feel more comfortable, can be misinterpreted as disrespectful. *Don* and *doña* + first name (usually used with *usted*), employed in colonial times to address the *patrones* or landowners on whose land the farmworkers labored and lived, survives today to show respect for those whom the speaker knows well but who are older or of a higher social status.

The most obvious contrast between Anglo and Hispanic nonverbal communication patterns when in the presence of authority figures is that of eye contact and head movement. Anglos are taught to look everyone in the eye when spoken to. In the Anglo tradition, eyes and head cast downward are signs of dishonesty, guilt, or disrespect, especially when one is spoken to or reprimanded by a superior.

In the Hispanic world, however, the *normal* behavior when one is being advised or scolded by a person in a position of power is to cast one's head and eyes downward. To respond to the authority figure with direct eye contact is considered challenging and disrespectful. Even when speaking informally to friends and family, prolonged eye contact, valued in the Anglo culture as a display of attention and understanding, may have a chilling effect on Hispanics, who tend to misinterpret such a gaze as a sign of anger or defiance.

The more common behavior is for Hispanics to shift their glance often and move their heads around to avoid making the conversational partner feel uncomfortable. It is especially important for males and females to avoid staring at each other when engaged in conversation. Prolonged eye gazing is reserved only for intimate relationships and may be misinterpreted as a desire to initiate such a relationship.

Another cultural difference concerns the type of behavior expected from those in authority. The Hispanic cultures are, by and large, much more formal in this respect than Anglo cultures. This is especially true in the business and professional world. Teachers, for example, are expected to act professionally and dress conservatively. Although helpful and caring about students, they maintain a distant and aloof posture. Formality abounds in the interaction between students and teachers. A Hispanic student would rarely consider calling a teacher or professor by a first name. This formality is also the rule in other business situations, although clients and professionals do display warmth and empathy for each other.

The importance of respect in the Hispanic culture cannot be underestimated. It has its basis in the sense of *dignidad,* or personal worth, regardless of the social class to which the individual belongs. Although this may seem paradoxical in view of the rather rigid social-class distinctions typical of most Hispanic countries, it really isn't. The fundamental belief is that each person's worth is an intrinsic birthright. To learn to operate in society according to the prescribed rule of social-class distinctions is to develop one's own sense of dignity, a high value for most Hispanics. Only by first respecting oneself, however lowly on the social ladder one is, can one then show respect for others and for one's country. One of the worst criticisms for a Latino is to be told *"Le falta respeto"* ("You lack respect").

Often the physical manifestation of respect demonstrated by Hispanic clients, especially those from low socioeconomic backgrounds, may be misinterpreted as passivity, acquiescence, nonchalance, or apathy by those from other cultures. In interactions with Anglos, some Hispanic clients may seem withdrawn or lacking initiative or assertiveness. In an Anglo culture where the dictum "the squeaky wheel gets the grease" governs much of the business and professional world, some Hispanic clients who seem more reserved may receive inadequate treatment or information. As a potential authority figure, you can adjust to your Hispanic clients' needs in this regard by:

1. Not making judgments about guilt or honesty on the basis of head and eye contact
2. Behaving in a formal, professional manner while still showing empathy and support
3. Treating all clients with the respect that is rightfully theirs, regardless of social class
4. Anticipating needs, questions, and instructions that the Hispanic client may be reluctant to mention
5. Gently helping clients to be aware of possible misinterpretations of their behavior toward authority
6. Helping clients to modify those behaviors that may be preventing them from receiving the services they seek

Putting it into practice

1. With the help of another member of the class, play the role of a teacher reprimanding a child for talking in class while the teacher is speaking in each of the following contexts. Pay special attention to head and eye movements.
    a. An Anglo teacher with an Anglo child
    b. An Anglo teacher with a Hispanic child
    c. A Hispanic teacher with a Hispanic child

2. Play the role of a Hispanic client from a low socioeconomic background whom a legal aid worker has identified as having experienced discrimination in applying for a job. Concentrate on nonverbal behavior as much as possible as the legal aid worker attempts to obtain details of the alleged discrimination.

3. What misinterpretations based on nonverbal cues might occur in the following situations:
    a. An Anglo judge who asks the Hispanic defendant if he is guilty of speeding?
    b. A young female Anglo professor who encourages her class, composed mostly of Hispanic males, to call her by her first name?
    c. An older Anglo male doctor who asks a young, single, female Hispanic patient if she uses birth control?

4. Decide whether **tú** or **usted** would be appropriate when you are addressing:
    a. A judge
    b. A client of the same age whom you've just met
    c. A client who seems nervous and whom you would like to put at ease
    d. A ten-year-old child
    e. A colleague you've just met

5. List at least three ways you can show *respeto* for your Hispanic clients:

    _____

    _____

    _____

Comunicándose en español

PRONUNCIACIÓN: Los diptongos 🔲

A diphthong is a combination of two vowels pronounced as one syllable. In Spanish, one of these vowels is *always* an unstressed **i** (or, at times, **y**) or **u**.

When **i** is the first vowel in a diphthong, it is pronounced as an English **y**:

gracias	bien	adiós	ciudadano
resfriado	siente	despacio	viudo

When **i** (or **y**) is the second vowel of the diphthong, it maintains its original sound:

hay	ley	estoy	muy
aire	seis	tiroide	fui

When **u** is the first vowel of the diphthong, it is pronounced like English *w*:

cuando	luego	individuo
situación	escuela	continuo

Note that the **u** in the combinations **gue, gui, que, qui** is silent:

guerra	guitarra	queda	Quiroga

When **u** is the second vowel in the diphthong, it maintains its original sound:

causa	neutral	ciudadana
bautista	Europa	viuda

Práctica 🔲

Practice the following sentences until you can say them without pauses. Pay close attention to vowels and diphthongs:

1. Entiendo bien la historia de Puerto Rico.
2. Europa no fue neutral en la Segunda Guerra Mundial.
3. Antonio es autor de un manual para trabajadores sociales.
4. ¿Qué quiere decir *bautista* en la lengua española?
5. Adiós, hasta luego. Saludos a la familia.
6. Eugenia Suárez es ciudadana de Guatemala.

Dictado 🔲

Write in Spanish the words you hear:

1. _____   4. _____

2. _____   5. _____

3. _____   6. _____

La trabajadora social me dice que Ud. habla muy bien el inglés, señora Gómez. ¿Por qué no me habla en inglés?

Pues, no es verdad. Lo hablo un poquito. No me siento cómoda hablando inglés.

Pero Ud. habla inglés, con la trabajadora social, ¿verdad?

Sí, porque ella no domina el español como Ud.

Comprendo, señora. ¿No quiere Ud. practicar el inglés? Es muy importante poder hablar inglés en los EE. UU.

Este . . . puedo expresarme mejor en mi lengua nativa, especialmente con una persona como Ud. que también comprende nuestra cultura.

¿Y Ud. no tiene simpatía con la trabajadora social?

No. Ella no aprecia ni nuestra lengua ni nuestra cultura. Ella me hace sentir inferior.

Entonces, ¿cómo se comunican?

Muy mal. Ella me pregunta algo en inglés y yo le contesto con "yes" or "no". Eso es todo.

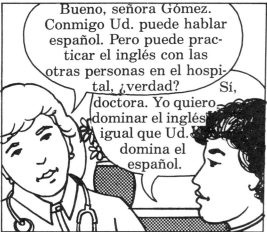

Bueno, señora Gómez. Conmigo Ud. puede hablar español. Pero puede practicar el inglés con las otras personas en el hospital, ¿verdad?

Sí, doctora. Yo quiero dominar el inglés igual que Ud. domina el español.

¿Ha entendido bien?

1. ¿Habla bien el inglés la señora Gómez?

2. ¿Habla bien el español la doctora?

3. ¿Quién habla mejor el español, la doctora o la trabajadora social?

4. ¿En qué lengua se comunican la doctora y la señora Gómez? ¿Y la trabajadora social y la señora Gómez?

5. ¿En qué lengua prefiere comunicarse la señora Gómez con la doctora? ¿Por qué?

6. ¿Cómo se siente la señora Gómez cuando habla con la trabajadora social? ¿Por qué se siente así?

7. ¿Con quién puede practicar el inglés la señora Gómez?

8. ¿Va a practicar el inglés la señora Gómez? ¿Por qué?

9. ¿Se siente Ud. cómodo/a hablando español? ¿Por qué?

10. ¿Es importante apreciar la lengua y la cultura de sus clientes? ¿Por qué?

INTRODUCTORY DIALOGUE: In the office (consultation room)

The doctor: The social worker tells me that you speak English very well, Mrs. Gómez. Why don't you speak to me in English?

The client: Well, it isn't true. I speak it a little. I don't feel comfortable speaking English.

D: But you speak English with the social worker, don't you?

C: Yes, because she doesn't speak (dominate) Spanish well like you.

D: I understand, ma'am. Don't you want to practice English? It's very important to be able to speak English in the United States.

C: Um . . . I can express myself better in my native language, especially with a person like you who also understands our culture.

D: And you do not have a good rapport with the social worker?

C: No. She doesn't appreciate either our language or our culture. She makes me feel inferior.

D: Then, how do you communicate?

C: Very poorly. She asks me something in English and I answer her with "yes" or "no." That's all.

D: Well, Mrs. Gómez. With me you can speak Spanish. But you can practice (your) English with the other people in the hospital, right?

C: Yes, doctor. I want to speak (dominate) English as well as you speak Spanish.

BASIC STRUCTURES I: At the reception desk

The receptionist (m.)	*The client (f.)*
María Cristina Díaz, please.	Here I am.
Mrs. Díaz, come with me.	Yes, of course.

(The two go into the office.)

Mrs. Díaz, sit down, please. I'm Ray Emerson. What can I do for you? (How may I serve you?)

I need to speak with the
- social worker (m/f).
- director (m/f).
- doctor (m/f).
- lawyer (m/f).
- manager (m/f).
- boss (m/f).

At the (this) moment (s)he is
- busy (m./f.).
- out of the office.
- in the consultation room.
- in a meeting.
- with another patient.

Can you wait for a while?	Sure. Where shall I wait?
Over there, please. You are the next client.	Thank you.

¿Sabe usted?

1. You may hear the following dialectal variations for **el/la jefe/a: el patrón, la patrona** (M.A.) **el/la bos** (Anglicism). **Jefito (jefecito)** and **jefita (jefecita)** in Mexican American dialect refer to one's parents.

2. Since most occupations were traditionally held by males, the feminine forms of certain professions (e.g., **jefa, gerenta**) have only recently been used colloquially in some countries and may not yet be found in all dictionaries.

3. Adjectives must agree in gender and number with the nouns they describe, even if the noun or pronoun is omitted from the sentence. **Está ocupado** refers to a male and **está ocupada** refers to a female.

ESTRUCTURAS BÁSICAS I: En la recepción ▣

El recepcionista	*La cliente*
María Cristina Díaz, por favor.	**Aquí estoy.**
Señora Díaz, venga conmigo.	**Sí, cómo no.**

(*Los dos entran en la oficina.*)

Señora Díaz, siéntese, por favor. Soy Ray Emerson. ¿En qué puedo servirle?

Necesito hablar con el/la {
trabajador/a social.
director/a.
doctor/a.
abogado/a.
gerente/a.
jefe/a.
}

En este momento está {
ocupado/a.
fuera de la oficina.
en el consultorio.
en una reunión.
con otro paciente.
}

¿Puede Ud. esperar un rato?   **Claro. ¿Dónde espero?**

Allá, por favor. Ud. es la próxima cliente.   **Gracias.**

Notas lingüísticas I

A. The verb **estar** is conjugated as follows:

yo	**estoy**	nosotros/as	**estamos**
tú	**estás**		
Ud., él, ella	**está**	Uds., ellos/as	**están**

In previous lessons, **estar** was used to express states of health (**¿Cómo *está* Ud.?**). In this lesson, it is used to locate (***está* en una reunión, *está* fuera de la oficina, *está* con otro paciente**) as well as to indicate a temporary condition (***está* ocupado**).

B. **Aquí** (*here*) and **allí** (*there*) are used to indicate specific locations. **Acá** (*over here*) and **allá** (*over there*) are used to indicate a more general area.

BASIC STRUCTURES II: In the office (consultation room)

The doctor (m.)	*The client (f.)*
Come in, Mrs. Díaz. Sit down. Are you comfortable?	Yes, I'm very comfortable, thank you, doctor.
First I need some personal information. María Cristina Díaz is your full name?	Well, my maiden name is Salazar.
Salazar is spelled *S-a-l-a-z-a-r*, isn't it?	Yes, that's how it's spelled.
This is the first time that you've come here?	No, it's the {second. / third. / fourth. / fifth. / sixth.}
When was the last time?	It was last week.
Who referred you?	A friend / The school / The court / The health department / The welfare agency / The minister of my church / The priest } referred me.
What religion are you?	I am {Catholic. / Protestant. / Baptist. / Seventh Day Adventist. / Jewish.} I don't go to any church.
Fine, Mrs. Díaz, now go into the waiting room again. I'll call you immediately.	Thank you. You are very kind.

¿Sabe usted?

1. You may hear the Anglicism **el departamento del welfare**.

2. The ordinal numbers **primero** and **tercero**, as well as the adjectives **ninguno** and **bueno**, drop the final **-o** before a masculine singular noun:

El *primer* doctor	La *primera* doctora
El *tercer* documento	La *tercera* oficina
No es *ningún* problema	No es *ninguna* molestia

3. The adjectives **protestante, adventista,** and **bautista** have only one singular form for both masculine and feminine:

   El abogado es **adventista.**   *La abogada* es **adventista.**

4. In Spanish, negative sentences follow this format:

No + verb: *No* **hablo español.**	I don't speak Spanish.
No + verb + negative expression:	
No **voy a** *ninguna* **iglesia.**	I don't go to any church.

ESTRUCTURAS BÁSICAS II: En el consultorio 🖭

El doctor	*La paciente*
Pase Ud., señora Díaz. Siéntese. ¿Está cómoda?	Sí, estoy muy cómoda, gracias, doctor.
Primero necesito ciertos datos personales. ¿María Cristina Díaz es su nombre completo?	Bueno, mi apellido de soltera es Salazar.
Salazar se escribe *S-a-l-a-z-a-r,* ¿verdad?	Sí, así se escribe.
¿Ésta es la primera vez que viene aquí?	No es la {segunda. / tercera. / cuarta. / quinta. / sexta.
¿Cuándo fue la última vez?	Fue la semana pasada.
¿Quién la refirió?	Me refirió {una amiga. / la escuela. / la corte. / el departamento de salud. / la agencia de bienestar público. / el ministro de mi iglesia. / el sacerdote.
¿De qué religión es Ud.?	Soy {católica. / protestante. / bautista. / adventista. / judía. No voy a ninguna iglesia.
Bien, señora Díaz, ahora pase Ud. otra vez a la sala de espera. Yo la llamo en seguida.	Gracias. Ud. es muy amable.

---

5. **Otro (otra, otros, otras)** is the equivalent of *other* and *another* in English. It is *never* preceded by the indefinite article **un** or **una** in Spanish.

   Está con *otro* paciente.

Notas lingüísticas II

A. Do not confuse the demonstrative **ésta** in the question *¿Ésta es la primera vez ...?* with the verb form **está.** Demonstratives are used to point out people and things with reference to the location of the speaker and/or listener; they may be used as adjectives or as pronouns (in which case they carry a written accent, as in the previous example). They agree in gender with the noun to which they refer:

este, esta, estos, estas	this, these	*near the speaker*
ese, esa, esos, esas	that, those	*near the listener*
aquel, aquella, aquellos, aquellas	that, those	*far from both speaker and listener*

The neuter forms **esto, eso,** and **aquello** refer to an idea, an action, or something whose gender is unknown:

| ¿**Qué es** *esto*? | What is this? |
| *Eso* **es muy importante.** | That (idea, situation, etc.) is very important. |

B. The English word *time* has several equivalents in Spanish, depending on the concept expressed. When referring to an *instance* of time, the word **(la) vez** is used:

| **Es la** *primera vez*. | It's the first time. |
| **Pase Ud.** *otra vez* **a la sala de espera.** | Go into the waiting room again (another time). |

C. The present tense in Spanish is used more extensively than in English. It is used:

1. To refer to something in progress (English often uses the progressive form):

   Trabajo **en la oficina.**   I'm working in the office.

2. To refer to a planned future occurrence (English prefers the future tense here):

   | ¿**Dónde** *espero?* | Where shall I wait? |
   | **La** *llamo* **en seguida.** | I'll call you (female) immediately. |

D. **Ser** and **estar,** both of which are the equivalent of the English *to be,* have different connotations when followed by an adjective:

ser + adjective = describes a norm or trait inherent in a person or thing

Yo *soy* **católico.**   I am a Catholic.

estar + adjective = describes a variable condition or a change from a norm or expected norm

Estoy **ocupada hoy.**   I am busy today.

Review the following uses of **ser** and **estar** already presented:

ser + noun (or pronoun) = identity of person or thing
ser + **de** = origin
estar + **en** = location

E. Direct object pronouns, which indicate the receiver of the action, *precede* the conjugated verb in Spanish. They are:

me	**me**		us	**nos**
you (fam.)	**te**			
you (form.), him, her, it	**lo, la**		you (pl.), them	**los, las**

¿**Quién** *la* **refirió?**   *Me* **refirió mi mamá.**

In a negative sentence, the following formula is used:

No + object pronoun + verb

No, no *lo* **hablo.**   No, I don't speak it.

F. Two past tense forms are introduced in this lesson:
1. **refirió**   You (formal)/he/she referred.
2. **fue**   You (formal)/he/she were, was or went.

(**Fue** is an irregular past tense form of *both* **ser** and **ir,** which are identical in this past tense.)

PRÁCTICA PRELIMINAR

Follow the guidelines for self-instructional practice given in the Preface.

A. Complete each sentence with the correct form of **estar** or **ser** according to context.

Ejemplo: Nosotros _estamos_ en la oficina.

1. Tú _____ ocupada.

2. Yo _____ con otro cliente.

3. La abogada _____ chilena.

4. Tú _____ muy amable.

5. Ella y yo _____ en una reunión.

6. Usted _____ mejor hoy.

7. Los García _____ simpáticos.

8. Señora Díaz, sus hijos _____ bien de salud.

9. Yo _____ su trabajador social.

10. Mi esposo y yo _____ adventistas.

B. Change the sentences in Exercise A to the negative.

Ejemplo: Nosotros estamos en la oficina.
Nosotros no estamos en la oficina.

C. Choose the correct adjective to complete each sentence.

Ejemplo: Las (estas (otras) esos) clientes están aquí.

1. El psicólogo necesita (ese   esos   esas) documentos.
2. La cita es con (este   esa   aquel) doctora.
3. La corte me refirió a (otra   otro   eso) abogado.
4. La directora tiene (otro   ese   otra) reunión hoy.
5. El recepcionista habla con (esta   esos   esas) mujeres.
6. (Eso   Estos   Otro) es muy importante para nosotros.
7. (Aquella   Eso   Ese) apellido se escribe M-o-n-t-e-s.
8. (Estas   Aquellos   Eso) señores son colombianos.
9. El jefe necesita hablar con (esto   este   esta) señora.
10. Necesito (estos   estas   aquel) datos personales.

A 1. estás 2. estoy 3. es 4. eres 5. estamos 6. está 7. son 8. están 9. soy 10. somos

B 1. Tú no estás ocupada. 2. Yo no estoy con otro cliente. 3. La abogada no es chilena. 4. Tú no eres muy amable. 5. Ella y yo no estamos en una reunión. 6. Usted no está mejor hoy. 7. Los García no son simpáticos. 8. Señora Díaz, sus hijos no están bien de salud. 9. Yo no soy su trabajador social. 10. Mi esposo y yo no somos adventistas.

C 1. esos 2. esa 3. otro 4. otra 5. esas 6. Eso 7. Ese 8. Aquellos 9. esta 10. estos

D. Rewrite each sentence, substituting the appropriate direct object pronoun for the noun in italics.

Ejemplo: Yo tengo *los documentos.*
            Yo los tengo.

1. Necesito *las solicitudes.*
2. No entiendo *al médico.*
3. Llamo *a la secretaria.*
4. Necesito *su nombre.*
5. ¿Tiene Ud. *los papeles?*
6. No domino *el inglés.*

E. Choose the appropriate direct object pronoun for *you,* using **te** when speaking to someone whose first name is given, or **lo, la, los,** or **las** when the formal **usted** form is indicated by the use of a title.

Ejemplo: Dr. Sánchez, _____*lo*_____ espera la secretaria.

1. Rafael, yo _____ llamo mañana.

2. Sra. Rodríguez, ¿quién _____ refirió?

3. Sr. Dávila, _____ busca su esposa.

4. Ana, _____ espera la doctora.

5. Don Felipe, _____ llaman por teléfono.

6. Bueno, señores, _____ veo mañana.

F. Complete the answers to the following questions by writing the appropriate direct object pronoun in the blank.

Ejemplo: ¿Quién la refirió (a Ud.)? _____*me*_____ **refirió la corte.**

1. ¿Quién llama al psicólogo? _____ llama el doctor.

2. ¿Quién me busca? _____ busca tu mamá.

3. ¿Tienes las solicitudes? Sí, _____ tengo aquí.

4. ¿Quién los refirió a Uds.? _____ refirió el sacerdote.

5. ¿Hablan Uds. español? _____ hablamos un poco.

6. ¿Quiénes te esperan? _____ esperan mis amigos.

D 1. Las necesito. 2. No lo entiendo. 3. La llamo. 4. Lo necesito. 5. ¿Los tiene Ud.? 6. No lo domino.
E 1. te 2. la 3. lo 4. te 5. lo 6. los
F 1. Lo 2. Te 3. las 4. Nos 5. Lo 6. Me

Combinándolo todo

PRÁCTICA COMUNICATIVA: Los datos personales

Conversación parcial

Practique Ud. oralmente la siguiente conversación. Cada raya (/) implica que falta una palabra. Es necesario conjugar cada verba *en bastardillas.*

Ejemplo: ¿Cómo / *sentir* Ud. hoy?   No / *sentir* bien.
¿Cómo se siente Ud. hoy?   **No me siento bien.**

La empleada	*El cliente*
1. Señor Gómez, ¿*dominar* / inglés?	Pues, / *hablar* un poquito, pero no / *entender* muy bien.
2. Pues, / Gómez, *necesitar* / datos / .	/ bien.
3. ¿Ésta *ser* / primera / que *venir* /?	No, *ser* la / vez.
4. ¿ / *ser* / última / ?	Fue la / pasada.
5. ¿Quién / *referir?*	/ refirió el / de / iglesia.
6. ¿ / qué / *ser* Ud.?	/ pentecostal.
7. ¿ / se *llamar* / ministro?	/ llama Raúl Domínguez.
8. ¿ / / *escribir Domínguez?*	Se / D-o-m-í-n-g-u-e-z.
9. ¿*Poder* Ud. esperar aquí / rato?	Sí, / no.

Pregunte Ud.

Dé Ud. oralmente las preguntas (o las respuestas) necesarias en la siguiente entrevista con un empleado de su agencia que llama a la puerta.

1. ¿Puedo pasar, señora?
2. Sí, señora, estoy muy cómodo, gracias.
3. Soy Ángel Morales, para servirle.
4. Lo hablo un poquito, pero no lo domino. Prefiero hablar español.
5. Pues, necesito hablar con el gerente de la agencia.
6. No, es la segunda vez que necesito hablar con el gerente.
7. Fue el primer día del trabajo.
8. Me refirió el jefe del departamento donde trabajo.
9. Trabajo en el departamento de relaciones públicas.
10. No, no puedo esperar. Es muy urgente.

Dígalo

Pregúntele a un/a compañero/a lo que le diga su profesor/a sobre los temas de los datos personales, el trabajo, las previas visitas a la agencia, y lo que necesitan los clientes.

Escuche bien

A. Ud. oirá seis nombres completos dos veces. Escríbalos en el espacio apropiado.

1. _____   4. _____

2. _____   5. _____

3. _____   6. _____

B. Ud. oirá a una persona que se describe usando oraciones que contienen el verbo **ser** o **estar.** Escriba:

A — si describe una característica inherente
B — si describe una condición que puede cambiar
C — si se refiere al origen de la persona
D — si se refiere a donde se encuentra la persona

1. _____   5. _____

2. _____   6. _____

3. _____   7. _____

4. _____   8. _____

Diálogos cortos

I. *La recepcionista*

_____ tardes, padre. ¿En

_____ puedo _____ ?

¿Cómo se _____ el

_____ ?

¿Es la primera _____ que

Ud. _____ a este hospital?

El sacerdote

Buenas _____ , hija. Quiero ver

a _____ paciente que _____ en este hospital.

_____ llama Carlos Santana Pietri.

No, la _____ vez _____ la semana _____ .

La recepcionista

Está en _____ segundo piso (*floor*). Pero no _____ hablar mucho, padre. No se _____ muy bien hoy.

Espere _____ momento, _____ Ud. _____. que llevar (*to take*) _____ tarjeta de entrada (*pass*).

El sacerdote

Gracias. Sólo voy _____ pasar _____ ratito _____ él.

Ah sí, claro, _____ . Gracias.

II. *La recepcionista*

_____ abogado _____ con otro cliente. ¿ _____ qué _____ servirle?

¿Es _____ primera _____ que viene _____ ?

Cálmese, señor. ¿ _____ se _____ Ud.?

¿ _____ ciudadano de _____ Estados Unidos?

¿ _____ tarjeta _____ ?

¿ _____ qué nacionalidad _____ ?

¿ _____ qué _____ Ud.?

El cliente

Buenas _____ . _____ hablar _____ el abogado que _____ español.

_____ problemas con mi jefe del _____ .

Sí. _____ muy nervioso.

Soy Evaristo Camacho.

No, señora, no soy _____ .

No ése es _____ problema.

_____ ecuatoriano.

Trabajo de mecánico.

La recepcionista   *El cliente*

¿Quién _____ refirió?   _____ refirió _____ amigo.

Ud. _____ que llenar   No, pero _____ llevo (*I'll take*) a

_____ formularios.   casa y mi _____ me
                                 ayuda (*will help*).

¿Entiende _____ ?

Ayude al cliente

You need to translate the following form from English to Spanish for your Spanish-speaking clients. At times it is better to avoid a direct translation and instead to use words and structures you have studied in previous lessons to translate the concept. You might also wish to adjust the form for relevant cultural information — for example, the full name of the client.

DEPARTMENT OF SOCIAL SERVICES

We need the following personal information for your next interview. Please fill out this form completely. You may write in Spanish, if you'd like.

Full name _____
                last name   first name

Maiden name _____ Name of spouse _____

Occupation _____ Place of employment _____

Occupation and place of employment of spouse _____

_____

Is this your first visit to the agency?   _____ yes   _____ no

Date of last visit _____

Source of referral _____

Religious preference: ____ Catholic ____ Jewish ____ Protestant ____ Other

U.S. citizen? _____ yes _____ no   Permanent resident? _____ yes _____ no

---

¿Comprende Ud.?

Llene Ud. el siguiente formulario según los datos personales de la señora que habla.

Full name _____
                        last name   first name

Married _____   Single _____   Maiden name _____

Seeks services of: _____ social worker   _____ physician

                    _____ legal aid employee   _____ dentist

Referred by _____   Previous visits _____

English proficiency _____   Other languages _____

U.S. citizen _____   National origin _____   Employed? _____

Piénselo

Prepárese para poder hablar con el/la profesor/a o con otros estudiantes sobre los siguientes temas, contestando las preguntas que le sugiera el/la profesor/a.

1. Cómo saber si el/la cliente se siente cómodo/a
2. Los varios servicios que se le ofrecen al/a la cliente
3. Lo que (*what*) pasa cuando el cliente viene a la agencia y la persona que quiere ver no está
4. Los problemas que ocurren en su agencia con los apellidos hispanos
5. La importancia de saber si es la primera visita a la agencia del/de la cliente

Imagínese

Estudie bien las fotos y conteste las preguntas:

A.

1. ¿De qué nacionalidad es este señor?
2. ¿Tiene esposa? ¿Cómo se llama ella?
3. ¿Dónde está este señor?
4. ¿En qué trabaja él?
5. ¿Quién lo refirió?
6. ¿Cómo se llama él?
7. ¿Qué lengua habla él?
8. ¿Cómo se siente hoy?
9. ¿Con quién necesita hablar?
10. ¿En qué puede Ud. servirle?

B.

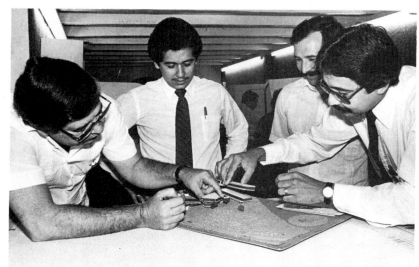

1. ¿En qué trabajan estos hombres?
2. ¿Hablan inglés o español?
3. ¿Cómo se llama cada uno de ellos?
4. ¿Están contentos con su trabajo?
5. ¿Es difícil (*difficult*) o fácil (*easy*) su trabajo?
6. ¿Es la primera vez que trabajan juntos? (*together*)?
7. ¿Quieren continuar con este trabjao?
8. ¿De qué nacionalidad son?
9. ¿Cuál es el jefe del grupo?
10. ¿Están muy ocupados hoy?

Haciendo el papel

Haga Ud. el papel de la persona indicada en las siguientes situaciones. Tenga en cuenta el posible mal entendimiento de las actitudes hacia la autoridad.

1. You are a doctor leaving the operating room of a hospital. A Latino man is waiting outside the door in a prohibited area. Ask if you may be of service to him. He answers in a low voice with head down that he is looking for his mother, María Acosta de Rojas. Ask him to repeat her name and spell it, since you do not understand or speak (*dominar*) Spanish very well. Ask him if Mrs. Rojas is a patient or if she works in the hospital. After he answers, tell him politely that he must go back to the waiting room and that a nurse who can help him will be there in a moment.

2. You are the school social worker. Mrs. Irene Vera de Matos, who wishes to speak to her son's teacher, has been referred to you by the principal. Ask her what her son's name is and what grade (*grado*) he's in. Ask her if her son has a problem. She says she prefers (*prefiere*) to speak with the teacher. Explain to her your role as a social worker and how you might be of service to her.

3. You are the director of a job program. An employee runs into your office. Ask him what's wrong. He says he has a problem with another employee. Ask him the name of the employee and where the employee is now. You sense that he is reluctant to tell you. Try to make him feel more comfortable and then ask him if you can call his boss.

4. Welcome your client, Mr. Pablo Iriarte, and introduce yourself, shaking hands. Ask him to sit down and tell him that you need some personal information in order to (*para*) process (*procesar*) his application. Then ask the appropriate questions in order to fill out the following form:

Name _____

Occupation _____

Name of spouse _____

Religious affiliation _____

Source of referral _____

Previous visits to agency _____

Current employment _____

REFLEJOS DE LA CULTURA: "Me matan si no trabajo"

The following song expresses the unhappiness of the majority of Latin American workers due to their extreme poverty and difficult working conditions. Just as the indigenous labor force was abused by the colonizing Spaniards, many of today's lower-class Hispanics continue to toil both in their native lands and in the United States, in the cities and in the countryside, in low-paying, backbreaking jobs. Many are subjected to inhumane treatment and a general lack of respect due to their poor economic conditions.

The words were written by Nicolás Guillén, a major Cuban poet of the twentieth century, and Daniel Viglietti, a singer and composer from Uruguay who is now living in exile. It was recorded by Grupo Raíz, a performing troup of musicians and singers who came together at La Peña Cultural Center in Berkeley, California, in 1980. Although their collective accent is Chilean, their music "begins in the Mapuche lands of southern Chile and extends across the Andes to the Atlantic plains and Caribbean coastline — island hops around Cuba and Puerto Rico — and absorbs the vibrance, pain and promise of Central America today."*

*From the description on the Monitor record jacket of the album *Amaneceres* recorded by Grupo Raíz.

The goals of this musical group are twofold: to present the music and culture of Latin Americans to others and to use their music to lend support to the resistance movement in Chile and to liberation movements in Latin America and other parts of the world.

ME MATAN SI NO TRABAJO

Me matan si no trabajo,
si trabajo me matan;
siempre me matan, me matan,
ay, siempre me matan.

Ayer vi un hombre mirando,
mirando el sol que salía.
El hombre estaba muy serio
porque el hombre no veía.

Ay, los ciegos viven sin ver
cuando sale el sol,
cuando sale el sol,
cuando sale el sol.

Ayer vi a un niño jugando
a que mataba a otro niño.
Hay niños que se parecen
a los hombres trabajando.

¿Quién les dirá cuando crezcan
que los hombres no son niños,
que no lo son,
que no lo son,
que no lo son?

Me matan si no trabajo,
y si trabajo me matan;
siempre me matan, me matan,
ay, siempre me matan.

THEY KILL ME IF I DON'T WORK

They kill me if I don't work,
If I work, they kill me;
They always kill me, and kill me,
Ay, they always kill me.

Yesterday I saw a man watching,
Watching the sun that was rising.
The man was very serious
Because the man didn't see.

Ay, blind men live without seeing
When the sun comes out,
When the sun comes out,
When the sun comes out.

Yesterday I saw a boy playing
At killing another boy.
There are children who resemble
Men working.

Who will tell them when they grow up
That men are not children,
That they are not,
That they are not,
That they are not?

They kill me if I don't work,
And if I work, they kill me;
They always kill me and kill me,
Ay, they always kill me.

LECCIÓN 4

Tengo la hora pero no tengo el tiempo

LOS OBJETIVOS

Raising awareness

1. To become aware of how people's differing perceptions of reality affect cross-cultural communication
2. To understand the Hispanic concept of time
3. To "break the time barrier" that often exists between Anglo professionals and their Hispanic clients

Comunicándose en español

1. To pronounce accurately stressed syllables in Spanish words
2. To use times and days of the week to make appointments with clients
3. To learn basic telephone etiquette in Spanish
4. To choose appropriate vocabulary and structures when referring to time
5. To use the indirect object construction with verbs that have an impersonal subject (e.g., **parecer**)

Combinándolo todo

1. To integrate the use of new vocabulary and structures presented in this lesson with those previously learned
2. To understand the Hispanic philosophical concept of time through the poetry of a Latin American woman

Raising awareness

OVERVIEW: What is cross-cultural communication?

Once you can see yourself as a product of both cultural conditioning and personal experiences, you are ready to apply this understanding directly to the cross-cultural communication process. In this chapter you will learn what other factors besides the language barrier affect you and your Hispanic clients as you try to understand each other.

Actually, these factors affect *all* communication between human beings, regardless of cultural background. An analysis of the components of the communication process leads to the following five observations. All of them influence cross-cultural communication enormously:

1. We perceive things differently.
2. Pure communication is impossible.
3. We communicate all the time.
4. We perceive things that do not exist.
5. We do not perceive things that do exist.

Let us explore each of these in depth.

1. *We perceive things differently; each of us has a unique way of sensing what is happening to us or around us.* For example, if two people are looking at the same coat, one may see a stylish red evening coat while the other may perceive an orange casual coat that is not in particularly good taste. In listening to a given song, one may hear loud music, unintelligible lyrics, and a deafening beat, while someone else may hear an evocative love song that elicits a deep emotional reaction. As the saying goes, "one man's meat is another man's poison."

2. *Pure communication is impossible.* No one can transfer fully what is in his or her mind to someone else's. Several factors may impede this 100 percent transfer.

Often what one says is not what one actually means. The words chosen do not accurately translate the thought they are meant to explain or clarify. Furthermore, the words you use have a meaning for you that may differ from their meaning for a friend of yours. As we have already seen, *meaning* is in people's perceptions and not in the words themselves. In addition, the emotional and experiential value (or *connotation*) that words have for each individual varies greatly. Thus what you *hear* me say may be very different from *what* I say.

The meaning of what is said or heard is further influenced by what can be called the *semantic environment* in which the speaker and/or the hearer find themselves. The communication rules that govern such semantic environments are most often dictated by cultural values and expectations. For example, you would respond differently to the question "How are you doing today?" when it is asked by a cab driver taking you to the airport than when it is asked by your surgeon the morning after you have had a major operation. Likewise, we have certain culturally determined expectations regarding the type of communication allowed in certain environments (e.g., elevators, doctors' offices, bars).

3. *We communicate all the time.* Nonetheless our verbal attempts to communicate our thoughts to others are often inaccurate and incomplete. Even when we say nothing we are communicating. Just as our minds are always engaged in some form of thought process, our external behavior sends off signals that are received and interpreted by others in our immediate environment. We may talk of getting "good vibes" or "bad vibes" from an individual that may contradict or belie the verbal message we are receiving. As living, breathing human beings, we are fields of energy which interact as soon as we come into reasonable proximity with each other. In addition, the emotional states we experience as either senders or receivers of verbal messages are evidenced in our bodies and their positions, affecting the communication process as much as the words spoken or heard.

4. *We perceive things that do not exist.* Our senses are bombarded by many different kinds of stimuli as we are involved in the communication process. These include input related to the message we are sending or receiving, as well as extraneous data which may distract our attention from that message. Hence, we select only what

we consider relevant enhancers to the message. We may even supply what is not there, using our own expectations regarding the message to fill in what is actually missing. For example, if someone makes a grammatical error, you may not really "hear" it but, rather, automatically supply or insert a corrected version (subconsciously, of course), thus perceiving something that is not really there.

5. *We often do not perceive things that do exist.* You may miss some cues that would enable you to better send or understand a message. As sender you may miss an obvious body-language cue that tells you that the receiver is closed to your message. Likewise, as receiver, you may not hear (or may not choose to hear) the underlying intonation that transforms an apparent compliment into a subtle hostile attack.

The following are illustrations of our inaccurate powers of observation:

If you did not notice the repetition of *the* in the figure on the left or the lack of the *i* in *smokng* in the right-hand figure, you are not unusual; you filled in what was missing and omitted unnecessary information in order to understand the message.

These five factors govern all attempts to communicate with others. They especially affect the exchange of information between people from different cultural backgrounds. The subjective aspect of our perceptions and our interpretations of outside reality is directly related to our success in understanding each other. When the difference between two individuals' subjectivity includes disparate culturally determined ways of viewing reality, the success of the communication process is even more in jeopardy. In summary, the following interaction between Sarah and Ramón is typical of the misunderstandings common to the cross-cultural communication process.

Applications

1. List five words that are emotionally charged for you, such as ethnic nicknames, physical or emotional descriptions, and "buzz" words.

2. What emotional reaction do you have when you hear each of the following:

fatso _____

queer _____

yuppie _____

3. Discuss what communication behaviors are culturally acceptable in the following semantic environments in the mainland United States: a movie theater, a subway, an open city/town council meeting, a business-oriented cocktail party.

4. How would you explain and/or analyze the following idiomatic expressions to a nonnative speaker of English: *to get with it, to let someone down, to beat around the bush, to take it easy, to sleep on it, off the top of my head,* and *get off my back?*

5. Working in pairs, express the following emotions nonverbally, using only gestures: anger, joy, hostility, fear, trust.

6. Working in pairs, take turns listening for one minute to your partner describing a very happy experience he or she recently had. Pretend you are a tape recorder and play back *exactly* what you heard your partner say. Now reverse roles and repeat the process. Verify the accuracy of each of the "recordings."

7. Which of the five factors affecting the cross-cultural communication process are operating in the situation illustrated on page 103?

Reflections

1. Compare your charged words with those of other members of the class. How are they alike? How do they differ? How much of your reaction to these words is determined by your cultural conditioning and how much to your personal experiences?

2. Compare your reactions to the words given in no. 2 above with those of other members of the class. What accounts for those who react more strongly than others to certain terms?

3. Do you agree with your classmates regarding the types of behaviors acceptable in each of the environments listed? What accounts for differences in opinion?

4. Did you have difficulty explaining the idiomatic expressions given? Are there others that you use often? How might these be misunderstood by nonnative speakers of English? Are there any Spanish idioms that are difficult for you to use and/or understand?

5. Were you able to express the emotions given easily without words? How did your mode of expression differ from that of your partner? Is it easier for you to express emotions verbally or nonverbally?

6. How accurately did you and your partner record each other?

7. What strategies do you suggest to improve the communication process between Sarah and Ramón depicted on page 103?

HISTORICAL PERSPECTIVE: The Hispanic day

The way we view time is dictated by the culture in which we live. For example, to most Americans February 13, 1983, meant nothing more than the eve of St. Valentine's Day nineteen hundred and eighty-three years after the birth of Christ. But to Chinese families living in China and other parts of the world, including the United States, it marked the first day of 4681, the Year of the Pig, according to the Chinese lunar calendar.

While Hispanics and Anglos *do* use the same calendar, there are differences in the perception of time. Although the movement of the sun and the moon determine the twenty-four-hour cycle of the day in both cultures, the division of those twenty-four hours is different in each.

First of all, in the United States, noon and midnight are used to divide time into A.M. (from the Latin *ante meridiem,* meaning *before noon*) and P.M. (from the Latin *post meridiem* meaning *after noon*). While noon (*mediodía*) and midnight (*medianoche*) are used to mark divisions in the Hispanic day, a third division marks the time between sunset and midnight and a fourth between midnight and sunrise. A.M. is reflected by both *de la madrugada* (midnight to 6:00 A.M.) and *de la mañana* (6:00 A.M. to noon) in Spanish, while P.M. is the equivalent of *de la tarde* until the sun goes down, after which *de la noche* is used. Furthermore, since the time of sunset may vary from one season to another, so does the use of *de la tarde* and *de la noche*. A party beginning at 7:00 P.M. in the winter, in some Hispanic countries is *a las siete de la noche*, while in the summer it starts *a las siete de la tarde*. In those countries near the equator, the variation is minimal. The following chart summarizes the differences between the two systems:

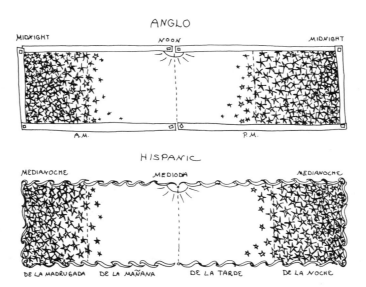

ANGLO

MIDNIGHT · NOON · MIDNIGHT · A.M. · P.M.

HISPANIC

MEDIANOCHE · MEDIODÍA · MEDIANOCHE · DE LA MADRUGADA · DE LA MAÑANA · DE LA TARDE · DE LA NOCHE

1. *Compare the division of the twenty-four-hour cycle of the American and Hispanic systems.*
2. *How do you determine when to use* de la madrugada *and* de la mañana? De la tarde *and* de la noche?

In addition to the formal divisions of the twenty-four-hour cycle, most cultures also use mealtimes as informal ways to divide up the working day. These food breaks not only provide nourishment and rest for the body but also provide the opportunity for "feeding" the emotions and "relaxing" the mind. Although this view of mealtimes is losing ground in the fast-paced efficient business and technical environment of the United States, this has not happened to the same extent in other cultures.

The Hispanic world has always emphasized the nurturing aspects of food and drink as much as the nutritional needs of the body. This is part of the heritage from Spain, which, like other Mediterranean countries including Portugal, Italy, and Greece, has always eaten the principal meal of the day in the early afternoon. This substantial meal (*la comida*), eaten at home with all family members present, has traditionally been followed by a rest or *siesta.* In the southern Mediterranean and tropical climates, this period coincides with the hottest part of the day. Business hours reflect this culturally accepted pattern, closing from noon or 1:00 until 4:00 or 5:00 in the afternoon and then reopening until 7:00 or 8:00 P.M.

As the Hispanic world is influenced by external cultures, especially in the field of business and technology, and by the realities of huge traffic jams four times a day, this "inefficient" (from the Anglo perspective) use of time is slowly being replaced. Eating a meal with friends or colleagues at a restaurant or cafeteria near one's place of work is becoming more common in some Hispanic cultures. The brown-bag sandwich lunch is not a popular option, although in some areas wives (or maids) may bring the man of the house a hot, home-cooked meal at work. Fast-food restaurants, while increasing in popularity in some Hispanic countries, are frequented more at snack times than during the traditional lunch break. Despite the Anglo influence, this midday rest-period is still longer and more leisurely in most

Spanish-speaking countries than it is in the United States. Cultural patterns, especially those dealing with food, seem to change slowly.

Regardless of the impact of the "efficiency" lunch break on Hispanic cultures, the after-work period still prevails as a time for socializing at home or in cafés. Drinking coffee, fresh juices, beer, or the local preferred beverage (wine in Spain, rum in the Caribbean, beer in many Hispanic countries) and snacking with friends or family commonly occurs at this time of the day. This is a time for people to get together, to drop in (often without calling first), and to take care of social obligations (visiting the sick or those in mourning). Men often use this time to meet with their male friends in small cafés in their neighborhood. Women and children tend to meet at the homes of friends or family members before the preparation of the evening meal.

This evening meal (*la cena* or *la merienda* in Mexico) tends to be lighter than the midday repast, unless family members have eaten *la comida* away from home. It is often served later in the evening than is the custom in the United States. Most of the day's activities end with this meal, although in some Latino cultures, concerts or theater, or visiting friends, occur in the evening after 8:30 or 9:00 P.M.

Since a large meal is eaten in the early afternoon and a late meal in the evening, breakfast is considered relatively unimportant for both physical and social needs. It usually consists of *café con leche* (equal parts of strong hot coffee and hot milk, to which sugar is usually added) and fresh bread with butter and/or jam, crackers, plain cookies, or sweet rolls (*pan dulce* in Mexico). It is not necessarily eaten with the entire family group present, and some people may omit it altogether. It is not uncommon to take a midmorning break later at school or work to have coffee (or even a light *aperitivo*) and a snack, usually with friends or colleagues.

This division of the day by mealtimes varies among Hispanic countries. In most cases, however, depending on the degree of industrialization and urbanization, Hispanic countries share the perspective that it is important to take the workday in small doses. A common saying in Spanish is that *"Los gringos viven para trabajar y nosotros trabajamos para vivir"* ("Americans live to work, while we work to live"). What may be judged as an inefficient use of time by an English-

speaking culture that values productivity above individual and social needs is seen by most Hispanics as the only real way to live.

The U.S. workday, with its deadlines and pressures, its schedules and appointments, its stresses and lack of emphasis on personal needs, seems strange to many Hispanics, who tend to view human needs as more important than efficiency and/or productivity.

Interestingly, both cultures are in a state of flux. The Anglo culture seems to be heading toward allowing more leisure time for consumption and recreation. On the other hand, Latino immigrants to the United States are often very highly motivated to work long hours and/or two jobs to get ahead. Recent studies in the Southwest show that many employers prefer to hire Hispanics, prizing them for their diligent work habits and punctuality.

---

3. *Describe how the divisions of the Hispanic day coincide with the meal breaks.*
4. *How does the division of the day reflect the difference between the Hispanic and Anglo views of work?*

NONVERBAL COMMUNICATION: Breaking the time barrier

A given culture's attitudes toward time are often reflected in its proverbs (*refranes* in Spanish). While both English and Spanish-speaking cultures share the maxim "Better late than never" (*"Más vale tarde que nunca"*), the similarities seem to end there.

The work ethic of the early settlers of the United States is evident in such axioms as "Don't put off until tomorrow what you can do today," "Time and tide wait for no man," "Time is money," "Time is of the essence," "A stitch in time saves nine," "Early to bed and early to rise makes a man healthy, wealthy, and wise," and "The early bird catches the worm." The message is the same — you must control time rather than let it control you. Time is viewed as a commodity to be saved and put to good use. It is seen as a force marching forward, needing to be harnessed for human success in the fast-paced world of modern technology. It is debatable, however, whether time is master or slave, especially in the large urban areas of the United States.

In the contemporary English-speaking world, socializing is often as scheduled as are business appointments. Friends must be called before we visit them in order to make sure they have the "time" to spend with us. Formal invitations to parties and other social events often include both

HISPANIC TIME   U.S. TIME

a starting and an ending time to make sure that guests do not outstay their welcome. Even one's physical exercise needs must find their place on the jam-packed calendar. Children are taught not to "waste time" and that "idle hands are the devil's workshop." Ironically, it is not uncommon for adults in the United States to schedule time even for "relaxation" and "stress-reduction" activities.

Hispanics, with their more casual attitude toward time, tend to view Anglos as obsessed with time. In Spanish, a watch doesn't *run*, it *walks* (*el reloj anda*). It is never *fast* or *slow*; it is merely *ahead* (*adelantado*) or *behind* (*atrasado*). Such adages as "*El que mucho corre, pronto para*" ("He who runs a lot, soon stops"), "*El tiempo todo lo trae y todo se lo lleva*" ("Time brings everything and also takes it away"), "*A su tiempo maduran las uvas*" ("Grapes ripen in their own time") and "*Procura lo mejor, espera lo peor y toma lo que viene*" ("Try your best, expect the worst, and take whatever comes") reflect a more relaxed and, perhaps, more respectful attitude toward time.

Unfortunately, this slower-paced lifestyle is often viewed stereotypically from the Anglo perspective. The *mañana* syndrome is often reflected in a derogatory way in cartoons, advertisements, television, and movies as typical of all Latinos. When measured according to the Anglo yardstick, this tendency to take life, and consequently time, as it comes may be judged as representing a lack of ambition or initiative, a fatalistic approach to life, or even disdain for the modern world of technology and efficiency.

In most Hispanic countries, the Anglo model of efficiency has made some headway, especially in the workday world of the large urban centers. In the rural areas, customs are slower to change. Few if any Spanish-speaking countries, however, reflect the true Anglo perspective on time.

In providing services to Hispanics living in the United States, the different cultural attitudes toward time may affect your interactions with your Spanish-speaking clients. Although you may be pleasantly surprised at the patience your Hispanic clients exhibit while waiting for professional services, you may also be quite dismayed when a client continually arrives late for appointments.

The following guidelines may help both you and your Spanish-speaking clients to adjust your different culturally determined attitudes toward time in order to "break the time barrier."

1. Remember to *explain* to your clients and not *lecture* them about why it is important for them to arrive on time for appointments.

2. Listen to a client's excuse for arriving late; in the Hispanic hierarchy of values, family needs will often take priority over scheduled appointments.

3. Whenever possible, be flexible in providing services to clients who have arrived late, even if they have missed their scheduled time slot.

4. Be careful not to make assumptions about your client's personal ambition and dependability based on his or her track record in punctuality.

5. Do not take literally such promises as *"mañana," "momentito," "inmediatamente"* (which can mean anytime in the not too distant future and not necessarily *tomorrow, in a moment,* or *immediately*). They do not translate according to the same time-measuring framework.

6. Relax when you are late for an appointment with a Hispanic client — tardiness is accepted as a natural event over which you have little control and will seldom produce an angry response from the person kept waiting.

7. Remember that attitudes toward time will vary from client to client, depending on both cultural factors and personal experiences. Latinos who have lived most of their lives in the United States will undoubtedly have assimilated more to the Anglo concept of time than those who have recently arrived.

Putting it into practice

1. Act out a scene between an English-speaking professional who has a stereotypic view of the Hispanic attitude toward time and his or her Hispanic client who arrives 45 minutes late for an appointment because he had to pick up his daughter at school.

2. Now act out the same scene, changing the role of the professional to someone who has a broader understanding of this Hispanic cultural phenomenon.

3. List three ways your life would be different if you lived according to the Hispanic concept of time. Would these changes be for the better or for the worse?

   a. _____

   b. _____

   c. _____

4. Complete the following statement according to your own value system:

   Time is: _____

   _____

5. How might your attitude toward time affect your interaction with Hispanic clients who may have a more relaxed attitude toward time in general and punctuality in particular?

Comunicándose en español

PRONUNCIACIÓN: La acentuación 🎞

Stress patterns in a language can affect meaning. Compare the following English words, in which the stressed syllables are italicized.

*im*port (noun)   im*port* (verb)
*con*vict (noun)   con*vict* (verb)

Now compare these words.

*és*ta (adjective: *this*)   es*tá* (verb: *is*)
*pa*pa (noun: *potato*)   pa*pá* (noun: *father*)

Notice the importance of stress in verb forms in Spanish.

hablo (*I speak*)   **habló** (*he spoke*)
trabaje (command: *work*)   **trabajé** (*I worked*)

Two simple rules govern stress in Spanish:

1. Words ending in a *vowel*, **n**, or **s**, are stressed on the *next to last* syllable.

   gus-to   pa-**pe**-les   tra-**ba**-jan   do-cu-**men**-tos
   tie-ne   es-**pe**-ran   com-**ple**-ta   en-fer-**me**-ra

2. Words ending in a *consonant* other than **n** or **s** are stressed on the *last* syllable.

   ver-**dad**   me-**jor**   pre-pa-**rar**   tra-ba-ja-**dor**
   pa-**pel**   mu-**jer**   ge-ne-**ral**   es-pa-**ñol**

Any exceptions to these rules will be indicated by a written accent mark over the syllable which should be stressed:

exceptions to rule 1	*exceptions to rule 2*
es-**tá** re-fi-**rió**	**Ló**-pez i-**nú**-til
des-**pués** **sién**-te-se	**cár**-cel Gon-**zá**-lez

A written accent is also used to distinguish words which are spelled alike but have different meanings:

si — *if*   sí — *yes*   mi — *my*   mí — *me* (with prepositions)
el — *the*   él — *he*   se — *himself*   sé — *I know*
de — *of*   dé — *give*   mas — *but*   más — *more*

A written accent is always placed on the stressed syllable of interrogative words such as *who* (¿quién?), *what* (¿qué?), *where* (¿dónde?), *how much* (¿cuánto?), *how* (¿cómo?), when used in questions.

Práctica 🎞

A. Underline the stressed syllable in each of the following Spanish words. Then pronounce each.

católico	general	teléfono	necesita
número	contador	continúa	trabajadora
inglés	Brasil	Panamá	Pérez
sígame	hable	trabajó	responsable

B. Read each of the following sentences without pausing. Pay particular attention to the stress patterns in the words. (It may help to underline the stressed syllable in each word.)

1. Necesito su número de teléfono.
2. ¿Por qué llegó Ud. tarde, señor Andoval?
3. El trabajador social no es católico.
4. Es importante hablar bajo en el hospital.
5. Señora Muñoz, ¿quién la refirió a esta agencia?

Dictado

Write the words your instructor pronounces, underline the stressed syllable, and write a written accent mark if the word is an exception to the two stress rules in Spanish.

1. _____   9. _____
2. _____   10. _____
3. _____   11. _____
4. _____   12. _____
5. _____   13. _____
6. _____   14. _____
7. _____   15. _____
8. _____

¿Ha entendido bien?

1. ¿Cómo se llama el cliente?

2. ¿Con quién tiene cita el cliente?

3. ¿A qué hora era la cita?

4. ¿A qué hora llegó el señor Ríos?

5. ¿Por qué llegó tarde para la cita?

6. ¿Dónde está el señor Henderson ahora?

7. ¿Qué tiene que hacer el señor Ríos para ver al señor Henderson?

8. ¿Qué quiere hacer el señor Ríos?

9. ¿La recepcionista le permite esperar al señor Henderson?

10. ¿Cuál es la opinión del señor Ríos acerca de "la hora exacta"?

INTRODUCTORY DIALOGUE: "On time"

Mr. Ríos: Excuse me, miss. I'm Joaquín Ríos and I have an appointment with Mr. Henderson.

Receptionist: I'm very sorry, but Mr. Henderson is in a meeting.

Mr. R: How can that be if I have an appointment with him?

R: At what time was the appointment?

Mr. R: I think it was at three o'clock.

R: But it's already three-thirty. You arrived very late for the appointment.

Mr. R: Yes, I know, but I had to take my wife to work first.

R: Well, you have to make an appointment for another day.

Mr. R: Can't I wait here for Mr. Henderson?

R: No, it's impossible. Here in the United States if you do not arrive on time, you lose the appointment.

Mr. R: I'll never be able to get used to this preoccupation that you (all) have with "(being) on time"!

BASIC STRUCTURES I: Speaking on the telephone

The employee (f.)

Hello. Herrera and Sons, at your service.

Who's calling, please?

Wait a moment, please.

The client (m.)

I would like to speak with Mrs. Ramos, please.

Rubén Acevedo.

Mrs. Ramos

Hello, Mr. Acevedo. This is Matilde Ramos speaking.

At what time is the appointment?

I won't be in the office tomorrow after three-thirty.

Just a moment. I have to check the (my) calendar.

The client (m.)

Mrs. Ramos, I have a problem with the appointment we have tomorrow.

It's at two-thirty. I can't arrive before four because I have to see the doctor at three.

Then, we have to change the appointment for next week. Are you free on Monday?

¿Sabe usted?

1. **Bueno** is used to answer the telephone in Mexico, **oigo** in Cuba and **aló, hola,** and **diga** in Puerto Rico. Diga is also heard in Spain and Cuba. **¿De parte de quién?** is asked to find out who's calling and is answered in third person (**Habla Matilde Ramos**). Calls may be answered by giving one's last name followed by **para servirle, a la orden,** or **a sus órdenes.**

2. **Y,** used to express *and* in Spanish, changes to **e** before a word beginning with an **i** or **hi** (e.g., **Herrera e hijos**).

3. **Si me hace el favor** is a formal expression of courtesy.

4. When the direct object of a sentence is a person, it is preceded by the preposition **a.** This a tells the listener that the person mentioned after it *receives* the action of the sentence.

   Tengo que ver *a mi esposa.*   I have to see my wife.
   ¿No puedo esperar *al señor Henderson?*   Can't I wait for Mr. Henderson?

5. **La semana que viene** is synonymous with **la próxima semana.**

ESTRUCTURAS BÁSICAS I: Hablando por teléfono

La empleada	El cliente
Aló. Herrera e hijos, a sus órdenes.	Quisiera hablar con la señora Ramos, si me hace el favor.
¿De parte de quién, por favor?	De Rubén Acevedo.
Espere un momento, por favor.	

La señora Ramos	El cliente
Aló, señor Acevedo. Habla Matilde Ramos.	Señora Ramos, tengo un problema con la cita que tenemos para mañana.
¿A qué hora es la cita?	Es a las dos y media. No puedo llegar antes de las cuatro porque tengo que ver al doctor a las tres.
Yo no voy a estar en la oficina mañana después de las tres y media.	Entonces, tenemos que cambiar la cita para la semana que viene. ¿Está libre el lunes?
Un momentito. Tengo que consultar el calendario.	

Notas lingüísticas I

A. Two-word prepositions are common in Spanish. The first word is usually an adverb; the second is usually **de**.

Preposition

No puedo llegar *antes de* las cuatro.	I can't arrive *before* four o'clock.
No voy a estar *después de* las tres.	I won't be (in) *after* three o'clock.

Adverb

Antes yo era maestro.	*Before,* I was a teacher.
Voy a casa *después.*	I'll go home *afterwards.*

B. Some verbs in Spanish are followed directly by the infinitive of another verb, while others need a linking word.

Followed directly by infinitive	Followed by linking word
querer + infinitive	ir + *a* + infinitive
poder + infinitive	tener + *que* + infinitive

Ejemplos:

Quiero hablar con Ud.	I want to speak with you.
Voy a llamar al doctor.	I'm going to call the doctor.
¿No *puede esperar?*	Can't you wait?
Ud. *tiene que volver* hoy.	You have to come back today.

C. Some Spanish words derived from Greek end in **-a** but are masculine: **el día, el problema, el programa, el sistema,** etc.

D. Review these one-word prepositions: **con** (*with*), **en** (*on, in,* or *at*), **de** (*of, from*), **a** (*at*), and **hasta** (*until*).

115

BASIC STRUCTURES II: Speaking on the telephone

Mrs. Ramos	*Mr. Acevedo*
Well, Mr. Acevedo, on Mondays I always have a meeting all afternoon. Can you come in the morning?	No, I can't because of (my) work.

How does
{ Tuesday / Wednesday / Thursday / Friday / Saturday / Sunday } seem to you? — Tuesday is best for me.

For me too. I'm free all afternoon. — Me, too.

Is
{ one o'clock / two o'clock / three o'clock / four o'clock / five-fifteen / six-twenty / seven-thirty / a quarter to eight / nine o'clock sharp / ten p.m. / eleven twenty-five / twelve o'clock } convenient? — (The time) seems perfect to me. Thank you very much, ma'am.

Don't hang up, Mr. Acevedo. I need your telephone number.	It's 5-14-13-16.
Let me see if I have it right. It's 5-14-13-17?	No, it's 5-14-13-*16*.
All right, I'll see you then.	Goodbye. See you Tuesday.

¿Sabe usted?

1. The names for the days of the week reflect the solar system. **Lunes** is derived from **luna** (*moon — lunar, lunatic* in English), just as *Monday* was originally *Moon day.* **Martes** refers to the planet *Mars;* **miércoles,** to *Mercury;* **jueves,** to *Jupiter;* and **viernes,** to *Venus.* **Sábado** refers to the *Sabbath,* while **domingo,** from the Latin *dominicus* or *Lord,* signals the *Lord's day.* The Spanish names of the days of the week are *not* capitalized except at the beginning of a sentence.

2. To express the concept *on a certain day,* use **el** + the day of the week: **Voy el jueves.** (*I'm going on Thursday.*) The plural article **los** + day of the week (adding *-s* to **sábado** and **domingo**) expresses the concept of a habitual action on that day:

    Siempre tengo reunión los   I always have a meeting on Monday afternoon.
    lunes por la tarde.

116

ESTRUCTURAS BÁSICAS II: Hablando por teléfono 🔲

La señora Ramos	El señor Acevedo
Bueno, señor Acevedo, los lunes siempre tengo una reunión toda la tarde. ¿Puede Ud. venir por la mañana?	No, no puedo por el trabajo.

¿Qué le parece el { martes? miércoles? jueves? viernes? sábado? domingo? }   El martes es mejor para mí.

| También para mí. Estoy libre toda la tarde. | Yo también. |

¿Le conviene { a la una? a las dos? a las tres? a las cuatro? a las cinco y cuarto? a las seis y veinte? a las siete y media? a las ocho menos cuarto? a las nueve en punto? a las diez de la noche? a las once y veinticinco? a las doce? }   Me parece perfecta (la hora). Muchísimas gracias, señora.

No cuelgue, señor Acevedo. Me hace falta su teléfono.	Es el 5-14-13-16. (cinco-catorce-trece-dieciséis).
A ver si lo tengo bien. ¿Es el 5-14-13-17 (cinco-catorce-trece-diecisiete)?	No, es el 5-14-13-*16*.
Bueno, nos vemos entonces.	Adiós. Hasta el martes.

---

3. To express the concept of *all day long, all morning long,* and so on, use the singular **todo/a** plus the definite article and time referent. *Every (day, Wednesday morning,* etc.) is expressed by **todos/as** followed by the plural definite article and the time referent.

Todo/a + el/la + time referent **Trabajo** *toda la tarde.*	All _____ (long). I work all afternoon.
Todos/as + los/las + time referent **Estoy libre** *todos los jueves.*	Every _____ . I'm free every Thursday.

4. Remember that **de la madrugada** and **de la mañana** are the equivalent of A.M., while **de la tarde** and **de la noche** are used for P.M. (see "Historical Perspective"

for a more complete explanation). These expressions are used *after* the hour (**La cita es a las ocho de la noche**). The expressions *in the wee hours, in the morning, in the afternoon,* and *in the evening* when used *without* a specific time, are translated by *por* **la madrugada,** *por* **la mañana,** *por* **la tarde,** and *por* **la noche** (**Hasta mañana por la tarde,** *Until tomorrow afternoon*).

5. Telephone numbers are given in pairs in Spanish whenever possible. With the seven-digit American system, the first digit is given separately, followed by the remaining numbers in pairs: **5-14-13-16.**

6. **A ver** (*let's see*) is often used when checking or verifying information.

Notas lingüísticas II

A. Several Spanish words are used to translate "time." The context determines which to select:

	Context	Example
tiempo	General concept of passage through time. **Pasar tiempo** (*to spend time*)	**No tengo tiempo.** I don't have time.
vez/veces	Instances of time. **una vez** (*once*), **muchas veces** (*often*), **algunas veces** (*sometimes*), **a la vez** (*at the same time*), **de una vez** (*once and for all*), **de vez en cuando** (*from time to time*).	**Es la primera vez.** It's the first time.
hora	clock time	**¿Qué hora es?** What time is it?
rato/ratito	a short period of time (a little while)	**Espere un ratito.** Wait a little while.

B. In telling time in Spanish, follow these simple rules:

1. Use the feminine article **la** before **una** and **las** before all other numbers. The article signals the reference to time.

    la una y media   one-thirty
    las tres menos diez   ten to three

2. Use **ser** to say what time it is. **Es** is used with **la una, son** with all other numbers.

    Es la una.   It's one o'clock.
    Son las nueve.   It's nine o'clock.

3. Use **y** to add on minutes from the hour to the half-hour.

    Son las nueve y veinte.   It's nine-twenty.
    Son las tres y media.   It's three-thirty.

4. Use **menos** from the half hour to the hour.

Son las seis menos diez.	It's ten to six.
Son las dos menos cuarto.	It's a quarter to two.

Or you can use:

Falta(n) + number of minutes + **para** + **la(s)** + next hour.

Faltan cinco para la una.	It's five to one.
Falta un minuto para las ocho.	It's one minute to eight.

5. Use **¿Qué hora es?** to ask the time and **¿A qué hora es?** to ask at what time something takes place. Use **a la(s)** to tell at what time something takes place.

¿Qué hora es?	What time is it?
Son las cuatro y cuarto.	It's four-fifteen.
¿A qué hora es la cita?	(At) what time is the appointment?
Es a la una y media.	It's at one-thirty.

C. The following diagram illustrates sequential day and night referents:

Current Time

lunes	martes	miércoles	jueves	viernes
anteayer day before yesterday	**ayer** yesterday	**hoy** today	**mañana** tomorrow	**pasado mañana** day after tomorrow
anteanoche night before last	**anoche** last night	**esta noche** tonight	**mañana por la tarde** tomorrow afternoon	**pasado mañana por la noche** night after tomorrow

D. Some verbs in Spanish use an indirect object construction similar to the verb **parecer** *to seem* (*to someone*).

Ejemplo: **¿Qué le parece a la una?** How does one o'clock seem to you?

Two other common verbs used like **parecer** include:

convenir to suit (someone) **hacer falta** to be lacking (to someone)

The indirect object pronouns used with these verbs are:

me	to me	**nos**	to us
te	to you (familiar)		
le	to you (formal), to him, to her	**les**	to you (plural), to them

In this construction, the indirect object refers to the person who is influenced by or affected by the action of the verb. The subject of the sentence refers to that which influences or affects the person, and it determines the verb ending.

¿Qué le parece el jueves?	How does Thursday seem to you?
Me hace falta su teléfono.	I need your number (your number is lacking to me).
¿Le convienen las citas?	Do the appointments suit you?

E. **Por** and **para** often are confusing to English speakers because they both, at times, translate the word *for*. Actually, they express very different concepts, as shown below.

<table>
<tr><th>Por</th><th>Para</th></tr>
<tr>
<td>

1. a cause = *because of*
   Llego tarde *por* mi esposa.
   I'm late because of my wife.

</td>
<td>

1. an objective = *in order to*
   Voy ahora *para* llegar a tiempo.
   I'm going now in order to arrive on time.

</td>
</tr>
<tr>
<td>

2. with time = *around*
   duration of time = *for*
   Vienen *por* las tres.
   They're coming around three.
   Siéntese *por* un momento.
   Sit down for a minute.

</td>
<td>

2. with time = *by* (a deadline)
   Lo necesito *para* el jueves.
   I need it by Thursday.

</td>
</tr>
<tr>
<td>

3. with **trabajar** = *for a cause,* or
   instead of
   Trabajo *por* mi familia.
   I work for my family (in their behalf).
   Tengo que trabajar *por* Carlos hoy.
   I have to work for Carlos today (in his place).

</td>
<td>

3. with **trabajar** = for a specific
   company or agency
   Trabajo *para* el estado.
   I work for the state.

</td>
</tr>
</table>

F. **Llegó**, the preterite (past) tense form of **llegar** (*to arrive*), appears in the "Diálogo introductorio." An accented **-ó** at the end of any verb tells you:
   a. it is an **-ar** verb;
   b. it is conjugated in the preterite (past);
   c. it is the third person singular (**Ud., él, ella**) form.

   Remember that **-ió** is the third person past of most **-er** and **-ir** verbs (e.g., **refirió**).

G. The form **era** is the imperfect past tense of **ser.** It is used in telling time in the past.

   ***Eran* las ocho cuando llegó.**   It was eight when he arrived.

   The differences between the preterite and the imperfect to describe past actions are discussed in subsequent chapters.

PRÁCTICA PRELIMINAR

Follow the guidelines for self-instructional practice given in the Preface.

A. Circle the correct form of the verb in each sentence.

Ejemplo: (Es (Son) Están) las cinco de la tarde.

1. (Estoy Eres Soy) Felipe Borrero y tengo una cita hoy.
2. La reunión de los directores de los programas de salud (es, era, son) esta noche a las seis.
3. ¿Cómo (es está era) su calendario hoy?
4. Ahora (es está son) las cuatro y cuarto.
5. La doctora (está era es) en su oficina hasta las ocho de la noche.
6. ¡(Está Es Soy) imposible acostumbrarme a hablar inglés!
7. Mi cita con el profesor (es son está) a la una de la tarde.
8. ¿A qué hora (es son era) la reunión mañana?
9. (Estoy Soy Es) aquí para mi cita con el gerente.
10. ¡(Es Son Está) las nueve de la mañana y no llegan los empleados!

B. Answer the questions with the time indicated in parentheses.

Ejemplo: ¿Cuándo vuelvo, señora? (after 4:00 P.M.)
   Vuelva Ud. después de las cuatro de la tarde.

1. ¿Cuándo es mi próxima cita? (Thursday at 2:30 P.M.)
2. ¿Cuándo quieres llegar? (after 10:00 A.M.)
3. ¿Hasta cuándo tengo que esperar? (until 3:15)
4. ¿Para cuándo tengo que hacer una cita? (Monday night)
5. ¿Cuándo vuelvo? (5:00 sharp)
6. ¿Cuándo tengo que llegar? (on time)
7. ¿A qué hora es la cita? (1:15 P.M.)
8. ¿Cuándo le conviene a Ud.? (tomorrow at 3:45)
9. ¿Qué hora era cuando llegó el doctor? (12:20 A.M.)
10. ¿Cuándo está Ud. libre? (all afternoon)

C. Choose the appropriate indirect object pronoun according to the context of the sentence.

Ejemplo: Rafael, ¿(les (te) me) conviene la hora?

1. Espere, señora, (me yo le) hace falta su nombre.
2. Señor Pérez, ¿qué (lo le te) parece mañana a las diez?
3. A mi esposa no (la le me) conviene una cita por la tarde.
4. Señora, ¿a sus hijos (les los le) parece importante la religión?
5. Yo quisiera hablar con la doctora Sánchez, si (me la le) hace el favor.

A 1. Soy 2. es 3. está 4. son 5. está 6. Es 7. es 8. es 9. Estoy 10. Son

B 1. Su próxima cita es el jueves a las dos y media de la tarde. 2. Quiero llegar después de las diez de la mañana. 3. Tiene que esperar hasta las tres y cuarto. 4. Ud. tiene que hacer una cita para el lunes por la noche. 5. Vuelva Ud. a las cinco en punto. 6. Ud. tiene que llegar a la hora exacta. 7. Es a la una y cuarto de la tarde. 8. Me conviene mañana a las cuatro menos cuarto. 9. Eran las doce y veinte de la madrugada cuando llegó. 10. Estoy libre toda la tarde.

C 1. me 2. le 3. le 4. les 5. me

6. Anita, ¿qué (te   la   le) parece la hora de la cita?

7. A mis empleados (los   les   me) hace falta llegar a la hora exacta.

8. A mi esposa y a mí no (nos   les   me) conviene hablar con el trabajador social.

9. Señorita Morales, ¿a qué hora (te   la   le) conviene la cita con el abogado?

10. Espere, señor, a Ud. (me   le   lo) hacen falta estos documentos.

D. Choose the correct direct or indirect object pronoun or verb as indicated in the following review exercise.

Ejemplo: ¿Qué ((le)   te   les) parece el viernes a las dos, señora?

1. Yo lo (espera   espere   espero) aquí, señor Guzmán.

2. Quiero hablar con el doctor, si (le   me   se) hace el favor.

3. (Me   Lo   Nos) siento mucho, pero la señora Ramos no está hoy.

4. ¿Qué le (pareces   parecen   parece) el viernes a las cuatro y media?

5. Nos (hacen   haces   hace) falta más datos.

6. Bueno, le (conviene   convienen   convienes) la cita a las dos.

7. (Nos   Los   Lo) espero a Uds. afuera.

8. La recepcionista le (hacen   hacemos   hace) una cita para las tres de la tarde.

9. Yo te (llamas   llamó   llamo) mañana a la una.

10. A ellos (los   le   les) parece buena la hora.

E. Write in the correct word from the following list to complete each sentence. If no word is needed, write *X* in the blank.

   a   que   por   para   X

Ejemplo: Tengo ____*que*____ volver mañana.

1. Usted tiene _____ hacer otra cita.

2. Voy _____ consultar el calendario.

3. Tengo unos documentos _____ la doctora.

4. Espere _____ un momento, por favor.

5. Faltan dos días _____ la cita.

C 6. te 7. les 8. nos 9. le 10. le
D 1. espero 2. me 3. Lo 4. parece 5. hacen 6. conviene 7. Los 8. hace 9. llamo 10. les
E 1. que 2. a 3. para 4. X 5. para

6. El doctor Sánchez vuelve _____ la madrugada.

7. ¿Puedo _____ ver a la señora Piñero?

8. La cliente quiere _____ esperar aquí.

9. Nos vemos _____ mañana a las cinco.

10. Es necesario llevar _____ mi esposa al hospital.

F. Translate each time referent to Spanish.

Ejemplo: *Tomorrow morning* vamos al hospital.
   Mañana por la mañana vamos al hospital.

1. Tengo que pasar mucho *time* con este señor.
2. ¿Cuándo fue la última *time* que la visitó?
3. *Yesterday* Ud. llegó muy tarde.
4. ¿Qué *time* tiene Ud.? ¿Las dos?
5. Lo voy a llamar *tonight.*
6. ¿A qué *time* llegó su marido ayer?
7. *Tomorrow afternoon* no voy a estar aquí.
8. ¿Ud. solamente trabajó allí *twice?*
9. ¿Por qué se fue Ud. *last night?*
10. Tiene que esperar aquí *a little while.*

G. Change the verb in the following sentences to the preterite.

Ejemplo: Llega a las tres.
   Llegó a las tres.

1. El director lo llama.
2. No trabaja mucho hoy.
3. ¿Quién la refiere?
4. ¿Dónde vive Ud.?
5. ¿Con quién habla la doctora?
6. La secretaria cambia la cita.
7. Él no lleva a su esposa.
8. ¿Por qué llega Ud. tarde?
9. ¿Le parece buena la hora?
10. ¿Cuánto tiempo espera Ud.?

E 6. por 7. X 8. X 9. X 10. a

F 1. tiempo 2. vez 3. Ayer 4. hora 5. esta noche 6. hora 7. Mañana por la tarde 8. dos veces 9. anoche 10. un ratito

G 1. llamó 2. trabajó 3. refirió 4. vivió 5. habló 6. cambió 7. llevó 8. llegó 9. pareció 10. esperó

Combinándolo todo

PRÁCTICA COMUNICATIVA: Datos numéricos

Conversación parcial

Practique oralmente la siguiente conversación. Cada raya (/) implica que falta una palabra. Es necesario conjugar cada verbo *en bastardillas.*

Ejemplo: ¿Qué / *parecer* / las dos?   No / *parecer* bien.
¿Qué le parece a las dos?   **No me parece bien.**

La empleada	*El cliente*
1. / tardes, / . ¿/ qué / servirle?	Quisiera / con la / social.
2. Lo / , pero / trabajadora / no / en la / ahora.	Pero *yo tener* / cita / ella.
3. ¿/ qué hora *ser* la /?	Era / / 10:15.
4. Pero Ud. *llegar* muy / . Son / 11:00.	Lo / mucho, señora. Pues, ¿*poder* hacer / cita / otro /?
5. / ver. ¿Qué / parece / martes?	¿A / hora?
6. ¿/ libre / las dos?	No, todos / martes *trabajar* / las 3:00.
7. ¿*Poder* venir Ud. / jueves / las 9:45?	/ *convenir* más después / / 10:30.
8. ¿/ *convenir* / las 11:00?	/ *parecer* perfecta.
9. / bien. / vemos el / a / 11:00.	Gracias, / . Hasta / jueves.

Pregunte Ud.

Ud. es el licenciado Cruz, un abogado. Ahora hable Ud. por teléfono con una nueva cliente que quiere hacer una cita con Ud. Primero Ud. necesita ciertos datos personales. Dé Ud. oralmente las preguntas y respuestas necesarias en la siguiente conversación.

Ejemplo: Me siento bien, gracias.
¿Cómo se siente Ud.?

1. Quisiera hablar con el licenciado Armando Cruz.
2. De Alicia Hernández.
3. Se escribe *H-e-r-n-á-n-d-e-z.*
4. Pues, quisiera hablar con Ud. sobre mi hijo Juan.
5. Sí, me parece mejor hacer una cita para hablar personalmente.
6. No, no me conviene el miércoles; trabajo todo el día. Para mí es mejor el jueves.
7. Estoy libre toda la mañana y después de las 3:30.

8. Me parece muy bien a las 9:30.

9. ¿Qué datos personales le hacen falta?

10. Es el 7-14-15-22.

11. Me refirió mi jefe de trabajo.

12. Gracias a Ud. Nos vemos el jueves, entonces.

Dígalo

Pregunte a un/a compañero/a de clase lo que le diga su profesor/a sobre los temas de las citas, de lo que le hace falta, de las horas del trabajo, de los días libres y ocupados, y cómo se dicen ciertas expresiones temporales.

Escuche bien

A. Ud. oirá diez citas (el día + la hora). Escriba Ud. *en inglés* el día y la hora de cada cita.

1. _____   6. _____

2. _____   7. _____

3. _____   8. _____

4. _____   9. _____

5. _____   10. _____

B. Ud. oirá a seis personas que describen parte de su horario (*schedule*). Escriba *en inglés* lo que dicen.

1. _____

2. _____

3. _____

4. _____

5. _____

6. _____

Diálogos cortos

(*Conversación telefónica*)

I. *La secretaria*   *El señor Rodríguez*

Diga.   Buenos días. ¿Está el señor Pérez?

No, no está _____ su   Pues, dígale que el señor Rodríguez lo
                                                             llamó hoy por la mañana.
oficina. ¿ _____ parte de

_____ , por favor?

Sí, cómo no. ¿ _____ es su   Es el 7-24-25-22. ¿Sabe Ud. cuándo
                                                             vuelve?
_____ ?

A _____ lo que dice en   Pues, dígale que yo espero su llamada
                                                             después de las tres de la tarde. Es muy
_____ calendario. Pues,   importante.

_____ una reunión a

_____ una y media. Va

_____ estar _____

después _____ las tres.

Bueno, _____ Rodríguez.   Gracias, señorita.

_____ señor Pérez

_____ va _____

llamar _____ tarde

_____ de las 3.

A _____ orden, señor.

II. *La paciente*   *La recepcionista*

Buenos días. El doctor Hernández   ¿Cuál _____ su nombre,
me espera.
                                          _____ favor?

Soy Eulalia Torres.   Su _____ se _____
                                          T-o-rr-e-z, ¿verdad?

La paciente	*La recepcionista*
No, se escribe T-o-rr-e-s.	_____ gracias. Pase _____ otro consultorio. Primero _____ enfermera tiene _____ hablar _____ Ud.
¿Cómo se llama ella?	Ella _____ llama Marta Muñoz.
¿Y a qué hora llega el doctor?	_____ doctora llega _____ la una.
Bueno, no puedo esperar mucho. Tengo que volver al trabajo para la una y media.	No se _____ , señora. Ud. va _____ llegar _____ tiempo.
Se _____ agradezco mucho.	_____ nada, _____ Torres.

Ayude al cliente

You must notify a Hispanic couple in writing regarding the details and schedule for the legal proceedings for them to adopt a foster child of theirs, Juan Gómez. Begin the letter with *Muy estimados señores Aguirre*. Then:

1. Tell them you are writing to them to inform them (*para informarles*) of their appointment on Wednesday, June 4th (*el cuatro de junio*) to talk about the adoption (*la adopción*) of Juan Gómez.

2. Tell them they have to arrive at 9:15 A.M. at your office to verify all the personal information that you have about the case (*sobre el caso*). Tell them that they then need to speak with Mrs. Marchese, the social worker, at 10:00. Tell them that you all (use *nosotros*) have to arrive in court (*a la corte*) by 10:30 sharp.

3. Ask them if these appointments are suitable for them. Tell them if there is a problem, they can call you on Monday after 2:00 P.M. Also tell them that everything seems perfect for the adoption.

4. End the letter with the reminder that you'll see each other on Wednesday. Close with *su seguro/a servidor/a* and sign your name.

¿Comprende Ud.? 📼

La secretaria de la oficina no está hoy y Ud. tiene que usar una máquina que contesta el teléfono (*telephone answering machine*) mientras (*while*) está con los clientes. A las 11:30, Ud. escucha la cinta (*the tape*) y escribe en inglés el nombre de las cuatro personas que llamaron (*called*), su número de teléfono y el mensaje que dejó cada uno/a (*the message that each left*).

1. nombre: _____   1. mensaje: _____

    _____   _____

    teléfono: _____

2. nombre: _____   2. mensaje: _____

    _____   _____

    teléfono: _____

3. nombre: _____   3. mensaje: _____

    _____   _____

    teléfono: _____

4. nombre: _____   4. mensaje: _____

    _____   _____

    teléfono: _____

Piénselo

Prepárese para poder hablar con el/la profesor/a o con otros estudiantes sobre los siguientes temas, contestando las preguntas que le sugiere el/la profesor/a:

1. la hora exacta y llegar tarde
2. hablar por teléfono en español
3. las citas
4. su calendario
5. su rutina diaria (*daily routine*)

Imagínese

Describa Ud. la situación que muestra cada foto, contestando las siguientes preguntas:

1. ¿Quién es esta persona?
2. ¿Qué hace en este momento?
3. ¿Con quién habla?
4. ¿Por qué?
5. ¿De qué hablan?
6. ¿Hablan en inglés o en español?
7. ¿Entiende lo que le dice la otra persona?
8. ¿A Ud. le parece que está contenta con la conversación?
9. ¿Cómo termina la conversación?

8:00	*reunión con el señor Mendoza*
9:45	*cita con el dentista*
10:30	*llamar a María Manzanares (532-6117)*
12:00	*almuerzo con Marcos*
2:30	*banco*
3:45	*visitar a la señora Vásquez*
4:30	*consultar con el director*
5:15	*buscar documentos importantes*

1. ¿Qué es esto? ¿De quién es?
2. ¿Qué pasa a las ocho?
3. ¿Cuál es el número de teléfono de María? ¿Por qué la llama?
4. ¿Con quién sale al mediodía? ¿Adónde van para almorzar?
5. ¿A qué hora tiene que visitar a la señora Vásquez? ¿Por qué la visita?
6. ¿Con quién tiene cita a las cuatro y media? ¿Para qué es la cita?
7. ¿Puede llegar a la cita a la hora exacta?
8. ¿Qué tiene que hacer a las cinco y cuarto?

Haciendo el papel

Haga Ud. el papel del/de la empleado/a en las siguientes situaciones. Sea cortés, especialmente cuando habla por teléfono.

1. You answer the telephone in the afternoon with the name of your agency; then say your name followed by "at your service." The caller wishes to speak with Marta Ramírez. Ask who is calling. Tell the caller that Mrs. Ramírez is speaking with someone else on another line (*línea*). Ask the caller her telephone number and ask her if it's convenient for Mrs. Ramírez to return the call in one hour.

2. You are the director of a social service agency. Politely ask your bilingual secretary to come to your office. Tell him where you will be this afternoon: at Doctor Ortega's office from 2:00 until 3:00, at the welfare department from 3:15 to 4:30, and at Mrs. Marino's house from 5:00 to 5:45. Tell him that you will be at home after that. Also tell him that if anyone calls you, you will return the calls tomorrow morning.

3. You are a doctor who is speaking on the telephone with a patient, Mr. Sebastián Monge, to discuss the results of some medical tests (*los resultados de unas pruebas médicas*). Verify that you have reached the right party. Give your name and explain why you are calling. Tell him that you want to see him again as soon as possible, since you prefer to discuss the results in person (*personalmente*). Mr. Monge seems very upset and wants to come in today. Tell him not

to worry, that everything is fine and that he can come in next Thursday. He asks if there isn't an earlier (*más temprano*) appointment. Tell him to wait a moment, that he can speak with the receptionist to see if he can have an appointment for this afternoon.

4. Entreviste a otro/a estudiante en español para completar el siguiente formulario:

Appointment: Day _____ Time _____ Arrived _____

Last name _____ First name _____

Spouse _____ Telephone number _____

Birthplace _____ Citizenship _____

Language spoken in the home _____

English language ability: Understand ____ Speak ____ Write _____

Profession _____ Place of employment _____

Name of supervisor _____

Supervisor's telephone number_____

Doctor's name _____

Source of referral _____

Last appointment: Day _____ Time _____

Next appointment: Day _____ Time _____

Name of interviewer _____ Title _____

REFLEJOS DE LA CULTURA: "Semanitas"

The traditional attitude toward time in Hispanic cultures reflects a belief in the cycle of life. The cycle is a spiritual one, beginning with birth, flourishing through life, passing through death, and continuing in life after death. This acceptance of death and the eternal life of the soul as a reality is very evident in Hispanic cultures. November 2nd, All Soul's Day, which passes virtually unknown in most churches in the United States, is a special holiday in Spanish-speaking countries for reverent commemoration of those loved ones who have passed away. In Mexico, for example, sweets in the shape of skulls are eaten to remind us that life on earth is only a temporary passage through the cycle of existence.

The traditional Hispanic value of the acceptance of one's fate is rooted in this deep spiritual belief in eternal life. It explains certain behaviors that can be perceived as stoic and fatalistic when viewed from an Anglo perspective. The misinterpretation of this traditional Hispanic value gives rise to certain stereotypes regarding Latinos. They are often seen as lacking in drive and initiative, unconcerned with achievement and success, and not planning sufficiently for the future. This stereotype contrasts sharply with the U.S. cultural backdrop, where the highly motivated, self-starting, future-oriented individual is most valued.

A more objective interpretation views the acceptance of one's fate as indicative of trust in the cycle of life, where all things come in their own time. To devote too much of one's time and energy to combat or control this life cycle seems foolhardy from the traditional Hispanic perspective.

At first glance, the following poem, entitled "Semanitas" seems an extreme example of *fatalismo*. Its overt pessimism gives little indication that the situation described can change. Without knowing more about its author, we might simply dismiss it from the stereotypic view of Hispanics as fatalists. We might empathize to some degree, remembering times when each day loomed darker than the one before because of specific circumstances in our lives.

Placing the poem in its political and social context sheds a different light on its interpretation. "Semanitas" was written by Teresa de Jesús, a pseudonym for a Chilean poet whose writings have been smuggled out of this militarily run country headed by General Augusto Pinochet. The coup he led in 1973 put an end to the constitutional presidency of Socialist Salvador Allende, who was assassinated. Organizations such as Amnesty International accuse Pinochet's military junta of murdering more than 20,000 Chilean dissidents and incarcerating thousands of others.

Teresa de Jesús portrays the sadness that grows as each day passes in a country where repression meets those who try to restore lost freedoms. The fact that she has dared to put these feelings into words in a country where freedom of speech is suppressed belies the stereotypic view of Hispanics fatalistically accepting the status quo. The risks she has taken to publish these words demonstrate the desire to bring the plight of contemporary Chile to the outside world in the hope of change. The activism demonstrated in such writings is typical of that expressed by other

contemporary Latin American writers and artists who use their creativity to promote the struggle for liberation from political and social repression.

Semanitas

Lo malo de domingo	The bad thing about Sunday
es que después es lunes;	is that after is Monday;
lo peor del lunes	the worst of Monday
es que es un día largo;	is it's a long day;
el martes es terrible	Tuesday is awful
porque es un día aciago;	because it's a luckless day;
el miércoles lo odio	Wednesday I hate
porque es igual a todos;	because it's like all the others,
pero el que más detesto	but what I detest most
es este día jueves;	is this day Thursday;
tan modoso, tan pulcro,	so circumspect, so tidy,
tan no comprometido;	so uncompromised;
el viernes no lo incluyo	Friday I don't include
pues no parece día	since it doesn't seem like a day,
entregándose al sábado	giving itself to Saturday
con gran coquetería;	with such coquetry;
y el sábado es un monstruo	and Saturday is a monster
que se cae a pedazos	that falls all to pieces
en las tiendas,	in the stores,
la feria,	the market,
las viejas empanadas,	the stale turnovers,
con su tarde tan corta	with its afternoon so short
y su noche tan larga . . .	and its night so long . . .

Evaluación del progreso—Lecciones 3–4

RAISING AWARENESS

A. Discuss the various factors that affect one's ability to communicate effectively across cultural boundaries.

B. Describe the differences in social classes between U.S. and Hispanic cultures and relate these differences to the history of the colonization of each region.

C. How can a Hispanic's behavior regarding respect for authority figures and attitudes toward time be misinterpreted by uninformed Anglo service providers?

COMUNICÁNDOSE EN ESPAÑOL

A. Pronunciación Write the words that your instructor dictates. Underline stressed syllables, write in accent marks as needed, and circle any diphthongs.

1. _____   6. _____

2. _____   7. _____

3. _____   8. _____

4. _____   9. _____

5. _____   10. _____

B. Discriminación auditiva Circle the letter of the most appropriate response to each oral question or statement you hear.

1. a b c   5. a b c   8. a b c

2. a b c   6. a b c   9. a b c

3. a b c   7. a b c   10. a b c

4. a b c

COMBINÁNDOLO TODO

A. Comprensión oral   Write down the name of each client, then, in English, the time of appointment, and the person he or she wishes to see.

	Name	*Time*	*Person he or she wishes to see*
1.	_____	_____	_____
2.	_____	_____	_____
3.	_____	_____	_____
4.	_____	_____	_____
5.	_____	_____	_____
6.	_____	_____	_____

B. La entrevista   Give the questions and/or responses needed in the following dialogue.

Recepcionista

Cliente

1. _____ ¿ _____ servirle?

   Buenas tardes. ¿Hablo con la Sra. Davis?

2. No, _____ .

   Necesito hablar con la Sra. Davis, si me hace el favor.

3. ¿_____ ?

   De Julia Marín.

4. Lo siento, pero la Sra. Davis _____ _____ .

   ¿Llamo más tarde o podría Ud. ayudarme? Necesito hacer una cita con ella.

5. ¿ _____ ?

   La semana próxima.

6. ¿ _____ ?

   No, el martes no puedo. ¿Ella está libre el miércoles?

7. _____ calendario.

   Me parece perfecto el jueves.

   No, _____ todo el día.

   ¿ _____ parece _____

   _____ ?

Recepcionista	*Cliente*
8. ¿ _____ mañana o _____ la tarde?	Prefiero ir por la tarde. Tengo que trabajar por la mañana.
9. ¿ _____ ?	Sí, está muy bien a las tres.
10. _____ , señora.	Sí, hasta el jueves, entonces.

C.   En acción   Choose one of the following situations and act it out with your instructor or another classmate.

1.   Set up an appointment with a client who calls for the first time, also finding out the source of referral.

2.   Initiate the first interview with a client, obtaining name, telephone number, prior history with the agency, source of referral, and religious preference.

3.   Call a client to change an appointment already set up. It is difficult to find a new day and time since both you and your client have busy schedules.

4.   Discuss a client's tendency to arrive late for his or her appointments, trying to arrive at a solution that validates both parties and their cultural conditioning.

LECCIÓN 5

Necesito ciertos datos personales

LOS OBJETIVOS

Raising awareness

1. To understand personal reactions to nonverbal cues
2. To be familiar with rural and urban cultural differences in Latin America
3. To become aware of the differences between Anglo and Hispanic cultures regarding physical space and touching

Comunicándose en español

1. To understand the Spanish system of linkage between spoken words in order to improve speaking and listening comprehension
2. To use vocabulary and structures relevant to hospital admission and medical insurance
3. To use and understand numerical data related to birth, age, telephone and social security numbers, and insurance policy identification
4. To form and recognize preterite tense forms of regular verbs

Combinándolo todo

1. To integrate all material from previous sections through extensive practice in work-related communication activities
2. To use and understand time references
3. To understand the unique migration experience of Puerto Ricans between the island and the mainland

Raising awareness

OVERVIEW: The importance of nonverbal cues

By now you are very much aware that the communication process is in no way a simple one. Whereas before you may have thought that it involved only words and sentences, you have learned that we communicate all the time, even when we are silent or asleep.

Learning to speak Spanish can enhance your ability to communicate with Hispanic clients, but you can become more proficient without speaking a word by simply focusing on nonverbal cues. These affect communication as much as or even more than words. Let us explore in more depth how nonverbal communication affects the way we relate across cultural boundaries.

We have already seen that we pick up messages by using our five senses (seeing, hearing, feeling, smelling, and tasting) as well as by a *sixth* or intuitive sense. Thus, if we focus on only *one* part of the message someone is sending us — most often on what we *hear* — we are limiting our conscious perceptual powers to less than their full capacity. Even without our conscious awareness, the other senses are busy picking up stimuli at a subconscious level, affecting how we receive and interpret the message. These subconscious impressions account for that slightly uneasy feeling we may experience at times. This, in turn, can give rise to a lack of confidence or trust as we try to communicate with someone raised in a different culture. By bringing our active, conscious attention to these subliminal cues, we can better understand the source of our feelings as they are triggered by nonverbal messages.

The kind of message registered by each of the senses varies a great deal. For the most part, the sense of taste can be excluded. However, idiomatic expressions such as "that left me with a bad taste in my mouth" manifest the physiological reality of emotional reactions. If you are experiencing dryness or a "bad taste" in the mouth as you listen or speak to someone from another culture, try to find the source of this sensation. It may be caused by fear, discomfort, anger, or some other emotion triggered by the cross-cultural communication process.

The sense of smell works closely with that of taste. The food we choose to eat may appeal to us more through our olfactory sense than through our taste buds. Also, the sense of smell seems to be linked to our feelings of nostalgia. Certain smells can take us back in time and permit us to reexperience both pleasant and distasteful events. When we communicate with someone in person, we are exposed to that individual's smells, both natural body odors and any perfumes, colognes, soaps, or mouthwashes that the person may have used. Even the cleanliness of that person's body or clothing will be evidenced by the odors we may sense.

Our reactions to these odors are again determined by our own personal upbringing in a given culture. Some cultures, for example, consider personal body odors as part of the intimate uniqueness of the individual and prefer to "smell the real person" rather than a series of artificial aromas produced to make us all smell different than we normally do and more like each other. Also, bathing practices vary among cultures and may express attitudes toward health as well as socioeconomic realities. The way one smells may be perfectly acceptable within one culture but offensive in another. If you sense that the odor emanating from the client you are interviewing is affecting the interaction, pause and refocus on maintaining your objectivity.

Another factor that may influence our feelings about another is the use of personal space. People in one culture may need more personal space or territory than those in another. If you have grown up in the mainland United States, you most probably have internalized the cultural norm of maintaining an imaginary bubble of space around yourself at least one foot thick. At a subconscious level, you perceive this space as inviolately your own. Anyone who enters that personal territory without your invitation will be viewed as an intruder, although you may not consciously understand why you are feeling hostile.

Other cultures, including those of Hispanic heritage, encourage more closeness among people, even among strangers in a crowd. If you ride a crowded bus in Mexico City or Bogotá, you may find people in very close contact as they press in to make more room for others, even when there

seems to be no space left from an Anglo perspective. A comparison with a crowded subway in Manhattan, where, despite "crowded" conditions, people still preserve as much of their personal space bubble as they can, illustrates the cultural differences regarding personal space.

It is not surprising that when a person from a culture that encourages closer contact between individuals attempts to communicate with someone raised in a culture that maintains more personal distance between speaker and hearer, mixed messages are sent and received *subconsciously* by each. The former may feel alienated and unaccepted by the latter, who in turn may feel invaded and not respected by the other.

Closely related to the concept of personal space is that of touching and, in general, the use of hands to communicate ideas and emotions. Each culture has certain hand signals that are commonly understood, if not used, by all its members. Sometimes the same gesture may mean different things in different cultures, again a potential source of misunderstanding. The use of the hand to touch another while speaking with that person again may reflect cultural conditioning as well as personal preference.

The importance of the message(s) sent by touch can be readily seen by focusing on the sensations received when shaking hands in the Anglo culture. If you offer your hand to someone who barely responds, offering only a limp, un-

feeling hand to your exuberant one, you may feel rejected, cautious, suspicious, or uninterested in further contact. However, someone who offers to shake hands with zest, enthusiasm, and warmth most likely gives you a feeling of trust, confidence, energy, and security. You may not think any of these thoughts consciously; yet the power of touch is there, sending very strong messages that interact with whatever words you hear.

What we visually observe as we speak or listen to another can greatly affect the message sent or received. Such body-language cues as sitting with legs and arms crossed (which, in the Anglo culture, indicates lack of openness and receptivity) will influence the degree of trust we share with our partner in the communication process. When sitting in such a closed position, we are blocking our own flow of energy. On a subconscious level we have decided to erect obstacles to our receptivity of the message we are hearing. We also may notice certain facial gestures, including eye contact (or lack of it), that send us messages regarding how we are being perceived by the other. Many of these may be the reflection of cultural conditioning. A gesture or use of eye contact that in one culture may be an indication of trust and respect may, in another, be seen as deviant, sneaky, or untrustworthy.

We also observe the way our communication partner moves his or her entire body while walking, standing, or sitting. Movements of the neck and head rarely escape our subconscious eye. In addition, we notice the way a person is dressed and groomed. This may also be an indicator of cultural conditioning. What may be considered in good taste in one culture or social class may be viewed as the opposite in another.

With the sense of hearing, we listen not only to the words that other people send our way but also to their grammatical arrangement. Both give us some indication of the level of education and/or language training that individual has had, be it in the native language or a foreign tongue. Even when we converse with people who share the same language background, the linguistic usage, including pronunciation and intonational patterns, gives us further clues to their social class, educational background, and geographical origin.

Often, when we hear a nonnative speaker communicating in English, we make judgments about that person's background based on his or her fluency and correctness in using the language. If you are struggling to learn Spanish, you may, at times, feel a natural sense of frustration at not being able to express the sophisticated thoughts and feelings you have because of your limited linguistic abilities in your new language. This phenomenon may convince you of the unfairness involved in making judgments about the intellectual capacity of others based on their fluency in speaking a second language.

If fluency in Spanish is your goal, you will find that, as you become more competent in the language, you will begin to "see" your native Spanish-speaking clients with limited abilities in English in a new light. You may better appreciate their depth of thought and sensitivity when they speak Spanish, as contrasted with the hazy, incomplete picture of their personality that may come across in English. As you realize that you will be heard differently when speaking Spanish than when speaking English, you may wish to concentrate on using some of the other body-language cues common to Hispanic cultures in order to communicate more fully across the linguistic and cultural barriers. The more fluent you become in the language, the more you will be expected to demonstrate cultural fluency as well.

Above all, when you experience that understandable frustration as your senses are bombarded by a wealth of stimuli when communicating with your Hispanic clients, remember to involve your entire being in the communication process. By first raising your awareness of the differences in sending and receiving messages dictated by the Spanish- and English-speaking worlds, you will soon be amazed at how easy this whole process of communicating across cultures can become. The key is to focus on the *essence* of the message being sent or received. This can occur only when you have overcome at a conscious level the interference caused by the differences in the verbal and nonverbal communication systems which you and your clients have learned as children. Despite the many differences that separate the cultural training each of you has received, you share many more similarities as human beings. Attention to the uniqueness of each client will help you to relax more and worry less about the exactness of the communication process. With practice and patience, you will soon reach your goal of communicating effectively with your Hispanic clients.

Applications

1. Try to experience within yourself, using any one or all of your physical senses plus your intuitive sense, each of the following concepts: *joy, fear, love, anger, trust*. Imagining a recent event that triggered these emotions for you may help.

2. Now try to convey each of these concepts to a partner nonverbally, using as many of your senses, including body position, as possible.

3. Try to use *only* words with little or no involvement of the rest of your body, facial gestures, hands, etc., to express the concepts listed here. Do not smile, frown, etc., but simply say whatever words you feel will most convincingly convey the message you wish to send while keeping your body "silent." You may use changes in your tone of voice to help.

4. Now do the same, using everything available to you,—senses, words, gestures, body, etc. — to convey these same five concepts.

Reflections

1. Which of the exercises was easiest for you? Which was the hardest? Why?

2. Do you feel comfortable using your body to convey certain messages, or do you feel tense and stressed when trying to do so? How might this affect your perceptions of someone who uses his or her body in a different way than you do to communicate?

3. Estimate what percentage of the message communicated in Exercise 4 above you conveyed by words. What percentage was conveyed by facial gestures? By body positions? By your intuitive sense? By other senses?

4. What was the greatest personal insight into your own way of communicating that you gained as a result of this exercise? How can you use this new awareness in communicating with your clients, both those who share your native language and cultural conditioning and those from Hispanic backgrounds?

5. Which area of the communication process would you like to develop further? What can you begin to do on a daily basis in order to begin to work on this development?

HISTORICAL PERSPECTIVE: Urban versus rural culture in the Hispanic world

Of all the aspects of Hispanic culture, the urban versus rural distinction is perhaps the most crucial. Whereas the farmer from Kansas may not have enough in common with an advertising executive from Manhattan to spend more than a few moments conversing at a political convention, both share, to some extent, the same culture. While their lifestyles may be very different, they are both products of growing up in the United States. At the convention they may find that this shared cultural background has led them to very similar political views despite the other differences separating their life experiences.

This situation, however, would be very different in the hypothetical case of a *campesino* from the Mexican countryside sitting down to dinner with an executive from PEMEX, the nationally owned petroleum company. Although both are *Mexican* — from the same country and perhaps even from the same geographical region — their shared experience and cultural conditioning would be much more limited than that of their counterparts in the United States. They might still be able to discuss politics, for example, but with very disparate levels of awareness. For the most part, the rural population of the Hispanic world in the Western Hemisphere has a culture all its own. Little of the sophistication of the urban environment makes its way to the rural areas commonly referred to in Spanish as the *interior*.

Of course, social-class differences also account for some of the lack of common ground shared by the hypothetical Mexican dinner partners. In fact, one of the basic differences between the rural dweller of the Hispanic world and that of the United States is primarily an economic one. The majority of those who reside permanently in the rural United States are middle-class farm or small business owners, or professionals. Although many farmers who own and work their own land are experiencing financial difficulties, these rural residents are still struggling to maintain their identity amid the growth of agribusinesses. The migrant farm workers who provide much of the seasonal labor in most farm regions north of the Rio Grande are an invisible labor force who are rarely considered when one thinks of the rural United States and its people.

This is not the case in Latin America. Although the per capita income of Hispanic countries is lower than that of the United States, the disparity between rural dwellers in both countries is much greater than that of their urban counterparts. Few Latin American rural workers own the land they farm. Most of the arable land is held by a wealthy few. Illiteracy is the norm among most rural laborers, although some may have attended several years of grammar school. Most *campesinos* live with their relatively large families in modest one- or two-room homes that may or may not have electricity or running water. Access to stores, medical facilities, entertainment centers, and other urban offerings is limited by lack of personal transportation, although most villages (*pueblos*) are served by inexpensive and timeworn interurban buses. Walking is the most common mode of transport — often on unpaved or dirt roads leading from the various *fincas* (farms) to the main roads. Consumer needs are simple — one pair of shoes, several changes of clothing, a few rudimentary cooking, eating, and farming utensils. The local store serves most buying needs. Few people own their own radios or television sets, although there are usually several to be found in the local town center. Farm instruments are often primitive — farming in most rural areas of Latin America is still more labor-intensive than mechanized.

It would be easy to romanticize the simplicity of the Hispanic rural life as free from modern-day tensions and worries. But this is an incomplete picture. Disease, malnutrition, high infant mortality rates, long workdays with little rest or relaxation, barely enough food for survival, lack of opportunity and incentive are also part of the *campesino's* lot. While inflation has raised the price of the few purchased commodities needed by the rural farm worker, farm wages have not kept pace. Often the owners of the large estates provide small loans to farm workers in times of need. This practice is little more than an indentured-servant system under which laborers may never free themselves from debt to their employer. Some of the more fortunate *campesinos* are given a small plot of land for family food needs.

1. *How are the "typical" rural resident of the United States and most Hispanic countries different?*
2. *Describe in general terms the life of a rural* campesino.

The crux of the problem is the lack of private ownership of the land. Historically its roots lie in

the colonial period. The land formerly owned communally by the indigenous populations was redistributed in large chunks to privileged colonizers who became the overseers for the Spanish Crown. After the independence struggles freed the land from this foreign domination, ownership simply reverted to those who once were its privileged caretakers. The source of wealth and social conflict in Latin America has always been the land. Large landed estates known as *haciendas* still abound, although some are now in the hands of U.S. corporations. There has been some attempt to redistribute the land to individuals or small farming cooperatives, but the overall picture has changed little since colonial times.

What little change there has been has occurred in recent years. Ironically, these changes have occurred in those countries that account for the largest migration of Hispanics to the United States: Mexico, Puerto Rico, and Cuba.

In 1910, the Mexican Revolution's primary aim was land reform. It was mainly in response to President Porfirio Díaz' common practice of attracting many foreign investors to buy into Mexico's future. Some small gains were made, although not enough to change the basic picture. Under President Lázaro Cárdenas in the 1930s, greater progress in distribution of the land was made, but, again, the countryside remained dominated by large estate and government holdings. As cities became more urbanized and industrialized, the rural–urban migration pattern increased dramatically. The growth of employment opportunities has not kept pace with the influx of *campesinos*. Shanty towns abound in many suburban and urban neighborhoods of the major cities, while the ever-increasing population of Mexico City has surpassed 17 million inhabitants.

The lack of jobs for the recent migrants have forced some to look elsewhere, primarily to Mexico's neighbor to the north. Most Mexican immigrants to the United States are originally from rural backgrounds. Some enter legally, while others do not. Recent estimates place the number of undocumented workers in the United States at one million, the majority of whom are Mexican. The irony is that the large majority of these illegal immigrants do find work either in factories or on farms. Employers are attracted to this cheap labor force whose illegal status frees the employers from adhering to strict federal regulations regarding minimum wage, working con-

ditions, and unemployment insurance. It is not uncommon for employers to contract with *coyotes*, bilingual entrepreneurs who charge for their services in facilitating illegal border crossings for a certain number of needed workers. Once here, however, the new arrivals are on their own, constantly trying to evade *La Migra* (immigration officers).

Recent legislation passed by the United States Congress imposes penalties on employers who knowingly hire illegal immigrants. It also grants amnesty to long-time residents without legal immigrant status. The impact of these laws on the undocumented worker-problem remains to be seen.

In the case of Puerto Rico, the alteration of the rural scene is due primarily to policy decisions made in the United States. Once sugar and coffee plantations dotted the countryside. As in other Latin American countries, the land was owned by a wealthy few and worked by farm workers known as *jíbaros*. With the takeover of the island, control shifted to U.S.-owned corporations who brought new technology to sugar production and virtually eliminated the coffee plantations. Later, when sugar prices dropped, its cultivation was also curtailed. These moves left a great number of *jíbaros* displaced and changed the overall economic picture of Puerto Rico.

Although agriculture was once the dominant economic base, today most foodstuffs, including coffee, must be imported, contributing to the high cost of living on the island. Since the 1950s, many U.S. companies have established industrial operations in Puerto Rico, primarily in pharmaceuticals and petrochemicals. Nevertheless, the unemployment rate continues to climb. Once some of the industries outlived the period of economic incentives offered to companies locating in Puerto Rico, they left the island in search of cheaper labor markets, adding to the ranks of the unemployed. Migration to the mainland is one alternative that has often been encouraged by the United States in times of need for a new labor source (during World War II, for example). While rural residents used to account for the majority of migrants seeking work primarily in the northeastern United States, urban workers and professionals abound in the most recent influx.

In the case of Cuba, one of the main objectives of the 1959 revolution led by Fidel Castro was redistribution of wealth and land. The land is now owned by the government, and the most basic needs of farm workers (*guajiros*) are met through government programs. Literacy rates have risen, but consumer goods are scarce.

The first wave of Cuban immigrants to the United States were those who were economically more comfortable and primarily from urban areas. In recent years, more and more working-class Cubans, both urban and rural, have come to the United States seeking better economic opportunities and a political alternative to Castro's totalitarian regime. The majority of Cuban exiles, like their counterparts from the other two Caribbean islands of Puerto Rico and the Dominican Republic, have been attracted to the large urban centers of the United States. The greatest numbers of Cuban emigrés are in the southeast, especially in Dade County, Florida.

Some of the newest Hispanic immigrants to the United States are from the Central American countries of El Salvador, Guatemala, and Nicaragua. Many of these are from rural backgrounds similar to those described earlier. In El Salvador, the conflict between the rebel forces and government occurs primarily in the countryside, driving *campesinos* from their homes for economic and/or political survival. In Guatemala, internal strife affects rural dwellers in the same way. Nicaragua's Sandinista regime is working to redistribute the land and to raise the literacy of its nationals. Those who have fled are predominantly from the wealthy, urban class.

---

3. *What historical facts account for the difference between rural Latin America and the rural United States?*
4. *How does the reality of rural Latin America affect the number of Hispanics residing in the United States?*
5. *What names are used to refer to rural farm workers in Mexico, Puerto Rico, and Cuba, respectively?*

In trying to understand the composite of Hispanics residing in the United States, it is important to be aware of the cultural differences between urban and rural lifestyles in the country of origin. Some recently arrived Hispanics may have come directly from the countryside to the mainland United States, crossing not one but *two* cultural boundaries: urban versus rural, as well as Hispanic versus Anglo. Others may have first made the adjustment to the urban environment in their homeland before emigrating. Those who were raised in the urban environment face a less drastic cultural adjustment than their rural counterparts.

You may experience linguistic problems in communicating with clients who have come directly from the *campo* in their homeland. Dialects vary from region to region and may account for differences in pronunciation, vocabulary, and/or structures used. Rural people may express themselves in more colloquial terms and be uncomfortable with the rigid, technical speech patterns common to professional settings in the United States. They may have a low literacy level, which may affect their ability to read and fill out forms and follow certain directions. Clients from those areas of Mexico and Central and South America where large indigenous populations abound may be bilingual, speaking an Indian tongue as their native language and Spanish as a second language used primarily to communicate within the urban culture.

Some of the same difficulties that occur in the mainland United States in providing services to Hispanic clients from rural backgrounds also occur in the countries of origin. Professionals with an urban upbringing often need special guidance in understanding their compatriot clients from the countryside. The cultural differences are vast, but not insurmountable.

In summary, the urban versus rural distinction is an important factor that can influence the success of communicating with Hispanic clients residing in the United States. Any attempt to better understand the background of an individual client can only serve to make the interaction easier and more pleasant for all involved.

---

6. *What type of cultural adaptations do Hispanics from a rural background have to make while trying to adjust to living in the United States?*
7. *What special problems may arise when trying to communicate in Spanish with clients from rural Latin America, and how can they be resolved?*

NONVERBAL COMMUNICATION: Personal space and touching

Perhaps the most subtle nonverbal cue to which we react is that of personal space. Many believe that our concept of how much space we need as a buffer zone between ourselves and others is derived from the territorial boundaries common in the animal kingdom. Others attribute it to the sensitivity of the energy field or "aura" that each individual has emanating from the nerve endings. Whatever its origin, we respond to violations of our personal space from a rather primitive, subconscious level. Our individual territorial boundaries are defined, to a large extent, by the culture in which we are raised.

Most cultures have a range of personal space needs, allowing a closer "invasion" for intimate contact. The Anglo-American culture prescribes rather rigid boundaries when in close proximity to others. Such expressions as "keeping one's distance," "keeping someone at arm's length," and "I wouldn't touch that with a ten-foot pole" are clues to the cultural value placed on preserving one's personal spatial domain. The amount of space necessary to prevent Anglos (and other northern Europeans) from feeling uncomfortable has been estimated at between 18 and 30 inches for nonintimate contact. Nontouching intimate encounters tolerate a 6- to 18-inch range. When two Anglos interact in a formal situation, each

encased in an imaginary personal air bubble, there may be as much as 4 or 5 feet of space between them.

Most Hispanics, on the other hand, have much less of a need to maintain substantial personal distance. If you observe your Hispanic clients as they talk to one another, you may notice that they stand much closer together than is common in the Anglo culture. This is true for both strangers and friends or acquaintances. It is also true, to some extent, for interaction with members of the opposite sex as well as with those of the same sex.

When an Anglo and a Hispanic interact personally, the former may feel invaded and intensely uncomfortable if the latter presses in too closely. The Anglo may (subconsciously, of course) view the Hispanic as being pushy or even too sexy, especially if the inner circle reserved for intimate contact (6 to 18 inches) is invaded. This may be particularly the case when an Anglo male stands near a Hispanic male. The Anglo culture is particularly rigid regarding personal space (and touching) among males: too intimate a contact may imply homosexuality, a threatening label to many heterosexual males. On the other hand, the Hispanic may feel that the Anglo is aloof, unconcerned, or even prejudiced if an attempt is made

to pull back. This subconscious attempt by the Anglo to preserve his or her spatial boundaries can be misinterpreted as cringing, a response to an unpleasant encounter.

The concept of personal space is extended to other aspects of culture as well. In the Anglo-American culture, it is very much in vogue to speak of "having one's space." The increase of efficiency and one-bedroom apartments and condominiums reflects the rise in popularity of living alone. Many individuals, especially those who work with people, feel a strong need to be alone to relax. These all illustrate the extension of the concept of *territorial domain*. Hispanics, however, tend to prefer to relax in large groups. They seem more open to receiving unannounced visitors and to accommodating friends and family in need of temporary housing than are their Anglo counterparts. Few Hispanics live alone: the extended family and other support networks common to Spanish-speaking cultures provide space for those who are experiencing economic, marital, or parental communication problems.

The use of the telephone to accomplish daily tasks rather than the personal visit is another indication of the Anglo view of personal distance. In the mainland United States it is easy to conduct almost all one's personal business by phone. We are, indeed, encouraged to "reach out and *touch* someone" via the telephone. Hispanics, on the other hand, have a long history of preferring personal contact to the impersonal use of the telephone for both business and pleasure. In most Hispanic countries it is virtually impossible to deal with most business matters over the telephone. Whereas an Anglo may consider it a waste of time to pay a bill in person or drop by an office to check on a routine business matter, the same behavior is the Hispanic expression of the high social value placed on the interpersonal contact. Many small stores in Hispanic areas of the United States flourish despite somewhat higher prices and limited selection when compared with the large Anglo chain stores precisely because they provide the opportunity for personal contact with the shopkeeper, who knows his or her customers well. Asking a relative or friend for a favor may have better results if the time is taken to pay a personal visit to the home.

The distancing effect that accompanies business phone calls and letter writing in the Hispanic world is evidenced in the rather formal, third-person speech patterns used to answer a phone (*¿De parte de quién?, Habla Carlos Ramírez*), address a letter (*Estimado señor,* esteemed sir), or end it (*De Ud. atento y seguro servidor,* your attentive and steadfast servant). Although some degree of formality governs the personal encounter in business environments, it is tempered by talking about one's personal life and family before getting down to business. The use of facial and hand gestures as well as close personal space and touch add warmth and vitality to most business interactions.

The use of touch is closely aligned with the concept of personal space. The United States shares with its northern European ancestors a rather reserved attitude toward personal touching. When in doubt, it seems, the rule is *do not touch* another human being. Although this custom may be changing somewhat, no doubt influenced by the warm hugging and kissing greeting behaviors common to TV talk show hosts and guests, the Anglo culture still refrains from punctuating conversation with touches to the other person's body. Hispanics, on the other hand, almost seem to consider touching as a way of talking. It is not uncommon for a Hispanic to touch the conversational partner's upper arm, hand, or even thigh with a finger, or a hand—the latter occasionally in a light slap. These touches are interspersed among many other hand gestures, adding an entire dimension to the communication process among Spanish speakers. Anglos, however, may view such uninvited touching of their bodies as insulting, threatening, or outrageous behavior. While they may understand perfectly the verbal message received, their subconscious reaction may misinterpret the intent, motivation, or honesty of its sender.

Of course, there is no right or wrong way to use personal space and touching in communicating with others. We are all culture-bound and find easiest and most comfortable those patterns learned in childhood. What is important is to be able to recognize the potential for misunderstandings and false judgments of behavior allowed and encouraged in one culture that is not accepted or condoned in another. Bringing the differences to a *conscious* awareness is half the battle. Learning not to let them influence our opinions of another human being is the other half.

Putting it into practice

1. Stand up. Now watch as another (Anglo) student approaches you from behind to speak with you. Notice how he or she gets your attention and how far away he or she stands from you.

2. Stand up. Now watch as another (Hispanic) student does the same as the student above. Again notice how he or she gets your attention and how far away from you he or she stands. Also notice your reaction to this invasion of personal space. What feelings does the encounter elicit?

3. You are trying to convince another student of something about which you feel very strongly. Say four or five sentences to him in the Anglo nontouching way. What devices do you use to get your point across (tone of voice, gestures, eye contact, etc.)?

4. Now do the same in Spanish, using *both* the Hispanic concept of space and touching behavior to convince your classmate of the truth of what you're saying. How did it feel to move in close and touch your listener? Ask your classmate how it felt to be talked to in this way.

5. What are the two most serious violations of your personal space and touching boundaries that you have experienced in your profession? How do you feel now about the person(s) who committed the transgression? What behaviors of your Hispanic clients trigger a similar response?

Comunicándose en español

PRONUNCIACIÓN: Enlace y ritmo 🎞️

In order to be able to understand your Spanish-speaking clients, you must be able to decipher word boundaries in the stream of speech. Although Spanish may seem to be spoken faster than English, this is not the case. Your years of experience speaking English have trained your ear to understand it when spoken at a rapid clip. When you hear "Wadjasay" in English, you know the person is asking you "What did you say?"

As you have more practice in listening to Spanish, you will have fewer and fewer problems in understanding words in the stream of speech. The following phonetic principles will help you.

We speak in breath groups, each consisting of several words linked together without a pause. In Spanish, when the same vowel ends one word and begins the next, the sounds often run together.

Está aquí	(es-*ta*-qui)	**su uso**	(*su*-so)
mi hijo	(*mi*-jo)	**¿Qué es?**	(ques)
la abogada	(la-bo-*ga*-da)	**¿no oye?**	(*no*-ye)

When an **i** or **u** sound (also spelled **hi** and **hu**) begins or ends a word in Spanish, a diphthong forms when the adjoining word begins or ends in a vowel sound.

¿Qué tiene usted?	(que-*tie*-neus-ted)	**a la una**	(a-*lau*-na)
la última vez	(*laul*-ti-ma-vez)	**mi amigo**	(mia-*mi*-go)
treinta y dos	(*trein*-tay-dos)	**su hijo**	(*sui*-jo)

When a word ends in a consonant followed by a word beginning with a vowel, the consonant tends to begin the syllable even across word boundaries.

el esposo	(e-les-po-so)	**es esta**	(e-ses-ta)
las horas	(la-so-ras)	**los años**	(lo-sa-ños)
en el hogar	(e-ne-lo-gar)	**mis hijos**	(mi-si-jos)

In Spanish, most syllables are stressed evenly, giving the language a rather staccato rhythm. Repeat the following sentences using the syllabification and stress patterns indicated in parentheses as your guide. The major stressed syllables are indicated in italics.

1. **Es un amigo de mi hijo.**   (E-su-na-*mi*-go-de-*mi*-jo)
2. **Tiene una infección seria.**   (*Tie*-neu-nain-fec-*cion*-se-ria)
3. **¿Cuál es su hijo?**   (Cua-*le*-sui-jo)
4. **¿Está libre el lunes?**   (Es-*ta*-li-bre-*lu*-nes)

Práctica 🎞️

Read the following semiphonetic transcriptions of statements containing words you've learned previously, using the proper linkage and stress patterns. Stressed syllables are indicated in italics. Practice until you can read them without pauses. Write the correct spelling of the sentence in the blank provided.

1. ¿*Cua*-le-su-*nu*-me-ro-de-te-*le*-fo-no?

2.   *Vuel*-va-la-*u*-na-si-me-*a*-cel-fa-*vor*.

_____

3.   ¿*Co*-mo-ses-*cri*-be-sua-pe-*lli*-do?

_____

4.   *E*-ra-*lau*-nay-*me*-dia-de-la-ma-dru-*ga*-da.

_____

5.   ¿A-que-*o*-ra-le-con-*vie*-ne-aus-*ted*?

_____

In case you experienced difficulties in deciphering, the correct spelling of the sentences follows:

1.   ¿Cuál es su número de teléfono?
2.   Vuelva a la una, si me hace el favor.
3.   ¿Cómo se escribe su apellido?
4.   Era la una y media de la madrugada.
5.   ¿A qué hora le conviene a usted? (Remember, no diphthongs form if one of the vowels is *not* **i, y,** or **u.**)

Now, without the semiphonetic guides, practice reading aloud the following until you can do so without pauses. Pay special attention to linking across word boundaries.

1.   ¿Cuántas horas trabaja usted cada semana?
2.   Su hijo se llama Eugenio, ¿verdad?
3.   El año pasado fui a vivir en Arecibo.
4.   Tengo una cita con el abogado.
5.   Me refirió una amiga de mi esposa.

Dictado 📼

Write the following short phrases and full sentences your instructor will dictate:

1.   _____   3.   _____

2.   _____   4.   _____

5.   _____

6.   _____

7.   _____

Señor Rivera, ¿qué hace Ud. por aquí? Ud. no tiene cita hasta la semana que viene.

Sí, lo sé. Estoy aquí para cambiar la cita. Voy a estar en Miami toda la semana que viene.

¿Por qué no me llamó por teléfono?

Es que prefiero hablarle personalmente.

Sí, pero, hombre, le cuesta mucho trabajo venir aquí. Se puede cambiar la cita en cinco minutos por teléfono.

Cuando vivía en Cuba siempre lo hacía así.

Comprendo, señor Rivera, pero aquí en los E.E.U.U. todos dependemos del teléfono para hacernos más fácil la vida.

Más fácil para Ud., tal vez, pero para mí es más fácil venir a hablarle personalmente. Como no domino bien el inglés, me pongo nervioso cada vez que tengo que hablar por teléfono.

Bueno, comprendo ahora, señor Rivera, porque a mí me pasa lo mismo cuando tengo que hablar por teléfono en español. Entonces, ¿quiere Ud. cambiar la cita que tiene?

Sí, prefiero venir la última semana del mes, si no es ninguna molestia.

¿Ha entendido bien?

1. ¿Para qué fue el señor Rivera a la oficina?
2. ¿Para cuándo era la cita?
3. ¿Dónde va a estar el señor Rivera la semana que viene?
4. ¿Por qué no llamó a la secretaria por teléfono?
5. ¿De qué país es el señor Rivera?
6. ¿Parece hispana la recepcionista? Explique.
7. ¿Para quiénes es más fácil usar el teléfono en los Estados Unidos?
8. ¿Por qué prefiere el señor Rivera hablarle personalmente a la recepcionista?
9. ¿Prefiere Ud. hablar inglés o español por teléfono?
10. ¿Se pone Ud. nervioso/a cuando tiene que hablar por teléfono en español?

INTRODUCTORY DIALOGUE: In person

Mrs. McNeil: What are you doing here, Mr. Rivera? You don't have an appointment until next week.

Mr. Rivera: Yes, I know. I'm here to change my appointment. I will be in Miami all next week.

Mrs. McN: Why didn't you call me on the telephone?

Mr. R: It's (just) that I prefer to speak to you in person.

Mrs. McN: Yes, but, sir, it's out of your way to come here (it costs you a lot of trouble). The appointment can be changed in five minutes by phone.

Mr. R: When I lived in Cuba I always did it this way.

Mrs. McN: I understand that, Mr. Rivera, but here in the United States we all depend on the telephone to make life easier for us.

Mr. R: Easier for you, maybe, but for me it's easier to come and talk to you in person. Since I do not speak (dominate) English well, I get very nervous each time I have to speak on the telephone.

Mrs. McN: Well, I understand now, Mr. Rivera, because the same thing happens to me when I have to speak Spanish on the telephone. Would you like to change your appointment, then?

Mr. R: Yes, I prefer to come the last week of the month, if that's no problem (trouble).

BASIC STRUCTURES I: I need some personal information

The employee (f.)	The client (m.)

(They're speaking on the telephone.)

Hello. Am I speaking with Mr. Silva?	Yes. Who is calling, please?
(This is) Miss MacGregor from Roosevelt Hospital speaking. You're coming here to check in tomorrow, right?	Yes, Miss, you are right.
Doctor Vermiglia will operate on you, correct?	Yes, Miss.
Mr. Silva, I need to ask you a few personal questions.	Yes, of course.
First of all, where do you live?	I live at { 36 Hudson Street. / 147 Buena Vista. / 68 Ford Street.
Is that here in the city?	{ Yes, it is. / No, it's in the Jackson Heights area.
And the zip code?	It's 2-7-3-8-4.
How long have you lived at that address?	(It's been) five years.
Your telephone number is still the same?	Yes, it's still 3-2-2-9-5-7-8.
What is your social security number?	It's 0-7-4-5-5-0-2-3-1.

¿Sabe usted?

1. In giving an address in Spanish, normally the type of street, road, etc., is given first, then its name, followed by the number. **En la Ford Street** is a commonly used anglicism.

2. The titles **señor, señora, señorita, maestro, licenciado,** etc., are used in direct address in Spanish. Some Hispanics may transfer this custom by addressing people in English as *Mister* (pronounced *Mihter*), *Mrs.* (pronounced *misi*), and *Teacher* without the surname.

3. **Barrio** in Spanish refers to *any* district of a city, *not* a ghetto as in English.

4. **Sigue igual** can be used in many contexts to indicate things are pretty much the same (**Todo sigue igual en casa**).

La empleada	*El cliente*
	(Hablan por teléfono.)
Aló. ¿Hablo con el señor Silva?	Sí. ¿Quién habla?
Habla la señorita MacGregor del Hospital Roosevelt. Ud. viene aquí mañana para internarse, ¿verdad?	Sí, señorita, tiene razón.
Le va a operar el doctor Vermiglia, ¿verdad?	Sí, señorita.
Señor Silva, necesito hacerle algunas preguntas personales.	Sí, cómo no.
Primero, ¿dónde vive?	Vivo en { la calle Hudson, número 36 (treinta y seis). la Buena Vista, número 147 (ciento cuarenta y siete). el 68 (sesenta y ocho) de la Ford (Street).
¿Eso es aquí en la ciudad?	{ Sí, lo es. No, está en el barrio de Jackson Heights.
¿Y la zona postal?	Es el 2-73-84 (dos setenta y tres ochenta y cuatro).
¿Cuánto tiempo hace que Ud. vive en esa dirección?	Hace cinco años.
¿Su número de teléfono sigue igual?	Sí, todavía es el 3-22-95-78 (tres veintidós noventa y cinco setenta y ocho).
¿Cuál es su número de seguro social?	Es el 0-74-55-0-2-31 (cero setenta y cuatro cincuenta y cinco cero dos treinta y uno).

---

5. **Internarse** is to be admitted to the hospital (**hospitalizarse** in Cuban dialect); **darle de alta** is to be released (**Me interné ayer; me van a dar de alta mañana**).

Notas lingüísticas I

A. **Ser** is used to *identify* the location of a building or event (¿**Es aquí donde puedo hacer una cita?**). Estar is used to actually locate something (**El hospital está en la calle Jefferson**).

B. **Lo es** is used as the equivalent of *that's right, that's it,* etc. The **lo** is considered neuter since it refers to an entire idea or concept. Its gender never changes.

C. To express the concept of duration of time **hace** + time + present tense is used: **Hace cinco años que vivo aquí.** It is literally translated as *It makes five years time that I live here.* English prefers the present perfect tense in the equivalent construction (*I have lived here for five years*).

BASIC STRUCTURES II: More personal information

The employee (f.)	*The client (m.)*

(They are still speaking on the telephone)

Where were you born?	I was born	on the island. in the capital. in Bogotá, Colombia. in El Salvador.

When were you born?	I was born on	January first. February second. March third. April fourth. May fifth. June sixth. July twenty-first. August twenty-second. September thirtieth. October thirty-first. November twelfth. December fifteenth.

In what year?	In 19	08. 23. 34.

How old are you, then?	I am	forty fifty sixty-six seventy eighty ninety one hundred	years old.

Do you have Blue Cross medical insurance?	Yes, I have (it).
What is your policy and group number?	It's T-1-6-0-7-3-A-1-5. The group is (number) 98.
Very well, sir, come to the reception office between two and four in the afternoon.	Yes. I have a favor to ask you. Can my wife accompany me in the operating room?
Well, you have to ask the doctor that. See you tomorrow, Mr. Silva.	Goodbye. See you later.

¿Sabe usted?

1. **La Isla** is commonly used by Puerto Ricans to refer to their homeland.

2. *To be* a certain age is expressed in Spanish by **tener x años.** To ask someone's age you may use either **¿Cuántos años tiene Ud.?** or **¿Qué edad tiene Ud.?** Responses may include **Tengo treinta años** or **Voy a cumplir treinta** (*I'm going to*

ESTRUCTURAS BÁSICAS II: Más datos personales

La empleada	El cliente

(Siguen hablando por teléfono)

¿Dónde nació Ud.?	Nací en	la Isla. la capital. Bogotá, Colombia. El Salvador.

¿Cuándo nació Ud.?	Nací	el primero de enero. el dos de febrero. el tres de marzo. el cuatro de abril. el cinco de mayo. el seis de junio. el veintiuno de julio. el veintidós de agosto. el treinta de setiembre. el treinta y uno de octubre. el doce de noviembre. el quince de diciembre.

¿En qué año?	En mil novecientos	ocho. veintitrés. treinta y cuatro.

Entonces, ¿cuántos años tiene Ud.?	Tengo	cuarenta cincuenta sesenta y seis setenta ochenta noventa cien	años.

¿Tiene Ud. seguro médico de Cruz Azul?	Sí, lo tengo.

¿Cuál es el número de la póliza y del grupo?	Es T-16-0-73-A-15 (T dieciséis cero setenta y tres A quince). El grupo es el 98.

Bueno, señor, venga mañana a la oficina de la recepción entre las dos y las cuatro de la tarde.	Sí. Tengo que pedirle un favor. ¿Me puede acompañar mi esposa en la sala de operaciones?

Bueno, tiene que preguntarle eso al doctor. Entonces, hasta mañana, señor Silva.	Adiós. Hasta luego.

---

be 30). One's *birthday* is **el cumpleaños**; one's *birthdate* is **la fecha de nacimiento**.

3. **Tener** is used in other idiomatic expressions: **tener miedo** = *to be afraid;* **tener razón** = *to be right;* **no tener razón** = *to be wrong.*

4. **Setiembre** may also be spelled **septiembre**; the p is not pronounced and consequently is commonly omitted.

5. The names of months in Spanish are not capitalized except at the beginning of a sentence.

6. The verb **nacer**, like **conocer** and **parecer**, has an irregular **yo** form in the present tense:

    nazco   conozco   parezco

Notas lingüísticas II

A. The numbers from 1 to 100 are as follows:

1 uno	11 once	
2 dos	12 doce	20 veinte
3 tres	13 trece	30 treinta
4 cuatro	14 catorce	40 cuarenta
5 cinco	15 quince	50 cincuenta
6 seis	16 dieciséis	60 sesenta
7 siete	17 diecisiete	70 setenta
8 ocho	18 dieciocho	80 ochenta
9 nueve	19 diecinueve	90 noventa
10 diez		100 cien

In combining numbers, these rules apply:

1. The numbers 16 to 29 are usually written as one word.

    dieciocho; veinticuatro

2. The combined numbers 31 to 99 are written as three words but are pronounced as a unit, since the **y** (pronounced *i*) forms a diphthong with the vowel at the end of the first number.

    treinta y cuatro   (trein-tai-cua-tro)
    sesenta y siete   (se-sen-tai-sie-te)

3. **Cien** is used in counting; **ciento** in combined forms. **Ciento** is *never* followed by the conjunction **y**.

    cien, ciento uno, ciento quince, etc.

B. When giving a date in Spanish:

1. Use **el** + number + **de** + month + **de** + year.

    el 3 de julio de mil novecientos cincuenta

2. Use **primero** for the first day of the month, the counting numbers (**dos, tres,** etc.) for subsequent days.

    el primero de octubre, el dos de mayo

3. Years in this century are read as **mil** + **novecientos** + two-digit number; they are *never* read as in English "nineteen forty."

    Nací el treinta de enero de mil novecientos veintidós.

C. To translate the concept of *to ask* in Spanish, three different verbs are used, depending on the context. The person asked is always referred to with the indirect object pronoun:

pedir	to ask *for* something
preguntar	to ask a *specific question*
hacer preguntas	to ask *questions* (*of someone*)

Tengo que pedirle un favor.	I have to ask you a favor.
Tengo que preguntarle dónde vive Ud.	I have to ask you where you live.
Tengo que hacerle algunas preguntas personales.	I have to ask you some personal questions.

D. Both direct and indirect object pronouns are commonly attached to the infinitive form of the verb, although they may precede the entire verb phrase:

Le **tengo que hacer una pregunta personal.**
Tengo que hacer*le* **una pregunta personal.** } indirect object
No *lo* **quiere hacer.**
No quiere hacer*lo***.** } direct object

E. You have learned that the third person singular form of the preterite tense of regular **-ar** verbs ends in **-ó** and that of **-er** and **-ir** verbs ends in **-ió**. The complete conjugations in the preterite of **-ar**, **-er**, and **-ir** regular verbs follow.

	llevar	*nacer*	*vivir*
yo	**llevé**	**nací**	**viví**
nosotros/as	**llevamos**	**nacimos**	**vivimos**
tú	**llevaste**	**naciste**	**viviste**
Ud., él, ella	**llevó**	**nació**	**vivió**
Uds., ellos/as	**llevaron**	**nacieron**	**vivieron**

F. Following are some of the verbs with irregularities in the preterite.

1. Verbs ending in **-gar** and **-car** have spelling changes in the preterite to maintain the consonant sound of the infinitive:

   a. **G** before **e** or **i** is pronounced like **j** unless silent **u** follows it.

llegar	yo	**lle***gué*
	tú	**llegaste**
	Ud., él, ella	**llegó**
	nosotros/as	**llegamos**
	Uds., ellos/as	**llegaron**

   b. **C** before **e** or **i** is pronounced like **s**; the **k** sound is represented by **qu** before **e** or **i**.

buscar	yo	**bus***qué*
	tú	**buscaste**
	Ud., él, ella	**buscó**
	nosotros/as	**buscamos**
	Uds., ellos/as	**buscaron**

2. Since **z** in Spanish appears only before **a, o,** and **u,** the same sound is represented by **c** before **e** and **i**. This spelling change occurs in the preterite **yo** form of verbs ending in **-zar.**

empezar		
	yo	**empe*cé***
	tú	**empezaste**
	Ud., él, ella	**empezó**
	nosotros/as	**empezamos**
	Uds., ellos/as	**empezaron**

PRÁCTICA PRELIMINAR

Follow the guidelines for self-instructional practice given in the Preface.

A. Give the present tense form of the verb **ser, estar,** or **tener** that correctly translates the English concept of *to be* in the following questions or statements that you might say to a client.

Ejemplo: ¿Cómo _*está*_ Ud. hoy?

1. ¿ _____ Ud. la señora Ramírez?

2. ¿A qué hora _____ la cita con la doctora?

3. Lo siento, pero ella no _____ en la oficina hoy.

4. Sí, señora, Ud. _____ razón; lo siento.

5. ¿Cuándo _____ Ud. libre la semana que viene?

6. El mejor día parece _____ el martes.

7. ¿ _____ bien a la tres?

8. Espere, señora, ¿cuál _____ su teléfono?

9. ¿Cuántos años _____ Ud., señora?

10. Usted _____ ama de casa, ¿verdad?

11. Entonces, su cita _____ el martes a las tres.

12. Sí, señora, la doctora va a _____ aquí.

A 1. Es 2. es 3. está 4. tiene 5. está 6. ser 7. Está 8. es 9. tiene 10. es 11. es 12. estar

B. Give the correct form of the Spanish verb that best translates the concept of *to ask* in the following statements you might make to a client.

   Ejemplo: **Señora, le tengo que** *hacer* **una pregunta personal.**

   1. Señor Robles, le quiero _____ una pregunta.

   2. Juanito, te van a _____ tu tarjeta verde.

   3. Señora Gil, le necesito _____ cuándo nació.

   4. Señor, le tengo que _____ su tarjeta de seguro.

   5. No, señora, no le voy a _____ muchas preguntas.

   6. Permiso, señor, le quisiera _____ qué hora tiene.

   7. La doctora le va a _____ si es ciudadano.

C. Practice asking the following questions orally, then answering them using the **hace + time + que** construction and the length of time given in parentheses.
   Ejemplo: ¿Cuánto tiempo hace que vive en la ciudad? (*2 months*)
           Hace dos meses que vivo en la ciudad.

   1. ¿Cuánto tiempo hace que Ud. no se siente bien? (*3 days*)
   2. ¿Cuánto tiempo hace que Ud. espera al trabajador social? (*an hour and a half*)
   3. ¿Cuánto tiempo hace que Uds. tienen problemas en casa? (*many years*)
   4. ¿Cuánto tiempo hace que su esposo no vive con Ud.? (*6 months*)
   5. ¿Cuánto tiempo hace que Ud. viene a esta agencia? (*4 years*)

D. Practice reading aloud the following sentences containing numerical information until you can say them without pausing.
   1. Mi teléfono es el 523-0731.
   2. No puedo llegar antes de las 4:15 P.M.
   3. El número de la póliza es 34-T-01903.
   4. Ud. nació el 13 de octubre de 1946, ¿verdad?
   5. Su número de seguro social es el 349-09-6311, ¿verdad?
   6. Su fecha de nacimiento es el 1 de julio de 1967.
   7. A ver si tengo bien su teléfono. ¿Es el 674-1252?
   8. Sigue igual mi número de teléfono; es el 921-0212.

B 1. hacer 2. pedir 3. preguntar 4. pedir 5. hacer 6. preguntar 7. preguntar
C 1. Hace tres días que no me siento bien. 2. Hace hora y media que lo espero. 3. Hace muchos años que tenemos problemas en casa. 4. Hace seis meses que mi esposo no vive conmigo. 5. Hace cuatro años que vengo a esta agencia.
D 1. cinco veintitrés cero siete treinta y uno 2. cuatro y cuarto (quince) de la tarde 3. treinta y cuatro T cero diecinueve cero tres 4. trece; mil novecientos cuarenta y seis 5. tres cuarenta y nueve cero nueve sesenta y tres once 6. primero; mil novecientos sesenta y siete 7. seis setenta y cuatro doce cincuenta y dos 8. nueve veintiuno cero dos doce

E. Give the correct direct or indirect object pronoun in the blank that corresponds to the word(s) in parentheses.

Ejemplo: Manolo __le__ quiere hacer unas preguntas. (*a ella*)

1. Mi hermano siempre _____ llama. (*a mí*)

2. El doctor _____ llamó a las dos de la tarde. (*al señor Fernández*)

3. La señorita Fonseca _____ habla muy despacio. (*a nosotros*)

4. ¿Tú _____ haces preguntas en español o en inglés? (*a la maestra*)

5. Mi madre _____ busca en el colegio. (*a mis hermanos*)

6. Él _____ refirió al doctor. (*a ti*)

7. ¿ _____ conviene hablar mañana? (*a su hijo*)

8. Esa señora _____ necesita. (*la póliza*)

9. El padre _____ pide volver esta noche. (*a ellas*)

10. Yo _____ tengo conmigo. (*los documentos*)

F. Answer the following questions in complete sentences using the information given in parentheses.

Ejemplo: ¿Cuándo puede Ud. volver? (*tomorrow at two*)
   Puedo volver mañana a las dos.

1. ¿A qué hora es su cita? (*11:30 A.M.*)
2. ¿Cuál es la zona postal? (*9-74-05*)
3. ¿En qué año nació Ud.? (*1957*)
4. ¿Cuántos años tienes tú? (*33*)
5. ¿Dónde vive Ud. ahora? (*40 Broad Street*)
6. ¿Cuándo nació su esposo? (*May 15, 1952*)
7. ¿Cuál es su número de seguro social? (*3-30-40-12-74*)
8. ¿Cuándo es su próxima cita? (*Friday, August 12th, at 1:30*)
9. ¿Cuál es su número de teléfono? (*5-22-7-0-31*)
10. ¿Cuánto tiempo hace que Ud. vive en Nueva York? (*25 years*)

E 1. me 2. lo 3. nos 4. le 5. los 6. te 7. Le 8. la 9. les 10. los
F 1. Mi cita es a las once y media de la mañana. 2. Es el nueve setenta y cuatro cero cinco. 3. Nací en mil novecientos cincuenta y siete. 4. Tengo treinta y tres años (de edad). 5. Vivo en el cuarenta de la calle Broad (en la calle Broad, número cuarenta). 6. Nació el quince de mayo de mil novecientos cincuenta y dos. 7. Mi número de seguro social es el tres treinta cuarenta doce setenta y cuatro. 8. Es viernes, el doce de agosto, a la una y media. 9. Mi número de teléfono es el cinco veintidós siete cero treinta y uno. 10. Hace veinticinco años que vivo en Nueva York.

G. Change the verb form from the present to the preterite in the following questions.

Ejemplo: ¿Cuándo llega su hermano?
             ¿Cuando *llegó* su hermano?

1. ¿Cuántas horas *trabajo* hoy?
2. ¿Quién te *espera* en la oficina?
3. *¿Hablas* inglés con la recepcionista?
4. *¿Necesitan* Uds. un abogado?
5. *¿Llamas* a la oficina esta mañana?
6. ¿Le *parece* buena la hora?
7. *¿Viven* Uds. aquí en la ciudad?
8. ¿Cuando *nace* el bebé?
9. *¿Escribes* las preguntas en español?
10. *¿Comprende* Ud. a la doctora?

H. Now answer the new questions in Exercise G with the verb in the preterite according to the answers that follow. Do not use subject pronouns in your replies.

Ejemplo: ¿Cuándo llegó su hermano? (*ayer a las 9 P.M.*)
             Llegó ayer a las nueve de la noche.

1. *ocho horas (Ud.)*
2. *el trabajador social*
3. *sí*
4. *no*
5. *sí*
6. *sí, muy buena*
7. *no*
8. *el 13 de agosto de 1986*
9. *no, en inglés*
10. *sí, muy bien*

I. Translate the sentences in Exercise H to English.

G 1. trabajé 2. esperó 3. Hablaste 4. Necesitaron 5. Llamaste 6. pareció 7. Vivieron 8. nació 9. Escribiste 10. Comprendió

H 1. Trabajó ocho horas hoy. 2. Me esperó el trabajador social. 3. Sí, hablé inglés con ella. 4. No, no necesitamos un abogado. 5. Sí, llamé a la oficina esta mañana. 6. Sí, me pareció muy buena la hora. 7. No, no vivimos en la ciudad. 8. Nació el trece de agosto de mil novecientos ochenta y seis. 9. No, las escribí en inglés. 10. Sí, la comprendí muy bien.

I 1. You worked eight hours today. 2. The social worker waited for me. 3. Yes, I spoke English with her. 4. No, we did not need a lawyer. (*also* we do not need) 5. Yes, I called the office this morning. 6. Yes, the time seemed very good to me. 7. No, we did not live in the city. (*also* we do not live) 8. (He or she) was born on August 13, 1986. 9. No, I wrote them in English. 10. Yes, I understood her very well.

J.   Fill in the missing verb forms.

	yo (present)	yo (preterite)	Ud. (present)	Ud. (preterite)
1.	hablo			
2.		viví		
3.			escribe	
4.		trabajé		
5.				comprendió
6.			espera	

J 1. hablo, hablé, habla, habló 2. vivo, viví, vive, vivió 3. escribo, escribí, escribe, escribió 4. trabajo, trabajé, trabaja, trabajó 5. comprendo, comprendí, comprende, comprendió 6. espero, esperé, espera, esperó

Combinándolo todo

PRÁCTICA COMUNICATIVA: Más datos numéricos

Conversación parcial

Practique oralmente la siguiente conversación. Cada raya (/) implica que falta una palabra. Es necesario conjugar cada verbo *en bastardillas.*

Ejemplo: ¿ / qué hora *ser* / cita?
¿A qué hora es la cita?

La empleada	El cliente
1. / tardes, / . ¿ / qué *poder* / ?	*Estar* aquí / cambiar / día / mi operación.
2. ¿ / qué no / *llamar* / teléfono?	/ *poner* nervioso / *tener* / hablar por / .
3. Bueno, / , ¿cuál / su nombre / ?	Es Vicente Varela Martínez.
4. / Varela, yo *tener* / / algunas preguntas sobre / operación.	Sí, / , cómo / .
5. ¿Quién / su doctor?	/ llama / doctor Reynolds.
6. ¿Cuándo / el día original / la / ?	Es / 13 / octubre.
7. ¿Por / *querer* Ud. / el / ?	Porque *ir* a / en San Juan toda / semana del 11 de / .
8. ¿ / *volver* Ud.?	*Volver* / 21.
9. ¿ / *convenir* / jueves, 28?	Sí, / / muy bien / mí.
10. Primero *necesitar* hablar / el doctor y entonces / llamo. ¿ / igual su / ?	Sí, todavía / / 5-34-09-66.

Pregunte Ud.

Usted tiene que obtener ciertos datos personales de Raúl Garay, un paciente de la doctora Mitchell, que no habla español. Dé Ud. oralmente las preguntas necesarias en la siguiente conversación por teléfono que tiene con él.

Ejemplo: No, no vivo en la ciudad.
¿Vive Ud. en la ciudad?

1. Sí, señora, me voy a internar el lunes que viene.
2. No, no sigue igual; ahora vivo en la calle Vernon, número 136.
3. Sólo hace un mes que vivo allí.
4. Antes viví en el 112 de la avenida Brook.
5. Mi doctora se llama Rebecca Mitchell; es cardióloga.
6. Tengo 57 años.
7. Nací el 1 de julio de 1930.
8. Sí, tengo seguro médico.
9. El número de la póliza es el 56-S-97035.
10. Sí, señora, voy a llegar el lunes antes de las ocho de la mañana.

Dígalo

Pregunta a un/a compañero/a lo que le diga su profesor/a sobre los temas de su uso del teléfono en el trabajo, sus experiencias en el hospital, sus planes futuros, su dirección, y su fecha y lugar de nacimiento.

Escuche bien

A. Escriba Ud. toda la información que le da cada una de las personas que lo/a llama por teléfono, dando el nombre y, *en inglés,* el tipo de información que le da (ej., número de seguro social) y los datos númericos que menciona.

	Nombre	*Tipo de información*	*Datos numéricos*
1.			
2.			
3.			
4.			
5.			

B. Ud. oirá a seis clientes que describen una parte de su vida. Escriba **pasado** si ya pasó, **presente** si está en progreso ahora, o **futuro** si va a pasar en el futuro. También escriba *en inglés* lo que describe y la referencia al tiempo que da.

	Pasado, presente, futuro	*Lo que es*	*Cuándo*
1.			
2.			
3.			
4.			
5.			
6.			

Diálogos cortos

I. *El cliente*   *La recepcionista*

Permiso, señora. ¿Dónde está la ofi-   Su oficina _____ en
cina del doctor Salas?

_____ segundo piso.

¿Sabe si el doctor Salas está en su   Sí, _____ esta mañana a
oficina?

_____ siete y media.

Otra cosa, señora. ¿Me puede ayu-   ¿Qué _____ pasa, señor?
dar?

Tengo un dolor de estómago muy   Espere _____ momento, señor,
fuerte y no puedo caminar (*walk*)
más.   y _____ allí. Yo _____

a llamar _____ la enfermera

que trabaja _____ el doctor
Salas.

Muchas gracias, señora.   _____ la orden, señor.

¿ _____ siente mejor?

Un poquito, pero tengo miedo.   No se _____ , señor. El doctor

Salas _____ muy bueno y va

_____ ayudarlo.

II. *El cliente*   *La empleada*

(*Por teléfono*)

¿Me permite hablar con la señora   Soy _____ . ¿Con
Lewis, por favor?

_____ hablo?

Habla Pedro Maldonado.   ¿Cómo _____ Ud., señor Mal-

donado? ¿En _____ puedo

_____ ?

El cliente

Voy a tener que cambiar la cita que tengo para mañana.

Sí, lo sé. Lo siento mucho pero, ¿Ud. no puede hacerme las preguntas ahora por teléfono?

No se preocupe, señora. Lo mismo me pasa a mí en inglés. Yo la ayudo. Dígame lo que necesita saber.

Vivo en la calle 112, número 336.

No, es el 10026.

Hace tres meses.

Nací en Cali, Colombia, el 27 de julio de 1952. Por favor, ¿a qué hora tengo que estar en la sala de recepción para internarme?

Señorita, ¡Ud. habla español mejor que yo!

La empleada

Pero _____ cita

_____ importante porque Ud.

_____ a internarse pasado ma-

ñana y yo _____ datos

_____ .

Pues, me _____ nerviosa

cuando _____ que hablar es-

pañol _____ teléfono.

Ud. _____ razón. Bueno, la

primera _____ que necesito

_____ le es dónde

_____ Ud.

¿Entonces, ¿la _____ postal

_____ 10025?

¿ _____ tiempo hace que

_____ en _____
dirección?

¿ _____ y cuándo nació?

Venga Ud. _____ las dos y

_____ cuatro _____
la tarde.

¡Gracias por su paciencia!

Ayude al cliente

A patient of yours is returning to the Dominican Republic to live. You need to write a letter in Spanish to her new doctor detailing her medical record and that of her two children. Begin the letter with the name and address of the doctor written in the Hispanic way and then address the doctor as *Distinguido/a doctor/a*.

1. Tell him or her that you have been Mrs. Margarita Canales's doctor for seven years, and that her first child, Armando, was born on June 19, 1979, and her second son, Carlos, on December 22, 1984.

2. Tell him or her that Mrs. Canales has had diabetes (*diabetes*) for four years. Add that she comes into the office once a month for a checkup (*un chequeo*) and that at times it is necessary to call her to make the appointment.

3. Mention that Armando was born with a birth defect (*un defecto congénito*) but that you operated on him in 1981 and that he is much better and continues in good health (*de buena salud*). Add that Carlos has no health problems.

4. Close the letter by stating that if you can be of service in any way (*de cualquier manera*) he or she can write you at this address: (give address).

5. End the letter with *su atento/a y seguro/a servidor/a* and sign your name.

¿Comprende Ud.?

Hace dos semanas que la computadora no funciona bien y el siguiente formulario de un paciente no está completo. Escuche lo que dice el paciente para completarlo con los datos necesarios.

Patient name: Silvia Morales

Address: 98th Street

Length of residence at current address:

Physician:

Scheduled date/time of operation: Feb. 15/

Phone: 251-

Next of kin: Fernández   Relation:

Social security: 041-93-

Birthdate: Sept. 3,   Birthplace:

Insurance:

Policy number: D97 31 07   Group:

Piénselo

Prepárese bien para poder hablar con el/la profesor/a o con otros estudiantes sobre los siguientes temas, contestando las preguntas que sugiera el/la profesor/a:

1. el proceso de internarse en el hospital
2. el ponerse nervioso/a
3. el teléfono
4. el tener razón

SITUACIONES DE LA VIDA REAL

Imagínese

Describa Ud. la situación que muestra cada foto, contestando las siguientes preguntas:

Señorita   Señor   Señor
A   B   C

1. ¿Es una foto del campo o de la ciudad?
2. ¿Qué ciudad es?
3. ¿En qué país se encuentran estas personas?
4. ¿Qué día es *día de damas* en el cine?
5. ¿Por qué hay muchas personas en esta calle?
6. ¿Qué hace la señorita "A"?
7. ¿Adónde va ella?
8. ¿Qué va a hacer el señor "B"?
9. ¿Dónde está el señor "C"?

1. ¿Cuántas personas hay en esta foto?
2. ¿Quiénes son estas personas?
3. ¿Qué edad tiene cada uno?
4. ¿Viven en una zona urbana o rural?
5. ¿El anuncio (*sign*) está bien escrito o no?
6. ¿Quién lo escribió?
7. ¿Qué hace el muchacho del centro?
8. ¿De qué nacionalidad son los muchachos?
9. ¿En qué mes del año están?

1. ¿Quién es esta señora?
2. ¿Adónde va?
3. ¿Qué trae? ¿Por qué?
4. ¿Vive en el campo o una ciudad?
5. ¿Cómo es el clima de este país?
6. ¿Por qué está seria la señora?
7. ¿Se siente bien?
8. ¿Cuántos años tiene ella?
9. ¿Dónde está su esposo?

Haciendo el papel

Haga Ud. el papel del empleado en las siguientes situaciones. Presten atención al espacio personal y al uso del toque.

1. You are a doctor's secretary. Call Mr. Fuentes to schedule his father's operation. Ask him if his father can be admitted to the hospital next Wednesday, October 21, at 9:30 A.M. Tell him that the operation will take place on Friday, October 22, at 7:00 A.M. Thank Mr. Fuentes.

2. You are the director of admissions at an urban U.S. college. Welcome Miss Montalvo to the college and ask if her flight (*vuelo*) arrived at 12:00 noon. Ask her where she wants to live — in a house, an apartment, or the dormitory (*residencia estudiantil*). Ask her if this is the first time that she has come to the United States. Tell her that you are going to Ecuador, her country, next year in March. Tell her that you don't speak Spanish very well and that you get nervous when you have to speak it when you are in a Spanish-speaking country. Ask her if she has the same problem in English.

3. You are a police officer helping someone locate a relative (*un pariente*). Ask the man if he is from this area (*de aquí*). Ask him if he has the address of the relative and if you can see it. Tell him that it says 22 South Street and that he must take (*tomar*) the number 7 bus (*autobús*) to Oakwood Avenue. Tell him he should ask the bus driver (*el chófer*) for further directions (*instrucciones*).

4. Work with a classmate to answer the following questions based on the information given in the calendar:

a. ¿En qué mes estamos?
b. ¿Cuántos días hay en este mes?
c. ¿En qué día va a haber luna llena? ¿Luna nueva?
d. ¿En qué día de la semana cae el 7? ¿El 23? ¿El 1? ¿El 19?
e. ¿En qué fecha cae el día de San Fermín? ¿El de Nuestra Señora del Refugio? ¿El de Santa Isabel?
f. ¿Qué signos zodiacales caen en julio? ¿Cuáles son las fechas de cada uno?
g. ¿En qué fechas caen los domingos de este mes? ¿Los viernes?
h. ¿Qué planes tiene Ud. para el primer fin de semana del mes?

REFLEJOS DE LA CULTURA: "El escritor en el exilio"

In speaking of Hispanics living in the United States, we are really talking about people who share strong cultural ties with two different countries. The question of homeland is not an easy one to answer for the more than 18 million U.S. residents whose heritage lies in Mexico, Puerto Rico, Cuba, Colombia, the Dominican Republic, El Salvador, or any of the other Spanish-speaking countries of the Western Hemisphere.

Of the various Hispanic groups living in the United States, the question is perhaps most complex for Puerto Ricans, whose country of origin has been altered to reflect the Anglo presence there. As U.S. citizens, Puerto Ricans have no need to think about visas or immigration quotas. Instead, their worries center more on national identity, the balancing act between adapting to the mainland culture while preserving those cultural behaviors and beliefs that are part of their proud heritage.

The ease of migration between the island and the mainland has its advantages and its disadvantages. Puerto Rico exists as much in the northeastern United States as it does in the Caribbean. While there may be a difference between growing up

Puerto Rican on the mainland and growing up Puerto Rican on the island, family and cultural ties are maintained despite the ocean that separates in a physical sense.

José Luis González, in the following essay, entitled "El escritor en el exilio," eloquently speaks of this phenomenon, using his own personal history as an example.

El escritor en el exilio

No exagero, en rigor, cuando afirmo que mi exilio empezó en el vientre de mi madre. Me explico: mi padre puertorriqueño, se casó con dominicana mientras vivía en Santo Domingo y allí nací yo, hace cincuenta años exactos. Nunca logró mi padre adaptarse a la inestabilidad y a la violencia siempre presentes en la vida de la Antilla hermana, y el mismo año de mi nacimiento (1926) intentó un nuevo trasplante, esta vez en Nueva York, donde ya residían su madre y tres hermanos menores. Mi madre y yo permanecimos en Santo Domingo, adonde no tardó mucho en regresar él después de sufrir un asalto a mano armada en plena calle neoyorquina . . .

Nos fuimos todos a Puerto Rico a fines de 1930.

En 1946, salí de Puerto Rico por la primera vez . . .

I do not exaggerate, in reality, when I state that my exile began in my mother's womb. I'll explain (myself): my Puerto Rican father married a Dominican when he lived in Santo Domingo and I was born there, exactly fifty years ago. My father was never able to adapt to the instability and violence always present in life in the sister Antille, (and) the same year I was born (1926) he attempted a new relocation, this time in New York, where his mother and three younger brothers were already living. My mother and I stayed in Santo Domingo, where, before long, he returned, after sustaining an armed robbery attack right in the middle of a New York street . . .

We all went to Puerto Rico at the end of 1930.

In 1946, I left Puerto Rico for the first time . . .

En Nueva York, donde pasé año y medio cursando una maestría en ciencias políticas y otro año y medio ejerciendo una aleccionadora variedad de oficios, descubrí, con fascinación y respeto que hasta hoy me duran, la existencia de la diáspora puertorriqueña.

Esa emigración, que hoy comprende más de un millón de seres humanos (mientras que en la Isla viven tres), representa uno de los hitos capitales de la experiencia nacional puertorriqueña. No hay aspecto de la vida del pueblo puertorriqueño en este siglo — social, económico, político, cultural y psicológico — que no esté marcado por las vicisitudes de ese éxodo en masa.

Y es que, a diferencia de otras emigraciones, ésta se caracteriza por el constante ir y venir de los emigrados, de su país de origen a la sede de su exilio y viceversa. Ese trasiego ininterrumpido ha dado lugar a un fenómeno también singularísimo: el mantenimiento de un vínculo extraordinariamente vivo entre la comunidad desterrada y la comunidad insular.

Pero el vínculo es, al mismo tiempo, dramáticamente conflictivo. El puertorriqueño emigrado, víctima del rechazo de la sociedad racista norteamericana, se aferra a su identidad nacional como único medio de supervivencia espiritual, personal y colectiva. Cierto puertorriqueño de la Isla, sin embargo, temeroso de la influencia "extranjerizante" que el emigrado pueda ejercer en la sociedad "matriz", tiende a rechazarlo con crueldad que sólo se explica en razón de su propia inseguridad, producto, a su vez, de su formación colonial.

In New York, where I spent a year and a half studying for a master's degree in political science and another year and a half working at an instructive variety of jobs, I discovered, with a fascination and respect which endure to this day, the existence of the Puerto Rican diaspora (widespread migration).

That emigration, that today comprises more than one million human beings (while three million live on the island), represents one of the major highlights of the Puerto Rican national experience. There is no aspect of the life of the Puerto Rican people in this century — social, economic, political, cultural, and psychological — that is not marked by the changing patterns of the mass exodus.

(And it is that), unlike other emigrations, this one is characterized by the constant going and coming of the migrants, from their country of origin to their seat of exile and vice versa. That uninterrupted displacement has also produced an extremely unique phenomenon: the maintenance of very active ties between the community in exile and the community on the island.

But the ties are, at the same time, dramatically conflicting (ones). The Puerto Rican migrant, a victim of rejection by the racist North American society, clings to his national identity as his only means of spiritual, personal, and collective survival. However, some Puerto Ricans on the island, fearful of the "foreignizing" influence that the migrant might exert on the "matrix" society, tend to reject him with a cruelty which can only be explained in view of their own insecurity, a product, in turn, of their own colonial formation.

LECCIÓN 6

El hombre y la mujer

LOS OBJETIVOS

Raising awareness

1. To learn how personal communication style affects cross-cultural communication
2. To understand the traditional cultural conditioning of Hispanic males and females
3. To be aware of how traditional Hispanic gender behaviors affect cross-cultural communication

Comunicándose en español

1. To understand and simulate Hispanic intonational patterns
2. To use and understand vocabulary and structures related to marital status, family members, and household composition
3. To use and understand the subjunctive mood to express desire and necessity

Combinándolo todo

1. To integrate all material from previous sections by applying the knowledge in work-related communication activities
2. To discriminate in the choice of verb form among the present indicative, present subjunctive, preterite, and infinitive
3. To understand references to family members in work-related comprehension activities
4. To appreciate the extent to which traditional Hispanic male–female roles influence daily life among Hispanics in the United States

Raising awareness

OVERVIEW: One's personal culture and communication style

In the preceding chapters you have been presented with many different aspects of what *culture* is and how cultural conditioning interacts with personal experience to form a unique, individual personality. One's personal verbal and nonverbal communicating style reflects that interaction. As you have raised your awareness on an intellectual level, you have also been asked to participate in certain exercises designed to ground this knowledge into the physical and emotional realms of your personality as well. All this was done so that you could truly learn to communicate with Hispanic clients whose cultural conditioning and personal experiences may be very different from your own.

Throughout the preceding chapters the recurrent theme of the raising awareness process has been: *The only effective strategy for communicating successfully across cultural boundaries is to see each individual as the unique person he or she is.* In order to carry out this strategy, you must first know yourself well. The following model for effective cross-cultural communication stresses the role of self-awareness in the sending and receiving of messages between people from different cultural and linguistic backgrounds.

As you can see from this diagram, the success of the cross-cultural communication process is dependent on the communication styles of *both* conversational partners. These styles reflect, to varying degrees, the following attributes:

1. The degree of self-awareness
2. Attitudes and knowledge regarding the cross-cultural communication process
3. The ability to understand and empathize with others

This personalized way of communicating is developed throughout one's lifetime. Both cultural conditioning and personal experience affect its development.

Obviously, the most effective communication will occur between individuals who are well matched on the self-awareness level, despite differences in their background. If, in addition, both partners in the communication process have a similar perspective on the complexity of the cross-cultural interaction, they will generally be more open and receptive toward each other. They will also tend to be more sensitive to their own subconscious blocks that may affect their ability to communicate across cultural boundaries.

PERSON A		MORE AWARE OF DIFFERENCES	PERSON B	
understanding others +	personal experience	MORE AWARE OF DIFFERENCES	personal experience +	understanding others
self-awareness +	communication style	MORE EFFECTIVE CROSS-CULTURAL COMMUNICATION	communication style +	self-awareness
understanding cross-cultural communication +	cultural conditioning		cultural conditioning +	understanding cross-cultural communication
		MORE CONTROL OVER THE COMMUNICATION PROCESS		

Although the ideal is for both partners to be equally well developed in these areas, this is seldom the case. Even when communication occurs between those who share very similar cultural backgrounds, individual communication styles may be at odds. In cross-cultural interactions, it is crucial that at least one of the partners be well aware of the complexities involved in order to avoid disastrous misunderstandings. As a well-educated professional whose clientele includes many Hispanics, it is to your own advantage and personal satisfaction to strive for a high level of self-awareness, the first step to effective communication across cultural boundaries. It seems natural that as you study the linguistic, cultural, and historical backgrounds of the various Hispanic groups that reside in the United States, you also use the opportunity presented here for personal growth and self-awareness in those areas that affect your personal communication style.

If your clients include many recently arrived Hispanics or those who, despite years of residence in the United States, are still not comfortable speaking English, it is up to you to provide access to greater communication and mutual understanding. Criticizing immigrants for their lack of assimilation or blaming them for not speaking English is not going to make your job any easier. Whatever your opinions regarding bilingualism in the United States, the everyday reality you will face is, in essence, that of communicating in a bilingual setting.

The first step is to see yourself as a product of the interaction of your various personal experiences and the cultural lessons you've learned throughout your lifetime, as shown below. All the

variables of cultural conditioning shown in the diagram form a composite of the different subcultures each of us experiences.

All these factors affect the cultural input an individual receives. Let us look at a fictitious cultural case history, that of "Joe Metzner."

Joseph Metzner is a male raised in the United States. He was born in 1947 in St. Cloud, Minnesota, where the winter lasts from mid-November until mid-May, with an average temperature of 15°F. The summer is short, from mid-June to early September. He lived there until he was twenty.

His parents, both of whom were born in Germany, owned a small farm in the outskirts of St. Cloud. They belonged to the lower middle class. They were both churchgoing Protestants. His father finished tenth grade in the United States and his mother sixth grade in Germany. They had strong family and friendship ties with other German Americans living in the area, limited contact with other English-speaking white Americans, and virtually none with people of other races or southern European backgrounds. English was spoken in the home. Joe attended a public elementary school and private high school in St. Cloud, graduating in 1965.

From this cultural profile of Joe, you have probably formed a pretty good idea of what he's like and how he would act in certain situations.

However, there are important elements of Joe's personal experiences that have been omitted. How would the following information affect your concept of Joe?

1.   His parents divorced when he was twelve and his father went back to Germany. His mother sold the farm, remarried, and moved to Minneapolis when Joe was sixteen.

2.   Joe spent three years in Vietnam and received a dishonorable discharge for drug abuse.

3.   Joe is now working as a case worker at the State Department of Income Maintenance (Welfare) in Chicago with a principally Spanish-speaking case load.

Although this expanded verbal portrait of Joe helps us know more about him by combining his personal experiences with his cultural background, we still don't really understand Joe.

Of course, you are not expected to analyze each of your Hispanic client's personal and cultural background to this extent, but it is important to learn to see each of your Hispanic clients as a unique individual. This will greatly enhance your communication style with *all* your clients, not just those of Hispanic heritage.

Applications

1.   Fill in the following details of your personal cultural history:

   a.   sex _____

   b.   country in which raised _____

   c.   ethnic/racial background _____

   d.   social class _____

   e.   geographical region and climate _____

   f.   urban, suburban, or rural upbringing _____

   g.   historical era in which born and raised _____

   h.   religious training _____

    i. educational training   _____

    j. contact with other cultures   _____

2. List the five most important personal experiences that have shaped your views and outlook on life:

    a. _____

    b. _____

    c. _____

    d. _____

    e. _____

3. Complete the following statements about yourself. Write down your first impulse, without censoring it. Then decide if the statement is a reflection of your cultural background or personal experiences.

    1. My family is _____

    2. I work because _____

    3. Friendships are _____

    4. My social life consists of _____

    5. To relax I _____

    6. In moments alone, I _____

    7. My diet consists mostly of _____

    8. My spiritual life is _____

    9. I get angry when _____

   10. I am happiest when _____

   11. What I want most from life is _____

   12. Alcohol and drugs are _____

   13. I like people who _____

   14. I dislike people who _____

   15. Time is _____

16. Money is _____

17. Before I die I would like to _____

18. I hope my children _____

19. Sex is _____

20. Life is _____

21. Death is _____

22. Men are _____

23. Women are _____

24. Older people are _____

25. Hispanics are _____

Reflections

1. Which of the foregoing questions was easiest to answer? Why? Which was most difficult? Why?

2. Did any of your answers surprise you? Which?

3. In looking over your responses, do you feel most of your values, attitudes, beliefs, norms, and behaviors are determined by cultural conditioning, personal experiences, or the interaction of the two? Can you pinpoint even further the source of most of your personal culture?

4. Do you think your answers would have been very different if you had been born in another country? Which ones and why?

5. Are any of these statements different from what you would have said five years ago? Which ones? What accounts for your changing views?

HISTORICAL PERSPECTIVE: Machismo and the role of women

Perhaps no other aspect of Hispanic culture has received such widespread attention and notoriety as that of *machismo*. The word itself has become part of the English language. It has given rise to such stereotypes as "Latin lover" and "hot-blooded Latin," which offer an incomplete and inaccurate portrayal of the traditional Hispanic male. In reality, machismo refers to a complex set of culturally condoned behaviors and beliefs regarding the role of both males and females in Hispanic societies. It is impossible to fully understand machismo without focusing on its relationship to the cultural conditioning of the traditional Hispanic female.

In Spanish, *macho* refers to the male of the animal species. Its female counterpart is *hembra*.

While there is no universally accepted single word that describes the corollary range of behaviors and beliefs for the Hispanic female, the term *marianismo* is often used to refer to her primary duty to follow Mary, the Mother of Christ, as the role model for passive, docile behavior. In addition, the term *hembrismo* (from *hembra*) is also used, particularly with reference to Hispanic women from the Caribbean, to describe the superior psychological stamina and spiritual strength attributed to women as "earth mothers." The seeming paradox implied by the two terms is resolved by the cultural portrayal of the Hispanic female as destined to a life of stoic passivity which she is, by nature, uniquely endowed to withstand.

The following guidelines describe the traditional role expectations of males and females raised in Spanish-speaking countries. The degree to which they typify a particular individual will reflect several factors. First, the socialization process varies among Hispanic nations. The more economically developed the country, the less traditional the role models become. Second, the social class into which one is born also affects the degree of traditionalism. Often, the lower the economic level, the more traditional the adherence to cultural norms. The rural–urban dichotomy also affects role expectations, with more options available to those born and raised in cities than to those from the countryside. Last, with regard to Hispanics now residing in the United States, the amount of contact with the majority culture, as well as the various socioeconomic realities of being a minority-group member, affect the degree of acculturation to Anglo values and norms.

---

1. *Define the terms* machismo, marianismo, *and* hembrismo *with respect to role expectations for Hispanic men and women.*
2. *What factors influence the degree to which an individual Hispanic will manifest traditional role behaviors?*

Historically, the legacy of machismo was inherited from the Spaniards, who, in turn, like other Mediterranean groups, were influenced by the Moslem culture's view of women.

The most salient characteristic of machismo is its paternalistic attitude toward women. They are seen as weaker and inferior to males, meant to serve men while needing to be taken care of and protected by them in return. Some theories attribute this paternalism to a fundamental belief that women are more like children than adult males. This implies an inability to take charge of their own lives or to keep in check their more basic needs, particularly their emotions or their sexual urges. The socialization process of males and females that has evolved in *machista* cultures centers on attitudes toward sexuality. Women are taught to repress their own sexual instincts while fending off the advances of males who have been taught that they have complete freedom of sexual expression. Although part of Moslem heritage, this attitude toward human sexuality has been reinforced by teachings of the Catholic church, which predominates in the Spanish-speaking world.

This double standard regarding sexual behavior does offer the Hispanic women a choice: the role of madonna or that of prostitute. The former status is the reward for following the cultural role assigned to her. It reflects the belief that true fulfillment as a female comes only through marriage and motherhood, preferably in that order. The woman who seeks a more sexually active role is labeled a prostitute (*prostituta* or *puta*). Any female who loses her virginity before marriage forfeits her right to the culturally sanctioned role of madonna. Her chances to marry a well-respected male are greatly reduced. She also is seen as easy prey for any and all male comers. The culture provides certain safeguards to aid women in making the correct choice. These, together with related role behaviors, are learned through the socialization process of both men and women. The three primary sources of instruction are (1) the home environment, (2) the extended family and friends, and (3) school, church, and other societal institutions.

---

3. *Describe the origin and basic beliefs inherent in countries that are characterized by ma-chismo.*
4. *Define the two categories into which ma-chismo classifies women and explain the qualities that characterize each.*

Culturally, the Hispanic woman's place has been in the home. According to Spanish proverbs, *"La mujer y la gallina, hasta la casa de la vecina"* ("The wife and the hen, only as far as the neighbor's house"), and *"El hombre en la plaza, y la mujer en casa"* ("The man in the town square, the woman at home"). Thus it has been the Hispanic mother, as primary caretaker, who has traditionally taught both girls and boys their respective role behaviors.

The female child learns quite early through both observation and direct instruction that her role is to please and serve the men in her family, including older and younger brothers. She learns to accept their dominance passively. She is trained to perform all household tasks competently and without complaint. Her lessons in stoicism begin early. She does learn that certain emotional expressions are allowed. These range from crying to, in extreme cases, the *ataque de nervios,* a display of histrionics culturally permitted to women as a safety valve in releasing the accumulated stress from continued self-repression.

The *varón,* or male child, however, learns that he is a privileged entity on whom special attention, especially from women, is showered. In contrast to his sister's passivity, he is encouraged to be active, to take risks, to be independent from an early age, and to be physically and verbally assertive and expressive. He is also taught a different kind of stoicism — the ability to withstand physical and emotional pain without crying. He learns to emulate the paternalistic guidance, instructions, and criticism that adult males provide females in the home with regard to household chores, personal grooming, and proper *marianista* behavior.

5. *Describe the cultural training the traditional Hispanic female receives as a child.*
6. *Contrast the training the traditional Hispanic male receives with that of the female.*

As the female child approaches adolescence, she becomes more aware of the importance placed on being physically attractive to males. Special attention is given to ultrafeminine dresses, high heels, makeup, nail polish, and frequent visits to the hairdresser, if affordable. In a culture that teaches the female that her highest pursuit in life is that of a husband who will provide her a good family life, this emphasis on physical adornment is not surprising. The more desirable a woman is to men, the more power she has in choosing her mate from a wider range of suitors than that available to an average or plain woman.

At the same time, she learns the paradoxical expectation that she should both attract males and repel their sexual advances. Sex education for the female is often limited to information regarding menstruation, with its implication that she is becoming physically prepared for motherhood. She is given little knowledge of her own anatomy but quickly learns that certain areas of her body are off limits for thoughts or touch. Most often her impressions of sex are those of her mother — mainly, that its primary purpose is procreation and her husband's sexual pleasure. Although it is culturally prized for a woman to *tener sal* (be "salty") — i.e., to be a lively, exciting partner for her mate, this is only acceptable within limits carefully prescribed by the latter. Any overt display of knowledge of sexual behavior prior to marriage may cast her in the role of prostitute.

The virgin bride learns about sex in her husband's bed.

The male adolescent learns quickly the cultural division of women into madonnas and prostitutes. The female members of his family are considered madonnas whose virtue he must protect at all costs. He knows that the worst insult that can be hurled at a man is an intimation that his "woman" (girlfriend, wife, or mistress) has been unfaithful to him (*cornudo* or *cuernudo*, accompanied by the hand gesture of horns formed by t..e extension of the index and pinky fingers). The second worst insult is to question the virtue of a man's mother. Any such innuendo may become grounds for a fight.

The male bases his fierce defense of the female family members on the cultural belief that both boys and girls are taught: "*Los hombre son así*" ("That's the way men are"). At the same time that he protects the women he loves, he views women outside the family as fair game. His socialization process has taught him, paradoxically, to respect women in their prospective role as mothers by extending basic courtesies and respect to them while, at the same time, assuming that they may, in reality, belong to the category of prostitutes unless they successfully pass the test of resisting his sexual advances. Part of his attainment of adulthood centers in his perfecting his techniques in the conquest of women. It is not uncommon for the Hispanic adolescent male to

have his first sexual encounter with a prostitute. He has also learned from other males in his family that frequent liaisons with prostitutes or other women after marriage are culturally acceptable and stoically tolerated by one's wife.

Relationships with peers afford both male and female adolescents further lessons in socialization. Young men reinforce each other's macho behavior. The dignity and respect due the male is both tested and fostered in these peer relationships. Beginning in adolescence, a type of bravado characterizes the gathering of males. Each is encouraged to demonstrate his physical strength and knowledge of the world. Long exhortations and pronouncements on life in general, politics, sports, and women are common. Boasts of one's personal experiences, especially with regard to the conquest of women, are the norm. Having a reputation as a *mujeriego* (woman chaser) is highly valued. The macho code of ethics also prescribes the ability to hold one's liquor and to refrain from showing emotional needs or expressing self-doubts, particularly in the company of other males.

The adolescent woman, though more restricted with regard to activities outside the home, also further socializes with her female peers. Friendship among them often centers in discussions of how to catch and keep a man. Emotional support is given to those who fail to attract the attention of a particular male, despite the competition that exists to *conseguir un marido* (catch a husband). Frank discussion about sex is usually discouraged, although advice on beauty and proper female behavior in other areas is freely given. Techniques for flirting and responding emotionally to love's intrigues are also shared.

7. *Compare the socialization regarding sexuality that traditional Hispanic males and females receive.*
8. *Discuss the influence of same-sex peer groups on the socialization process of Hispanic adolescents.*

Ways of interacting with members of the opposite sex other than those in one's family are important lessons learned during adolescence. In more traditional homes, one-on-one male–female dates are discouraged except when the male's intentions are seriously focused on marriage. At this point, such excursions are permitted but are chaperoned. In more modern homes, group male–female excursions replace the restricted role of the chaperone. Dating in the Anglo sense is a relatively new phenomenon, both in Latin America and in Spanish-speaking areas of the United States. Where it does exist, pressure is often created in the household between the parents' adherence to the traditional values governing courtship and the young woman's desire to conform to a more modern approach to getting to know members of the opposite sex.

Adolescents also learn that in public places traditional male–female interaction is still governed by rather rigid role behaviors. It is the male's prerogative to observe and attempt to make eye contact with any woman who passes by. He is also free to comment on her appearance or sex appeal with a *piropo*. This can range from a compliment to a woman's beauty (*"Si cocinas como caminas, me caso contigo,"* "If you cook like you walk, I'll marry you'') to an obscene comment with a sexual intent. Any acknowledgement, including eye contact, on the part of the female is forbidden and can be construed as an invitation to further sexual contact. Many less traditional Hispanic women often have conflicts with regard to this male prerogative. While they may welcome the praise that affirms their adherence to cultural values, they may resent the often sexually explicit comments as offensive.

---

9. *Explain the traditional male–female courtship patterns in Hispanic cultures and how they conflict with Anglo values.*
10. *Discuss the behavior of traditional Hispanic men and women in public, pointing out how it compares and/or contrasts with similar behavior in Anglo cultures.*

As Hispanic adolescents grow into adulthood, the pressure for women to marry and for men to establish themselves in their line of work becomes very strong. Although more and more Hispanic women are seeking higher education and entering the work force, the conservative male-female role expectations continue to reign. The cultural pastime of *amores* (love affairs) may still dominate. Since it is difficult for the traditional Hispanic male to conceive of platonic relationships with women, his male pride may require at least a verbal allusion to a potential sexual relationship with women at work. The flirtatious behavior and dependence on men taught the adolescent girl is difficult for the adult professional woman to unlearn. Since a woman's success outside the home is contradictory to the socialization of both males and females, conflicts may result. The male employee may have a difficult time accepting a woman in a position of authority. Women may experience conflicts as they learn to be more assertive and independent in response to the demands of their jobs. Any female who achieves a high level of success in a business or profession that has been traditionally closed to women may be subjected to gossip or innuendo suggesting that she has used her feminine charms to get ahead. Whatever her role in the world outside the home, inside it she is still viewed as primarily responsible for the cooking, cleaning, and caretaking.

Hispanic women from the lower social classes have had a rather unique experience in that their economic straits have commonly required them to work outside the home, almost always at menial, low-paying jobs. There are many women with children who have been abandoned by their mates who find themselves in a constant struggle for subsistence. Often regular or intermittent prostitution is their only means of survival.

---

11. *Describe how the traditional socialization of Hispanic males and females may affect the workplace.*
12. *Describe the economic reality of the Hispanic woman from the lower socioeconomic classes.*

As adults, Hispanic males and females continue to prove their worth by conforming to cultural expectations. The *respeto* (respect) from society at large, expressed by what members of the community think about the individual and the family, is of primary importance. As already mentioned, the female earns *respeto* by attending to her duties as wife and mother, regardless of her work outside the home. She must also continue to maintain her virtue by avoiding behaviors, situations, or people that may jeopardize her reputation as a faithful and loving wife. Her social activities are mostly limited to daytime conversations with female friends or large social events attended by the entire family. She rarely goes out alone and when she does must take care to inform her husband of her whereabouts. Any transgression is grounds for *celos* (jealousy), which can result in her husband's anger and even violent behavior, both of which are, at times, culturally justifiable responses.

The adult Hispanic male is expected to provide for his family and to be generous with relatives and friends in need. He also should spend time with his children (including those conceived through extramarital relationships). He is encouraged to express tenderness toward them and their mother, although the culture does allow the male to express anger as part of his role in maintaining a proper household. It is he who makes the major decisions governing his household, although he may often seek counsel from his wife or mother (viewed in the role of wise earth mother). His relationships with other males expand on the type of bravado that characterizes the gatherings of male adolescents. His active participation in political campaigns and religious festivals also marks his coming of age in the community, especially in rural areas.

---

13. *Discuss the concept of* respeto *with regard to the reality of the traditional adult role of Hispanic males and females.*
14. *Explain the term* celos *and its relationship to traditional Hispanic males' view of women.*

To what extent are these strictly defined behavioral models for males and females in the Hispanic world changing? To what extent have they been influenced by such current phenomena as feminism, unisex styles of dress, greater educational and employment opportunities for women, revolutionary movements in Latin America, and the international influence of music, movies, and television? As the Hispanic female gains some economic power and becomes less dependent on men, she experiences more freedom and greater self-expression. Nevertheless, social mores and values are slow to change.

It is interesting to note that the number of divorces in those Hispanic countries where divorce is allowed has risen sharply, with the majority of them initiated by women seeking greater parity in their marriages. (In Puerto Rico and the Dominican Republic, recent statistics show one divorce for every three marriages.) Divorced women, however, are a recent cultural phenomenon and still face the socially undesirable and economically difficult position of being a single woman and, most often, mother in a more traditional couples-oriented society. A divorced woman may seek the "protection" of returning to the home of a parent or other family member, since women living alone are still somewhat suspect with regard to their virtue.

Interestingly, the single female head of household is becoming exceedingly common in some Hispanic neighborhoods in the United States, especially those with large numbers of Puerto Ricans, Cubans, and Dominicans. Although in practice, pre- and extramarital sex have become more acceptable for the individual woman, the need to keep up appearances and preserve her reputation is still an important one. This strong cultural value continues to impede frank and open discussion among females, except between very close friends. In addition, although the reporting of rape, incest, and physical abuse for both Hispanics and Anglos has increased in recent years, known statistics are still considered low in relation to the number of actual incidents. The cultural conditioning of the individual woman to tolerate her man's idiosyncrasies still predominates.

With regard to Hispanic women living in the United States and their incorporation into the women's movement, many feel caught in a double bind as members of two minorities, Hispanic and female. Supporting some of the premises inherent in the North American female liberation movement may mean rejecting some of their own cultural attitudes or feeling somewhat alienated when issues relating to ethnocentrism and racism are excluded from the struggle for women's rights. Involvement in the feminist movement implies challenging Hispanic males and their values regarding the role of women while at the same time working with them to eliminate discrimination and racism toward Hispanic minorities of either sex.

Among Hispanic groups residing in the United States, there is also a strong drive to preserve their cultural heritage amid the influence of the predominant Anglo society. This presents a paradox — maintaining cultural values while striving to change them regarding the lack of parity in male and female roles.

The economic realities faced by Hispanics residing in the United States also take their toll on traditional role behaviors. The Hispanic woman may more easily find and keep employment than her husband, owing to the greater availability of low-paying menial jobs traditionally done by women (housekeeping, washing, ironing, and working in light manufacturing, especially in the garment industry and electronic assembly). This can undermine the male's role as provider in the family, lowering his self-respect. When this phenomenon is added to the already difficult adjustment process of living in a new culture, it may seriously affect the family unit and the mental and emotional well-being of its members.

The differences regarding the socialization of children may also be at odds. Often, Hispanic adolescent females struggle to attain the "equal rights" of dating, more freedom of movement, and fewer restrictions that she sees her Anglo schoolmates enjoy. This produces more friction in the family and also can trigger conflict for the mother, who may secretly acknowledge her own repression and empathize with her daughter's desire for freedom, while at the same time feeling bound by cultural mores to discourage it.

Obviously, the cultural roles of Hispanic men and women are in a transitional phase, one that is compounded by living in the United States. It is a complex situation with no easy answers.

What is important is to keep in mind these culturally determined perspectives and behaviors when providing services to Hispanic male and female clients. Effective communication and appropriate counseling or care must take into account the effect it may have on gender-prescribed behaviors and beliefs.

15. *What evidence is there of changing role expectations for Hispanic males and females?*
16. *What effects can the experience of living in the United States have on traditional Hispanic male and female roles?*

NONVERBAL COMMUNICATION: Male–female behavioral patterns

It is not only internal attitudes and beliefs that are determined by sex-role conditioning, but also observable behaviors. What is acceptable behavior for men and women in one culture may be completely unacceptable in another.

Perhaps the most overt behavior governed by culturally determined sex-role conditioning is the way we move our bodies. Anglo cultures stress the rather rigid posture of moving the entire trunk, from the shoulders to the buttocks, as one unit. The "shoulders back, chest out, stomach in" military stance with the buttocks tucked in tightly is appropriate behavior learned by both sexes. It is particularly important for women in English-speaking cultures to walk with a rigid trunk. Excessive movement of the buttocks and/or swaying of the hips is discouraged and regarded as too overtly sensual for well-mannered "ladies."

Hispanics in general, and Hispanic women in particular, learn a much less rigid way of holding and moving their bodies. As they move, their body movements are less restricted, including more mobility in neck and shoulder muscles. Most Hispanic women tend to move the various parts of the trunk as they walk, twisting the waist, and with a greater swaying of the hips and more movement of the buttocks than is common in Anglo cultures. The range of movement is even more pronounced in the Spanish-speaking Caribbean

cultures, where the African heritage has left a legacy of much greater freedom of body movement.

Hispanic men also walk with a similarly freer gait. While they do not twist as much at the waist or sway their hips as do women in their culture, they tend to take longer strides and move their buttocks more than is the norm for Anglo males. They, too, usually have a greater range of motion in their neck and shoulder muscles which is often

evidenced in their personal gait. The effect is similar to the strut immortalized by Tony Manero in the film *Saturday Night Fever*.

Culturally determined ways of holding and moving one's body are at play as we walk, sit, stand, bend, and dance. Latin rhythms are danced to in a style that may be termed provocative by Anglo standards. Although current dances popular among adolescents and young adults in the United States may also be seen in that light, they tend to seem more sexual than sensual, with their emphasis on pelvic thrusts. The rigidity common to other Anglo movement patterns is still evident here, with the entire trunk manipulated as a single unit. Hispanics dance to their music with more rotation of the hips and movement of the shoulders and knees, although the popularized U.S. ballroom versions of such dances as the conga and the rhumba still emphasize rigidity of the upper part of the body.

There is a great potential for misinterpreting and misjudging an individual's attitude toward sexuality based on the different movement patterns learned in the Anglo and Hispanic cultures. An Anglo male or female may subconsciously view a particular Hispanic female as extremely sexy, and perhaps even lewd or promiscuous, based on her way of walking. An Anglo female may sense that a Hispanic male is trying to relate to her in a sexual way because of his physical bearing as he approaches her. An Anglo male may feel threatened or challenged by the typical Hispanic male's overtly aggressive movement patterns.

Hispanics, on the other hand, may assume that Anglos are all "up-tight" or repressed in their sexuality because of the rather rigid movement patterns learned in childhood. Hispanics may view an Anglo female as unfeminine, harsh, and unfeeling based solely on a subconscious evaluation of her way of moving and sitting. They may view an Anglo male as effeminate or unmanly because of his more controlled, subdued movements.

There are other less-obvious sex-typed behaviors that may be misinterpreted across cultural boundaries. The greatest margin for error exists in interactions between members of opposite sexes.

An Anglo male may expect a greater degree

of personal freedom from a Hispanic woman than may be the case. He may view her as excessively modest or reticent in talking about intimate details of her life even though professional circumstances may warrant such frankness. He may be insensitive to her need to protect her reputation and/or virginity, especially in the case of medical examinations. At the same time he may find her rather flirtatious.

He may also be annoyed or offended by her husband's interference in or insistence on being present during personal interviews and physical examinations or may misunderstand the cause of the latter's jealous reactions. He may inadvertently touch the Hispanic woman inappropriately or use other nonverbal behaviors that seem too intimate by Hispanic cultural standards.

An Anglo female may experience personal embarrassment and discomfort when interviewing or examining a Hispanic male client. She may observe his glance or remarks as somewhat lascivious and may respond inappropriately with direct eye contact or an involuntary smile because of her nervousness and loss of composure. In situations where an Anglo female holds a responsible position, she may become frustrated or angry when she interprets the physical behavior of a Hispanic male as challenging to her authority when it may, instead, be a sign of his respect or discomfort.

The limited personal freedom and autonomy experienced by more traditional Hispanic women may be overlooked in offering them professional or personal counseling. Making major life decisions may be a new experience, because of the degree of dependence they have had on the males in their lives. Advice that may be appropriate in the English-speaking culture may have much more serious implications in the Hispanic cultures. Leaving one's mate, having an abortion, going back to school, seeking a job, moving to a new apartment, seeking help from a battered women's shelter, and in general relying on institutions to provide aid and support that the family may have provided in the past — all are at odds with cultural norms. Effective guidance must take this cultural dimension into account.

The need to preserve one's dignity and reputation as a man may also be ignored or disdained when providing services to Hispanic males. This is especially true among Hispanic men living in the United States, where chronic unemployment, changing roles for women, and loss of identity may have already greatly affected their self-image. Some social problems such as drug and alcohol abuse and/or mistreatment of their wives and children may often be expressions of their inability to cope with the changes in their lives and the modifications of their role as head of the household. Effective counseling techniques will attempt to aid the male in reestablishing his self-image.

Often, female professionals have more success by adopting a maternal approach in providing services to their Hispanic male clients, since it is culturally permissible for men to seek advice from mother figures. This can remove sexual tension and help them gain the men's confidence and trust. This strategy may also be effective in dealing with male children and adolescents. On the other hand, it may be difficult for a Hispanic man to open up to an Anglo male, since revealing personal weaknesses or failures to another male is against machismo's code of ethics. Older males may have more success in establishing rapport with male clients, since Hispanic cultures value the wisdom of elders and condone seeking their advice in personal matters.

It is equally important to try to refrain from making value judgments regarding the culturally prescribed male and female roles in the Hispanic world. Although there is some sign that they are changing, it is *not* appropriate or ethical for non-Hispanics to prescribe what course those changes should take. You are, of course, entitled to your own opinions regarding the ideal way in which men and women should behave. You may offer choices to your clients, outlining the cultural and personal consequences of alternative actions. In doing so, you can reeducate male and female clients to understand how some of their culturally defined value systems may be inconsistent with their present-day reality.

As long as you try, first, to understand and, second, to operate from an informed cultural perspective as you interact with Hispanic men and women, you will be able to provide services more effectively. When in doubt, confer with your Hispanic colleagues. It may be best to refer certain cases to them. To underestimate the nonverbal nuances of culturally determined male–female conditioning is a grave error.

Putting it into practice

1. Observe as an Anglo male and female walk in front of the class in their normal movement style. Now observe as they attempt to emulate the Hispanic Caribbean movement styles. What differences do you notice? What impressions come to mind as you watch the second exercise? How do the two "actors" seem to feel as they move in this new way?

2. What misconceptions or stereotypes may arise from observing body movements of Hispanic clients in the following situations?
   a. a Hispanic female who is in court seeking a divorce and custody of her children
   b. a Hispanic male arrested for "loitering" on the street with his friends
   c. a Hispanic male who wants to accompany his wife into the doctor's examining room
   d. a twelve-year-old Hispanic female who may be pregnant

3. What cross-cultural communication strategies would you recommend for professionals in the following situations?
   a. an Anglo male doctor giving a young Hispanic woman her first pelvic examination
   b. an Anglo female teacher disciplining a ten-year-old male student for fighting on the playground
   c. an Anglo female social worker processing a claim for unemployment from a Hispanic male with a wife and five children
   d. an Anglo male social worker who suspects that his Hispanic female client has been physically abused by her husband

Comunicándose en español

PRONUNCIACIÓN: La entonación 📼

Just as a song is a combination of words and music, a language is a combination of words, structures, and intonational patterns. Intonation is often the first thing you notice in listening to a foreign language and one of the last things truly mastered by nonnative speakers of any language. Intonational patterns enhance a language with added clues to the intent of the speaker. Foreign-language learners should be aware that these patterns are different for every language. If you have ever listened to nonnative speakers of English using the intonational patterns of their native tongue, you may have been confused by the double messages they seem to be sending.

To illustrate the importance of intonation for meaning, read the following sentence in English, adjusting the intonation cues to match the intent:

Come over here. (sweetly)
Come over here. (sternly)
Come over here. (angrily)

Unless you learn the proper intonational patterns of Spanish as you learn vocabulary and structures, you may find yourself speaking Spanish with an English rhythm. This is similar to singing the words of the national anthem to a jazz rhythm—it just doesn't fit the intent of the message! More important, it can lead to confusion, misunderstandings, and even mistrust when speaking with your Spanish-speaking clients.

Each phrase has its own intonational pattern, a combination of *stress* (the relative prominence of syllables in the stream of speech), *pitch* (highness or lowness of tone), and *terminal junctures* (features that signal pauses). The greatest difference between the Spanish and English intonation systems is that English has *four* pitch levels, whereas Spanish has *three*. Since both languages tend to use the highest pitch level relatively infrequently for special emphasis, Spanish generally is spoken with much less variation in tone than English. This contrast can be expressed by the following musical intonation:

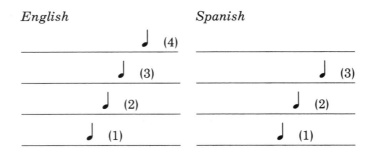

Spanish phrasing is quicker than in English, with less variation in pitch, alternating principally between levels (1) and (2). This gives Spanish a flatter, less emotional, staccato rhythm. When heard by someone used to English's more colorful three-level pitch variation and less rapid phrasing, the two-pitch level of the Spanish speaker may connote anger, insistence, uninterest, or lack of emotion.

191

When native speakers of English learn Spanish, they tend to avoid duplicating Spanish intonation because they subconsciously "hear" that pattern as expressing anger or disgust, so they may force Spanish intonation into the English pattern, with which they are more comfortable. By paying special attention to the correct intonation patterns, you can overcome this negative transfer of your English-speaking habits to Spanish.

Práctica

1. Repeat the following sentences in English and Spanish after the tape or your instructor. The numbers above each syllable indicate pitch level, the arrows indicate rising or falling intonation at the end of the utterance, and the slashes indicate a pause where a comma appears.

2 2 4 3 3		2 2 2 2 2
Is Carl leaving now?	question	¿Ya se va Carlos? ↗
2 / 1 1 4 3 3		2 2 2 / 2 2
Carl, are you leaving now?	question	¿Ya se va, Carlos? ↘
3 / 2 3 1 2		2 2 3 / 1 1
Carl, she's leaving now.	statement	Ya se va, Carlos. ↘
2 1 3 2 2		2 2 2 1 1
Carl is leaving now.	statement	Ya se va Carlos. ↘

2. Repeat the following groups of utterances, following the intonation guide given in parentheses.

a. Statements and information questions end with falling intonation in both English and Spanish:

Spanish (1211)	English (231)
¿Cómo se siente hoy?	How are you feeling?
¿Cuántos años tiene Ud.?	How old are you?
¿De dónde es Ud.?	Where are you from?
Tengo cincuenta años.	I'm fifty years old.
Mi esposo es de Cuba.	My husband is from Cuba.

b. Yes-no questions end with a rising intonation in both Spanish and English:

Spanish (1222)	English (233)
¿Puede Ud. volver mañana?	Can you come back tomorrow?
¿Se siente mejor?	Are you feeling better?
¿Es Ud. casado?	Are you married?
¿Quisiera sentarse?	Would you like to sit down?
¿Le conviene a las dos?	Does two o'clock suit you?

c. Commands usually end with a falling intonation in both Spanish and English:

Spanish (2211)	English (232)
Siéntese, por favor.	Sit down, please.
Vuelva Ud. a la una.	Come back at one o'clock.
Llame Ud. a este número.	Call this number.
Favor de no fumar.	No smoking, please.
¡No cuelgue!	Don't hang up!

   d. Greetings end with a falling intonation in Spanish, but most often with a rising intonation in English:

Spanish (1221 or 1231)	*English (232 or 322)*
Adiós.	Good-bye.
¿Cómo le va?	How's it going?
Mucho gusto en conocerlo.	Pleased to meet you.
Buenos días.	Good morning.
Hasta mañana.	See you tomorrow.

3. Read the following sentences, paying special attention to Spanish intonation patterns:

   a. Buenas tardes, señora Meléndez. ¿Cómo está?

   b. ¿Cuántos años hace que vive en los Estados Unidos?

   c. Señor Sotomayor, su hijo se siente mucho mejor hoy.

   d. ¿Es usted la señorita Rodríguez?

   e. Adiós, señora. Nos vemos pronto.

   f. ¿Qué le parece el martes a las cinco y media?

Dictado

Write each sentence you hear and indicate with an arrow whether it ends in a rising or falling intonation pattern.

1. _____

2. _____

3. _____

4. _____

5. _____

¿Ha entendido bien?

1. ¿Quién llama a la casa de los Jiménez?

2. ¿Quién contesta el teléfono?

3. ¿Qué recado le deja a Marta la señora Mason?

4. ¿Por qué cree el señor Jiménez que la señora Mason está equivocada?

5. ¿Cuándo es la entrevista? ¿Para qué puesto es?

6. ¿Quiere el señor Jiménez que su esposa trabaje fuera de la casa? ¿Por qué piensa así?

7. Según la señora Mason, ¿por qué busca trabajo la señora Jiménez?

8. Según el señor Jiménez, ¿quién es el que manda en su casa? ¿Cree Ud. que él tiene razón?

9. ¿Qué obligación tiene la señora Mason?

10. ¿Qué factores culturales son evidentes en este diálogo?

INTRODUCTORY DIALOGUE: I'm the one who gives the orders

Ms. Mason: Good afternoon. Is Marta Jiménez (there), please?

Mr. Jiménez: Who's calling, please?

Ms. M: (It's) Jean Mason from the Employment Office speaking.

Mr. J: Well, she's not at home at the moment. Would you like to leave her a (some) message?

Ms. M: Well, tell her that I got an interview for her for the position of receptionist tomorrow at 10:00.

Mr. J: You must be mistaken. I'm her husband and I know that she is not looking for work.

Ms. M: I don't know what to say to you. She told me that you (both) need money. Now that the children are in school, it's not necessary that your wife spend all day at home.

Mr. J: Well, ma'am, you have a right to express your opinion, but in this house I'm the one who gives the orders. If I say that my wife is not going to work, that's the way it's going to be. My wife always does what I tell her (to).

Ms. M: Anyway, I have the obligation of informing your wife about the interview. Please tell her to call me as soon as possible.

Mr. J: I'll tell her, but first she and I have to talk about this. It seems incredible to me that she's looking for work without first consulting me.

BASIC STRUCTURES I: Are you married?

The employee (m.)	*The client (f.)*
Alicia Hernández, would you like to come into the office for a moment?	Of course.
Be seated, please. Before starting (we start), I want you to answer a few personal questions for me.	What do you want (desire) to know?
Are you married?	Yes, I've been married three years. (I "carry" three years of marriage.) I'm single. / a widow. I'm engaged. / divorced. / separated from my husband.
How many children do you have?	I don't have any. I have three, two sons and a daughter. I have two. The older (one) is a boy (male) and the younger (one) a girl (female).
How many people are there in your family?	There are (we are) five of us: my husband, my three children, and I.

¿Sabe usted?

1. Since dating many different people before marriage is *not* the norm in most Hispanic countries, Spanish lacks words relating to that custom. **Salir con** (*to go out with*) may be used. **Novio** implies a serious suitor and not a boyfriend in the Anglo sense (**novios** also refers to newlyweds; **el noviazgo** is the formal premarriage period). Hispanic women who do date may use the English term *boyfriend* to refer to a dating partner, since **amigo** (*male friend*) implies a platonic relationship.

2. It is important to be culturally sensitive when referring to various living arrangements between Hispanic couples. Church marriages are more highly valued than those performed by civil authorities. Although common-law marriages (described by the term **vivir en concubinato**) are even less prestigious, all norms for married behavior (fidelity, child rearing, setting up house, etc.) apply to them. The terms **esposo/esposa** usually reflect a legally sanctioned marriage, while **marido/mujer** may refer to a common-law relationship in some cultures.

3. Verbs describing relationships include **comprometerse (con)**, *to become engaged to;* **casarse (con)**, *to get married* (*to*); **divorciarse (de)**, *to divorce (someone)*; **separarse (de)**, *to separate (from someone)*. Nouns include **el compromiso (matrimonial)**, *engagement;* **la boda**, *wedding;* **el matrimonio**, *marriage* (also *the married couple*); **el divorcio**, *divorce;* **la separación**, *separation;* **el estado civil**, *marital status.*

ESTRUCTURAS BÁSICAS I: ¿Es usted casada?

El empleado	*La cliente*
Alicia Hernández, ¿quisiera Ud. pasar a la oficina por un momento?	Claro que sí.
Siéntese, por favor. Antes de empezar, quiero que me conteste algunas preguntas personales.	¿Qué desea saber?
¿Es usted casada?	Sí, llevo tres años de casada. Soy { soltera. / viuda. Estoy { comprometida. / divorciada. / separada de mi esposo.
¿Cuántos hijos tiene?	No tengo ninguno. Tengo tres, dos hijos y una hija. Tengo dos. El mayor es varón y la menor es hembra.
¿Cuántas personas hay en su familia?	Somos cinco: mi esposo, mis tres hijos y yo.

---

4. **Hijos,** *children,* when the relationship to parents is inferred; **niños,** *children,* in the general sense. **Nene/nena** is commonly used in Puerto Rico and elsewhere to refer to small children; **chamaco/a** is a Mexican term referring to children. While **varón** is commonly used, **hembra** is not, perhaps reflecting the cultural value placed on male children. **Hombre (hombrecito)** and **mujer (mujercita)** are common in Mexican dialects to designate sex of children.

Notas lingüísticas I

A. In speaking of marital status, **ser** is used with **soltero/a** and **viudo/a** because they are *nouns.* **Estar** is normally used with the adjectives **separado/a** and **divorciado/a,** implying a change from the norm **casado.** Clients may use the verb **ser** if divorced or separated long enough for it to become their "normal" state. Use **ser casado/a** unless a change from the norm or expected norm is implied: **Ahora estoy casada por segunda vez** (*I'm now married for the second time.*)

B. The infinitive is the only form of the verb that can follow a preposition: **antes de empezar, después de divorciarse.**

C. **Llevar** + time expresses duration of time: **Llevo tres años de casada.**

D. Remember the double negative rule: **no tengo ninguno; ninguno = ni uno** (*not even one*) and, consequently, is used in the singular.

BASIC STRUCTURES II: What's your family like?

The employee (m.)	*The client (f.)*

Does anyone else live in your house?

My { mother / father / uncle / father-in-law / brother-in-law / cousin (f.) / grandmother / niece / granddaughter } also lives with us.

Who supports you?

{ My husband supports us. / I support the family. }

Who raised you?

{ My grandmother / My grandparents / My parents / My uncle and aunt } raised me.

Where do your parents live?

{ My father died last year and my mother lives with my older sister. / They both died two years ago. }

Fine, ma'am (Mrs.), it is necessary that you come here next week with your husband to speak more about the mortgage you are applying (for).

Um ... first I have to speak with him. I don't think he can come because of work.

Well, tell him to call me tomorrow morning. I hope he can come because it is very important that I speak with him.

Fine, sir, my husband will call you tomorrow morning at about ten. I appreciate it very much.

You're welcome.

¿Sabe usted?

1. **Familia** connotes the extended family; **parientes** are *relatives*, **padres** are *parents*. The masculine plural of kinship words indicates the male and female (**abuelos**, *grandparents*; **tíos**, *uncle and aunt*; **hermanos**, *brothers and sisters*). **Tengo tres hijos** can mean either *I have three children* or *I have three sons*. Usually, more information is given to clarify.

2. **Mamá** is more common than **madre** to refer to one's own mother.

3. **A eso de + la hora** is used to express approximate time: **a eso de las tres**, *at about four o'clock*.

198

ESTRUCTURAS BÁSICAS II: ¿Cómo es su familia?

El empleado	La cliente

¿Hay otras personas que viven en su casa?

También vive con nosotros mi
- mamá.
- papá.
- tío.
- suegro.
- cuñado.
- prima.
- abuela.
- sobrina.
- nieta.

¿Quién los mantiene a Uds.?

- Mi esposo nos mantiene.
- Yo mantengo a la familia.

¿Quién la crió a Ud.?

- Me crió mi abuelita.
- Me criaron
  - mis abuelos.
  - mis padres.
  - mis tíos.

¿Dónde viven sus padres?

- Mi papá murió el año pasado y mi mamá vive con mi hermana mayor.
- Los dos murieron hace dos años.

Bueno, señora, es necesario que venga aquí la semana que viene con su esposo para hablar más sobre la hipoteca que buscan Uds.

Este . . . primero tengo que hablar con él. No creo que él pueda venir por el trabajo.

Pues, dígale que me llame mañana por la mañana. Ojalá que pueda venir porque es muy importante que yo hable con él.

Bueno, señor, mi esposo lo va a llamar mañana a eso de las diez. Se lo agradezco mucho.

No hay de qué.

---

4. **Menor** and **mayor** are both comparative (**Ramón es menor que Paco**, *Ramón is younger than Paco*) and (when used with the definitive article) superlative forms (**Marisol es la menor de los tres hijos**, *Marisol is the youngest of the three children*).

5. **Este** . . . and **pues** . . . are interjections used to fill time while thinking, rephrasing, etc.

6. **Ojalá**, from the Arabic meaning *may Allah grant that*, is considered an entire clause. It is *not* conjugated as a verb and is always followed by the subjunctive mood. (See "Notas lingüísticas II," H.)

Notas lingüísticas II

A. Like *all* adjectives in Spanish, possessive adjectives agree with the noun they describe. They have two forms, singular and plural, except **nuestro**, which has four:

yo	**mi hijo**	**mi hija**	**mis hijos**	**mis hijas**
nosotros/as	**nuestro hijo**	**nuestra hija**	**nuestros hijos**	**nuestras hijas**
tú	**tu hijo**	**tu hija**	**tus hijos**	**tus hijas**
Ud., él, ella	**su hijo**	**su hija**	**sus hijos**	**sus hijas**
Uds., ellos/as	**su hijo**	**su hija**	**sus hijos**	**sus hijas**

Since **su hija** can mean *your, her, his,* or *their daughter,* **la hija de usted, la hija de ella,** etc., can be used instead for greater clarity.

B. **Hace** + time + **que** is used to express both *duration of time* and *time ago*. The difference in meaning is determined by the tense of the verb following **que**. Compare:

Hace + time + **que** + *present*	=	duration of time (length of time something has been going on)
Hace tres años que vivo aquí.		I've been living here 3 years.
Hace + time + **que** + *preterite*	=	time ago (time since something occurred).
Hace tres años que él murió.		He died three years ago.

C. **Hay** is an irregular form meaning *there is* or *there are*. It is used to locate non-specific nouns (**hay un hombre aquí, hay documentos en la oficina,** etc.) and nouns used with numbers (**hay tres personas en la lista**). **Estar** is used to locate specific nouns (**Su esposo está allí**).

D. Avoid the English speaker's tendency to use a preposition after the verbs **buscar** (*to look for*), **pedir** (*to ask for*), and **mirar** (*to look at*). These verbs are completed by a direct object to express what is looked *for*, asked *for*, or looked *at*. Of course, as always, the preposition **a** precedes the name or title of a person used as the direct object of the sentence.

Busco un empleo.	I'm looking for a job.
Busco al contador.	I'm looking for the accountant.
Miro la televisión.	I'm looking at TV.
No me mire así.	Don't look at me that way.

Pedir is used with a direct object referring to *what* is requested, and an indirect object referring to the *person* from whom it is asked:

El cliente no me pidió permiso.   The client did not ask me for permission.

E. **Empezar** + **a** + infinitive means *to begin to do something*.
Hoy empiezo a hablar español.   Today I begin to speak Spanish.

F. Stem-changing verbs of the **-ar** and **-er** conjugations *do not* change in the preterite. However, **-ir** stem-changing verbs (e.g., **pedir, seguir, sentir, dormir,**

morir) do change from **e** to **i** or **o** to **u**, *only* in the third-person singular and plural preterite forms.

	empezar	**volver**	**pedir**	**dormir**
yo	empecé[1]	volví	pedí	dormí
tú	empezaste	volviste	pediste	dormiste
Ud., él, ella	empezó	volvió	*pidió*	*durmió*
nosotros/as	empezamos	volvimos	pedimos	dormimos
Uds., ellos/as	empezaron	volvieron	*pidieron*	*durmieron*

G. The verbs **ser** and **ir** share the same irregular preterite forms. Meaning is obvious by content:

ser, ir

yo	**fui**	nosotros/as	**fuimos**
tú	**fuiste**		
Ud., él, ella	**fue**	Uds., ellos/as	**fueron**

Yo fui al hospital.   I went to the hospital.
Ud. fue el jefe, ¿verdad?   You were the boss, right?

H. The command forms learned earlier are actually the **usted**-forms of the present tense of the subjunctive mood. Whereas *tense* refers to *time, mood* refers to the *type* of verb information given. The two basic moods in Spanish are the *indicative* and the *subjunctive,* each of which has several different tenses. You have already learned two tenses of the indicative mood, the present and the preterite. In this lesson you will work with the present tense of the subjunctive mood.

1. For regular verbs, the present tense of the subjunctive is formed as follows:
   a. Start with the **yo**-form of the present tense, indicative mood.
   b. Drop the **-o** to form the stem.
   c. Add the endings **-e, -es, -e, -emos, -en** to the stem if the verb belongs to the **-ar** conjugation; **-a, -as, -a, -amos, -an** if it belongs to the **-er** or **-ir** conjugation.

Regular Verbs	*Presente del subjuntivo*				
	yo	tú	Ud., él, ella	nosotros/as	Uds., ellos/as
hablar hablo/habl-	hable	hables	hable	hablemos	hablen
comer como/com-	coma	comas	coma	comamos	coman
vivir vivo/viv-	viva	vivas	viva	vivamos	vivan

---

1. Spelling change from **z** to **c** does not affect pronunciation. The combination **ze** does not exist in Spanish.

d. For stem-changing verbs, follow the same steps, but note that the stem of the **nosotros/as** form of **-ar** and **-er** verbs has the same vowel as the infinitive, not the vowel change of the **yo-** form of the present indicative. For stem-changing verbs ending in **-ir, e** changes to **i** and **o** changes to **ue** in all forms, except the **nosotros/as** form of **-ir** verbs, in which **o** changes to **u**:

Stem-changing verbs	Presente del subjuntivo				
	yo	tú	Ud., él, ella	nosotros/as	Uds., ellos/as
volver vuelvo/vuelv-	vuelva	vuelvas	vuelva	volvamos	vuelvan
dormir duermo/duerm-	duerma	duermas	duerma	d*u*rmamos	duerman
pedir pido/pid-	pida	pidas	pida	pidamos	pidan

e. These verbs have irregular forms in the present subjunctive:

	yo	tú	Ud., él, ella	nosotros/as	Uds., ellos/as
ser	sea	seas	sea	seamos	sean
estar	esté	estés	esté	estemos	estén
haber	haya	hayas	haya	hayamos	hayan
ir	vaya	vayas	vaya	vayamos	vayan
saber	sepa	sepas	sepa	sepamos	sepan

2. The following diagram illustrates the differences between the indicative and the subjunctive moods.

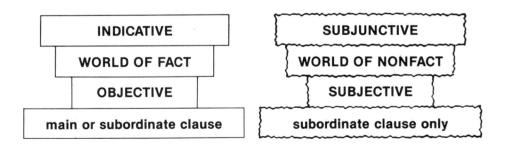

There are many times in Spanish when it is essential to use the more ''subjective'' subjunctive mood. In this chapter its use in *noun clauses* (a clause used as a noun in the sentence) is highlighted. The following sentences contain noun clauses:

Noun	*Noun clause*
Me parece muy bien *la hora*.	**Me parece bien que *vienen*.**
(**la hora** is the subject)	(**que vienen** is the subject)
The hour seems fine to me.	(The fact that) they're coming seems fine to me.
Yo quiero *una tarjeta verde*.	**Yo quiero *que vengas hoy*.**
(**una tarjeta verde** is the direct object)	(**que vengas hoy** is the direct object)
I want a green card.	I want you to come today.

3. The choice of the subjunctive mood in noun clauses is governed by three rules:

   a. The subjunctive is used only in the subordinate (secondary) clause of two-clause sentences. The subordinate noun is always introduced by **que** (*that*) except after **ojalá,** where **que** is optional.

Main clause		*Subordinate clause*
Es importante	**que**	**vuelvas.**
It's important	(that)	you come back.
Ana no quiere	**que**	**su hijo se case.**
Ana doesn't want		her son to marry.
Ojalá	**(que)**	**Ud. se sienta bien.**
I hope (May God grant)	(that)	you're feeling better.

   Notice that in English, introducing the subordinate noun clause with *that* is optional. In Spanish the **que** is *always* used (optional only after **ojalá**).

   b. The subjunctive is used after a verb or impersonal expression in the main clause that reflects a subjective attitude toward the content of the subordinate clause rather than stating (confirming) that what is said in the second clause is fact. Nonconfirming main clauses (requiring the subjunctive) are essential to the meaning of the sentences, whereas confirming clauses could be omitted without altering the message.

Confirming		*Nonconfirming*	
ser verdad	to be true	**ser importante**	(expresses opinion)
ser cierto	to be certain	**ser necesario**	(expresses influence)
ser evidente	to be evident	**querer**	(expresses desire)
estar claro	to be clear	**esperar**	(expresses hope)
parecer	to seem	**pedir**	(expresses request)
creer	to believe	**no creer**	(expresses doubt)

   Compare the following sets of sentences. The first sentence of each set contains a *confirming* element which states more clearly the speaker's point of view regarding the truth of what follows in the subordinate clause. The *indicative* is used in the subordinate clause. Notice that the confirming element could be eliminated without affecting the meaning of the sentence. The second sentence of each set contains a nonconfirming expression requiring *subjunctive* in the subordinate clause.

Confirming	*Nonconfirming*
(Es verdad que) vienen. (It's true that) they're coming.	**Es importante que vengan.** It's important that they come.
(Es evidente que) lo hace. (It's evident that) he does it.	**Espero que lo haga.** I hope he does it.
(Me parece que) trabaja. (It seems to me) he works.	**Pido que trabaje.** I ask him to work.
(Creo que) están aquí. (I believe) they're here.	**No creo que estén aquí.** I don't believe they're here.
(Está claro) que es mejor. (It's clear that) it is better.	**Quiero que sea mejor.** I want it to be better.

When confirming expressions are used *in questions to express doubt,* they are often followed by the *subjunctive.*

¿Cree Ud. que *venga* hoy?   Do you think he'll come today?

c. The subjunctive is used only when the subject of the subordinate clause is different from that of the main clause; if there is no change in subject, the infinitive is used:

    1. **Es necesario verlo.**   **Es necesario que Ud. lo vea.**
       It's necessary to see it.   It's necessary that you see it.

    2. **Espero volver temprano.**   **Espero que vuelvas temprano.**
       I hope to return early.   I hope you return early.

d. In summary, use the subjunctive in noun clauses according to the following formula:

> subject$_1$ + verb$_1$ + **que** + subject$_2$ + verb$_2$
>   *nonconfirming*   *subjunctive*
> (expresses
> personal opinion
> about subject
> and verb$_2$)

PRÁCTICA PRELIMINAR

Follow general guidelines for self-instructional practice.

A. Choose the expression that best completes each sentence.

    Ejemplo: Me comprometí ((con) de a) él en marzo.

    1. Yo (divorcio   me divorcié de   divorcié) mi esposo el año pasado.

    2. Pues, estoy (soltera   viuda   divorciada) ahora.

    3. Mi esposa y yo (me   nos   se) divorciamos en 1976.

4. No quiero casarme (a   de   con) él.

5. (El matrimonio   La boda   Se casa) va a ser en junio del año próximo.

6. ¿Cuál es su estado (matrimonio   civil   de boda)?

7. ¿Por qué quieren Uds. (separar   separarse   se separan)?

8. Yo (casé   case   me casé) con Lupe dos años después del divorcio.

9. Mi novio y yo llevamos dos años de (comprometer   comprometidos).

10. ¿Por qué quieren Uds. (divorciar   divorciarse   a divorciar)?

B. Give the appropriate form of **mejor, peor, mayor,** or **menor** according to the context of the sentence.

Ejemplo: Alba tiene ocho años. Su hermano ___*menor*___ tiene seis.

1. Ayer tenía dolor de cabeza, pero hoy no lo tengo. Me siento mucho

    _____ .

2. La _____ tiene siete años y el _____ tiene dieciséis.

3. Los _____ de edad tienen más de veintiún años.

4. El paciente sufrió otro ataque anoche. Por eso se siente _____ hoy.

5. Yo tengo cuarenta y dos años. Mi esposo es _____ ; él tiene cincuenta.

6. Mis tres hijos _____ van a la escuela; la _____ empieza el año que viene.

7. Me parece _____ mañana a las tres porque mi hermana puede estar con mi hija.

8. Mi hijo _____ nació en 1968; el _____ nació en 1982.

C. Give the appropriate possessive form that corresponds to the subject in each sentence (or object in 5, 6, and 7).

Ejemplo: Vivo con ___*mis*___ abuelos.

1. El esposo mantiene a _____ hermana también.

2. Vivimos con _____ padres.

3. La cuñada vive sola con _____ dos hijas.

A **1.** me divorcié de **2.** divorciada **3.** nos **4.** con **5.** La boda **6.** civil **7.** separarse **8.** me casé **9.** comprometidos **10.** divorciarse

B **1.** mejor **2.** menor, mayor **3.** mayores **4.** peor **5.** mayor **6.** mayores, menor **7.** mejor **8.** mayor, menor

C **1.** su **2.** nuestros **3.** sus

4. La abuela vive con _____ hijo menor.

5. ¿ _____ hijos viven con Ud.?

6. Me criaron _____ abuelos.

7. ¿Te crió _____ mamá?

8. Yo también mantengo a _____ hermana menor.

9. Nosotros no podemos comprar _____ casa.

10. ¿Quisieras hablar con _____ hijos?

D. Give the appropriate form of the verb **ser, estar, tener,** or **haber** according to the context of the sentence.

Ejemplo: Mi hijo mayor ___*es*___ soltero.

1. ¿Cuántas personas _____ en su familia?

2. Mi mamá _____ viuda.

3. Yo _____ la menor de la familia.

4. ¿ _____ Ud. casado, señor Reyes?

5. ¡Mi abuela _____ ciento dos años!

6. Yo no _____ hijos; _____ soltera.

7. ¿Cuánto tiempo hace que Uds. _____ divorciados?

8. Yo no _____ esposo; _____ viuda.

9. ¿ _____ otras personas que viven en su casa?

10. _____ cinco: mi esposo y yo y nuestros tres hijos.

E. Formulate questions beginning with ¿**Cuánto tiempo hace . . .**? to ask the client how long it's been that something has been going on or since something happened, according to the English cue.

Ejemplo: . . . that you've been a widow?
            ¿**Cuánto tiempo hace que** *Ud. es viuda?*

C 4. su 5. Sus 6. mis 7. tu 8. mi 9. nuestra 10. tus
D 1. hay 2. es 3. soy 4. Es 5. tiene 6. tengo, soy 7. están 8. tengo, soy 9. Hay 10. Somos

1. . . . since you (Uds.) got married?

2. . . . that your daughter has been engaged?

3. . . . that your mother has been living in your house?

4. . . . since you and your husband got divorced?

5. . . . that you've been in the hospital?

F. Now answer the questions in Exercise E using the expression **llevar** plus the time indicated.

Ejemplo: ¿Cuánto tiempo hace que Ud. es viuda? (dos años)
  Llevo dos años de viuda.

1. trece años

2. un mes

3. año y medio

4. muchos años

5. tres días

G. Give the missing forms of the following verbs.

presente del indicativo	presente del subjuntivo	pretérito
1.	hablen	
2. cambio		
3.		vivió
4.	seamos	
5.	vea (yo)	
6. llamas		
7.	vuelvan	
8.		empezó
9. va		
10.	pidas	

E 1. ¿Cuánto tiempo hace que Uds. se casaron? 2. ¿Cuánto tiempo hace que su hija está comprometida? 3. ¿Cuánto tiempo hace que su mamá vive en su casa? 4. ¿Cuánto tiempo hace que Ud. y su esposo se divorciaron? 5. ¿Cuánto tiempo hace que Ud. está en el hospital?

F 1. Llevamos trece años de casados. 2. Lleva un mes de comprometida. 3. Lleva año y medio (de vivir) en mi casa. 4. Llevamos muchos años de divorciados. 5. Llevo tres días en el hospital.

G 1. hablan, hablen, hablaron 2. cambio, cambie, cambié 3. vive, viva, vivió 4. somos, seamos, fuimos 5. veo, vea, vi 6. llamas, llames, llamaste 7. vuelven, vuelvan, volvieron 8. empieza, empiece, empezó 9. va, vaya, fue 10. pides, pidas, pediste

H.   Decide which, if any, of the criteria for using the subjunctive is evident in each sentence, according to the following key: **(a)** sentence contains subordinate noun clause; **(b)** main clause does not confirm content of second clause; **(c)** the subject of the main clause is not the same as that of the second.

Ejemplo: I want you to go tonight.
   a, b, c

1.   It's impossible to go tonight.
2.   We want to get a divorce.
3.   I hope your daughter is feeling better.
4.   It's true that my son got married.
5.   It's easy to say so (it).
6.   I don't believe he's engaged.
7.   Is it true you are seventy years old?
8.   I ask that we not talk about that.
9.   How does six o'clock seem to you?
10.   It's clear that they are separated.

I.   Now translate the sentences from English to Spanish, using subjunctive only in those sentences that meet all three criteria.

J.   Choose the appropriate verb form according to context.
   Ejemplo: Es importante que (vienen (vengan) vinieron) mañana.

1.   No quiero (ir   vaya   va) al hospital.
2.   No es evidente que lo (saber   sepan   saben).
3.   Ojalá que mi hijo no (tener   tiene   tenga) un resfriado.
4.   Me parece que el doctor (es   ser   sea) muy competente.
5.   Es necesario que Uds. (volver   vuelven   vuelvan) mañana a las tres.
6.   Yo entiendo que Ud. (necesita   necesite   necesitó) ir al hospital la semana que viene.
7.   Te pido que no (venir   vienes   vengas) aquí más sin tu esposo.
8.   Quiero que Ud. (va   vaya   ir) a casa hoy.
9.   Es verdad que la doctora no (estar   esté   está) en la oficina hoy.
10.   Es importante siempre (decir   dice   diga) la verdad.

H 1. a, b 2. a, b 3. a, b, c 4. a, c 5. a, b 6. a, b, c 7. a, b, c 8. a, b, c 9. x 10. a, c

I 1. Es imposible ir esta noche. 2. Queremos divorciarnos (un divorcio). 3. Espero (Ojalá) que su hija se sienta mejor. 4. Es verdad que mi hijo se casó. 5. Es fácil decirlo. 6. No creo que él esté comprometido. 7. ¿Es verdad que Ud. tenga setenta años? 8. Pido que no hablemos de eso. 9. ¿Qué le parece a las seis? 10. Está claro que están separados.

J 1. ir 2. sepan 3. tenga 4. es 5. vuelvan 6. necesita 7. vengas 8. vaya 9. está 10. decir

Combinándolo todo

PRÁCTICA COMUNICATIVA: Relaciones familiares

Conversación parcial

Practique Ud. oralmente la siguiente conversación. Cada raya (/) implica que falta una palabra. Es necesario conjugar cada verbo *en bastardillas*.

El empleado	La señora Carranzo
1. Señora Carranzo, ¿*poder* Ud. / a / oficina / momentito?	Sí / , ¿me *poder* acompañar / hijos?
2. No, señora, yo *preferir* / ellos *esperar* en / sala / espera.	Bueno, / bien.
3. Antes / empezar, yo *querer* / Ud. me *contestar* algunas / .	Sí, / no.
4. ¿ / personas / en / familia, señora?	/ cuatro. Yo / / tres / .
5. ¿ / *vivir* / esposo?	Yo / viuda. / esposo *morir* / un accidente / 1979.
6. ¿ / *mantener* / / familia?	Yo *mantener* / toda / familia.
7. ¿Hay / personas / *vivir* / su / ?	/ , la hermana / mi esposo.

Pregunte Ud.

Haga Ud. las preguntas necesarias en la siguiente entrevista con la señora Ortega, que busca hipoteca.

1. Pues, ahora estoy separada de mi esposo.
2. Hace cinco meses que estamos separados.
3. Somos seis: mi esposo y yo y nuestros cuatro hijos.
4. Ahora él vive en San José.
5. El mayor vive con mi esposo y las tres menores viven conmigo.
6. También vive con nosotros mi suegra.
7. Me criaron mis padres.
8. Mi mamá murió y mi padre vive con mi abuela.
9. Hace seis años que ella murió.
10. Quiero que Ud. me ayude a solicitar una hipoteca.

Dígalo

Pregunte a un/a compañero/a de clase lo que le diga su profesor/a sobre los temas del estado civil, la familia, las personas que viven en la casa, los padres, y el mantener a la familia.

Escuche bien

A. Ud. oirá a seis personas que hablan de las personas que viven en su casa. Escriba Ud. el número de personas que viven en la casa y, entonces, quiénes son. Escriba en inglés.

Number in household	Identification
1.	
2.	
3.	
4.	
5.	
6.	

B. El señor y la señora Martínez hablan de su familia. Escriba Ud. en español el miembro de la familia que describen en cada oración. Después, escriba *sí* si la persona que habla "confirma" la información, empleando el indicativo, y *no* si expresa un aspecto más subjetivo, empleando el subjuntivo en la cláusula subordinada. Entonces, ponga una *X* en la columna apropiada, *indicativo o subjuntivo*.

Miembro de la familia	¿Confirma?	Indicativo	Subjuntivo
1.			
2.			
3.			
4.			
5.			
6.			

Diálogos cortos

I. *El doctor*

Siéntese, señora Ríos. Necesito _____ algunas _____ personales.

La paciente

Pues . . . está bien. ¿Qué quiere saber?

I. *El doctor*   *La paciente*

¿ _____ Ud. casada?   Sí, pero ahora estoy separada de mi es-
                                              poso.

¿ _____ tiempo hace   Nosotros llevamos cinco meses de se-
_____ Uds. _____   parados.
separados?

¿ _____ fue la última vez   Pues, doctor, esa es una pregunta muy
que Ud. tuvo (*had*) relaciones sex-   personal. ¿Por qué me lo pregunta?
uales?

Pues, _____ posible que Ud.   No entiendo, doctor. ¿Qué quiere decir
_____ una infección ve-   *venérea?*
nérea.

Quiere _____ "transmi-   Este . . . eso, pues . . . no puede ser. ¡Ay,
tida por contacto sexual."   Dios mío!

II. *La trabajadora social*   *El señor Álvarez*

(*Hablan por teléfono*)

¿Es ésta _____ casa de   Sí, lo es. ¿Con quién hablo?

la _____ Álvarez?

_____ Lois Mallory   Sí, soy yo. ¿En qué puedo ayudarla, se-
                                              ñora?
del _____ de _____

sociales. ¿ _____ Ud. Vi-

cente Álvarez, _____

esposo _____ Margarita?

Pues, _____ seis meses   Eso no puede ser. Yo soy su esposo y yo
                                              no sé nada de esto. Nosotros podemos
que _____ esposa viene   resolver nuestros problemas sin la ayuda
                                              de Ud.
_____ para hablar de

_____ problemas matri-

moniales. Ahora _____

importante que Ud. _____ a
hablarme, también.

La trabajadora social	El señor Álvarez
Pero _____ esposa me _____ que Ud. no quiere _____ con ella de _____ problemas. Por eso, viene _____.	Pues, mire, señora, en mi casa yo soy el que manda. Aquí nosotros no tenemos ningún problema.
Señor Álvarez, es _____ que Ud. y _____ esposa _____ sobre esto. ¿Por qué no _____ con ella a mi _____ mañana a _____ tres y media?	Bueno, yo voy a hablar con Margarita esta noche. Pero no quiero hablar de nuestros problemas personales con personas fuera de la familia. ¿Entiende Ud.?

Ayude al cliente

You need to write a short report in Spanish to the parents of Juan Castaños, who is receiving treatment in an adolescent treatment facility. He has made a great deal of progress and is now scheduled to be released within a month. After talking with Juan about his release, you have discovered that he has some apprehensions about returning to live at home. You need to verify some of the facts about his living conditions before going ahead with his release.

Begin the letter with *Muy estimados señores Castaños*.

1. Tell them that it is possible that you (plural) will be releasing Juan next month. Tell them you think that Juan is much better. Then tell them that before releasing him (*antes de darlo de alta*) you want to verify (*verificar*) some personal information about the family.

2. Ask them how many people are living in the house and who they are. Then tell them that you need to know who supports the family. Then ask them if it's true that Juan's Uncle Carlos still lives in the house. Ask them if they think that Juan and his Uncle Carlos get along well (*se llevan bien*).

3. Tell them that it is important that you talk with everyone who lives in the house by next Friday. Ask them if a Wednesday evening appointment at 7:30 at their house is convenient for them.

Close with *muy atentamente* and sign your name.

¿Comprende Ud.?

Recientemente se murieron los padres de Antonio Miranda, que tiene cinco años. Usted tiene que entrevistar a varios parientes de Antonio para decidir cuál sería la persona más apropiada para criarlo. Escuche bien lo que dice cada persona; escriba Ud. el nombre de cada uno y, en inglés, su parentesco con Antonio y los datos relevantes de su vida que puedan influir en la decisión. Después, decida Ud. cuál cree que debe criarlo.

	Name	*Relationship*	*Relevant details*
1.			
2.			
3.			
4.			
5.			
6.			

Piénselo

Prepárese para poder hablar con el/la profesor/a o con otros estudiantes sobre los siguientes temas, contestando las preguntas que le sugiera el/la profesor/a.

1. el noviazgo y el matrimonio
2. la separación y el divorcio
3. los problemas de tener y criar hijos
4. el trabajo fuera de casa para las mujeres que tienen hijos
5. la familia en casa
6. la cortesía por teléfono

Imagínese

1. ¿Cree Ud. que este mensaje dice la verdad? Explique su respuesta.
2. ¿Cree Ud. que hay ciertos trabajos o profesiones donde la *peor* alternativa pueda ser una mujer (o un hombre)? ¿Cuáles son? ¿Por qué lo cree Ud.?
3. ¿Es común que las mujeres hispanas trabajen fuera de la casa? Explique su respuesta.
4. ¿Qué problemas pueden ocurrir en una casa hispana si la esposa trabaja fuera de la casa, pero su esposo no tiene empleo?
5. ¿Qué problemas pueden resultar entre un empleado y su jefa del trabajo si los dos son hispanos? ¿Si él es hispano y ella es de origen anglo? ¿Si ella es hispana y él no lo es?
6. ¿Prefiere Ud. trabajar para un hombre o para una mujer o le da igual?

1. ¿Cómo se llama la novia? ¿Y el novio?
2. ¿Cuántos años tienen? ¿Cuál es mayor?
3. ¿Cuánto tiempo hace que se conocen?
4. ¿En qué trabaja él? ¿Y ella?
5. ¿Los dos van a trabajar fuera de la casa después de casarse?
6. ¿Van a tener luna de miel (*honeymoon*)? ¿Dónde?
7. ¿Quién va a ser el/la que manda en la casa?
8. ¿Quieren tener hijos? ¿Cuántos?
9. ¿Cree Ud. que es el primer matrimonio para los dos?
10. ¿A Ud. le parece que va a ser un matrimonio feliz?

> **MENSAJE DEL GOBERNADOR DE PUERTO RICO**
>
> **HON. CARLOS ROMERO BARCELÓ**
>
> **EN HONOR A LAS MADRES PUERTORRIQUEÑAS**
>
> **La madre es la expresión más sublime de amor y sacrificio que conocemos, y hoy dedicamos un día especial para honrarla. Los que la hemos perdido aquilatamos aún más el recuerdo de lo que sus enseñanzas y consejos significaron para nuestra formación como adultos.**
>
> **Quiero extender a todas las madres de Puerto Rico un mensaje de cariño y admiración genuina. Admiración que se merecen porque han demostrado su gran capacidad como mujeres que saben trabajar y contribuir al desarrollo de nuestro pueblo, sin que por ello se debilite su esencial labor de preservar la unidad de la familia, de lo que depende, a fin de cuentas, todo el bienestar de la sociedad puertorriqueña.**
>
> **A ti, madre puertorriqueña, mi cariño y mi respeto.**

1. ¿Por qué escribió el gobernador de Puerto Rico este mensaje?
2. ¿Es común que el presidente de los Estados Unidos escriba un mensaje de este tipo? Explique su respuesta.
3. Según el gobernador Romero Barceló, ¿cuáles son las cualidades de la madre puertorriqueña?
4. Según él, ¿de qué depende el bienestar de la sociedad puertorriqueña?
5. ¿Cree Ud. que el papel de la madre es más importante en los países hispanos que en los Estados Unidos? Explique.
6. ¿Cree Ud. que el señor de la foto le expresa bien su cariño y su respeto a su mamá? Explique.

1. ¿Qué pasa en esta fotografía?
2. ¿Por qué no hay ningún hombre en la foto?
3. ¿En qué trabajan las mujeres?
4. ¿Los hijos están en casa o en otro lugar?
5. ¿Qué hace el payaso (*clown*)?
6. ¿Tienen hijos todas las mujeres? Explique su respuesta.
7. Según el reloj (*clock*), ¿qué hora es?
8. ¿Qué otras cosas observa Ud.?

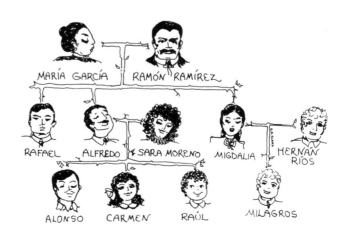

1. ¿Cuál es el parentesco entre María y Alonso?
2. ¿Es casado Alfredo? ¿Y Rafael?
3. ¿Cuántos hijos tienen Alfredo y Sara? ¿Son todos varones?
4. ¿Cuál es el nombre completo de la abuela de Milagros?
5. ¿Cuál es el parentesco entre Raúl y Milagros?
6. ¿Cómo se llama el suegro de Hernán?
7. ¿Son hermanos Alfredo y Migdalia?
8. ¿Cuántas nietas tienen María y Ramón?
9. ¿Cómo se llaman los tíos de Milagros?
10. ¿Cuántas personas hay en la familia? ¿Viven todos juntos?

Haciendo el papel

Haga Ud. el papel del empleado en las siguientes situaciones. Use la comunicación sin palabras cuando sea apropiada.

1. You are a social worker who has just begun working at a new agency. You are going through the file of a client named Lilia Ortiz, who is 39 years old. The file contains the names and ages of the other members of the household, but not the family relationship. They are: Ana López (59), Samuel Ortiz (42), María Ortiz (19), Carlos Santiago (21), Juana Santiago (6 months), Raúl Ortiz (16), and Felipe López (25). Ask Lilia questions regarding the family relationship among the members of the household (e.g., *¿Ana López es su mamá?*).

2. You are a young female lawyer defending a seventeen-year-old Hispanic male accused of assault and battery (*asalto y agresión*). In your first interview ask him his name, family and household composition, and other relevant data. He tells you that he's the oldest of six children, all of whom live with his mother, that his parents are divorced, his father is living in California with another woman, and he's the man of the house now. You sense that he is being rather flirtatious with you. Continue to interview him in a way that discourages the flirtation while treating him with *respeto y dignidad.*

3. You are a male psychiatrist interviewing Magdalena Montalvo, a thirty-year-old Hispanic mother of four children, ages three months, eighteen months, three years, and five years. She has been brought to the emergency room of the hospital where you work by her common-law husband, Fernando Candelas. She is suffering from an *ataque de nervios,* a culturally accepted way for Hispanic women under stress to gain temporary relief from their family and household responsibilities. You need to talk with the patient alone, but her husband insists that he be with her throughout the interview. Explain why you must speak with her alone to him in a way that respects his manhood as defined by cultural role expectations. Then interview Magdalena, again showing cultural sensitivity to the importance of carrying out her duties as mother and wife even though you suspect that the stress of these duties is responsible for her current physical and emotional state.

REFLEJOS DE LA CULTURA: "La triste historia de mi vida oscura"

The novel *La triste historia de mi vida oscura* was written in 1978 by Armando Couto, a Cuban who states his main objective as that of escaping from the *barrio humilde* of Havana where he was born in 1918. He succeeded by becoming a script writer for radio and a specialist in public relations. His rise to wealth and fame was interrupted by the Castro revolution, and he once again found himself living in poverty, this time in the United States, which he describes as "an industrialized country where poverty is intolerable."

Couto affirms that now, in exile, nostalgia colors his memories of the barrio he once hated. He describes the protagonist of this novel as a composite of the various men among whom he was raised. The Cuban sense of humor pervades the following description of an encounter with an old flame. While the episode is related with tongue in cheek, its first-person narrative style reveals some of the inner thoughts of a fictitious Cuban male now living in Miami. It portrays both the traditional and the changing mores of male–female behaviors in the modern Hispanic world.

—¡Lupita!—le grité y le di un abrazo. Y nos besamos los dos en las mejillas. Tomados de las manos nos miramos. Yo no sé lo que ella pensaba de mí, pero yo estaba haciendo mis cálculos mentales y me decía: "Carijo, todavía está rebuenísima y por lo que parece, tiene los senos tan parados como cuando tenía diecisiete años."

"Lupita!" I exclaimed and hugged her. And we kissed each other on the cheek. Holding hands, we looked at each other. I don't know what she was thinking about me, but I was calculating mentally and saying to myself: "Damn, she still looks great and from what I can see, her breasts are as firm as when she was seventeen."

—¿Qué haces?

"What are you doing?"

—Trabajo como forlady y gano buena plata.

"I work as a forelady and make a good living."

—¿Te casaste?

"Did you get married?"

—Sí . . . pero . . .— Comprendí que estaba separada. Decidí no preguntar. Esperé, seguro de que me haría la confesión.

"Yes . . . but . . . " I understood that she was separated. I decided not to ask. I waited, certain that she would confide in me.

—Mi marido se me echó a perder en Miami. Aquí todos los hombres se corrompen fácilmente. Tuve que divorciarme.

"My husband got into trouble in Miami. All men are easily corrupted here. I had to get a divorce."

—¿Vives sola?—le pregunté ya con la malicia perversa del hombre que busca la aventura.

"Do you live alone?" I asked then with the perverse malice of a man seeking adventure.

—Con mi hermana Petra. . . . ¿Y tú? ¿Cómo te va?

"With my sister, Petra. . . . And you? How's it going?"

Le conté muy por arriba la trágica historia de mi vida oscura. Exageré mis sufrimientos y los defectos de Andrea. Me presenté como el marido bueno, sufrido, santón, pero no aguantón, que perdona y espera. Aunque añadí: "Siento un vacío en el alma que necesito llenar cuanto antes o me volveré loco". (Como ven ustedes, yo la estaba atacando con todos mis hierros. Pero, bueno, ¡yo soy así y nadie me puede hacer cambiar!)

Ella me miró sonriendo, con esa sonrisa de crueldad feroz, que sólo algunas mujeres son capaces de emplear y me dijo con pérfida alegría: "Éste es el justo castigo por todo lo que me hiciste sufrir, chico".

—Yo no te hice nada—le respondí con la voz apagada.

—¿Te parece poco que fueras mi novio durante diez años y no te casaras conmigo? ¡Eso no tiene perdón de Dios!

Claro que no lo tenía. Lo confieso, fue una infamia. Una verdadera infamia, pero debo decir para disculparme, que éramos muchos los que por aquella época lo hacíamos en La Habana.

Por parte mía, no había amor. Había sexo. Ya en aquella época, estaba de noviecito de Andrea, que era la que de verdad me volvía loco. Como siempre fui hábil, pude llevar los dos noviazgos sin que Lupita se enterase. En cuanto a Lupita, a los pocos meses, después que conocí todo el paisaje maravilloso de su cuerpo, ya me aburrió, como me aburre comer arroz con picadillo todos los días . . .

Todo hombre tiene siempre un complejo de culpa con alguna mujer. Y Lupita era como una espina clavada en mi corazón.

I recounted very superficially the tragic story of my gloomy life. I exaggerated my sufferings and the defects of Andrea. I presented myself as the good, long-suffering, saintly, but impatient husband, who forgives and waits. Although I did add: "I feel a void in my heart which I must fill soon or I will go crazy." (As you can see, I was already attacking her with all my weapons. Well, but that's how I am and no one can make me change!)

She looked at me smiling, with that fiercely cruel smile which only a few women are capable of using, and she said with perfidious pleasure: "This is your just punishment for all that you made me suffer, man."

"I didn't do anything to you," I answered in a meek voice.

"Isn't it enough that you were my fiancé for ten years and you didn't marry me? That's unpardonable!"

Of course it was. I admit it; it was despicable. Truly despicable, but I must say to excuse myself, that there were lots of us who used to do it in Havana at that time.

On my part, there was no love. There was sex. At that time, I was already dating Andrea, who was really the one I was crazy about. Since I've always been clever, I was able to continue dating them both without Lupita finding out. With regard to Lupita, after a few months, after I became familiar with the whole marvelous landscape of her body, she began to bore me, just as it bores me to eat rice with Cuban hash every day.

Every man always has a guilt complex about some woman. And Lupita was like a thorn pricking my heart.

Evaluación del progreso—Lecciones 5–6

RAISING AWARENESS

A. Discuss why the cross-cultural communication process may be affected by the misinterpretation of nonverbal cues.

B. Why is it important to understand one's personal culture when communicating with people from other cultures?

C. Discuss how Hispanics from rural areas of Latin America may differ from those born and raised in the rural United States.

D. Mention the most important aspects of traditional Hispanic cultures regarding the roles of men and women and how they relate to the reality of Hispanic men and women living in the United States.

E. Explain what gender-related problems Anglo providers may face when dealing with Hispanics of the same or the opposite sex.

F. Discuss the concept of personal space in traditional Hispanic and Anglo cultures, emphasizing behaviors that reflect culturally different values.

COMUNICÁNDOSE EN ESPAÑOL

A. Pronunciación   Write the sentences your instructor dictates, being careful to indicate word boundaries. Underline the stressed syllables you hear and decide where written accent marks are necessary.

1. _____

2. _____

3. _____

B. Discriminación auditiva   Circle the letter of the most appropriate response to each oral question or statement you hear.

1. a b c   5. a b c   8. a b c

2. a b c   6. a b c   9. a b c

3. a b c   7. a b c   10. a b c

4. a b c

COMBINÁNDOLO TODO

A. Comprensión oral   Write the numerical information you hear, indicating in English the type of information it is (e.g., telephone number, birthdate).

1. _____

2. _____

3. _____

4. _____

5. _____

6. _____

B. La entrevista   Give the questions and/or responses needed in the following interview with a client who would like to buy medical insurance for his family.

La empleada	*El cliente*
1. Buenas _____ .	Necesito seguro médico para mi familia.
¿ _____ ?	
2. Bueno, primero _____ _____ .	Cómo no. ¿Qué necesita preguntarme?
3. ¿ _____ ?	Sí, soy casado.
4. ¿ _____ ?	Llevamos quince años de casados.
5. ¿ _____ ?	Es ama de casa, pero también trabaja un poco de enfermera privada.
6. ¿ _____ ?	Sí, tenemos tres hijos.
7. ¿ _____ ?	Sí, los tres viven con nosotros.
8. ¿ _____ ?	Los varones tienen 8 y 10 años y la hija tiene 13.
9. ¿ _____ ?	Somos seis: mi esposa y yo, los tres hijos y mi mamá, que es viuda.
10. ¿ _____ ?	Ella vino a vivir con nosotros hace dos años, después de que murió mi padre.

	La empleada	*El cliente*

11. ¿ _____ ?   Sí, señora, yo mantengo a la familia, pero mi esposa también ayuda con los gastos (*expenses*) de la casa.

12. Gracias. _____   No sé si entiendo. ¿Tengo que llevar estos papeles a casa para que mi esposa los _____ . firme?

13. Sí, señor, _____ .   Bueno, señora, yo vuelvo mañana con los papeles firmados.

C. En acción Choose one of the following situations and act it out with your instructor or another classmate.

1. Calling a patient to ask preliminary questions needed before she is admitted to the hospital next week for an operation.

2. Interviewing a couple who has come to you for marriage counseling over problems that have arisen since the wife began working as a secretary two months ago.

3. Trying to convince a client to phone you with information rather than coming in to the office when it is not necessary to do so.

4. Explaining what you want a female client to do in order to tell her husband that she has been secretly looking for a job for two months.

5. Trying to set up an appointment for a home visit when all members of the household are present.

LECCIÓN 7

Bienvenido a mi hogar

LOS OBJETIVOS

Raising awareness

1. To understand culture shock and how to deal with it effectively
2. To become aware of the intrinsic support system of the Hispanic family as a resource in providing services
3. To interpret the behavior of Hispanic children from a culturally aware perspective

Comunicándose en español

1. To hear and pronounce the consonants **b**, **v**, and **p**
2. To elicit and understand information regarding clients' residences and housing needs
3. To use and understand the Spanish pronoun system with ease and clarity

Combinándolo todo

1. To master vocabulary and sentence composition with increased accuracy in use of present and past tenses as well as object pronouns
2. To gain increasing independence from the written word in eliciting and responding to information in work-related activities
3. To understand the isolation common to Latino women in the United States who do not often venture alone outside the Hispanic *barrio*

Raising awareness

OVERVIEW: What is culture shock?

Now that you have a clearer idea of who you are as a culturally defined personality and of how the various cultures you live in have influenced your values, attitudes, beliefs, and behaviors, you are better prepared to communicate with your Hispanic clients. The next step in the process is to understand the phenomenon of *culture shock*, which is commonly experienced by those who work or live with people from other cultures. The term *culture shock* describes the feelings of alienation, disorientation, and confusion that one experiences when operating in a foreign culture. A closer look shows us that:

1. Culture shock is really the cross-cultural adjustment process that an individual experiences in order to function effectively without alienation in a setting that does not recognize some or all of the assumptions and behavioral patterns that he or she takes for granted.

2. Culture shock affects both the newcomer to the culture and the resident who interacts with someone from another cultural background.

3. This adaptation process varies from one individual to another.

4. The adjustment is a continuous, ongoing process that never ends.

5. *All* realities are changed by the process — that is, the setting as much as the individuals living and/or working there.

6. The successful process allows the individual to achieve personal goals and find satisfaction while fulfilling the expectations of the larger societal structure.

7. There is a fine line between adjustment and alienation when functioning in a cross-cultural setting.

8. A major concern for any culture is how to encourage individual expression while maintaining the right degree of uniformity and stability.

9. All individuals and organizations have their own definitions of *adjusted* and *nonadjusted.*

10. Successful adaptation requires the practice of conflict resolution.

The following hypothetical situation illustrates how these components interact: Suppose you suddenly become the only female player on a previously all-male basketball team. It would not be enough for you to learn only the rules of men's basketball. You would need to adjust also to the behaviors, values, attitudes, and norms expected of players on the team, regardless of their sex. Your first time in the locker room might be very traumatic as you experience a conflict between your conditioning as a female regarding modesty and the locker-room antics of the male members of the team.

You would not be the only one to feel discomfort or anxiety. The males would also have to adjust to the new situation caused by your presence. Although they might not necessarily change any of their behaviors, the "invasion" of someone from an "alien" (in this case, female) culture, would force them to experience the conflict between two culturally determined ways "to be" a basketball player. Nevertheless, the onus of adjustment would primarily be on you as the newcomer. The larger society changes less than its individual members do. To adapt to your new environment, you must learn to resolve the conflicts that arise in order to derive satisfaction from your new situation.

This analogy is fairly accurate in describing what happens when a Hispanic client comes to you for professional services. The "team" — in this case, the workplace — has become accustomed to following certain rules, ways of operating, and norms for the behavior of its clients. When a new "player" walks in with a different set of rules and expectations regarding the interaction about to take place, the scene is set for culture shock for both the Hispanic client and the Anglo professional. Of course, past experiences for both will shape the interaction. A client who has sought services before from the same or a similar agency or a professional who has served

Hispanic clients from the same cultural background will be less affected by culture shock. Nonetheless, cultural adjustment is an ongoing process for all involved, for the newcomers who seek services as well as the natives who dispense them, regardless of previous experience. The potential for growth, learning, and resolving conflicts in a way that leaves both communication partners satisfied and understood is ever present when people from different cultures interact.

It is essential to the effectiveness of the cross-cultural communication between Anglo professionals and their Hispanic clients to recognize that *both*, to some degree, experience culture shock. Both are prone to the symptomatic feelings of confusion, bewilderment, frustration, and uneasiness. If not acknowledged, these feelings can interfere with the client's success in seeking needed services and with that of the professional in providing them in a way that engenders trust and satisfaction.

Unfortunately, few individuals who work with Hispanic clients are trained to master the process of cross-cultural communication with which they are constantly confronted. The lack of awareness of the complexity of the task and the opportunity for personal growth and self-actualization it offers leave such professionals feeling stuck with the emotional reactions of culture shock, with no remedies at hand. If they are feeling threatened and insecure, they may behave in a defensive, resistant, and hostile manner toward their Hispanic clients. This is fertile breeding ground for the growth of stereotypes and stress. Such situations endanger the well-being of the professional, the client, the agency where the interaction occurs, and the society at large.

A more constructive way to deal with culture shock is to acknowledge it as the process of adjustment of both parties involved in the cross-cultural interaction. Of course, the newcomer bears the greater burden in this regard, since every aspect of daily living in the new culture requires continuous adaptation. Even such apparently routine matters as taking a bus, mailing a letter, making a telephone call, paying a bill, or buying a loaf of bread require conscious effort to learn the new culture's mores. Only after living in another culture in a role other than that of tourist can one truly appreciate the emotional toll such constant adjustment takes.

Added to the new cultural experiences is the reality of functioning in a new language environment. The stress that results from this highly charged emotional experience tends, in general, to constrict muscles and the operation of the nervous system. This, in turn, compounds the difficulties of speaking a new language. If you think back to the first time you had to say something in Spanish, even pronouncing a Hispanic client's name, you will empathize more easily. The more tense you are, the harder it is to form new sounds and remember the words you need.

Once you understand how difficult it is to adjust as a foreigner to the new culture, you can extend more empathy to your clients and assume your responsibility in the process of cultural adaptation involved in providing services to Hispanic clients. By taking the time to explain the procedures by which services are offered, what you personally will do, and what is expected of clients in return, you will aid their understanding of the workings of this one aspect of the new culture.

Your responsibility, however, does not end here. The procedures by which you operate are not necessarily the "correct" ones — they are simply those decided on by other human beings as the most appropriate for your organization. There is always room for flexibility and change. Sometimes the needs of individual clients may require some alteration of procedures in order to adequately provide services to them.

By knowing something about the clients' backgrounds as reflected in those values, attitudes, assumptions, beliefs, norms, and behaviors defined as *Hispanic culture,* you may find a better or easier way to provide services for them. You can then integrate this knowledge into a course of action which is most suitable to the task at hand.

Remember, *both* perceptions of reality will, of necessity, be changed to some degree by the process of cross-cultural communication. The result is a totally new version of reality which can leave both employees and clients better adjusted and less alienated from each other. The key is to resolve the conflicts presented by cultural differences in a way that leaves both sides satisfied. In subsequent chapters you will be given techniques that use the culture shock or adjustment process as a constructive, creative opportunity for growth and personal satisfaction.

The following diagram outlines how the experience of culture shock can be transformed into the constructive process of adjustment. It reflects a learning process that begins with *knowledge*, which is applied to the development of *skills*, which then affect certain *values* and *assumptions* that are expressed by observable *behaviors*.

Key learning areas	*Culture shock*	*Adjustment process*
Knowledge	To become aware of the existence of culture shock and its consequences	To understand some of the key aspects of the adjustment process
Skills	To be able to recognize culture shock and its symptoms	To be able to apply a set of core skills in order to ease the adjustment process
Values/assumptions	Culture shock exists and affects our attitudes, behavior, and performance	The adjustment process can be eased and used to an advantage
Behaviors	To avoid, to flee, to fight, to become too dependent, and to adjust are possible coping strategies	To demonstrate a capacity to select the right reactions when confronted with an unusual or ambiguous situation

Applications

Four people volunteer to form a group or "culture," in this case an agency providing a service, using only nonverbal interaction. A fifth volunteers to be the "outsider" and leaves the room while the other four decide on the "rules" governing the obtaining of the service. The remaining students function as observers. (It is best to have the four seated in a circle with the observers forming a larger circle around them.) The group decides the following:

1. Which concrete object represents the "service" provided by the agency

2. The role of each member of the group in dispersing the service

3. The "correct" way of getting the service (who refers the "client" to whom, when, how, etc.)

4. One *physical* way to show unity as a group

5. One acceptable way for a newcomer to break through the physical unity of the group in order to be accepted as a seeker of the service

The fifth volunteer returns and, through trial and error, approaches each member of the group until he or she finds the right person to initiate the procedure for obtaining the service. The trial-and-error method continues until the seeker obtains the service.

Reflections

1. If you were one of the four group members, how did you feel about the outsider?

2. If you were the outsider, how did you feel as you tried to "break the code" and get the service?

3. If you were an observer, did you find yourself empathizing with the outsider or the group members? What did you observe happening among the group members? Between the group members and the outsider?

4. How does this relate to the phenomenon of culture shock as experienced in the cross-cultural communication process involved between Anglo professionals and their Hispanic clients?

5. Have you ever traveled or lived outside the United States? Did you experience culture shock? Describe what you felt and the circumstances that triggered the feelings. How did you resolve the situation?

6. What evidence of culture shock have your Hispanic clients demonstrated when seeking services at your agency? What has been (or could be) done to ease their adjustment process? What evidence of culture shock on the part of the employees dispersing services to Hispanics have you observed? What coping mechanisms have been employed? How successful have they been?

HISTORICAL PERSPECTIVE: The family and other
support systems

Hispanics everywhere enjoy a legacy of strong family and friendship ties. These are inherited from the social systems of both the indigenous populations and Spanish-speaking colonizers. Despite the effects of migration within Hispanic countries and immigration to the United States, family ties remain strongly rooted in the culturally determined value system. The sustained support of the family for those individual members of the household who are forced by economic or political need to leave loved ones and homeland in search of a better life is as much a part of the Hispanic heritage as the Spanish language or Christianity.

The family unit in Spain has always been a strong one. The reliance of family members on each other for material support, counsel, and aid extends far back into history. This support system includes both the extended family and friends as well as the special ties engendered in the *compadrazgo* system, through which family members or friends become godparents to a child. The par-

ents and the godparents now are *coparents* (*compadres* and *comadres*) with a special kinship bond between them, just as there is between the child and his or her *padrino* (godfather) and *madrina* (godmother).

At the time of the colonization of Latin America, Spain still followed the primogeniture system of bequeathing the father's entire estate to the first-born son. This forced the younger sons to seek alternative ways of making their fortune. The primary motivation of many of the original colonizers and settlers of Latin America was precisely this need to establish themselves outside of the family economic structure while maintaining close emotional ties.

Through the colonization process, the legacy of the strong family-based Spanish social ties became interwoven with the communal social system that typified the more highly developed indigenous populations in Latin America. Each member of society had a specific role to play. In return, the society met all the individual's basic needs. All members of the community shared the common purpose of sustaining and developing the welfare of the society as a whole. Though based on a strong hierarchy with rather rigid social class delineations, the system engendered a sense of harmony and serenity. Since these civilizations were based on religious beliefs which governed their socio-political organization, following the established guidelines to achieve one's purpose in life brought fulfillment on both the material and the spiritual planes.

1. *What are the origins of the strong sense of family ties common to Hispanic cultures?*
2. *How were these ties strengthened by the communal lifestyle typical of many of the indigenous populations of Latin America?*

This combined heritage explains the values that typify most Hispanic families. A Hispanic is more likely to be defined first as a member of a given family rather than by his or her individual identity. The concept of *self* most often takes a back seat to the concept of *family representative*. One's actions reflect on the family's reputation as much as, if not more than, on one's own. An individual's behavior is circumscribed by the fear of bringing disgrace or dishonor to the family. Personal needs are given less priority than those of the family unit.

In exchange for this loyalty and responsibility, the individual relies on the family to provide material and moral support. Whether in need of financial assistance or emotional sustenance, an individual is expected to turn first to the family. Rarely, if ever, will the family refuse to meet these needs. To be unable to succor or support family members in need is an affront to the family's collective sense of pride and dignity.

3. *What is the relationship between* self *and* family *in the Hispanic cultures?*
4. *What does the Hispanic family offer its individual members?*

The Anglo society's dependence on impersonal institutions and agencies to provide mate-

rial aid and emotional support is at odds with the culturally defined role of the Hispanic family. The sense of independence and personal pride in making it on one's own that typify the U.S. social and economic structure conflict with the Hispanic hierarchy of values, in which the family's welfare receives top priority. Many professionals providing services to Hispanics living in the United States see the symbiotic relationship among family members as pathological overdependence when viewed from the perspective of the Anglo culture. They are often bewildered and frustrated when they observe Hispanics with limited economic means sending money to family members back home or sharing their scarce resources with relatives and friends who are even more in need.

Anglo professionals often criticize other family practices that are defined by Hispanic cultural values. An individual whose behavior brings disgrace or dishonor to the family name may be disowned by the family, and the family may refuse to participate in efforts to rehabilitate the deviant individual.

At the other extreme, when an individual member suffers a crisis at the hands of fate, family members rally to the cause. Illness, accidents, death, acts of God, and other calamities elicit the support of the entire family. Anglo professionals in hospitals or other agencies providing services to these victims of tragedies often express frustration due to their futile efforts to keep the family "out of the way." The Anglo hospital rule of two visitors per patient conflicts with the need of the entire family to lend moral support with their physical presence to loved ones in pain. Of course, joyous events such as weddings, baptisms, and celebrations of all kinds also bring the family together in full force. Children of all ages are included both in the celebration of happy events and in the sadness that accompanies tragedies.

5. *How do the Anglo and Hispanic cultures differ with regard to the relationship between the individual and the family?*
6. *What behaviors of Hispanic families are often misunderstood by Anglo professionals?*

The interrelationship among extended family members and *compadrazgo* ties are also often misunderstood by Anglos. Although the norm of both the Anglo nuclear and the Hispanic extended family is changing because of such sociological phenomena as divorce and geographic mobility, the two cultures still reflect different concepts of what constitutes *the family*. Hispanics consider grandparents, aunts and uncles, cousins and *compadres* as part of the family support system. The relationships within this extended family unit are intimate — the only way to describe a relationship as *close* in Spanish is to declare the person to be *como familia* (like family). It is not uncommon to have a household consisting of the nuclear family plus one or more relatives, including unmarried aunts, cousins, sisters, or grandparents. Relatives and close friends who have recently arrived in the United States may spend months or years at the home of a family member until financially able to establish their own household.

The *compadrazgo* system is a particularly strong bond. The most common way to become a *compadre* or *comadre* is to serve as a sponsor at the baptism of a child. Although the *compadres* promise to raise the child as their own in case of the death or other tragedy of the parents, the real relationship is between the adults — parents and coparents. Accepting the privilege of being a *compadre* brings with it the responsibility common to blood relatives. A father might ask the child's *padrino* for a loan, a place to stay, or help in finding a job. A mother might ask the child's *madrina* for advice on housekeeping or on wifely duties, or for food or money to tide the family over until the next payday.

Friendships (*amistades*) are also important elements of the Hispanic's support system. They may take time to develop, but the bonds are there for life. Some Hispanics are puzzled by the immediate closeness and intimate details of their life that Anglos seem to share quite readily, even with virtual strangers. Such *confianza* (intimate rapport) is never established overnight. Once a friendship bond is formed, the commitment is similar to that shared by the extended family. It affords the same privileges and responsibilities.

Refusing a friend in need, despite the personal sacrifice it might entail, is a rare phenomenon.

---

7. *Describe the importance of the* compadrazgo *support system.*
8. *How are friendships formed in Hispanic cultures, and what role do they play in the life of the individual?*

One instance of how the extended family and friendship network fulfills a society need that is handled by formal institutions in the Anglo culture is seen in the *hogar de crianza,* a practice common in the Spanish-speaking Caribbean. This is an informal adoption process through which a family member or friend will raise a child whose parents either cannot provide an adequate home life or need to be away from the home for an unspecified length of time. Although similar to the foster home concept in the Anglo society, it differs in that the child is not uprooted from the larger network of family and friends. In addition, the arrangement is not formalized through the courts or other civil institutions. Nor is the person who cares for the child formally remunerated, although the parents may, at times, offer whatever financial assistance they can. The *hogar de crianza* is illustrative of the sharing and caring based on kinship and friendship in times of need.

Other support systems abound in the Hispanic cultures and have been transplanted to U.S. soil. The local grocery store (*tienda de abarrotes* in Mexico, *bodega* in Cuba, and *colmado* in Puerto Rico) is a mainstay in Spanish-speaking neighborhoods. Here the owner provides native foods (often at higher prices because of lower volume), newspapers, information regarding local events and people, and, often, credit. This social center is as much a place to make contact with friends and neighbors as it is to purchase needed items for daily living.

Religion provides another source of support to many Hispanics. Although the majority are Christian, not all are Catholic. In recent years Protestant, Pentecostal, and other fundamentalist denominations have been increasing their membership. They are particularly successful in attracting U.S. Hispanics who find Catholic and other Christian rituals rather conservative and alienating in their emphasis on doctrine. The Pentecostal churches especially, like the Charismatic movement within the Catholic church, provide an atmosphere of community participation, with an emphasis on music and personal spiritual expression. The Catholic churches provide some outlet for community involvement through such organizations as *Los Caballeros del Santo Nombre* (Knights of the Holy Name), *Las Damas del Rosario* (The Ladies of the Rosary), and *Las Hijas de María* (Daughters of Mary). Almost all churches located in Spanish-speaking areas of the United States are involved in serving the community, particularly with regard to basic needs such as food and shelter, in addition to pastoral counseling. It is not uncommon for priests and ministers to become involved in aiding their Hispanic parishioners with political and social issues regarding human rights.

The *espiritistas, curanderos,* and *santeros,* traditional folk healers, also serve as an alternative source for dealing with physical and psychological problems. In addition, they often offer counseling with respect to marital, family, and other personal relationships.

Hispanic cultures provide a wealth of inherent systems to take care of human needs. In coming to the United States, Hispanics may find that the values on which these systems are built clash, at times, with the Anglo emphasis on the development of the individual and the reliance on more formal institutions and agencies that provide services to meet those needs. A balance can be met, however. Anglo professionals who are aware of the various culturally defined support systems might be able to incorporate them into the services they provide. Hispanics, on the other hand, might learn more about how the Anglo system could meet some needs while not conflicting with their cultural values. Unless attempts are made to merge the two systems, frustration, confusion, and misunderstandings will hinder the adequate delivery of services to Hispanics living in the United States.

---

9. *What other support systems exist in Hispanic cultures?*
10. *How can an awareness of the Hispanic support systems aid you in the delivery of services to your Hispanic clients?*

NONVERBAL COMMUNICATION: Children's behavior

Children are considered one of the greatest resources in the Hispanic world. Their upbringing reflects all aspects of cultural conditioning, since it is as children that individuals learn to conform to the norms of the society into which they are born.

The way children are raised in Hispanic cultures is a reflection of both social-class differences and the male–female dichotomy. In upper- and middle-class families, children tend to be more pampered than in the lower classes, where often they are considered an important economic resource and may need to go to work at an early age. In all economic classes, however, girls are protected more than boys and are encouraged to stay close to home and to learn domestic chores. Little boys, on the other hand, are taught to develop their macho image from infancy. They are allowed more freedom in their comings and goings, especially after the onset of puberty.

The Hispanic home is often described as child-centered, since both parents tend to be indulgent and permissive with younger children. Yet disrespectful or frivolous behavior is not tolerated either within the home or with authority figures outside the family structure. Proper behavior when in the presence of elders is learned at a very early age in the Hispanic household. Silence, shyness, avoidance of direct eye contact, and passivity are nonverbal ways that Hispanic children show respect for adults.

Both boys and girls are expected to assume some responsibilities within the home. These may range from taking care of younger brothers or sisters to actually working outside the home, in the fields in rural areas or in menial, low-paying jobs in the city. Often these activities are truly needed for the support and well-being of the entire family. As is the case with the other members of the family, the welfare of the family unit is more important than that of the individual members. There appears to be less sibling rivalry in the Hispanic family, perhaps because of the emphasis placed on the status attached to fulfilling one's special role in the family unit.

Contrary to what many Anglos may believe, Hispanic parents highly value education and the opportunities it presents. What often happens is that the public school system in the United States is seen as a threat to the family unity that is the cornerstone of security in the Hispanic cultures. The distance between Hispanic children educated in the Anglo system and their parents grows much larger than the normal generation gap experienced by all parents and their children. The gains afforded the individual in the Anglo educational system can result in losses for the family, with children becoming "foreigners" to their own parents.

Hispanic children in the United States face many conflicts when confronted with the differences between the values taught in the Anglo school system and those learned at home. One of the most striking contradictions is that between the more authoritarian structure of the home environment and the more democratic ideals taught in the schools. Here again, the emphasis on the individual's goals and aspirations is at odds with the higher priority Hispanics place on the good of the family unit. Often, Anglo teachers find Hispanic children unaggressive and uncompetitive. The values of cooperation learned at home may be transferred to the classroom setting, as when Hispanic children share information and help each other follow directions and perform learning activities. The teacher, accustomed to the more individualistic, competitive classroom behavior of Anglo students, may misinterpret such behavior as cheating.

The language factor contributes further to the difficulties Hispanic children encounter in the Anglo school system. Those from Spanish-dominant households may be ridiculed or embarrassed for not speaking correct English or for speaking it with a strong accent. Their limited practice in English may result in frustration at their inability to share their more intimate thoughts and feelings with their Anglo schoolmates. In schools that do not have a true bilingual program — one with instruction in *both* English and Spanish — they may experience conflicts in the Spanish as a Second Language classroom. Often they are criticized for their colloquial speech patterns and lack of grammatical expertise by teachers unfamiliar with the dialectal variations common to those from different Spanish-speaking backgrounds.

Such conflicts can erode the self-esteem of

Hispanic children, especially in schools with few Spanish-speaking role models. Often the self-identity problem is aggravated if the child's name is translated into English, with Carlos called Charles and Ana, Ann by the classroom teacher. Many respond to the conflicts by choosing to speak only English in order to avoid further embarrassment or ridicule. This can further impede communication in the home if the parents are not comfortable speaking English. Parents, moreover, may worry that their children are losing other aspects of their Hispanic heritage, since language is one of the strongest elements of cultural solidarity.

Another conflict arises when Hispanic boys encounter many female teachers in the schools. They often have a difficult time relating to Anglo women whose behavior may be so radically different from that of the Hispanic women in their lives. This is especially true with authoritarian, businesslike women who do not display the warmth and nurturing the Hispanic boy has come to expect from women through his experiences in the home environment. Although the child may have a difficult time taking a woman seriously who is in a position of authority, the situation may become more volatile if the female teacher dismisses his macho behavior as cute or criticizes him for being disrespectful.

Hispanic girls encounter other conflicts in the Anglo school system. They may view their need for an education as secondary to their future role as wife and mother. Absenteeism may result if the girl is needed at home to care for younger brothers and sisters during a family crisis. She may also miss school if her brother–protector does not attend because of illness or other family obligations. After the age of puberty, girls and their virtue are protected very strictly. Fathers may prefer that their daughters cut short their education rather than run the risk of their being too highly influenced by the more relaxed dating patterns and contact with boys that Anglo teenage girls enjoy.

The high increase of teenage pregnancy among low-income Hispanics in the United States is attributable to many factors. The Hispanic male adolescent, who has been taught to exert his machismo from an early age, often pressures his girlfriend(s) to engage in sex in order to prove his manhood. The teenage female, on the other hand, is faced with both the narrow options for women prescribed by Hispanic cultures and the lack of frank discussion of sex and birth control given girls in the Hispanic home. Even though premarital sex is highly discouraged for Hispanic women, pregnancy, in effect, redeems the loss of virtue and raises the young woman to the most revered status available to her — motherhood. Starting her own family is an instant avenue to adulthood and an exit from parental restrictions that may conflict with the greater freedom allowed women in the Anglo society.

Perhaps the greatest challenge facing Hispanic children who live in the United States is that of finding out who they are as they try to integrate two different cultures with disparate lifestyles. The identity crisis faced by all adolescents is particularly complex for Hispanic youth. The predominance of strong group ties among young teens, particularly males, is, in part, an attempt to resolve some of the conflicts presented by their bicultural experience. The problems faced are compounded by low socioeconomic status, high unemployment, and racial discrimination that many Hispanic youths encounter in the Anglo society. Because of their generally greater exposure and experience in English-speaking environments, children often become the bridges between their Hispanic parents and the Anglo culture. The most common expression of this intermediary role is that of interpreter when the Spanish-speaking parent must interact with the Anglo-speaking society. This places the Hispanic child in a very precarious position, caught in the middle between two authority figures, a parent and an English-speaking professional. Each may ask the child to relay a message that results in a conflict with the values of courtesy, good manners, and respect learned since infancy. The Spanish-speaking parent may encourage the child to be more assertive in presenting the problem than is natural for a young Hispanic who interacts with an authority figure. The Anglo professional may want the child to ask the parent a rather intimate personal question or to reprimand the parent for some inappropriate behavior, both of which would seem rude and disrespectful to the youth. The emotional conflict inherent in such a situation is difficult for the child to resolve. Deliberate misinterpretation or silence may result.

Often professionals unaware of such Hispanic cultural values as *respeto* and *cortesía* compound the problem by virtually ignoring the non-English-speaking parent and communicating directly and exclusively with the child. This is an affront to the dignity of the parent, particularly that of the father. Such insensitive behavior can force the child–interpreter to assume a role reserved for adults in the Hispanic culture while, at the same time, witnessing the parent's loss of pride and personal dignity. The emotional consequences may be even greater when a daughter acts as interpreter for her father.

Using any interpreter greatly diminishes the personal contact that is so crucial for establishing rapport in the Hispanic culture. When children serve as interpreters for their parents, the emotional trauma they may experience may impede the communication between the professional and the client to an even greater extent. An awareness of the culturally charged role of the child–interpreter can help to lessen the potential risks inherent in this less than perfect way of communicating with Hispanic clients.

Putting it into practice

1. Describe the contact you have with Hispanic children in your professional capacity.

2. What specific culturally determined behaviors of Hispanic children have you observed that have affected or could affect the cross-cultural communication process?

3. Describe the potential misunderstandings that may arise from the culturally based behaviors of the Hispanic children involved in the following situations:

   a. A ten-year-old Hispanic boy who is being reprimanded by a female Anglo teacher for talking with a Hispanic girl in the class during an examination.

   b. A twelve-year-old Hispanic male who is being questioned by a female Anglo police officer for "hanging out" on the corner with a group of Hispanic youth thought to be a "gang."

   c. A thirteen-year-old Hispanic girl who thinks she may be pregnant. Her father has brought her to an Anglo male doctor's office to be examined.

   d. An eight-year-old Hispanic girl who is serving as an interpreter for her mother, who needs the birth certificate of a son born in a common-law marriage with a man who is not the girl's biological father.

4. Now role-play the situations described here with other members of the class, using nonverbal communication as much as possible.

Comunicándose en español

PRONUNCIACIÓN: Las consonantes b, v, p 🔲

In Spanish, the letters **b** and **v** are pronounced alike. Just as some Spanish speakers who have learned English have a difficult time distinguishing between the two different sounds represented by these letters in their new language, English speakers learning Spanish may find it takes a great deal of practice to overcome the tendency to pronounce **b** and **v** differently. The following rules govern the pronunciation of both **b** and **v**:

1. At the beginning of a breath group and after **m** and **n**, the **b** and **v** are similar to the English *b* in *boy*; both lips meet and stop the flow of air. This is called a *stop* **b**. However, no aspiration (puff of air) accompanies the separation of the lips to form the sound as it does in English. (Note: *n* before *b* is pronounced like *m*.)

voy	bien	banco	hombre	un bebé
venga	veinte	viernes	hembra	un varón

2. In all other instances, which include the majority of cases, **b** and **v** in Spanish are pronounced differently from **b** in English. Although both lips meet in the corners of the mouth, they do not come together to block the flow of air, but instead let it flow through. The sound is *not* formed by both lips meeting and stopping the flow of air (as in no. 1) or by the upper teeth meeting the lower lips as in English *v* but by the partially closed lips. This is called a *fricative* **b**.

abuela	cabeza	abogado	el bebé	está bien
nueve	avenida	sirve	la verdad	nos vemos

   Spanish **p** is similar to the English *p* as in *spoil*. No aspiration accompanies the Spanish **p** as it does in English when *p* does not follow *s*. (To illustrate the phenomenon of aspiration, pronounce *paper* in English while holding your hand in front of your mouth. You will notice the explosive release of air when the *p* is pronounced. It takes practice to learn *not* to release the air when pronouncing Spanish **p**.)

peor	padres	esposa	problema	apartamento
poco	parece	papá	posible	comprometido

   The only difference between Spanish **b/v** and **p** is that the former sound is *voiced* (vocal cords vibrate) whereas the **p** is not. You may have difficulty distinguishing between these two sounds because: (1) both the stop **b** and **p** are pronounced by the closing of the lips, and (2) you no longer hear the puff of air that has helped you distinguish English *b* and *p*. Pronounce the following:

boca/poca	beso/peso	baño/paño

Práctica 🔲

Pronounce the following sentences in Spanish. It may help to underline those instances of **b** and **v** pronounced with the lips slightly open:

1. Mi esposa y yo vivimos en la avenida Vargas.
2. Voy a visitar a un vecino, el señor Varela.
3. Mis padres no se sienten bien en el nuevo apartamento.
4. Nos vemos el viernes que viene.
5. El trabajador social está preocupado por el problema.
6. Bernarda, ¿puedes venir aquí mañana a las nueve y veinte?

Dictado 🔲

Now write the words and sentences your instructor dictates:

1. _____   3. _____   5. _____

2. _____   4. _____   6. _____

7. _____

8. _____

9. _____

Mrs. Martínez? I'm Doctor Johnson.

Mucho gusto, doctor.

Oh, you don't speak English?

No, no speak. Mi hijo habla inglés. Dile eso, Ramón

She says I'll speak for her.

Good. Now, the problem?

Mamá, el doctor quiere saber cuál es el problema.

Dile que tengo mucho dolor en la barriga y que estoy sangrando mucho.

She says she has stomach pains and is bleeding a lot.

Where, from the urethra or the vagina?

Ramón, ask her where she's bleeding from.

Ramón, ¿qué dice? ¡Dime!

Ramón, do you understand the question?

No lo entiendo, mamá.

Yes.

Well, ask her.

Ramón, ¿qué dice el doctor? Dile que te lo explique.

Mamá, no puedo. ¡No puedo!

Well, Ramón, if you won't ask her, I'll just have to examine her. Tell her to get undressed.

236

¿Ha entendido bien?

1. ¿Qué idioma(s) habla Ramón?
2. ¿Qué edad tiene Ramón?
3. ¿Se comunican bien el doctor y la señora Martínez? Explique su respuesta.
4. ¿Quién sirve de intérprete (*acts as an interpreter*)?
5. ¿Por qué no contesta Ramón la pregunta del doctor?
6. ¿Qué le pregunta la señora Martínez a su hijo?
7. ¿Por qué no le hace Ramón la pregunta a su mamá?
8. ¿Cómo se siente la señora? ¿El doctor? ¿Ramón?
9. ¿Sirve Ud. de intérprete a veces en su trabajo?
10. ¿A Ud. le es fácil o difícil ser intérprete? ¿Por qué?

INTRODUCTORY DIALOGUE: The interpreter

Dr. Johnson: ********

Woman: Nice to meet you, doctor.

Dr. J: ********

W: No, I don't speak. My son speaks English. Tell him that, Ramón.

Ramon: ********

Dr. J: ********

R: Mamá, the doctor wants to know what the problem is.

W: Tell him I have a lot of pain in my stomach and that I am bleeding a great deal.

R: ********

Dr. J: ********

Dr. J: ********

W: Ramón, what is he saying? Tell me!

R: I don't understand him.

Dr. J: ********

R: ********

Dr. J: ********

W: Ramón what's the doctor saying? Tell him to explain it to you.

R: Mamá, I can't. I can't!

Dr. J: ********

The employee (f.)	*The client (m.)*
Mr. Echeverría, you recently moved, didn't you? Well, I need some information on your new home. Where is your house?	Yes, I changed houses. The new one is larger than the old one. It is on Quincy Avenue, near Saint Ann's Church.
That is the Linda Vista area, right?	It is not too far from there, but it is really (better yet it is found) in the San José area. But I have many friends that live in the Linda Vista area.
Do you live in a house or in an apartment?	It is ⎰ a small house. / the first floor of a three-story building. / an apartment.
Is the house yours or are you renting it?	We are ⎰ buying it. / renting it.
How much do you pay for the ⎰ mortgage? / rent?	We pay three hundred and fifty per month.
Is the house insured?	Yes, the insurance costs us sixty dollars per month.
How much do they charge you for taxes on the house?	More or less seventeen hundred per year. / The owner of the house pays them.

¿Sabe usted?

1. To nominalize (make a noun out of) an adjective, place the appropriate definite article in front of it: **la nueva** = *the new one* (f.).

2. **Quedar** (*to remain*) and **encontrar(se)** (*to find/to be found*) are commonly used as synonyms for **estar** with the meaning of *to be located*.

3. **Planta baja** is the common term for *ground floor*. **El primer piso** refers to *the first story* — i.e., what is called *the second floor* in English.

4. **Más bien** (*rather, actually*) is used to indicate more specific information.

5. **La renta** (*the rent*) and **rentar** (*to rent*) are commonly used anglicisms.

Notas lingüísticas I

A. **Estar** + gerund (the **-ndo** form of the verb, the equivalent of *-ing* in English) is used to emphasize actions in progress. In general, Spanish prefers simple present tense even where English uses the progressive forms for habitual actions:

Siempre habla por teléfono. (habitual action)	He is always talking (He always talks) on the phone.
Está hablando por teléfono. (in progress)	He is talking on the phone.

La empleada	*El cliente*
Señor Echeverría, hace poco Ud. se mudó, ¿verdad? Pues, me hace falta cierta información sobre su nuevo hogar. ¿Dónde queda la casa?	Sí, cambié de casa. La nueva es más grande que la vieja. Queda en la avenida Quincy, cerca de la Iglesia Santa Ana.
Ése es el barrio Linda Vista, ¿verdad?	No queda muy lejos de allá, pero más bien se encuentra en el barrio San José. Pero tengo muchas amistades que viven en Linda Vista.
¿Viven Uds. en una casa o en un apartamento?	Es { una casa pequeña. / la planta baja de un edificio de tres pisos. / un apartamento.
¿Es suya la casa o la alquilan?	La { estamos comprando. / estamos alquilando.
¿Cuánto pagan de { hipoteca? / alquiler?	Pagamos trescientos cincuenta al mes.
¿Está asegurada la casa?	Sí, el seguro nos cuesta sesenta dólares al mes.
¿Cuánto les cobran en impuestos sobre la casa?	{ Más o menos mil setecientos al año. / El dueño de la casa los paga.

To form the gerund of **-ar** verbs, drop the **-ar** ending of the infinitive and add **-ando**; for **-er** and **-ir** verbs, drop that ending and add **-iendo**. Only **-ir** *stem-changing* verbs change from **e → i** and **o → u** in this form.

trabajar − ar + -ando = trabajando
entender − er + -iendo = entendiendo
escribir − ir + -iendo = escribiendo
p*e*dir − ir + -iendo = p*i*diendo
d*o*rmir − ir + -iendo = d*u*rmiendo

B. **Mío** = *mine*, **nuestro** = *ours*, **tuyo** = *yours* (familiar), **suyo** = *his, hers, theirs, yours*, (formal and plural) are special possessive adjectives. They have four forms to agree with the object possessed in gender and number and are used when the ownership of an object is emphasized in the sentence:

1. *After* a noun, they are the equivalent of *of mine, of yours*, etc.:

   una amiga mía   a friend of mine

2. After **ser**, they are used to identify ownership of the object.

   ¿Son tuyos estos papeles?   **No, no son míos; son de Ana.**
   Are these papers yours?   No, they're not mine; they're Ana's.

3. **Suyo,** like the short possessive form **su,** can refer to something belonging to **él, ella, usted, ellos, ellas, ustedes.** For emphasis or clarity **de** + the appropriate pronoun is used:

   ¿Es suya la casa?   **No, no es mía; es de ella.**
   Is the house yours?   No, it's not mine; it's hers.

BASIC STRUCTURES II: More on home life

The employee (f.)	*The client (m.)*
How many rooms are there?	There are six: the living room, the kitchen, the dining room, three bedrooms, and two bathrooms.
Does the {house / apartment} come furnished?	No, all the furniture is mine.
Are the electric appliances yours, too?	Well, the {stove / dryer / washing machine} is mine. the {refrigerator / dishwasher / freezer} is mine.
When did you buy {it (f.)? / it (m.)?}	I bought {it (f.) / it (m.)} two years ago.
Who sold {it (f.) / it (m.)} to you?	The former owner of the house sold {it (f.) / it (m.)} to me.
Did you buy {it (f.) / it (m.)} with cash or on the installment plan?	I bought {it (f.) / it (m.)} with a credit card.
Do you need any furniture or appliances?	I need {an armchair. / a couch. / a television. / an air conditioner. / a table. / a crib. / a sewing machine. / a vacuum cleaner.} some {chairs / beds / lamps.}
Is the house in good condition?	The {kitchen sink / bathtub / toilet / plumbing} doesn't work well. The {ceiling (roof) / heating system} isn't good for anything.
How much does the {telephone / gas / electricity} cost you?	It's not very expensive. It varies between thirty and fifty per month.
Is any (one) of the bills outstanding?	No, they are all {up to date. / current.}
Do you like the {house? / apartment?}	How could I not like it? It's my home.

La empleada	*El cliente*
¿Cuántos cuartos hay?	Hay seis: la sala, la cocina, el comedor, tres dormitorios y dos baños.
¿Viene { amueblada la casa? / amueblado el apartamento?	No, todos los muebles son míos.
¿Los aparatos eléctricos también son suyos?	Pues, { la { estufa / secadora / lavadora } es mía. / el { refrigerador / lavaplatos / congelador } es mío. }
¿Cuándo { la / lo } compró Ud.?	{ La / Lo } compré hace dos años.
¿Quién se { la / lo } vendió?	Me { la / lo } vendió el antiguo dueño de la casa.
¿{ La / Lo } compró al contado o a plazos?	{ La / Lo } compré con tarjeta de crédito.
¿Le hacen falta algunos muebles o aparatos eléctricos?	Me hace falta { un { sillón. / sofá. / televisor. / acondicionador de aire. } / una { mesa. / cuna. / máquina de coser. / aspiradora. } }
	Me hacen falta unas { sillas. / camas. / lámparas. }
¿Está en buenas condiciones la casa?	Pues, no funciona bien { el fregadero. / la bañera. / el inodoro. / la tubería. }
	No sirve para nada { el techo. / la calefacción. }
¿Cuánto les cuesta { el teléfono? / el gas? / la electricidad? }	{ No es muy caro/a. / Varía entre treinta y cincuenta al mes. }
¿Está atrasada alguna de las cuentas?	No, todas están { al día. / corrientes. }
¿Le gusta { la casa? / el apartamento? }	¿Cómo no me va a gustar? Es mi hogar.

¿Sabe usted?

1. The names for rooms of the house and furnishings often vary among Spanish dialects. The following is a list of common variations:

bedroom	**recámara** (M.A.), **pieza** (M.), **alcoba** (Sp.), **cuarto de dormir, habitación** (various dialects), **dormitorio** (various dialects)
bedspread	**cubrecama** (C.), **colcha** (P.R.), **sobrecama** (various dialects)
blanket	**colcha** (C.), **cobija** (M.A.), **frisa** (P.R.), **manta** (various dialects)
bathroom	**excusado** (M.A.), **cuarto de baño** (P.R.), **servicio** (various dialects)
bathtub	**tina** (M.), **bañadera** (C.), **bañera** (P.R.)
washbasin	**lavamanos** (M.A., P.R.), **bandeja** (C., M.), **lavabo** (various dialects)
armchair	**butaca** (C., P.R.), **sillón** (M.A. and various dialects)
closet	**ropero** (C., M.), **guardarropa** (various dialects), **armario** (various dialects), **clóset** (Anglicism)
refrigerator	**nevera** (P.R.), **hielera** (M.A.), **frigorífico** and **refrigeradora** (various dialects)
stove	**estufa** (C., P.R.), **cocina** (various dialects)
faucet	**grifo** and **llave (de agua)** (various dialects), **pila** (C.), **pluma (de agua)** (P.R.)
appliances	**enseres eléctricos** (P.R.), **aparatos eléctricos** (various dialects)

2. You may also hear **la luz** for **la electricidad** and **el caliente** for **la calefacción.**

3. Commonly heard anglicisms include **la furnitura** (*los muebles*), **furnido** (*amueblado*), and **el rufo** (*el techo*). **El techo** is both *roof* and *ceiling.*

4. While **funcionar** is the most appropriate equivalent of *to work* when referring to machinery, **trabajar** may be heard colloquially. **Servir** is often used to refer to the adequacy of something or someone (**Esta silla sirve**); **no servir (para nada)** indicates *worthlessness* (**Ese carro no sirve para nada**).

5. Some words that are singular in English have plural equivalents in Spanish. Common examples include **muebles,** *furniture;* **buenas condiciones,** *good condition;* **las vacaciones,** *vacation.*

6. Do not confuse the words **dolor** (*pain*) and **dólar** (*dollar*).

7. **Antiguo** means *former* when it precedes the noun it modifies and *ancient* when it follows it. **Nuevo** means *new,* with regard to the owner, when it precedes the noun (**mi nueva casa,** *my new house,* e.g., *new* for me), and *brand new* when it follows (**Vamos a comprar una casa nueva,** *We're going to buy a brand new house*).

8. **Hacer falta** (literally, *to make a lack*), in addition to its use to express *need,* also means *to miss emotionally* (**Me hace falta mi esposo,** *I miss my husband*). **Faltar** is the equivalent of *to be missing* (**Faltan los documentos,** *The documents are missing*). It is also used for *to miss an engagement, work, school,* etc. (**Ud. faltó a la cita de ayer,** *You missed the appointment yesterday*).

9. The opposite of **caro** is **barato.**

Notas lingüísticas II

A. It may help to learn numbers greater than one hundred by reviewing the derivational patterns for all numbers:

0	cero						
1	uno	11	once				
2	dos	12	doce	20	veinte	200	doscientos
3	tres	13	trece	30	treinta	300	trescientos
4	cuatro	14	catorce	40	cuarenta	400	cuatrocientos
5	cinco	15	quince	50	cincuenta	500	quinientos
6	seis	16	dieciséis	60	sesenta	600	seiscientos
7	siete	17	diecisiete	70	setenta	700	setecientos
8	ocho	18	dieciocho	80	ochenta	800	ochocientos
9	nueve	19	diecinueve	90	noventa	900	novecientos
10	diez			100	cien(to)	1,000	mil

1. The *hundreds* agree with the noun they quantify:

    Me hacen falta doscient**as** sill**as** para la fiesta.
    I need two hundred chairs for the party.

    Me cobraron seiscient**os** dólar**es**.
    They charged me six hundred dollars.

2. Two-digit numbers ending in **uno** also agree with the noun to which they refer. **Uno** changes to **un** before a masculine noun and **una** before a feminine noun:

    Tengo veinti**ún** años.
    I'm twenty-one years old.

    Compré treinta y *una* tarjetas.
    I bought thirty-one cards.

3. **Cien** is used in counting and as a single form adjective. **Ciento** is the combined form used with other numbers; it is followed directly by the next number without a conjunction:

    Me costó *cien* dólares.
    It cost me $100.

    Faltan *ciento* diez dólares.
    $110 are missing.

4. **Mil** is used without the indefinite article and has only the one form when used in numbers. The plural noun **miles** is followed by **de** when used to express *thousands*.

    Pago *mil* quinientos al año.
    I pay $1,500 a year.

    Gano veinte *mil* dólares.
    I earn $20,000.

    Hay *miles de* problemas.
    There are thousands of problems.

B. **Gustar** (literally, *to please*), **faltar**, and **hacer falta** follow the pattern of such verbs as **parecer** and **convenir**, introduced in Lección 4: the person affected is expressed by the indirect object, and that which causes the reaction becomes the subject. (Remember, there is no subject pronoun for *it* in Spanish.)

    No nos gusta la casa.
    The house doesn't please us. (We don't like the house.)

    Te hacen falta dos camas.
    Two beds are lacking to you. (You need two beds.)

    Me falta mucho que hacer.
    Much is lacking for me to do. (I have a lot left to do.)

    A Carlos no le gusta.
    It is not pleasing to Carlos. (Carlos doesn't like it.)

C. The indirect object pronouns **le** and **les** have several possible referents (**le,** *to him, to her, to you,* formal; **les,** *to them, to you,* plural). As a result, the prepositional form of the pronoun (**a él, a ella, a Ud., a ellos/as, a Uds.**) is often added for clarity or emphasis. It may not, however, be used *instead of* the indirect object pronoun:

¿(A Uds.) les gusta la casa?	Do you (all) like the house?
Sí, nos gusta mucho (a nosotros).	Yes, *we* like it a lot.
(A él) le hace falta dinero.	He needs money.
(A ti) no te gusta, ¿verdad?	*You* don't like it, do you?

D. The indirect object in Spanish expresses more than the English equivalents of *to whom* or *for whom* the action is done. It refers to a person who is involved *indirectly* in the action. With the verb **comprar,** it can refer to the person *for whom* or *from whom* something is purchased.

Te voy a comprar el sofá.	I'm going to buy the sofa for (from) you.
Nadie nos compra nada.	No one is buying anything for (from) us.

E. When both the direct and indirect objects are expressed as pronouns, the normal order is *indirect* before *direct*:

Me los vendió mi cuñado.	My brother-in-law sold them to me.
¿Quién te la compró?	Who bought it for (or from) you?

However, the *indirect* object **le** or **les** becomes **se** before the direct object pronouns **lo, la, los, las.** In this case **se** is *not* the reflexive form; it can be the equivalent of **a él, a ella, a Ud., a ellos, a ellas,** or **a Uds.** For clarity or emphasis this longer form may be added to the sentence:

¿Quién se lo vendió (a Ud.)?	Who sold it to you?
Se las compré (a él).	I bought them for (from) him.

The following chart summarizes the Spanish pronoun system:

	Subject	*Reflexive object*	*Indirect object*	*Direct object*	*Object of preposition*
Functions	Do-*er* of action; determines ending of the verb	Used when direct or indirect object refers to same person as subject	Indicates person involved in the action other than *do-er* or *done-to*	Signals the *done-to* or receiver of the action	Used after any preposition (most commonly **a, en, de, con, por, para**)
Forms	**yo**	**me**	**me**	**me**	**(a) mí**
	tú	**te**	**te**	**te**	**(a) ti**
	usted	**se**	**le**	**lo, la**	**(a) usted**
	él	**se**	**le**	**lo**	**(a) él**
	ella	**se**	**le**	**la**	**(a) ella**
	nosotros/as	**nos**	**nos**	**nos**	**(a) nosotros/as**
	ustedes	**se**	**les**	**los, las**	**(a) ustedes**
	ellos	**se**	**les**	**los**	**(a) ellos**
	ellas	**se**	**les**	**las**	**(a) ellas**

Remember:

1. Subject pronouns are often omitted or placed at the end of the sentence. There is no subject pronoun for English *it*; it is expressed in the third person verb form.

2. A plural reflexive pronoun and verb form often indicates the reciprocal reflexive (to each other):

   Nos vemos el lunes.   We'll see each other on Monday.

3. In some dialects, **le (les)** replaces **lo/la (los/las)** as the **usted, él,** and **ella** singular and plural direct object forms.

4. There are two special pronoun forms that combine with the preposition **con: conmigo** (*with me*), **contigo** (*with you*, familiar). To refer to other persons, use the regular pronoun forms that follow a preposition:

   ¿Quiere Ud. ir conmigo?   Do you want to go with me?
   No quiero ir con usted.   I don't want to go with you.

PRÁCTICA PRELIMINAR

Follow general guidelines for self-instructional practice.

A. Substitute the appropriate form of the synonym for **estar** given in parentheses.
   Ejemplo: El doctor no está en su oficina. (encontrarse)
   El doctor no se encuentra en su oficina.

   1. La clínica está en el quinto piso. (quedar)
   2. ¿Dónde están los documentos? (encontrarse)
   3. El departamento de salud está en la calle Colón. (quedar)
   4. ¿Cómo estás hoy? (encontrarte)
   5. Espero que su esposa esté mejor. (encontrarse)

B. Answer each question about your housing situation in the affirmative, using the appropriate form of the verb **ser, estar,** or **hay,** according to context.
   Ejemplo: ¿La casa? ¿En la calle Main?
   Sí, está en la calle Main.

   1. ¿La casa? ¿En buenas condiciones?
   2. ¿Ocho cuartos? ¿En la casa?
   3. ¿Uds.? ¿Alquilando la casa?
   4. ¿Los muebles? ¿Suyos (de Ud.)?
   5. ¿Los muebles? ¿Asegurados?
   6. ¿La estufa? ¿Suya (de Uds.)?
   7. ¿El Sr. Ramos? ¿El dueño de la casa?
   8. ¿Las otras cuentas? ¿Al corriente?

A 1. queda 2. se encuentran 3. queda 4. te encuentras 5. se encuentre
B 1. Sí, está en buenas condiciones. 2. Sí, hay ocho. 3. Sí, la estamos alquilando. 4. Sí, son míos. 5. Sí, están asegurados. 6. Sí, es nuestra. 8. Sí, es el dueño de la casa. 8. Sí, están al corriente.

C. Practice the following questions that might be made regarding possession of household goods to a client who is sharing an apartment with a female friend. Then answer the questions, using the English cue given in parentheses as a guide.

Ejemplo: ¿Es suya la casa? (no, hers)
            No, no es mía; es suya (de ella).

1. ¿De quién es la estufa? (mine)
2. ¿Son de Ud. los muebles? (yes)
3. ¿El refrigerador es de su amiga? (no, not hers, mine)
4. ¿También son de Ud. la lavadora y la secadora? (no, not mine, hers)
5. ¿De quién es el televisor? (hers, too)
6. Y los aparatos eléctricos, ¿de quién son? (some mine, some hers)

D. Read aloud the following sentences containing numbers until you can do so easily, without hesitation.

1. Mi esposa tiene 51 años.
2. Me hacen falta 500 sillas.
3. Me faltan 100 dólares.
4. Vivo en el 115 de la calle Bay.
5. Pago 700 dólares mensuales.
6. Me cuesta 1,900 dólares al año.
7. Este mes la calefacción me costó 161 dólares.
8. Hay 400 casas en el barrio.
9. Me cobraron 675 dólares por los muebles.
10. El alquiler nos cuesta 550 dólares.

E. The Oliveros family has just moved into the area. Ask the following questions of the family members indicated regarding what they like about their new home and what they need to make it feel like home.

1. Ask Mr. Oliveros if he likes . . .
    a. el vecindario
    b. los muebles
    c. su nueva casa

C 1. Es mía. 2. Sí, son míos. 3. No, no es suyo; es mío. 4. No, no son mías; son suyas. 5. Es suyo también. 6. Algunos son míos y algunos son suyos.

D 1. cincuenta y un 2. quinientas 3. cien 4. ciento quince 5. setecientos 6. mil novecientos 7. ciento sesenta y un 8. cuatrocientas 9. seiscientos setenta y cinco 10. quinientos cincuenta dólares

2. Ask Mr. and Mrs. Oliveros if they like . . .
   a. la ciudad
   b. la estufa nueva
   c. los muebles nuevos

3. Ask their eight-year-old son Pepito if he likes . . .
   a. su nueva escuela
   b. su dormitorio
   c. sus nuevos amigos

4. Ask Mrs. Oliveros if her twenty-year-old daughter Irene likes . . .
   a. vivir cerca de su trabajo
   b. la cocina moderna
   c. los dormitorios

5. Ask Mr. and Mrs. Oliveros if they need . . .
   a. un lavaplatos nuevo
   b. más muebles
   c. más lámparas

F. Now answer the questions you formed in Exercise E in the **affirmative**, as if you were the family member(s) indicated.

G. Change the infinitive of the verb to the **present** or to the **present progressive**, according to the context.

   Ejemplo: Nosotros *vivir* en el barrio Linda Vista.
   Nosotros *vivimos* en el barrio Linda Vista. (habitual action)

   Hoy yo *trabajar* en casa.
   Hoy yo *estoy trabajando* en casa. (in progress)

   1. Ud. me *cobrar* mucho por el lavaplatos, amigo.
   2. ¿Cuánto le *costar* el gas?
   3. Bueno, la estufa nunca *funcionar* bien.
   4. En este momento el doctor *hablar* con otro paciente.
   5. Normalmente mi esposo *trabajar* de maestro, pero hoy *trabajar* en la nueva casa.
   6. ¿Qué está haciendo el abogado ahora?
      Buscar la hipoteca del cliente.
   7. ¿Cuánto tiempo hace que Uds. *vivir* en el vecindario?
   8. Yo *llamar* a mi mamá dos o tres veces a la semana.

E 1. a. ¿Le gusta el vecindario? b. ¿Le gustan los muebles? c. ¿Le gusta su nueva casa? 2. a. ¿Les gusta la ciudad? b. ¿Les gusta la estufa nueva? c. ¿Les gustan los muebles nuevos? 3. a. ¿Te gusta tu nueva escuela? b. ¿Te gusta tu dormitorio? c. ¿Te gustan tus nuevos amigos? 4. a. ¿A Irene le gusta vivir cerca de su trabajo? b. ¿A Irene le gusta la cocina moderna? c. ¿A Irene le gustan los dormitorios? 5. a. ¿Les hace falta un lavaplatos nuevo? b. ¿Les hacen falta más muebles? c. ¿ Les hacen falta más lámparas?

F 1. a. Sí, me gusta. b. Sí, me gustan. c. Sí, me gusta. 2. a. Sí, nos gusta. b. Sí, nos gusta. c. Sí, nos gustan. 3. a. Sí, me gusta. b. Sí, me gusta. c. Sí, me gusta. 4. a. Sí, le gusta. b. Sí, le gusta. c. Sí, le gustan. 5. a. Sí, nos hace falta. b. Sí, nos hacen falta. c. Sí, nos hacen falta.

G 1. Ud. me está cobrando mucho por el lavaplatos, amigo. 2. ¿Cuánto le cuesta el gas? 3. Bueno, la estufa nunca funciona bien. 4. En este momento el doctor está hablando con otro paciente. 5. Normalmente mi esposo trabaja de maestro, pero hoy está trabajando en la nueva casa. 6. Está buscando la hipoteca del cliente. 7. ¿Cuánto tiempo hace que Uds. viven en el vecindario? 8. Yo llamo a mi mamá dos o tres veces a la semana.

H. Practice reading aloud the following questions and answers between a social worker and a client regarding the financial details of furnishing the latter's new living quarters. Then translate the client's responses into English.

Ejemplo: ¿Quién le vendió la estufa?
Me la vendió mi tío.

My uncle sold it to me.

1. ¿A quién le compró Ud. los muebles?
   Se los compré a mi hermano.

2. ¿Quién le vendió la secadora?
   Me la vendió mi cuñada.

3. ¿Quién le compró las camas?
   Me las compró mi mamá.

4. ¿Se compró Ud. la lavadora nueva?
   Sí, yo me la compré.

5. ¿A quién le vendió Ud. la lavadora antigua?
   Se la vendí a mi primo.

6. ¿Le pagó Ud. la renta al dueño?
   No, se la voy a pagar hoy.

7. ¿Quién le pagó el depósito?
   Me lo pagó mi papá.

8. ¿Quién le vendió el televisor?
   Me lo vendieron mis abuelos.

I. You miss your old apartment, so you answer all of the following questions about your new apartment *in the negative*. Use complete sentences, replacing all italicized nouns with pronouns and making any other changes necessary.

Ejemplo: ¿Le explicaron a Ud. *la hipoteca?*
No, no me *la* explicaron.

1. ¿A Uds. les gusta el nuevo apartamento?
2. ¿A sus hijos les parece bueno el vecindario?
3. ¿Les hacen falta muebles?
4. ¿Les compró Ud. *la estufa* a sus cuñados?
5. ¿Les paga *la calefacción* el dueño?
6. ¿Ud. y el dueño se hablan mucho?
7. ¿Le vendió Ud. *los antiguos muebles* a su hermana?
8. ¿Les cobraron mucho por la cuna?
9. ¿Ud. le cobra *el alquiler* a su hijo?

H 1. I bought them from (for) my brother. 2. My sister-in-law sold it to (for) me. 3. My mother bought them from (for) me. 4. Yes, I bought it for myself. 5. I sold it to my cousin. 6. No, I'm going to pay it to him today. 7. My father paid it for me. 8. My grandparents sold it to (for) me.

I 1. No, no nos gusta. 2. No, no les parece bueno. 3. No, no nos hacen falta. 4. No, no se la compré (a ellos). 5. No, no nos la paga. 6. No, no nos hablamos mucho. 7. No, no se los vendí. 8. No, no nos cobraron mucho. 9. No, no se lo cobro (a él).

Combinándolo todo

PRÁCTICA COMUNICATIVA: Cosas del hogar

Conversación parcial

Practique oralmente el siguiente diálogo entre un oficial del banco y una cliente que busca una hipoteca. Cada raya (/) implica que falta una palabra; el verbo *en bastardillas* indica que es necesario conjugarlo.

Ejemplo: ¿ / *pagar* Uds. / / seguro?

¿Cuánto pagan Uds. por el seguro?

El oficial del banco	La cliente
1. / tardes, / . / secretaria / dice / Ud. *buscar* / hipoteca.	Sí, / , yo *querer* / una / nueva.
2. ¿ / *vivir* Ud. ahora?	*Vivir* / / calle Marsh, / 136.
3. ¿*Ser* / la casa o / *alquilar*?	La alquilamos.
4. ¿ / personas *vivir* / la / ?	*Ser* cuatro: / hermana y yo, y / dos nenas / ella.
5. ¿ / las *mantener* a Uds.?	Mi / y yo nos *mantener*.
6. ¿ / *costar* la / que Ud. *querer* / ?	*Costar* $87,000.
7. ¿ / *poder* Ud. pagar / depósito?	*Poder* pagar $10,000.
8. ¿*Saber* Ud. / *ser* / impuestos?	*Creer* / *ser* $1,200 / año.
9. Pues, / , *tener* / llenar estos / .	¿Cuándo / *necesitar* Ud.?
10. / *necesitar* mañana / / tarde.	Mil / , señor.

Pregunte Ud.

Usted tiene una entrevista con Magdalena Escovar, que ahora vive con su familia en una nueva casa. Haga Ud. oralmente las preguntas necesarias en la siguiente conversación con ella sobre su nuevo hogar.

Ejemplo: La casa queda en el barrio Linda Vista.

¿Dónde queda la casa?

1. Vivimos ahora en una casa alquilada de seis cuartos.
2. No, no me gusta mucho el nuevo vecindario.
3. Pagamos $525 de renta. Es bastante cara, ¿verdad?
4. La calefacción varía entre $65 y $90 al mes.
5. No, no tenemos que pagar la luz; el dueño nos la paga.
6. Los muebles son míos, pero los aparatos eléctricos vienen con el apartamento.

7. No, los muebles no están asegurados. ¿Es importante?

8. Sí, me compré un televisor nuevo; me costó $250.

9. También le compré dos sillones a mi primo, Javier.

10. El me cobró solamente veinte dólares.

11. Sí, nos hacen falta una cama y una cuna.

12. Pues, está en buenas condiciones con la excepción de la tubería que no sirve para nada.

Dígalo

Pregunte a un/a compañero/a de la clase lo que le diga su profesor/a sobre los temas de su vecindario, su hogar, los gastos del hogar, lo que le hace falta en casa, y las posesiones del hogar.

Escuche bien

A. Ud. oirá a una persona que describe su vida, con referencias a su hogar. Escriba:

A—si la oración indica que la persona necesita ayuda emocional o financiera con su hogar;

B—si la oración indica que todo está bien con su hogar;

C—si la oración no se refiere al hogar.

1. _____   3. _____   5. _____   7. _____   9. _____

2. _____   4. _____   6. _____   8. _____   10. _____

B. Ud. oirá a una persona que describe lo que compró y vendió cuando cambió de casa. Escriba Ud. *en inglés* el mueble o el aparato eléctrico del cual habla la persona, el precio del artículo, si lo compró o lo vendió, y la persona a quién se lo compró o se lo vendió.

	El artículo	*Precio*	*Comprar o vender*	*La persona*
1.				
2.				
3.				
4.				
5.				
6.				

Diálogos cortos

I. *El representante del departamento de salud*

La señora Meléndez

Señora Meléndez, Ud. reportó problemas _____ el dueño del _____ ¿verdad?

Sí. El apartamento está en muy malas condiciones y el dueño no quiere hacer nada.

¿ _____ problemas _____ Ud. con el _____ ?

El fregadero y el inodoro no sirven para nada y hace dos semanas que no funciona la calefacción.

¿Cómo _____ llama el _____ ?

Se llama Paul Merton.

¿Llamó Ud. al _____ por _____ ?

Sí, lo llamé tres veces. Él me dice que va a venir, pero nunca viene.

¿Cuántos _____ hay en el _____ ?

Hay cinco: tres dormitorios, la sala, la cocina y el baño.

¿ _____ personas _____ en el apartamento?

Somos tres: mis dos hijas y yo. No quiero seguir viviendo aquí sin calefacción. Mi hija menor ya tiene resfriado.

Bueno, señora, yo _____ a llamar _____ señor Merton _____ tarde.

Mil gracias, señor. Se lo agradezco mucho.

II. *El empleado de la compañía telefónica*

El señor Acevedo

(Conversación telefónica)

¿Aló?

Luis Acevedo, por _____ .

Soy yo. ¿Con quién hablo?

El empleado de la compañía telefónica	*El señor Acevedo*
Le _____ el señor Wright de la compañía _____ .	Es que ya no tengo trabajo. No puedo pagar la cuenta porque no tengo el dinero. ¿Cuánto es la cuenta total?
Señor Acevedo, _____ dos meses que Ud. no _____ la cuenta de teléfono. ¿ _____ le pasa?	
Ahora _____ de $153. ¿No puede Ud. _____ nada este mes?	Es posible que pueda pagar unos $25 para el 15 del mes.
Si Ud. no puede _____ la _____ muy pronto, va a _____ necesario cortarle el servicio _____ .	Se la quisiera pagar, pero no puedo trabajar porque me estoy recuperando de una operación muy seria.
Lo _____ mucho, _____ Acevedo, pero es _____ que Ud. pague la _____ .	¿Cómo la voy a pagar si me falta el dinero?

Ayude al cliente

Your client, Mr. Marco Montalvo, has just received the following letter from his landlord. Since he does not read English, he has sent the letter to you. Translate the letter into Spanish so that you can return it to him. If you wish, you may add a note recommending what Mr. Montalvo should do about the situation.

Mr. Marco Montalvo
139 Canyon Drive
Denver, CO.

Dear Mr. Montalvo:

I am writing to you to inform you that you have not paid your rent for three months. Since the rent is very much in arrears, I must refer this matter (*asunto*) to my lawyer, Attorney Samuel Stenson.

Mr. Stenson will call you or write to you this week in order to ask you when you can pay the $1,260 you owe (*deber*) for the rent for November, December, and January.

If you cannot pay the rent that is in arrears by the first of February, I will have to ask you to vacate (*abandonar*) the house.

If you or your attorney have any questions, you can call me at my office. The number there is 535–7809.

Sincerely,
John S. Reilly

¿Comprende Ud.?

Lea Ud. los cinco anuncios que describen casas o apartamentos para alquilar. Después Ud. oirá descripciones de cinco clientes que buscan un nuevo hogar. Escriba Ud. el número del/de la cliente al lado del anuncio que más le conviene.

_____ A. Familia ofrece para alquilar a soltero un apartamento no amueblado; segundo piso en casa privada; dormitorio, baño, estudio; barrio tranquilo cerca de todo transport público; 200 pesos mensuales.

_____ B. Casa, dos baños, cuatro dormitorios, sala, comedor, patio, garaje; barrio excepcional; todos aparatos de cocina; $880 alquiler mensual con opción de comprar a $125,000.

_____ C. Cuarto semi-amueblado (cama y tocador) con aire acondicionado en pensión para señoritas; baño completo privado; sexto piso (con ascensor); barrio céntrico; $75/semana.

_____ D. Apto. 2 dormitorios, parcialmente amueblado con juego de comedor y muebles de sala y dormitorio; aparatos de cocina; $500/mes sin calefacción eléctrica ni a/c.

_____ E. Pequeña casa amueblada de 2 dormitorios; cocina viene con refrigerador/congelador/lavaplatos/estufa; $325 al mes, incluye gas y electricidad.

Piénselo

Prepárese para poder hablar con el/la profesor/a o con otros estudiantes sobre los siguientes temas, contestando las preguntas que le sugiera el/la profesor/a.

1. Los gastos de alquiler vs. los de comprar una casa
2. Los aparatos "indispensables" del hogar
3. Los métodos de comprar
4. Los gastos de las utilidades

SITUACIONES DE LA VIDA REAL

Imagínese

a

1

b

2

c

3

d

4

1. Escoja Ud. la foto de la(s) persona(s) que vive(n) en cada una de las casas. Describa Ud. la vida del hogar de cada casa, contestando las preguntas siguientes.
   a. ¿Cómo se llama la familia?
   b. ¿Cuántas personas viven en el hogar?
   c. ¿Cuánto tiempo hace que viven allí?
   d. ¿Es suyo/a el apartamento (la casa) o lo/la alquilan?
   e. ¿Cuánto pagan por el alquiler (la hipoteca)?
   f. ¿Cuánto pagan por la electricidad? ¿Por el gas? ¿Por la calefacción? ¿Por el teléfono?
   g. ¿Está amueblado/a?
   h. ¿Qué muebles (aparatos eléctricos) les hacen falta?
   i. ¿En qué condiciones está la casa (el apartamento)?
   j. ¿Les gusta vivir allí o buscan otro hogar?

Ahorre $60
en lavadora de 2 ciclos, 3 temperaturas

399⁹⁹

- Ciclo especial Perma Prest, evita arrugas.
- 3 niveles de agua.
- Precio regular $459.99.

Ahorre $60
en secadora con 3 ciclos

299⁹⁹

- Ciclo de aire solamente para ropa delicada.
- Filtro en la parte superior.
- Precio regular $359.99.

Ahorre $100
en nevera de 17 P.C., no hace escarcha

599⁹⁹

Acepta "Ice Ma-ker", no incluido. Montada sobre ruedas. Regular $699.99.

FREGADERO DOBLE STAINLESS STEEL, CON FITTINGS

Reg. $75.00

Especial $55.00

INODOROS
Y tanque americano

Reg. $85.00

Inodoros en colores

$59.00

Ahorre $60 en estufa eléctrica de 21"

369⁹⁹

Regular $429.99.

Ahorre $50 en estufa de gas de 21"

329⁹⁹

Regular $379.99.

Ahorre $120 en congelador de 15 P.C., horizontal o vertical

449⁹⁹ cada uno

Regular de cada uno $569.99.

ABANICO GIRATORIO DE 12"
MODELO DE LUJO.

16.⁹⁰

Reg. 29.95

Ahorre desde $70 hasta $130
en acondicionadores de aire

2. Use Ud. los anuncios ilustrados para contestar las siguientes preguntas.
   a. ¿Cuánto cuestan la secadora y la lavadora? ¿Cuál es el precio normal de cada una? ¿Cuánto se ahorra si se compran ahora?
   b. ¿Es grande o pequeña la nevera? ¿Qué quiere decir *escarcha*? ¿Y *montada sobre ruedas*? ¿Cuánto cuesta normalmente? ¿Cuánto se ahorra si se compra ahora?
   c. ¿Cómo se dice *freezer* en español? ¿Cuánto cuesta ahora? ¿Prefiere Ud. que sea horizontal o vertical? ¿Por qué?
   d. ¿Prefiere Ud. la estufa eléctrica o la da gas? ¿Por qué cree que ésa es mejor? ¿Cuál cuesta más?
   e. ¿Cuál cuesta más, el fregadero o el inodoro?
   f. ¿Sabe Ud. el precio del acondicionador de aire? ¿Es más caro o más barato que el abanico giratorio? ¿Qué quiere decir *modelo de lujo*?

Haciendo el papel

1. Usando el siguiente anuncio de guía, explíquele al señor Rafael Monegal los detalles de la casa que está en venta. Después, hágale las preguntas necesarias para ver si tiene interés en comprar la casa y si califica para conseguir la hipoteca.

¡¡¡ULTIMAS UNIDADES!!!
¡RESIDENCIAS LISTAS PARA ENTREGA INMEDIATA!
— 13 1/4% INTERÉS ANUAL —

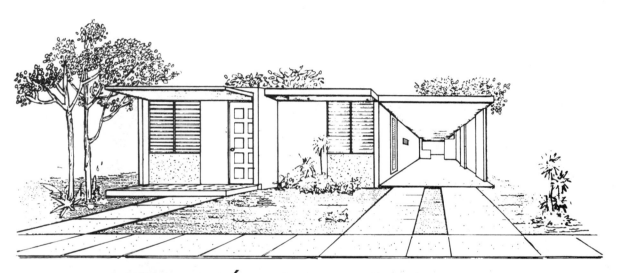

SI SU COMPOSICIÓN FAMILIAR E INGRESOS ANUALES es como sigue, usted puede cualificar;

2 personas.....................	De $12,000. a $15,200.
3 personas.........................	De $12,500. a $16,000.
4 personas.........................	De $12,700. a $16,500.
5 personas.........................	De $13,500. a $17,000.

GRANDES VENTAJAS:

- Cómodas residencias de 3 cuartos y un baño, marquesina, piso terrazo, laundry y balcón.
- Parque softball, cancha baloncesto, cancha tennis, centro recreativo.

- Cerca Playa Puerto Nuevo de Vega Baja
- Tres fachadas a escoger
- Solares desde 300 metros

2. La señora Carmen Vega viene a hablarle a Ud. porque necesita ayuda económica para comprar uno de los muebles o aparatos eléctricos que se ven en el anuncio. Pregúntele por qué lo quiere comprar, si quiere comprarlo al contado o a crédito, si tiene tarjeta de crédito y cuál es el límite.

Juego de Cuarto

Mesa de Noche Reg. $99.	Esp. **$64.**
Cabezal Twin Reg. $79.	Esp. **45.**
Gavetero Sencillo Reg. $159.	Esp. **109.**
Tablillero Reg. $119.	Esp. **79.**
Gavetero Doble Reg. $199	Esp. **149.**
Espejo Reg. $69.	Esp. **39.**
Escritorio Reg. $159.	Esp. **99.**
Tablillero Reg. $129.	Esp. **89.**

Ahorre $90 en
T.V. a color de 5" diagonales
369⁹⁹

Sintonizador electrónico. Filtro en la pantalla para ver bajo el sol. Regular $459.99.

Ahorre $40 en radio
AM/FM, tocacasetes
Regular $219.99. **179⁹⁹**

Ahorre $40
en gabinete para la máquina
Regular $130 . . . . **$90**

Ahorre $80 en
máquina de coser de 6 puntadas

179⁹⁹

- 4 puntadas de utilidad y 2 estirables.
- Ojalador empotrado,
- Base parcialmente removible para costuras tubulares.
- Precio regular $259.99.

Ahorre $80
en equipo estereofónico compacto

269⁹⁹

Radio AM/FM. Toca y graba casetes y cintas de 8 pistas. Regular $349.99.

3. Entreviste Ud. a otro/a estudiante de la clase para completar el siguiente formulario para ver si califica para recibir una tarjeta de crédito.

Solicitud para Tarjeta de Crédito

Nombre _____ No. de s.s. _____

Dirección _____ Teléfono _____

Edad _____ Fecha de nacimiento _____

Profesión _____ Empleo actual _____

Estado civil _____ Nombre de esposo/a _____

Número de hijos _____ _____

Nombre	*Sexo*	*Edad*	*Fecha de nacimiento*

Otras personas que viven en el hogar:

Nombre	*Parentesco*

Número de cuartos _____ Número de dormitorios _____

Gastos del hogar

La hipoteca _____ El alquiler _____

Los impuestos _____ El seguro _____

La electricidad _____ El gas _____ El teléfono _____

La calefacción _____ Otros gastos _____

REFLEJOS DE LA CULTURA: "La nochebuena"

The tendency to live in an area of a city or town populated by others from the same cultural background has marked the adaptation process of most, if not all, immigrant groups to their new country of residence. For Hispanics residing in the United States, the Spanish-speaking *barrio* becomes an important extension of the support systems enjoyed in the country of origin.

Newcomers are drawn to the *barrio* by the advantages of speaking the native language, buying foods and other items from the homeland, and feeling comfortable with the customs and people who think the same. It is possible for them to live completely engulfed in a Spanish-speaking lifestyle in the *barrios* of most U.S. cities with a large Hispanic population. The most obvious disadvantage is the lack of contact with the Anglo culture. The fears associated with dealing with the unknown aspects of the majority culture may be intensified by years of avoiding interaction with Anglos and their culture.

The following selection, entitled "La nochebuena" ("Christmas Eve") is from Mexican American author Tomás Rivera's collection of short fiction, . . . *y no se tragó la tierra.* It illustrates how one woman, the wife of a migrant farm worker, decides to venture forth into the Anglo world of the city in which her family is currently residing. Her fears, doubts, and lack of self-confidence are clearly illustrated in this poignant segment. They stem from both the isolation of the home which affects many Hispanic women who venture out only in the company of male family members, as well as from the general lack of contact with the Anglo society.

The author has added to the realism of the story by including the Mexican American dialectal variations in grammar and vocabulary listed below. Studying these may make your reading of the passage in Spanish easier.

alzar	= *ahorrar*	to save
Crismes	= *Navidad*	Christmas
pos	= *pues*	well . . .
ándale		Aw, come on . . .
voltear	= *doblar, virar*	to turn the corner
traques	= *la vía*	train tracks
nomás	= *solamente*	only
viejo/a		term of endearment for one's spouse

. . . se decidió a comprarles algo. Pero no tenían dinero para gastar en juguetes. Su esposo trabajaba casi las diez y ocho horas lavando platos y haciendo de comer en un restaurante. No tenía tiempo de ir al centro para comprar juguetes. Además tenían que *alzar* cada semana para poder pagar para la ida al norte. Ya les cobraban por los niños aunque fueran parados todo el camino hasta Iowa. Así que les costaba bastante para hacer el viaje. De todas maneras le propuso a su esposo esa noche, cuando llegó bien cansado del trabajo, que les compraran algo.

—Fíjate, *viejo,* que los niños quieren algo para *Crismes.*

—¿Y luego las naranjas y las nueces que les traigo?

—*Pos* sí, pero ellos quieren juguetes. Ya no se conforman con comida. Es que están más grandes y ven más.

—No necesitan nada.

—¿A poco tú no tenías juguetes cuando eras niño?

—Sabes que yo mismo los hacía de barro — caballitos, soldaditos . . .

—*Pos* sí, pero aquí es distinto, como ven muchas cosas . . . *ándale* vamos a comprarles algo . . . yo misma voy al Kres.

—¿Tú?

—Sí, yo.

—¿No tienes miedo (*de*) ir al centro? ¿Te acuerdas allá en Wilmar, Minnesota, cómo te perdiste en el centro? ¿'Tas (*Estás*) segura que no tienes miedo?

—Sí, sí me acuerdo pero me doy ánimo. Yo voy. Ya me estuve dando ánimo todo el día y estoy segura que no me pierdo aquí . . . De veras que no estaría difícil.

. . . she decided to buy something for them. But they didn't have any money to spend on toys. Her husband worked almost eighteen hours washing dishes and cooking in a restaurant. He didn't have time to go downtown to buy toys. Furthermore, every week they had to save money to pay for the trip to the north. They had to pay the children's fare now even if they had to stand up all the way to Iowa. So it was very expensive for them to make the trip. In spite of all this, that night when her husband arrived tired from work she suggested that they buy something for them.

"Look, father, the children would like something for Christmas."

"What about the oranges and nuts that I bring them?"

"Well, yes, but they want toys. They won't settle for food. They're older now, and they are aware of more things."

"They're not in need of anything."

"Don't tell me you didn't have any toys when you were a child."

"You know I used to make them myself, out of clay. I'd make little horses, little soldiers. . . . "

"Well, yes, but it's different here since they see many things . . . come on, let's go buy something for them . . . I'll go to Kress myself."

"You?"

"Yes, me."

"Aren't you afraid to go downtown? Don't you remember what happened in Wilmar, Minnesota, when you got lost downtown? Are you sure you're not afraid?"

"Yes, yes, I remember, but I'll try to get up my courage. I'll go. I've been building up courage all day and I'm sure that I won't get lost here . . . It really won't be difficult at all."

—*Pos* sí. Bueno, te voy a dejar dinero sobre la mesa cuando me vaya por la mañana. Pero tienes cuidado, *vieja,* en estos días hay mucha gente en el centro.

Era que doña María nunca salía de casa sola. La única vez que salía era cuando iba a visitar a su papá y a su hermana quienes vivían en la siguiente cuadra. Sólo iba a la iglesia cuando había difuntito y a veces cuando había boda.

Pero iba siempre con su esposo así que nunca se fijaba por donde iba. También su esposo le traía siempre todo. Él era el que compraba la comida y la ropa. En realidad no conocía el centro aun estando solamente a seis cuadras de su casa . . .

El siguiente día se levantó, como lo hacía siempre, muy temprano y ya cuando había despachado a su esposo y a los niños, recogió el dinero de sobre la mesa y empezó a prepararse para ir al centro. No le llevó mucho tiempo.

—Yo no sé por qué soy tan miedosa yo, Dios mío. Si el centro está solamente a seis cuadras de aquí. *Nomás* me voy derechita y luego *volteo* a la derecha al pasar los *traques.* Luego, dos cuadras, y allí está Kres. De allá para acá ando las dos cuadras y luego *volteo* a la izquierda y luego hasta que llegue aquí otra vez. Dios quiera y no me vaya a salir algún perro. Al pasar los *traques* que no vaya a venir un tren y me pesque en medio . . . Ojalá y no me salga un perro . . . Ojalá y no venga un tren por los *traques.*

"All right, I'll leave you some money on the table when I leave in the morning. But be careful, mother, there are a lot of people in town these days."

The fact was that Doña María never went out of the house by herself. The only time she left the house was when she visited her father and her sister who lived a block away. She went to church only when someone passed away or sometimes when there was a wedding.

But she always went with her husband, so she never noticed where she was going. Also, her husband always brought everything to her. He was the one who bought food and clothing. In reality she had never been downtown even though it was only six blocks away from her house. . . .

The following day she got up very early, as she always did, and after she had sent off her husband and the children she picked up the money from the table and started to ready herself to go downtown. It didn't take her very long.

"I don't know why I'm so timid, my God. Downtown is only six blocks away. I just go straight and I turn right when I cross the tracks. Then two blocks and there is Kress. On the way back I walk two blocks and then I turn left and then straight home. God willing I won't meet any dogs on the way. I'll be careful when I cross the tracks, or a train might come along and catch me in the middle of the tracks. . . . I hope I don't meet any dogs. . . . I hope there is no train on the tracks."

LECCIÓN 8

La educación y el trabajo

LOS OBJETIVOS

Raising awareness

1. To evolve strategies for dealing with stress resulting from the cross-cultural communication process
2. To understand how the historical perspective on employment and education in the Hispanic world affects the current socioeconomic reality of U.S. Hispanics
3. To learn how to interpret Hispanic styles of dress that may differ from Anglo standards

Comunicándose en español

1. To pronounce and interpret Spanish **t** and **d**
2. To elicit information regarding work skills, experience, educational background, salary, and other details regarding employment
3. To use and understand preterite and imperfect tenses, and subjunctive mood in adjectival and adverbial clauses

Combinándolo todo

1. To integrate present and past tenses, indicative and subjunctive mood in work-related communication activities
2. To develop increased conversation skills in response to oral and written stimuli in professional contexts
3. To understand the difficulty some Hispanic children have adapting to the Anglo monolingual school system

Raising awareness

OVERVIEW: Experiencing cross-cultural confrontations and conflicts

Now that you understand culture shock as the natural adjustment process that occurs when one enters a new culture or communicates with someone from a different cultural background, you are ready to evolve strategies for dealing with it. By viewing this adaptation process as a positive experience, you become more aware of the potential for growth it offers.

Recent psychological theories encourage us to know our true feelings and to express them in a constructive way to others. From this perspective, conflict and confrontation are not seen as bad, unnatural, or frightening, but rather as normal, natural human experiences that can greatly enhance our effectiveness in communicating with others.

In this context, there are no *good* or *bad* conflicts or confrontations. It is not the fact that they occur but, rather, the way they are resolved that counts. In a *good* resolution of a conflict, both parties leave feeling at least partially satisfied and secure in their own worth as human beings. This outcome depends on the mutual validation of each other's right to perceive reality in a way that is appropriate to each. In a *bad* resolution of a conflict, one or both of the parties feels attacked, defensive, or even hostile. This occurs when one attempts to prove his or her version of reality as *right*, implying, of course, that the other's must be *wrong*. There is a winner and a loser. In reality, both lose ground in learning to communicate openly, honestly, and effectively in a way that validates both parties' right to be as they are.

The same is true of *confrontation*. It can be defined as the attempt to resolve conflicts between individuals with different perceptions of reality via direct communication between them. In a *good* confrontation, an issue is raised in such a way as to allow both individuals the right to feel or think as they do. A *bad* confrontation arises when accusations, attacks, and prejudgments are used. These tend either to alienate or to force the other party into a posture of defensiveness or counterattack.

As you may have noticed, many of the strategies for effective cross-cultural communication differ very little from successful communication techniques between any two individuals, regardless of their cultural backgrounds. The main difference lies in the wider variation among perceptions of reality that can clash when people from different cultural backgrounds attempt to communicate. The intensity of the conflict is stronger than if both had remained protected within their own cultural boundaries.

Let us examine in more detail the steps to the positive resolution of conflict generated in the cross-cultural communication process.

When one first experiences a conflict between one's own view of reality and that of someone from another culture, one of the first symptoms is a feeling of stress or anxiety coming from various sources. When meeting a new Hispanic client, you may feel that (1) the client's behavior does not make sense to you, (2) *your* behavior does not produce the results you have come to expect from past experiences with non-Hispanic clients, or (3) the interaction presents you with new demands or problems for which you have no pat answers.

In addition, you may experience any or all of the following emotions: (1) embarrassment at not knowing what to do, (2) frustration at not being able to communicate effectively, (3) disappointment at the difficulty of what you anticipated as an exciting new experience, (4) anger at your communication partner for perceiving things differently than you do, or (5) guilt for not being able to stay in control of the situation. Even your self-image may suffer if your communication partner appears more self-confident than you do.

In order to free yourself from feelings that may accompany the initial symptoms of the experience, you must first accept them as natural and real, rather than good or bad. It is normal to feel discomfort when confronting a new perception of reality that challenges one's own. Unless these feelings are accepted, they cannot be dealt with effectively. Instead, they remain ghosts locked away in the closet of the subconscious, ready to haunt and hamper all future cross-cultural interactions.

Once you have accepted and experienced the initial feelings of culture shock, you are better able to select an appropriate strategy for dealing with them. The following options are neither good nor bad; the focus is on choosing the most appropriate course of action for the personalities involved. You can choose, then, (a) to avoid the situation, (b) to move against it, or (c) to move with it. Any one of these three options can, under the right conditions, prove to be either a real learning experience or merely a way of relieving the stress.

For example, in avoiding the situation, you could choose to *run from* the cross-cultural experience. You may opt to leave the conflict because the effects are too painful for you to deal with or to try to understand. For someone whose self-awareness is limited, this could be the appropriate response. If one is not at a stage of personal evolution that leads to empathy across cul-

tural boundaries, it may be wiser for that individual not to continue serving Hispanic clients.

A more adaptive mode of the avoidance strategy is to withdraw, to give yourself the time and opportunity to understand the situation you are experiencing and the feelings it has aroused in you. Later, when you are more in touch with those feelings, you can return to the cross-cultural experience. In this case, the avoidance strategy is part of the learning process.

The option to *move against* the stress-producing intercultural experience implies two extremes — aggressiveness and assertiveness. In the first, the attitude most often is: "I'm right — you're wrong; I want the process to move *my* way at all possible costs." This approach does not validate the other person's right to his or her perceptions of reality. Instead, the communication partner is forced to take it or leave it. A more constructive use of the moving-against approach in experiencing the conflict is the assertiveness

c) MOVE WITH THE SITUATION

b) MOVE AGAINST THE SITUATION

a) AVOID THE SITUATION

COPING STRATEGIES

mode. One may actually initiate a confrontation, but in a way that allows both parties to express their views and to have them heard and respected. This type of "we're both right" approach opens up avenues for negotiation. You may still opt to have the process move "your way" as in the aggressive style. The difference is that you have acknowledged the validity of the other's point of view and, consequently, his or her worth as a human being. The risk of alienation for both parties is greatly reduced.

The third option, that of *moving with*, also implies two extremes. The first is to give up. This "you win" approach is a one-way process in which the other gets exactly what he or she wants from the interaction while you impose no limits or resistance of any kind. It is characterized by a "just tell me what you want and I'll conform" attitude that negates your own self-worth while falsely inflating that of the other. The opposite extreme is adjustment—effective negotiation of both persons' needs in order to create a new version of reality acceptable to both. Limits are set and acknowledged by both parties. Each individual is validated as a unique human being.

In addition to these basic strategies, other guidelines can help to lessen the impact of culture shock and speed the adjustment process.

1. Be aware that culture shock is a reality. It does exist and it can affect you despite your familiarity with other cultures.

2. Talk about the symptoms of culture shock as you experience them with supportive friends, colleagues, and counselors. Establish a support system with others who interact with clients of other ethnic backgrounds.

3. Try to identify as accurately as possible: (a) your assumptions about things, ideas, and people as determined by your own cultural conditioning and personal experiences, (b) the assumptions common to your Hispanic clients that may affect the delivery of services to them, and (c) the clashes that may arise between these two sets of assumptions and possible resolutions of these conflicts.

4. Keep your focus on the positive aspects of the adjustment process and the potential for personal and professional growth it offers.

5. Clarify the expectations of your clients and inform them in a constructive way of how the reality of the delivery of services in your agency differs from their expectations.

6. Go slowly; take things one step at a time. Do not expect to become an expert in cross-cultural communication skills overnight.

7. Always strive to establish a two-way communication system with your Hispanic clients. Remember that each is a unique individual, so that what worked with one Hispanic client may not with another. Also remember that the degree to which culturally determined behaviors, beliefs, and the like are evidenced in individual members of the culture will vary. Avoid stereotyping at all costs.

8. Check with your Hispanic clients to see if they are understanding you and if they have any questions. Remember that the degree of openness and frankness in such interaction may vary among individuals because of both cultural conditioning and personal communication styles.

9. Try to ask clients open-ended questions that begin with an interrogative word (*how, who, what,* etc.) rather than relying exclusively on simple yes–no questions that may omit pertinent information from the interview.

10. Always try to keep your sense of humor. Be ready and able to laugh at yourself when you have made a mistake or misunderstood your client. However, be sensitive to your clients' feelings if the error is on their part. Remember that a smile can help to establish rapport when words and other attempts to communicate fail.

Applications

1. Rank order the following list of values in order of personal importance to you, with number 1 reflecting the most important, and so on.

———— Family life	———— Physical exercise and activity
———— Professional achievement	———— Sharing with a mate
———— Financial security	———— Efficient use of time
———— Time alone	———— Being in touch with one's feelings
———— Peace of mind	———— Intellectual growth
———— Interaction with others	———— Relaxation
———— Spiritual development	———— Travel to other places

2. Share your list with another member of the class and listen as that person shares his or her list with you. Try to negotiate a new rank-ordered list that is acceptable to both of you. Do this in a way that validates the other person's perspectives as well as your own.

3. Now share your combined list with another pair's list. Try to negotiate a new rank-ordered list acceptable to all four people. Again, validate all parties involved as well as their points of view.

Reflections

1. What was the easiest part of this exercise for you? The most difficult? How different is the last list negotiated from your original one? How do you feel about that?

2. What techniques did you use to validate the perspectives of the others? What techniques did they use with you?

3. What feelings did you experience throughout the process? Were you aware of these at the time? How did you deal with these feelings? Did you use any of the strategies discussed earlier? Which worked best for you?

4. How do you think the others felt during the process? Did your feelings affect theirs? Vice versa?

5. What one communicating tool did you learn from this exercise that you can use when dealing with your Hispanic clients?

6. Have you experienced culture shock either while traveling in another country or while communicating with someone from another culture? What symptoms did you experience? What strategies did you use to deal with the symptoms?

7. Which of the strategies listed for dealing with culture shock while delivering services to Hispanic clients seems most appropriate to your personality? Do you feel comfortable in using any one of the three, depending on the situation? Why or why not?

HISTORICAL PERSPECTIVE: Education and the labor force

In order to understand the role of education and work in Hispanic cultures, one must look back to colonial times in Latin America. The interaction of the church, the representatives of the Spanish Crown, and the natural resources and indigenous social institutions that awaited the Spanish *conquistadores* explains much of the present-day socioeconomic reality of Latin America.

Colonies in Latin America began springing up in the early 1500s, predating those to the north by nearly a century. As mentioned earlier, the differences between the colonization of the United States and of Latin America account for much of the current socioeconomic disparity between the two.

Settlers came to the Northern Hemisphere with families to begin a new way of life, unlike the adventurers, missionaries, and colonizers who came to the Southern Hemisphere to strengthen Spain's hold on the newly annexed territories. Success in the latter endeavor brought wealth, power, and prestige to these individuals and to Spain, Europe's greatest power at that time.

The values of sixteenth-century Spain were reflected in the development of the economy and the educational system of the New World. At the time of the conquest of the new lands, Spain was emerging from a period marked by the *Reconquista* (Crusades against the Moors in Spain to recover the land taken by them), the *Inquisición* (the Inquisition, a severe interrogation process designed to discover and punish heresy and to assure strict adherence to Catholicism throughout the recently united autonomous regions of Spain), and the expulsion of the Jews from Spain.

The "typical" Spaniard of the period and "typical" Spanish attitudes toward work and education are interestingly described by the Italian historian and diplomat, Francesco Guicciardini (1483–1540), the representative of Florence in the court of King Ferdinand at the time of the conquest of the New World.

Spaniards are generally regarded as ingenious and astute people, but they have little taste for the mechanical or liberal arts. Almost all the artisans in the royal court are from France or some other foreign country. Nor do Spaniards devote themselves to commerce, for they think it shameful, and all give themselves to the airs of an hidalgo *(nobleman). They would rather eat the meager fare of a soldier, or serve some grandee, suffering a thousand privations and inconveniences . . . than devote themselves to commerce or some other work. . . .*

There is great poverty in Spain, and I believe this arises less from the quality of the country than from the nature of its people, who lack the inclination to devote themselves to industry and trade. The problem is not that Spaniards leave their country, but that they prefer to export the raw materials that the kingdom yields and buy them back in the form of finished goods. . . . Aside from a few grandees of the realm, who live sumptuously, the Spaniards live in very straitened circumstances. . . . Although they can manage with very little, they are not free from greed for gain. . . .

They are not given to letters. One finds little knowledge of Latin among the nobility or among the rest of the population. . . . In demonstrations and outward show they are very religious, but not in fact. . . . [1]

This rather unflattering, stereotypic view of sixteenth-century Spaniards highlights two qualities that apparently were operant in the conquest and colonization of the new lands: the disdain for manual labor and the desire for wealth in order to live as noblemen. Both are evidenced by the exploitation of the indigenous populations during the colonial period in Latin America.

The poorly developed industrial scene in sixteenth-century Spain described by Guicciardini came at a time when the Industrial Revolution was beginning in other parts of Europe. The New World soon became the major source of the raw materials that Spain sold to other countries for industrial use. Using the labor force provided by the indigenous population and its civilization based on communal work for the greater good, Spanish overseers in Latin America extracted the rich natural resources from the mines. Although the Spaniards lacked enthusiasm for working with their hands, the indigenous populations were accustomed by their political and religious beliefs to hard manual labor. The present-day stereotype of the poor *campesino* sitting under the tree saying *"mañana"* is far removed from the reality of the work life of most Hispanics.

1. Francesco Guicciardini, "Relazione di Spagna," in *Opere*, edited by Vittorio de Caprariis (Milano, 1961), pp. 29–31.

1. *How do the differences in the colonization patterns of Latin America and the United States affect the present-day socioeconomic system of each?*
2. *What details of Guicciardini's description of the "typical" Spaniard may account for the classification of most of Latin America as third world?*

The Spaniards' disdain for working with one's hands has left a legacy in the economy of Latin America. While the middle class in the United States is populated by both blue- and white-collar workers, the small, but growing, middle class in Latin America is composed primarily of bureaucrats, technocrats, small business owners, and professionals in the fields of law, medicine, accounting, architecture, and engineering. (Interestingly, the field of social work is relatively unknown in Latin America.)

Whereas in the United States a plumber may earn more than a teacher, this seldom happens in Latin America. The early *conquistador*'s dream of living like a nobleman has now been replaced by the desire for a white-collar position. Yet very few of those whose ancestors have lived through five centuries of colonization can conceive of such a dream as even a remote possibility for themselves or their children. There are few Horatio Alger myths in Latin America.

Another legacy of Spain in Latin America was the virtual exclusive control of education exercised by religion. Despite Guicciardini's assess-

ment of the Spaniards as "not given to letters," the first two universities in the New World, the universities of Lima, Peru, and Mexico City, were both established in 1551 by the Spanish Crown. Their primary objective was to train clergy and scholars. These universities were modeled on the medieval University of Salamanca, Spain, with its emphasis on metaphysical debates, rote memorization, and knowledge of the ancients. Censorship regarding what was taught in universities in the New World was a carry-over from the Spanish Inquisition. Needless to say, the universities were restricted to the conquerors and their children. The natives and mixed castes had long been relegated to a life of poverty and illiteracy.

In many areas of the Hispanic world, things have changed very little from colonial times. According to recent figures from the Interamerican Development Bank, the literacy rate for El Salvador and Honduras is 40 percent; for Bolivia, 63 percent; for the Dominican Republic, 66 percent; for Mexico, 78 percent. More industrialized countries such as Chile and Argentina, whose population is mostly of European origin, enjoy a literacy rate of 94 and 93 percent, respectively. These rates measure only the ability to read and

write and not the level of *functional literacy* — the ability to function in a technological society requiring sophisticated skills of reading, writing, analyzing, and synthesizing.

Nor has the educational system in most of Latin America evolved greatly since colonial times. (By contrast, the educational system in Puerto Rico, with its direct U.S. influence, is very similar to that on the mainland.) Although there are national universities not dependent upon the church for support or sanction, teaching methods have not changed much from the medieval style of rote memorization. Most professors are not employed full-time as academics but, rather, are professionals employed outside the university who come to the university to *dar clases* (give classes). Although these government-run universities technically are open to all students and charge little or no tuition, few students have the necessary academic background to benefit fully.

Two separate educational tracks exist — public and private. The former is mostly concentrated at the primary level, teaching basic skills up to the sixth grade, the terminal point for most students fortunate enough to attend. Some may continue on to low-level vocational schools or to public secondary institutions or other special schools, similar to the normal schools formerly prevalent in the United States, in order to become elementary teachers in the same system in which they were educated. This limited education cycle is all that is offered to students from the lower socioeconomic classes, although more of them are finding ways to attend universities.

The middle and upper classes rely primarily on private elementary and secondary schools called *colegios,* where, in grades seven to twelve, students receive an academic background broader than that commonly taught in U.S. public high schools. The *colegios* offer many of the courses that compose the liberal arts programs in U.S. colleges and universities. Their graduates are the students who enter the universities.

The division between graduate and undergraduate studies common in the United States is virtually unknown in Latin America. University students enter directly into the school (*facultad*) of their chosen profession (*carrera*) and graduate with a title such as *licenciado* (licensed, usually a law degree), *químico* (chemist), or *ingeniero civil* (civil engineer), designating their field of study.

In this century, university students have often been the most progressive elements in Latin America, often championing the cause of the working class and criticizing government policies by going on strike and demonstrating. Many of the liberal and radical movements for social and economic change have arisen among university students.

---

3. *Describe how the Spaniard's view of education relates to the present-day literacy rates of Latin American countries.*
4. *Describe the differences between the educational systems of the United States and Latin America, emphasizing their impact on the socioeconomic system.*

The colonial economic policy of exporting raw materials and agricultural products and importing manufactured goods still typifies Latin America, thus classifying most Spanish-speaking nations as belonging to the third world. After the independence movements of the nineteenth century, the developmental needs of countries lagging far behind the industrialized neighbors to the north soon brought in a new ruler — foreign capital. As we approach the twenty-first century, it is the multinational corporations who condone and promote the economic status quo of Latin America.

Some countries — for example, Argentina, Brazil, Mexico, and Venezuela — have made some economic gains through industrialization in the last few decades. Their progress has been hampered, however, by the ever-growing population among the lower socioeconomic classes, as well as by their increasing foreign debts and by the current instability and unpredictability of the world economic system.

It is from this economic situation that the great majority of Spanish speakers have come to the United States seeking economic survival or a better job. Low levels of literacy and formal education compound the problem for many Hispanics seeking to work in the United States. Many Hispanics with agricultural skills have found intermittent work along the migrant farm routes that run from south to north in the United States, but the resulting transience offers little hope for a stable home life or expanded educational opportunities for their children.

In the cities of the United States, Hispanics often find themselves on the lowest rungs of the employment ladder. Unemployment rates swell among Hispanic groups, who lack the required educational background and/or vocational training needed for most blue-collar jobs. Even those who are literate may not know enough English or may not have had the appropriate educational background to compete in a job market where functional literacy is required.

---

5. *What socioeconomic factors in Latin America account for the exodus of Hispanics and their subsequent arrival in the United States?*
6. *Describe the socioeconomic reality that most Hispanic immigrants and migrants meet upon arrival to the United States.*

Many Americans whose own ancestors have come from Europe criticize the current wave of recently arrived Hispanics for failing to assimilate and "make it" as their parents or grandparents did. These critics often do not see the differences between the Hispanic immigration of the last four decades and those of other ethnic groups in the late nineteenth and first half of the twentieth century. These include:

1. The basic historical differences between the poorer classes of industrialized Europe and those of colonized Latin America

2. The different economic climate during which the earlier migrations occurred, when unskilled labor was both needed and welcomed

3. The increased educational background required for most current employment opportunities

4. The discrimination often faced by Hispanics because of their mixed racial backgrounds

5. The impact that U.S. economic and political policies have had on the development (or lack of it) in Hispanic countries in the nineteenth and twentieth centuries

6. The accessibility of the homeland and the continued contact with the mother culture through the perpetual arrival of *compatriotas* (fellow countrymen) and the return visits to family and friends back home

7. The inability, economic or otherwise, of most Hispanics to leave the *barrio hispano* in order to integrate into the majority culture

8. The pride in ethnicity that has evolved in the United States since the 1960s, encouraging the maintenance of cultural mores

One possible answer to many of the contemporary problems faced by Hispanics in the United States is bilingual education. Ever since the westward expansion of the United States in the mid-nineteenth century, Hispanics have been underserved by the educational system because of the language barrier. Bilingual education is not a new phenomenon in the United States, since it has been traditionally available to other ethnic groups via private, often religious, sources. What is new is its incorporation into the public education system.

In recent years the topic of bilingual education has triggered much debate. Critics of bilingual education, like their counterparts who criticize Hispanics for not assimilating, often are unaware of the complex differences between the influx of Hispanics and the immigration of other ethnic groups. First of all, the Spanish language and Hispanic heritage are part of the history of this country, particularly in the Southwest. In addition, unlike the countries of European immigrants, which lie on the other side of the Atlantic Ocean, the geographic accessibility of Mexico, Central America, and the Caribbean strengthen the linguistic and cultural ties of Hispanics in the United States with their homelands. The political status of Puerto Rico as a commonwealth provides for unrestricted travel and two-way migration between the mainland and this Spanish-speaking island. The fact is that Spanish and English coexist as the predominant languages of the Western Hemisphere, and therefore Spanish is linked inextricably to both the history and the future of the United States.

The language barrier that many Hispanic youths face in the U.S. public school system is often considered the primary reason for the high dropout rate and lack of academic success among Hispanic groups. The fundamental concept of bilingual education is to provide instruction in the native language in the basic subjects until the Spanish-speaking students learn enough English in order to be instructed in that language. An adult professional who is learning Spanish as a second language might appreciate the difficulty of having to learn complex material in a foreign language if that individual were forced to study law or medicine in Spanish.

A secondary goal of bilingual education is that of preservation and appreciation of the Spanish language and the cultural values it reflects. It seems incongruous that the United States encourages the learning of a foreign language at the high school or college level as the mark of an educated person while at the same time discouraging native speakers of a language other than English from speaking and perfecting their native tongue.

Finally, it is important to realize that the word *educación* itself has a different cultural connotation in the Spanish-speaking world. It refers to one's *upbringing*, the training that children receive in dealing with others. The Hispanic culture places a good deal of emphasis on becoming *bien educado,* which is demonstrated by showing respect for others at all times. Specific behaviors include the formal greeting system, respect for elders and the family, respect for authority, and other nonverbal behaviors described in this text. A good formal education *(buena preparación)* is also valued. Those with university training are described as *bien preparados* (well-prepared) and are well respected for their academic accomplishments. Those who are *bien preparados* are also expected to be *bien educados.* It is important for English-speaking professionals to remember the need for seeing all clients as *bien educados,* whether or not they are *bien preparados.* Mutual respect can bridge the language and culture gap between the English-speaking provider of services and his or her Hispanic clients.

---

7. *What factors account for the differences surrounding the ability of European and Hispanic newcomers to assimilate to the U.S. socioeconomic mainstream?*

8. *What are the goals of bilingual education in the United States? What accounts for the debate about its value?*

NONVERBAL COMMUNICATION: Do clothes make the person?

In the workaday world of the United States, one's image is of utmost importance. The "dress for success" look of the 1980s reflects the renewed significance given appearances in the business world. The higher up one is on the corporate ladder, the more one is encouraged to conform to an approved dress code, to look the part as much as to act it. Countless books and courses guide prospective employees in developing a marketable image.

Although the recent emphasis in the United States has been on dressing up for work, North Americans are still noted for their casual, relaxed appearance at play. Wearing jeans to go to a restaurant, a party, the movies, or shopping has become the norm. It seems that across the United States, there is a growing awareness of the political and social statement one's appearance makes. Conformists opt for designer clothes even at play, while self-proclaimed nonconformists prefer the casual, carefree look even in the workplace and the classroom.

Women in particular have been reexamining the external image they wish to present. Their personal choices include wearing pants or skirts, high-heeled shoes or more comfortable flats, makeup or the natural look. Despite the efforts of the advertising media to promote conformance to culturally acceptable norms regarding appearance, people are often unsure which image they wish to project.

Although other countries are also experiencing instability regarding culturally determined dress norms, especially with the proliferation of the jeans and T-shirt syndrome, Spanish-speaking countries seem to be adhering to traditional standards more than elsewhere. Hispanics tend to be very concerned about the way they look, whether at work or at play. One's appearance is a reflection of one's self-respect, sense of modesty and refinement, consideration for others, and role in the family and the community. Following the latest style of dress is less important than being neat and clean, with no ragged hems, missing buttons, or specks of dirt.

In the Hispanic cultures, a dirty or unkempt appearance indicates negative feelings about oneself. This is true at all social-class levels, although one's economic status is reflected in the type and quality of the clothing worn. Nonetheless, the extreme disparity between the upper and lower classes explains much of the emphasis on one's external appearance in the Spanish-speaking world. The wealthy class prefers to follow a more conservative, European way of dressing, as do members of the middle class, to the extent that their economic means allow. Those with limited income are still concerned with portraying the best-dressed image possible. Generally, the only people who opt for the colorful native dress so popular in foreign boutiques in the United States are those of indigenous ancestry. Naturally there seems to be a stricter adherence to dress norms in cities than in the rural areas of Latin America.

It is especially important in the workplace for Hispanic employees to pay particular attention to their physical appearance. A professional who is not dressed in a respectable way may not be taken seriously. One's appearance in all public places, even in such informal situations as shopping and going to the movies, is expected to adhere to traditional standards of neatness and cleanliness. Even workers who wear uniforms in their job may dress like executives on the way to work.

Hispanic women, both those pursuing a career outside the home and those following a more traditional model, are very conscious of their appearance. Dresses are still more the norm than pants. Fashions that accentuate the female figure are favored, although modesty regarding the amount of bare skin that may show is more stringent than in the Anglo culture. Special attention is given to makeup, hair care, and well-manicured fingernails. It is rare for a Hispanic woman to leave her home without being dressed up. Few Hispanic females have been influenced by feminists' belief that excessive attention to their physical attractiveness encourages men to view them as sex objects.

Differences in attitudes toward clothing may present difficulties for Hispanics living in the United States. Hispanic clients may have a hard time taking seriously professionals who do not dress appropriately for work. There may be con-

flicts between Hispanic parents and their children, who are influenced by the more casual dress style of their Anglo peers. Hispanics may be seen as overdressing, especially when they wear more formal attire even in hot weather. Physical discomfort is less important than maintaining the cultural standards of modesty and self-respect. Hispanic women may be viewed as sexier because of their propensity for traditionally feminine dress styles, makeup, and high-heeled shoes. The importance that Hispanics place on all members of the family being well dressed may be judged by Anglo standards as an excessive need for clothing and personal toiletries, especially among families on fixed or limited incomes or government subsidies. In addition, members of the dominant culture in the United States may feel ill at ease with Hispanics whose appearance varies from the accepted norm.

The pressure to conform with regard to appearance has affected all U.S. immigrant groups. Those of northern European ancestry have had the least difficulty in assimilating to the majority culture because of their tendency to be fair-skinned. Those from southern Europe, Asia, Africa, and the Middle East, for the most part, have been less successful in adapting the way they look to conform to U.S. cultural standards since they do not easily blend into the WASP image. In the case of Latin Americans, whose heritage includes varying mixtures of Indian, Caucasian, and Ne-

gro races, assimilation has been even more difficult. Their difficulty is often proportional to the degree of racially different physical characteristics they manifest. In a society where racism is still evident, skin color, hair texture, and facial features are often more determinant in making superficial judgments about an individual's worth than the clothes that the individual is wearing.

The increasing influx of minorities living in the United States has triggered attempts to classify them by means of demographic studies. Many of these attempts have proved more cumbersome than helpful in trying to define the Hispanic population residing on the U.S. mainland. Some of the greatest inaccuracies arise from the questions used in surveys and on application blanks to ascertain racial background information. Hispanics are faced with a dilemma when they have to choose among "white, black, Native American, Asian, or Hispanic" as identity options. This error comes from confusing ethnicity with race.

Because of the rich intermingling of the various cultures, Hispanics may be both black and Hispanic. However, dark-skinned Latinos may view themselves as Hispanic rather than black, especially in the United States, where their Spanish-speaking culture distinguishes them from blacks from the United States or the English-speaking Caribbean. Some who express pride in their Indian heritage face a difficult choice — are

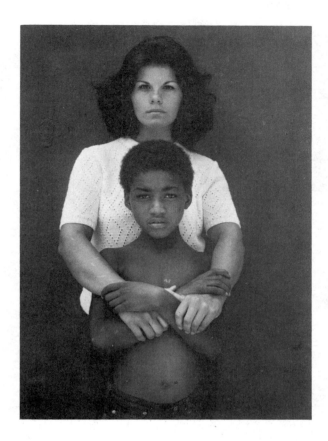

to those in the U.S. culture who are labeled non-white. Many people of Asian descent, whose families have lived in the Spanish-speaking world long enough to have assumed a Hispanic identity, face a similar dilemma when asked to classify their racial background.

The term *Spanish-surnamed* has often been used to fine-tune data gathering. In actuality, however, it compounds the problem further. There are many Hispanics with such non-Spanish-sounding surnames as O'Reilley, Mueller, Curt, Chang, and Scarletti, derived from their ancestors who immigrated from Europe or Asia to Latin America generations ago.

However Hispanics are classified and viewed from the Anglo perspective, the great majority demonstrate pride in their ethnic background, their cultural heritage and their personal appearance. Many leaders of Hispanic advocacy groups declare the myth of the melting-pot theory and advocate instead the beauty of the tossed-salad model of cultural diversity in the United States. Yet the pressures to conform are felt by all generations, especially the young. Often, those who exert such pressures have had little contact with people from culturally diverse groups and may simply fear the unfamiliar.

Whatever you personally may feel about cultural pluralism in the United States, you can best serve your clients' needs and your own professional growth by remembering the English proverb, "You can't judge a book by its cover." Regardless of appearance, every person deserves the opportunity to show the individual personality within. Your receptivity to each client's uniqueness allows that individual to shine through.

they Native American as well as Hispanic, or is the former term reserved only for North American Indian groups? Those whose Caucasian ancestry is most apparent may prefer to identify themselves as white rather than Hispanic. Their choice may stem from their realization of the inaccuracy of the identifying instrument as well as from their knowledge of the inferior status given

Putting it into practice

1. List below whatever images regarding personal appearance (physical characteristics as well as dress patterns) the following terms evoke:

   a. executive _____

   _____

   b. waitress _____

   _____

    c. doctor _____

_____

    d. migrant worker _____

_____

    e. welfare mother _____

_____

    f. Korean female _____

_____

    g. Greek male _____

_____

    h. Puerto Rican male _____

_____

    i. Mexican female _____

_____

    j. Cuban male _____

_____

    k. Spanish-surnamed _____

_____

    l. Hispanic _____

_____

2. What assumptions might each of the following professionals make regarding the Hispanic client described in each case history? Indicate where different cultural norms may lead to misinterpretations.

    a. An Anglo doctor examining a Hispanic woman who is dressed in an expensively tailored suit, with matching leather shoes and handbag

    b. An Anglo female lawyer interviewing a Hispanic male neatly dressed in a pair of dark trousers and brightly colored patterned shirt, who is seeking to file suit against an insurance company for an automobile accident

    c. A male social worker for Aid to Dependent Children interviewing a Hispanic female client who is wearing a nice cocktail dress and whose three children are dressed in Sunday-best clothes

3. List below the adjectives that define your own personal style of dressing:

_____

_____

Now circle the following statements that apply to your own personal grooming and dress standards:

    neat   clean   casual   sporty   trendy   preppy   tailored

    individual   fashionable   dress-for-success   bright-colored

    comfortable   appropriate-to-climate   attractive   sexy   stylish

    whimsical   frilly   exotic   attention-getting   practical

    easy-to-care-for   feminine   masculine   flashy   expensive

    subdued   tasteful   professional

4. List below images that come to mind regarding the personal appearance of your Hispanic clients:

_____

_____

_____

5. Decide what aspects of your Hispanic clients' physical appearance are similar to your own standards for personal appearance and which are different:

alike _____

different _____

How might these differences influence your attitude toward your Hispanic

clients? _____

_____

Comunicándose en español

The Spanish **t** is pronounced with the front of the tongue touching the back of the upper teeth, unlike the English initial *t* as in *tone*, which is pronounced with the front of the tongue touching the alveolar ridge (bumpy ridge above the front teeth). Spanish **t** is closer to the *t* sound in the English blend *st* as in *stone*. The Spanish **t** is not accompanied by the aspiration (puff of air) common to the English initial *t*.

Practice the following pairs of English words, comparing the sound of *t* when in initial position and when following the *s*. Also notice the aspiration accompanying initial *t*.

tab/stab   tub/stub   tone/stone   two/stew

Now practice the following words in Spanish, remembering to pronounce the **t** with the tongue touching the back of the upper teeth and *without* aspiration.

tu	trece	respeto	falta
tío	treinta	techo	aparato

Spanish **d** at the beginning of a breath group — that is, after a pause — and also after **l** or **n**, is similar to the English *d*. However, this Spanish *hard* **d** is dental, pronounced with the front of the tongue touching the back of the upper teeth, while in English *d*, the tongue touches the alveolar ridge.

The difference between the Spanish **t** and **d** is that the latter is voiced — that is, the vocal cords vibrate. You can feel this vibration by placing your fingers on your larynx (the bony part of your throat) as you pronounce **d**. You may have difficulty, at times, hearing the difference between Spanish **t** and **d**, since the lack of aspiration with Spanish **t** makes it harder to distinguish it from Spanish **d**. Compare:

tos/dos   te/de   ti/di   teme/deme

Pronounce these Spanish words with the *hard* **d** sound:

donde	ven**d**e	el **d**octor	un **d**ía
duerme	compren**d**e	el **d**ormitorio	un **d**olor

In all other instances, Spanish **d** is similar to English *th* as in *that*. This includes words beginning with **d** that are *not* after a pause but rather in the middle of a breath group. At the end of a word, Spanish **d** is pronounced like a very weak *th* and at times disappears entirely. In colloquial Spanish, the **d** sound in the combinations **-ado** and **-ido** may disappear (e.g., **separado** is pronounced **se-pa-ra-o**).

Pronounce these words with Spanish *soft* **d**:

na**d**a	ver**d**ad	la **d**octora	una **d**emocracia
to**d**o	uste**d**	la **d**irección	**d**ivorcia**d**o

Práctica

Pronounce these sentences in Spanish. It may help to underline those instances in which **d** is pronounced like English *th,* which are more frequent than the Spanish *hard* **d** sound:

1. La doctora Salgado está divorciada.
2. ¿Es usted el licenciado Torres?
3. ¿Cuántos tíos tiene Migdalia?
4. Buenas tardes, Doctor Dávila. ¿Se siente Ud. bien hoy?
5. Tengo que decirte la verdad, David.

Dictado

Now write the phrases and sentences your instructor dictates:

1. _____   4. _____

2. _____   5. _____

3. _____   6. _____

7. _____

8. _____

9. _____

Señor Marcarenas, me dice la secretaria que Ud llegó recientemente de México.

Sí, me casé con una americana que estudiaba en la Universidad Autónoma. Decidimos vivir aquí porque hay más oportunidades.

¿Qué oficio tenía Ud. en México?

Soy licenciado en derecho y trabajaba de abogado en una compañía exportadora.

¿Y qué tipo de empleo le interesa a Ud. ahora?

Bueno, me gustaría seguir trabajando en el campo de derecho.

Hay pocas posibilidades sin el inglés y sin graduarse de una facultad de derecho de aquí.

Pero asisto a clases de inglés en la escuela nocturna. Necesito establecerme pronto.

Comprendo, señor, pero el único trabajo que le puedo ofrecer es el de conserje en una fábrica. Pagan cuatro cincuenta la hora.

Pues, vengo de mi país bien preparado. Prefiero trabajar usando la cabeza y no las manos.

Lo siento mucho, señor Marcarenas, pero no hay nada más que yo pueda hacer. Avíseme para mañana si quiere el puesto o no.

No sé. Tengo que pensarlo.

280

¿Ha entendido bien?

1. ¿Por qué vive ahora el señor Marcarenas en los Estados Unidos?

2. ¿Qué preparación formal tiene él en derecho?

3. ¿En qué campo quiere trabajar ahora?

4. ¿Cree el señor Livingston que el señor Marcarenas pueda trabajar fácilmente en ese campo? Explique su respuesta.

5. ¿Qué puesto le ofrece el señor Livingston? ¿Cuánto paga?

6. ¿Le interesa el puesto al señor Marcarenas? Explique su respuesta.

7. ¿Cree Ud. que el señor Marcarenas debe aceptar el puesto? ¿Por qué?

8. ¿Ve Ud. otra alternativa para el señor Marcarenas?

9. ¿Qué factores culturales pueden afectar la decisión del señor Marcarenas?

10. ¿Quisiera Ud. vivir en un país hispano y buscar trabajo allí? Explique su respuesta.

INTRODUCTORY DIALOGUE: In the employment office

Mr. Livingston: Mr. Marcarenas, the secretary tells me that you recently arrived from Mexico.

Mr. Marcarenas: Yes, I married an American (woman) who was studying at the Autonomous University (of Mexico). We decided to live here because there are more opportunities.

Mr. L: What occupation did you have in Mexico?

Mr. M: I have a law degree and I worked as a lawyer in an export company.

Mr. L: And what type of work interests you now?

Mr. M: Well, I would like to continue working in the field of law.

Mr. L: There are few possibilities without English and without having graduated from a law school here.

Mr. M: But I am attending English classes at night. I need to establish myself here soon.

Mr. L: I understand, sir, but the only job I can offer you is as a (that of) janitor in a factory. The pay is four-fifty an hour.

Mr. M: Well, I come from my country well prepared. I prefer to work using my head and not my hands.

Mr. L: I am very sorry, Mr. Marcarenas, but there is nothing else I can do for you. Let me know by tomorrow if you want this position or not.

Mr. M: I don't know. I have to think about it.

BASIC STRUCTURES I: What do you do (for a living)?

The employee (f.)	*The client (m.)*
Trinidad Valbuena, please.	That's me. (I am he.)
Come in, Mr. Valbuena, and sit down.	Thank you, ma'am.
I understand (have it understood) that you are currently unemployed, true?	Unfortunately it is true.
How long have you been out of work?	More than two months.
Where was your last job (where were you working before)?	I worked for the Hall Company.
What were you doing (in what were you working)?	I worked as { a mechanic. / an electrician. / a plumber. / a carpenter. / a janitor. }
How long did you work for that company?	I spent six years with them.
Did you like the work you had?	Well, I did not like it much (a great deal). I would like to learn another skill (occupation).
How much were you earning?	I started with a salary of $4.50 an hour. When they let me go, they were paying me $6.73.
Do you currently receive (any) financial aid from the state?	I receive $250 monthly from { welfare. / social security. / unemployment. / food stamps. }

¿Sabe usted?

1. Whereas English colloquially uses the object pronouns after *it's* (*it's me, is it him?*), Spanish *always* uses **ser** + the subject pronouns: **Soy yo. Son ellos.**

2. **Trabajar + de** = *to work as a(n)* + name of profession. **Trabajar como** is used metaphorically (**Trabaja como un caballo**, *He works like a horse.*)

3. **Época** is used for a period of time consisting of days, weeks, months, or years. **Rato** refers to a shorter period of time, usually a few moments or hours.

4. You may also hear **salario, estipendio,** and **pago** for *sueldo.*

5. **Empleo, trabajo,** and **puesto** are commonly used for *job.*

6. **Anual, mensual,** and **semanal** are adjectives meaning *yearly, monthly,* and *weekly.* **Al año, al mes, a la semana, al día,** and **a la hora** are also commonly used.

282

La empleada	El cliente
Trinidad Valbuena, por favor.	Soy yo.
Pase, Sr. Valbuena, y siéntese.	Gracias, señora.
Tengo entendido que Ud. está desempleado durante esta época, ¿verdad?	Desgraciadamente es verdad.
¿Cuánto tiempo hace que Ud. está sin trabajo?	Hace más de dos meses.
¿Dónde trabajaba anteriormente?	Trabajaba para la compañía Hall.

¿En qué trabajaba?　　Trabajaba de

- mecánico.
- electricista.
- plomero.
- carpintero.
- conserje.

¿Cuánto tiempo hacía que trabajaba para esa compañía?	Llevaba seis años con ellos.
¿Le gustaba el trabajo que tenía?	Pues, no me gustaba mucho. Quisiera aprender otro oficio.
¿Cuánto ganaba?	Empecé con un sueldo de $4.50 (cuatro cincuenta) la hora. Cuando me dejaron ir, me pagaban $6.73 (seis setenta y tres).

¿Recibe Ud. ayuda económica del estado actualmente?　　Recibo $250 mensuales de

- bienestar público.
- seguro social.
- desempleo.
- cupones de alimento.

---

7. You may also hear the anglicism **el welfare**. **Estampillas** (rather than **cupones**) **de alimento** is often used by Mexican Americans.

Notas lingüísticas I

A. *More/less than* is expressed by **más/menos** + **de** + number. In other comparisons, **más/menos** is followed by **que**. The expression **no más que** means *only*.

Tengo más de dos dólares.	I have more than two dollars.
No quedan más que dos días.	There are only two days (left).
Trabaja más que su hermano.	He works more than his brother.
Tiene menos empleados que yo.	He has fewer employees than I do.

B. Adverbs in Spanish are most commonly formed by adding **-mente** to the feminine singular form of the adjective:

desgraciada		desgraciadamente
anterior	+ mente =	anteriormente
posible		posiblemente

BASIC STRUCTURES II: What's your educational background?

The employee (f.)	*The client (m.)*
	I got up to (reached) { sixth / seventh / eighth / ninth / tenth } grade.
What's your educational background? (How many years of schooling do you have?)	I graduated from { high school. / a private high school. / high school. }
	I have a high school diploma.
	I finished a year at (of) the university.
When did you leave school (your studies)?	I left (it, them) nine years ago.
Why did you leave your last job?	I left (it) because they fired me (from the position). I wasn't getting along well with the supervisor.
What did you like most about your last job?	I liked { the atmosphere / the money / the responsibility / the people I worked with } most.
What type of work are you looking for now?	I want a job where I { can earn more. / learn English. / have more contact with people. }
Would you like to enter into a special training program?	It depends. What programs are there?
There are several. Perhaps this paramedic program interests you.	Do they pay while you are in the training program?
Well, they pay you a low salary the first month and then they increase it each month.	How long does it last?
It lasts a year. Does it interest you?	Of course it interests me. Where can I get more information about the program?
When you leave here, go see Mr. Robinson, the person in charge of these programs.	That's fine. Thank you very much (a thousand thanks), ma'am.
Don't mention it.	

ESTRUCTURAS BÁSICAS II: ¿Cuántos años de escuela tiene Ud.?

La empleada	*El cliente*
	Llegué hasta el { sexto / sé(p)timo / octavo / noveno / décimo } grado.
¿Cuántos años de escuela tiene Ud.?	Me gradué { de la secundaria. / del colegio. / de la escuela superior. }
	Tengo el bachillerato.
	Terminé un año de la universidad.
¿Cuándo dejó sus estudios?	Los dejé hace nueve años.
¿Por qué dejó Ud. su último empleo?	{ Lo dejé porque me echaron del puesto. / No me llevaba bien con el supervisor. }
¿Qué le gustaba más de su último trabajo?	Me gustaba más { el ambiente. / el dinero. / la responsabilidad. / la gente con quien trabajaba. }
¿Qué tipo de trabajo busca Ud. ahora?	Quiero un trabajo donde { pueda ganar más. / aprenda inglés. / tenga más contacto con la gente. }
¿Le gustaría entrar en un programa de adiestramiento especial?	Depende. ¿Qué programas hay?
Hay varios. Tal vez le interese éste de paramédico.	¿Le pagan a uno mientras esté en el programa de adiestramiento?
Pues, le pagan un salario bajo el primer mes y después lo aumentan cada mes.	¿Cuánto tiempo dura?
Dura un año. ¿Le interesa?	Claro que me interesa. ¿Dónde puedo conseguir más información sobre el programa?
Cuando salga de aquí, vaya a ver al señor Robinson, la persona encargada de estos programas.	Está muy bien. Mil gracias, señora.
No hay de qué.	

¿Sabe usted?

1. You may also hear **grado** + cardinal number: **Terminé el grado seis,** *I finished the sixth grade.*

2. **Graduarse** is always used reflexively: **Mi hijo se graduó de la escuela superior.**

3. **Colegio** refers to a private, usually secondary, school. Since there is no Spanish equivalent for *college,* **colegio** may be heard to refer to that type of institution. In most Hispanic countries, **bachillerato** refers to the secondary school preparation for university studies and not to a *bachelor's degree.* Upon completion of university studies in a given area **(carrera),** the student becomes **licenciado** *(licensed* or *titled)* in that professional field and may use either **licenciado** or **doctor** with the surname, although not actually possessing a doctorate degree. In Puerto Rico, however, **bachillerato** refers to the university degree.

4. **Dejar** means *to leave behind, to leave off* or *stop* (often followed by **de** + the infinitive) and *to allow* or *let,* and, therefore, can take direct and indirect objects. **Salir** means *to leave a place* (or *to go out)* and is followed by **de** + place when the latter is mentioned:

Mi esposo me dejó en mayo.	My husband left me in May.
Dejé mis estudios en 1982.	I left school in 1982.
Me dejaron ir en junio.	They let me go in June.
Dejé de fumar el domingo.	I stopped smoking on Sunday.
Salí temprano anoche.	I left early last night.
Salgo del trabajo a las dos.	I leave work at two.

5. **Llevarse bien** (literally, *to carry each other well)* is a reciprocal reflexive used to describe getting along with another person: **Mi supervisor y yo nos llevamos muy bien,** *My supervisor and I get along very well.*

6. **Echar,** literally *to throw* or *fling,* is used in many idiomatic expressions. In this lesson it means *to fire.* **Botar** *(to throw out),* **despedir** *(to say good-bye to),* and **dejar ir** *(to let go)* are also used. You may hear the anglicism **me dieron el layoff.**

7. **Entrenamiento** may also be heard for *training,* although **adiestramiento** (from **diestro,** *skilled)* is technically more appropriate.

8. **La gente** is used to refer to *people* in a general sense (**Me gusta trabajar con la gente). Persona(s)** is used in a specific sense: **Hay dos personas que quieren verlo,** *There are two people who want to see you.* It is always a feminine noun, even when referring to a man: **Carlos es una persona inteligente.** *Carlos is an intelligent person.*

Notas lingüísticas II

A. There are two past tenses in Spanish, the preterite and the imperfect. You have learned the forms for regular verbs in the preterite. To form the imperfect, drop the **-ar, -er,** or **-ir** of the infinitive, and add the following endings.

	-ar verbs	*-er and -ir verbs*	
	trabajar	hacer	salir
yo	trabaj*aba*	hac*ía*	sal*ía*
tú	trabaj*abas*	hac*ías*	sal*ías*
Ud., él, ella	trabaj*aba*	hac*ía*	sal*ía*
nosotros/as	trabaj*ábamos*	hac*íamos*	sal*íamos*
Uds., ellos/as	trabaj*aban*	hac*ían*	sal*ían*

There are only three irregular verbs in the imperfect:

	ser	ir	ver
yo	era	iba	veía
tú	eras	ibas	veías
Ud., él, ella	era	iba	veía
nosotros/as	éramos	íbamos	veíamos
Uds., ellos/as	eran	iban	veían

Ejemplos: **Yo *trabajaba* en una fábrica.**
Mi esposo *recibía* desempleo.
¿A Ud. le *gustaba* el trabajo que *tenía*?
Me *pagaban* cuatro sesenta la hora.
***Íbamos* a la Oficina de Desempleo.**

B. Both the preterite and imperfect tenses are used to describe actions that occurred in the past. At a specific moment in the past, an action could have
begun, ended, or been in progress. The beginning or ending of an action is
described by the preterite. Actions in progress are described by the imperfect.
The imperfect is also used to refer to habitual, repeated actions in the past.
Compare the following:

Beginning of the action:
Anoche yo *cené* a las seis.   Last night I ate (began to eat) at six.
El jefe me *habló* a la una.   The boss spoke (began to speak) to me
                                          at one o'clock.

Action in progress:
Anoche a las seis yo *cenaba*.   Last night at six I was eating (in the
                                          process).

A la una yo *hablaba* con él.   At one I was speaking (in the process)
                                          with him.

End of the action:
Usted *llegó* tarde hoy.   You arrived late today (act of arrival
                                          over).

Me *gradué* del colegio en 1978.   I graduated from the school in 1978.

Habitual action:
Yo siempre *llegaba* tarde.   I always used to arrive late (habitual
                                          action).

De niño siempre me *gustaba* el   As a child, I always liked algebra.
álgebra.

In a narrative in the past, the imperfect provides the setting (e.g., time, place, atmosphere) while the preterite describes the events that took place:

Eran las dos de la madrugada.	It was two in the morning.
Todos *dormían* tranquilamente.	Everyone was sleeping peacefully.
De repente, alguien *llamó* a la puerta.	Suddenly, someone knocked at the door.
Salí del dormitorio para investigar.	I left the bedroom to investigate.

Verbs that describe *internal* states (mental, physical, and emotional), such as **querer, ser, estar, tener, saber, creer, pensar, doler,** are *usually* in the imperfect tense in the past unless the sentence describes the *beginning* or *end* of the condition, most often as a reaction to a stated or implied cause:

Yo **estaba** muy nerviosa.	I was very nervous. (imperfect)
Hasta que hablé con el doctor **estuve** nerviosa.	Until I spoke with the doctor I was nervous. (preterite—end of being nervous)

C. The **hace** + *time* expression can be used at the end of a sentence in the preterite to refer to *time ago.*

Dejé el empleo hace tres meses.	I left the job three months ago.

Desde hace + *time* can be used at the end of a sentence in the present tense to refer to *duration of time.*

Estoy sin trabajo desde hace tres meses.	I've been without a job for three months.

Hacía + *time* + **que** + *imperfect* is used to indicate how long something was going on in the past.

Hacía tres meses que buscaba trabajo.	I had been looking for a job for three months.
Hacía dos años que nos conocíamos cuando nos casamos.	We had known each other for two years when we got married.

D. The subjunctive mood can be used in both adjectival and adverbial clauses.

1. An adjectival clause is one that describes a person or thing. The verb in the adjectival clause is in the *indicative* mood if the clause describes a specific, definite referent, and in the *subjunctive* if it describes an ideal, conceptual, or nonexistent person or thing. Compare:

Indicative:

Tengo un empleo que *paga* bien.	I have a job that pays well. (describes a specific job)
Busco al jefe que *sabe* inglés.	I'm looking for the boss who knows English. (describes a specific boss, one you know)

Subjunctive:

Quiero un empleo que *pague* bien.	I want a job that pays well. (describes an ideal job)
Busco un jefe que *sepa* inglés.	I'm looking for a boss who knows English. (describes a boss who may or may not exist)

2. An adverbial clause usually describes the verb by telling how, when, or where something takes place. The decision between indicative and subjunctive in the adverbial clause depends on the following criteria:

    a. Certain adverbial conjunctions are *always* followed by the subjunctive. The most common of these are the **CASPA** (*dandruff*) conjunctions (the first letter of each spells **caspa**).

*C*on tal que	provided that
*A*ntes (de) que	before
*S*in que	without
*P*ara que	in order to, so that
A menos que	unless

Trabajo para que la familia tenga una vida buena.	I work so that the family has (may have) a good life.
Prefiero dejar el puesto antes de que me boten.	I prefer to leave the position before they fire me.

    b. Adverbial *time* conjunctions are followed by the *subjunctive* when they describe an event in the *future* and by the *indicative* when they describe a *habitual action* or a *past experience*. The most common time conjunctions are:

cuando	when		**después (de) que**	after
mientras	while		**tan pronto como**	as soon as
hasta que	until			

Indicative:

Hablo inglés cuando *trabajo.*	I speak English when I work. (habitual action)
Recibí desempleo después que me *botaron* del puesto.	I received unemployment after they fired me. (past action)

Subjunctive:

Voy a hablar inglés cuando *trabaje.*	I'm going to speak English when I work. (in the future)
Voy a recibir desempleo después de que me *boten* del puesto.	I'm going to receive unemployment after they fire me. (future act)

    c. If there is no change in subject in the subordinate clause, the infinitive is used after the prepositions **sin, para, hasta, antes de,** and **después de.** Compare:

Subject 1 different from subject 2:

Trabajo **para que** *tengamos* una vida mejor.	I work so that we'll have a better life.
Yo *voy a comer* **antes de que** *salgamos.*	I'll eat before we leave.

Subject 1 same as subject 2:

Trabajo **para** *ganar* dinero.	I work to make money.
Yo *voy a comer* **antes de** *salir.*	I'll eat before leaving (I leave).

d. Other adverbial clauses follow the same criterion of adjectival clauses: the *indicative* is used when a specific, definite action is described; the *subjunctive* is used when an unspecific, nonexistent, or indefinite action is described. Several common adverbial conjunctions are:

como(quiera)	how(ever)
aunque	although
donde(quiera)	where(ver)

Indicative:

Lo *escribí* como Ud. lo *quería*.	I wrote it the way you wanted it.
Se lo *digo* aunque *es* difícil.	I'll tell it to him although it is difficult.

Subjunctive:

Lo *escribo* como Ud. lo *quiera*.	I'll write it however you (may) want it.
Se lo *digo* aunque *sea* difícil.	I'll tell it to him although it may be difficult.

e. The expressions **tal vez** and **quizás** (*perhaps*) and **ojalá (que)** (*may God grant that*) are usually followed by the subjunctive:

¿Tal vez le *interese* este empleo?	Perhaps this job interests you?
Quizás *vengan* más tarde.	Perhaps they'll come later.
Ojalá (que) *encuentre* Ud. un buen trabajo.	I hope (may God grant that) you find a good job.

PRÁCTICA PRELIMINAR

Follow general guidelines for self-instructional practice.
A. Write the appropriate *preterite* form of **salir** or **dejar** as needed by context.

Ejemplo: Juan ___salió___ para el trabajo.

1. Ayer (yo) _____ el cheque en la oficina.

2. José _____ a su esposa el año pasado.

3. ¿Cuándo _____ (tú) de fumar?

4. ¿A qué hora _____ Uds. anoche?

5. (Nosotros) _____ del trabajo a las cinco.

6. Paco _____ con su novia anoche.

7. Ayer (yo) _____ temprano a buscar empleo.

8. Mis padres no me _____ trabajar.

A 1. dejé 2. dejó 3. dejaste 4. salieron 5. salimos 6. salió 7. salí 8. dejaron

B. Choose **de** or **que** as needed by context.

Ejemplo: Quiero que me des más (que (de)) cinco dólares.

1. No hay más (que   de) dos trabajadores en la oficina, Jorge y Carlos.

2. Las secretarias trabajan más (que   de) los jefes.

3. Cuando me dejaron ir, ganaba menos (que   de) $5.50 (cinco cincuenta) la hora.

4. Hace más (que   de) dos meses que estoy sin empleo.

5. Busco un empleo donde pueda ganar más (que   de) $20,000 (veinte mil) al año.

6. Ahora que me siento bien, puedo trabajar más (que   de) la semana pasada.

7. No tengo nada más (que   de) decirle.

8. No puedo comprar ese libro porque cuesta tres dólares y no tengo más (que   de) $2.40 (dos cuarenta).

C. Fill in the blank, translating the English adverb given in parentheses.

Ejemplo: Necesito *exactamente* (exactly) cinco dólares.

1. Ella puede hacer el trabajo _____ (easily).

2. Escriba Ud. su dirección _____ (clearly).

3. _____ (possibly) tenemos un empleo que le guste.

4. _____ (unfortunately) no domino el inglés.

5. _____ (naturally) es necesario volver al trabajo.

6. Yo dejé el puesto _____ (freely).

7. Es difícil conseguir empleo, _____ (especially) en esta época.

8. La secretaria me dijo que Ud. quería hablar conmigo _____ (personally).

B 1. que 2. que 3. de 4. de 5. de 6. que 7. que 8. que

C 1. fácilmente 2. claramente 3. Posiblemente 4. Desgraciadamente 5. Naturalmente 6. libremente 7. especialmente 8. personalmente

D. Give the preterite and imperfect forms of the verb.

		Pretérito	*Imperfecto*
Ejemplo:			
yo	llamar	*llame*	*llamaba*
1. nosotros	llegar		
2. ella	conocer		
3. tú	entender		
4. tú	trabajar		
5. yo	empezar		
6. Uds.	vivir		
7. él	escribir		
8. tú	salir		
9. Ud.	ser		
10. yo	pagar		
11. nosotras	aprender		

E. Translate from Spanish to English the following sentences that a client might use to describe the past.

Ejemplo: Yo salí a las seis mientras mi hijo veía la tele.
I left at six o'clock while my son was watching TV.

1. Mi hijo se graduó del colegio en 1978.
2. Yo trabajaba para mi hermano en esa época.
3. Nos llevamos bien hasta que llegó el nuevo jefe.
4. De niño, siempre me gustaba salir con mi papá.
5. Me dejaron ir la última semana de agosto.
6. Llegué hasta el sexto grado.
7. Yo terminaba el bachiller cuando murió mi mamá.
8. Cuando me despidieron, ganaba $6.60 (seis sesenta) la hora.
9. Yo trabajé seis años de mecánico.
10. Siempre llegaba tarde al trabajo.

D 1. llegamos; llegábamos 2. conoció; conocía 3. entendiste; entendías 4. trabajaste; trabajabas 5. empecé; empezaba 6. vivieron; vivían 7. escribió; escribía 8. saliste; salías 9. fue; era 10. pagué; pagaba 11. aprendimos; aprendíamos

E 1. My son graduated from (the private) high school in 1978. 2. I was working for my brother at that time. 3. We got along well until the new boss arrived. 4. As a child, I always used to like to go out with my dad. 5. They let me go the last week of August. 6. I went up to the sixth grade. 7. I was finishing high school when my mother died. 8. When they fired me, I was earning $6.60 an hour. 9. I worked six years as a mechanic. 10. I always used to arrive late at my job.

F. Indicate if the italicized verbs should be in the preterite or imperfect.

From 1978 until 1982 I (1) *worked* for Suárez Imports, Inc. I (2) *used to like* my job very much. But one day everything (3) *changed* when the new boss (4) *arrived.*

He (5) *used to work* for a company in California. His former boss (6) *recommended* him, saying that Mr. Becker (7) *was* very creative.

So, what (8) *happened* when Mr. Becker (9) *arrived* at Jason Imports? His first day on the job he (10) *decided* to change all our systems. He (11) *started* by changing our record keeping, which (12) *used to be* very efficient, just because he (13) *didn't like* it. The biggest change (14) *was* the worst—he (15) *fired* me, saying that my services (16) *were* no longer *needed.* So now I'm unemployed, thinking about the way things (17) *used to be.*

G. Now fill in each blank with the appropriate past tense verb form as determined by context.

Desde el 1978 hasta el 1982, yo (1) _____ (*trabajar*) para la Compañía Importadora de Suárez. A mí me (2) _____ (*gustar*) mucho el trabajo. Pero un día todo (3) _____ (*cambiar*) cuando (4) _____ (*llegar*) el nuevo jefe.

Antes (5) _____ (*trabajar*) para una compañía en California. El otro jefe lo (6) _____ (*recomendar*), diciendo que el señor Becker (7) _____ (*ser*) muy creativo.

Entonces, ¿qué (8) _____ (*pasar*) cuando (9) _____ (*llegar*) el señor Becker a la Compañía Importadora de Suárez? El primer día en el trabajo (10) _____ (*decidir*) cambiar todos nuestros sistemas. (11) _____ (*empezar*) por cambiar nuestro sistema de archivo, el cual (12) _____ (*ser*) muy eficaz, simplemente porque no le (13) _____ (*gustar*). Pero el mayor cambio (14) _____ (*ser*) el peor—él me (15) _____ (*botar*), diciendo que él ya no (16) _____ (*necesitar*) mis servicios. Y ahora estoy sin empleo, pensando en como (17) _____ (*ser*) las cosas antes.

F 1. preterite 2. imperfect 3. preterite 4. preterite 5. imperfect 6. preterite 7. imperfect 8. preterite 9. preterite 10. preterite 11. preterite 12. imperfect 13. imperfect 14. preterite 15. preterite 16. imperfect 17. imperfect

G 1. trabajé 2. gustaba 3. cambió 4. llegó 5. trabajaba 6. recomendó 7. era 8. pasó 9. llegó 10. decidió 11. empezó 12. era 13. gustaba 14. fue 15. botó 16. necesitaba 17. eran

H. Translate from Spanish to English the following description of Rosa Álvarez'
search for a bilingual secretary. Pay special attention to the use of the subjunctive in the narrative.

1. Hace seis meses que yo busco una secretaria que domine bien el inglés y
el español.

2. Necesito una persona que también sepa mucho de la educación bilingüe.

3. Es importante que la secretaria que trabaje para mí se lleve bien con los
niños que asisten a esta escuela.

4. Mis colegas me dicen que me hace falta una buena agencia de empleo para
que no tenga que pasar tanto tiempo entrevistando a candidatas.

5. Es posible que tengan razón. Sin embargo, es difícil encontrar una agencia
que tenga personal que hable español.

6. La semana que viene, cuando tenga más tiempo libre, voy a buscar una
agencia que tenga personal que hable español.

I. Indicate whether the italicized verbs should be in the indicative or subjunctive
mode or remain in the infinitive. If the verb should be in an indicative past
tense, indicate whether it should be in the preterite or imperfect.

For many years I've been looking for a job that (1) *pays* well, where I (2)
can do my work however I (3) *like.*

I work because I (4) *want* to contribute something important to life. Therefore, I need a position that (5) *gives* me the opportunity to make the world
better.

I know that there are not many jobs that (6) *allow* the individual (7) *to do*
all that he or she (8) *may want.* Although I (9) *may be* an idealist, I think it
(10) *is* important that all workers (11) *have* more control over their work environment.

When I (12) *graduated* from the university, I (13) *believed* that it (14) *was
going* to be easy to get my ideal job. Now I know very well that I (15) *am* not
going to find it until I (16) *have* enough money to (17) *start* my own company.

J. Now fill in each blank with the appropriate indicative tense, present subjunctive, or infinitive as needed by context.

Hace muchos años que busco un empleo ideal. Quiero un empleo que (1)

_____ (pagar) bien, donde yo (2) _____ (poder) hacer mi tra-

bajo como me (3) _____ (gustar).

H 1. I have been looking for six months for a secretary who speaks English and Spanish very well. 2. I need a person
who also knows a lot about bilingual education. 3. It's important that the secretary who works for me get along
well with the children who go to this school. 4. My colleagues tell me that I need a good employment agency so
that I don't need to spend so much time interviewing candidates. 5. It's possible that they're right; nevertheless,
it's difficult to find an agency that has Spanish-speaking personnel. 6. Next week, when I have more free time, I'm
going to look for an employment agency that has Spanish-speaking personnel.

I 1. subjunctive 2. subjunctive 3. subjunctive 4. indicative 5. subjunctive 6. indicative 7. subjunctive 8. subjunctive
9. subjunctive 10. indicative 11. subjunctive 12. indicative-preterite 13. indicative-imperfect 14. indicative-imperfect
15. indicative 16. subjunctive 17. infinitive

Yo trabajo porque (4) _____ (*querer*) contribuir algo importante a la vida. Por eso, me hace falta un puesto que me (5) _____ (*dar*) la oportunidad de mejorar el mundo.

Yo sé que no hay muchos empleos que (6) _____ (*permitir*) que la persona (7) _____ (*hacer*) todo lo que (8) _____ (*querer*). Aunque yo (9) _____ (*ser*) idealista, creo que (10) _____ (*ser*) importante que todos los trabajadores (11) _____ (*tener*) más control sobre el ambiente en que trabajan.

Cuando yo me (12) _____ (graduar) de la universidad yo (13) _____ (*creer*) que (14) _____ (*ir*) a ser fácil conseguir mi empleo ideal. Ahora sé muy bien que yo no lo (15) _____ (*ir*) a encontrar hasta que yo (16) _____ (*tener*) suficiente dinero para (17) _____ (*empezar*) mi propia compañía.

K. Choose the phrase that best completes the first part of the sentence according to both context and the criteria for choosing the indicative or subjunctive.

1. Si es urgente, tal vez (tú) . . .
2. Ud. puede trabajar donde . . .
3. Tengo una casa que . . .
4. Es verdad que mi jefe y yo . . .
5. Espere aquí hasta que (yo) . . .
6. Busco una casa que . . .
7. No puedo comprar muebles a menos que . . .
8. No dejé el puesto hasta que (yo) . . .
9. Es importante que los empleados . . .
10. El médico dice que puedo volver al trabajo cuando me . . .

a. encontré otro empleo.
b. nos llevamos muy bien.
c. los compro a plazos.
d. tenga cuatro dormitorios.
e. vamos a México.
f. vuelva.
g. sienta mejor.
h. se lleven bien.
i. quiera.
j. me gusta.
k. puedes ver al jefe hoy.
l. puedas hablar con el jefe hoy.
m. los compre con tarjeta de crédito.
n. habla español.

J 1. pague 2. pueda 3. guste 4. quiero 5. dé 6. permiten 7. haga 8. quiera 9. sea 10. es 11. tengan 12. gradué 13. creía 14. iba 15. voy 16. tenga 17. empezar
K 1. l 2. i 3. j 4. b 5. f 6. d 7. m 8. a 9. h 10. g

Combinándolo todo

PRÁCTICA COMUNICATIVA: La escuela y el trabajo

Conversación parcial

Practique Ud. oralmente la siguiente conversación. Cada raya (/) implica que falta una palabra. Es necesario conjugar cada verbo *en bastardillas.*

La empleada	*El cliente*
1. *Tener* / que Ud. *buscar* empleo.	Sí, señora, me *hacer* / un / .
2. ¿En / *trabajar* Ud. mientras *vivir* / Cuba?	Yo *trabajar* / plomero / seis años.
3. ¿ / *gustar* ese / .	No, no / *gustar* mucho.
4. ¿Cuál *ser* su último / aquí / los EE.UU.?	*Trabajar* / conserje.
5. ¿Cuándo *dejar* Ud. / puesto?	/ *dejé* hace / meses.
6. ¿ / *ganar* Ud. cuando lo *dejar.*	*Ganar* seis cincuenta / hora.
7. ¿*Recibir* Ud. desempleo ahora?	No. No / *solicitar* porque (yo) *dejar* el / .
8. ¿Qué / de / *buscar* Ud. ahora?	*Querer* / empleo / *pagar* bien.
9. ¿*Querer* seguir trabajando / conserje?	Pues, prefiero / empleo donde *poder* trabajar / la gente.
10. ¿ / años / escuela *tener?*	*Llegar* / el noveno / .
11. / ver. Yo *tener* / consultar / lista / empleos / ver si hay uno / le *convenir.*	Bueno, / . ¿*Esperar* o *volver* / tarde?
12. *Esperar* / , por / .	Gracias.

Pregunte Ud.

Haga Ud. oralmente las preguntas necesarias en la siguiente entrevista con Amelia González, una señora de cuarenta y dos años que quiere empezar sus estudios universitarios el año que viene. Ayúdela a decidir qué carrera le conviene más.

1. Me gradué del colegio hace 24 años.

2. Pues, en el colegio me gustaba mucho la biología.

3. Cuando estaba en el colegio quería ser enfermera, pero me casé a la edad de 18 años y tuve cuatro hijos.

4. No, nunca trabajé fuera de casa hasta que mi hija menor se graduó del colegio el año pasado.

5. Conseguí un trabajo de ayudante (*aid*) en un hogar para ancianos.

6. Pues, al principio a mi esposo no le gustaba la idea, pero ahora ve que es importante que yo tenga una carrera.

7. Quisiera ser dentista, pero yo sé que soy muy vieja para esa carrera.

8. No sé. ¿Qué otras carreras hay en el campo de la salud?

9. Quiero un trabajo donde pueda ayudar a la gente.

10. Tal vez Ud. tenga razon. Es posible que me convenga ser enfermera practicante. ¿Dónde puedo conseguir más información sobre esta carrera?

Dígalo

Pregunte a un/a compañero/a de clase lo que dice su profesor/a sobre los temas del trabajo, el salario, la educación formal, el trabajo ideal, y el estar sin trabajo.

Escuche bien

A. Ud. oirá a seis clientes que describen un empleo. Escriba *pasado* si describe un empleo del pasado y *actual* si describe un empleo actual (de ahora).

1. _____ 4. _____

2. _____ 5. _____

3. _____ 6. _____

B. Ud. oirá a seis clientes que describen un empleo. Escriba Ud. *ideal* si describe un empleo ideal que busca el cliente y *actual* si es un empleo que ya tiene.

1. _____ 4. _____

2. _____ 5. _____

3. _____ 6. _____

Diálogos cortos

I. *Sara Borges, la jefa*   *Máximo Gómez, el empleado*

                                                      ¿Se puede, señora?

Adelante, señor Gómez. ¿En que   Bueno, señora, tengo un problema con
                                                      mi nueva supervisora.
_____ servirle?

¿ _____ es _____   No creo que a ella le gusten los hispanos.
 problema?   Ella no se lleva bien con ninguno de no-
                                                      sotros.

Pues, _____ Gómez,   Puede ser, pero yo quiero que Ud. hable
                                                      con ella lo más pronto posible.
_____ posible _____

usted _____ equivocado.

Señor Gómez, _____ cinco   Sí, señora, y es la primera vez que tengo
                                                      un problema de este tipo.
años _____ Ud. trabaja

_____ nosotros, ¿verdad?

Entonces, voy _____   Mil gracias, señora.

hablar _____ ella hoy
mismo.

II. *El empleado*   *La cliente*

Sra. Carrera, ¿ _____   Ya hace más de tres semanas.

tiempo hace _____ Ud.

_____ desempleada?

¿En _____ trabajaba?   Era oficinista en la compañía de gas.

¿Cuánto _____ hacía que   Llevaba tres años allí.

_____ allí?

¿ _____ gustaba ese   Cuando empecé el trabajo, me gustaba
                                                      bastante, pero después no me llevaba
_____ ?   bien con mi jefe.

¿Fue por eso que _____ el   Sí, señor. Por eso lo dejé.
empleo?

¿ _____ ganaba Ud.?   Me pagaban 12 000 dólares el año.

El empleado	La cliente
¿ _____ tipo de _____ busca ahora?	Quisiera aprender a trabajar con computadoras.
¿ _____ interesa entrar _____ un _____ de adiestramiento?	Sí, estoy muy interesada. ¿Cómo puedo obtener más información?

Ayude al cliente

You need to write a short note to Jesús Romero, the supervisor of your patient (client) Migdalia Moreno, explaining how her back problems affect her work. Begin the letter with *Muy estimado señor Romero.*

1. Tell him your name and your professional relationship with the client, mentioning her name. Tell him that you are writing to him to inform him of the physical (*físicos*) problems that Mrs. Moreno has.

2. In a new paragraph, tell him that Mrs. Moreno has been suffering from back problems (*sufrir de problemas de la espalda*) for more than two years. Add that they began to get worse (*empeorarse*) six months ago when she changed jobs.

3. Tell him that you believe that she cannot continue to work in the kitchen of the hospital because it hurts her back (*le hace daño a la espalda*). Tell him it's important that she have a job where she can be seated (*estar sentada*) most (*la mayor parte*) of the day.

4. Thank him for his help in finding her a new position in the hospital which will help her to get better. Tell him he can call you if he has any questions and give your phone number.

5. End the letter with *Su seguro/a servidor/a* and sign your name.

¿Comprende Ud.?

Escuche bien las calificaciones de los cuatro hispanos que buscan trabajo. Escriba la letra del (de los) programa(s) de adiestramiento que mejor le convenga(n) a cada uno. Es posible que más de uno les convenga.

_____ 1. Gonzalo Rivera

_____ 2. Sonia Ramírez

_____ 3. Marta Cruz

_____ 4. Alberto Medina

a. secretary
b. social worker assistant
c. paramedic
d. police officer
e. teaching assistant
f. interpreter (Spanish-English)
g. accountant
h. paralegal assistant
i. office machinery repair apprentice

Piénselo

Prepárese para poder hablar con el/la profesor/a o con otros estudiantes sobre los siguientes temas, contestando las preguntas que le sugiera el/la profesor/a:

1. El estado actual de la economía
2. Los programas de adiestramiento
3. La ayuda económica del estado
4. La educación formal y el trabajo
5. Los beneficios del trabajo

SITUACIONES DE LA VIDA REAL

Imagínese

1. ¿En qué trabajan estos hombres?
2. ¿Son todos hispanos?
3. ¿Cuál es el jefe? ¿Cómo se llama? ¿De dónde es?
4. ¿Cuánto tiempo hace que él es el jefe?
5. ¿Cuánto gana el jefe? ¿Y los empleados?
6. ¿Se llevan bien los empleados y el jefe?
7. ¿Por qué no hay mujeres en el grupo?
8. ¿Tienen los empleados mucho interés en lo que les dice el jefe?
9. ¿Son profesionales los empleados? ¿El jefe?
10. ¿Están bien vestidos (*well-dressed*) todos en el grupo?

1. ¿De dónde es este señor?
2. ¿Cómo se llama? ¿Cuántos años tiene?
3. ¿Le gusta su trabajo? Explique su respuesta.
4. ¿Dónde vende la guitarra que produce? ¿Es cara o barata?
5. ¿Le gusta al señor trabajar con las manos (*hands*)?
6. ¿A Ud. le gusta trabajar con las manos? Explique su respuesta.
7. ¿A Ud. le gusta comprar cosas hechas a mano (*handmade*)?
8. ¿Es posible ganar mucho dinero fabricando guitarras a mano aquí en los Estados Unidos? Explique su respuesta.
9. ¿Trabaja el señor para otra persona o por su propia cuenta (*on his own*)?
10. ¿Cuáles son algunas ventajas (*advantages*) de trabajar por su propia cuenta? ¿Hay desventajas?

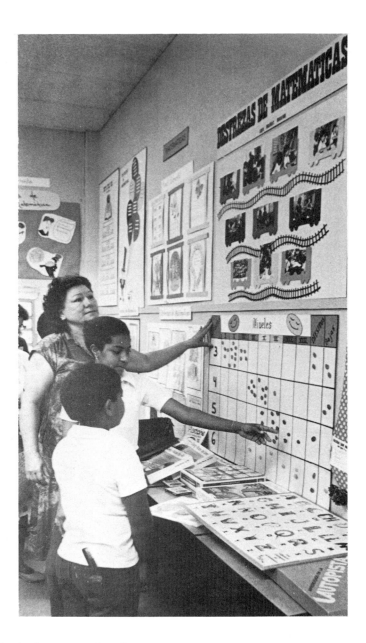

1. ¿De qué nivel es esta clase?
2. ¿Cómo se llama la maestra? ¿De dónde es?
3. ¿Domina la maestra el inglés y el español?
4. ¿De dónde son los estudiantes?
5. ¿Cuántos años tienen?
6. ¿Cuánto tiempo hace que viven en los Estados Unidos?
7. ¿Qué lengua(s) dominan?
8. ¿Qué materia (*subject*) aprenden?
9. ¿Quisiera Ud. aprender matemáticas o ciencias en español? ¿Por qué?
10. ¿Cree Ud. que es una ventaja o una desventaja ser bilingüe? Explique su respuesta.

Lea Ud. la siguiente carta. Aunque contiene mucho vocabulario nuevo, use la imaginación para entenderla. Después, conteste las preguntas que siguen.

Querido hermanito mío,

Llevo ya tres meses aquí en Nueva York. Todavía no tengo empleo. Gracias a Dios que nuestro primo Miguel y su esposa Ramona están aquí. Ellos son tan buenos conmigo, dejándome vivir en su casa, sin que les pague nada. Pero no sé cuánto tiempo más puedo tolerar estar desempleado.

Cada día paso de cinco a ocho horas caminando de oficina en oficina buscando trabajo. Yo creía que hablaba muy bien el inglés después de estudiarlo por seis años en el colegio. Pero casi no entiendo nada de lo que me dice la gente. ¡El acento con el cual hablan aquí no se parece en nada al acento de los maestros del colegio!

También es peligroso caminar por las calles de la ciudad, especialmente de noche. Hay muchos crímenes a mano armada. ¡Anoche la hermana de Ramona fue atacada y casi violada en su propio apartamento! Afortunadamente, su esposo llegó a casa y sorprendió al canalla.

Pues, no sé que más decirte. A veces me siento arrepentido de haber dejado mi bella isla por este ambiente tan frío y poco cómodo. Tal vez sea mejor ser pobre y feliz en su propio país que rico y miserable aquí. Espero quedarme hasta diciembre. Si no encuentro ningún trabajo, entonces vuelvo a Santo Domingo. Saludos a todos.

Te echa de menos,
Carlos

1. ¿Cuánto tiempo lleva Carlos en Nueva York?

2. ¿Con quién vive? ¿Cuánto paga de alquiler?

3. ¿Tiene trabajo Carlos?

4. ¿Cuántos años de escuela tiene?

5. ¿Según él, es fácil encontrar trabajo en Nueva York?

6. ¿Le gusta el ambiente de la ciudad?

7. ¿Qué quiere decir *crímenes a mano armada*? ¿Qué quiere decir *violar*?

8. ¿De qué se siente arrepentido Carlos? ¿Por qué?

9. ¿Cree Ud. que Carlos va a quedarse en Nueva York? Explique su respuesta.

Haciendo el papel

1. Ud. es el único supervisor que habla español en la compañía donde trabaja. Hoy tiene que hablar con Santos Salgado, un empleado de hace seis meses, sobre la primera evaluación oficial de su trabajo. Use el siguiente formulario que completó el supervisor del señor Salgado para informarle de los varios comentarios sobre su trabajo. Mencione los factores culturales que tal vez influyan en la evaluación.

Employee Evaluation of Santos Salgado

Strengths

1. Good worker

2. Seems to get along well with co-workers

3. Seems interested and enthusiastic about his job

Weaknesses

1. Habitually arrives ten to fifteen minutes late for work

2. Seems reluctant to ask questions of supervisor regarding work

3. Tends to indicate that he has understood instructions, even when

    he has not

---

2. Usted es un/a trabajador/a social en una escuela donde 20 por ciento de la población es hispana. La escuela no tiene programa de educación bilingüe. Usted

está hablando con Magdalena León, la mamá de Enrique, que tiene doce años y está en el sexto grado. La familia sólo lleva cinco meses en los Estados Unidos. La maestra de Enrique dice que Enrique no presta atención (*doesn't pay attention*) en la clase y parece ser una persona solitaria que no quiere estar con los otros estudiantes en la clase. Ud. cree que los problemas de Enrique son debidos a las dificultades de adaptarse a la nueva lengua y cultura. Hable con la señora León sobre la familia, el proceso de adaptarse, y las habilidades lingüísticas de Enrique.

3. Ud. es un/a consejero/a en una universidad del estado. Una estudiante que se llama Elena Salcedo quiere hablar con Ud. sobre el siguiente anuncio de la Reserva del Ejército. Conteste sus preguntas sobre las ventajas y desventajas de esta manera de financiar sus futuros planes educativos.

HAZ ALGO ESTE VERANO, QUE TE PAGUE DURANTE TODO EL AÑO

Llegó el tiempo de buscar trabajo de verano! Si estás en escuela superior sabes que estos trabajos están al borde de la extinción.

Pero... vamos a suponer que encontrarás un trabajo de verano, a tiempo completo... que te brinde la oportunidad de viajar, que te enseñe un oficio que puedas usar en la vida civil... y que te pague y te mantenga trabajando sólo un fin de semana al mes durante el año escolar, sin afectar tus estudios.

Un trabajo de verano en la Reserva del Army, te ofrece ésto y más. Te ganarás sobre $1,100 en sólo ocho semanas durante tu entrenamiento inicial. Además, te ganarás otros $1,200 al año mientras sirves en una unidad de la Reserva del Army en tu área, un fin de semana al mes. Y lo mejor de todo es que puedes aprender un oficio de provecho en tu comunidad.

Ahora tenemos vacantes disponibles en los campos de mantenimiento de equipos mecánicos, transportación y comunicaciones.

En adición a todo ésto, ya tendrás un trabajo asegurado para el siguiente verano, además de otros $1,100 más.

Si quieres saber más,

visita a tu reclutador de la Reserva más cercano.

ARMY RESERVE. BE ALL YOU CAN BE.

4. Ud. trabaja en una agencia que tiene los siguientes puestos disponibles.

SE SOLICITA PERSONA CON BBA O EQUIVALENTE EN EXPERIENCIA EN ADMINISTRACION Y VENTAS, CON CONOCIMIENTO DE PINTURA.

Carro propio, preferiblemente que resida en área de Mayagüez. Salario a discutirse y beneficios marginales.

Patrono con igualdad oportunidad de empleos.

GANE MUCHO DINERO COMO JEFE DE GRUPO

Requisitos:
*Deseos de progresar.
*Habilidad para trabajar con jóvenes mayores de 12 años.
*Conocer Area Metropolitana
*Vehículo en buenas condiciones (preferible Van o Station Wagon)

Centro de Empleos

22-PROFESIONALES
FARMACEUTICO GRADUADO: Para turno de noche y fin de semana.

5-21

24-GENERALES

NECESITO URGENTE: Pintor con experiencia en neveras y equipo doméstico.

¿LE INTERESA hacer comerciales? Necesitamos niños, adultos y adolescentes para comerciales de T.V. Inscripción $25,00 y adiestramiento.

SE SOLICITA Estilista con experiencia, si no tiene experiencia no llamar. Buen sueldo.

ACADEMIA NECESITA Part-Time Maestros de Ballet, Bailes generales, Maestra de Canto, Modelaje. Maestro clases Música Instrumental.

SE SOLICITA repostero con experiencia para panadería en Dorado. Si no tiene experiencia no solicite.

SE NECESITA Bookkepper typing, bilingüe, viva área de Puerto Nuevo. Experiencia importante.

SI ESTAS desempleado o necesitas aumentar los ingresos, esta es tu oportunidad. Para entrevistas

Entreviste a un/a compañero/a de clase en español para completar la siguiente solicitud. Después, hable con él/ella sobre el/los puesto/s que mejor le convenga/n según sus calificaciones.

Careers Unlimited, Inc.

Name _____ Soc. Sec. No. _____

Address _____ Phone _____

Age _____ Birthdate _____ Birthplace _____

Languages spoken: _____

Educational background:

Type of program	Dates attended	Degree	Major

Employment history:

Type of job	Location	Dates	Salary

Special skills, interests, aptitudes:

_____

_____

Type of position sought, salary requirements:

_____

_____

References:

Name	Address	Relationship

REFLEJOS DE LA CULTURA: "No saco nada de la escuela"

Many believe that education is the key to economic and social progress for Hispanics living in the United States. Yet many Hispanic children have experienced barriers to educational success, resulting in a higher high school dropout rate for Hispanics than for Anglo or black students. The greatest barrier may be language. It is this problem which bilingual education hopes to resolve.

An equally important barrier to success in the Anglo educational system is often the lack of cultural awareness on the part of non-Hispanic teachers. The main goal of any public educational system is to encourage students to conform to the social values of the majority culture. These, however, may be at odds with the cultural values learned by children in Hispanic homes.

The following *Acto*, a short dramatization from the collection of Chicano playwright Luis Valdez' *Teatro Campesino*, provides a satirical look at how an Anglo teacher's lack of respect for and understanding of the minority culture may act as a barrier to the educational success of Hispanic children. The message is loud and clear: "Conform if you want to succeed in the Anglo culture." Yet the corollary is also evident: "Such gains are not without some loss." In this instance, the loss is one of personal identity and integrity.

The *Actos* are meant to be performed before live audiences. In the words of Valdez, *"El Teatro Campesino* . . . is putting all the joys, sorrows, history and culture of *La Raza* on stage to be examined, to be remade, to pass on to others and to show others that there are answers, that things don't have to be this way." The power of dramatization is evident in this portrayal of Chicano life in the Anglo school system.

(**Scene:** *An elementary school classroom, somewhere in the Southwest*)

Teacher: Who's next. Moc . . . Moc . . . (*She can't pronounce his name.*) Ramirez!

Monty: Yes, teacher?

Teacher: How do you pronounce your name?

Monty: Moctezuma.

Teacher: What?

Monty: Moctezuma?

Teacher: Oh! What a funny name! (*She laughs and class joins her. Teacher stomps foot and shuts them up.*) Class! (*To Moctezuma.*) And what does it mean?

Monty: He was an emperor in the times of the Indians. He was a Mexican like me.

Teacher: Oh! You mean Mon-tezuma.

Monty: No, Moc-tezuma.

Teacher: *Mon*tezuma.

Monty: *Moc*tezuma.

Teacher: *Mon*tezuma!

Monty: *Moc*tezuma!

Teacher: Montezuma! (*Begins to march up and down stage singing "Marines Hymn."*) "From the halls of Monte-zoo-oo-ma to the shores of Tripoli." (*Using her oversized pencil as a bayonet, she stabs Monty, who falls forward with head and arms hanging.*) Now what's your name, boy? (*Lifts his head.*)

Monty: Monty.

Teacher: Do your ABC's.

Monty: A is for airplane, B is for boat, and C is for . . . ah, C is for . . . for . . . cucaracha!

Teacher: What!

Monty: (*Crying.*) Cuca—cuca-qui-qui.

Teacher: (*Twisting his ear*) What you meant to say was *cock-a-roach*, right?

Monty: Sí.

Teacher: What? (*Twists his ear even more.*)

Monty: Yes!

Teacher: Yes, what?

Monty: Yes, teacher!

Teacher: Sit down. (*He sits down crying.*) And shut up! Let's see who's next. Oh, yes, Francisco.

Francisco: ¿Qué?

Teacher: Oh! Another one that can't speak English! Why do they send these kids to me? You can't communicate with them. Is there anybody here that can speak Spanish?

Monty: I can, teacher.

Teacher: Tell him to do his ABC's.

Monty: Dice que digas tus ABC's.

Francisco: Dile que no las sapo[a] en inglés, nomás en español.

Teacher: Oh, sit down! This has been a most trying day! Class dismissed . . . (*Students start to run out cheering.*) except (*They freeze.*) for Monty and Franky. (*Points to them. The rest of the class runs out.*)

. . .

Teacher: Now look, boy. Tell him his name is no longer Francisco, but Franky.

Monty: Dice que tu nombre ya no es Francisco, es Franky.

Francisco: No, es Francisco . . . Panchito.[b]

Monty: Hey, teacher, he said his name is still Francisco. (*Francisco punches him in the back.*)

Teacher: Look, boy, Francisco—no, Franky—yes.

Francisco: No, Francisco.

Teacher: Franky!

Francisco: Francisco.

Teacher: Franky!

Francisco: O.K. (*As teacher begins to walk away—to audience.*) Francisco.

Teacher: It's Franky!!!

Francisco: (*Grabs sign and throws it on the ground.*) Es Francisco, ya stufas.[c]

Teacher: Oh! You nasty boy! (*Beats him over the head twice.*) Remember the Alamo! (*Hits him again.*) And just for that, you don't pass!

Monty: Teacher, teacher, do I pass? (*Picks up sign, and hands it to her.*)

Teacher: I suppose so. You are learning to speak English. (*To audience.*) They shouldn't place these culturally deprived kids with the normal children. No, no, no. (*She leaves—stomps out. Monty begins to follow.*)

Francisco: (*Getting up from floor.*) Oye, Moctezuma. ¿Qué dijo esa vieja, chaparra y panzona? (*old, short, fat lady*)

Monty: Dijo que tu no pasates[d]; you don't pass.

Francisco: Y tú pasates.

Monty: Sure, I pass. I speak good English, and besides, my name isn't Moctezuma anymore . . . it's Monty.

Francisco: No, es Moctezuma.

Monty: Monty.

Francisco: Moctezuma.

Monty: It's Monty. See, you stupid? You never learn. (*Sticks his tongue out at him and leaves.*)

Francisco: (*Crying.*) Entonces dile a tu teacher que coma chet![e] (*Leaves crying.*)

---

[a]Incorrect form of *sé*.

[b]Diminutive form.

[c]Obscenity.

[d]Ungrammatical form for *pasaste*.

[e]*Chet = shit.*

Evaluación del progreso—Lecciones 7–8

RAISING AWARENESS

A. Discuss how one's attitude toward culture shock can influence whether or not it is a bad experience or an opportunity for personal growth.

B. Discuss how strategies of avoidance, moving against, and moving with can be used to resolve cross-cultural communication conflicts.

C. Discuss the support system of the Hispanic family and how it may be used in providing services to Hispanics in the United States.

D. How does the socioeconomic reality of Hispanics in the United States reflect traditional attitudes toward work and education among the various social classes in Latin America?

E. Discuss the identity problems faced by many Hispanic adolescents living in the United States and how these may affect the delivery of services to them and to other members of their families.

F. Discuss what misinterpretations can arise from initial judgments made regarding Hispanics in the United States based on superficial visual cues.

COMUNICÁNDOSE EN ESPAÑOL

A. **Pronunciación** Write the sentences your instructor dictates. Underline instances of *soft* **b**, **v**, and **d**.

1. _____

2. _____

3. _____

B. **Discriminación auditiva** Circle the letter of the most appropriate response to each oral question or statement you hear.

1. a b c	5. a b c	8. a b c
2. a b c	6. a b c	9. a b c
3. a b c	7. a b c	10. a b c
4. a b c		

COMBINÁNDOLO TODO

A.   Comprensión oral   Write the name of the client and, in English, what the client needs and the monetary amount mentioned.

	Name	*Needs*	*Amount of money*
1.			
2.			
3.			
4.			
5.			
6.			

B.   La entrevista   Give the questions and/or responses needed in the following dialogue.

	El empleado	*La cliente*
1.	_____ datos _____.	Muy bien. ¿Qué necesita saber?
2.	¿ _____ ?	Vivimos en el 52 de la calle 13.
3.	¿ _____ ?	Queda en Brooklyn, entre la quinta y sexta avenidas.
4.	¿ _____ o _____ ?	Es un apartamento en el tercer piso de una casa.
5.	¿ _____ ?	Hay cuatro: dos dormitorios, la sala, y la cocina.
6.	¿ _____ personas _____ ?	Somos tres: mis dos hijas y yo.
7.	¿ _____ ?	Pagamos 375 pesos mensuales.
8.	¿ _____ ?	No, no viene con muebles. Todos los muebles son míos.
9.	¿ _____ ?	Yo nos mantengo.
10.	¿ _____ ?	Ahora no puedo trabajar porque tengo problemas de salud.
11.	¿ _____ ?	Sí, recibo $125 a la semana de desempleo.
12.	¿ _____ ?	No, no recibo cupones de alimento, pero me hacen falta.
13.	¿ _____ ?	Mi último trabajo fue de costurera (*seamstress*) en una factoría en Manhattan.

14. ¿ ———————————— ?   No, no sé cuándo pueda volver al tra-
                                       bajo. El doctor me dice que quiere verme
                                       en dos semanas y no quiere que vuelva
                                       a trabajar antes de esa cita.

15. Muy bien, señora. ——————   Mil gracias, señor. Yo lo llamo el viernes,
    cupones de alimento.   si está bien.

C. En acción Choose one of the following situations and act it out with your
instructor or one of your classmates.

1. Discussing the lack of response from the landlord of the client's apartment regarding needed repairs

2. Interviewing a client to see if he or she qualifies for a mortgage

3. Teaching a recently arrived Hispanic couple with limited economic resources
   what to buy and how in order to set up their household

4. Using the ten-year-old male child of a female client as an interpreter, discussing
   the client's dismissal from her job, which she thinks is due to discrimination
   and sexual harassment

5. Interviewing a young Hispanic adolescent who dropped out of school in the
   tenth grade regarding getting his equivalency diploma and enrolling in a training program for paramedics

6. Counseling a female college freshman regarding possible career opportunities
   for her

LECCIÓN 9

Hay que divertirse

LOS OBJETIVOS

Raising awareness

1. To understand the psychological dimensions of effective cross-cultural communication reflected in Gestalt theory
2. To appreciate the traditional Hispanic attitudes toward celebrations, holidays, sports, eating, and drinking
3. To interpret correctly Hispanic cultural norms regarding noise levels, leisure activities, laughter, and smiles

Comunicándose en español

1. To pronounce and comprehend **r** and **rr**
2. To use and understand structures and vocabulary to discuss clients' eating habits and dietary needs
3. To use and understand negative structures and changes in meaning between preterite and imperfect tenses

Combinándolo todo

1. To integrate all material from previous sections and lessons by engaging in more challenging professional activities in Spanish
2. To use and understand nuances of differences indicated by verb tense and mood
3. To understand the nostalgic association between foods and one's native culture through the view of an exiled Cuban

315

Raising awareness

OVERVIEW: Dealing effectively with cross-cultural conflict and confrontation

In the last chapter we discussed the importance of letting yourself experience both culture shock and its resultant conflicts and confrontations, accepting them as a natural and inevitable part of the process of cross-cultural communication. Until you allow yourself to feel the confusion, the ambivalence, the doubts, and the frustrations that come your way as you attempt to adjust to the new cultural environment in which you find yourself, you will be unable to deal effectively with these feelings. This process has no room for guilt or self-denigration or for "shoulds" or "musts." Nor can anyone give you a simple set of guidelines that defines how to communicate effectively across cultural boundaries. The approach presented here reflects a Gestalt orientation to the intercultural understanding as developed in Pierre Casse's *Training for the Cross-Cultural Mind*. It evolves from one basic premise — "in cross-cultural communication there is no rule with the exception of one: there is no rule. That's the rule" (p. 119).

This revelation may be disappointing to you. It may seem an amorphous approach to resolving cross-cultural conflicts and confrontations. You may feel that you've been brought so far along the path of raising your awareness and then left at an intersection without guideposts.

Yet raising awareness leads to an indefinite conclusion precisely because of the uniqueness of each individual. What works for one may not work for another. By knowing more about oneself and the cross-cultural communication process, each of us can then find the most appropriate way to resolve a conflict with someone from a different cultural background.

Although the Gestalt approach to resolving intercultural misunderstandings offers no rules, it is based on the following assumptions.

1. Each individual takes responsibility for him or herself. This implies that each person possesses strength and power. It avoids a "taking care of" syndrome in which those who view themselves as stronger take responsibility for the behavior and feelings of others. Actually, those who accept and shoulder so much responsibility often suffer from a weak self-concept and low self-esteem.

This assumption correlates with our earlier view of each individual as unique. We all have the same human needs but differ in how we get those needs met. The "I am responsible for my actions and you for yours" approach assumes the basic equality of all men and women. This assumption underlies all effective communication, regardless of the cultural backgrounds involved.

2. It is also important that both partners share a common focus on the situation at hand, the goals of each, and the needs and feelings that surface. If one is focused on the past, including prior experiences of a similar nature, one's awareness of the present interaction will be less accurate and more prone to distortion.

3. As mentioned earlier, conflicts and confrontations in intercultural communication are creative opportunities for learning and growth. Since there are no rules for resolving these conflicts, each individual must learn to choose an appropriate strategy. By consciously observing how a given strategy works for you in a variety of encounters, you can become more aware of when and how to use it to your best advantage. The resolution of each conflict will depend on the situation, the individuals involved, and the other variables related to the encounter.

4. Throughout the communication process one's awareness should be focused on one's own feelings, both physical and emotional. By relying on one's own intuition to receive internal feedback, one can choose the appropriate communication strategy. Authentic communication requires greater emphasis on self-awareness and one's own responses than on the communication partner and his or her needs. Since one can control only one's own actions and reactions, not those of others, it is important to stay in touch from within. In this way one exercises one's own

personal strength by choosing wisely the best strategy for resolving the conflict.

5. The autonomy of each partner is paramount to effective cross-cultural communication. Just as each is encouraged to take responsibility for his or her own actions and feelings, it follows that each has the capability to choose his or her course of action. This approach may be fearsome to people who prefer predictability and tight control. Those who have used techniques in the past to successfully manipulate the behavior of others and their responses through intimidation, giving orders, and the like, may feel uncomfortable about relinquishing control. Nonetheless, authentic communication respects the autonomy of both parties and consequently leaves both feeling better about themselves.

6. Being honest as one communicates is viewed as healthy in the Gestalt model. Sometimes such honesty about how one feels may reveal a closed attitude toward the interaction. This is not judged as bad behavior but, rather, as a genuine feeling. As long as one is self-aware enough to acknowledge it and can communicate this in a way that validates the other person's right to be, this is effective communication.

7. Closely related to this honest approach is the principle of authentic behavior, which leads to more genuine relations between people. To be authentic means nothing more than both people allowing each other to be who they are. Role playing, masks, and the like are dropped.

8. The primary goal of the Gestalt approach is to increase the individual's competence regardless of his or her cultural background. The model encourages people to know and understand what it is they want, how they keep themselves from getting what they want, and what alternatives they have available to them to fulfill their needs. This model discourages game playing and manipulation in exchange for direct interaction that validates self and others despite divergent viewpoints and cultural backgrounds.

9. The strategy of withdrawing, as mentioned earlier, is accepted in the model as a healthy, positive choice in certain situations. For example, it is appropriate when an individual needs time away from the direct stimulation of the cross-cultural communication process in order to evaluate what is happening, recharge energy, and develop new strategies for dealing with the process of intercultural contact. Other strat-

egies outlined here are equally positive options. Self-awareness is the key to choosing wisely.

10. The model equally values both unity and separation in the cross-cultural communication process. It regards differences and feelings at odds with the situation as natural, essential parts of the full life experience. It is unrealistic to expect to feel happy and fulfilled, at one with one's environment and the people in it, *at all times.* Although we all strive for such feelings of unity, it is equally important to feel one's separateness at times without imposing value judgments on this feeling. Were we locked into one state or the other (i.e., always at one with others or always apart), we would then need to start worrying about our emotional health. Being able to experience both with acceptance and understanding is a sign of maturity in the Gestalt model applied to cross-cultural communication.

Applications

1. List at least five fears you have regarding the cross-cultural communication process you experience with your Hispanic clients. Then list at least five positive expectations you have for this same process. Share your hopes and fears with others in the class.

2. Use the following checklist to evaluate how your cross-cultural communication style coincides with the Gestalt model outlined earlier.

    a. As I talk with Hispanic clients, am I caught up in the role I play at work, or am I authentic as myself?

    b. Do I tell the client what he or she *should* do, or do I listen to the client so we can arrive at a solution together?

    c. Do I say *I cannot* when I really mean *I will not* (in Spanish, *no puedo* instead of *no quiero*)?

    d. Do I focus on past experiences and stereotypes regarding Hispanic clients or on the present, seeing each client as an individual?

    e. Do I hide behind such words as *we* or *they* or *it isn't possible,* when I am really speaking for myself and mean *I*?

    f. Do I say *no* when I mean *no* or do I express myself in an ambivalent manner that may confuse the client?

    g. Do I send mixed signals in other ways, including body language, tone of voice, and the like?

    h. Do I allow myself to withdraw from the cross-cultural communication process when it feels right to do so?

    i. Do I try to be honest with my comments, or do I play games, expressing half-truths, leaving things unsaid, or giving false reasons that really do not explain what I mean or want to communicate?

    j. Do I personalize my interactions with others? That is, do I interpret a client's response as a reaction to me as a person, or do I see each client as a separate individual reacting from his or her own cultural conditioning or personal experiences?

3. According to the Gestalt model as it applies to intercultural understanding, the following are six ways of preventing oneself from making contact with another person. As you read each, decide if you use any of them to impede communication with your Hispanic clients:

a. *Introjection:* allowing values imposed on you by your cultural environment to prevent meaningful interaction

b. *Retroflection:* feeling guilty about what you say or do

c. *Attribution:* the opposite of retroflection; making everyone else responsible for what you feel

d. *Confluence:* preventing real contact with other people by agreeing with everything the other person says

e. *Projection:* saying things about others that are really true of yourself

f. *Deflation:* not responding to what the other person says to you

Reflections

1. In Exercise 1 in the "Applications" section, what is your greatest fear regarding communicating with your Hispanic clients? Do your fellow students share this fear? How can you deal with this fear so that it does not keep you from communicating effectively with Hispanic clients?

2. What has been your greatest positive expectation regarding communicating with your Hispanic clients? Has this proved to be true in your actual experience, or have you been disappointed at times? Why? How does this relate to the Gestalt model for cross-cultural communication?

3. In Exercise 2 in the "Applications" section, did you identify one specific behavioral style that impedes your effective communication with your Hispanic clients? How can you change it? Practice with someone else in the class so that you establish a new way of interacting that eliminates this behavior.

4. Give an example from your experience in working with Hispanic clients for each of the six ways listed in Exercise 3 in the "Applications" section that prevent making contact with another person. If you cannot remember any examples from past experiences, apply what you have learned so far regarding Hispanic culture to imagine a situation in which an Anglo professional might avoid real contact with his or her clients by adopting each of these behavior patterns.

HISTORICAL PERSPECTIVE: Celebrations, diversions, food, and drink

One of the most revealing aspects of a culture is the way people play. It is not just the workaday world that reflects values regarding time, money, social status, productivity, and human resources. The predominant attitudes of a culture toward the use of leisure time are directly related to how that culture looks at play. In contrasting Anglo and Hispanic cultures, a common saying in Spanish best sums up the differences: *"Los gringos viven para trabajar y los hispanos trabajan para vivir"* ("Anglos live to work and Hispanics work to live"). One of the most impressive aspects of Hispanic cultures is the high value placed on celebrating the joy of living through holidays, parties, sports, diversions, eating, and drinking.

Holidays in the Spanish-speaking world are many and varied. Most celebrate religious events, while the rest commemorate important dates in national history. The reverence for religious feast days has a rich legacy, inherited from the indigenous inhabitants, the Spanish *conquistadores,* and the African influx.

The predominant Indian civilizations that greeted the Spaniards were political–religious cultures, with no separation of church and state. In addition, they were evolving agricultural societies, which paid tribute to the religious entities that controlled the all-important weather conditions as well as other aspects of life. Their calendars were frequently punctuated with religious celebrations to worship these deities in order to ensure the productivity of the land and the prosperity of its inhabitants.

The Spaniards came bearing a love for religious ritual and celebration. In addition, the regionalism prevalent in Spain was steeped in the tradition of local feast days marked by colorful dances and festive activities.

Similarly, African cultures have historically placed religious ritual and celebration high on their scale of values. For the most part, they resemble the indigenous cultures of pre-Columbian Latin America in their view of multiple deities responsible for providing and sustaining life forces.

It was inevitable that the blending of these three cultural backgrounds would yield present-day societies that continue to value religious ceremonies and celebrations. Despite the diversity and heterogeneity characterizing the Hispanic world, the religious unity forged by the overlay of Christianity on the Indian and African religious cultures is most visible in the religious observances of *días festivos* (holy days) and in the celebration of *días feriados* (national holidays).

---

1. *Do you agree that the way a culture* plays *is as indicative of its value system as the way it* works? *Explain.*
2. *Describe the various legacies regarding religious celebrations in the modern Spanish-speaking world.*

All Hispanic cultures consider the Christmas and Easter seasons the most important celebration times of the year. Beginning with *Nochebuena* (Christmas Eve) through *Navidad* (Christmas, also called *Pascuas*) and on to *El Día de Reyes* (Three Kings' Day or Epiphany), families reunite to celebrate the birth of Christ. In Mexico, the custom of *las posadas* (the inns) commemorates Mary and Joseph's search for lodging as the time for birth approached. Each evening beginning December 16, children carrying candles and singing a litany go from house to house requesting lodging. Each night they are admitted to a predetermined house, where there is great merrymaking, refreshments, and the breaking of a *piñata,* a figure made of brittle pottery that is covered with papier-mâché and filled with fruit, *jícamas* (a vegetable root often eaten raw), peanuts, and sugarcane. It is hit with a stick by each child until it is broken. In Puerto Rico, a similar Yuletide custom called *la parranda* is a less formal surprise visit to someone's house by adults and children carrying musical instruments. Once inside the home, they sing, dance, eat, and drink. The host family then departs with the group to launch more surprise *asaltos* (attacks) on other unsuspecting families. These visits can occur anytime during the holiday season, which officially ends on January 6, *El Día de Reyes,* the day Hispanic children traditionally receive their gifts.

A few weeks later, the solemn season of *Cuaresma* (Lent) begins on *Miércoles de Ceniza* (Ash Wednesday), preceded by *Martes de Carnaval* (Shrove Tuesday or Mardi Gras), the last of four nights of celebration. This time of year is a preparation for *La Pascua Florida* (Easter). One of the most solemn days of the year is *Viernes Santo* (Good Friday), traditionally the day when one atones for past transgressions to prepare for the joys of the Resurrection. It is observed by processions through the streets that reenact Jesus' walk to Calvary and his subsequent crucifixion. This solemn period ends the next evening with *Sábado de Gloria* (Holy Saturday). Although midnight marks the actual beginning of the rejoicing, *Sábado de Gloria* often includes dances and parties beginning in early evening. *La Pascua Florida* is celebrated with religious services and special foods.

Although there are other church holy days and feast days through the spring and summer, their commemoration is not usually marked by special celebrations, although June 24, *El Día de San Juan* (St. John's Day), is observed in some Hispanic countries. On the eve of this holy day, bonfires whose flames reputedly reveal the name of one's future mate are found scattered throughout the city and countryside.

Although Halloween is not a typical Hispanic holiday, it is celebrated in Puerto Rico. November 1, *El Día de Todos los Santos* (All Saints' Day), and November 2, *El Día de los Difuntos* (All Souls' Day) are more important feast days. On the latter, families pay special tribute to loved ones who have passed away. Visits to the cemetery during the day are concluded by celebrating life in the evening with food, drink, singing, and dancing.

In addition to these universal religious feast days, there are also national, local, and individual celebrations that reflect the deep sense of spirituality common to most Hispanics. Some countries pay homage to a particular saint or the Virgin Mary through a special veneration. The most famous example is *La Virgen de Guadalupe,* the patron saint of Mexico, whose legendary appearance as a dark-skinned virgin to an Indian *campesino* is commemorated. In addition, each urban and rural locale usually has its patron saint, whose feast day is celebrated on a par with other national holidays. In remote rural areas of Latin America where customs have not changed since the preconquest era, the political–religious social order remains intact. Adult men are still expected to contribute a year of their life to either civil or religious duties. Often their primary responsibility is sponsorship of the annual celebration of the patron saint of the community.

The life cycle of the individual also revolves around religious celebrations. In more traditional Hispanic countries, the *día del santo* (saint's day), the feast day of the saint after whom one is named, is celebrated more than the individual's birthday. In addition, the *bautismo* (baptism) rite marks the infant's entry into the Christian community. The *quinceañera* is a special celebration of a female's fifteenth birthday, her rite of passage to the adult world of marriage and motherhood. In most Hispanic countries, tradition dictates that civil weddings be sanctioned by a religious ceremony. Funeral rites are almost exclusively handled through the Christian churches.

Although most festivities reflect the strong religious heritage of both the conquerors and the conquered, there is one universal nonreligious Hispanic holiday called *El Día de la Raza* (The Day of Race, or Columbus Day), the October 12 commemoration of Columbus's arrival in the Western Hemisphere. In addition, each country demonstrates its national pride through the commemoration of various holidays recalling the struggle for independence. For example, while Mexico's actual *Día de Independencia* (Independence Day) is *el 5 de mayo* (May 5), other important national events, such as the November 20 celebration of *el Aniversario de la Revolución Mexicana* (the anniversary of the Mexican Revolution), are also observed.

Religious and national occasions are not the only occasions that bring Hispanic people together. There are two major cultural pastimes. The first is *fútbol* (soccer), one of the most popular sports among Hispanic people. The matches are attended by both men and women, and much media coverage is given them. The *aficionados* (fans) closely follow team scores and favorite players. The playoff games are marked by intense rivalry, which often triggers passionate anger as well as jubilant celebration, not only among players and fans at the stadium but throughout entire cities and countries. Interestingly enough, American football (*fútbol americano*) is considered to be an excessively brutal sport and is not popular among Hispanics.

In the Caribbean, baseball (*béisbol*) is the most popular sport, provoking animated behavior among the spectators as soccer does in other Latin countries.

The *corrida de toros* (bullfight) is not really considered a sport in the Spanish-speaking world. Although more popular in Spain, this drama or art form has traditional significance for Hispanics in Mexico and some other Latin American countries (although not in the Spanish-speaking Caribbean) and represents human victory over brute force. Both men and women attend the bullfights, which are normally held on Sunday afternoons.

There are other diversions popular among Hispanic males. *Peleas de gallos* (cockfights) attract groups of men who are fond of betting on the outcome. Another traditional male pastime is

playing dominoes (*dominó*), especially in the Spanish-speaking Caribbean. It is a favorite hobby of older men who have retired.

---

3. *Name the two most important national sports in the Hispanic world and describe their cultural relevance.*
4. *How do some Hispanics view* la corrida de toros*? Do you agree with their view?*

Whatever the occasion that brings Hispanics together, food (and lots of it) and drink are constant companions. It is not uncommon for soccer, baseball, and bullfight *aficionados* to bring to the stadium or the arena baskets of food and containers of alcoholic beverages. In some countries, however, it is illegal to bring in glass bottles, since these can be used as weapons as passions increase, especially in soccer games. Food is also the focus of *fiestas* (parties) held in private homes to which all members of the family are invited. The "peer party," to which only people of the same age group are invited, is relatively rare in the Hispanic world. *Fiestas* are usually filled with music—live bands if the host's family can afford one, amateur musicians, records, or the radio. Everyone dances, from the youngest to the oldest. No one is expected to arrive at the time stated for the party to begin, nor is there a set time for it to end. *Fiestas* beginning in the early hours of the afternoon may go on to the wee hours of the morning. At the end of hours of dancing and drinking, a substantial meal is usually served.

Following the tradition of male–female relationships, the women in the family generally serve the male guests first.

With regard to alcoholic beverages, there is no legal drinking age in Hispanic countries. Children grow up learning to drink at their parents' side. The most popular alcoholic drinks are local beers and, depending on the country, certain national beverages. The Caribbean, of course, is noted for its rum, produced from sugarcane. Mexico's tequila, made from the *maguey* plant, needs no introduction. There are also home brews, fermented beverages sold by entrepreneurs in rural areas, such as Mexican *pulque*.

One of the most popular nonalcoholic beverages of both adults and children in the Hispanic world is *el café* (coffee). In most countries, *el café* is strong, similar to Italian *espresso*. It is served in a variety of ways, almost always with sugar. For breakfast, it is frequently served as *café con leche*, equal amounts of strong black coffee and hot milk to which sugar is added. *Mate* is a strong tea common in Argentina. Chamomile tea (*té de manzanilla*) is an herbal tea often drunk after a meal to aid digestion. *Chocolate* (hot chocolate) was indigenous to Mexico and is still popular there, particularly with children. Another common Mexican drink is *atole,* a mixture of cornmeal, milk, cinnamon, and raw sugar. In addition, most Hispanic countries serve *batidas* (*batidos* in Cuba), mixtures of milk and tropical fruits whipped together in a blender. Soft drinks (*refrescos* or *gaseosas*) are also favorites, particularly American brands. Especially in the Spanish-speaking Caribbean, *malta,* a nonalcoholic malt drink, is a favorite.

---

5. *Describe the importance of food to social and sporting events in the Hispanic world.*
6. *What type of drinks, both alcoholic and non-alcoholic, are common in the Hispanic world? Are you personally familiar with any of them? If so, describe your reaction to them.*

Foods (and the names used to refer to them) in the Spanish-speaking world are as varied as the people who eat them. For example, a *tortilla* in Spain (and in some Latin American countries) is an omelette with potatoes and onions, whereas in

Mexico it is the staple bread source, a type of pancake made out of ground corn or wheat flour. A *taco* in Mexico is a fried *tortilla* folded over a mixture of meat, vegetables, and special sauces. In Puerto Rico, however, a *taco* is a round piece of dough on which a meat mixture is spread, then rolled up in cigar fashion and deep-fried.

Foodstuffs indigenous to Latin America have made their way to cuisines the world over. For example, the tomato, a prime ingredient in the cooking of the Mediterranean region and elsewhere, is native to Mexico. The name itself is originally a Nahuatl Indian word, as is the word *chocolate.* The potato, a staple of many northern cultures, is indigenous to the Andean region, where it is still a staple today.

While it is impossible to list all the varieties of food found in the Hispanic world, general guidelines on the kinds of foods eaten by Hispanics and the role food plays in Hispanic cultures may be helpful. Despite the variety that abounds, the lack of economic resources still condemns many Hispanics to malnutrition.

An interesting aspect of the Hispanic diet is the amount and types of protein eaten. Again variety is the key word. In well-developed countries, such as Argentina, beef is a mainstay and eaten frequently by all social classes. In other countries meat, especially beef, is a luxury, reserved for those with moderate to high incomes. In some countries, chicken is also a special commodity. Many rural (and some urban) families throughout Latin America raise pigs and goats for their own consumption. Especially in those countries with a seacoast, fish and seafood are plentiful and relatively inexpensive. There are many varieties of *mariscos* (seafood) that may seem exotic to the

American palate, such as *pulpo* (octopus) and *calamares* (squid). Other animal sources of protein include eggs and cheese. Eggs (*huevos*) are not eaten as frequently for breakfast as they are in the United States but are reserved more often for the late evening *cena*. Local cheeses (*quesos del país*) are usually readily available, although those on higher incomes may prefer processed and imported cheeses.

---

7. *What accounts for the variety of foods available and eating habits among Hispanic countries?*
8. *Compare the kinds of animal protein eaten in the Hispanic world with those eaten in the United States.*

Many Hispanics rely on vegetable sources of protein because of both custom and economic reality. Often vegetables are eaten in combinations that form complete proteins: Mexican corn tortillas with refried beans (*refritos*), Puerto Rican rice and pink beans (*arroz con habichuelas*), Cuban black beans and rice (*frijoles negros con arroz*).

The Hispanic world uses many root vegetables that are either unknown or unpopular in the United States, such as yucca, (*yuca*), common in tropical and temperate regions. Green vegetables such as broccoli and brussel sprouts are not prevalent in the Spanish-speaking world, although salads with cabbage (*col*) or lettuce (*lechuga*) are eaten. A salad (*ensalada*) either comes already "dressed" with vinegar and oil or is brought "undressed" to the table, accompanied by cruets of vinegar and oil. Rice, a daily staple in most Hispanic countries, is often served at both the midday and evening meals.

Many non-Hispanics think of all Hispanic cuisine as hot or spicy (*picante*). Hispanic cuisine is not always spicy, although some areas do favor hot condiments: Mexico, parts of Central America, and Peru, for example, rely heavily on *ají* and *chile* (varieties of hot peppers). Other common condiments include garlic (*ajo*), and onion (*cebolla*). Coriander (*cilantro*) is a common seasoning in the Spanish-speaking Caribbean, where a special mixture of condiments called *sofrito* is used as the basis for most cooking.

---

9. *How does the concept of vegetables and side dishes differ between the Hispanic world and the United States?*
10. *Discuss the variety of seasonings and condiments used in Hispanic countries.*

Desserts are not usually served at the end of each meal as in the United States. They are served as formal or informal snacks and tend to be quite sweet. Fruits are peeled and eaten with a knife and fork, not with the hands, as they tend to be in the United States.

An interesting difference between Hispanics and Anglos revolves around behavior at the dining table. Many Hispanics follow the European way of eating with the fork always in the left hand and the knife in the right. In families of moderate to high income, the cooking is done usually by servants, although the *señora* of the house may provide guidance. Men, not women, are served first. In some homes the woman of the house may be so busy tending to details of food preparation and serving that she rarely eats with the rest of the family.

Another difference is the question of eating in and eating out. Hispanics, in general, prefer to eat as many meals as possible in the home environment. Although fast-food chains are finding their way into the Spanish-speaking world, eating out is still a relatively rare event for most families.

It is important to remember that what is a balanced diet in American terms may be very foreign to Hispanics, whose native environment provides an abundant source of proteins, vitamins, and minerals in foodstuffs not readily available in the United States. The variety of tropical fruits, including, for example, mango, soursop (*guanábana*), and papaya, provide many nutrients needed for good health. Hispanics coming to the United States often encounter difficulties in trying to adapt their eating habits to foods available here.

Another important cultural difference is the Hispanic tradition of classifying foods according to their effect on maintaining health and curing specific illnesses. The so-called hot–cold theory regarding foods is common. It has nothing to do with either the temperature at which food is served or its degree of spiciness. Instead, certain illnesses are classified as "hot" and, as such, are treated with foods or beverages deemed "cold" by tradition. For example, *empacho,* a childhood affliction resulting in nausea, vomiting, and/or diarrhea, is considered a "cold" disease to be treated by such "hot" substances as castor oil, cinnamon, chocolate, cornmeal, or evaporated milk.

Having a knowledge of your clients' eating and drinking habits and their leisure activities gives you a broader base from which to provide services. Trying to change these important cultural patterns may be futile as well as unethical.

Understanding them, however, affords you and your clients a better opportunity to resolve cultural differences that might otherwise jeopardize professional interaction.

---

11. *What differences exist between the Hispanic and Anglo cultures regarding table behavior and eating habits?*
12. *What specific knowledge about Hispanic customs of food and leisure activities may be helpful to you in providing services to your Hispanic clients?*

NONVERBAL COMMUNICATION: Laughter, smiling, and play

As has been pointed out, there is a basic difference in the attitudes of Anglos and Hispanics toward life. The Anglo emphasis is on work, while that of the Hispanic is on living. When viewed from the Anglo perspective, steeped in the Puritan work ethic, Hispanic cultures may seem inefficient, unproductive, and underdeveloped in their attitudes toward work and play. Of course, this is an ethnocentric value judgment, an opinion that measures a different cultural value system using one's own cultural norms as the yardstick.

This basic cultural difference regarding the purpose of life is manifested in important nonverbal ways. Perhaps the greatest potential for nonverbal misunderstanding between Anglos and Hispanics relates to the love of laughter and play that typifies most Spanish-speaking cultures. The high cultural value placed on enjoyment of the lighter side of life prevails in every aspect of living—in the home, in the workplace, in schools, and on the streets. To a certain extent, the formality that characterizes interactions with authority figures, strangers, or mere acquaintances is tempered by the laughter and joking that typifies relationships with friends and family. Yet, whether a serious or playful interaction occurs among Hispanics, it is always marked by *respeto,* respect for each person's human dignity.

This love of laughter and play may be misinterpreted by an Anglo professional as "juve-

nile," "immature," or "irresponsible." For example, an Anglo social worker may misunderstand a Hispanic client's need to throw a party to celebrate a happy family event, even though the client is experiencing financial difficulties. An Anglo teacher may also find it exasperating to try to "discipline" Hispanic children who continually talk and laugh with each other when they are expected to be working on their own. An Anglo health-care worker may feel frustrated in the attempt to persuade a Hispanic patient that peace and quiet are necessary for recovery, when the latter may feel the need for spirited *fiestecitas* (little parties) to celebrate the success of the medical treatment.

An Anglo employer may view as excessive the joking and kidding that go on among Hispanic employees. In addition, although the Anglo professional world provides time off from work via sick days, personal days, and vacation time, it still highly values perfect attendance records at work and school. This value may conflict with the Hispanic view that "off" time is designed to meet human needs, whether physical, mental, emotional, or spiritual. The latter may tend to use this time as the need arises, rather than striving for good attendance records that are often viewed by Anglos as evidence of dedication to one's job.

Many Anglos experience guilt or discomfort if not engaged in some "worthwhile" activity, even when at leisure. Time off is often viewed as necessary primarily to regain one's energy and well-being in order to return to "meaningful activity." Hispanics, on the other hand, acknowledge their need to play, to party, to sing and dance, or just "to hang out" as intrinsically important to their well-being. Consequently, Hispanics attending Anglo social gatherings may find them boring and subdued, characterized by a lot of talking. This is especially true of work-related social activities, company cocktail parties, and the like. Even when laughing and joking do occur at an Anglo party, it is usually devoid of the gaiety and frolicking, the music-making, singing, and dancing that characterize the "Latin" party.

The Anglo party may seem subdued to the Hispanic guest for another reason — the difference in noise levels common to each culture. Anglo adults may prefer low-key, Muzak-type background noise, or silence when at work, at home, or at play. A Hispanic may be struck by the silence that prevails in apartment corridors, office buildings, doctors' offices, and restaurants in the Anglo environment. On the other hand, an Anglo visiting a Hispanic country or even a Hispanic area of a U.S. city would immediately notice the noise level. The visitor may reinforce his or her stereotypic view of Hispanics as "not ever being quiet or serious about work," while the Hispanic may typify Anglos as "uptight and always taking things too seriously."

Neither of these lifestyles is right or wrong. They represent different approaches to living which the individual learns at an early age and may never really be able to change, despite pressure from others. It seems that the Anglo has a need for personal space, privacy, and silence in order to concentrate on the task at hand and achieve ultimate productivity. On the other hand, the Hispanic seems to seek human energy in the form of bodies and voices in order to feel at ease. In the more "sterile" Anglo environment, the Hispanic may feel depressed and incapable of operating at full creative capacity. Anglos tend to recharge their vital energies alone and in silence. Hispanics do the same in the presence of others and their human noises.

Another nonverbal cue that can be misunderstood is the Hispanic smile. Although the smile is a universal facial expression, its meaning and use vary from culture to culture. In the Anglo culture, smiling seems reserved for friendly exchanges, but rarely in contexts where serious activities are being carried out, such as working, teaching, learning, or attending religious services. The more relaxed, less formal, smiling and joking atmosphere that characterizes similar activities in Hispanic countries, especially in the Caribbean and coastal areas of Latin America, is not typical in the United States.

Like their Anglo counterparts, Hispanics do smile at their friends, whom they may also touch often during conversation. But Hispanics also use the smile with strangers to communicate *nonverbally* what the Anglo uses words to achieve — for example, in asking information, addressing clerks, and responding to kindnesses extended them. The Hispanic smile may be "saying": "May I help you?" "Could you tell me where . . . ?" "Please." "Thank you." "You're welcome." "Hi." The Hispanic, when speaking English, may enter an office, smile, and ask the receptionist, "Where's the personnel office?" which seems rude by Anglo standards. The English speaker in the same situation would probably establish eye contact and, with a serious expression, ask "Excuse me, but could you please tell me where the personnel office is?" A Hispanic receptionist might acknowledge the presence of either visitor by a simple lifting of the head and a smile instead of the Anglo receptionist's verbal "May I help you?"

In a similar way, Hispanics often substitute a smile as a response to a compliment or service performed for them, particularly in place of "*gracias.*" The ubiquitous "Thank you" the Anglo offers to the waiter each time a service is performed or that the Anglo professional offers in exchange for each response a client makes to intake interview questions may seem extremely formal and distancing to Hispanics, especially to those from the Caribbean and other tropical climates. Although formality and respect typify human interactions in Hispanic cultures, certain behaviors can carry the extreme to the point of nonverbally conveying "I do not wish to be open or accessible to you."

The Hispanic smile may reflect another message — "I am embarrassed." The context and other nonverbal behaviors will provide clues, such as downcast eyes, fidgety body movements, and obvious discomfort. Unless an Anglo professional is aware of this possible interpretation of the Hispanic's smile, it may be read instead as flippant or disrespectful.

The smile is also used in Hispanic cultures to accompany the unofficial ritual that typifies the offering and accepting of food or beverages. The Hispanic guest is expected to show reticence by refusing food or drink when it is offered the first time, saying *"No, gracias"* with a smile. The host then offers again, smiling, coaxing, perhaps using a term of endearment. The guest again is expected to decline with a smile. A third or even fourth exchange may occur before the guest succumbs to the host's urging to partake of the refreshments. In the Anglo culture, which encourages frankness and respects the individual's right to decline food or drink, refreshments are offered once. If refused, they are usually not offered again, much to the consternation of the Hispanic guest who may expect a different scenario.

Not all Hispanics will use the smile in the same way. Those who have acculturated more to Anglo norms may have learned that verbal expressions are taken more seriously than facial gestures in the English-speaking world. In addition, some areas of the Hispanic world do follow more formal patterns of interaction, particularly large urban areas such as Bogotá, Colombia, and La Paz, Bolivia. Anglo professionals who learn from their Hispanic clients by observing their behaviors and adapting their own communication style to reflect this awareness of nonverbal messages will be more successful in the cross-cultural communication process.

Putting it into practice

1. Identify the cultural differences that may be operant in the following situations and the misinterpretations that may arise:
    a. An Anglo teacher who spots two Hispanic children laughing while she is giving instructions to the class
    b. An Anglo social worker on a home visit to a Hispanic family who must speak loudly to be heard over the radio, two children playing, and two visiting neighbors who are talking and laughing
    c. An employer who notices that his Hispanic secretary has taken every sick day and vacation day to which she is entitled and now needs a week off for important surgery
    d. An Anglo employee who is invited to the christening party of her Hispanic colleague's baby
    e. A doctor who finds out that the patient for whom she has prescribed complete rest and ten-minute hospital visits once a day from his spouse has a small Christmas party in his room, with eight visitors who have somehow evaded hospital visitation procedures

2. Construct short dialogues in English or Spanish reflecting the following situations in which a smile would be used instead of specific verbal expressions:
    a. An intake interview
    b. Being served a meal in a restaurant
    c. Asking someone to come in and sit down
    d. Meeting a client at a social gathering where you can't get close enough to speak
    e. Asking for instructions from a receptionist

3. Practice offering coffee to a Hispanic client who has just entered the office:
    a. In the "Anglo" way
    b. In the "Hispanic" way

Comunicándose en español

PRONUNCIACIÓN: r, rr 🔲

The Spanish **r** sound exists in English, although it is associated with a different spelling. The sound of Spanish **r** between vowels or before a consonant other than **l**, **n**, or **s** is similar to the sound in English represented by a double *d* or *t*, as in the words *ladder* and *butter*. To produce this sound, the upper part of the front of the tongue taps once against the ridge above the front teeth. Pronounce these words in English:

la*dd*er	E*dd*ie	ri*dd*le	Be*tt*y	bu*tt*er

Now say in Spanish:

hora	tarde	creo	directo	preparado
para	madre	claro	hermano	divorciado

Spanish **rr** and **r** at the beginning of a word or after **l**, **n**, or **s**, are trilled; that is, the tongue taps quickly several times against the ridge above the front teeth. At the end of a word, **r** is often pronounced this way as well. If you're having trouble making this sound, practice repeating *cut it up* rapidly.

These Spanish words contain the trilled **r** sound. Practice pronouncing them.

rico	Israel	barrio	arroz	tomar
reloj	Enrique	corre	arriba	comer

Failure to distinguish between the **r** and **rr** sounds can result in misunderstandings. Practice the following paired words:

pero/perro   caro/carro   ahora/ahorra   coro/corro

In some Puerto Rican dialects, **r** is pronounced as **l**, and **rr** as the **j** (heavy *h*) sound, so that **tarde** sounds like **tal-de** and **arroz** becomes **a-jos**.

If Spanish soft **d** is mispronounced as an English hard **d**, it will sound very much like Spanish **r**, possibly confusing the listener. Practice making the distinction in the following pairs:

toro/todo   cara/cada   parece/padece   hora/oda

Práctica 🔲

Practice the following sentences aloud, without pauses.

1. Creo que sus padres están separados.

2. El barrio puertorriqueño está cerca del teatro.

3. Buenas tardes, señor Rodríguez. ¿Se siente mejor hoy?

4. Enrique le compró el carro a su primo Ramón.

5. Es peor correr después de comer.

Dictado 📼

Now write the words and sentences your instructor dictates:

1. _____   4. _____

2. _____   5. _____

3. _____   6. _____

7. _____

8. _____

9. _____

¿Ha entendido bien?

1. Describa Ud. a la señora Ortiz y a su familia.

2. ¿Parece ser ella una mujer contenta? Explique su respuesta.

3. ¿Qué piensa Ud. de la manera en que el doctor le habla a la señora Ortiz?

4. ¿Cree Ud. que el doctor es delgado o gordo (*fat*)? ¿Por qué lo cree?

5. ¿De qué sufre la señora Ortiz?

6. ¿Qué instrucciones le da a ella el doctor?

7. ¿Quiere la señora Ortiz cambiar de dieta? Explique.

8. ¿Qué argumentos ofrece la señora Ortiz para no seguir las instrucciones del doctor? ¿A Ud. le parecen válidos? Explique.

9. ¿Por qué dice la señora Ortiz "nunca hay que decir de esa agua no beberé"? ¿Puede Ud. pensar en otro contexto donde sea apropiado este refrán?

10. ¿Cree Ud. que el doctor y la señora Ortiz se comprenden y se llevan bien? ¿Ve Ud. algunos factores culturales que afectan esta conversación? ¿Cuáles son?

INTRODUCTORY DIALOGUE: Eat and live

The doctor: Mrs. Ortiz, the laboratory tests indicate that you have diabetes. You have to change your diet, lose (reduce) thirty pounds, and give yourself insulin injections.

Sra. Ortiz: O my! My mother died of diabetes at the age of fifty (years).

D: Diabetes can be handed down from parents to children. You have to eliminate sugar and sweets.

Sra. O: I can't. I have a sweet tooth (am fond of sweets) and I must eat candy from time to time.

D: But you should think about your health.

Sra. O: Doctor, I'm already an old lady. I'm a widow and my children are married and have their own families. I have no other pleasure (no pleasure is left for me) in life other than eating.

D: At the age of sixty, you have a lot of life ahead of you. Don't you want to get better and be thin?

Sra. O: For what? No, I prefer to continue enjoying my food and live fewer years but happier.

D: I'm never going to be able to understand that attitude of living to eat instead of eating to live.

Sra. O: Look, doctor, as the proverb says, "you should never say that I won't drink from that water." I've spent all my life taking care of others and now I'll take care of myself in my own way.

BASIC STRUCTURES I: Don't you like hospital food?

The dietitian (f.)

Mrs. Espinosa, I'm Rosaura Cárceres, the dietitian. The nurse told me that yesterday you refused to eat anything.

Is it because (that) you don't like American food?

Me either. Why didn't you ask for something else to eat?

What's the difference? The important thing is that you get better as soon as possible. Unless you eat well, you're not going to get better.

I don't know. Wait a moment. I'll be right back.

The patient (f.)

Well, it's just that the meals that they serve here take my appetite away. I could not (manage to) eat that awful stuff that they brought me last night.

That's it. I don't like American dishes at all.

I didn't know that it was possible to do it. Besides, it embarrasses me to ask for special favors.

Well, you're right. And now I am very hungry. Could you bring me a meal that I'd like better?

¿Sabe usted?

1. Singular feminine nouns beginning with stressed **a** are preceded by the masculine definite or indefinite article, although any adjective that modifies these nouns is feminine (**el hambre; Tengo mucha hambre**).

2. **¿Qué más da?** (*what difference does it make?*), **¿qué importa?** (*what does it matter?*), and **¿qué va?** (*go on*, expressing disbelief) are useful responses.

Notas lingüísticas I

A. The following verbs have irregular stems in the preterite that combine with a special set of endings, none of which is accented:

tener:	**tuv-**	venir:	**vin-**		yo	tuve
estar:	**estuv-**	querer:	**quis-**		tú	tuviste
andar:	**anduv-**	hacer:	**hic-**[1]	Ud., él, ella	tuvo
poder:	**pud-**	decir:	**dij-**[2]	nosotros/as	tuvimos
poner:	**pus-**	traer:	**traj-**[2]	Uds., ellos/as	tuvieron

B. **Dar** is completely irregular in the preterite: yo **di**, tú **diste**, Ud., él, ella **dio**, nosotros/as **dimos**, Uds., ellos/as **dieron**.

---

1. Changes to hiz- in the third person singular: **hizo.**

2. Drops the i after j in the third person plural: **dijeron, trajeron.**

ESTRUCTURAS BÁSICAS I: ¿No le gusta la comida del hospital?

 La dietista

La paciente

Señora Espinosa, soy Rosaura Cárceres, la dietista. La enfermera me dijo que ayer Ud. no quiso comer nada.

Pues, es que me quitan el apetito las comidas que se sirven aquí. Yo no pude comer esa porquería que me trajeron anoche.

¿Es que no le gusta la comida americana?

Eso es. No me gustan nada los platos americanos.

Ni a mí tampoco. ¿Por qué no pidió otra cosa de comer?

No sabía que era posible hacerlo. Además, me da vergüenza pedir favores especiales.

¿Qué más da? Lo importante es que Ud. se mejore lo más pronto posible. A menos que coma bien, no se va a mejorar.

Pues, tiene razón. Y ahora tengo mucha hambre. ¿Me puede traer una comida que me guste más?

No sé. Espere un momento. Vuelvo en seguida.

C. Certain verbs are irregular in the preterite in the *third-person singular and plural forms only:*

1. In regular verbs whose stem ends in a vowel (e.g., **creer, leer, caer, oír**), the **i** changes to a **y** before the third person endings. The **i** in the other forms receives a written accent to avoid the formation of a diphthong: **creí,** creíste, *creyó,* creímos, *creyeron;* oí, oíste, *oyó,* oímos, *oyeron*

2. In **-ir** stem-changing verbs (such as **pedir, seguir, dormir**) **e** changes to **i** and **o** to **u** (*in the third person singular and plural only*). Note that **-ar** and **-er** stem-changing verbs have no stem changes in the preterite: **pedí, pediste,** *pidió,* pedimos, *pidieron;* dormí, dormiste, *durmió,* dormimos, *durmieron*

D. Some verbs referring to "internal actions" take on a special meaning in the preterite. **Querer, poder, saber, conocer,** and **tener** express more of a physically observable phenomenon, an action which occurred and was completed at a given moment, when rendered in the preterite. Compare the use of the preterite in these sentences with the use of the imperfect to describe an ongoing past action.

El paciente no quería comer.	The patient didn't want to eat.
El paciente no quiso comer.	The patient refused to eat.
Yo no podía ir al hospital.	I couldn't go to the hospital.
Yo no pude ir al hospital.	I didn't make it to the hospital. (implies effort)
Yo sabía que era verdad.	I knew it was true.
Yo supe que era verdad.	I found out it was true.
Me conocían antes de ayer.	They knew me before yesterday.
Me conocieron antes de ayer.	They met me before yesterday.
Yo tenía una idea magnífica.	I had a wonderful idea. (I was thinking about it)
Yo tuve una idea magnífica.	I had a wonderful idea. (it occurred to me)

BASIC STRUCTURES II: What do you like to eat?

The dietitian (f.)	*The patient (f.)*
Mrs. Espinosa, we have permission to prepare you special meals. Let's see, what kind of food do you like to eat?	I like { tasty / hot (spicy) / Cuban / Mexican / Puerto Rican } food.
What do you normally eat for breakfast?	For breakfast I eat { cereal with milk. / toast. / bread and butter. / coffee with milk. / hot chocolate. }
Is lunch the principal meal for you?	Yes, it is.
Then, what do you eat for lunch?	The main dish can be { a steak. / stewed meat. / fried fish. / baked chicken (chicken in the oven). / cheese enchiladas. / roast pork. / Cuban hash. }
Do you also eat some vegetables?	Yes, I eat { rice with beans. / black beans with rice. / refried beans. / fried plantains. / tortillas with hot sauce. }
Do you eat salads or greens very often?	Well, at times I eat them, but not very often.
What vegetables do you like best?	I like { potatoes. / carrots. / onions. / spinach. / peas. / mushrooms. / peppers. / lettuce. / squash. / celery. / corn. }
What do you like to eat for supper?	Something light, for example { two fried eggs. / soup. / some plantains. / some meat pies. / a Spanish omelette. }
And for dessert, what do you prefer?	I prefer { custard. / guava fruit (paste) with cheese. / peaches in heavy syrup. }

334

La dietista	*La paciente*		
Señora Espinosa, tenemos permiso para prepararle comidas especiales. A ver, ¿qué tipo de comida le gusta más?	Me gusta la comida	{	sabrosa. picante. cubana. mexicana. puertorriqueña.
¿Qué come Ud. normalmente en el desayuno?	Para el desayuno como	{	cereal con leche. pan tostado. pan con mantequilla. café con leche. chocolate caliente.
¿Para Ud. es el almuerzo la comida principal?	Sí, lo es.		
Entonces, ¿qué come para el almuerzo?	El plato principal puede ser	{	un bistec. carne guisada. pescado frito. pollo al horno. enchiladas de queso. lechón asado. picadillo.
¿También come Ud. algunos vegetales?	Sí, como	{	arroz con habichuelas. frijoles negros con arroz. frijoles refritos. tostones. tortillas con ají.
¿Come ensaladas o verduras con mucha frecuencia?	Pues, a veces las como, pero no muy a menudo.		

¿Qué legumbres le gustan más?	Me gustan	las {
		
		los {
			papas.
			zanahorias.
			cebollas.
			espinacas.
			guisantes.
			hongos.
			pimientos.

	Me gusta	la { el {	lechuga. calabaza. apio. maíz.
¿Qué le gusta comer para la cena?	Algo ligero, por ejemplo	{	dos huevos fritos. una sopa. unos plátanos. unas empanadas. una tortilla española.
Y de postre, ¿qué prefiere?	Prefiero	{	flan. guayaba con queso. melocotones en almíbar.

335

Do you eat a lot of sweets?	No, I almost never eat them. I prefer to eat fresh fruits.
Which fruits do you like best?	I like { pineapple. soursop. mangos. apples.
What drinks do you have with meals?	I drink { beer. wine. milk. tomato juice. soda pop. iced tea.
Are you used to eating something between meals?	Normally I don't eat anything, but at times I eat { (an) ice cream. fried pork rinds. candies.
Well, Mrs. Espinosa, I'm going to send you a tray with a meal that you'll like.	Thank you, Mrs. Cárceres. Talking about the foods I like made me extremely hungry (gave me a ferocious hunger). Now I really feel like eating!
It's obvious (it is seen) that it's not at all easy to change one's diet. I wouldn't want to do it either.	No one knows how difficult it is until it's his turn (it touches one).

¿Sabe usted?

1. **Tener** + noun is used in many idioms describing human conditions which are the equivalent of English *to be* + adjective:

tener sed	to be thirsty	(have thirst)
tener hambre	to be hungry	(have hunger)
tener frío	to be cold	(have coldness)
tener calor	to be hot	(have heat)
tener ganas de	to be in the mood to	(have the desire to)
tener la culpa	to be at fault	(have the blame)
tener miedo	to be afraid	(have fear)
tener prisa	to be in a hurry	(have haste)
tener vergüenza	to be embarrassed	(have embarrassment)
tener razón	to be right	(have "reason")
no tener razón	to be wrong	(not have "reason")

These same nouns also follow the verb **dar** to express the cause of the condition, usually translated in English as *to make someone* + adjective. Compare:

Tengo vergüenza.	I'm embarrassed.
Tienen hambre.	They're hungry.
Tenías miedo de mí.	You were afraid of me.
Tengo ganas de bailar.	I feel like dancing.

¿Come muchos dulces?	No, casi nunca los como. Prefiero comer frutas frescas.

¿Qué frutas le gustan más?

Me gusta { la piña. / la guanábana. }
gustan { los mangos. / las manzanas. }

¿Qué bebidas toma Ud. con las comidas?

Tomo { cerveza. / vino. / leche. / jugo de tomate. / refrescos. / té helado. }

¿Suele Ud. comer algo entre comidas?

Normalmente no como nada, pero a veces como { un helado. / chicharrones. / caramelos. }

Bueno, señora Espinosa, voy a mandarle una bandeja con una comida que le guste.

Gracias, señora Cárceres. Hablar de las comidas que me gustan me dio un hambre feroz. ¡Ya tengo ganas de comer!

Se ve que no es nada fácil cambiar de dieta. Yo tampoco quisiera hacerlo.

Nadie sabe lo difícil que es hasta que le toca a uno.

Hablar del sexo me da vergüenza.	Speaking about sex makes me ashamed.
Ese bistec les da hambre.	That steak makes them hungry.
Te daba miedo estar solo.	Being alone made you afraid.
Esa música me da ganas de bailar.	That music makes me feel like dancing.

2. While **tener** + **frío/calor** (tengo frío hoy) is used to describe body temperature, **hacer** + **frío/calor** (hace calor en San Juan hoy) is used to describe air temperature. In describing the temperature of foods, **ser** + **frío/caliente** (the adjectives are used to describe the normal temperature of foods (**el helado es frío**, *ice cream is cold*), while **estar** is used with the adjective forms to describe a change from the normal temperature (**la sopa está fría ahora**, *the soup is cold now*).

3. The opposite of **ligero** is **pesado**. Both refer to *weight* or *quantity*. **Claro** means *light* regarding *color;* its opposite is **oscuro**.

4. The names for foods, what is eaten, and the way in which foods are prepared vary a great deal in the Spanish-speaking world. The following discussions regarding the food mentioned in "Estructuras básicas II" may help:
   a. **La comida cubana**—similar to the cuisine found in Puerto Rico, the Dominican Republic, and other Caribbean countries. **Frijoles negros** (black beans) are preferred to the Puerto Rican **habichuelas rosadas** (pink beans). They are a staple, eaten with a separate plate of white rice, or mixed with it in a dish called **moros y cristianos** (Moors and Christians). Beans and rice are

eaten as a side dish with the main meal, which usually consists of **carne, pollo,** or **pescado.** The food is not hot (**picante**), although it is well seasoned. Picadillo (spicy ground beef with olives and raisins) is popular. **Plátanos** (plantains, a banana-like fruit that is cooked like a vegetable) are also a staple; they are prepared in a variety of ways, including **tostones** (fried slices of green plantain) and **maduros** (ripe plantains, which have a sweeter taste).

b. **La comida puertorriqueña**—similar to the above, except for its preference for **habichuelas rosadas. Frituras** (fried foods) are favorites, including **rellenos** (fried mashed-potato balls stuffed with meat), **alcapurrias** (a mixture of plantain and meat which is fried), and **pastelillos** (fried dough filled with seasoned meat). **Lechón asado** (roast pork) is a main dish eaten on special occasions. **Sancocho** is a stew made with a variety of meat, poultry, and tropical root vegetables. **Tostones** are also common, as are root vegetables such as **ñame** and **yuca** (yucca).

c. **La comida mexicana**— a typically **picante** (hot) cuisine based on **maíz** (corn), **frijoles** (pinto beans), and **chiles verdes** (green chili peppers). The **tortilla,** made of either **harina** (wheat flour) or **maíz,** is the staple used in many dishes and as an accompaniment to most meals. A **taco** is a fried tortilla that is folded and filled with **carne** or **refritos** (refried beans) and often topped with **lechuga, cebolla, tomate y varias salsas** (lettuce, onion, tomato, and various sauces). A **tostada** is similar except that it is a fried flat tortilla. **Enchiladas** are soft tortillas filled with **carne, pollo** or **queso,** topped with a sauce, and baked. **Las salsas** (sauces) are many and varied, ranging from those with a tomato base to the exotic **mole,** a blend of peanuts, chocolate, chilies, and other spices.

5. Following is a list of other foods eaten in the Spanish-speaking world, along with lexical variants for their names.

Nombres y regiones   *En inglés*

CARNES

la carne de res	beef
la ternera	veal
el cordero	lamb
el cerdo, el puerco	pork
el hígado	liver
el jamón	ham
el tocino, la tocineta (PR)	bacon
el pavo, el guajalote (M)	turkey

PESCADOS Y MARISCOS

las almejas	clams
las gambas, los camarones	shrimp
los langostinos	prawns
el bacalao	codfish
el lenguado	flounder
las sardinas	sardines
el atún, el bonito (C)	tuna fish
el pargo, el chillo (PR), el huachinango (M)	red snapper

Nombres y regiones   *En inglés*

VEGETALES

las judías, los ejotes (M), las habichuelas tiernas (MA)	green beans
la col, el repollo (PR, C)	cabbage
el betabel (M, O), la remolacha (PR, C)	beet
la batata (PR, O), el camote (M, MA), el boniato (C)	sweet potato
la mazorca de maíz, el elote (M, MA)	corn on the cob
los hongos (PR, O), los champiñones (Spain, M), las setas (PR, C)	mushrooms
la aceituna	olive
el aguacate	avocado
los guisantes, los chicharos (M, MA)	peas
el cacahuete, el cacahuate (M, MA), el maní (C, PR)	peanut

FRUTAS

el albaricoque, el chabacano (M)	apricot
la cereza	cherry
la manzana	apple
el melocotón, el durazno (M, MA)	peach
la naranja, la china (PR), la naranja china (C)	orange
la papaya, la lechosa (PR, O), la fruta bomba (C)	papaya
el plátano, el guineo (C, PR)	banana
la uva	grape
la sandía, el melón de agua (C)	watermelon
el limón	lemon
la fresa	strawberry
la ciruela	plum, prune

MISCELÁNEO

la torta, el pastel (C, M, O), el queque (MA), el bizcocho (PR)	cake
la galleta (M, MA, PR), la galletica (C), la galletita (PR)	cookie, cracker
los bocadillos (C, PR, O), la botana (M), los entremeses (C, PR, O)	hors d'oeuvres
los panecitos (C, PR, O), los bollos de pan (PR), los bolillos (M, MA)	rolls/buns
las empanadas (C, M), los pasteles (C), los pastelillos (PR)	turnovers

Notas lingüísticas II

A. The neuter form **lo** is used to refer to an entire preceding idea, rather than a specific person or thing.

   1. **Lo que** is translated as *that which* or *what.* It is normally used in two-clause sentences:

Lo que Ud. me dice es difícil de comprender.	What you are telling me is difficult to understand.

El médico no entiende lo que le digo en inglés.	The doctor doesn't understand what I say to him in English.

2. **Lo** + adjective is used to describe a concept or action:

Lo más importante es no comer azúcar.	The most important (thing) is not to eat sugar.
Lo bueno es que Ud. pueda comer todo lo que quiera.	The good (thing) is that you can eat everything you want.

3. **Lo** is also used with the verb **ser** in response to an inquiry regarding an idea or action:

¿Es el almuerzo su comida principal? Sí, lo es.	Is lunch your main meal? Yes, it is (my main meal).

B. The third person reflexive form of many verbs is used in the passive voice, that is, to describe situations where the *object of the action is expressed* as the subject of the sentence without mention of the agent(s) responsible. Compare:

Los dietistas sirven buenas comidas. (active voice)	The dietitians serve good meals.
Se sirven buenas comidas. (passive voice)	Good meals are served.

Often, the third person singular reflexive is used to express the impersonal subject *one* (or unspecific *you* or *they*):

Yo veo que Ud. está mejor hoy.	I see that you are better today.
Se ve que Ud. está mejor hoy.	One sees (it is seen) that you are better today.
No se come bien en este hospital.	You don't eat well in this hospital.

C. Remember that in Spanish, once a sentence is in the negative, all subsequent references in the sentence must also be negative. Here is a list of affirmative-negative pairs:

algo / **nada**	something	/ nothing
alguien / **nadie**	someone	/ no one
alguno[1] / **ninguno**[1,2]	some, any	/ none, not any
siempre / **nunca**	always	/ never
o . . . o / **ni . . . ni**	either . . . or	/ neither . . . nor
también / **tampoco**	also	/ neither, not . . . either

Note that the negative word can precede or follow the verb. If it follows the verb, the word *no* must be inserted before the verb.

***Alguien* me llamó.**	Someone called me.
No me llamó *nadie*. ⎫ ***Nadie* me llamó.** ⎬	No one called me.
Siempre me dan *algo*.	They always give me something.
No me dan *nada nunca*. ⎫ ***Nunca* me dan *nada*.** ⎬	They never give me anything.

Nada is often used as an adverb to modify an adjective, meaning *not at all:*

Esta comida no es nada picante.	This food isn't at all hot.
No es nada fácil comer menos.	It's not at all easy to eat less.

---

1. Before masculine singular nouns, the forms are **algún** and **ningún**.

2. Usually used only in the singular.

PRÁCTICA PRELIMINAR

A. Choose the verb in each sentence that best translates the concept of "to be" in Spanish.

Ejemplo: Cuando la bandeja llegó al cuarto, la sopa ya (era tenía (estaba)) fría.

1. El niño no puede dormir porque (es está tiene) hambre.
2. La típica comida mexicana (está tiene es) picante.
3. Mi hermano (era tenía estaba) miedo de hablar inglés cuando llegó a los Estados Unidos.
4. En los países tropicales (hay es están) más variedad de frutas que en otros países.
5. ¿(Es Estás Tienes) frío? (Hace Es Está) mucho frío en la casa, ¿verdad?
6. ¿(Hay Está Es) preparada la comida?
7. Mi hermano (tiene es está) la culpa de estar tan gordo (*fat*), pues come demasiado.
8. ¿Dónde (hacías eras estabas) anoche?
9. No (hacemos tenemos estamos) prisa para comer.
10. ¿Cuántos pacientes (hay hacen son) en el hospital?

B. Translate the following sentences from Spanish to English.

Ejemplo: Yo no sabía nada de lo que se hablaba.
I didn't know anything about what was being said.

1. El año pasado conocí a una mexicana que siempre tenía ganas de comer.
2. Lo importante es que Ud. no coma mucha comida frita.
3. Ojalá que se sirva una comida fuerte porque tengo un hambre feroz.
4. Ayer almorcé en casa pero cené en un restaurante que queda cerca del trabajo.
5. Yo quise ir a la fiesta, pero no pude terminar todo el trabajo.
6. Nadie sabe lo difícil que es eliminar el azúcar de la dieta.
7. Se dice que es mejor para la salud comer más pollo y pescado y menos carne.
8. A mí no me gustaban los mariscos, ni a mi esposo tampoco; ahora nos encantan.

A 1. tiene 2. es 3. tenía 4. hay 5. Tienes; Hace 6. Está 7. tiene 8. estabas 9. tenemos 10. hay

B 1. Last year I met a Mexican woman who always was in the mood to eat. 2. The important thing is that you not eat a lot of fried foods. 3. I hope a substantial meal is served because I'm *really* hungry. 4. Yesterday I ate lunch at home, but I had dinner at a restaurant (that is) near work. 5. I tried (really wanted) to go to the party, but I couldn't (manage to) finish all the (my) work. 6. No one knows how difficult it is to eliminate sugar from one's diet. 7. It is said (they say) it's better for your health to eat more chicken and fish and less meat. 8. I never used to like seafood, nor did my husband; now we love it.

C. Translate the missing part of each sentence.

Ejemplo: Those tacos make me hungry.

Esos tacos me _____.

1. Not being able to speak English makes me feel ashamed.

   El no poder hablar inglés me _____.

2. Are you (*tú*) in the mood for rice and beans tonight?

   ¿_____ de comer arroz con habichuelas esta noche?

3. Does that make you thirsty?

   ¿Eso le _____ a Ud.?

4. I'm cold now.

   _____ ahora.

5. That cake makes me hungry.

   Esa torta me _____.

6. Yesterday I felt like eating chicken enchiladas instead of tostadas.

   Ayer _____ de comer enchiladas de pollo en vez de tostadas.

7. I'm in a hurry; my wife is waiting for me.

   _____ ; mi esposa me está esperando.

8. I felt ashamed about asking for special favors.

   _____ de pedir favores especiales.

9. I get the urge to dance when I hear music.

   Me _____ de bailar cuando oigo música.

10. It's not my fault that dinner isn't ready.

    Yo no _____ de que la comida no esté lista.

D. Conjugate the following verbs in the person indicated.

		Preterite	*Imperfect*	*Present indicative*	*Present subjunctive*
(*yo*)	tener	tuve	tenía	tengo	tenga
1. (*nosotros*)	estar				
2. (*ellos*)	ser				
3. (*yo*)	hacer				

C 1. da vergüenza 2. tienes ganas 3. da sed 4. Tengo frío 5. da hambre 6. tenía ganas 7.Tengo prisa 8. Tenía vergüenza 9. da ganas 10. tengo la culpa

D 1. estuvimos; estábamos; estamos; estemos 2. fueron; eran; son; sean 3. hice; hacía; hago; haga

			Preterite	Imperfect	Present indicative	Present subjunctive
4.	(*él*)	poner				
5.	(*tú*)	dar				
6.	(*Uds.*)	dormir				
7.	(*yo*)	poder				
8.	(*Ud.*)	creer				
9.	(*tú*)	llamar				
10.	(*yo*)	venir				
11.	(*ellas*)	decir				

E. Give the correct forms of the verb indicated to complete each paragraph.
Ejemplo: **comer**

Ayer yo ___*comí*___ arroz con pollo. De niño yo lo ___*comía*___ todos los domingos. Hace más de diez años que no lo ___*como*___. El médico prefiere que yo no lo ___*coma*___ más.

1. **hablar**

La semana pasada mi mamá _____ con el nuevo doctor en español, como lo hacía cuando vivía en Cuba donde le _____ todos los días. Desde que vive en Hartford, no _____ español casi nada, pues, aquí todos los americanos prefieren que ella _____ inglés.

2. **llegar**

Ayer yo _____ tarde al trabajo. Cuando vivía cerca del trabajo, siempre _____ temprano. Ahora _____ tarde a menudo. Mi jefe quiere que yo _____ temprano todos los días.

D 4. puso; ponía; pone; ponga 5. diste; dabas; das; des 6. durmieron; dormían; duermen; duerman 7. pude; podía; puedo; pueda 8. creyó; creía; cree; crea. 9. llamaste; llamabas; llamas; llames 10. vine; venía; vengo; venga 11. dijeron; decían; dicen; digan
E 1. habló; hablaba; habla; hable 2. llegué; llegaba; llego; llegue

3. **escribir**

Mi madre le _____ una carta a mi hermano en México la semana

pasada. Ella le _____ más a menudo cuando no trabajaba fuera

de casa. Ahora le _____ una vez al mes. Para él es importante que

ella le _____ frecuentemente.

4. **hacer**

Anoche mi esposo nos _____ una comida mexicana en casa. Fue

igual a las que nos _____ mi mamá cuando vivíamos en

México. Ahora que yo trabajo hasta las seis los lunes, mi esposo siempre

_____ la comida en casa ese día. Pero cuando mamá nos visita,

ella no quiere que el hombre de la casa _____ la comida.

5. **saber**

Ayer yo _____ que mis amigos me van a dar una fiesta el sábado

que viene. Mi hermana ya lo _____ pero no me dijo nada. Ahora

que yo _____ que me la van a dar, no puedo esperar. ¡Ojalá que

lo _____ todos mis amigos!

F. Choose the most appropriate vocabulary item needed by context.
   Ejemplo: La ((guayaba) aceituna   ternera) es una fruta tropical.

   1. Muchos hispanos toman (lechón asado   jugo de tomate   café con leche) en el desayuno.
   2. Un plato típico de México consiste en (arroz con habichuelas   frijoles negros con arroz   enchiladas).
   3. Entre las frutas nutritivas está la (ternera   lechuga   guanábana).
   4. Los (guisantes   melocotones   mariscos) son un plato favorito en las islas del Caribe.
   5. La fruta que más me gusta es (la manzana   la cebolla   el cerdo).
   6. En esta dieta no se puede comer comida pesada como (pescado   ensalada   carne guisada).
   7. Los vegetarianos nunca comen (postre   frijoles   carne).
   8. En Cuba se come mucho el (mole   chile   picadillo).

E 3. escribió; escribía; escribe; escriba 4. hizo; hacía; hace; haga 5. supe; sabía; sé sepan

9. Un ejemplo de una fritura en Puerto Rico es la (alcapurria   china   galleta).

10. La comida (mexicana   cubana   puertorriqueña) suele ser muy picante.

G. Translate the missing expressions to complete each sentence.

Ejemplo: I didn't meet anyone at the party.

No conocí a ___*nadie*___ en la fiesta.

1. I never drink either beer or wine.

Yo _____ tomo _____ cerveza _____ vino.

2. No one told me anything.

_____ me dijo _____ .

3. I want dessert after supper, too.

Despuésde la cena quiero postre _____ .

4. I don't want anyone to speak with the nurse.

_____ quiero que _____ hable con la enfermera.

5. Does anyone want rice?

¿ _____ quiere arroz?

6. He didn't eat either.

El _____ comió.

7. We always eat lunch at 1:00 P.M.

_____ almorzamos a la una de la tarde.

8. She never goes to the doctor's alone.

_____ va al médico sola.

9. I don't feel like eating either meat or fish.

_____ tengo ganas de comer _____ carne _____ pescado.

10. There's nothing I like better.

_____ hay_____ que me guste más.

F 1. café con leche 2. enchiladas 3. guanábana 4. mariscos 5. la manzana 6. carne guisada 7. carne 8. picadillo 9. alcapurria 10. mexicana

G 1. nunca/ni/ni 2. Nadie/nada 3. también 4. No/nadie 5. Alguien 6. tampoco 7. Siempre 8. Nunca 9. No/ni/ni 10. No/nada

Combinándolo todo

PRÁCTICA COMUNICATIVA: Comer y beber

Conversación parcial

Practique Ud. oralmente la siguiente conversación. Cada raya (/) implica que falta una palabra. Es necesario conjugar cada verbo *en bastardillas*.

El trabajador social	La cliente
1. / médico me *decir* que Ud. *necesitar* ayuda para mejor alimentar (*to feed*)/ la familia.	Sí, señor; ayer / doctor *saber* que / hijos *estar* sufriendo / malnutrición.
2. ¿Por / *creer* Ud. que ellos *tener* problemas con la nutrición?	No *saber;* / posible que *comer* demasiados dulces.
3. ¿ / tipo / comida *comer* Uds. cuando *vivir* en México?	*Comer* mucha comida / y / frutas.
4. ¿No se *poder* conseguir / mexicana aquí?	Sí, / puede, pero *costar* muchísimo más / lo que *costar* en México.
5. ¿A / hijos / *gustar* la comida americana?	Pues, / *gustar* / hamburguesas y / papas / pero *ser* / caras.
6. ¿*Recibir* Ud. cupones de / ?	No, pero *querer* / .
7. ¿*Recibir* / económica / estado.	Sí, $425 / mes de /.
8. ¿*Saber* Ud. preparar / baratas con carne y legumbres?	No, no *saber* nada de cómo / preparan / comidas baratas de aquí.
9. Yo *ir* / recomendar que Ud. *asistir* / unas clases / nutrición que / *ofrecer* aquí / el hospital.	Bueno, / *interesar* mucho. *Querer* que / hijos *estar* bien de / .

Pregunte Ud.

Dé Ud. oralmente las preguntas necesarias en la siguiente entrevista con Mirta Maldonado, una cliente que necesita rebajar treinta libras por razones de la salud. Ayúdela a entender qué comidas más le convenga para rebajar.

1. Sí, el médico me dijo que tengo que rebajar treinta libras.

2. Pues, no, no sé qué comidas debo comer para perder peso.

3. Para el desayuno suelo comer pan con mantequilla y mermelada y café con leche y azúcar.

4. Generalmente como la comida principal a las dos de la tarde.

5. Normalmente como un poco de carne y arroz con habichuelas.

6. No, no me gustan nada las ensaladas. Nunca las como.

7. Las legumbres que más me gustan son las papas.

8. Tengo el hábito de cenar a las nueve de la noche, antes de dormir.

9. Pues, sí, me encantan los dulces.

10. Me gustan algunas frutas, pero no se consiguen por acá.

11. No, no me gusta nada el pescado ni el pollo; prefiero comer carne de res.

12. Pues, no quiero cambiar mucho mi manera de comer; me gusta mucho comer.

Dígalo

Pregúntele a un/a compañero/a de clase lo que le diga su profesor/a sobre los temas de los hábitos de comer, la comida que le gusta más, el comer dulces, las bebidas que toma, y el cambiar de dieta.

Escuche bien 📼

A. Ud. oirá ocho listas; cada una contiene cuatro nombres de varios comestibles. Escriba el nombre que no les convenga a los otros de la lista, y explique por qué es diferente.

	Nombre del comestible	*¿Por qué es diferente?*
1.		
2.		
3.		
4.		
5.		
6.		
7.		
8.		

B. Ud. oirá a seis clientes que describen acciones en el pasado relacionadas con la comida. Escriba:

A — si la acción comenzó en el pasado
B — si la acción terminó en el pasado
C — si la acción estaba en progreso

1. _____   3. _____   5. _____

2. _____   4. _____   6. _____

Diálogos cortos

I. *La doctora*

Entre, señorita Rodríguez.

Tenemos que _____ sobre su dieta.

¿Ud. sabe que _____ alta presión (*high blood pressure*)?

Pues, Ud. tiene que _____ su dieta. _____ importante que no _____ nada de sal.

Exacto, como no _____ buena para su _____ .

_____ preferible que Ud. no _____ grasas (*fats*).

Claro. _____ mejor que _____ comida _____ ligera.

La paciente

Gracias, doctora.

Muy bien, doctora.

Sí, me lo dijo la enfermera.

¿No puedo comer sal en las comidas?

¿Hay algo más que debo hacer?

¿Eso incluye las comidas fritas?

Bueno, doctora, yo voy a hacer todo lo que Ud. me dice.

II. *La señorita Viera*

_____ días, _____ Ocampo. _____ llamo María Viera. _____ intérprete. ¿En _____ servirle?

Sí, _____ mucho gusto. Primero yo _____ saber si Ud. _____ una dieta especial.

¿Qué _____ Ud. en _____ desayuno, té o café?

El señor Ocampo

Buenos días, Señorita Viera. Sé un poco de inglés pero no lo leo bien. El menú que me trajeron es en inglés y no entiendo nada. ¿Podría ayuudarme a descifrarlo?

Sí, señorita. La doctora me dice que padezco de la vesícula (*gall bladder*) y no quiere que coma comidas grasosas.

¿No hay chocolate caliente?

La señorita Viera

Sí, pero Ud. no _____ tomarlo.

Así es. ¿ _____ Ud. cereal

o _____ tostado con margarina?

_____ siento, señor.

_____ platos _____

son malos para _____

salud. Ud. puede _____

pollo pero solamente _____

horno. ¿A Ud. _____

gusta el arroz _____ habichuelas?

No, porque Ud. _____

leche en _____ desayuno.

¿Quisiera _____ jugo

_____ tomate?

Sí, señor.

Lo _____ , señor. Nosotros no lo _____ permitir.

¿Qué _____ parece

_____ fresca?

El señor Ocampo

Entonces, que me traigan un buen café con leche. Supongo que sólo me permiten tomar leche descremada, ¿verdad?

Si no puedo poner mantequilla en el pan ¡no lo quiero! ¿Qué se sirve para el almuerzo? ¡Las ganas que tengo de comer pollo frito con tostones!

Parece que no hay más remedio. ¿Puedo tomar un vaso de leche?

Ay, Dios. ¿No puedo tomar leche más que una vez al día?

Sí, como no. Estoy resignado a todo. Me permiten tomar postre, ¿no?

Entonces, voy a pedirle a mi esposa que me traiga un flan.

¡No! Ya basta con las frutas frescas y las ensaladas y leche descremada. En este hospital no curan a los pacientes. ¡Los matan (*they kill*) de hambre!

Ayude al cliente

Your patient, Francisco Silverio, is leaving the hospital after an operation to remove part of his stomach. Write a note in Spanish that he can take home to his wife describing what he should and should not eat for the next four weeks. Begin the note with: *Muy distinguida señora Silverio.*

1. Tell her that you are writing to give her instructions about the type of food her husband should eat while he is recuperating (*recuperarse*) from the operation. Tell her that it is very important that she follow the instructions carefully (*con cuidado*); otherwise (*si no*), her husband will not get better.

2. Start a new paragraph and tell her that Mr. Silverio should not eat spicy foods at all. Mention that it is better that he not drink coffee or tea, but a little milk twice a day is fine. State that it's better that he eat five or six small meals a day. Tell her that he should not eat anything fried or greasy, and that baked chicken and fish are better than beef. Mention that he may eat some fresh fruit and vegetables, but not too many. Also state that you prefer that he eat eggs no more than three times per week.

3. Close the letter telling her that a dietitian will be visiting the house next week to see if she has any questions about the diet. Tell her to call you if there is any change in her husband's condition.

4. Close the letter with *su seguro/a servidor/a* and sign your name.

¿Comprende Ud.?

Escuche bien a los cinco clientes que describen su dieta regular. Después de escuchar a cada uno, Ud. va a hacer recomendaciones para que cada uno mejore la salud. (Es posible que algunos clientes tengan más de una recomendación.) Escriba primero la edad de la persona y después:

   A — si se le recomienda comer menos dulces.
   B — si se le recomienda comer más proteína.
   C — si se le recomienda comer una dieta de bajo colesterol.
   D — si le parece bien la dieta.

		Edad	*Recomendación*
1.	Magdalena Casal Rodríguez	_____	_____
2.	Carlos Segreda	_____	_____
3.	Rafael Carrasco Robles	_____	_____
4.	Norma Rosado	_____	_____
5.	Jorge Ruiz Romano	_____	_____

Piénselo

Prepárese para poder hablar con el/la profesor/a o con otros estudiantes sobre los siguientes temas, contestando las preguntas que le sugiera su profesor/a.

1. Los platos típicos de los EE.UU.
2. Los platos típicos de los varios países hispanos
3. La importancia del desayuno
4. La persona que prepara las comidas en casa
5. La dieta perfecta
6. Las dietas especiales

Imagínese

1. ¿Cómo se llama la quinceañera (la señorita)?
2. ¿Cuándo se celebró el quinceañero? ¿Dónde?
3. ¿A qué hora empezó la fiesta según la invitación?
4. ¿A qué hora llegaron los invitados?
5. ¿Qué se dijo en la invitación?
6. ¿Qué edad tenían los invitados?
7. ¿Qué se sirvió para la comida?
8. ¿Cómo se sentían los padres y la familia?
9. ¿Celebró Ud. su año quinceañero? ¿De qué manera?
10. ¿Quisiera Ud. tener quince años otra vez? Explique su respuesta.

1. ¿Según el anuncio, ¿cuándo es el baile?
2. ¿Cree Ud. que vaya mucha gente al baile? ¿Por qué?
3. ¿Qué van a servir para comer?
4. ¿Qué va a tomar la gente?
5. ¿Va a bailar mucho la gente? Explique su respuesta.
6. ¿Qué tipo de música se va a tocar (*play*)?
7. ¿Cuánto cuesta la entrada?
8. ¿Hay que hacer reservaciones? ¿Dónde?
9. ¿Tiene Ud. ganas de ir a este baile? Explique su respuesta.
10. ¿Le gustan más los bailes hispanos o los americanos? ¿Por qué?

Lea Ud. la siguiente carta y conteste las preguntas que siguen. Hay algunas palabras nuevas, pero el contexto le va a ayudar a entenderlas.

Querido José,

Ya llevo tres meses en Milwaukee y la verdad es que no entiendo a estos americanos. Aquí todo se hace de prisa, hasta comer. La mayoría de la gente casi nunca come en casa porque nadie tiene tiempo de cocinar. Hay muchos restaurantes de comida ligera, como los llaman ellos, donde se venden hamburguesas, pollo frito, etc. ¡Allí se puede comer en menos de quince minutos — imagínate! Ni toman la siesta. ¡Hay personas que nunca salen de la oficina para almorzar! Llevan un "sandwich" a la oficina o compran algo ligero en la cafetería y lo comen sentados a su escritorio. ¡Qué barbaridad!

No sabes cuánta falta me hacen nuestras costumbres — comer en casa con la familia, sin prisa, y después, la siesta para poder volver al trabajo bien descansadito. También extraño mi comida criolla — los frijoles, las enchiladas suizas, el mole, las chalupas, etc. Por aquí la comida mexicana que se sirve en los restaurantes no tiene nada en común con lo que comía en casa de mamá.

No te puedes imaginar lo difícil que es el tener que cambiar de dieta. Así que decidí aprender a cocinar. ¡Sí, yo, cocinando! Ya se ve que es la única solución. Bueno, hermano, te dejo en esa nota.

Hasta la próxima,
Víctor

1. ¿Cómo se siente Víctor en Milwaukee?
2. ¿De dónde es?
3. ¿Cuánto tiempo hace que está en Milwaukee?
4. ¿Qué describe él en su carta a su hermano?
5. ¿Le gustan a Víctor las costumbres americanas relacionadas con la comida? Explique su respuesta.
6. ¿Qué le hace falta a Víctor?
7. ¿Qué decidió hacer Víctor para sentirse mejor?
8. ¿Qué quiere decir *extraño* en la carta?
9. ¿Come Ud. de la manera que describe Víctor? Explique su respuesta.
10. ¿Quisiera Ud. cambiar su manera de comer? ¿De qué manera?

1. ¿Qué día cree Ud. que es?
2. ¿Qué hora del día (o de la noche) es?
3. ¿Quiénes están en el restaurante?
4. ¿Son todos amigos o parientes?
5. ¿Están tomando algo? Explique su respuesta.
6. ¿Qué están celebrando?
7. ¿Ya comieron o van a comer más tarde?
8. ¿Cuánto tiempo hace que están en el restaurante?
9. ¿Quién está tocando un instrumento musical?
10. ¿Quisiera Ud. estar con ellos en el restaurante? ¿Por qué?

Haciendo el papel

1. Ud. es un/a enfermero/a visitante que tiene que ayudar a un cliente mexicano de 69 años, a cambiar su dieta porque tiene una úlcera. Usted sabe que al paciente le gusta la comida picante, la cual no debe comer. ¿Cómo puede Ud. ayudar al paciente, teniendo en cuenta los factores culturales?

2. Usted es trabajador/a social y va a ayudar a una señora que llegó a los Estados Unidos hace dos meses a planear su visita al supermercado. La idea es poder conseguir mucha comida buena por poco dinero, empleando los siguientes

anuncios. Los cinco hijos de la señora suelen comer comida de tipo "fast foods" porque le parece a ella más barata. También, no puede conseguir la comida que solía cocinar ni tampoco sabe cómo se preparan muchos de los vegetales que se ven en el supermercado. ¿Cómo puede Ud. ayudarla?

3. Escriba Ud. un menú del hospital que les guste a sus clientes hispanos, escogiendo comidas regionales que les convengan. Escriba dos alternativas para cada parte de cada comida.

	Desayuno	*Almuerzo*	*Cena*
proteína	_____	_____	_____
	_____	_____	_____
vegetales o ensaladas	_____	_____	_____
	_____	_____	_____
postre	_____	_____	_____
	_____	_____	_____
bebidas	_____	_____	_____
	_____	_____	_____

Ahora haga Ud. el papel del/de la dietista con un/a compañero/a que haga el papel del paciente para ver si le conviene el menú.

REFLEJOS DE LA CULTURA: "En Cuba no falta nada"

The consequences of the Cuban revolution are many and varied. The most obvious result is the change in the social system, which, prior to Castro's overthrow of the Batista government, was a typical oligarchy, with a small percentage of "haves" and the majority of the population "have-nots." Although the previous *clase popular* now has more access to adequate housing, education, employment, and the finer things of life, the continued economic difficulties on the island have resulted in a shortage of manufactured goods and foodstuffs.

The following satirical poem, written by José Sánchez-Boudy in his *anti-novela* entitled *Lilayando pal tu* (*mojito y picardía cubana*), highlights the loss of typical Cuban foods enjoyed prior to the revolution. It is critical of the regime, as evidenced by the term *maricón* (a derogatory term for homosexual, a strong insult in Hispanic cultures). The rich vocabulary reflects both the variety of foods enjoyed in Cuban cuisine and the pride and nostalgia that foods from one's native land evoke. The English interpretation of the poem is a clear example of something lost in the translation—the descriptions of the foods in English do not do justice to the images evoked in Spanish for a Cuban who has left the island.

Era la isla más bella
descubierta por Colón,
y vino este maricón
e hizo una mierda con ella.

Se acabó la mortadella,
la malta, la condensada,
el queso y la jamonada,
el dulce y el salchichón
y dice este maricón
que en Cuba no falta nada.

Ya no hay tomate ni ají,
no hay papas, falta el anís
no hay quien chupe un pirulí,
ya no se come congrí.

No hay azúcar, no hay panqué,
no hay ajiaco, no hay fabada,
ya no hay carne entomatada,
no hay zapote, no hay anón;
y dice este maricón
que en Cuba no falta nada.

It was the most beautiful island discovered by Columbus and (then) along came this "homosexual" and turned it into excrement.

You can no longer find mortadella (sausage), malt (drink), condensed (milk), cheese, and pork sausage, candy, and pepperoni, and yet this "homosexual" says there is nothing lacking in Cuba.

There's no longer tomato or hot pepper, there are no potatoes, anise isn't around, (and) no one sucks lollipops, nor are rice and red beans eaten.

There's no sugar, or muffins, there's no soup or white bean stew, nor is there meat in tomato sauce, no marmalade fruit or other fruits and (yet) this "homosexual" says there's nothing lacking in Cuba.

No hay especias, no hay comino,
falta la sal, no hay tostadas,
ya nadie come ensalada,
no hay cebollas, no hay tocino,
no hay cerveza, ron ni vino,
no hay garbanzos ni empanadas,
piñas, mango ni melón;
y dice este maricón
que en Cuba no falta nada.

Se acabaron las tortillas,
falta el pan y las galletas,
no hay ya las ricas chuletas,
no hay ajos ni empanadillas,
se acabaron las saladas
y el sabrosito lechón;
y dice este maricón
que en Cuba no falta nada.

Trece años muy fatales,
sin arroz ni bacalao,
ya no hay coquito quemao,
no hay manteca, no hay tamales,
se acabaron los panales,
las cremas azucaradas,
las paticas rebozadas
que nunca admiten disputas;
y dice este hijo de fruta
que en Cuba no falta nada.

Ya no se ven golosinas,
ya no se ven los quequés,
ni un frijol,
no hay azafrán, no hay bijol,
no hay aceite, no hay sardinas,
se terminó hasta la harina
que antes estaba botada,
la carne está racionada
en todita la nación;
y dice este maricón
que en Cuba no falta nada.

No hay vergüenza, no hay
honor, no hay virtud,
no hay sensatez,
no hay respeto ni honradez,
ni escrúpulos, ni pudor,
ni alivio para el dolor
de mi patria atormentada,
de esta Cuba acorralada
llena de desilusión;
y dice este maricón
que en Cuba no falta nada.

There are not spices, or cumin, you can't find salt, there's no toasted bread, no one ever eats salad anymore, there are no onions, no bacon, no beer, no rum or wine, there are no chickpeas or meat pies, pineapples, mangos or melon; and yet this "homosexual" says that in Cuba nothing is lacking.

They have done away with tortillas, you can't find bread or crackers, there are no longer the delicious pork chops, there's no garlic or little pastries, salt meats have disappeared, as has the scrumptious roast pork, and yet this "homosexual" says that nothing is lacking in Cuba.

Thirteen very fatal years without rice or codfish, there are no longer any macaroons, there's no lard, no tamales, honeycombs have disappeared, as have candies made from sugared cream, and the breaded pig's feet that knew no rival; and yet this son of a fruit says that in Cuba nothing is lacking.

You no longer see delicacies, nor do you see cakes, not even a bean, there's no saffron, or other spice(s), there's no oil, there are no sardines, even the flour that before was overabundant has been used up; meat is rationed all over the country; yet this "homosexual" says that in Cuba nothing is lacking.

There's no shame, there's no honor, there's no virtue, there's no good sense, there's no respect or honesty, no scruples, or modesty, no relief for the pain of my tormented fatherland, this fenced-in Cuba full of disappointment; and yet this "homosexual" says that in Cuba nothing is lacking.

LECCIÓN 10

Lo que dice la ley

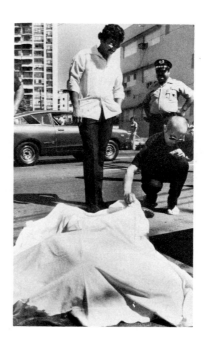

LOS OBJETIVOS

Raising awareness

1. To improve interaction with Hispanic clients by analyzing one's communication style as a reflection of personality
2. To understand the cultural significance and implications of **personalismo**
3. To contrast attitudes toward money common to Hispanic cultures with those typical of the U.S. culture

Comunicándose en español

1. To pronounce and comprehend words containing **h, g, gu,** and **j**
2. To use and understand vocabulary and structures common to legal and law-enforcement situations
3. To use and understand vocabulary and structures relating to emotions and interpersonal relationships

Combinándolo todo

1. To integrate all material from previous sections and lessons, applying it to challenging professional activities
2. To use and understand formal commands and negative constructions
3. To appreciate the role of the **coyote** as a reflection of **personalismo**

357

Raising awareness

OVERVIEW: Communicating styles

Previous chapters have shown that effective cross-cultural communication is a creative process, demanding practice, patience, self-awareness, and specific skills. Another dimension of cross-cultural communication is an awareness of communication styles and how they reflect the individual's personality, regardless of cultural background.

There appear to be four basic communication styles reflecting four distinct personality types. Although an individual may possess characteristics of all four personality types, usually one dominant personality style characterizes the way that individual communicates with others.

Style 1 is typical of the *action*-oriented personality. People who rely heavily on this style of communicating are achievers who like to be ac-

tively involved in solving problems and improving the status quo. *Style 2* reflects the *process*-oriented personality. It is the dominant mode of communicating for people who like facts, organizing, structuring, setting up strategy, and planning tactics. *Style 3* is typical of the *people*-oriented personality, which is prone to focus on inner actions, social processes, teamwork, social systems, and the motivation behind actions. *Style 4* is characteristic of the *idea*-oriented personality. People who use this approach to communication are fond of concepts, theories, intellectualizing, exchanging ideas, innovation, and creativity.

An individual's personality type seems to be influenced by inherent qualities, cultural background, past experiences, and the present envi-

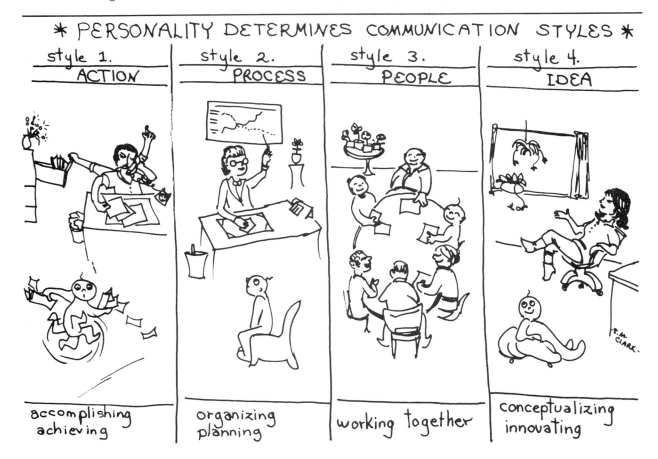

* PERSONALITY DETERMINES COMMUNICATION STYLES *

style 1. ACTION	style 2. PROCESS	style 3. PEOPLE	style 4. IDEA
accomplishing achieving	organizing planning	working together	conceptualizing innovating

ronment. Since most people evidence all four personality types to some extent, the choice of communication style can change in accordance with the particular situation. It is possible to switch from one personality channel to another. So-called well-rounded individuals are often viewed as such precisely because of the ease with which they can shift from one communication style to another. But although they may be seen as balanced personalities, their lack of predictability may be confusing to those who communicate with them often. Most individuals prefer the one style of communicating that best reflects their predominant personality traits, especially in situations of crisis or stress.

By exploring each of the four styles, you can develop strategies for coping with partners who employ each. You will be able to classify the communication style of each individual you meet if you focus on both content and process. For example, in style 1, action-oriented people talk about results, efficiency, moving ahead, achievements, and performance. They tend to be pragmatic and direct, energetic, at times impatient, and prone to jumping from one idea to another. Style 2 communicators, with their focus on process, tend to discuss procedures, planning, details, observations, and analyses. They often give the impression of being systematic, logical, factual, unemotional, and talkative. People-oriented style 3 communicators speak of people and their needs and motivations, beliefs and values, understanding, cooperation, and self-development. Their personality would be most often described as warm, perceptive, sensitive, spontaneous, and somewhat subjective. Idea-oriented communicators, typical of style 4, focus their messages on concepts, issues, problems, alternatives, and opportunities. Style 4 communicators are often perceived as charismatic, unrealistic, creative, provocative, and even difficult to understand.

The following guidelines may be helpful for coping with each of these communication styles.

A. *Communication with the action-oriented person is usually most successful if one:*
   1. Focuses on the results from the beginning
   2. States the best recommendation
   3. Is as brief as possible
   4. Emphasizes the practicality of the recommendation
   5. Uses visual aids of some kind

B. *When communicating with a process-oriented person, it is important to remember to:*
   1. Be precise by stating the facts
   2. Organize your presentation in a logical manner
   3. Include all alternatives with pros and cons
   4. Give the communication partner sufficient time
   5. Outline your proposal, using numbers whenever possible

C. *In communicating with a people-oriented person, it is often best to:*
   1. Leave time for small talk and initiate the discussion with it
   2. Stress the relationships between your proposal and the people concerned
   3. Demonstrate how well similar ideas have worked with other people in the past
   4. Indicate support from a well-respected person
   5. Use an informal style in writing and speaking

D. *Communicating with an idea-oriented person implies a need to:*
   1. Allow enough time for discussion
   2. Not get impatient when he or she goes off on tangents
   3. Try to relate the topic to a broader range from the beginning of the discussion
   4. Stress the uniqueness of the idea at hand
   5. Focus on the future impact that the idea will have

As you work with your Hispanic clients, you can apply the insights gained from the different communicating styles, but you must also keep in mind that:

1. You cannot solve the client's problem; you can best provide services by facilitating an environment that allows the *individual* to resolve the problem at hand.
2. What is appropriate for one Hispanic client may be inappropriate for another.

3. What is effective in one situation may be counterproductive in another, especially when dealing with cultural variables.

4. Being open to each new client as an individual and trying to understand his or her cultural background provides the best chance for success.

Just as there are different communication styles, there are also different ways of listening. Each can be effective, depending on personality, cultural conditioning, and personal experiences.

1. You can be *interpretive* in your listening by explaining what the problem is and *not* giving advice. This is particularly useful in helping the other realize the impact of what has just been said, and it may lead to a constructive confrontation.

2. A *supportive* response is sent to reassure the other person and to reduce anxiety by showing support for what has already been said or done. This is a useful tool when the person demonstrates a need for acceptance as well as for support and reassurance.

3. A *probing* style of listening and replying elicits information by asking questions and provoking discussion to clarify the issue. This is an effective means of defining the problem and aids in exploring the full implications of any decision made.

4. An *understanding* listening style is characterized by periodically providing the other person with paraphrases of what he or she has said in order to check the accuracy of your understanding. This listening style helps the other person to expand ideas and feelings. It also increases the accuracy of communication between partners.

5. An *evaluative* response shows that the listener has assessed the problem and may indicate possible courses of action for the other person. This is most effective when the listener has been asked directly to disclose his or her feelings, attitudes, or values.

Remember that all these listening styles are valid and appropriate, depending on the people and situations involved.

It has been shown that when working with clients, especially those from different cultural backgrounds, the overuse or underuse of any one style may prevent adequate communication. In addition, the failure to select the appropriate response is often the cause of many miscommunications. The understanding response, in particular, is a very powerful one, especially in the beginning of the communication process. It is wise to avoid giving an evaluative response at the early stages of the interaction, since this may block further communication and often results in one value judgment leading to another.

As you apply any of these communicating or listening styles in your interactions with Hispanic clients, be aware of any nonverbal cues you are sending as well. In addition, to be most effective, your way of questioning and soliciting information should respect cultural norms. This is especially true when asking Hispanic clients personal questions. It takes time to set up the close rapport needed to ask questions that the Hispanic client may regard as overly personal and/or intrusive. Remember that silence is also a response, as are eye contact and head movements. The direct approach, which may work well with Anglo clients, may be completely ineffectual with Hispanics. Developing a sense of timing and awareness of how your style affects your Hispanic clients comes with practice. If you continue to be open and observe the impact your own style has on clients, you will greatly increase your own self-knowledge as well as your skill in the cross-cultural communication process.

Applications

1. Select *in each pair* of attributes the *one* most typical of your personality. Make your choice as spontaneously as possible. There is no right or wrong answer. The pattern that develops will help you be more aware of your personal communicating style.

1. I like action.
2. I deal with problems in a systematic way.

3. I believe that teams are more effective than individuals.
4. I enjoy innovation very much.

5. When I start something, I like to go through it until the end.
6. I want to set up my own objectives.

7. I basically try to understand other people's emotions.
8. I do challenge people around me.

9. I look forward to receiving feedback on my performance.
10. I find the step-by-step approach very effective.

11. I like creative problem solving.
12. I think I am good at reading people.

13. *Cooperation* is a key word for me.
14. I use logical methods to test alternatives.

15. I like to handle several projects at the same time.
16. I always question myself.

17. I learn by doing.
18. I believe that my head rules my heart.

19. I can predict how others may react to a certain action.
20. I do not like details.

21. I enjoy reading very much.
22. I perceive myself as a facilitator.

23. I like to focus on one issue at a time.
24. I like to achieve.

25. I usually make decisions without thinking too much.
26. Emotions create problems.

27. I like to be liked by others.
28. I can put two and two together quickly.

29. I find abstractions interesting and enjoyable.
30. I am patient with detail.

31. I like brief, to-the-point statements.
32. I feel confident in myself.

Circle the numbers below that correspond to those circled above.

Style 1 =	1	6	9	15	17	24	25	31
Style 2 =	2	5	10	14	18	23	26	30
Style 3 =	3	7	12	13	19	22	27	32
Style 4 =	4	8	11	16	20	21	28	29

Compare your responses with those of another member of the class.

2. You are a professional whose Hispanic client has consistently been late for appointments. You feel this has caused many problems in scheduling other appointments and has deprived you of time to deal with this client's needs. In English or Spanish, write what you would say to this client, depending on what you perceive to be his or her main communicating style.

a. *Client appears to use Style 1 (Action)*

_____

_____

_____

b. *Client appears to use Style 2 (Process)*

_____

_____

_____

c. *Client appears to use Style 3 (People)*

_____

_____

_____

d. *Client appears to use Style 4 (Idea)*

_____

_____

_____

Now role-play the same situation with four members of the class, each representing a different communication style.

3. A Hispanic client whom you've known well for the past six months has come in to tell you that he or she is homesick, is unable to function in the Anglo environment, and wants to go home as soon as possible. In English or Spanish, write what you would say in each of the following types of responses:

a. Understanding response: _____

_____

_____

_____

b. Probing response: _____

_____

_____

_____

c. Supportive response: _____

_____

_____

_____

d. Interpretive response: _____

_____

_____

_____

e. Evaluative response: _____

_____

_____

_____

Now role-play the same situation with five members of the class, using a different type of response with each.

Reflections

1. Were you surprised to discover what your dominant communicating style is? How do you feel your personal style has affected your ability to communicate with your Hispanic clients? Based on your experiences, do you feel one communication style has worked better than another with Hispanic clients? If so, which one? What cultural factors may account for this?

2. In role playing the situation in which you discussed with the Hispanic client the problems regarding tardiness for appointments, with which communicating style did you feel most comfortable? Was it difficult for you to switch from one style to another? Why?

3. Which type of response do you feel typifies your listening style? With which style did you feel most comfortable? Least comfortable? Do you overuse one specific listening style with your Hispanic clients? Do you find it difficult to use a specific listening style with your Hispanic clients? Is this due to your personality, cultural factors, or both?

HISTORICAL PERSPECTIVE: *Personalismo*

A corollary to the value Hispanic cultures place on the personal dignity and respect due human beings is the importance of *personalismo*. It can be defined as the trust placed in an *individual,* especially one in a position of power, believing more in his or her personal sense of integrity and honesty, rather than in the role, position, or institution that endows the individual with authority. It is at odds with the Anglo culture's trust in systems and institutions that govern everyday life. That trust continues despite the occasional breaches of faith triggered by individuals who abuse the system. Understanding this contrast is crucial to you as a provider of services to Hispanic clients. In addition, it will aid your comprehension of contemporary political and socioeconomic developments in Latin America that may have played an important role in your clients' decision to come to the United States.

Personalismo has its origins in both the indigenous societies of Latin America and in the code of ethics of the Spanish *conquistadores.* Members of the well-developed indigenous societies were accustomed to following the dictates of the leader of the group. The Spaniards brought to these highly organized groups their code of personal ethics based on the concepts of *honor* (the respect afforded one through the reputation that has been earned) and *honra* (one's own self-respect based on the adherence to moral principles). Although much of the Spaniards' conduct with regard to the indigenous populations may seem abhorrent from a present-day perspective, the importance of the concept of *honor* was evident in the debates that went on in Spain regarding the ethics of conquest and colonization.

The Indian populations soon saw that they were expected to transfer loyalties from their own leaders to the newly arrived Spaniards. They learned that their survival and treatment depended more on the personality of their overseers than on any formal institutionalized practices. Absolute power over their lives lay in the hands of these "lords of the lands." The Indians' sense of impotence over their own life could be relieved only through the personal benevolence of their masters. The paternalism of the Spaniards encouraged the indigenous labor force to look to the individual rather than to the now defunct social system that had once provided for individual and societal needs. Dependence on the *dueño* (owner) for material needs set the tone for viewing all authority figures as lords worthy of respect but also capable of responding personally to an individual's requests. The likelihood of an affirmative response depended on the individual leader's personal integrity and sense of honor. Appealing to that sense of ethics has been the main resource accessible to the disempowered lower classes.

---

1. *Define* personalismo *and explain how it contrasts with the Anglo "systems and institutions" approach to life.*
2. *Discuss the origins and development of* personalismo *in the Hispanic cultures.*

Through the years, *personalismo* has evolved into a complex concept. It explains the cult of certain individuals, heroes of the independence movements, revolutionary figures such as the Mexicans Emiliano Zapata and Pancho Villa, the Cuban Fidel Castro, the Nicaraguan Augusto Sandino, and even the veneration of certain saints. Life for the individual in Hispanic cultures revolves around the concept of *personalismo*. If one views the individual and family as the nucleus of a web, it becomes apparent that part of the task of living involves establishing as many links as possible on that personal network in order to survive life's inevitable crises and traumas. It contrasts sharply with the Anglo concept of *individualism*, a belief that society's systems and institutions provide the individual with all the opportunities for success. In Anglo terms, it is up to the individual to make the most of what is available, to play by the rules of organized society, in return for success in the material world. Personal needs are likewise met by the various institutions, including the family, work, organized religion, social services, educational institutions, health-care facilities, legal institutions, and the like. The two systems are contrasted in the following diagram:

For the individual Hispanic, the web of *personalismo* is centered in the individual's sense of honor and integrity and that of his or her family. The two are tightly interwoven. One's own reputation both reflects and stems from that of the family. In addition, the individual's personal dignity is deeply rooted in a sense of ethics derived mostly from Christian principles. Hispanics also tend to cultivate a personal devotion to God, either directly or via an intermediary such as the Virgin Mary or one of the saints.

Conduct within the extended family unit is the most immediate area in which the principles of *personalismo* are evident. The *compadrazgo* (godparenting) system provides another arena in which *personalismo* operates. One adult male may choose another to be the *padrino* (godparent) of his child on the basis of the added support this new relationship will bring to him and his family. The relationship is primarily between the adults, who now address each other as *compadres* (co-parents), although the child's welfare is now the concern of both parents and godparents.

3. *Compare* personalismo *and* individualism *with regard to how individuals in Hispanic and Anglo cultures view their life.*
4. *Define the components of* personalismo *that affect the individual in the intimate aspects of life.*

On the local level, individual priests, military figures, merchants, and politicians are revered or scorned (at least in private), according to their adherence to the code of honor and their concern for those less fortunate. In the world of business and law, *personalismo* is also evident. Those entering a legal contract or business arrangement must share mutual respect for each other. The *palabra de honor* (word of honor) is as important, if not more so, than the actual documents signed by each. Maintaining one's personal reputation as an *hombre honrado* (an honorable man) is paramount to success in business and professional endeavors. This is as true for the vendor at the marketplace as it is for the president of a large corporation. A change in ownership and/or management may affect the success of a business until the new leader has established a solid personal reputation.

When Hispanics need help, they prefer to use their own personal network of friends, relatives, and acquaintances for services and/or referrals, rather than impersonal institutions. Often, friends and relatives are the first recourse for advice on personal, marital, financial, legal, and health problems. Women, particularly in their role as mothers, are looked to as counseling sources for men and women. Seeking help outside the personal circle is often viewed as a last resort, especially if it implies going to strangers for advice or aid. It may cause problems within the family, since revealing intimate details of family life to outsiders is not culturally acceptable. This is in direct conflict with the Anglo tendency for individuals to resolve their own problems and not to rely on family or friends to do so except in cases of extreme need.

On the political level, *personalismo* typifies Latin America. It explains the political upheaval in some Latin American countries and the long decades of left- and right-wing dictatorships in others. Although other factors influence the politics of each country, *personalismo* plays an important role. Its legacy encourages politicians who feel they know what is right for their countries to instigate a *coup* or revolution and/or to stay in power for as long as they are able. The Hispanic cultures' belief in the *person* and not the *system* condones such personalistic politics. For U.S. Anglos steeped in the institutional approach to society and proud of their democratic system, the political paradoxes of Latin American countries are sometimes incomprehensible.

---

5. *How does* personalismo *affect the business and professional worlds in Hispanic cultures?*
6. *What effect has* personalismo *had on the political situations in some Hispanic countries?*

Another distortion of Hispanic cultural values when viewed from the Anglo perspective is that of honesty and integrity. The Anglo stereotypic view of Hispanics as untrustworthy or dishonest often stems from limited contact and knowledge of Hispanic cultures as well as from misrepresentation of Hispanics in the media. In reality, both Hispanics and Anglos place a high value on personal honesty. In practice, however, the concept is evidenced in culturally different ways.

Anglo tourists who visit Spanish-speaking countries are often impressed by the willingness to bargain (*regatear*) for goods and services. Later, however, they are often dismayed to find that what they thought was a bargain is, in reality, available more cheaply from other sources. This leads to the feeling of being "ripped off," which reinforces the misconception of Hispanics as dishonest. In effect, this type of exchange is another aspect of *personalismo*. Whereas Anglos are accustomed to fixed prices, which imply equal treatment for all (typical of their pride in democracy), Hispanics tend to value the personal exchange as much as the monetary one. When entering into a bargaining position with a prospective buyer, the merchant affords the buyer all due respect and dignity by assuming that he or she knows the value of the merchandise or service. Reaching a mutually agreeable price affirms both partners in the exchange on a personalistic basis. The buyer feels personally valued by the seller's willingness to give a special price. The seller is personally gratified by the purchaser's decision to buy from him or her. Future transactions will build on this personal relationship.

When Anglo tourists arrive on the scene, they often are unaware of the nuances involved in the bargaining exchange. They may be in a hurry, may not speak the language well (if at all), and may see the intent of bargaining as trying to outwit the vendor, emphasizing more the competitive edge than the *personalismo* aspect of the interaction. The tourist, not knowing the value of the merchandise or service *in that country*, may base his or her offers on comparable expenditures in the United States. Thus what seems a bargain for the Anglo tourist may be a much higher price than the vendor normally receives. Yet the vendor is culturally justified in not offering the more common lower price because the tourist has not come properly prepared. In addition, the tourist is usually viewed as rich, since in most Hispanic countries only the very well-to-do are capable of traveling to other countries. In the Hispanic cul-

tural view of honesty, the tourist is naive for not knowing the value of the purchase and, furthermore, can afford the loss; thus the higher price is justified.

A similar situation may exist with regard to street crime and petty thefts in Hispanic countries. Despite the large numbers of economically disadvantaged citizens, most Spanish-speaking countries enjoy a rather low crime rate compared with the United States. However, tourists are often prime targets for pickpockets and petty theft, since they are seen as naive for not knowing how to take proper precautions as well as able to afford the loss.

---

7. *What accounts for the misconceptions that Anglos may have about Hispanics and the value they place on honesty?*
8. *Explain the cultural differences that operate when the Anglo tourist bargains with a Hispanic merchant.*

Another misinterpretation of Hispanics' honesty stems from the common use of tips (*propinas*) and bribes (*sobornos;* in Mexico, *la mordida*) offered for services rendered in Spanish-speaking areas. A fine line separates the two, and it is most often drawn in accordance with cultural values. In Hispanic cultures, these practices stem from the emphasis on *personalismo* in all interactions among people. When an individual who usually depends on the personal network of friends and family to take care of needs is suddenly in a position of needing something from strangers, it is not uncommon to establish a personal connection to assure preferential treatment or to show appreciation for a special favor by using money. It may be offered to office workers, civil servants in bureaucratic positions (remember, "systems" in Latin America are not highly prized or always effective mechanisms), or law-enforcement officers when a special favor is needed. In some ways, it is an extension of the practice of tipping for services rendered. Since many civil servants are paid relatively low wages, the extra money is accepted as a necessary recompense to earn a just wage, just as tips supplement the low wages paid restaurant workers. Although many governments have attempted to change this practice, it continues to reign in many areas of institutionalized life in Hispanic cultures.

Anglos may also have difficulty understanding another Hispanic cultural interpretation of honesty — the tendency to say what is expected in a given situation, even if it is not exactly true. This is a manifestation of the need to save face, maintaining one's personal and familial reputation to the outside world, which is important from the perspective of *personalismo.* For example, when Hispanics are asked information or directions that they do not know, they may give a false reply rather than admit their ignorance. In interviews conducted by an authority figure, Hispanic clients may try to anticipate what the investigator wants to hear rather than reveal the truth, especially if it is perceived as contradictory to the expectations of the interviewer. In addition, the need to preserve the name and honor of the family may prevent some Hispanics from giving truthful answers to questions about the intimate details of their private lives, particularly when the questions are asked by relative strangers.

The misperceptions of many Anglos regarding honesty among Hispanics are also due to the misrepresentations of Spanish speakers in textbooks and the media. Portraits of Mexicans in history books stress the banditlike qualities of such national heroes as Zapata and Villa, overlooking the fact that the American forces were invading what was Mexican territory. The "Frito Bandito" character (in Spanish, the word is actually *bandido*) is another example of how the image of Hispanics as dishonest is reinforced. Newspapers in U.S. cities with large Spanish-speaking populations often stress reports of crimes committed by Hispanics, without equal time for the many contributions these residents bring to their environment. Ironically, such accounts provide the only contact many Anglos have with Hispanics, whose human dignity and respect for others are best appreciated through personal encounter.

Anglo professionals are fortunate in having the opportunity to apply their understanding of *personalismo* to their interactions with Hispanic clients. In these interactions, it is helpful to remember that establishing personal contact with the client is the best way to assure effective communication. It is helpful to inform Hispanic clients when there will not be continuity in the personnel providing services, although admittedly rotation of personnel is less than ideal. Hispanics may need assurances that the system will meet their needs even if a different person will be attending them. The loyalty and appreciation Hispanics may shower on Anglo professionals who attempt to incorporate *personalismo* into their communication style is indicative of the high value their cultures place on truly caring about others.

---

9. *What areas of human activity demonstrate the culturally determined views of honesty for Anglos and Hispanics?*
10. *What specific guidelines reflective of* personalismo *might Anglo professionals keep in mind when dealing with Hispanic clients?*

NONVERBAL COMMUNICATION: Money matters

Perhaps no other topic is as sensitive to discuss as money. An individual's attitudes toward this commodity are deeply ingrained by personal experiences and habits and cultural conditioning. Both the Anglo and Hispanic cultures are subject to misconceptions regarding the role money plays in everyday life. Hispanics, like other ethnic groups, often view Anglos as worshipping the dollar, whereas Anglos may extend the *mañana* stereotype to explain what they view as Hispanics' tendency to use money to live for today and worry about it tomorrow. Both generalizations do an injustice to the respective cultures and oversimplify the complex attitudes and behaviors involving money operant within each group.

A look at proverbs from each culture highlights more similarities than differences and dispels some common misconceptions. *"Poco vale ganar sin guardar"* ("Earning without saving is worthless"), *"Dinero llama dinero"* ("Money calls money"), *"Quien dineros tiene hace lo que quiere"* ("He who has money does what he wants") are counterparts to the English maxims "A penny saved is a penny earned," "Money makes money," and "Money talks." Indeed, both cultures value money and recognize its importance. In fact, the significance of money in Hispanic cultures may be even more overt because of the rigid class divisions between the haves and have-nots.

Despite the analogous cultural sayings, there is a definite difference in the way the Anglo and the Hispanic handle money matters, particularly in public. Although both cultures encourage appearances that reflect financial security and comfort, Hispanic cultures tend to place a higher value on such outward manifestation of economic resources. At the same time, Hispanics are conditioned to demonstrate a balanced attitude toward money and material possessions, viewing them as neither a means nor an end, but merely a circumstance of life. This complex attitude is expressed in several subtle ways.

The Hispanic cultures encourage individuals to refrain from being overly concerned about money. It is particularly important not to appear stingy (*tacaño*). This quality is referred to nonverbally by hitting the elbow of the arm bent upward with the palm of the hand or the fist several times. There is no equivalent gesture in English-speaking cultures, where frugality is considered a virtue, although Scroogelike miserliness is disdained. It is, perhaps, this contrast that gives rise to the mutual misconceptions regarding Anglo and Hispanic attitudes toward money.

The *macho* code of ethics is strict regarding how men should handle money in the company of others. The male is expected to pay for all expenses when inviting a female out—"dutch treat" dating is virtually nonexistent. In fact, the female might feel embarrassed or humiliated if her male companion did not offer to pay or did not have enough money to do so. In Hispanic cultures women rarely pay for expenses when a man is present, just as it is not as common as in the United States for a Hispanic woman to be alone or in the exclusive company of females in restaurants, movies, theaters, and other public places where money is spent for entertainment or socializing.

When two or more Hispanic men are out together, with or without females present, each feels the culturally instilled need to pay the entire bill for everyone. A "real" man will make all visible efforts to do so, including loud discussions and forcing the waiter to take "his" money rather than that of his friend(s). All this is expected by cultural norms. Only if the group has decided ahead of time to go dutch, often called *a la gringa* (*gringo*-style) or *a la americana* (the American way) in some Hispanic countries, will each pay his own way.

The need to appear generous with regard to money (and other commodities) is essential for both Hispanic men and women, particularly regarding lending money to a friend in need. Small sums of change or a dollar or two are usually given with no expectation that they will be returned. To ask for the return of such small sums would be an insult to the borrower's integrity. Likewise, to give back a quarter or a dollar to the lender or to remind that person that you haven't forgotten the debt is an insult, since it implies that the lender needs the money and/or is stingy. The reaction might be one of hurt or anger. Anglos, on the other hand, tend to feel uncomfortable borrowing money from each other, doing so only when in dire straits. They will often go out of their way to return even small amounts of money as soon as possible. Should the Anglo borrower forget to do so, the lender may feel insulted and the relationship could be affected.

While Hispanic cultures stress generosity as an expression of disinterest in money and material possessions, they also emphasize the social obligations incurred by mutual giving and receiving. The dollar lent to a Hispanic might not be returned in currency, but it will be repaid in some way at some future time. The phrases "*Le estoy obligado; le estoy en deuda por sus muchas atenciones*" ("I'm obligated to you/him/her; I'm indebted to you/him/her for your/his/her many thoughtful acts") express the high value placed on not forgetting the special kindnesses and favors someone extends to you. One of the worst feelings for Hispanics is that of being *en deuda* (in someone's debt) and not being able to do something for or give something to that person to settle the score. Reminding the debtor of his or her obligations to you is taboo in Hispanic cultures, an affront to the other's personal dignity by *echándoselo en cara* (throwing it up in his or her face). The repayment may take various forms— sharing food, visiting the person during illness, helping in time of a family crisis, and giving small

presents, particularly at Christmas. It is considered offensive to seem hurried or pressed (as is expected in Anglo cultures) to settle a debt.

The heart of the cultural role assigned to money is really the balance between justice and charity. A fine line separates the two in all cultures. Money matters essentially deal with the individual's sense of integrity and with feelings of human solidarity. In that light, money can be viewed as merely an "energy" form exchanged for goods or services. It may or may not be a just exchange, just as it may or may not be tempered by charity—that is, love for one's fellow human being. Since most professional services provided to Hispanic clients involve money in some way, the different cultural values surrounding the role of money will naturally come into play. Your awareness of the contrasts, as well as of the client's personal dignity and your connection as human beings (justice + charity), can make the difference between a mutually satisfactory interaction and a mutually offensive one.

Putting it into practice

1. Indicate the cultural values regarding money that may be operating in the following interactions and suggest a strategy for dealing with whatever cross-cultural conflicts might arise.

   a. A Hispanic client brings in small gifts and home-baked pastries to her Anglo social worker who has, on several occasions, bent the rules of the agency to accommodate the client's special needs.

   b. A Hispanic male client and his Anglo male lawyer go out to lunch together.

   c. A Hispanic male asks his Anglo coworker to lend him two dollars for gas for his car.

     d. An Anglo female schoolteacher observes one of her Hispanic male students consistently buying snacks for his Anglo male friend.

     e. An Anglo female doctor suggests that she and her Hispanic female assistant go out to lunch together.

     f. An Anglo social worker finds out that her Hispanic male client who is receiving food stamps and welfare is sending thirty dollars per week to his family back home.

     g. An Anglo policeman stops a Hispanic male for speeding only to have the latter offer him a ten-dollar bribe.

2. Act out the following scene with each person reacting according to Anglo cultural norms, and then according to Hispanic cultural guidelines.

     Over a period of two weeks, Bernardo, a bilingual teacher in a predominantly Anglo school, borrows stamps, pens, and small change for the vending machines from Harold, who teaches math at the school. Bernardo makes no attempt to repay or return anything he has borrowed.

Comunicándose en español

Spanish **h** is *always* silent. Practice the following words:

hay	hogar	mi hermano	ahora
hace	horrible	mi hijo	alcohol

Spanish **j**, before any vowel, and Spanish **g**, before *e* and *i*, are pronounced alike; the sound does not exist in English, but is similar to the *heavy h* sound in the name of the German composer *Bach*. In rapid speech, it may sound like English *h* accompanied by a slight aspiration (puff of air). The sound is produced at the back of the mouth, in the same position as the English *k* in *kite*. For the English *k*, however, unlike the Spanish **j**, the back of the tongue touches the roof of the mouth, blocking the passage of air. By lowering the back of the tongue to allow the air to pass you will automatically pronounce the **j** sound. Practice the following pairs:

co/jo   ca/ja   coco/cojo   oco/ojo   hico/hijo

Now pronounce these words with the **j** sound:

juez	abajo	jueves	gente	religión
jugo	viejo	jefe	general	biología

Spanish **g** is pronounced similar to English *hard g* as in the word *go* when it is followed by *a, o,* or *u, and* preceded by *n,* or a pause.

gusto	con gusto	gracias	guardia
gana	tengo	global	ninguno

In all other positions, *except* before *e* or *i,* Spanish **g** is much softer than English **g**. The back of the tongue does not touch the roof of the mouth, so air is allowed to escape. The sound is so soft that, until your ear becomes accustomed to it, you might not hear it between vowels.

pago	salgo	luego	estómago
haga	traigo	llega	mucho gusto

When this **g** sound occurs in combination with *e* or *i,* it is written as **gue** or **gui**, since **ge** and **gi** are pronounced with the **j** sound. The *u* in these combinations is only a spelling aid and is not pronounced:

pague	en se**gui**da	**Gui**llermo
lle**gue**	**gui**tarra	**gui**sado

When the *u* is to be pronounced between **g** and *e* or *i,* forming a diphthong with the following vowel, it is written **güe** or **güi**; the **ü** sounds like **w** as in other diphthongs:

vergüenza   averigüe   güiro   bilingüe

Práctica 🔲

Pronounce the following sentences:

1. Mi hermano Guillermo llegó de Caguas el jueves pasado.
2. Yo no pagué la cuenta del gas del mes de junio.
3. La señora Gómez tiene vergüenza de lo que dijo su hijo.
4. Me gusta mucho la carne guisada con arroz y habichuelas.
5. ¡No hay nadie que toque la guitarra como Héctor!
6. A Jaime le gustan todas las bebidas alcohólicas, especialmente la ginebra.

Dictado 🔲

Now write the words and sentences your instructor dictates:

1. _____   4. _____

2. _____   5. _____

3. _____   6. _____

7. _____

8. _____

9. _____

¡Licenciado Cruz! ¡Cuánto me alegro de verlo!

¡Me han acusado de robar y matar al dueño de una tienda de licores! Salí tarde del trabajo. Tenía prisa. No me fijé en que sobrepasaba el límite de velocidad. Un policía me detuvo.

¿Estaba a solas en el carro, señor Ibáñez?

Sí. Pues, el policía me preguntó algo en inglés sobre el fuego que no comprendí. Entonces, me pidió la licencia de conducir y la matrícula del vehículo. Se las di en cuanto me di cuenta de lo que quería.

RULES
1.
2.
3.
4.
5.

Según el reporte, Ud. trató de sobornar al policía.

Me entró un pánico. No comprendía nada. Decidí entregarle un billete de veinte junto a la licencia. En mi país es una práctica común.

Y el policía se acordó del reporte del asesinato de ese señor y se dio cuenta de que Ud. se parecía a la descripción dada por un testigo.

Pero el reporte describe a un hispano joven que mide seis pies y que pesa doscientas libras. ¡Yo sólo mido cinco pies con seis y peso ciento cuarenta!

¿Ha entendido bien?

1. ¿De qué le acusaron al señor Ibáñez?

2. ¿Por qué se alegra de ver al licenciado Cruz el acusado?

3. ¿Por qué detuvo el policía al acusado?

4. ¿Qué le pidió el policía?

5. ¿Qué le entregó el acusado al policía?

6. ¿Por qué trató de sobornar al policía?

7. ¿Cómo reaccionó el policía?

8. ¿Qué evidencia hay en contra del acusado?

9. ¿Cree Ud. que el acusado es el que robó y mató al dueño de la tienda de licores? Explique su respuesta.

10. ¿Qué factores culturales operaban en el encuentro entre el policía y el acusado?

INTRODUCTORY DIALOGUE: I don't understand it

The accused: Attorney Cruz! How happy I am to see you!

A: They've accused me of robbing and killing the owner of a liquor store. I left work late. I was in a hurry. I didn't notice that I was exceeding the speed limit. A policeman stopped me.

The public defender: Were you alone in the car, Mr. Ibáñez?

A: Yes. Anyway, the policeman asked me something in English about a fire that I didn't understand. Then he asked me for my driver's license and the car registration. I gave them to him as soon as I realized what he wanted.

PD: According to the report, you tried to bribe the officer.

A: I panicked (panic entered me). I didn't understand anything. I decided to give him a twenty dollar bill together with the license. In my country it's (that's) a common practice.

PD: And the policeman remembered the report of the murder of that man and he realized that you looked like the description given by a witness.

A: But the report describes a young Hispanic who is six feet tall and weighs two hundred pounds. I am only five feet six and I weigh one hundred and forty!

BASIC STRUCTURES I: In jail

The lawyer (m.)	*The client (m.)*
Are you Ramón Carrión?	Yes, that's my name.
I'm attorney Manuel Colón, Legal Services representative. The court appointed me to defend you. When did they arrest you?	They arrested me yesterday { morning. afternoon. evening.
What did they charge you with?	They charged me with { robbery. theft. assault and battery. rape. selling drugs. murder.
Were you carrying a weapon?	Yes, I was carrying { a revolver. a pistol. a knife.
Were there witnesses?	No, there were none.
What happened yesterday in the preliminary hearing?	I pleaded guilty.
Did they explain all of your rights to you?	Yes, but in English. I didn't understand very well. What rights do I have under the law?
During the interrogation you have the right to have a lawyer present, and if you don't have one you can ask that they appoint one for you.	I didn't realize that.
Also you have the right to remain silent and to terminate the interview at any moment; any statement you make can be used against you.	I didn't know that. Last night the detectives interrogated me for three hours and I told them everything I knew. They advised me to plead guilty.

¿Sabe usted?

1. **Detener** (*to detain*, conjugated like **tener**), **arrestar**, and **parar** (*to stop*) are all used to mean *to arrest*.

2. **Llevar** (*to carry*) also means *to wear* (*clothing*): **llevarse** means *to get along with.*

3. **Juicio** (*trial*), **el juez** (*the judge*), **el prejuicio** (*prejudice*, i.e., *pre + judge*), and **juzgar** (*to judge*) are derived from the same root.

4. **Darse cuenta de** may be followed by a noun, pronoun, or clause beginning with **que**; it is always used reflexively and means *to realize* (*become aware of*).

5. The English word *right* has several Spanish equivalents: **tener razón** (*to be right*); **derecho** (*a legal right*); **a la derecha** (the direction *to the right*).

ESTRUCTURAS BÁSICAS I: En la cárcel 🎞

El abogado	*El cliente*
¿Es Ud. Ramón Carrión?	Sí, así me llamo.
Yo soy el licenciado Manuel Colón, representante de Servicios Legales. La corte me nombró para defenderlo. ¿Cuándo lo detuvieron?	Me detuvieron ayer { por la mañana. / por la tarde. / por la noche.
¿De qué lo acusaron?	Me acusaron de { robo. / hurto. / asalto y agresión / violar a una mujer. / vender drogas. / asesinato.
¿Llevaba arma?	Sí, llevaba { un revólver. / una pistola. / una navaja.
¿Había testigos?	No, no había ninguno.
¿Qué pasó ayer en el juicio preliminar?	Me declaré culpable.
¿Le explicaron a Ud. todos sus derechos?	Sí, pero en inglés. No los comprendí muy bien. ¿Qué derechos tengo bajo la ley?
Durante el interrogatorio tiene el derecho de tener presente a un abogado y, si no tiene uno, puede pedir que se le nombre uno.	No me di cuenta de eso.
También tiene el derecho de quedarse callado y de terminar la entrevista en cualquier momento; cualquier declaración que dé puede usarse en su contra.	No lo sabía. Anoche los detectives me interrogaron por tres horas y yo les dije todo lo que sabía. Me aconsejaron a declararme culpable.

Notas lingüísticas I

A.   Most verbs that can take a direct object can also be used reflexively, when the subject and the direct object are the same person. Compare:

La llamo todos los días.	I call her every day.
Yo lo declaro culpable.	I declare him (to be) guilty.

Me llamo Ana.	I call myself (my name is) Ana.
Yo me declaro culpable.	I plead (declare myself) guilty.

B.   The infinitive is the only form of the verb that can follow a preposition:

Ud. tiene el derecho de quedarse callado.	You have the right to remain silent.
Me acusaron de vender drogas.	They charged me with (accused me of) selling drugs.

377

BASIC STRUCTURES II: Is this your first offense?

The lawyer (m.)	*The client (m.)*
Mr. Carrión, before proceeding with the case, I need some personal information. How old are you?	I'll be nineteen on the fifteenth of October.
Is it your first offense?	No, they arrested me in May of last year for possession of drugs.
Did they put you in jail?	No, they put me on probation for two years.
Then you're still on probation?	Yes, I have nine months left to go (nine months are left to me to fulfill).
Do you use (any) drugs now?	I still use: barbituates. / amphetamines. / tranquilizers. / cocaine. / heroin.
Do you smoke marijuana?	Yes, I like "grass" a lot ("grass" enchants me).
Do you drink alcoholic beverages?	I have a few drinks to calm my nerves.
What do you drink?	I drink either whiskey or rum.
How often (with what frequency) do you drink?	I drink a little every day.
Do you get drunk frequently?	From time to time but not very often.
Do you believe that you have problems with drugs or alcohol?	No, they are a part of life and I know how to control myself.
Were you drunk or under the influence of drugs when they arrested you yesterday?	Possibly. I don't remember now.
What did you drink yesterday?	I forget.
Do you remember what happened yesterday?	Hell, no! I don't remember anything before finding myself here in jail.
According to the police report, you were intoxicated and incoherent when they arrested you.	(It's a) Lie! I didn't drink too much yesterday.
Tell me all of yesterday's events that you remember.	I returned from work (got home from work) at 2:00 P.M. I found my wife at home talking with my cousin (m.). I got angry and I became jealous. She and I began to fight. I hit her several times and I went out into the street to drink.
And then what happened?	That's all I remember (that is everything that I remember).

El abogado	*El cliente*
Señor Carrión, antes de seguir con el caso, necesito ciertos datos personales. ¿Qué edad tiene Ud.?	Cumplo diecinueve (años) el 15 de octubre.
¿Es su primera ofensa?	No, me detuvieron en mayo del año pasado por posesión de drogas.
¿Lo encarcelaron?	No, me pusieron en probatoria por dos años.
Entonces, ¿todavía está en probatoria?	Sí, me quedan nueve meses por cumplir.

¿Usa Ud. drogas ahora? Todavía uso
- barbitúricos.
- anfetaminas.
- tranquilizantes.
- cocaína.
- heroína.

¿Fuma Ud. marihuana?	Sí, "la yerba" me encanta.
¿Toma Ud. bebidas alcohólicas?	Tomo unos tragos para calmarme los nervios.
¿Qué toma Ud.?	Bebo o "whiskey" o ron.
¿Con qué frecuencia lo bebe?	Tomo un poco todos los días.
¿Se emborracha frecuentemente?	De vez en cuando, pero no muy a menudo.
¿Cree Ud. que tenga problemas con las drogas o con el alcohol?	No, son una parte de la vida y yo sé controlarme.
¿Estaba Ud. borracho o bajo la influencia de drogas cuando lo arrestaron ayer?	Posiblemente. No recuerdo ahora.
¿Qué tomó ayer?	Se me olvida.
¿Se acuerda Ud. de lo que pasó ayer?	¡Coño, no! No me acuerdo de nada antes de encontrarme aquí en la cárcel.
Según el reporte de la policía, Ud. estaba intoxicado e incoherente cuando lo arrestaron.	¡Mentira! No tomé demasiado ayer.
Dígame todos los sucesos de ayer que recuerde Ud.	Regresé del trabajo a las dos de la tarde. Encontré a mi esposa en casa hablando con mi primo. Me enojé y me puse celoso. Ella y yo empezamos a pelear. Yo le di varias veces y salí a la calle a tomar.
Y después, ¿qué sucedió?	Eso es todo lo que recuerdo.

Well, Mr. Carrión. I would like to try to get you out on bail, but I don't think it's possible since you're on probation and you pleaded guilty.

Calm down a little, Mr. Carrión. I'm going to speak with the judge. We're going to do everything possible to help you in this matter.

What does it matter! Don't bother. It's not worth the trouble. Damn! I'm a miserable wretch. Bad luck follows me wherever I go.

There's no one that can help me. Life here is shit and it's driving me crazy.

¿Sabe usted?

1. **Cumplir** is used in the sense of *to carry out, to keep a promise, to fulfill,* and *to reach one's birthday;* **cumplir con** is used in the sense of *to observe a law:*

   Ayer cumplí lo que me pidió. — Yesterday I carried out what you asked me (to).

   Jaime no cumplió su promesa. — Jaime didn't keep his promise.
   Hay que cumplir con la ley. — One has to observe the law.
   Me quedan dos meses para cumplir la condena. — Two months are left for me to fulfill my sentence.
   Cumplo cuarenta años en enero. — I'll be forty in January.

2. **Darle** and **pegarle** both mean *to hit,* although the latter refers more to a spanking. Notice that the indirect object pronoun is used to indicate the person who is hit.

   ¿Le pegó Ud. a su hija? — Did you hit your daughter?
   El me da cuando está borracho. — He hits me when he's drunk.

3. **Recordar (ue)** and **acordarse (ue) de** are synonyms meaning *to remember.* **Recordar** is *never* used reflexively, while **acordarse** *must* be used reflexively, followed by **de**. **Olvidar** and **olvidarse de** (*to forget*) are synonyms, the latter following the same pattern of usage as **acordarse**. The action of *forgetting* may also be expressed by a special impersonal reflexive construction of **olvidar** and the indirect object pronoun (**olvidársele a uno**):

   Se me olvidó su nombre. — I forgot his name. (His name "forgot" itself to me.)
   No se te olvide comprar leche. — Don't forget to buy milk. (Don't let buying milk "forget" itself to you.)

4. Slang names for **la marihuana** include **la yerba, el pasto, la mota. Meterse la aguja** (*to stick the needle in oneself,* or *to shoot up*) is a slang expression for heroin use. **Bombillas** (PR) (*"light bulbs"*) is slang for amphetamines.

5. **La policía** can mean either *the police* (force) or *the policewoman;* **el policía** refers to *the policeman.*

Bueno, señor Carrión. Quisiera tratar de sacarlo bajo fianza, pero no creo que sea posible como Ud. está en probatoria y se declaró culpable.

Cálmese un poco, señor Carrión. Voy a hablar con el juez. Vamos a hacer todo lo posible para ayudarlo en este asunto.

¡Qué importa! No se moleste Ud. No vale la pena. ¡Carajo! Soy un desgraciado. La mala suerte me sigue dondequiera que vaya.

No hay nadie que me pueda ayudar. La vida de aquí es una mierda y me vuelve loco.

---

6. Certain obscenities, while appearing quite vulgar when translated literally, are really the equivalent of mild expletives such as *hell, damn, shit,* and the like. The following are the obscenities most commonly used, mostly by men:

   ¡Coño! (*female genital area*) **¡Carajo!** (*damn*)
   ¡Pendejo! (*male genital area*) **¡Hijo de puta!** (*bastard*)
   ¡Mierda! (*shit*)

   The verbs **joder** (C, PR, O) and **chingar** (M, MA) are slang expressions referring to sexual intercourse and are used in many colloquialisms.

7. False cognates are words in two languages that look alike but have different meanings. For example, **suceso** is an *event; success* in Spanish is **éxito,** used with the verb **tener;** *exit* in Spanish is **salida.**

Notas lingüísticas II

A. As you learned in *Lección 4,* when two verbs in Spanish are combined in one clause and both refer to the same subject, the first is conjugated and the second remains in the infinitive form. Some verbs are followed directly by the infinitive, while others require a connecting word:

   1. Verbs followed directly by infinitive: **querer, poder, olvidar, recordar, saber, pedir**

      Quiero ver al abogado. I want to see the lawyer.
      ¿Sabes manejar? Do you know how to drive?

   2. Verbs followed by **a** + infinitive: **ir, venir, aprender, empezar, ayudar, salir** (*to go out to do something*)

      *Empezó a hablar*me en inglés. He began to speak to me in English.
      Aprendí a manejar en Cuba. I learned how to drive in Cuba.

   3. Verbs followed by **que** + infinitive: **tener, hay**

      Tuve que llamar a la policía. I had to call the police.
      Hay que decir la verdad. One has to tell the truth.

4. Verbs followed by **en** + infinitive: **insistir, consistir**

   Insisto en verlo ahora.   I insist on seeing him now.

5. Verbs followed by **de** + infinitive: **tratar, dejar** (*to stop doing something*), **acordarse, alegrarse, olvidarse, enojarse**

   Dejé de fumar pasto.   I stopped smoking "pot."
   *Me alegro de ver*te.   I'm happy to see you.

B. There are various ways of expressing emotions in Spanish, each with its own nuances:

   1. When verbs of emotion are used reflexively, they imply the *beginning* of the feeling, usually translated by *to get* (*happy, sad,* etc.) and are usually followed by **de** + infinitive or noun to express the cause of the emotion:

enojarse	to get angry
alegrarse	to be happy
Me enojo de mi esposo.	I get angry at my husband.
¿Te alegras de estar aquí?	Are you happy to be here?

   2. **Ponerse** + adjective expressing emotion is also used to indicate *becoming* + *emotion:*

Me puse celosa cuando lo vi con otra mujer.	I got angry when I saw him with another woman.
Se puso furioso cuando el policía lo detuvo.	He got furious when the policeman stopped him.

   3. **Volver(se) loco(a)** is an idiom meaning *to go crazy.*

      Me estoy volviendo loca en este trabajo.   I'm going crazy in this job.

   4. When verbs of emotion, **poner** + emotion, or **volver loco(a)** are used non-reflexively, the emphasis shifts from the person *experiencing* the emotion to the person or situation *causing* the reaction:

Mi esposa siempre me enoja.	My wife always makes me angry.
Me animó mi hijo.	My son cheered me up.
Su mamá lo puede calmar.	His mother can calm him (down).
Este juez me vuelve loco.	This judge is driving me crazy.

   5. When the cause of the emotion is an action expressed in a dependent clause, the verb in that clause is in the subjunctive:

Me alegro de que estés aquí.	I'm glad that you are here.
Él se enoja de que yo trabaje fuera de la casa.	He gets angry about (the fact that) I work outside the home.

C. When using expressions that express physical, emotional, and/or intellectual relationships between people, listen for clues that tell you who did what to whom, and try to understand the nuances expressed by the various ways of describing events. Compare:

Mi esposo me enojó.	My husband made me angry.
Me enojé de que se fuera.	I got angry at his leaving.
El hablar con mi papá me puso triste.	Talking with my father made me sad.
Al hablar con mi papá, me puse triste.	Upon talking with my father, I became sad.

1. Remember that the **a** used before a direct object referring to a person is another clue as to who did what to whom:

Yo no vi al testigo.	I didn't see the witness.
El testigo no vio al policía.	The witness didn't see the police officer.

2. Word order in Spanish is more flexible than in English because of the number of grammatical cues in Spanish telling who did what to whom. Since the end of the Spanish sentence receives the most emphasis, it is common to place the most important information in that slot, even if it means stating the subject after the verb, if the subject is emphasized. If the new word order moves the *direct object* before the verb, a *redundant direct object pronoun* is inserted between the direct object and the verb to signal this word order:

   a + direct object + redundant pronoun + verb + subject

   Compare:

El mató a su esposa. (objective statement)	He killed his wife.
A su esposa la mató él. (emphatic statement)	*He* killed his wife.
Un testigo vio al asesino. (objective statement)	A witness saw the murderer.
Al asesino lo vio un testigo. (emphatic statement)	A *witness* saw the murderer.

D. Notice that the **usted, ustedes** command forms learned earlier are nothing more than the **usted, ustedes** forms of the present subjunctive. Remember that object pronouns (direct, indirect, and reflexive) are attached to *direct affirmative commands* but precede the verb in *direct negative commands:*

Affirmative commands		*Negative commands*	
Hábleme.	Talk to me.	**No me hable.**	Don't talk to me.
Díganmelo.	Tell it to me.	**No me lo digan.**	Don't tell it to me.
Démelo.	Give it to me.	**No me lo dé.**	Don't give it to me.
Acuérdese.	Remember.	**No los olvide.**	Don't forget them.
Llámenme.	Call me.	**No me llamen.**	Don't call me.

PRÁCTICA PRELIMINAR

Follow general guidelines for self-instructional practice.

A. Translate the following sentences from Spanish to English.

Ejemplo: Me lo dio mi hermano.
My brother gave it to me.

1. No me acordé de hacerlo.
2. Yo tuve que declararme culpable.
3. Al testigo no lo vi yo, pero él me vio a mí.
4. No me di cuenta de lo que Ud. me dijo.
5. Él me acusó de violarla.
6. El policía se puso violento.
7. Casi me volví loco en la cárcel.
8. A mí me vuelven loca mis hijos.
9. Nunca le doy a mi mujer.
10. Olvídese de eso.

B. Translate the following sentences from English to Spanish.

Ejemplo: I was (became) happy to see him.
Me alegré de verlo.

1. I tried to call a lawyer after they arrested me.
2. Were you (Ud.) happy to get out on probation?
3. Did you (Ud.) tell the judge what happened to you?
4. He insisted on seeing me again.
5. Calm down, sir; I'm going to help you (Ud.)
6. This case is driving me crazy.
7. He couldn't remember what happened that night.
8. I got angry and I hit him.
9. I forgot my (the) license.
10. Did they charge you (masc.) with carrying a weapon?

C. Choose the word from the following list that is needed to complete the sentence. Write X if none is missing.

a   en   de   que   X (= nada)

Ejemplo: Tengo ___*que*___ hablar con el juez.

1. Quiero _____ ir _____ ver _____ la juez.

A 1. I didn't remember to do it. **2.** I had to plead guilty. **3.** I didn't see the witness, but he saw me. **4.** I didn't realize what you said to me. **5.** He accused me of raping her. **6.** The policeman became violent. **7.** I almost went crazy in jail. **8.** My children are driving me crazy. **9.** I never hit my wife. **10.** Forget that.

B 1. Traté de llamar a un abogado después de que me arrestaron. **2.** ¿Se alegró de salir en probatoria? **3.** ¿Le dijo al juez lo que le pasó? **4.** Él insistió en verme otra vez. **5.** Cálmese, señor. Yo lo voy a ayudar. **6.** Este caso me está volviendo loco/a. **7.** Él no pudo recordar (acordarse de) lo que pasó esa noche. **8.** Me enojé y le di. **9.** Olvidé (Se me olvidó) la licencia. **10.** ¿Lo acusaron de llevar arma?

2. Hay _____ tener fe *(faith)*.

3. ¿Puedes _____ ayudarme _____ salir bajo fianza?

4. ¿Te alegras _____ verme?

5. El policía insistió _____ interrogarme toda la noche.

6. ¿Se acuerda Ud. _____ cómo se llaman los testigos?

7. No pude _____ venir _____ verlo más temprano porque tuve

   _____ hablar con el juez.

8. ¿ _____ qué te enojaste?

9. Se me olvidó _____ decírtelo.

10. Tengo _____ salir _____ hablar con el policía que lo arrestó.

D. Write the indicated form of each verb.

		Preterite	Imperfect	Present indicative	Ud. command
(yo)	tener	*tuve*	*tenía*	*tengo*	*tenga*
1. (él)	dar				
2. (ella)	decir				
3. (Ud.)	cumplir				
4. (ellos)	venir				
5. (nosotras)	saber				
6. (tú)	detener				
7. (ella)	tomar				
8. (Ud.)	seguir				
9. (tú)	salir				
10. (yo)	recordar				

C 1. X, a, a 2. que 3. X, a 4. de 5. en 6. de 7. X, a, que 8. de 9. X 10. que, a

D 1. dio; daba; da; dé Ud. 2. dijo; decía; dice; diga Ud. 3. cumplió; cumplía; cumple; cumpla Ud. 4. vinieron; venían; vienen; venga Ud. 5. supimos; sabíamos; sabemos; sepa Ud. 6. detuviste; detenías; detienes; detenga Ud. 7. tomó; tomaba; toma; tome Ud. 8. siguió; seguía; sigue; siga Ud. 9. saliste; salías; sale; salga Ud. 10. recordé; recordabas; recuerdo; recuerde Ud.

386 LECCIÓN 10 LO QUE DICE LA LEY

E. Choose the appropriate word needed by context.

Ejemplo: No me informaron de mis ((derechos) derechas juicios)

1. Sólo me queda un año para (detener cumplir llevar) la condena.
2. Me arrestaron por tener (una derecha una navaja un testigo) en el carro.
3. El policía no se (acordó dio cuenta recordó) de informarme de mis derechos.
4. El (juez juicio interrogatorio) es un amigo mío.
5. Voy a tratar de sacarla bajo (juicio testigo fianza).
6. Me (pude volví puse) celosa cuando vi a mi esposo hablando con la vecina.
7. El (cárcel juicio testigo) vio muy bien el accidente.
8. Ayer mi mamá (tuvo cumplió fue) sesenta años.
9. Creo que la oficina del abogado queda a la (derecho razón derecha).
10. El abogado ganó el caso y celebró su (éxito salida suceso).

F. Respond to the following questions or statements from a client with the *affirmative* usted-command of the verb indicated by context.

Ejemplo: ¿Le puedo hablar en español?
Sí, *hábleme* en español.

1. ¿Debo llamarlo mañana?

   Sí, _____ a las nueve.

2. ¿Dónde me puedo sentar?

   _____ , allí, señora.

3. ¿Cuándo debo volver?

   _____ el lunes a la una.

4. ¿Le puedo decir la verdad?

   Claro, _____ .

5. Me estoy poniendo nerviosa.

   Pues, _____ , señora.

6. ¿Le debo dar este documento?

   Sí, _____ , por favor.

7. ¿Puedo pagar la cuenta ahora?

   Sí, _____ al contador.

E 1. cumplir 2. una navaja 3. acordó 4. juez 5. fianza 6. puse 7. testigo 8. cumplió 9. derecha 10. éxito
F 1. llámeme 2. Siéntese 3. Vuelva 4. dígamela 5. cálmese/no se ponga nerviosa 6. démelo 7. páguela

G. Respond to the following questions or statements from a client with the *negative* **usted**-command of the verb indicated by context.

Ejemplo: ¿Debo ir a la corte hoy?
             No, no *vaya* hoy.

1. Eso me enoja.

   Pues, no _____ , señor.

2. Es posible que me olvide.

   Pues, señor, no _____ .

3. ¿Puedo llamarla mañana?

   No, no _____ mañana.

4. Me emborracho muy a menudo.

   Pues, no _____ el día del juicio.

5. ¡Voy a darle a Ud!

   Por favor, señor, no _____ .

6. Estoy preocupada por el caso.

   Señora, no _____ .

7. ¿Cuándo puedo hablar con Alicia?

   No _____ antes del juicio.

8. ¿Le puedo explicar a Ud. lo que pasó?

   No, no _____ ahora.

H. Write the form of the verb needed by context.

Ejemplo: **ir**

Anoche yo ___*fui*___ a ver a un cliente que estaba en la cárcel. No sabía

que ___*iba*___ a ser tan difícil verlo. Hace más de dos años que yo no

___*voy*___ a verlo. Espero que no ___*vaya*___ a ser tan difícil la pró-

xima vez.

G 1. se enoje 2. se olvide 3. me llame 4. se emborrache 5. me dé 6. se preocupe 7. le hable 8. me lo explique

1. **hablar**

La semana pasada ＿＿＿＿＿＿ con mi abogada sobre el caso. Ella me dijo que iba a ＿＿＿＿＿＿ con los testigos. Yo quiero decirle que también ＿＿＿＿＿＿ con mi esposa, pues la noche del suceso, yo estaba en casa con ella.

2. **querer**

El acusado ＿＿＿＿＿＿ que tengamos el juicio la semana que viene, pero el juez ＿＿＿＿＿＿ que sea mañana. No me gustó cuando me dijo que iba a ser mañana porque yo ＿＿＿＿＿＿ más tiempo con los testigos. Ojalá que el acusado por fin ＿＿＿＿＿＿ darme el nombre de la mujer con quien estaba esa noche para que ella pueda ayudarlo.

3. **ver**

Ayer tuve un accidente muy serio. Lo ＿＿＿＿＿＿ dos testigos. Uno de ellos lo ＿＿＿＿＿＿ todo. El otro me dijo, "Yo ＿＿＿＿＿＿ que la otra señora tenía la culpa." Espero que el representante de la compañía ＿＿＿＿＿＿ que la culpa no es mía.

4. **pagar**

Mis cuñados normalmente ＿＿＿＿＿＿ el alquiler a plazos. Ahora el superintendente quiere que lo ＿＿＿＿＿＿ todo a la vez. Mis cuñados no lo pueden ＿＿＿＿＿＿ porque no tienen el dinero. Ayer yo les ＿＿＿＿＿＿ el alquiler de este mes para que no tengan problemas con la vivienda.

H 1. hablé; hablar; hable 2. quiere; quiere; quería; quiera 3. vieron; vio; vi; vea 4. pagan; paguen; pagar; pagué

Combinándolo todo

PRÁCTICA COMUNICATIVA: Servicios legales

Conversación parcial

Practique Ud. oralmente la siguiente conversación. Cada raya (/) implica que falta una palabra. Es necesario conjugar cada verbo *en bastardillas*.

La abogoda	El cliente
1. / Vargas, *ser* / licenciada Cruz, de / oficina del defensor / .	Mucho / , señora Cruz. Me *hacer* falta / ayuda. La policía / *acusar* / violar / una / .
2. Anoche / el juicio, ¿Ud. / *declarar* culpable?	Pues, anoche yo no / *dar* cuenta / lo que yo *decir*.
3. Un / lo *identificar* ayer por / fotografía.	Pero yo no *tener* la / . ¡Yo no *violar* / nadie!
4. ¿*Llevar* Ud. / pistola / el carro cuando / policía / *detener*?	Pues, sí, pero no *ser* / . *Ser* de / hermano.
5. ¿ / *explicar* / Ud. todos / derechos?	Creo / sí, pero no / *acordar*. Ayer *estar* / poco borracho.
6. ¿ / cuántas horas / *interrogar* los / ?	Me *interrogar* / más / cuatro / . Ellos / aconsejaron a / culpable.
7. ¿ / su / ofensa?	No, me / el / pasado / asalto.
8. ¿ / *encarcelar*?	No, / *declarar* inocente.
9. Yo *ir* / tratar / sacarlo / fianza.	Gracias, / . Me *alegrar* / que Ud. *ser* mi / .

Pregunte Ud.

Dé Ud. las preguntas necesarias en la siguiente entrevista con Carmen Lozano, la víctima de asalto y agresión, sobre lo que le pasó.

1. Regresé a mi casa a eso de las nueve de la noche.
2. No, no me acuerdo de la hora exacta.
3. Sí, estaba a solas en casa esa noche.
4. Me di cuenta de que alguien trataba de entrar por la ventana *(window)*.
5. Sí, a la policía la llamé yo inmediatamente.
6. Pues, vi a un hombre que entraba por la ventana.
7. Sí, llevaba una navaja.

8. Me dijo, "No diga nada si quiere seguir viva."

9. Me puse muy nerviosa y empecé a gritar *(to shout)*.

10. En ese momento la policía llegó a la puerta y salió el hombre por la ventana.

Dígalo

Prepárese para hacer el papel del defensor o el del acusado, según las instrucciones que le dé su profesor/a.

Escuche bien

A. Ud. oirá a algunas personas hablando de los detalles de un crimen, la defensa u otras cosas legales. Decida quién habla y escriba:

AC — si habla la persona acusada del crimen
AB — si habla el/la abogado/a
V — si habla la víctima

1. _____   4. _____   7. _____   9. _____

2. _____   5. _____   8. _____   10. _____

3. _____   6. _____

B. Ud. oirá a diez clientes que describen lo que pasó. Escriba Ud. en inglés *who did what to whom*.

	who	did what	to whom
1.			
2.			
3.			
4.			
5.			
6.			
7.			
8.			
9.			
10.			

Diálogos cortos

I. *La policía*   *Un joven de dieciocho años*

(Una policía detiene a un joven)

La policía	El joven
Buenas _____ , señor.	Sí, bastante, ¿por qué?
¿ _____ mucha prisa?	
Pues, Ud. _____ el límite de _____ .	No, señora, no puede ser. Yo sólo iba a treinta millas por hora.
Lo _____ , señor, pero el radar indicaba que Ud. _____ a cuarenta _____ por hora, y es _____ zona de veinticinco.	¡Dios mío! No me di cuenta. Lo siento.
¿Tiene Ud. su _____ de conducir?	Claro . . . a ver. Pues, no la encuentro. ¡Tiene que estar aquí! ¡Ay, Dios mío!
Pues, _____ , señor.	¡Coño! Ay, perdone, señora.
Está _____ . Pues, ¿Ud. _____ tiene o no?	No sé lo que le pasó. Creo que se me olvidó en casa.
Pues, Ud. _____ que acompañarme al cuartel (*headquarters*).	Señora, ¿puedo llamar a mi papá para que me la traiga?

II. *El abogado*   *El acusado*

El abogado	El acusado
Yo _____ el licenciado Francisco Leal. La corte _____ nombró para _____ . ¿Cuándo _____ detuvieron?	Me detuvieron anoche como a las ocho.
¿De _____ lo _____ ?	Me acusaron de secuestrar (*kidnap*) a mi hijo. Mi esposa y yo estamos divorciados y yo sé que mi hijo Miguel no está bien en la casa de ella.

El abogado	*El acusado*
¿Ud. _____ arma?	Claro que no. Yo no soy criminal.
¿ _____ testigos?	No, sólo mi hijo y yo.
¿A Ud. le _____ sus derechos?	Creo que sí. Es que estaba tan aturdido (*confused*) que apenas los recuerdo. ¿Cuáles son?
Durante el _____ Ud. tiene el _____ de _____ presente un _____. Si no _____ , la corte _____ nombra uno.	¿Esa persona es Ud. entonces?
Sí, y _____ a ayudarlo.	

Ayude al cliente

In order to better serve your Hispanic clients, you need to translate into Spanish the following statement. Begin with *A todo nuevo cliente:*

We would like to tell you that now that we are your legal representatives (*representantes legales*) we will do everything we can to provide you with (*proporcionarle*) the best possible service. In order to do this, we need your cooperation. We ask that you follow these instructions:

1. It's important to tell your lawyer the whole truth. S/he must know all the facts (*hechos*) in order to help you.

2. When we ask you to come to the office, please try to arrive on time. If you cannot make (*cumplir con*) the appointment, please call us as soon as possible to make another one.

3. If you change (*cambiar de*) your address or phone number please advise (*avisar*) us so that we can maintain (*mantener*) communication with you.

4. Please do not discuss (*hablar de*) your case with anyone until there is a decision on the case. You may tell anyone who asks you questions that s/he should discuss the case with your lawyer and not with you.

Thank you for your cooperation. We are happy to be able to serve you.

¿Comprende Ud.? 🔲

Ud. oirá a tres personas que describen encuentros con la policía. Llene Ud. el siguiente formulario con la información que den.

1. Name _____

   Address _____

   Age _____ Birthdate _____

   Charged with _____

   Witnesses _____

   Previous offenses _____

2. Name _____

   Address _____

   Age _____ Birthdate _____

   Charged with _____

   Witnesses _____

   Previous offenses _____

3. Name _____

   Address _____

   Age _____ Birthdate _____

   Charged with _____

   Witnesses _____

   Previous offenses _____

Piénselo

Prepárese para poder hablar con el/la profesor/a o con otros estudiantes sobre los siguientes temas, contestando las preguntas que le sugiera el/la profesor/a.

1. El conducir a alta velocidad
2. Los sobornos
3. Los términos legales
4. La encarcelación
5. Los testigos

Imagínese

1. ¿Cómo se llama este joven?
2. ¿Por qué está entrando en el Juzgado?
3. ¿Cree Ud. que es un juez, un abogado, un testigo, o un acusado? ¿Por qué?
4. Describa Ud. el caso.
5. ¿Cuándo ocurrió el incidente? ¿Dónde?
6. ¿Es el juicio preliminar?
7. ¿Qué otras personas van a ir al Juzgado para el caso?
8. ¿Quién cree Ud. que sea el/la culpable?
9. ¿Cómo cree Ud. que se vaya a resolver el caso?
10. ¿Quisiera Ud. asistir al juicio? Explique su respuesta.

MALTRATO Y VIOLENCIA EN EL HOGAR

¿Qué derechos tengo si mi esposo, compañero o cualquier hombre me maltrata?

La agresión física o maltrato es un delito contra la integridad corporal. El Código Penal de Puerto Rico tipifica como delito la agresión.

"Toda persona que emplease fuerza o violencia contra otra para causarle daño . . . " (Artículo 94 Código Penal de Puerto Rico).

"La agresión o maltrato se considerá agravada cuando se cometiere por un varón adulto en la persona de una mujer o niño . . . " (Artículo 95 Código Penal de Puerto Rico).

Si tú o tus hijos son maltratados físicamente por tu esposo, compañero o cualquier hombre puedes denunciarlo inmediatamente a la policía de P. R., Departamento de Servicios Sociales, la División de Relaciones de Familia, Casa Protegida Julia de Burgos al teléfono 772-2977, a la Comisión para los Asuntos de la Mujer, para que lo procesen criminalmente ante los tribunales competentes. Este delito está sujeto a sanción penal de reclusión y/o multa.

¿Qué derechos tengo si abandono mi hogar por temor de ser agredida o maltratada por mi esposo o compañero?

Si tú o tus hijos son víctimas de una agresión física, tienes derecho a defenderte y denunciar a la policía de Puerto Rico dicha agresión.

Si el agresor fuera tu esposo, el NO podría alegar como causa para el divorcio el abandono de su esposa toda vez que la causa del abandono fue su propia conducta.

¿Qué puedo hacer si no tengo recursos para mantenerme, ni sitio o lugar donde vivir?

Si no tuvieras sitio donde vivir, ni dinero para proporcionarte una vivienda, el Tribunal puede ordenar a tu esposo que abandone la casa del matrimonio, dejándote a tí y tus hijos en ella, hasta que se divorcien. El Tribunal puede ordenar que tu esposo te pase una pensión alimenticia para ti y tus hijos durante el período que duren los trámites del divorcio.

¿Qué derechos tengo respecto a mis hijos si abandono el hogar?

Si el abandono es por razón justificada, tienes todos los derechos de madre respecto a tus hijos. NO pueden quitarte la custodia o la patria potestad sin mediar razón justificada en relación a tu conducta como madre. En todos los casos el Tribunal competente determinará quien tendrá consigo la custodia y patria potestad a base del mejor bienestar e interés del menor.

1. ¿Qué derechos tiene una mujer en Puerto Rico si su esposo, compañero o cualquier hombre la maltrata?
2. ¿Puede la mujer denunciar a su esposo si le da a ella o a sus hijos?
3. ¿Qué derechos tiene la mujer maltratada por su esposo o compañero si ella abandona su casa?
4. ¿Qué puede hacer si ella no tiene dónde vivir o si no tiene dinero?
5. Si la mujer abandona el hogar sin llevar a sus hijos, ¿le pueden quitar la custodia de sus hijos? Explique su respuesta.
6. ¿Cree Ud. que la mujer maltratada en Puerto Rico tenga más o menos derechos que la mujer maltratada en uno de los cincuenta estados? ¿Por qué?
7. ¿Cree Ud. que la mujer maltratada en otros países hispanos tengan los mismos derechos que tiene la mujer puertorriqueña? Explique su respuesta.
8. ¿Cree Ud. que sea más o menos difícil abandonar el hogar por problemas domésticos para una mujer hispana que para una mujer "anglo"? ¿Por qué?

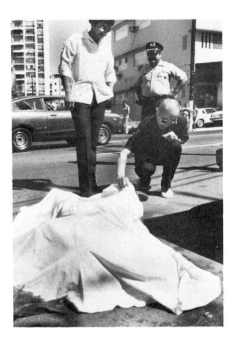

1. ¿Quién murió?
2. ¿Cómo se llamaba?
3. ¿Qué edad tenía?
4. ¿Cómo murió? ¿Fue un asesinato, un accidente, o una muerte natural?
5. ¿Había testigos? ¿Cuántos?
6. ¿Cuándo sucedió?
7. ¿Llegó en seguida la policía? Explique su respuesta.
8. ¿La policía arrestó a alguien?
9. ¿De qué lo/la acusaron?
10. ¿Qué otros detalles de la muerte sabe Ud.?

POLICÍA
MANUEL RÍOS DUARTE

Miembro de la Unidad de Operaciones Tácticas de la Policía de Puerto Rico, quien en cumplimiento de su deber ofreció su vida obedeciendo la ley y el orden para mantener en alto el sentido de la Democracia en su tierra.

El Departmento de la Vivienda se une en estos momentos de dolor a su esposa, Lourdes Vargas Matos, a sus hijos Manuel y Nelson, a sus padres, Wilfredo Ríos y Marta Duarte, y a sus compañeros de la Unidad de Operaciones Tácticas de la Policía de Puerto Rico.

Que Dios le reciba en su Gloria.

1. ¿Quién murió?
2. ¿Qué edad cree Ud. que tenía?
3. ¿Cómo sucedió? ¿A qué hora? ¿Por qué?
4. ¿Cuánto tiempo llevaba en el cuerpo policíaco?
5. Describa Ud. a la familia del muerto.
6. ¿Cómo se sienten la esposa y la familia?
7. ¿Qué responsabilidades tenía el policía muerto?
8. ¿Cómo cree Ud. que se sienten sus compañeros del trabajo?
9. ¿Murió el policía cumpliendo su deber? Explique su respuesta.
10. ¿Es fácil ser la esposa de un policía (o el esposo de una policía)? ¿Por qué (no)?

Haciendo el papel

1. Ud. es el/la abogado/a de un joven hispano acusado de robar una farmacia. El acusado dice que sólo estuvo en la farmacia por un momento cuando entraron los ladrones. Es la primera vez que está arrestado y tiene mucho miedo. Entrevístelo y trate de calmarlo.

2. Ud. habla con una hispana que cree que tal vez su esposo sea alcohólico. Hágale preguntas que puedan ayudarla a saber si lo es y sugiera varias alternativas para ayudarla con la situación.

3. Usando la "Miranda warning" que sigue, explíquele sus derechos a una hispana a quien detuvieron anoche.

MIRANDA WARNING

1. Ud. tiene el derecho de tener un abogado presente para que le aconseje, ya sea antes de ser interrogado o durante el interrogatorio.
2. Que si no es posible ocupar a un abogado tiene el derecho de que se le nombre un abogado para que le aconseje antes o durante algun interrogatorio.
3. Ud. tiene el derecho de quedarse callado y no dar una declaración, cualquier declaración que dé puede usarse en su contra en cualquier juicio o juicios sobre la ofensa u ofensas por la que esté dando la declaración y cualquier declaración que dé puede usarse en su contra en el juzgado.
4. Ud. tiene el derecho de terminar esta entrevista a cualquier momento.

4. Ud. es un/a doctor/a que examina a una joven hispana que fue violada. Acordándose de los valores culturales que puedan afectar la comunicación, trate de obtener los detalles del caso de la manera más inofensiva.

REFLEJOS DE LA CULTURA: "Coyotes"

Perhaps the greatest barriers to equal justice under the laws of the United States are ignorance of the system and linguistic and cultural differences. Many Hispanics face all three obstacles when dealing with the democratic process and its resulting bureaucracy.

To reduce these impediments, more social and legal service agencies have been established in the United States to offer greater access to the rights and privileges for residents, whatever their ethnic or racial background. Nevertheless, cultural traditions still wield their magic, especially with regard to Hispanics and their tendency to believe more in the person than in the institution. This often results in underutilization of the "system" and excessive dependence on specific individuals who have greater access to it.

Hispanic communities throughout the United States are growing in their awareness of the power inherent in self-directed groups organized to deal with the problems faced by their constituents. In addition, individual Hispanics, recognizing the cultural preference for individual leaders who inspire confidence, have become ardent spokespersons for the needs and rights of their ethnic group.

There are also some people, including Hispanics, who, capitalizing on their knowledge of both the Anglo and Hispanic cultural systems, see power as an end rather than a means. This type of person has lost sight of the need of the community at large as he or she focuses more on self, even to the extent of exploiting Hispanics with limited knowledge of Anglo institutions. While definitely in the minority, these "Tío Tacos" (the Hispanic equivalent of "Uncle Toms") will continue to surface as long as the need for help and guidance exists.

The following sketch (*estampa*) of life in a Mexican American community was written by Rolando Hinojosa, one of the most respected contemporary Chicano authors. It appears in his bilingual edition of *Estampas del valle y otras obras*. It captures the essence of the Hispanic expression of *personalismo*, as well as the difficulties faced by Spanish-speaking residents in dealing with Anglo institutions and value systems. In this short vignette, Hinojosa has confronted a part of Hispanic culture that is not easily understood by those raised in the Anglo system. The accompanying English translation is by Hinojosa himself.

Coyotes

. . . se les llama a esos que se dejan ver en la sede del condado, el county court house, como quien dice. No son empleados aunque lo parezcan: se visten de camisa blanca y corbata o, si son mujeres, de zapato con tacón alto y media larga. Afanan en los pasillos diariamente y viven de lo que le suelten al pobre que se asome en la corte con algún negocio. Tampoco son abogados pero como hablan inglés, claro es, ya tienen ventaja. Están al tanto de cualquier runrún en la corte y como desconocen la vergüenza, se ponen botas con cada inocente que les caiga. La gente que no sabe nada de nada se asusta de cualquier sobre con sello oficial y por eso es ganado bastante fácil para los coyotes.

Adrián Peralta, coyote, es de Edgerton y viaja de allí a Klail de diario. Trigueño, sombrero de petate a la moda, camisa blanca y corbata con ganchito de donde salta un pez vela, sonrisa en la boca que no en los ojos, bigote fifí, con ese par de ojos mencionados que si no han visto todo poco les falta. Como tiene la piel curtida ya no le entran ni indirectas ni insultos. Tiene buena representación y mejor voz ya que hasta la fecha nadie le ha rompido [sic] las narices. Es muy democrático, según él, y allí se puede ver saludando a todo el mundo, altos y bajos, hembras y machos, jueces y reos, putas y queridos, etc.

—¿En qué puedo servirle?

—Psss, verá usté, aquí traigo este papel . . . me cayó por correo y como dice Court House . . . aquí estoy, ya ve.

—Adrián Peralta, un servidor. ¿Su gracia?

—Marcial de Anda, señor. (Don Marcial debe tener unos 70 años: es dulcero de profesión. . . .)

. . . is the name given to those who hang around the county seat, the county court house, as some people refer to it. They aren't employees although they seem to be: they wear a white shirt and tie or, if they happen to be women, high heels and nylons. They scurry through the hallways daily and live off of what they can shake from the poor who might appear at the court house on some business. They aren't lawyers either but since they speak English, they obviously have an advantage. They are always on top of any rumor at the court house and since they are shameless, they pounce on any unsuspecting soul who happens to come along. People who are ignorant of bureaucracy are frightened by any envelope bearing an official seal and for that reason are easy prey for *los coyotes.*

Adrián Peralta, *coyote,* is from Edgerton and drives from there to Klail daily. Dark, wearing a fashionable straw hat, a white shirt and a tie with a pin in the shape of a sailfish, a smile on his lips but not in his eyes, a thin mustache, with that pair of eyes which, if they haven't seen everything, soon will. Since his skin is so thick, neither snide remarks nor insults bother him. He presents a good appearance and an even better voice since so far no one has broken his nose. By his own report, he is very democratic and there he is, always greeting everyone, tall, short, men, women, judges, defendants, whores, queers, etc.

"And what can I do for you?"

"We-eelll, you see, I got this here paper . . . came by mail and since it sez Court House . . . Here I am."

"Adrián Peralta, at your service. And your name?"

"Marcial de Anda, sir." (Don Marcial must be about 70 years old; he's a confectioner by trade. . . .)

—¿Me permite?

—Sí, señor. . . .

—Amigo de Anda, voy a arreglarle este asunto en un dos por tres. Hablando de un dos por tres, ¿me puede pasar un par de dólares para hacer andar la maquinaria? Ya sabe que sin grasa no se puede caminar.

Coge el dinero, le vuelve el sobre y antes de despedirse le señala una ventanita. — Allí mero — dice, — pregunte por Miss Espinoza, una muchacha bien peinada. — Como es de la raza y no tiene pena de serlo, Miss Espinoza sonríe a don Marcial y le saluda en español. Es la oficina del County Tax Assessor y a don Marcial le han nombrado para el jurado; no, no tiene que presentarse ahora; no, que no se reunirán hasta el fin de año; no, no me debe nada que aquí estamos para servirlo . . . Miss Espinoza le advierte que no ande dando dinero a los coyotes.

Como don Marcial no tiene que pagar nada se siente feliz — tanto que ni se acuerda ya de los dos billetes que le sacó el coyote; ni por pienso que vaya a seguir el consejo de la muchacha. Don Marcial vuelve a su casa en paz, hasta la próxima.

Peralta ahora está tomando café en el *coffee lounge*. Está de pie, por si acaso. Como ya hizo la cruz con don Marcial se siente a gusto y está listo para caerle encima a otro inocente que venga a la corte con ese susidio de la raza tan conocido. . . .

"May I see the letter?"

"Yessir." . . .

"Anda, my good friend, I'm going to straighten out this matter in short order. Speaking of being short, can you give me a couple of dollars to make the machinery run? You know it can't function properly without grease."

He takes the money, returns the envelope, and before saying good-bye points out a little window. "That's the place," he says, "ask for Miss Espinoza, the girl with the stylish hairdo." Since she is *de la raza* and not ashamed of it, Miss Espinoza smiles at Don Marcial and greets him in Spanish. It's the County Tax Assessor's Office and Don Marcial has been asked to serve on jury duty; no, you don't have to show up now; no they won't meet until the end of the year; no, you don't owe me anything, we're here to serve you . . . Miss Espinoza warns him against giving money to the coyotes.

Since Don Marcial doesn't have to pay anything, he's overjoyed, so much so he no longer remembers the two bucks *el coyote* got out of him; nor will he recall the advice the girl gave him. Don Marcial goes home content, until the next time.

Peralta is now having coffee in the cafeteria. He's on his feet, just in case. Since he finished off Don Marcial, he feels at ease and ready to pounce on the next innocent that comes to the court house with that well-known anxiety of *la raza.* . . .

Evaluación del progreso—Lecciones 9–10

RAISING AWARENESS

A. What strategies exist for effectively dealing with cross-cultural conflicts and confrontations?

B. How do the communication styles of the persons involved in cross-cultural communication affect the process?

C. How do the Hispanic and Anglo cultures differ with regard to foods, recreation, and the role of diversion in one's life?

D. What are the advantages and disadvantages of *personalismo* when applied by Hispanics seeking services in the United States?

E. What cultural factors regarding social gatherings might be misinterpreted by an Anglo at a Hispanic party and a Hispanic at an Anglo get-together?

F. What Hispanic cultural values regarding money might be misinterpreted by Anglo providers of services?

COMUNICÁNDOSE EN ESPAÑOL

A. **Pronunciación**   Write the following sentences your instructor dictates:

1. _____

2. _____

3. _____

B. **Discriminación auditiva**   Circle the letter of the most appropriate response to each oral question or statement you hear.

1. a b c   5. a b c   8. a b c

2. a b c   6. a b c   9. a b c

3. a b c   7. a b c   10. a b c

4. a b c

COMBINÁNDOLO TODO

A. Comprensión oral Circle **sí** if the client's statement indicates a problem needing intervention and **no** if it does not. Write the problem in *English* when one is indicated.

Problem?   *State the problem*

1. sí no _____

2. sí no _____

3. sí no _____

4. sí no _____

5. sí no _____

6. sí no _____

7. sí no _____

8. sí no _____

9. sí no _____

10. sí no _____

B. La entrevista Give the questions and/or responses needed in the following dialogue that takes place in an attorney's office.

El Lic. Carduña

La señora Jiménez

¿Es Ud. el licenciado Carduña?

1. Sí, _____ . ¿ _____ ?   Quiero divorciarme.

2. ¿Su esposo _____ ?   No, él se puso furioso cuando yo le dije que iba a hablar con Ud. sobre el proceso del divorcio.

3. ¿Por qué _____ ?   Hace más de tres años que no nos llevamos bien. Siempre peleamos.

4. ¿ _____ ?   Peleamos sobre la comida, los hijos, la casa, su falta de trabajo. A veces me pega cuando toma mucho. ¡Ya no puedo más!

5. Pues, _____ difícil cuando _____ .   Comprendo, pero no me importa. Tengo miedo de él y no puedo seguir viviendo en la misma casa con él.

6. Entonces, ¿ _____ ?   Sí, quiero una separación inmediata-
                                       mente. ¿Cuánto tiempo tengo que es-
                                       perar para divorciarme?

7. Eso depende. _____ .   Entonces, ¿me va a ayudar?

8. Claro _____ .

C. En acción Choose one of the following situations and act it out with your instructor or another classmate.

1. Helping a client to change his or her diet for medical reasons
2. Explaining to a client how to buy and prepare foods that are culturally unfamiliar
3. Helping a client choose meals for the next day from a hospital menu
4. Interviewing a witness about a crime or accident he or she saw
5. Interviewing a Hispanic victim of a crime
6. Explaining the legal process to a Hispanic client

LECCIÓN 11

Problemas de salud

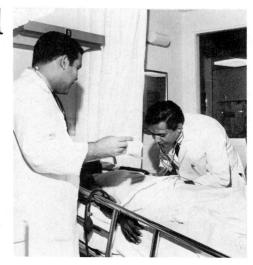

LOS OBJETIVOS

Raising awareness

1. To learn to create empathy between Hispanic clients and Anglo professionals despite cultural differences
2. To understand the Hispanic holistic views of physical and mental health as well as the range of community services available to Hispanics in the United States seeking health care
3. To apply cultural sensitivity to the delivery of health care services

Comunicándose en español

1. To pronounce and comprehend **ch, qu, c, z,** and **s**
2. To use and understand basic medical vocabulary needed to obtain a medical history
3. To use and understand the present perfect and future tenses

Combinándolo todo

1. To integrate all material from previous sections and lessons in more challenging professional activities
2. To perfect use of commands, present and past tenses in the indicative and subjunctive in varied contexts
3. To understand the cultural differences Hispanics may encounter when seeking health care services in the United States

Raising awareness

OVERVIEW: Building empathy across cultural boundaries

We each see the world through our own mind's eye. That inner camera has sharpened its focus through years of cultural conditioning and personal experiences. As we watch and listen to others, we experience their world through our own interpretation of what they present to us. We constantly try to see and understand how others perceive, discover, and interact with their inner and outer worlds. The ability to do so accurately is called *empathy*.

Even when we try to guess what other people are feeling and thinking, we often guess wrong because we assume their thinking is identical to our own psychic processes. It is easy to forget that none of us thinks exactly the same way. At times the differences are great, especially when people from two distinct cultural backgrounds interact. This does not mean that we should forget about being empathetic; instead, we should continue to attempt to empathize in a way that recognizes and takes advantage of the very differences that separate us. As we become more adept at practicing empathy, we enrich ourselves and expand our awareness of our own world views and those of others.

In practicing empathy, we need to become more aware of both outward expressions (words and actions) and the meaning behind them. For example, a coworker may come up to you and say, "It is a terrible day, isn't it?" As you hear his words, you may also notice that his face is sad, his shoulders stooped, and his general energy level low. If you respond only to the words he uses, you might simply say, "It certainly is. It doesn't look like it's going to clear up, either." However, if you look to the meaning behind the words, as evidenced by the nonverbal clues, you might perceive that what your colleague is trying to tell you is that *he* has had a particularly difficult time and is feeling upset. Your response would then be much different, perhaps a probing "Why, what's happened?" or an interpretive "Sounds like you've had a rough day," both of which are more empathetic responses.

You may find that your Hispanic clients are particularly prone to dropping verbal and nonverbal clues to what they really mean, rather than speaking openly of feelings that are normally expressed only to close family and friends. This may be especially true when they are experiencing difficulties, since the culture highly values keeping up appearances even when things are not going well.

For example, a Hispanic client may sit in your office rather silent, head and eyes down, and respond with a nonenthusiastic *regular* or a hesitant *bien* when asked "*¿Cómo le va?*" ("How's it going?"). This is a good indication that there are problems. An Anglo attempting to empathize with another Anglo in an analogous situation might probe directly by asking "Is something wrong?" to which the other would probably respond with more information. This direct approach might seem offensive or too forceful to a Hispanic client.

A more appropriate way to encourage Hispanic clients to reveal their feelings would be to ask specific questions about various aspects of life, starting with those valued most highly—home and family. If this does not seem to be the problem area, one could then ask questions about friends, work, school, money, and so on down the Hispanic cultural values scale. Care must be taken to seem interested while not appearing too "nosy." Establishing rapport with Hispanics often takes more time than it does with Anglos but is usually rewarded with strong, loyal commitments. In the concrete example just given, one might follow "*¿Cómo le va?*" with "*Y la familia, ¿qué tal?*" ("And how's the family?"), "*¿Todo va bien con el trabajo?*" ("Everything all right at work?"), and so on.

When the Anglo professional and the Hispanic client try to understand each other, the following five interpersonal dimensions govern the exchange:

1. How different are the two individuals psychologically and culturally?
2. How does each perceive him- or herself?
3. How does each perceive the other?
4. How does each *think* the other perceives him or her?
5. How does each perceive the relationship between them?

The illustration above shows how these five dimensions can affect the cross-cultural communication process, in this example probably with negative results.

Some of the problems these hypothetical characters are experiencing in trying to empathize with each other are due to stereotyping. This is a real danger in communicating with people from different cultural backgrounds. When we lack *firsthand* knowledge of how growing up in a different cultural environment affects the individual, we must rely on our *perceptions* of cultural conditioning gained from books, movies, television, newspapers, and what we learn from others, including members of that culture. It is easy to fall into the trap of false generalizations and/or oversimplifications. Even highly sensitive individuals with the best intentions are not immune to such pitfalls.

Authentic cross-cultural communication demands a conscious effort to avoid stereotyping. The problems inherent in exchanges between people from different cultural backgrounds warrant special attention to the process of building empathy. The following guidelines can help:

1. Listen with understanding, trying not to make judgments about the other person or what is said.

2. Make sure you understand the other's frame of reference about the topic under discussion. Verify your comprehension periodically by using the *understanding* response mode, paraphrasing and restating as necessary.

3. Employ the *interpretive* and *evaluative* modes of responses with great caution, so that you avoid jumping to conclusions, solving the other's problems as *you* perceive them, or working from a stereotypic perspective.

4. Exercise the *probing* response with care, so as to allow the other to reveal only as much as he or she wishes at any given time.

5. Use the *supportive* response mode often enough to let the other person know that you are actively listening and affirming his or her perceptions of the issue at hand.

Immediate and/or total empathy between two people is rare. Just as it takes time to truly know and understand oneself, feeling empathy with a stranger, especially one from a different cultural background, requires both conscious effort and sufficient contact to experience various aspects of the other's individuality. It is a complex undertaking, made more so by the fact that we are all constantly changing and evolving. Yet achieving empathy and authentic communication in the intercultural exchange can be one of the most challenging and rewarding human activities we may ever experience.

Applications

1. Review the cartoon on page 407, pointing out the conflicting views that may reflect the cultural background of each. Discuss what historical factors may be operating and suggest strategies that enable both to achieve mutual empathy.

2. Based on your readings of the historical perspectives and nonverbal communication sections of previous chapters, work with another individual to role-play a work-related situation in which it is important for an Anglo professional and a Hispanic client to achieve mutual empathy. Then role-play the same situation between a Hispanic professional and an Anglo client.

3. Identify possible stereotypes of Hispanics that may affect the Anglo professional's ability to empathize with the following Spanish-speaking clients:

   a. A forty-year-old female who arrives late for her appointment

   b. A group of adolescents who arrive together for an appointment that one of them has

   c. A fifteen-year-old female bringing a baby to a doctor's office for an appointment

   d. A good-looking extroverted male who, while waiting to see a lawyer, makes small talk with the female secretary

   e. The middle-aged husband of a woman receiving counseling who is silent and reticent during the first interview the counselor has requested with him

   f. A divorced twenty-five-year-old female who expresses the desire to return to her homeland

Reflections

1. Based on your responses to number 1 of "Applications," do you think that some Hispanic cultural behaviors and attitudes are less understood by Anglos than others? If so, which ones? What strategies for building greater empathy would you suggest to deal with them?

2. Compare your role-playing experiences in number 2 of "Applications" with those of other members of the class. Can you identify three main areas of your personal interaction with Hispanic clients in which you need to make a more conscious effort to establish empathy?

3. Do you subconsciously operate from any of the stereotypic views of Hispanics you identified in number 3 of "Applications"? If so, which ones? Can you identify other cultural values or personal situations that may be operating in the interactions outlined that are very different from the stereotypic images that came to mind? What does this exercise show regarding the process of achieving empathy with your Hispanic clients?

HISTORICAL PERSPECTIVE: Seeking medical and psychological aid in the Spanish-speaking world—a wide spectrum

The holistic approach to the practice of medicine currently in vogue in the United States is not new. Treating the whole patient rather than individual parts has prevailed in medical care in many cultures since the beginning of time. Only recently has the Western model of health care resulted in the compartmentalization of the human being into body, mind, emotions, and spirit, each served by a different type of practitioner and/or institution. The sophistication and technology that characterize the state of the art of medical and psychological services in Western medicine have given rise to a high degree of specialization. The cardiologist treating the heart patient who also has bladder cancer may never speak with the latter's urologist. The social worker working with a client in the group process may never consult the priest from whom the client is receiving spiritual and psychological counseling. On the other hand, the team approach to working with patients experiencing physical and psychological problems is a growing phenomenon designed to bring the parts of the whole person and the practitioners treating those parts into harmony.

In addition to the holistic and specialization approaches that coexist in contemporary U.S. society, many alternative sources of physical and psychological care and healing are available through naturopathic, homeopathic, and chiropractic services, herbalists and nutritionists, self-help and spiritual healing groups, intuitive counselors, faith healers, mind- and stress-control activities, biofeedback, and such Eastern practices as meditation, massage therapy, and acupuncture. When one examines the wide range of health care available in the United States and the various philosophic and psychological belief systems represented, it becomes apparent that the wide spectrum of health care beliefs, attitudes, and practices in Hispanic cultures is not so unusual after all.

The diversity of health care available in the United States and Latin America reflects the heterogeneity of their populations. Researchers indicate that no one theory of disease and its cures is accepted by *all* Hispanics. The mixture of Indian, Spanish, and African races has produced a syncretic or overlapping blend of spiritual, psychological, and physical attitudes, beliefs, and practices that govern the individual's sense of self, including health and its maintenance. Other factors that influence daily life in Hispanic cultures, such as the urban–rural dichotomy, socioeconomic class, and male–female roles, also affect the individual's belief system in relation to personal health.

1. *Compare and contrast Hispanic and U.S. cultures with regard to the diversity of belief systems affecting the range of health care services available.*
2. *Define your own theory regarding health and how it is maintained. Are your views traditional or unorthodox in the framework of your own cultural conditioning? Explain your answer.*

The belief system regarding health held by a Hispanic in Latin America or the United States may have been influenced by any or all of the following sources:

1. Indigenous beliefs and practices
2. Traditional medical practices handed down through the family
3. Homeopathic therapy, which involves taking small amounts of herbs and/or drugs that, if given in more concentrated doses, would cause symptoms similar to those of a specific disease
4. Spiritual beliefs ranging from Christianity to spiritism that attribute the causes and cures of specific afflictions to supernatural intervention
5. The Western biomedical model
6. Patent medicines
7. The same holistic health care practices gaining popularity in the United States.[1]

Often the Hispanic client who deviates in any way from the scientific view of modern medicine is immediately classified from the Anglo perspective as believing exclusively in what it terms unorthodox folk medicine. This is an oversimplification and in most cases an erroneous conclusion. Many Hispanics share similar concepts of illness and health with their Anglo neighbors. However, most Hispanics expand on these concepts to include some or all of the following dimensions:

1. The religious perspective, which sees life stemming from Divine Providence and suffering sent by God as a learning experience, with healing dependent on His will; illness may also be seen as a result of failure to live a good spiritual life; however, these views do not preclude actively seeking cures or relief from illness and pain.

2. The sociological perspective, which considers traditional Hispanic cultural values deeply rooted in faith in God and consequently attributes illness to an excessive adherence to overly materialistic Anglo lifestyles thought to violate the family-centered Hispanic tradition.

3. The supernaturalistic view, based on the acceptance of good and evil spiritual influences; it affirms the power of mind over matter and that of wishes and desires in creating material reality; it also believes that communication with the dead is possible and that the latter can influence life on earth.

4. The naturalistic view, which acknowledges the importance of maintaining the body in a state of harmony and balance by following specific practices, including diet, protection from the elements, hygiene, and moderation in all activities involving the body; it also views nature as providing cures in the form of foods, herbs, and other sources.[2]

---

3. *How are Hispanic beliefs and attitudes regarding illness and health syncretic? What sources have contributed to those beliefs?*
4. *What are the four perspectives that contribute to the Hispanic belief system about health?*

One of the main differences between the Anglo and Hispanic views of health is directly linked to cultural differences regarding the role of the individual in society. Previous discussions have typified Anglo society as based on the independence of the individual and the impersonality of the "institutions approach" to meeting human needs. This also characterizes the delivery of health-care services to the majority of Anglos. The individual is seen as responsible for his or her health through choices involving smoking, diet, exercise, work, and coping with life's problems. Allowances are made for the unexpected, impersonal hand of fate in choosing its victims; statistical analyses and predictions explain how two people with identical lifestyles may experience very different states of health. When one be-

---

1. Kelz, Rochelle. *Conversational Spanish for Medical Personnel.* New York: John Wiley and Sons, p. 184.

2. Fabrega, Horacio and Carol Anne Wallace. "Value Identification and Psychiatric Disability: An Analysis Involving Americans of Mexican Descent" in Hernández et al., *Chicanos: Social and Psychological Perspectives,* 2nd ed., pp. 253–261.

comes ill, an "expert" is consulted. The type of ailment will determine the kind of help sought. The expert gives the diagnosis and decides on a cure, usually in the form of medicine and/or restrictions or prescriptions involving lifestyle (lose weight, stop smoking, eliminate salt, get more exercise, etc.).

The Hispanic environment, however, stresses the importance of family and friendship ties over the interests and desires of the individual. It is not surprising, then, that Hispanics see health and illness as part of that network of relationships between the individual and God, nature, and other human beings, living and dead. From that perspective, modern medicine is simply another resource available alongside home remedies (*remedios caseros*), folk healers, over-the-counter medicines, and the advice of family and friends, particularly women in their role as mother and sage in health matters.

Beliefs pertaining to mental health reflect the same cultural differences as do those pertaining to physical health. What is deemed healthy and acceptable social behavior in one culture may be viewed as pathological in another. The high value Hispanics place on the needs of the family over those of the individual may seem unhealthy to the therapist trained in Anglo society, with its cult of the individual. The scientifically based Anglo psychiatrist might look for biochemical imbalances in the Hispanic client who "hears voices" and "talks to the saints." The psychiatric social worker might view an unhappily married Hispanic woman as masochistic for not wanting to leave her husband because she values her children's need for a two-parent home more than her personal happiness. Yet each of these behaviors would be acceptable by traditional Hispanic cultural norms.

The advice or treatment commonly given to Anglo clients in similar situations may result in the creation of more problems than it solves for Hispanic clients, since treatment models reflect Anglo cultural values. For the Hispanic to "get better," changes reflective of more Anglo-like thinking and behaviors might be suggested by the Anglo professional. Although this will make the Hispanic more acceptable to the mainstream U.S. culture, it can cause confusion and concern in the traditional Hispanic environments of home and family.

5. *What cultural differences between Anglo and Hispanic societies influence common attitudes toward health care?*
6. *How might the Anglo psychotherapeutic model misinterpret and mistreat behaviors considered normal in Hispanic cultures?*

In the delivery of physical and mental health services to Hispanics living in the United States, the degree of effectiveness of the Anglo model depends mostly on the degree of acculturation of the Hispanic client. Many Hispanics differ very little from mainstream Anglos in their acceptance of the modern scientific model of health care; usually they have accepted other Anglo values as well. The degree of acculturation tends to correlate positively to socioeconomic class, educational level, English-speaking ability, and, to a lesser extent, the length of time the individual has lived in the United States. Those living in rural areas or Spanish-speaking *barrios* generally retain traditional cultural values longer than do those in urban and suburban communities in the United States. Research indicates, however, that even well-educated Hispanics who demonstrate a high degree of acculturation may retain folk beliefs and attitudes regarding health care, although they may be more reluctant to admit this to Anglo peers.

The most widespread of the "nonscientific" views is the belief that outside forces can influence health. The resultant illnesses are often best cured by folk healers, usually thought to channel the healing power of God. Each of three major Hispanic groups in the United States has a preference for a specific type of folk healing.

Curanderismo is prevalent in Mexican, Mexican American, and Chicano communities. The *curandero/a*, a trusted member of the community, is seen as highly religious and spiritually motivated. *Curanderos* are expected not to charge for their services. Although they may accept unsolicited payment, they are expected to treat free of charge anyone unable to offer a contribution. Their healing consists primarily of prayers, usually before an altar in their home. They may also prescribe remedies to aid the recovery process.

Espiritismo is the most common form of folk healing in Puerto Rican communities. The *espiritista* is considered a gifted psychic able to identify illnesses and their source, usually attributed to evil spirits who may be sent by other members of the community. The *espiritista* is thought to be able to feel the pain the client is experiencing in the same place in his or her own body. The client is cleansed of the evil spirit through a series of rituals involving herbs, potions, music, movements, and other paraphernalia.

Santería is found throughout the Caribbean (as is *espiritismo*) but predominates in Cuba. It is related to *espiritismo* in that spirits possess the healers, only in this case, it is the spirits of saints who cure the illness.

Several common folk illnesses are attributed to external forces. They include *mal (de) ojo* (evil eye), *susto* (illness from fright), *empacho* (a lump of undigested food clinging to the stomach wall), *mal puesto* (sorcery), *ataque de nervios* (attack of nerves), and *mal humor* (being in a bad mood).

Mal (de) ojo is believed to be caused by excessive admiration, desire, or envy. The resultant condition may depend on what was overly admired or desired; for example, the loss of hair, eyesight, health, or boyfriend may be considered as caused by someone's envy. Its symptoms include fatigue, an overall ill feeling, and a severe headache. Babies and children are thought to be especially susceptible. It is common when admiring a child to bless the child to prevent the evil spirits from causing the illness. An *amuleto* (amulette) may be worn to ward off *mal (de) ojo*.

Susto is attributed to an emotionally traumatic experience which results in restlessness, loss of energy, and general inertia. The soul is believed to be lost to the body as a reaction to the trauma experienced. It is most common in Mexican cultures.

Empacho is believed to result from bad-quality food that may or may not have been intentionally prepared to cause harm. The food is thought to form a ball that clings to the stomach wall and is prevented from being properly digested. It is often accompanied by a burning sensation in the digestive tract.

Mal puesto is considered a consequence of either a lover's quarrel, unrequited love, or envy between close friends or family members. It results in dramatic mania, during which the person is aware of being possessed by another individual. It can become chronic and resistant to healing from any source. It is most predominant in Mexican cultures.

The *ataque de nervios* is a culturally acceptable means of coping with anxiety. It results in a display of histrionics, most often by women, and can be misdiagnosed as epilepsy. It affords the sufferer relief from an anxiety-producing situation and enlists the aid and support of others in the family.

Mal humor can be a chronic condition evidenced by an angry disposition. It is thought to result in such physical conditions as acne. This state of involuntary irritability may be temporary in a female experiencing a menstrual period or pregnancy. Also, males and females may be in a bad mood (*estar de mal humor*) for no acknowledged reason. Treatment is usually to let the person work out of the state without probing its cause.

Many folk healers in Hispanic communities often refer their clients to the more orthodox medical establishment. More and more health care workers are participating in such professional reciprocity, sending their patients to folk healers when modern medicine isn't quite enough. Many clinics and hospitals have doctors and folk healers working together in teams, treating the whole patient within the specialized area of each. This culturally expanded holistic approach is worth considering as an alternative to the exclusively scientific model.

---

7. *Describe some of the common illnesses attributable to external nonorganic sources in Hispanic cultures.*
8. *What strategies are recommended for the traditional health care practitioner whose Hispanic clients profess belief in alternative theories regarding the causes and cures of illness?*

NONVERBAL COMMUNICATION: The therapeutic touch

The personal interaction between the individual seeking services and the health practitioner is as important to recovery as an accurate diagnosis or appropriate prescription. While a medical worker's bedside manner is important with all clients, it is particularly so in Hispanic cultures.

The delivery of health-care services is probably the most intimate interaction sanctioned between two strangers, the professional and the client. Because of this intimacy, health-care professionals may need even greater sensitivity, awareness, and understanding of their Hispanic clients than professionals in other fields. In treating the whole person, aspects of cultural conditioning come into play in two ways: (1) in the cross-cultural communication process itself and (2) in understanding those Hispanic clients who believe in and use alternative health-care resources.

The communication process in the medical setting may be most affected by the cultural concepts of *personalismo, respeto, machismo*, the role of the family, and interaction with authority figures. Disregarding their importance can result in incorrect diagnosis and sabotage treatment and recovery.

Personalismo is at odds with the operation of most U.S. medical facilities, which are staffed by efficient but often impersonal practitioners, technicians, and support personnel. Hispanics coming into a hospital, clinic, or doctor's office are conditioned to look for a personal connection, especially in times of stress and crisis. When instead they find a well-oiled machine that seems not to distinguish between processing papers, laboratory tests, and people, they may feel disoriented, anxious and/or distrustful. Hispanic patients or family members may "pester" health care workers for information when long waiting times are involved.

A more successful approach with Hispanic patients is to provide one person as a resource with whom they can identify and who will offer continuity to their medical experience. Of course, it is best if this person is bilingual and biculturally aware, so that he or she can intervene when language or cultural barriers surface.

Closely linked to *personalismo* is the concept of *respeto* for the patient's needs and beliefs. Often when there is a language or culture barrier, professionals who are not fluent in Spanish or are not culturally aware may ignore the Hispanic client's "humanness" and focus only on physical symptoms and the task at hand, which is construed as a deep affront to the patient's personal dignity. The personal resource staff member can serve to guide the patient through the process, explaining what is happening and encouraging the non-Spanish-speaking staff to interact in an appropriate nonverbal manner with their Spanish-dominant patients.

Respeto also implies nonjudgmental acceptance of such culturally determined health attitudes and behaviors as dietary habits, resistance to change from traditional values, female modesty, protectiveness toward females by male members of the family, self-diagnosis and use of home remedies, and spiritual beliefs and practices that overlap with maintaining health. An aware practitioner will adapt treatment to reflect the Hispanic patient's cultural beliefs rather than dismiss them as "primitive" or "unimportant."

Machismo and its corollary role expectations for Hispanic women have important implications in health care. Generally speaking, female practitioners are more successful in examining Hispanic female patients than males, especially when gynecological exams are required. Female counselors may encounter less resistance than male counselors with males seeking psychological or medical advice, since the Hispanic culture views women as the dispensers of such knowledge. A Hispanic male may have a difficult time admitting his "weakness"—that is, his emotional needs—to another male, since this is contrary to the Hispanic male's code of ethics. On the other hand, certain subjects are only discussed *de hombre a hombre* (man to man) and may be avoided in talking with female professionals.

When treating Hispanic female patients, it should be realized that the culture places great emotional demands on its women. The Hispanic woman forced by economic necessity to work outside the home may be under even greater stress than her Anglo counterpart, since she is often still the sole caretaker of home and family needs. More Hispanic women than men use health care facilities, most likely for two reasons: (1) the culture allows women to admit their "weaknesses" and seek help more openly; (2) the repression of self in the role of self-sacrificing mother and wife may lead to physical symptoms that can mask depression or other emotional problems.

Birth control and childbearing are particularly sensitive areas of health care interaction. The Anglo norm of two children per family may not coincide with the Hispanic perspective. The Catholic Church's ban on artificial birth control is respected by many Hispanics. Males may see the number of children they sire as evidence of their manhood, and women take their role as childbearer quite seriously. A woman who wishes to practice birth control may find her husband resistant, which can affect the choice of methods. Respect for the individual's rights and an awareness of the cultural implications of specific med-

ical events (miscarriage, vasectomy, etc.) is crucial for Anglo professionals.

When treating the Hispanic patient, the role of the family should not be overlooked. The behavior of the patient is defined, to a large extent, by the family circle. This may include behaviors that have contributed to the illness and that need to be modified for the patient's welfare. For example, discussing dietary changes only with the male, and not with the female of the family who does the cooking, could sabotage the treatment. The health practitioner who takes the time to talk to the family about the diagnosis, prognosis, and treatment can count on greater cooperation than one who ignores this important element.

It is also normal for the entire family and close friends to want to be near the patient. The presence of a group of Hispanics "hanging around" can be a source of conflict for Anglo professionals accustomed to less intrusive behavior from relatives, but it is often a source of comfort for the patient. Recovery may be faster when surrounded by loved ones than when left alone in a sterile, quiet environment. Negotiating a compromise may ease tensions on both sides.

Hispanic modes of interacting with authority figures may play a critical role when transferred to Anglo health care systems. Doctors, especially, may be treated by Spanish-speaking patients with deference and acquiescence. Answers to important questions may be geared to what the patient thinks the doctor wants to hear, rather than the actual details. Since traditional Hispanics tend to be less assertive than Anglos, they may be reluctant to question treatment, point out

extenuating circumstances, ask for clarification of instructions, or say no to something the Anglo authority figure suggests, even if they have no intention of following through. An adept health care professional will accommodate this behavior with nonpatronizing attempts to verify information and to encourage more open discussion.

Even though the Hispanic patient may view the doctor, nurse, or technician as an authority figure, there are limits to how much the professional is allowed to interfere with the client's life. When help is sought for a particular problem, the expectation is that a resolution to the problem stated will be given. Hispanics may view recommendations to change lifelong habits or aspects of their personal life (work, sexual activities, etc.) as beyond the jurisdiction of the health-care worker. This is especially true among Hispanics who view illness as caused by external forces rather than their personal lifestyle.

In addition, many Hispanics respond best to examinations, diagnoses, and treatments that are tangible. The practitioner who spends time with clients, treating them as "whole persons," touching the body as part of the examination process, and prescribing specific medications and detailed treatment (rather than simply "rest" or "eat lightly") is most likely to achieve positive results.

In summary, Anglo health care practitioners who treat the Hispanic client as an individual, who are sensitive to traditional Hispanic cultures, and who adapt the delivery of services to reflect those cultural values, beliefs, and behaviors the patient manifests will have a greater chance for success of treatment.

Putting it into practice

1. Decide which of the cultural values discussed above may account for the following conflicts involving health care (more than one may be operant in a given situation):

   a. A Hispanic sixty-year-old male client assures the doctor he's been taking his medication for high blood pressure for the last two weeks and eliminating salt from his diet; the doctor doesn't understand why there is no visible change in the patient's condition.

   b. A well-dressed Puerto Rican woman denies to her doctor that she believes in *espiritismo*, although she wears several strings of colored beads around her neck; she is not responding to treatment for lower back pain.

c. A twenty-five-year-old Chicana woman refuses to use artificial birth control even though her Anglo doctor has warned that future pregnancies might result in a dangerous aggravation of the varicose veins she developed after her last pregnancy.

d. A forty-year-old married Cuban male visits an Anglo male psychologist because he is in love with another woman and wants to divorce his wife but does not want to lose his children; he is reluctant to talk about any other aspect of his life, although the therapist feels there is more to the matter than this problem.

e. A thirty-eight-year-old Dominican female has been suffering *ataques de nervios* for the last two years, since she began working as a secretary at an insurance company; her doctor and social worker recommend that she change her home life so that she may receive more help from her husband and children in taking care of the home.

2. Suggest strategies to help resolve each of the cross-cultural conflicts just described.

3. Now role-play the situations with other members of the class. Contrast the uninformed Anglo approach with a more flexible one that adapts treatment to the cultural needs of the Hispanic client.

Comunicándose en español

PRONUNCIACIÓN: ch, qu, c, z, s 🔲

Spanish **ch** is similar to English *ch* as in *chair*.

fecha	mucho	cheque
lecho	rancho	chico

In Spanish, **c** before a consonant or before *a, o,* or *u* is pronounced like English *c* in *score*. This is also the pronunciation of **qu** before *e* or *i*, as well as **k**, which appears in words of foreign origin. No aspiration accompanies this sound in Spanish as it does in English, especially at the beginning of a word, as in *candy*.

que	cama	cuatro	quieto	kilo
quince	poco	como	quedar	kilómetro

In Latin American Spanish, **s** and **z** in all positions and **c** before *e* or *i* are pronounced like the English *s* in *say*. In Spain, the **z** and **c** before *e* or *i* are pronounced like English *th* as in *thirty*. In many rural dialects and in the Spanish-speaking Caribbean, final **s** often is dropped or pronounced as an aspirated *h*.

celoso	cinco	juez	sobrino
cenar	cerca	razón	zapatos

Práctica 🔲

Practice the following sentences aloud, without pauses.

1. Mi dirección es la calle Diez, número ciento cincuenta.
2. Quisiera saber dónde queda la oficina del señor López.
3. Usted tiene razón; hay diez personas en la oficina.
4. El juez empezó a las dos y diez.
5. ¿Qué quiere decir "quítese los zapatos"?

Dictado 🔲

Now write the words and sentences your instructor pronounces:

1. _____   4. _____

2. _____   5. _____

3. _____   6. _____

7. _____

8. _____

9. _____

Sra. Ibáñez, ¿se ha recuperado de la monga?

Sí. Estoy aquí para otra cosa.

Dígame.

Pues, mi esposo y yo queremos tener otro hijo. Pero no he podido salir encinta porque después de que nació mi nena, me operaron para que no tuviera más hijos.

¿Dónde y cuándo tuvo lugar la operación?

En Puerto Rico en el '83. Ya tenía tres hijos. Casi me volvía loca al pensar en salir en estado otra vez, así que la operación me pareció buena idea.

¿Pero no le explicaron que iba a ser imposible tener más hijos?

No, sólo me dijeron que era la manera más segura de no salir encinta. Como en La Isla ya estaba "de moda" la operación, yo decidí hacerlo.

¿Habló Ud. sobre esto con su esposo antes de tomar la decisión?

No, doctora, no le dije nada. A él no le gusta la idea de intervenir con el destino.

Bueno, voy a examinarla, pero francamente, creo que Ud. nunca va a poder tener otro hijo.

¿Cómo puede ser? ¿Y qué le voy a decir a Víctor?

¿Ha entendido bien?

1. ¿Por qué visita a la doctora la señora Ibáñez?

2. ¿Por qué no ha salido encinta la señora?

3. ¿Cuándo y dónde tuvo lugar la operación?

4. ¿Por qué no quería más hijos la señora Ibáñez en 1983?

5. ¿Le explicaron a la señora Ibáñez todas las consecuencias de la operación? ¿Por qué (no)?

6. ¿Por qué no habló la señora Ibáñez con su esposo sobre la decisión de tener la operación?

7. ¿Cree Ud. que esto les ha pasado a muchas otras mujeres hispanas? ¿Por qué (no)?

8. ¿Cree Ud. que la doctora tenga buena manera de comunicarse con la señora? Explique su respuesta.

9. ¿Qué factores culturales han contribuído a la situación en la cual se encuentra ahora la señora Ibáñez?

10. ¿Cómo cree Ud. que vaya a reaccionar el esposo cuando sepa por qué no sale embarazada su esposa?

INTRODUCTORY DIALOGUE: I want to have a baby

The doctor: Mrs. Ibáñez, have you gotten over the flu?

The patient: Yes, doctor. I'm here about something else.

D: Go ahead. (Tell me.)

P: Well, my husband and I want to have another child. But I haven't been able to get pregnant because after my little girl was born, they operated on me so that I would not have any more children.

D: Where and when did the operation take place?

P: In Puerto Rico in '83. I already had three children. I was almost going crazy thinking about winding up pregnant again, so that the operation seemed like a good idea to me.

D: But didn't they explain that it was going to be impossible to have more children?

P: No, they only told me that it was the safest way not to get pregnant. Since the operation was "in style" on the island, I just decided to do it.

D: Did you speak to your husband about this before making a decision?

P: No, doctor, I didn't tell him anything. He doesn't like to mess (intervene) with fate.

D: Well, I'm going to examine you, but frankly, I think you are never going to be able to have another child.

P: How can that be? And what am I going to tell Victor?

BASIC STRUCTURES I: In the emergency room

The doctor (f.)	*The patient (f.)*
Mrs. Sotomayor, I am Dr. Anderson. How are you feeling?	Oh, doctor, my whole body hurts me so much!

Where is it that it hurts (you)?

My
- head
- nose
- mouth
- shoulder
- ear
- eye
- stomach

} hurts

- hands
- hips
- legs
- knees
- teeth
- shoulders
- feet
- ankles

} hurt

me.

How long has it (have they) been hurting you?

Since
- yesterday.
- this morning.
- two days ago.
- (For the last two days.)

Besides (forgetting for a moment) that pain, do you feel well in general?

Well, I feel
- sad.
- depressed.
- tired.
- very alone.
- without energy.

Well, take off your
- clothes.
- blouse.
- dress.
- bra.
- pants.
- shoes.

Shall I put on this hospital gown?

Yes, put it on. I will return immediately to examine you.

¿Sabe usted?

1. The definite article (**el, la, los, las**), rather than the possessive adjective, is usually used with parts of the body and articles of clothing.

2. **Mano** is a feminine noun, even though it ends in **-o.**

3. **El oído** refers to the inner ear; **la oreja** is the outer ear.

4. Humans have **pies,** but animals and furniture have **patas.**

5. **Rendido/a** or **agotado/a** (*exhausted*) may also be heard instead of **cansado(a).**

6. **Triste** (*sad*) may describe depression, as may the Anglicism **tengo un "down."**

La doctora

La paciente

Señora Sotomayor, soy la doctora Anderson. ¿Cómo se siente?

Ay, doctora, ¡cuánto me duele todo el cuerpo!

¿Dónde es que le duele?

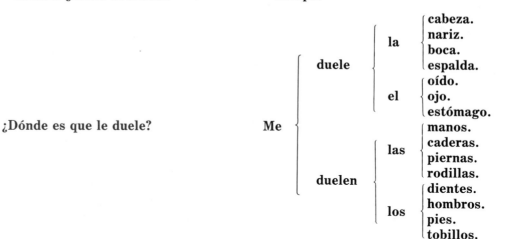

Me
- duele
  - la
    - cabeza.
    - nariz.
    - boca.
    - espalda.
  - el
    - oído.
    - ojo.
    - estómago.
- duelen
  - las
    - manos.
    - caderas.
    - piernas.
    - rodillas.
  - los
    - dientes.
    - hombros.
    - pies.
    - tobillos.

¿Desde cuándo le duele(n)?

Desde
- ayer.
- esta mañana.
- hace dos días.

Olvidando por un momento ese dolor, ¿se siente bien en general?

Pues, me siento
- triste.
- deprimida.
- cansada.
- muy sola.
- sin fuerzas.

Bueno, quítese
- la ropa.
- la blusa.
- el vestido.
- el sostén.
- los pantalones.
- los zapatos.

¿Me pongo esta bata?

Sí, póngasela. Regreso en seguida para examinarla.

Notas lingüísticas I

A. The **se** in **quítese** and **póngasela** is a reflexive form indicating that the indirect object is the same as the subject.

Quítese la ropa.	Take your clothes off (yourself).
Póngase la blusa.	Put your blouse on (yourself).

B. The **-ndo** form of the verb can be used to introduce a verb phrase to refer to the subject.

Olvidano ese dolor, ¿se siente bien?	Forgetting that pain, do you feel well?

BASIC STRUCTURES II: The medical history

The doctor (f.)

Does it hurt when { I touch your chest? / you cough? / you go to the bathroom?

Have you had { a burning (sensation) upon urination? / difficulty breathing? / fatigue when walking?

Have you experienced { shortness of breath? / a lot of phlegm? / swelling in your feet? / dizziness? / vomiting of blood? / vision difficulties? / fainting spells?

What other symptoms have you noticed?

Have you had { measles? / scarlet fever? / rheumatic fever? / whooping cough? / tonsilitis? / asthma? / anemia? / allergies?

Are your parents still living?

What did your mother die of?

The patient (f.)

Yes, it hurts me quite a bit.

It burns me a lot. / It's difficult for me to breath. / I get tired (tire myself) easily.

Yes, I have experienced { it (f.). / it (f.). / it (m.). / it (m.). / them (m.). / them (m.). / them (m.).

I have had { nausea. / itching. / muscle cramps. / weakness. / mucous. / nervousness. / tingling. / a rash. / insomnia.

No, I have not had any of those illnesses.

No, both of them died.

She died of cancer of the { rectum. / liver. / pancreas. / skin. / vagina. / bladder. / gall bladder. / uterus. / lungs. / kidneys. / intestines. / bones. / breasts. / ovaries.

La doctora   *La paciente*

¿Le duele cuando { le toco el pecho?
tose?
Ud. va al baño? }   Sí, me duele bastante.

¿Ha tenido Ud. { ardor al orinar?
dificultad al
  respirar?
cansancio al
  caminar? }   Me { arde mucho.
es difícil respirar.
canso fácilmente. }

¿Ha experimentado { falta de aire?
mucha flema?
hinchazón en
  los pies?
mareos?
vómitos de
  sangre?
trastornos en
  la vista?
desmayos? }   Sí, { la
la
la

los
los

los

los } he experimentado.

¿En qué otros síntomas se ha fijado Ud.?   He tenido { náuseas.
picazón.
calambres.
debilidad.
mucosidad.
nerviosidad.
hormigueo.
erupción.
insomnio. }

¿Ha tenido Ud. { sarampión?
escarlatina?
fiebre reumática?
tos ferina?
amigdalitis?
asma?
anemia?
alergias? }   No, no he tenido ninguna de esas enfermedades.

¿Todavía viven sus padres?   No, murieron los dos.

¿De qué murió su mamá?   Murió de cáncer { del { recto.
hígado.
páncreas. }
de la { piel
vagina.
vejiga.
vesícula.
matriz. }
de los { pulmones.
riñones.
intestinos.
huesos.
senos.
ovarios. } }

| And your father? | He died of $\left\{\begin{array}{l}\text{leukemia.}\\ \text{a stroke.}\\ \text{a heart attack.}\\ \text{tuberculosis.}\\ \text{pneumonia.}\end{array}\right.$ |

Have you ever been hospitalized?

$\left\{\begin{array}{l}\text{Yes, they operated on me last year.}\\ \text{Yes, when I gave birth to my son.}\\ \text{No, I have never been hospitalized.}\end{array}\right.$

Have you received psychiatric treatment?

No, I have never received it.

Have you ever suffered with nerves?

Yes, I have had "nerve attacks" since I had children.

In general, do you feel in good health?

Well, $\left\{\begin{array}{l}\text{I suffer from}\left\{\begin{array}{l}\text{migraines.}\\ \text{diarrhea.}\\ \text{constipation.}\end{array}\right.\\ \text{I get up exhausted.}\\ \text{I lack energy.}\\ \text{I have little appetite.}\end{array}\right.$

I want you to have a medical exam with laboratory tests and X-rays. As you leave, tell the nurse to make you another appointment for Monday.

In the meantime, what do you recommend that I do?

Well, get dressed now. I will give you a prescription for some medicine. Take the pills with a lot of liquid. I want you to stay in bed for a couple of days. When I get the results of the tests I will have a better idea of what you have.

Well, doctor, thanks a million. I'll go to bed as soon as I get home. See you soon.

¿Sabe usted?

1. The following noun-verb pairs are common medical terms:

la tos	toser	la hinchazón	hinchar(se)
el ardor	arder	la picazón	picar
los vómitos	vomitar	el desmayo	desmayar(se)
la sangre	sangrar	el mareo	marear(se)
el ataque	atacar	el cansancio	cansar(se)
el dolor	doler	la orina	orinar
la respiración	respirar	la debilidad	debilitar(se)
la operación	operar	el examen	examinar
la receta	recetar	el sufrimiento	sufrir
el tratamiento	tratar	el resultado	resultar
la muerte	morir(se)	la recomendación	recomendar

¿Y su papá?	Murió de { leucemia. / un ataque al cerebro. / un ataque al corazón. / tuberculosis. / pulmonía.
¿Ha estado Ud. hospitalizada alguna vez?	{ Sí, me operaron el año pasado. / Sí, cuando di a luz a mi hijo. / No, nunca he estado hospitalizada.
¿Ha recibido Ud. tratamiento psiquiátrico?	No, nunca lo he recibido.
¿Ha sufrido Ud. de los nervios?	Sí, he tenido ataques de nervios desde que tuve hijos.
En general, ¿se siente Ud. de buena salud?	Pues, { padezco de { jaquecas. / diarrea. / estreñimiento. } / me levanto rendida. / me falta energía. / tengo poco apetito.
Quiero que se haga un examen médico, con pruebas de laboratorio y radiografías. Al salir, dígale a la enfermera que le haga otra cita para el lunes.	Mientras tanto, ¿qué me recomienda Ud. que haga?
Bueno, vístase ahora. Le daré una receta para una medicina. Tome las pastillas con mucho líquido. Quiero que Ud. guarde cama por un par de días. Cuando yo reciba los resultados de las pruebas, tendré mejor idea de lo que tiene.	Bueno, doctora, un millón de gracias. Yo me acuesto en cuanto llegue a casa. Nos vemos pronto.

---

2. **Tocar** is *to touch* as well as *to play a musical instrument.*

3. **Experimentar** means both *to experiment* and *to experience.*

4. **Fijarse en** is used reflexively meaning *to notice;* **notar** is a synonym.

5. **Rayos-x** and **placas** may also be used for **radiografías.**

6. **Examen médico** may also be described as **examen físico** or **reconocimiento,** from **reconocer** (*to recognize*), which is conjugated like **conocer.**

7. **Guardar** means *to keep or preserve;* **guardar cama** is an idiom.

8. **Medicina** and **medicamentos** are synonyms.

9. **Síntoma,** like other Spanish nouns ending in **-ma (problema, drama, clima, sistema, telegrama, programa,** etc.) is *masculine* in Spanish, as it was in the original Greek.

10. **Vestir(se) (e-i)** is conjugated like **pedir.**

11. **Acostarse (o-ue)** is the equivalent of *to go to bed;* **dormirse (o-ue),** *to fall asleep.*

Notas lingüísticas II

A. The present perfect tense (the equivalent of *have/has* + past participle in English) is used to refer to an action that has occurred from some point of time in the past to the moment of speaking. It contrasts with the preterite and imperfect, which focus on a specific point in the past *with no reference to present time.* Compare:

He comido mucho hoy.	I've eaten a lot today. (since I've been up)
Comí a las dos.	I ate at two o'clock. (specific past time)
¿Ha tenido asma?	Have you had asthma? (sometime in your life)
¿De niño, tenía asma?	As a child, did you have asthma? (specific time)

1. The present perfect tense is formed by the present indicative of **haber (he, has, ha, hemos, han)** with the past participle. To form the past participle, drop the **-ar, -er, -ir** ending from the infinitive and add **-ado** to the stem of **-ar** verbs and **-ido** to the stem of **-er** and **-ir** verbs (estar — **estado;** comer — **comido;** sufrir — **sufrido**). The past participle always ends in **-o.**

yo	**he**	
tú	**has**	
Ud., él, ella	**ha**	+ { **estado**
nosotros/as	**hemos**	**comido**
Uds., ellos/as	**han**	**sufrido**

The following verbs have irregular past participles:

decir:	**dicho**	ir:	**ido**
hacer:	**hecho**	romper:	**roto**
escribir:	**escrito**	poner:	**puesto**
describir:	**descrito**	resolver:	**resuelto**
ver:	**visto**	volver:	**vuelto**
abrir:	**abierto**	morir:	**muerto**

Verbs whose stems end in **a, e,** or **o** require an accent mark when **-ido** is added to form the past participle:

traer: **traído**   creer: **creído**   oir: **oído**

2. When used to form the perfect tenses, the past participle does not change form to show gender or number agreement:

¿Ha venido su esposa?	Has your wife come?
Vicente y Lola se han casado.	Vincent and Lola have gotten married.

3. When the past participle is used as an adjective, it agrees in gender and number with the noun it modifies, like other adjectives:

Señora, ¿ha estado Ud. hospita-lizad*a* antes?	Ma'am, have you been hospitalized before?
Mi hermana casad*a* sufre de diabetes.	My married sister suffers from diabetes.

B. The future tense in Spanish is formed in the same way for **-ar, -er,** and **-ir** verbs. The endings **-é, -ás, -á, -emos, -án** are added to the infinitive. Notice that these are the same vowel endings as for the present tense of **haber,** except for the accent marks for all forms except **nosotros/as.**

	Future	**haber** (*present indicative*)
yo	estar*é*	h*e*
tú	estar*ás*	h*as*
Ud., él, ella	estar*á*	h*a*
nosotros/as	estar*emos*	h*emos*
Uds., ellos/as	estar*án*	h*an*

The following verbs have irregular stems in the future, but they use the same endings as regular verbs:

Ejemplo: tener: **tendr-, tendré, tendrás, tendrá, tendremos, tendrán**

venir:	**vendr-**	poner:	**pondr-**	decir:	**dir-**
salir:	**saldr-**	poder:	**podr-**	hacer:	**har-**
saber:	**sabr-**	valer:	**valdr-**	querer:	**querr-**

C. Verbs that describe daily habits, such as **levantar(se), acostar(se),** and **ves-tir(se),** are usually used reflexively, since each person normally takes care of his or her personal needs. However, these verbs can also take a direct object that is *not* the same person as the subject:

Yo *me* visto antes de desayunar.	I get dressed before having breakfast.
Yo visto *a mi hija* primero.	I dress my daughter first.
Anoche *me* acosté a las diez.	Last night I went to bed at ten.
Acosté *al bebé* a las ocho.	I put the baby to bed at eight.

This is also true for the verbs **quitar** and **poner.** For example, when one person helps another to dress or undress, the indirect object is used to refer to the latter. Compare:

Yo *me* pongo los zapatos.	I put on my shoes (on myself).
Yo *le* pongo los zapatos.	I put on his shoes (for him).
Ella *se* quitó la chaqueta.	She took off her jacket.
Yo *le* quité la chaqueta.	I took off her jacket (for her).

D. When both an indirect and a direct object pronoun are used in the same sentence, the indirect precedes the direct.

Juan *me* quitó *la chaqueta.*	Juan took off my jacket (for me).
Juan *me la* quitó.	He took it off for me.
El doctor *te* manda *los resultados.*	The doctor sends you the results.
El doctor *te los* manda.	The doctor sends them to you.

However, the indirect object pronouns **le** and **les** cannot be used before **lo, la, los, las** and are replaced by **se**:

Yo *le* pongo *los zapatos.*	I put his shoes on for him.
Yo *se los* pongo.	I put them on for him.
El doctor *les* manda *la cuenta.*	The doctor sends you the bill.
El doctor *se la* manda.	The doctor sends it to you.

In this instance, **se** is *not* a reflexive. Any ambiguities that result when **se** appears in a sentence can be resolved by adding **a sí mismo (a, os, as)** to indicate reflexive usage, or **a Ud. (él, ella, Uds., ellos, ellas)** in nonreflexive usage.

Ella se la quitó.	{ She took it off (herself). { She took it off (someone else).
Ella se la quitó a sí misma.	She took it off (herself).
Ella se la quitó a él.	She took it off (him).

PRÁCTICA PRELIMINAR

A.   Answer each question with an affirmative **usted** command. Replace all nouns with pronouns where possible.

Ejemplo: ¿Me quito la blusa?
              Sí, quítesela.

1.   ¿Debo acostarme al regresar a casa?
2.   ¿Me pongo los zapatos ahora?
3.   ¿Debo acostar a mi hija?
4.   ¿Debo levantarme?
5.   ¿Le quito los pantalones a mi hijo?
6.   ¿Le doy los resultados a la paciente?
7.   ¿Le puedo poner la blusa a mi hija?
8.   ¿Me puedo vestir ahora?
9.   ¿Le digo a la enfermera que venga?
10. ¿Le doy a Ud. las pastillas?

B.   Now answer the same questions with a negative **usted** command.

Ejemplo: ¿Me quito la blusa?
              No, no se la quite.

A 1. Sí, acuéstese. 2. Sí, póngaselos. 3. Sí, acuéstela. 4. Sí, levántese. 5. Sí, quíteselos. 6. Sí, déselos. 7. Sí, póngasela. 8. Sí, vístase. 9. Sí, dígaselo. 10. Sí, démelas.
B 1. No, no se acueste. 2. No, no se los ponga. 3. No, no la acueste. 4. No, no se levante. 5. No, no se los quite. 6. No, no se los dé. 7. No, no se la ponga. 8. No, no se vista. 9. No, no se lo diga. 10. No, no me las dé.

C. Write the indicated forms of the following verbs.

		Preterite	Present perfect	Future	Present subjunctive
(Ud.)	salir	salió	ha salido	saldrá	salga
1. (nosotros)	ir				
2. (tú)	venir				
3. (ella)	morir				
4. (Ud.)	decir				
5. (yo)	tener				
6. (Ud.)	hacer				
7. (tú)	creer				
8. (nosotras)	ver				
9. (Uds.)	vestir				
10. (yo)	saber				
11. (él)	querer				

D. Choose the verb form needed by context.

Ejemplo: Ud. me lo (ha dicho (dijo) dirá) ayer.

1. Yo no (vi he visto veré) al doctor desde la operación.
2. Mi hija (ha vuelto volverá vuelva) al trabajo después de dar a luz el mes que viene.
3. (Tome Ha tomado Tomó) Ud. estas pastillas con leche o jugo, por favor.
4. ¿(Ha seguido Seguiré Siga) Ud. las instrucciones que le dio el médico?
5. No se (ha puesto ponga pondrá) Ud. la ropa hasta que venga la enfermera.

C 1. fuimos; hemos ido; iremos; vayamos 2. viniste; has venido; vendrás; vengas 3. murió; ha muerto; morirá; muera 4. dijo; ha dicho; dirá; diga 5. tuve; he tenido; tendré; tenga 6. hizo; ha hecho; hará; haga 7. creíste; has creído; creerás; creas 8. vimos; hemos visto; veremos; veamos 9. vistieron; han vestido; vestirán; vistan 10. supe; he sabido; sabré; sepa 11. quiso; ha querido; querrá; quiera
D 1. he visto 2. volverá 3. Tome 4. Ha seguido 5. ponga

6. Perdón, doctor, pero todavía no me (escriba ha escrito escribirá) la receta.

7. ¿Cuánto tiempo hace que Ud. (ha tenido tiene tenga) fiebre?

8. ¿Le (duela duele ha dolido) cuando le toco el estómago?

9. ¿(Ha tenido Tenía Tuvo) dificultad al caminar desde que lo operaron?

10. (Recibo He recibido Recibí) tratamiento psiquiátrico desde hace dos años.

11. Cuando me sienta mejor, mi esposo y yo (fuimos iremos vayamos) a México.

12. ¿No hay ninguna medicina que me (puede pueda podrá) ayudar, doctor?

E. Write the medical term needed to complete each sentence.

Ejemplo: Ella tenía una ___*fiebre*___ muy alta; su temperatura llegó a ciento cuatro grados.

1. El _____ conecta el pie con la pierna.

2. El cardiólogo trabaja con enfermedades del _____ .

3. Tengo náuseas con ganas de _____ .

4. La _____ es un cáncer de la sangre.

5. El sarampión es una _____ de la infancia.

6. El esqueleto (*skeleton*) del cuerpo humano consiste en un sistema de _____ .

7. Los órganos que eliminan los líquidos del cuerpo humano son los _____ y la vejiga.

8. Se le puede tomar la temperatura a alguien con un termómetro puesto o en la _____ o en el _____ .

9. El sistema reproductivo de la mujer consiste en la vagina, la _____ y los _____ .

D 6. ha escrito 7. tiene 8. duele 9. Ha tenido 10. Recibo 11. iremos 12. pueda
E 1. tobillo 2. corazón 3. vomitar 4. leucemia 5. enfermedad 6. huesos 7. riñones 8. boca, recto 9. matriz, ovarios

10. Si una persona tiene problemas con los _____ , puede sentir dificultad al respirar.

11. Si una persona experimenta mareos, es posible que se _____ .

12. Si Ud. siente ardor al _____ , debe ver a un urólogo.

F. Answer the following questions in the negative. Replace any direct and indirect objects with pronouns.

Ejemplo: ¿Ha comido la carne?
   No, no la he comido.

1. ¿Han visto Uds. al médico?
2. ¿El doctor ha examinado a su hija?
3. ¿Le ha hablado a Ud. la enfermera?
4. ¿Se ha puesto Ud. la bata?
5. ¿A Ud. le ha escrito la receta el doctor?
6. ¿Le ha dicho la verdad a su esposo?
7. ¿Han leído Uds. las instrucciones?
8. ¿Se ha quitado Ud. los zapatos?

G. Now answer the questions in Exercise F beginning your answer with *no,* then give an affirmative statement using the future tense and the time indicated.

Ejemplo: ¿Ha comido la carne? (esta noche)
   No, la comeré esta noche.

1. más tarde
2. mañana a la una
3. la semana que viene
4. después de levantarme
5. esta tarde
6. cuando estemos a solas
7. esta tarde
8. antes de acostarme

E 10. pulmones 11. desmaye 12. orinar

F 1. No, no lo hemos visto. 2. No, no la ha examinado. 3. No, no me ha hablado. 4. No, no me la he puesto. 5. No, no me la ha escrito. 6. No, no se la he dicho. 7. No, no las hemos leído. 8. No, no me los he quitado.

G 1. No, lo veremos más tarde. 2. No, la examinará mañana a la una. 3. No, me hablará la semana que viene. 4. No, me la pondré después de levantarme. 5. No, me la escribirá esta tarde. 6. No, se la diré cuando estemos a solas. 7. No, las leeremos esta tarde. 8. No, me los quitaré antes de acostarme.

Combinándolo todo

PRÁCTICA COMUNICATIVA: Recomendaciones para la salud

Conversación parcial

Practique oralmente la siguiente conversación. Cada raya (/) implica que falta una palabra. Es necesario conjugar cada verbo *en bastardillas.*

La doctora	El señor Chavela
1. / tardes, / Chavela, / mucho que no nos *ver.*	Buenas /, doctora. Sí hace más / seis /.
2. ¿Cómo / *sentir* hoy?	Pues, no / bien. Siempre / cansado y / *doler* / pecho cuando *respirar.* ¿ / *quitar* toda / ropa?
3. No / *quitar* Ud. / pantalones; yo sólo *querer* examinarle / pecho.	/ bien.
4. ¿*Tomar* Ud. / medicina que / receté la / vez?	/ *tomar* hasta / mes pasado.
5. ¿Y por qué *dejar* / tomarla?	Porque / *sentir* mejor y no / *parecer* necesaria.
6. Pues, / *hacer* falta / pruebas del /. *Esperar* Ud. / la / de espera.	¿Cuándo *tener* Ud. los / de las / ?
7. Yo / *llamar* cuando / *tener.*	Gracias, doctora. Ha *ser* un placer verla otra /.
8. Bueno, / Chavela, *querer* / Ud. *guardar* / hasta que *tener* los / .	Claro / sí. Ud. *ser* la /.

Pregunte Ud.

Ud. está entrevistando a una nueva paciente, Miriam Rodríguez. Dé Ud. oralmente las preguntas necesarias al tomar su historial médico.

1. Pues, no muy bien. Me levanto rendida y me falta energía.
2. Sí, he experimentado falta de aire al caminar.
3. Sí, tengo otros síntomas; se me hinchan los tobillos.
4. Hace más de cinco semanas que me siento tan débil.
5. No, nunca he padecido de asma.

6. Sí, padezco de estreñimiento muy a menudo.

7. Sí, sufro mucho de los nervios.

8. Vi al psiquiatra por dos años después de que nació mi tercer hijo.

9. Tengo cinco; el mayor tiene doce años y la menor, dos.

10. ¿Internarme? ¿Para qué? Sólo he estado hospitalizada para dar a luz. No puedo, doctor. ¿No me puede dar una inyección?

Dígalo

Pregúntele a un/a compañero/a lo que le diga su profesor/a sobre los temas de cómo se siente, el historial médico del individuo, el historial médico de la familia, y las instrucciones para el/la paciente.

Escuche bien

A. Ud. oirá a doce personas que describen algún aspecto de la vida. Escriba Ud.:
   A—si se describe una condición física o una enfermedad
   B—si se describe un tratamiento físico o un procedimiento (*procedure*) diagnóstico
   C—si lo que se describe no está relacionado con la salud

1. _____   4. _____   7. _____   10. _____

2. _____   5. _____   8. _____   11. _____

3. _____   6. _____   9. _____   12. _____

B. Ud. oirá nueve oraciones habladas por varias personas en el hospital. Escriba:
   REF —si la oración contiene un complemento directo o indirecto que es reflexivo
   NO —si la oración no es reflexiva
   AMB—si la oración puede ser reflexiva o no, dependiendo del contexto en el cual se use

1. _____   4. _____   7. _____

2. _____   5. _____   8. _____

3. _____   6. _____   9. _____

Diálogos cortos

I. *La enfermera*   *El paciente*

(*Hablan por teléfono*)

_____ de radiografías. Dí-   Aló. Soy Ramón Guzmán. Soy paciente
game.   del doctor King.

Sí, _____ Guzmán. Yo   El año pasado el doctor me sacó una ra-
                                               diografía del pecho.
_____ acuerdo de Ud.

¿ _____ qué puedo

_____ hoy?

Déjeme ver, señor. Espere un   Bueno, he solicitado un empleo donde re-
                                               quiere que tenga una radiografía del
_____ . (*Un minuto*   pecho anualmente. ¿Cree Ud. que ésa
                                               sirve?
después) Sí, _____ ra-

zón. Fue _____ diez de

agosto.

Bueno, ahora _____ en   Está bien. ¿Me la puede mandar (*send*)
                                               lo más pronto posible?
marzo. Ya hace _____ de

un año. Yo creo _____ sí.

Sí, cómo _____ .   Mil gracias, señora.

_____ la mando mañana

_____ la mañana.

No _____ de qué.

II. *La doctora*   *El paciente*

Sr. Quiñones, _____ la   Bueno, doctora, no me siento bien.

Dra. Feld. ¿Cómo _____
siente?

¿En _____ síntomas se   Primero empezó con diarrea.

_____ fijado?

¿Desde _____ tiene   Desde hace una semana.
diarrea?

La doctora	El paciente
¿ _____ dolor ahora?	Dolor, no. Pero me siento cansado, sin fuerzas.
¿ _____ apetito?	No, no tengo ganas de comer nada.
¿ Le _____ la cabeza?	Bueno, sí. Me duele todo el cuerpo. Al principio creí que tenía la gripa, nada más.
¿ _____ duele cuando _____ ?	No, eso no.
Señor Quiñones, ¿ _____ viven _____ padres?	Mi madre, sí. Mi padre murió hace dos años.
¿ _____ qué _____ ?	De un ataque al cerebro.
¿Ha _____ Ud. hospitalizado?	Sí, una vez. Me operaron del estómago. Me dijeron que tenía una úlcera.
Primero Ud. _____ algunas pruebas _____ laboratorio. Cuando yo reciba los _____ , lo llamaré.	

Ayude al cliente

Your client, Matilde Ramírez, is pregnant. She needs to travel to Guatemala to visit her mother, who is very ill. You need to write a letter to a doctor there describing her pregnancy and special needs. Begin the letter with *Muy estimado/a colega:*

1. Introduce yourself, stating the length of time you have been Mrs. Ramírez' physician. Tell the doctor that she is eight months pregnant and that you think she will give birth on the twenty-first of next month.

2. Tell the doctor that Mrs. Ramírez has had many problems with this pregnancy: excess fluids (*líquidos*) in the blood resulting in swollen legs, feet, and hands, a lot of fatigue, extreme back pain, and high blood pressure. State that you prefer that she not take any medication while she is pregnant, since you feel it may harm the fetus (*puede hacerle daño al feto*). Mention that you have recommended that she go to bed for three or four hours every afternoon and that she have a physical examination every week.

3. Tell the doctor that he or she can call you if he or she has questions. Close with *Su seguro/a servidor/a,* and sign your name.

¿Comprende Ud.?

Escuche bien mientras los siguientes pacientes describen sus problemas de salud. Después, indíquele a cuál de los siguientes especialistas debe consultar según los problemas que experimente.

A — psychologist	D — dermatologist	G — pediatrician
B — cardiologist	E — gynecologist	H — orthopedic surgeon
C — pharmacist	F — ophthalmologist	I — gastroenterologist

1. _____   3. _____   5. _____   7. _____

2. _____   4. _____   6. _____

Piénselo

Prepárese para poder hablar con el/la profesor/a o con otros estudiantes sobre los siguientes temas, contestando las preguntas que le sugiera el/la profesor/a:

1. La operación
2. Los síntomas
3. Cómo evitar problemas de salud
4. El hablarle al paciente de problemas de salud

SITUACIONES DE LA VIDA REAL

Imagínese

1. ¿Quién es el paciente? ¿Qué edad tiene?
2. ¿De qué padece?
3. ¿Cuánto tiempo hace que está enfermo?
4. ¿Cuáles fueron los síntomas?
5. ¿Se mareó primero o sintió dolor en el pecho?
6. ¿Dónde estaba el paciente cuando esto ocurrió?
7. ¿Qué está haciendo el doctor en la foto?
8. ¿Quién es el otro señor?
9. ¿Cuánto tiempo estará el paciente en el hospital?
10. ¿Se recuperará mejor en casa o en el hospital? Explíquese.

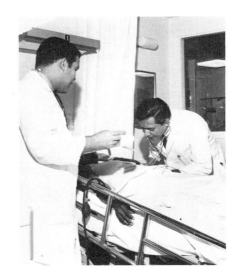

RECOMENDACIONES SOBRE EL USO ADECUADO DE LAS MEDICINAS

1. Evite el uso regular y permanente de medicinas que puede obtener sin receta médica.
    * *Estas sólo deben ser usadas para aliviar dolencias menores y sólo temporalmente.*

2. Informe a su médico y a su farmacéutico sobre las medicinas que está tomando, así como las reacciones adversas que puedan desarrollarse al tomar determinado medicamento.
    * *En esta forma su médico y su farmacéutico podrán advertir y evitar posibles efectos de la combinación entre dos o más drogas.*

3. Tome su propia medicina y no comparta su medicina con otra persona.
    * *La medicina que su médico le receta es para usted únicamente. Síntomas similares a los de otra persona pueden ser de diferentes enfermedades.*

4. No tome más de la dosis recetada ni más de la dosis recomendada, en el caso de una medicina que se puede obtener sin receta.
    * *Una cantidad excesiva de medicina no le cura más rápidamente, lo que más bien puede ocasionarle es daño.*

5. Consuma las medicinas en sus envases originales, firmemente cerrados.
    * *Cada medicina está envasada en el recipiente adecuado para protegerle de la luz, humedad o de otras condiciones ambientales. Nunca ponga dos medicinas en un mismo envase; pueden reaccionar una con la otra.*

6. Deseche las medicinas viejas o con fecha de expiración vencida.
    * *Las medicinas con el tiempo cambian su potencia o se deterioran.*

7. Guarde las medicinas en sitio seguro fuera del alcance de los niños.
    * *Guárdelas en un sitio alto y cerrado que sea fresco, seco y obscuro.*

8. Proteja a sus niños. Enséñeles a respetar las medicinas.
    * *Evite tomar medicinas frente a ellos. Nunca se refiera a las medicinas como dulces. Explíqueles el propósito de una medicina.*

9. Mantenga en su hogar algunas medicinas para usar en casos de dolencia o accidentes leves.
    * *En su botiquín tenga: antisépticos (para cortaduras, quemaduras, etc.), aspirina incluyendo la dosis para niños (para dolores de cabeza y fiebre), antiácido (para malestar estomacal), gotas oftálmicas (para irritación en los ojos), laxante (para estreñimiento ocasional), jalea de petroleo-vaselina (para ampollas y lubricación), alcohol (para fricciones), espíritu de amonia (para desmayo), vendaje adhesivo, vendajes de gasa estériles, algodón absorbente, aplicadores, termómetro, pinzas, imperdibles y tijeras.*

---

1. ¿Se debe tomar medicinas regularmente?
2. ¿Es importante saber las reacciones adversas de la medicina que se está tomando? ¿Por qué?
3. ¿Puedo yo compartir (*share*) mi medicina con otra persona si tiene la misma enfermedad que yo?
4. Para aliviarme más rápidamente, ¿puedo tomar la medicina doble?
5. ¿Puedo poner dos o más medicinas en un envase?
6. ¿Por qué es importante mantener cerrados los envases de medicina?
7. ¿Cómo puedo evitar que mis hijos tomen las medicinas?
8. ¿Qué medicinas debo tener en mi casa?

BOTÁNICA
ORULA
209 Main Street

Botánica en general. Se vende toda clase de bebidas, leche a precio de oferta, perfumes, cassettes, discos, figuras decorativas, productos alimenticios, gran variedad de dulces. Se da teléfono y dirección para una consulta de espiritismo. Estamos ubicados donde funcionaba anteriormente Caridad del Cobre.

1. ¿Ha estado Ud. en una botánica?
2. ¿Qué clase de figuras decorativas venden? ¿Para qué son?
3. ¿Venden hierbas y frascos de perfumes? ¿Para qué sirven?
4. ¿Qué es una consulta de espiritismo?
5. ¿De qué tipo de problemas o enfermedades se hablan en la consulta?
6. ¿Cree Ud. que este servicio ayude al paciente? Explique su respuesta.
7. ¿Quisiera participar en una consulta de espiritismo? Explíquese.
8. ¿Qué tipo de problema quisiera Ud. presentar en la consulta?

La experiencia de la enfermedad

Todos somos humanos delante de la enfermedad, incluso los profesionales de la medicina, y llevamos con nosotros a la habitación del paciente nuestras actitudes, miedos, necesidades y recuerdos. La mayoría sentimos incomodidad y puede que angustia.

La nueva situación dispara una respuesta emocional inesperada, las defensas pueden perderse o endurecerse, una relación puede romperse, un modelo familiar puede cambiar, podemos sentir:

Incompetencia: ''Todos me dicen lo que tengo que hacer. He perdido el control de mi vida y me siento como si fuera un niño''. Un paciente.

Ineptitud: ''No sé qué hacer o qué decir cuando voy a verle, me siento desválido''. Un hombre con un amigo seriamente enfermo.

Falta de humanidad: ''Siento que necesito que se me cuide como a una persona y no como un objeto numerado y sin valor''. Un paciente de hospital.

Vulnerabilidad: ''La gente dice que soy fría. No puedo soportar comprometerme emocionalmente. No puedo hacerme cargo''. Una enfermera.

Miedo: ''Me da miedo quedarme solo. ¿Por qué me dejan solo? Quiero a mi mamá''. Un niño en el hospital.

Enojo: ''Me peleaba con todo el mundo . . . mi debilidad me enojaba''. Un paciente después de una operación a corazón abierto''.

1. ¿Cuáles son las emociones que expresan los pacientes cuándo se dan cuenta de que están enfermos?
2. ¿Se ha sentido Ud. incompetente alguna vez debido a una enfermedad? Explíquese.
3. ¿Ha visto a algún paciente enojado porque tiene miedo a una operación? Explique su respuesta.
4. ¿Ha muerto algún familiar de Ud.? ¿Cómo fue la experiencia?
5. ¿Cómo se comportó Ud. ante (*regarding*) la muerte? ¿Y su familia?
6. ¿Cómo ve Ud. a los doctores y a las enfermeras, como compasivos o como indiferentes?
7. ¿Qué otra emoción ha sentido Ud. al estar enfermo/a?
8. ¿Es Ud. buen/a paciente cuando está enfermo/a? Explíquese.

Haciendo el papel

1. Ud. es un/a doctor/a que tiene que avisarle a la señora Meléndez que tiene cáncer del seno. Ella tiene cuarenta y cinco años y es casada con cinco hijos. El menor tiene siete años. Ella nunca ha pasado un sólo día en el hospital. Parece tener mucha fe en Dios. Explíquele los síntomas, el tratamiento y las varias maneras de tratarla.

2. Usando la siguiente descripción de ''la abstinencia,'' explíquele a un joven hispano por qué no debe comer o tomar ciertas cosas. Como Ud. cree que no siga sus instrucciones, es importante tratar de convencerle de cambiar su dieta. Hable primero de lo que le gusta comer para establecer cierta confianza.

LA ABSTINENCIA

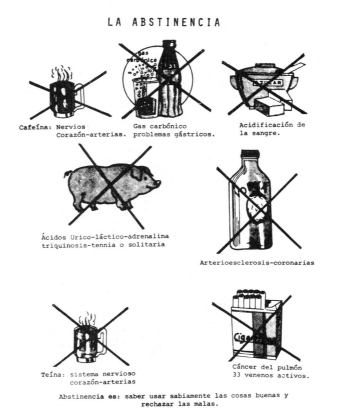

Cafeína: Nervios
Corazón-arterias.

Gas carbónico
problemas gástricos.

Acidificación de
la sangre.

Ácidos Urico-láctico-adrenalina
triquinosis-tennia o solitaria

Arterioesclerosis-coronarias

Teína: sistema nervioso
corazón-arterias

Cáncer del pulmón
33 venenos activos.

Abstinencia **es**: saber usar sabiamente las cosas buenas y
rechazar las malas.

3. Ud. es una enfermera que toma el historial médico de una joven de quince años. Es evidente que está embarazada. Es su primer hijo. Ella vive en casa con sus padres y sus cinco hermanos menores. A ella le gusta comer los ''fast foods''. Las pruebas del laboratorio indican que sufre de malnutrición. Háblele, tomando en cuenta su formación hispana, sobre la importancia de comer bien para la salud del bebé. Hágale una cita para el mes que viene e insista Ud. en la importancia de venir para un examen todos los meses que esté encinta.

4. Tome Ud. el historial médico de uno/a de sus compañeros/as, fijándose en las siguientes categorías: datos personales, problemas actuales de salud, enfermedades de niño, otras enfermedades previas, el historial médico de la familia, incluyendo las causas de la muerte de padres y/o hermanos y previo tratamiento psiquiátrico.

REFLEJOS DE LA CULTURA: "El doctor y los rayos X"

Life for someone new to a culture is often a series of one adaptation and adjustment after another. Experiences that natives to a culture take for granted become for the newcomer never-ending opportunities for learning about oneself and new cultural mores. However, this learning process may be accompanied by bewilderment and physical, psychological, or, at times, even financial distress.

The following episode describes the feelings of disorientation that an immigrant from the Dominican Republic experiences when seeking a rather routine medical procedure in the United States. Although he finds little to criticize in the medical treatment, the personal interaction surrounding the delivery of services leaves him confused and alienated. His sense of personal dignity is violated by the lack of trust extended him despite the personal referral he has received.

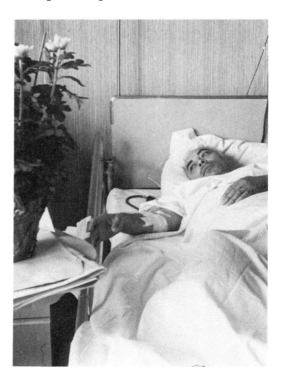

It is always interesting to see ourselves through the eyes of others. What we may perceive as an efficient, well-run office may seem very different when seen through eyes trained in another culture. The author of this vignette refers to himself simply as "Leni." The work in which it appears is entitled *Nueva York (EE.UU.): El falso paraíso.*

Al cabo de dos años y medio de estar residiendo en Nueva York empecé a sufrir de un problema intestinal que los entendidos llaman constipación pero que en la República Dominicana denominamos comúnmente estreñimiento y de otras formas más. . . .

At the end of two and a half years of living in New York I began to suffer from an intestinal problem that those in the know call *constipación*, but that in the Dominican Republic we commonly refer to as *estreñimiento* among other names. . . .

Cuando llevaba el tiempo antes dicho residiendo allí, disponía de cierta libertad económica que me permitía pedir cualquier buen plato en un restaurante, sin que importara su categoría ni la especialidad. Pero de nada me valía visitar estos establecimientos porque no podía echarle gran cosa al estómago puesto que los intestinos estaban, casi siempre, llenos como longanizas. Así me sentía. Debo decir que el estreñimiento me hacía sufrir más porque tenía como meta saborear la comida de todos los países del mundo, cuyos platos típicos aparecen por todos los lados en Nueva York.

Pues, así como saltaba de un restaurante a otro, iba de un médico a otro hasta que un conocido—médico también, con un historial bastante sucio entre los hispanos—me recomendó un amigo suyo especialista en las vías digestivas. Recuerdo que me concertó él mismo la cita para un sábado por la mañana.

Allí estuve bien temprano sin desayunar (como lo había recomendado) y tan pronto llenaron el récord, una enfermera se encargó de mí haciéndome pasar de un cuarto a otro, donde no solamente me hacía tomar un líquido especial para ponerme los rayos, sino que también me ponía enemas del mismo líquido. Un tanto rosado, si mal no recuerdo.

Tuve de mala esa mañana, pues algunas placas no salieron muy bien y había que repetirlas. Fue necesario hartarme nuevamente de la insípida sustancia.

Terminada la tortura, siguiendo instrucciones de la enfermera, pasé al despacho de la secretaria, informándome ésta que podía volver en la tarde para que el doctor diera los resultados de los estudios. Todavía no lo había visto pero me dio opción de regresar el lunes.

When I was living there at the time I mentioned, I had a good deal of economic freedom that allowed me to order any good entrée in the restaurant, without its price or uniqueness being of any importance to me. But visiting these establishments was of little value to me since I could not put a lot of food into my stomach since the intestines were, almost always, stuffed as sausages. That's the way I felt. I should say that the constipation made me suffer more because I had as an objective to savor the food from every country in the world whose typical dishes appear everywhere in New York.

Well, that's the way I bounced from one restaurant to another, going from one doctor to another until an acquaintance of mine, who was also a doctor with a rather dirty reputation among Hispanics, recommended to me a friend of his who was a specialist in the digestive tract. I remember that he himself made the appointment for one Saturday morning.

I was there bright and early without eating breakfast (as had been recommended) and as soon as they filled out the record, a nurse took charge of me, making me go from one room to another, where she not only made me drink a special liquid for taking the X-rays, but she also gave me enemas with the same liquid. (It was) a little pink, if my memory doesn't fail me.

I had bad luck that morning, since some of the X-rays did not come out all right and had to be taken over. It was necessary to fill me up again with the insipid substance.

Once the torture was over, following the instructions from the nurse, I went into the secretary's office who told me I could return in the afternoon for the doctor to give me the results of the tests. I still had not seen him, but she gave me the option to return on Monday.

Dicho lo anterior agregó la secretaria: — Todo cuesta 85 dólares. — Saqué la cartera pasándole 25 dólares y le dije que pagaría el resto en dos partidas dándole la primera parte cuando regresara a ver al doctor. Pero ésta me contestó: —No se puede . . . el pago hay que efectuarlo completo ahora.

Me resistí a creer lo que oía de labios de la mujer, ya que me había recomendado alguien bien conocido por ellos. Por eso me lo recomendó. No le puse mucho caso a lo que acababa de oír, por lo que llamé a la enfermera que había hecho las placas. Le expliqué la situación para que ella a la vez se la comunicara al doctor. La norsa accedió gentilmente, pero la respuesta no se hizo esperar:—Dice el doctor que lo siente mucho, pero esos aparatos (los de rayos X) no son de él.

No tuve otra alternativa, pagué los 85 dólares requeridos, pero antes hice que me buscaran las placas—aquí no vuelvo—dije. Así se lo hice saber a la secretaria.

En lo que aparecían las radiografías llamé al médico que me había recomendado su colega y lo enteré de lo que estaba ocurriendo. Éste me dijo por teléfono que llamaría inmediatamente para resolver el asunto. En nada cambiaron las cosas. No sé si porque la llamada prometida no se produjo o porque hubo intransigencia.

Al cabo de diez o quince minutos recibía lo que me costó 85 dólares sin ningún resultado positivo. Por fortuna, eso ocurrió un sábado por la mañana, yo había cobrado el viernes anterior y andaba con cerca de 100 dólares en los bolsillos.

Once that was said, the secretary added: "Everything comes to eighty-five dollars." I took out my wallet, (and) handing her twenty-five, I told her I would pay the rest in two installments, giving her the first when I returned to see the doctor. But she answered: "You can't do that . . . payment must be made in full right now."

I couldn't believe what I heard from that woman's lips, since someone well known to them had recommended me. That's why he recommended him to me. I didn't pay too much attention to what I had just heard, so I called the nurse who had taken the X-rays. I explained the situation to her so that she, in turn, could tell it to the doctor. The nurse kindly agreed, but in no time at all the answer came back: "The doctor says that he's very sorry, but these (X-ray) machines are not his."

I had no other alternative, (so) I paid the required eighty-five dollars, but before I did I made them hunt up my X-rays. "I'm not coming back here," I said. That's how I made it known to the secretary.

As I waited for the X-rays to appear, I called the doctor who had recommended his colleague to me and I filled him in on what was happening. He told me on the phone that he would call at once to settle the matter. Things didn't change in the least. I don't know if it was because the promised phone call didn't take place or because there was no room for compromise.

After ten or fifteen minutes, I received what cost me eighty-five dollars with no positive results. Luckily, it all happened on a Saturday morning, (and) I had gotten paid the Friday before and I was walking around with about one hundred dollars in my pockets.

LECCIÓN 12

Hay que tener fe

LOS OBJETIVOS

Raising awareness

1. To analyze and relate levels of consciousness to behaviors and attitudes regarding cross-cultural communication
2. To understand the experience of being Hispanic in the United States as contrasted with that of previous immigrant groups
3. To learn how the Hispanic cultural value of anticipating needs conflicts with Anglo values of frankness and directness

Comunicándose en español

1. To pronounce and comprehend **m, n, ñ, l, ll,** and **y**
2. To use and understand vocabulary and structures that express faith and despair within a spiritual context
3. To express and understand hypothetical situations employing past subjunctive, past perfect, and conditional tenses

Combinándolo todo

1. To integrate all material presented in text by applying it to increasingly more challenging professional activities
2. To make and understand subtle distinctions in vocabulary and language structures relevant to spiritual beliefs, emotional distress, and wishes and desires
3. To understand the philosophical and psychological dimensions of migrating to the United States via segments of the script from the movie *El norte*

443

Raising awareness

OVERVIEW: Putting it into practice

Throughout this text, you have come to see yourself as a product of cultural conditioning and personal experiences. At the same time, you have expanded your awareness of how people from other cultural backgrounds may differ from you in their perceptions of reality. You have learned that culture shock is inevitable when two or more people with different cultural backgrounds interact. You've also discovered that it can be a positive experience for all concerned.

While you may have begun your study of Spanish and Hispanic culture trying to understand Hispanics, by now you have probably realized that the key to successful cross-cultural communication lies in understanding yourself. The rich experience of working and/or living in an intercultural arena presents a unique opportunity for self-growth. As you become open to understanding and accepting another culture's point of view, you also open up to comprehend the depth of your own experience as a culturally conditioned human being.

In this last chapter, you will take a closer look at yourself and the various levels of consciousness of the psyche. As you examine the ways in which you operate at each level, you will also become more aware of how these behaviors affect your success as a cross-cultural communicator.

Pierre Cassé in *Training for the Cross-Cultural Mind* presents the following theoretical construct from which to view the psyche. He identifies five key states of consciousness that govern our intercultural interactions. Each has its own set of characteristics, which translate into specific behaviors, reactions, and strategies for coping across cultural boundaries. He sees the individual's awareness as sliding up and down a sort of scale, stopping at times at various identifiable positions. In this construct the highest level is termed *nirvana*, followed by *satori*, the middle *analytical* state, followed by the *functional* level and the *neurotic* level. This scale can be illustrated as follows:

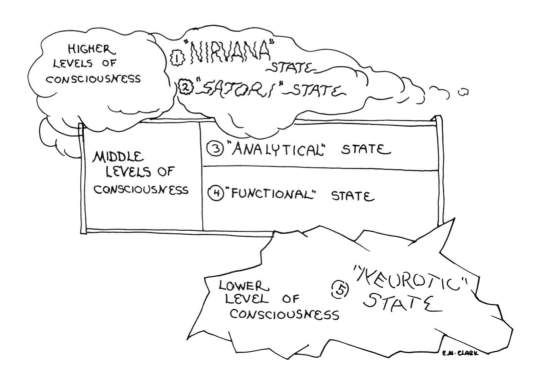

By using the neutral *analytical* state (Level 3) as a reference point, the higher and lower levels of consciousness may be more easily understood. At this neutral level of consciousness, information is received from the inner and outer worlds and is processed in an objective, systematic, and analytical way. The individual in this state feels neither good nor bad. The focus is on the here and now. It is an open, exploratory state, which can accept ambiguity, is receptive to seeing all aspects of an object or situation, and is probing, inquiring, and understanding.

The two lower levels of consciousness are typified by pain and difficulty. The *functional* state (Level 4) is characterized by the individual's ability to perform, to carry out what he or she is expected to do or wants to do, but with feelings of guilt, boredom, loneliness, annoyance, or general malaise. The individual is prone to judge, categorize, compare, and evaluate with an eye toward generalizing. People who often function at this level are prone to self-pity, egocentrism, headaches, and insomnia. They may feel they are constantly battling with disappointments, frustrations, doubts, fears, inhibitions, tensions, and insecurities.

Level 5, the *neurotic* state, can be termed an extremely dangerous experience, typified by extreme suffering and pain. Unlike someone operating at Level 4, the individual in the neurotic state can no longer function in any way. There is a blockage of energy resulting in loneliness, hopelessness, alienation, and loss of objectivity. Behaviors stemming from this state may range from self-destructive activities to extreme aggression, from obsessions, panic, and paranoia to passivity, submissiveness, and depression.

On the other hand, Levels 1 and 2 provide the individual with rewarding and enjoyable experiences. In the *satori* state the individual seems to perform without any effort, as life is perceived as flowing naturally and spontaneously. It is typified by feelings of peace, harmony, and authenticity. The individual seems well adjusted and

Level	Source	Behavior	Intercultural reaction
1. *Nirvana*	The need to outgrow one's own life and reality, to belong to the whole	Both passive and active, thinking and feeling, receptive and creative	Creative interaction with the new cultural environment, personal expression and growth
2. *Satori*	The need to be, to experience the here and now	Flowing with the forces around, in tune with the situation at hand, letting be	Seeing the differences and being able to enjoy them (multicultural approach)
3. *Analytical state*	The need to be aware, understand, and control	Being a witness, watching and drawing conclusions from factual observations	Controlled adjustment (understanding one's own reactions, "their" reactions, and the interactions)
4. *Functional state*	The need for security, sensation, and power	Fleeing, fighting, withdrawing, giving up, being afraid, frustrated, bored, hostile, intimidated	Adjustment, but constant criticism of the behavior of those from another culture
5. *Neurotic state*	The need for exploring the deep shadow of one's own personality	Behaving in a way that does not make sense to others, may be viewed as "evil"	Rejection of the new culture and those from that culture

centered and gives total attention to the task or person at hand, with an innate ability to be effective in whatever situation arises.

The highest level of consciousness attainable is Level 1, the *nirvana* state. It is an exceptional feeling, characterized by total integration, transcendence, and bliss. The individual experiences inner peace as well as a sense of unity with the world. This metaphysical plane, where the creative forces of imagination, intuition, and revelation are experienced, is characterized by a sense of truth and wholeness.

Each individual has the ability to experience all five states of consciousness. Each state may be triggered by a specific situation in which the individual is involved. It also seems possible for the individual to control the psychic processes and choose whether to operate at a given level. Although the five states seem universal, their definition can be culturally biased.

A closer look at the sources of the various psychic states and their identifiable behaviors can help to define the reaction typical of each state to the cross-cultural communication process.

In more specific terms, an individual stuck in the neurotic state when dealing with people from another culture will find it impossible to communicate with them, reacting with secretiveness, mistrust, and possibly aggression. The pose is one of "I'm O.K., but *you* certainly are not." Any attempt to bridge the communication gap at this level is doomed to failure.

The individual functioning at Level 4 will be able to communicate well enough with those from another culture in order to carry out duties and obligations. However, this will be done in a way that validates only the Level 4 functioner and not the person from the other culture. The behavior will be manipulative, and the person stuck at this level may seem provocative, forceful, or pushy, giving the same "I'm O.K., but you're not" message as the Level 5 personality.

Someone operating from the level 3 position will be noticeable by his or her controlled behavior. The tone during the interaction will be factual and low-key, since being "O.K." or not is irrelevant to the analytical perspective. The person from another culture is accepted and observed in a detached, unemotional way, and elements of the interaction will be perceived and analyzed for their impact on the situation.

An individual exhibiting Level 2 behaviors would be best termed spontaneous and authentic. This individual recognizes and appreciates cultural differences and is eager to learn more about them, approaching cross-cultural communication as a process of cooperation and negotiation in a way that validates both parties. It is reflective of the "I'm O.K. and so are you" approach to life.

The individual operating from the Level 1 nirvana state brings the best of the creative process to intercultural interaction. The exchange is synergistic, tapping into the best in the other. The differences that separate disappear, while the focus is fixed on the human essence shared by each. *Transcendental* is the word that most aptly describes the process, characterized by "the whole world is O.K." as an approach to life.

There is some polemic regarding how much the individual can control his or her awareness at a given moment. Some feel that we can choose our level of consciousness by an act of will. Others postulate that an individual can work psychologically through one state and move to the next, although the motivational force behind this is unclear. It is also hypothesized that it is natural to move among the five states, since staying at only one state exclusively would be boring and ultimately nonproductive.

The idea that individuals can consciously select how to perceive and interact with their environment has optimistic implications for the cross-cultural communication process. One can hope that the innate human ability for growth and self-actualization will flourish in the opportunities afforded by the intercultural process.

The key to growth in self-awareness while communicating with those from another culture lies in how you perceive cultural differences. An appropriate analogy might be that of yoga, in which the individual muscles are stretched and emphasized in order to later be forgotten, so that the psyche can transcend the limitations of the body. By first focusing intensely on the differences that separate, you are then freer to reach the state in which the previously misunderstood behaviors and attitudes are appreciated and, ultimately, fade into irrelevancy. What might have at one time annoyed, angered, or provoked eventually becomes a source of joy, peace, and harmony. As you begin to understand yourself and your Hispanic clients as unique individuals, cultural conditioning ceases to be an obstacle to intercultural communication. Only when the focus shifts from what separates us to what we have in common as human beings can we truly communicate across cultural boundaries.

Applications

1. Circle the adjectives that best describe how you feel when you are communicating with your Hispanic clients:

   angry   annoyed   frustrated   guilty   helpful   interested   observant   patronizing   misunderstood   panicked   effortless   rational   peaceful   detached   alienated   hostile   curious   frightened   unprepared   critical   painful   harmonious   validated   unsure   anxious   nervous   excited   whole   happy   selfless   compassionate   humble   neutral   liberal   tense   genuine   effective   imaginative   honest   ambivalent

2. Circle the state of awareness that typifies the way you feel most of the time that you spend with your Hispanic clients:

Nirvana	*Satori*	*Analytical*	*Functional*	*Neurotic*
1	2	3	4	5
_____	_____	_____	_____	_____
_____	_____	_____	_____	_____
_____	_____	_____	_____	_____

3. Now write under the appropriate heading the adjectives that you circled above that best fit the description given for each of the above states.

4. Describe the specific behaviors and attitudes that might be displayed by an Anglo professional operating from each of the five states in the following situations:

   a. A Hispanic client recently arrived from his native country comes into the office. He speaks very little English. He needs to get some forms to fill out in order to seek the services the agency provides.

   b. A young female Hispanic client who is very shy has come to the agency for the first time. She has brought her boyfriend along to help her through the initial interview, even though she speaks English rather well.

Reflections

1. How did your choice of "typical" state in dealing with Hispanic clients correlate with the adjectives you circled? Which feelings that you experience when providing services to Hispanics would you most want to change? What strategies can you suggest to change them?

2. In describing the various reactions to the two situations regarding Hispanic clients typical of each of the five states of consciousness, did you recognize your own behaviors? In which state? How does this correlate with your self-assessment in numbers 2 and 3 of "Applications"?

3. Do you know anyone who is particularly successful in dealing with Hispanic clients? What behaviors and/or attitudes does he or she exhibit? To what do you attribute the effectiveness of this person? What can you learn from this person?

4. List below four goals that you would like to achieve regarding your interactions with Hispanic clients as well as specific strategies to attain them.

	Goals	*Strategies*
1.		
2.		
3.		
4.		

HISTORICAL PERSPECTIVE: Being Hispanic in the United States

The "Historical Perspective" sections of this text have traced the cultural value systems shared by Hispanics to earlier roots in history. For most of Latin America, these roots go back to the indigenous, European, and, in some areas, African cultures. Life for most Hispanics in the Western Hemisphere since the *Conquista* has been a constant process of adaptation to the way of thinking of a different source of power. The degree of acculturation has varied, ranging from those who view their lifestyle as similar to that of educated Europeans and North American Anglos to those whose way of life has changed very little from precolonial times.

While this text has emphasized the cultural similarities of the various Hispanic groups, an attempt has been made to point out the diversity of the Spanish-speaking world. This heterogeneity may be seen as both an asset and a liability.

For English-speaking North Americans, the rich diversity of their Spanish-speaking neighbors to the south often goes unappreciated amid the tendency to look at those from other cultural backgrounds as "different." This reflects a subjective *we-they* world view, with anything that is not *we* seen as foreign, strange, and incongruent with the "American way of life." It leaves little room for a more objective perspective that notes *both* similarities and differences. We can spend so much time trying to understand how Hispanic clients deviate from the Anglo cultural value system that we never take the time to examine how much we have in common.

1. *What evidence of heterogeneity among Hispanic groups have you observed or learned about through this text? What are the roots of this diversity?*

2. *Do you agree that North American Anglos tend to miss the nuances of diversity among peoples from other cultures? To what can this be attributed?*

The experience of being Hispanic in the United States is directly affected by this tendency of U.S. Anglos to think of the rest of the world as "different." Being different somehow is an affront to the collective psyche. The pressure to assimilate, to become part of the melting pot, is felt by all newcomers. A resident of the United States whose appearance, thoughts, or actions do not conform to cultural norms is often viewed as insulting the values on which this country was established, even though one of the principles of democracy is freedom of choice. The "America, love it or leave it" mentality prevails in the hearts of many Anglos, regardless of their ancestry. Often the most vehement voices urging Hispanics to conform or get out are those of immigrants (and their children) who have come to the United States from other parts of the world. In some instances, this message suggests an undercurrent of "I gave up my roots to live in America, so you must do the same."

While it may appear that the push to assimilate is a desire for integration, a closer look at history reveals that it is an attempt at elimination or segregation. The European adventurers and colonizers considered the native populations either a barrier to attaining their objectives, as in North America, or a resource to be manipulated, as in much of Latin America. The Native Americans of the north were either exterminated or pushed out, later to be given their own territories separate from the new colonies. The indigenous populations to the south provided a large, unsophisticated labor force on which the colonizers depended for survival and prosperity. When they were wiped out by disease and exploitation in some areas of Latin America, Africans were brought in to replace them in the lower social strata.

The continued resistance to change in the social order, typical of most Hispanic countries, is predicated on the same need for a captive lower class to meet the demands of the more prosperous and powerful. Similarly, just as the early colonizers of North America sought to eliminate the native populations or relegate them to a separate area and, in the process, to second-class citizenship, those who advocate the "assimilate or leave" policy really encourage the elimination or segregation of ethnic and racial diversity.

---

3. *Do you agree that the foregoing statements describe the Anglo view of ethnic and racial differences? Explain your answer.*

4. *What parallels can be drawn between the interaction of the early colonizers of North and South America with the indigenous populations and the contemporary socioeconomic reality of both areas?*

Until the 1800s, most of the present-day southwestern United States was sparsely populated Mexican territory. The westward-ho colonization movement of Texas, California, and other western states by Anglos seemed to be spearheaded by the same attitude toward the indigenous populations as that of the early settlers of the original colonies — "get out or give up." Although Mexican citizens who chose to stay in these territories were granted U.S. citizenship, it came stamped "second class." Many of these people lost title to their land as well as the right to be culturally different. The reins of control shifted from the conquered to the conquerors in such matters as language and cultural behaviors. While Mexican Americans were given the option of assimilating to the majority culture, this proved a more difficult task for them than for other European immigrants, whose less mixed racial identity blended more easily into the Anglo mainstream.

A historical look at Puerto Rico also illustrates how the United States has colonized lands occupied by an indigenous population. Since 1898 Puerto Rico has been a colony of the United States; it was given full commonwealth status in 1952. Much of the present economic power on the island resides in the hands of American businesses whose upper-management personnel are primarily mainland Anglos living in English-speaking enclaves on the island. The indigenous population is economically manipulated by a small group of U.S. businessmen. Economically, the "colonization" pattern of the United States in Puerto Rico is but a twentieth-century replay of that of the Spaniards in Latin America. The difference, however, is that there is little racial mixture between the Anglos and the Puerto Ricans. Much like the pattern on the U.S. mainland, the prevailing attitude is that of we–they, except that in this case the *we* is the controlling minority. Attempts have been made to encourage the island residents to assimilate to the linguistic and cultural norms of the United States, but the majority of the indigenous population have been unwilling to abandon their ethnic heritage completely. Thus the "separate" rather than "assimilate" command is issued by the dominant minority.

Those who direct the "assimilate or leave it" demand at Puerto Ricans residing on the mainland often forget three things:

1. Puerto Ricans are U.S. citizens with as much "right" to migrate between the island and the mainland as a resident of Ohio has to move to California.
2. The United States, through its economic involvement in the island and the political control it exerts there, has inextricably linked the destiny of the two countries.
3. The fact that Puerto Ricans exhibit characteristics of the Indian, Spanish, and African racial blend adds to the difficulty they encounter in assimilating to the Anglo majority culture on the mainland.

The identity distinctions made in the United States on the basis of race put the assimilation question regarding Hispanics into a different perspective. Of course, it would be unfair to single out the United States as the only country in which racial discrimination exists; it seems to occur in most countries with racially mixed populations. In fact, one of the legacies of the colonial period in Latin America is that different racial categories are assigned to people of mixed races, and importance is attached to these categories. One historical difference, however, defines the way racial distinctions are made in the United States and Latin America. In the U.S. colonies, there was little or no intermarriage among the Anglo colonizers and either the indigenous populations or the African slaves brought in later. Thus the three races have remained relatively unmixed for a large proportion of the population. Since the majority population in the United States is still "white," residents from other racial backgrounds are classified as "nonwhite" in the we–they terms described above.

In Latin America, however, very few women accompanied the original colonizers. Thus racial mixtures among Caucasians, Indians, and, in some areas, Africans, became more the norm than they did in the north. To varying degrees in different countries, depending on the numbers of the

indigenous populations that survived the *Conquista* and the numbers of Africans who were brought in, the majority of Hispanics are racially mixed. Although being "white" is considered a favorable characteristic in the Spanish-speaking world, the reality is that racial mixtures exist in most families. Hence the racial issue is treated differently in Hispanic countries than in the United States. No clear dichotomy is evident, such as that presented by the white–nonwhite distinction prevalent in the United States.

---

5. *How can the U.S. colonization of the Mexican territories and Puerto Rico compare with the attitude of the early colonizers of the United States toward the indigenous populations they encountered?*
6. *How does the basis for making racial distinctions differ between the United States and the Spanish-speaking world? How can this difference be explained from a historical perspective?*

Another issue regarding the ability and desirability of Hispanics to assimilate to the Anglo way of life is language. Most immigrant groups to the United States from Europe and Asia have lost their native language by the second or third generation of offspring. Since immigration from Europe has declined since the early part of this century, there are no large waves of newcomers from the motherland to maintain linguistic contact with the native tongue. Nonetheless, most large urban centers with ethnic populations have small shops and services where "foreign" languages are spoken.

Few people become truly bilingual in all contexts. Regardless of the amount of time spent learning and speaking a second language, even in an environment where that language predominates, people feel most comfortable expressing themselves in their native tongue. Children who learn two languages as infants have the best chance of becoming equally fluent and expressive in each, although they may always feel at a disadvantage when forced to rely exclusively on one language, especially in times of stress, anxiety, fear, or any other strong emotional context.

Another phenomenon of bilingualism is that a person who speaks two languages with apparent fluency may be more comfortable speaking the second language in contexts reflecting the environment in which it was learned. For example, a Hispanic from a Spanish-speaking home who learned English in school may feel more comfortable doing mathematical calculations in English rather than in Spanish but may prefer to discuss personal feelings or family matters in Spanish.

An important factor affecting the bilingualism of many Hispanics living in the United States is the historical and geographical connection between Spanish and English in North America. Unlike immigrants from Europe, Asia, or other distant continents who left their birthplace and its language far behind, Hispanics have always had continued access to the homeland. This is especially true for Mexican Americans, Puerto Ricans, and, to a lesser extent, Cubans. The geographic proximity as well as the historical links between the Spanish and English-speaking neighbors of this hemisphere have forged a linguistic bond that shows few signs of weakening. The ease of travel between the mainland and both Mexico and the Spanish-speaking Caribbean encourages return visits as well as new migrations among family members. Maintenance of Spanish is a natural result of the continued contact.

---

7. *What aspects of language acquisition affect the degree of bilingualism of a given individual? Do you consider yourself bilingual? Do you know anyone who is? How do your personal experiences with bilingualism correlate to the various aspects discussed in this section?*
8. *How do history and geography affect the bilingualism of Hispanics living in the United States?*

The complexity of learning a second language is often ignored by monolingual Anglos who feel that everyone should speak English in America. Since English has been the predominant language in this country, it goes without saying that anyone living in the United States who does not have command of the English language will have a difficult time functioning in the mainstream culture. Non–English speakers usually face limited access to employment, education, and socioeconomic mobility. Nevertheless, adult immigrants, including those from European backgrounds in the last century, have been faced with the challenge of mastering English to the point of being able to speak, understand, read, and write it as well as an educated native speaker in order to succeed economically. Not all have been able to do so. Those who have usually were from middle-class backgrounds where access to quality education and an awareness of the international culture are the norm.

Many Hispanic immigrants, however, have come from the economically and socially oppressed classes in Mexico, Central America, and the Spanish-speaking Caribbean. Those from rural backgrounds have usually had an even more parochial experience in terms of education and awareness than their urban *compatriotas* (those from the same country). These newcomers have come to the United States with few skills that translate into the highly sophisticated Anglo economic world. Learning English may not be easy for those whose education has primarily come from the land and its people. For the *campesino,* acquiring a second language based on unfamiliar cultural concepts presents a far greater challenge than it does for the Hispanic lawyer or schoolteacher.

Even Hispanics who attain fluency in English may not easily assimilate into the Anglo linguistic mainstream if they retain any semblance of a Spanish accent. Since the large majority of Anglos are monolingual, many are unaware of the difficulty adults have in learning to speak a second language accent-free. Accented English, regardless of its fluency and accuracy, places the individual in the category of *other* for those who see all "foreigners" as different from themselves.

Some Hispanics and Anglos see bilingualism in both English and Spanish as a worthwhile objective. Some proponents of bilingual education advocate fluency in both languages *at the level of an educated native speaker* as a legitimate educational objective. They find it incongruous that a country that has advocated foreign language learning at the primary, secondary, and university levels discourages those who already speak Spanish from studying it formally.

In summary, Hispanics living on the United States mainland must deal with their racial back-ground, ethnic heritage, and linguistic preferences on a daily basis. Most recognize assimilation as a myth. Some have succumbed to the pressure not to be different; they may have changed their last name, intermarried with Anglos, speak only English, and consider their Hispanic heritage a thing of the past in order to blend into the majority culture. Others cling to their Hispanic heritage as their birthright and dedicate their lives to gaining equal opportunities and access to political and economic power for all Hispanics. They proclaim the beauty of the "tossed salad" description of the United States, a pluralistic perspective that recognizes the advantages of cultural diversity.

The vast majority fall somewhere between the two extremes, compromising on some issues, holding steadfast on others. Some Hispanics make a concerted effort to speak English and may resist any attempt made to speak to them in Spanish. Others may feel ashamed of their "street" Spanish when asked to speak it with those who have learned their language in an academic environment. Others may pursue the study of Spanish at the university level only to find that their "Spanish" is branded inferior to that spoken in Spain or Latin America. And still others take pride in their bilingualism, "code switching" (changing from one language to another in a conversation) at will in order to express an idea in the language best suited to the situation.

Each Hispanic resident of the United States will have made choices at a conscious or unconscious level about how much ethnicity to retain. These decisions are not made overnight. Rather, they are the process of a lifetime lived as a minority in a culture where the majority is, at times, ignorant, intolerant, or prejudiced with regard to those it views as different.

9. *How does the question of native language maintenance differ between those who have come from Mexico and the Spanish-speaking Caribbean and those from Europe, Asia, or other continents?*
10. *Describe the various aspects of the English–Spanish language polemic in the United States. How do you personally feel about it?*

NONVERBAL COMMUNICATION: Anticipating needs

One of the most important cultural differences that affects the cross-cultural communication process between Anglos and Hispanics is the degree to which the individual is taught to anticipate the needs of others. In the individualistic Anglo culture, the values of independence, self-reliance, frankness, and assertiveness condition people to "look out for number one." While some Anglos are very adept at perceiving and tending to the needs of others, in professional settings in the United States it is generally expected that each person will take responsibility for getting his or her own needs met. In Hispanic cultures, men and women are taught to perceive the needs of those who come to their homes, offices, stores, and restaurants for social and professional exchanges. Women are usually the direct caretakers in these situations. Men, too, are trained to observe those around them and anticipate their needs, although they usually refer the need to a woman to fulfill (except, often, in the case of mixing and serving drinks).

Hispanics, then, are used to being observed by sensitive eyes and ears that take in their message-laden movements, sighs, and facial gestures. When in their own cultural environment, they are secure in the knowledge that these signals will be perceived and correctly interpreted and their needs taken care of. This awareness makes it unnecessary for Hispanics who have grown up in their native environment to develop such Anglo-prized skills as assertiveness and directness.

Hispanics coming to the United States may experience confusion when the signals and gestures that in their own country brought instant recognition and attention to their needs go unnoticed and ignored. This is particularly true in sterile professional settings, where efficiency requires seekers of services to state their needs overtly. Such an atmosphere leaves little time for the professional to experience the human element in the exchange, including the client's nonverbal messages.

On the other hand, Hispanic residents of the United States need to develop the ability to speak frankly and request their needs directly to survive in the mainstream culture. This learning process requires time and guidance, since to state

one's needs forcefully, to criticize, or to ask for clarification of instructions goes against the cultural grain of *respeto*, especially in dealings with professionals seen as authority figures.

Anglos providing services to Hispanic clients are in a position to effect a mutual reeducation process in nonverbal communication for themselves and their clients. The following guidelines can help Anglos learn a new way of looking at their clients and perceiving their needs, as well as guide the latter in learning to derive the fullest benefit from living in the Anglo environment.

1. Pay close attention to eye contact. Eyes cast down usually indicates respect to a Hispanic. It may also signal the need for reassurance to discuss a personal, embarrassing, or distasteful matter. Another interpretation is that the individual feels ashamed of something he or she has done or that has been done to his or her family.

2. Remember that Hispanics tend to be reticent in accepting food, drink, small gifts, and favors. When hearing *"No, gracias,"* offer again, perhaps two or three times, making sure the client understands that this is not an inconvenience and that you really want him or her to accept what is offered. But don't press the issue if the Hispanic client seems not to want what is offered.

3. A client's silence in response to a question or suggestion may imply that you as a professional have overstepped your bounds and that you are treading on intimate territory. It may indicate a reluctance to discuss the matter in the immediate environment, particularly if other people are in listening range. It may also signal a lack of understanding or reluctance to ask for a repetition of instructions. Find out the reason for the silence by gentle probing. It is best to anticipate the need with specific questions such as "Would you rather discuss this at another time?" rather than with direct, open-ended questions such as "Why don't you answer me?"

4. Avoid a paternalistic attitude which treats the client as a child for demonstrating certain Hispanic cultural traits that, in the Anglo environment, are considered childlike behavior (e.g., lack of assertiveness, silence). Respecting the in-

dividual's sense of personal dignity is a crucial strategy for success in dealing with Hispanic clients.

5.   Be sensitive to the culturally different Hispanic value systems, particularly male–female relationships, the role of the family, and the like. In giving advice, *anticipate* the cultural impact of your suggestions and discuss it directly with your clients.

6.   Encourage your clients to be more frank and direct with you. Let them know you expect certain behaviors from them which have your approval. Explain the specific expectations they will meet in Anglo professional contexts. Discuss the cultural differences that may keep them from obtaining adequate services.

7.   Do not be afraid to be open with your clients about how their culturally determined behaviors affect you — for example, that you feel frustrated when they don't follow your instructions. Clients will try harder to do what you personally expect of them because of the role of *personalismo*. Remember, however, that in Hispanic cultures authority figures are expected to maintain a professional demeanor, so that an overly personal approach may not always be appropriate.

8.   Maintain a sense of humor, but be discreet; what is funny in one culture may not be at all humorous in another. Try to keep the rapport light enough so that the client feels comfortable. At the same time, do not make light of the client's behavior or problems to the point that you give the impression of not taking the situation seriously.

By paying special attention to how your Hispanic clients express their needs nonverbally, you will develop more sensitivity to *all* clients, regardless of their cultural background. You will also expand your ability to switch cultural channels, to select the appropriate way of behaving in a specific cross-cultural exchange. As you take the time to guide your clients through the Anglo-valued behaviors expected and rewarded in professional contexts, you will help them to become more aware of how many of their frustrations and those of the personnel who serve them are due to intercultural misunderstandings. This awareness will enrich both the Hispanic clients and the Anglo practitioners who deliver services to them.

Putting it into practice

1. Discuss what needs the Hispanic client may be demonstrating by each of the following nonverbal clues:

    a. Reluctance to respond to specific personal questions on an intake interview form

    b. An *ataque de nervios* that a young Hispanic mother of three small children is suffering

    c. A smile that a young Hispanic male uses to respond to the Anglo doctor's question regarding sexual intercourse

    d. The reluctance of a client to transfer to another social worker when the one to whom she had been going for services is promoted to another position

    e. The apparent lack of attention that a young adolescent displays when questioned about his activities

    f. The suspected lack of compliance with certain medical instructions a patient has been given

2. Suggest strategies for dealing with the above behaviors as well as for guiding the clients to a better awareness of the effect their cultural conditioning may have on the delivery of services they seek.

3. Role-play each of the situations described above with another classmate.

Comunicándose en español

PRONUNCIACIÓN: m, n, ñ, l, ll, y 📼

Spanish **m** is similar to the English *m* in *mess*.

mano	miedo	vemos	tiempo	fumado
mamá	matriz	tenemos	muebles	dormir

Spanish **n** is similar to the English *n* in *now*.

nada	nuevo	nadie	nunca	funciona
nota	nuestro	varón	encinta	condición

However, Spanish **n** sounds like **m** before consonants formed with both lips (**b, v, m, p**).

un poco	un varón	un profesor
un beso	un macho	inmediatamente

Spanish **ñ** is similar to English *ny* in *canyon*.

año	señor	riñon	compañía
niña	dueña	mañana	español

Spanish **l** is pronounced similar to the English *l* as in *lake*, except that the tip and the front of the tongue come into contact with the ridge behind the upper teeth (much like English *d*). It is important to maintain this position in pronouncing final **l**.

al	blanco	salgo	fiel	legal
del	solo	Julio	final	dolor

Spanish **ll** and **y** are pronounced alike; however, the way they are pronounced will vary depending on the speaker's native country. For most Latin Americans, this sound is similar to the English *y* in *you*. Argentinians pronounce it as *zh*, while Puerto Ricans prefer the pronunciation of *j* as in *jet*. Spaniards tend to pronounce it as *ly* as in *million*. It is perhaps easiest for you to pronounce the **ll** as **y**. If Hispanic speakers in your area have a different pronunciation of this sound, you may wish to practice it with your instructor.

millón	ella	calle	creyó	ya
llega	allí	pollo	oyeron	yo

Práctica 📼

Practice the following sentences aloud until you can say them without pauses.

1. Quiero un poco de pollo.
2. Mi yerno y yo nos llevamos bien.
3. Mi cuñado salió a la calle a las dos de la mañana.
4. La niña llegó tarde anoche.
5. Ya se lo llevaron.
6. Matilde está encinta; va a dar a luz en abril.
7. Necesito investigar la situación.

Dictado 📼

Now write the words and sentences your instructor will pronounce.

1. _____   4. _____

2. _____   5. _____

3. _____   6. _____

7. _____

8. _____

9. _____

Rafael, mi sentido pésame por la muerte de tu esposa.

Gracias, Padre. Ud. ha sido muy amable.

Me dice tu hija que Uds. piensan volver a la patria para enterrarla.

Sí. Milagros siempre ha querido ser enterrada allá... nunca se ha creído "americana".

Eso me sorprende. Me parecía que ya se había acostumbrado a la vida de los EE.UU.

La verdad es que se sentía harta de lo difícil que es ser hispano en este país.

¿A qué te refieres?

Pues, aquí hay que luchar por todo si es hispano. No importan ni los grados ni los títulos ni el dinero ni el poder hablar inglés. Si uno no parece "americano" o si habla inglés con acento hispano, lo consideran ciudadano de segunda clase.

Algunos, sí, miran de reojo a los que tengan otra manera de vivir pero hay americanos que tratan de comprenderlos.

Pero me da pena pensar en las muchas veces en que Milagros sufrió por ser trigueña. A veces me pregunto si hice bien en traerla aquí.

Digas lo que digas de lo que sufrió tu esposa, la querían mucho. ¡Cuántos han venido a despedirse de ella!

Es verdad que ha venido muchísima gente, tantos anglos como hispanos. Quisiera creer que todos se acordarán de lo buena que era.

458

¿Ha entendido bien?

1. ¿Dónde piensan enterrar a Milagros? ¿Por qué?
2. Según su esposo, ¿de qué se sentía harta a veces la difunta?
3. ¿Cómo describe el señor Padilla la vida de un hispano que vive en los Estados Unidos? ¿Cree Ud. que él tiene razón? Explique su respuesta.
4. Según el sacerdote, ¿cómo miran los "americanos" a los hispanos?
5. ¿Qué le da pena al señor Padilla? ¿Qué es lo que se pregunta?
6. ¿Cómo era la señora Padilla? ¿Cree Ud. que su esposo era más o menos trigueño que ella? Explique su respuesta.
7. ¿Qué dice el sacerdote para animar al señor Padilla?
8. ¿Tiene él algún remordimiento? ¿Cuál(es) es (son)?
9. ¿Ha sido Ud. víctima de prejuicio? ¿De qué manera?
10. ¿Cree Ud. que en su comunidad los "americanos" aceptan a los hispanos sin problema? Explique su respuesta.

INTRODUCTORY DIALOGUE: At the wake

The priest: Rafael, my deepest condolences on the death of your wife.

Mr. Padilla: Thank you, Father. You have been very kind.

P: Your daughter tells me that you're planning to return to your homeland to bury her.

Mr. P: Yes. Milagros has always wanted to be buried there . . . she has never felt (believed herself to be) American.

P: That surprises me. It seemed to me that she had already gotten used to life in the United States.

Mr. P: The truth is that she felt fed up with how difficult it is to be Hispanic in this country.

P: What are you talking about? (To what do you refer?)

Mr. P: Well, here one has to fight for everything if one is Hispanic. Neither degrees nor titles nor money nor being able to speak English matters. If one does not look "American" or if one speaks English with a Spanish accent, they consider you a second-class citizen.

P: Some *do* look down at those who have another way of living, but there are Americans who try to understand them.

Mr. P: But it pains me to think about the many times that Milagros suffered because of being dark-skinned. At times I ask myself if I did the right thing in bringing her here.

P: You may say what you want to about how your wife suffered, (but) many loved her. How many have come to say good-bye to her!

Mr. P: It is true that a lot of people have come, Anglos as well as Hispanics. I would like to believe that everyone will remember how good she was.

BASIC STRUCTURES I: How sad!

The social worker (f.)	*The client (m.)*
Mr. Lebrón, you seem (see yourself) very sad today. What has happened to you?	Well, ma'am, my dear wife died last week.
I don't believe it (you don't say to me)! I extend my deepest sympathy. Was it something sudden?	Yes, she had (suffered) a heart attack. I had her in my arms and I couldn't do anything to save her.
How sad! It must be very difficult for you. It is a tremendous loss.	Yes, ma'am, I am (find myself) so depressed and disoriented since the wake. I don't know what to do.
Are you a religious person?	Well, they baptized me as a Catholic, but I almost never go to church. My wife always went and prayed for the whole family.
Do you believe in God? religion? Catholicism? Spiritism?	I used to (before) have a lot of faith, but now it doesn't console me nor does it satisfy me. I know that this life is not all that there is, but now I don't have faith in any religion.
Would you like to speak to a minister? priest? rabbi? spiritist?	I would like to speak to someone who could help me to understand why I feel so disillusioned.
I know someone who can help you. Would you like me to call him?	It's fine, ma'am. I trust (have confidence) in you.

¿Sabe usted?

1. **¡No me diga!** expresses disbelief, **¡Qué pena!**, empathy for someone's sad news. **Darle pena (a alguien)** can mean *to cause someone sorrow* or *to embarrass someone.*

2. **Rezar** and **orar** both mean *to pray.* Una **plegaria** or **una oración** refers to *a prayer.*

3. A priest is also known as **un cura** or **un padre.** A preacher is called **un predicador,** from the verb **predicar** (*to preach*).

4. The word **fe** is the root for several derivatives dealing with trust:

fiarse de **confiar en**	to rely on, to trust	**ser de fiar**	trustworthy
		tener confianza en	to trust
confiado/a	trusting (person)	**tener confianza con**	to be on close terms with
confianza	faith, confidence		
en confianza	confidentially	**hacerle (a alguien)**	to confide in
confidencial	confidential	**confidencias**	(someone)

5. **Engañar** means *to deceive;* **desengañar,** the opposite, *to "undeceive"* (*set right*).

6. **Satisfacer** is derived from the same root as **hacer** and has all the same irregularities in its conjugation (e.g., **satisfago** = *I satisfy*).

460

ESTRUCTURAS BÁSICAS I: ¡Qué pena!

La trabajadora social	*El cliente*
Señor Lebrón, Ud. se ve muy triste hoy. ¿Qué le ha pasado?	Pues, señora, se murió mi querida esposa la semana pasada.
¡No me diga! Le doy mi más sentido pésame. ¿Fue algo repentino?	Sí, sufrió un ataque cardíaco. Yo la tenía en mis brazos y no pude hacer nada para salvarla.
¡Qué pena! Será muy difícil para Ud. Es una pérdida tremenda.	Sí, señora, me encuentro tan desanimado y desorientado desde el velorio. No se qué hacer.
¿Ud. es una persona religiosa?	Pues, me bautizaron católico, pero casi nunca voy a la iglesia. Mi esposa siempre iba y rezaba por toda la familia.
¿Cree Ud. en { Dios? la religión? el catolicismo? el espiritismo?	Yo antes tenía mucha fe, pero ahora no me consuela ni me satisface. Yo sé que esta vida no es todo lo que hay, pero ahora no me fío de ninguna religión.
¿Quisiera Ud. hablar con un { ministro? sacerdote? rabino? espiritista?	Me gustaría hablar con alquien que me pudiera ayudar a comprender por qué me siento tan desengañado.
Yo conozco a alguien que lo puede ayudar. ¿Quisiera que lo llamara?	Está bien, señora. Yo tengo confianza en Ud.

---

7. **Consolar (o-ue)** also means *to comfort;* the noun form is **el consuelo.**

8. Colloquially you may hear **¿Quisiera que lo *llame?*** instead of **llamara.**

Notas lingüísticas I

A. The future tense is often used to express conjecture, wonder, or probability about something in the *present;* it is the equivalent of **probablemente** + *present tense* and **deber** (*present tense*) + *infinitive* (*must* expressing probability).

Será difícil el cambio.
El cambio *debe ser* difícil.
El cambio *probablemente es* difícil.
} The change must be (probably is) difficult.

B. The past subjunctive is used when the main clause requiring the subjunctive mood in the subordinate clause contains a past verb, usually *preterite* or *imperfect.* It is formed from the *third person, plural* form of the *preterite* tense, dropping the **-on** and adding **-a, -amos, -as, -a, -an:**

hablar—hablar**on**: hablara, habláramos, hablaras, hablara, hablaran
vivir—vivier**on**: viviera, viviéramos, vivieras, viviera, vivieran
decir—dijer**on**: dijera, dijéramos, dijeras, dijera, dijeran

Do not confuse the *first and third person singular, past subjunctive forms* of **-ar** verbs with *the third person singular future form,* with an accented final **á.**

461

BASIC STRUCTURES II: Speaking about life and death

The spiritual counselor (m.)

Mr. Lebrón, the social worker told me that you feel very down and grief-stricken since your wife passed away.

Mr. Lebrón, you have to try to understand that it is natural to be so full of grief after one's wife dies (affecting him).

Listen to me well, Mr. Lebrón. You do not have the right to decide who will live or who will die. Everything is in God's hands.

Would you like to talk more about that?

She must have already forgiven you everything. It is you who have to forgive yourself.

If she were here right now, I know that she would tell you that she forgives you for everything.

Just (here) between us, Mr. Lebrón, you are going to get ill if you don't leave the past in peace.

Suicide doesn't resolve anything. It takes more courage to keep on living than to take one's life.

You have no other recourse (there is no other remedy) than to tell it to her now. Human relations do not end with the grave.

The client (m.)

Yes, it's true. I spend all day thinking about her. I wish I could die too.

Look, (you). Don't speak to me about what is or isn't natural. It should have been me (I) who died, not her (she).

But God has not been just. I am the sinner. She has always been so kind and understanding with me. And I hurt her and offended her so much.

No, they're private things between her and me. And she will never be able to forgive me for them. I don't deserve either her forgiveness or God's.

I would like to forget everything I made her suffer, but we wretches are condemned to go through hell here on earth.

She would have told me that a thousand times while she was living if I had asked her, but I couldn't do it. I am so egotistical and proud!

I'm telling you confidentially that it doesn't matter to me whether I live or die. If I weren't such a coward, I would kill myself.

If I had been braver, I would have told my wife how much I appreciated her and loved her.

I know one has to have faith, but it's so hard for me. I need a lot of help to believe. Can you help me?

¿Sabe usted?

1. **Pensar (e-ie)** literally means *to think* (in the intellectual sense), and *to plan to* when followed by the infinitive. **Pensar en** means *to think about someone or something* (*to have it on one's mind*). **Pensar de**, *to think of,* expresses *an opinion about someone or something*. **Creer** is more commonly used to express *a belief,* although it is commonly translated as *to think*.

El consejero espiritual

Señor Lebrón, me dijo la trabajadora social que Ud. se siente muy desanimado y desconsolado desde que falleció su esposa.

Señor Lebrón, tiene que tratar de comprender que es natural sentirse tan desolado después de que se le muere a uno la esposa.

Óigame bien, señor Lebrón. Ud. no tiene el derecho de decidir quien vivirá y quien morirá. Todo está en manos de Dios.

¿Quisiera hablar más de eso?

Ella ya le habrá perdonado todo. Es Ud. el que tiene que perdonarse.

Si ella estuviera aquí ahora mismo, yo sé que le diría que le perdona todo.

Acá entre nosotros, señor Lebrón, Ud. se va a enfermar si no deja en paz el pasado.

El suicidio no resuelve nada. Toma más valentía seguir viviendo que quitarse la vida.

No hay más remedio que decírselo ahora. Las relaciones humanas no terminan con la tumba.

El cliente

Sí, es verdad. Paso todo el día pensando en ella. Ojalá pudiera morir yo también.

Mire Ud. No me hable de lo que es o no es natural. Debiera haber sido yo el que murió, no ella.

Pero Dios no ha sido justo. Soy yo el pecador. Ella siempre ha sido tan buena y comprensiva conmigo. Y yo la herí y la ofendí tanto.

No, son cosas privadas, entre ella y yo. Y ella nunca me las podrá perdonar. Yo no merezco ni el perdón de ella ni el de Dios.

Me gustaría olvidarme de todo lo que la hice sufrir, pero los desgraciados estamos condenados a pasar por el infierno aquí en la tierra.

Me lo habría dicho mil veces mientras vivía si yo se lo hubiera pedido, pero no pude hacerlo. ¡Tan egoísta y orgulloso soy!

Le digo en toda confianza que no me importa si vivo o muero. Si no fuera tan cobarde, me mataría.

Si hubiera sido más valiente, le habría dicho a mi mujer cuánto la apreciaba y la quería.

Yo sé que hay que tener fe pero me es tan difícil. Necesito mucha ayuda para creer. ¿Puede Ud. ayudarme?

Yo no puedo *pensar.*
Pensamos volver a la Isla.
Sigo *pensando en* mi esposa.
¿Qué *piensa* Ud. *del* catolicismo?
Creía que tú venías hoy.

Creo que sí.

I can't think.
We plan to return to the island.
I'm still thinking about my wife.
What do you think of Catholicism?
I thought (believed) you were coming today.
I think (believe) so.

2. **Fallecer** is an equivalent of *to pass away;* it appears often in obituary listings and when speaking of the dead in a reverent way. **El/la difunto/a** is used as a noun referring to the deceased.

3. **Desolado/a, desconsolado/a,** and **afligido/a** all describe the state of being grief-stricken.

4. **Parecer** is the equivalent of *to seem;* **aparecer** means *to appear (physical presence);* **parecerse a** means *to resemble (someone, etc.).*

   Parece que no sufrió nada.   It seems that he didn't suffer at all.
   De repente, *apareció* Gilda.   Suddenly, Gilda appeared.
   Sara *se parece* mucho *a* mi mamá.   Sara looks a lot like my mom.

5. **Mire** and **oiga** are formal commands often used to get someone's attention, especially at the beginning of a sentence. **Óigame bien** emphasizes even more the importance of what follows. The equivalent **tú** command forms are **mira, oye,** and **óyeme bien.**

6. **Herir(e-ie)** is used to speak of inflicting either physical or emotional pain; **ofender** refers only to the latter. **Hacerle daño (a alguien)** is also used to describe something causing either great physical or emotional pain (**daño,** *harm, damage*). It is often used reflexively.

   Mi novia me *hirió* mucho.   My fiancée really hurt me.
   No te *ofendas,* papi.   Don't get hurt (upset), dad.
   ¿Se *hizo daño?*   Did you hurt yourself?

7. **No hay más remedio** is a useful phrase indicating that there is no alternative other than that being discussed.

Notas lingüísticas II

A.   The definite articles (**el, la, los, las**) are often used as pronouns followed by **de** or **que**; in this usage they are the equivalent of *that of, the one(s) with* (**de**), *the one(s) who, that* (**que**).

   No merezco ni el perdón de ella ni   I don't deserve her forgiveness, or
     el de Dios.   God's (that of God).
   La del vestido blanco es la hija del   The one with the white dress is the
     difunto.   deceased man's daughter.
   Los que no se perdonan no ten-   Those who don't forgive themselves
     drán perdón de Dios.   won't have God's forgiveness.

B.   The conditional tense describes what *would happen* in the future in a hypothetical situation. It is also the "future" of the past. It is formed by adding the endings of the *imperfect indicative* for **-er** and **-ir** verbs (**-ía, -ías, -ía, -íamos, -ían**) to the same stem used to form the *future indicative tense* (see Lesson 11). Here is the conjugation of **ser,** regular in the future and conditional, and **tener,** which has an irregular stem in these tenses.

	Future		Conditional	
yo	ser*é*	tendr*é*	ser*ía*	tendr*ía*
tú	ser*ás*	tendr*ás*	ser*ías*	tendr*ías*
Ud., él, ella	ser*á*	tendr*á*	ser*ía*	tendr*ía*
nosotros/as	ser*emos*	tendr*emos*	ser*íamos*	tendr*íamos*
Uds., ellos/as	ser*án*	tendr*án*	ser*ían*	tendr*ían*

Future of the present axis:
Ella dice que vendrá temprano.

She says she will come early.

Future of the past axis:
Ella dijo que vendría temprano.

She said she would come early.

Future hypothetical situation:
Yo no lo haría así.

I wouldn't do it that way.

C. Besides the *present perfect*, other common perfect tenses in the indicative mode are the *past perfect* (**pluscuamperfecto**), formed with the *imperfect* of **haber** and the *conditional perfect* formed with the *conditional of* **haber**. In the subjunctive mode, the most common are the *present perfect*, formed with the *present subjunctive* of **haber**, and the *past perfect*, formed with the *past subjunctive* of **haber**. Although you may not use them all, you should be able to understand them.

	INDICATIVE		SUBJUNCTIVE	
	Present Perfect			
yo	he		haya	
tú	has		hayas	
Ud., él, ella	ha	+ escrito	haya	+ escrito
nosotros/as	hemos		hayamos	
Uds., ellos/as	han		hayan	
	(I have written, you have written, etc.)			
	Past Perfect			
yo	había		hubiera	
tú	habías		hubieras	
Ud., él, ella	había	+ escrito	hubiera	+ escrito
nosotros/as	habíamos		hubiéramos	
Uds., ellos/as	habían		hubieran	
	(I had written, you had written, etc.)			
	Conditional Perfect			
yo	habría			
tú	habrías			
Ud., él, ella	habría	+ escrito		
nosotros/as	habríamos			
Uds., ellos/as	habrían			
	(I would have written, you would have written, etc.)			

D. An outline of the verb tense system in Spanish may be helpful in understanding how these new tenses relate to those you already know in both the indicative and subjunctive modes. It is organized around two principal points of reference, the *present axis,* which refers to the moment of speaking expressed by the *present* (or *present progressive*) tense, and the *past axis,* which refers to a specific point of time in the past, expressed by either the *preterite* or the *imperfect.* Each axis has both a future and past relative to these main reference points. In the following chart the time reference is indicated *above* the time line, the tense used to express it *below.* The verb **comer** is used as an example.

INDICATIVE   **SUBJUNCTIVE**

PRESENT AXIS

Past	Moment of speaking	Future	Past	Moment of speaking	Future
PRESENT PERFECT	**PRESENT** or **PRESENT PROGRESSIVE**	**FUTURE**	**PRESENT PERFECT**	**PRESENT**	**PRESENT**
he comido	*como* *estoy comiendo*	*comeré*	*haya comido*	*coma*	*coma*

PAST AXIS

Past	Reference point	Future	Past	Reference point	Future
PAST PERFECT	**PRETERITE** or **IMPERFECT**	**CONDITIONAL**	**PAST PERFECT**	**PAST**	**PAST**
había comido	*comí* *comía*	*comería*	*hubiera comido*	*comiera*	*comiera*

E. It is important to keep in mind the present and past axis when working with contexts that require the subjunctive in the subordinate clause.

1. A present-axis verb in the main clause that requires subjunctive in the dependent clause is followed by *present perfect subjunctive* when the *time* referred to in the dependent clause is *prior to* that in the main clause; *present subjunctive* is chosen if the *time* referred to in the dependent clause is *simultaneous to* or *after* that of the main clause:

Prior action:	*Present perfect subjunctive:*
Me alegro de que lo *hayas hecho*.	I'm happy that you did it.
Simultaneous action:	*Present subjunctive:*
Es natural que te *sientas* triste.	It's natural that you feel sad.
Future action:	*Present subjunctive:*
Quiero que *vuelvas* en dos semanas.	I want you to return in two weeks.

2. In colloquial usage, the *past subjunctive* is often used to express a *prior action* with a present axis verb in the indicative:

Me alegro de que me lo $\begin{cases}\text{dijeras.}\\\text{hayas dicho.}\end{cases}$　I'm glad you told me.

No me gusta que lo $\begin{cases}\text{haya hecho.}\\\text{hiciera.}\end{cases}$　I don't like that he did it.

3. A past-axis verb in the main clause that requires subjunctive in the dependent clause is followed by *past perfect subjunctive* when the *time* referred to in the dependent clause is *prior* to that in the main clause; *past subjunctive* is chosen if the *time* referred to in the dependent clause is *simultaneous to or after* that of the main clause:

Prior action:
No me gustó que lo *hubieras hecho.*

Past perfect subjunctive:
I didn't like your having done it.

Simultaneous action:
Era natural que te *sintieras* triste.

Past subjunctive:
It was natural that you felt sad.

Future action:
Quería que *volvieras* en dos semanas.

Past subjunctive:
I wanted you to return in two weeks.

F. Hypothetical situations are those that one speculates about, although they may not really take place. Certain types of hypothetical situations in the present and past employ the *past* and *past perfect* subjunctive verb tenses *nonsystematically* — that is, to specify *not* time sequence but rather *meaning*. Follow these guidelines in creating sentences to describe such situations and in understanding those described to you:

1. The hypothetical situation sets up a condition. It is expressed in a clause beginning with si or the conjunctions **en caso de que** (*in case*) or **con tal que** (*provided that*).

2. The result clause states the outcome of the fulfillment of the hypothetical situation.

3. Clauses beginning with **ojalá** and **como si** (*as if*) also describe hypothetical situations.

4. The types of hypothetical situations can be classified as those having:
   a. a 0 percent chance of fulfillment in the *past,* because they are contrary to what already happened.
   b. a 0 to 5 percent chance of fulfillment in the *present or future.*
   c. a 50 percent chance of fulfillment in the *present or future.*

5. The *past perfect subjunctive* is used nonsystematically to describe hypothetical situations in the *past* with a 0 percent chance of fulfillment; the *conditional perfect* is usually used in the result clause:

0% chance in past (contrary to what actually happened)	*Hypothetical clause* Past perfect subjunctive	*Result clause* Conditional perfect

Si me lo hubieras dicho, yo te lo habría arreglado.

If you had told me, I would have fixed it for you.

Con tal que te lo hubieran hecho, lo habrías terminado.

Provided they had done it, you would have finished it.

| Ojalá se lo hubiera dicho. | I wish I had told it to her. |
| Me mira como si me hubiera visto antes. | He looks at me as if he had seen me before. |

6. The *past subjunctive* is used nonsystematically to describe hypothetical situations in the *present or future* with a 0 to 5 percent chance of fulfillment. The *conditional* is used in the result clause:

0–5% chance in present or future	*Hypothetical clause* Past subjunctive	*Result clause* Conditional

Si lo hiciera, ella me ayudaría.	If I were to do it, she would help me. (I probably won't.)
Con tal que lo hicieran, podríamos salir hoy.	Provided they were to do it, we would be able to leave today. (They probably won't.)
Ojalá ella estuviera aquí.	I wish she were here. (She isn't.)
Tú hablas como si fueras hombre.	You're talking as if you were a man. (You're not.)

7. Objective hypothetical situations, those with a 50-50 chance of fulfillment, follow two patterns, depending on how the hypothetical clause begins:

a. si clauses introducing a 50-50 proposition are followed by *present indicative* (si is *never* followed by present subjunctive)

b. All other hypothetical clauses introduced by **en caso de que, ojalá,** or **como si** are followed by *present subjunctive*

c. The *result clause* of all 50-50 hypotheses usually contains a verb in the *future indicative*

50–50 chance in present or future	*Hypothetical clause* Si + Present indicative Others + Present subjunctive	*Result clause* Future

Si me dices la verdad, te ayudaré.	If you tell me the truth, I will help you.
En caso de que se sienta mal, no iremos hasta el viernes.	In case he feels bad, we won't go until Friday.
Ojalá que me lo traigan.	I hope they bring it to me.

8. Notice the different interpretations of **ojalá** according to the verb tense that follows it:

a. Hoping for something that can happen (present subjunctive)

b. Wishing for something in the *present* to be different than it really is (past subjunctive)

c. Wishing for something in the *past* to be different than it was (past perfect subjunctive)

9. The following chart summarizes those nonsystematic verb tenses in hypothetical situations:

		Hypothetical clause	*Result clause*
a.	50–50 chance in present or future	Si + Present indicative Others + Present subjunctive	Future
b.	0 to 5 percent chance in present or future	Past subjunctive	Conditional
c.	0 percent chance in past (contrary to what actually happened)	Past perfect subjunctive	Conditional perfect

PRÁCTICA PRELIMINAR

Follow general guidelines for self-instructional practice.

A. Translate the following expressions from Spanish to English.

1. ¡ ＿＿＿＿＿＿＿ (*Don't tell me*) Ud. que ha fallecido!

2. El espiritista es una persona ＿＿＿＿＿＿＿ (*trustworthy*).

3. Nunca he tenido ＿＿＿＿＿＿＿ (*much faith in*) el cura.

4. Ya sabe Ud. que puede ＿＿＿＿＿＿＿ (*rely on*) mí.

5. Quisiera ＿＿＿＿＿＿＿ (*confide in*) a Ud.

6. No ＿＿＿＿＿＿＿ (*fool yourself*) Ud.

7. Siempre ＿＿＿＿＿＿＿ (*I think about*) mi mamá.

8. Tu hija ＿＿＿＿＿＿＿ (*looks like*) tu esposo.

9. ¿Qué ＿＿＿＿＿＿＿ (*do you think of*) la nueva consejera? (*tú*)

10. Si Ud. quiere, puedo hablar con el juez. Yo ＿＿＿＿＿＿＿ (*am on good terms with*) él.

11. Mi esposo me ＿＿＿＿＿＿＿ (*hurt*) mucho la semana pasada.

12. ＿＿＿＿＿＿＿ (*There's no other alternative*) que tratar de animarse.

A 1. No me diga 2. de fiar; de confianza 3. mucha confianza en 4. fiarse de; confiar en 5. hacerle confidencias 6. se engañe 7. pienso en 8. se parece a 9. piensas de 10. tengo confianza con 11. hirió; ofendió 12. No hay más remedio

B. Give the indicated forms of the verbs.

| | | Indicative | | Subjunctive | |
		Future	Conditional	Present perfect	Past
(ella)	tener	*tendré*	*tendría*	*haya tenido*	*tuviera*
1. (yo)	venir				
2. (Uds.)	estar				
3. (él)	morir				
4. (yo)	decir				
5. (Ud.)	dar				
6. (nosotros)	hacer				
7. (ella)	ir				
8. (ellos)	ser				
9. (tú)	saber				
10. (yo)	querer				
11. (tú)	poder				

C. Change each sentence in the following short dialogues from the present to the past.

Ejemplo: Quiero hacerlo antes de que vengan.
          Quería hacerlo antes de que vinieran.
          Es imposible hacerlo.
          Era imposible hacerlo.

1. *El doctor:* Es posible que muera pronto.
    La enfermera: No hay más remedio que decírselo a la familia.
2. *La cliente:* Todavía no he visto al médico.
    La espiritista: No me gusta que no lo hayas visitado.
3. *El cliente:* Si ella me perdonara, estaría contento.
    El consejero: Si le hablara, te perdonaría.
4. *El abogado:* No me fío de que lo hagan.
    La cliente: Me dicen que lo harán.

B 1. vendré; vendría; haya venido; viniera 2. estarán; estarían; hayan estado; estuvieran 3. morirá; moriría; haya muerto; muriera 4. diré; diría; haya dicho; dijera 5. dará; daría; haya dado; diera 6. haremos; haríamos; hayamos hecho; hiciéramos 7. irá; iría; haya ido; fuera 8. serán; serían; hayan sido; fueran 9. sabrás; sabrías; hayas sabido; supieras 10. querré; querría; haya querido; quisiera 11. podrás; podrías; hayas podido; pudieras

C 1. Era posible que muriera pronto. No había más remedio que decírselo a la familia. 2. Todavía no había visto al médico. No me gustaba que no lo hubieras visitado. 3. Si ella me hubiera perdonado, habría estado contento. Si le hubiera hablado, te habría perdonado. 4. No me fiaba de que lo hicieran. Me dijeron que lo harían.

D. Choose the verb form that is needed by context.

Ejemplo: Era imposible que ella lo (sabría (supiera) sabía).

1. El médico me dijo que (coma comiera comería) menos para poder recuperarme.

2. Si yo (fuera sería era) más valiente, yo le diría la verdad.

3. Buscábamos un médico que (dominaba dominará dominara) el español.

4. Es verdad que mi esposa (era fuera sea) respetada por muchos.

5. Queríamos regresar a la Isla antes de que (teníamos tuviéramos tengamos) hijos.

6. Lo más importante es que (tengas tuvieras tendrás) confianza en mí.

7. Era natural que yo lo (ayudaba ayude ayudara) con sus problemas.

8. El sacerdote quería que (volvemos volviéramos volvamos) en dos semanas.

9. Yo te lo dije para que (comprendes comprendas comprendieras) algo del pasado.

10. Vivimos con mi familia hasta que (tuvimos tuviéramos tenemos) suficiente dinero para comprarnos una casa.

E. Choose the result clause in the left-hand column that best completes each hypothetical situation.

1. Si no toma la medicina,
2. Si la conociera mejor,
3. Si me lo hubieran dicho,
4. Si ellos estuvieran vivos,
5. Si le parece bien,
6. Si yo fuera tu médico,

a. me lo perdonarían todo.
b. puedo hacerlo esta noche.
c. no se va a mejorar.
d. la invitaría a la fiesta.
e. te operaría.
f. los habría podido ayudar.

F. Give the form of *haber* needed to complete each sentence.

Ejemplo: Yo nunca la _____ visto antes de anoche.

1. Yo no _____ visto al sacerdote desde ayer.

2. El padre me dijo que todavía no _____ podido hablar con la trabajadora social.

3. Yo no me di cuenta de que Uds. todavía no la _____ visitado.

D 1. comiera 2. fuera 3. dominara 4. era 5. tuviéramos 6. tengas 7. ayudara 8. volviéramos 9. comprendieras 10. tuvimos
E 1. c 2. d 3. f 4. a 5. b 6. e
F 1. he 2. había 3. habían

4. Me da pena que sus padres _____ muerto.

5. Si ellos me lo _____ pedido anoche, yo se lo _____ dado con mucho gusto.

6. No comprendo cómo tú lo _____ hecho tan rápido.

7. ¿ _____ tenido Ud. problemas de salud anteriormente?

8. Ojalá yo lo _____ sabido antes.

9. Siento mucho que no _____ más remedio.

10. Si no _____ llamado, tendrán una buena razón.

G. Write the appropriate verb form needed by the context of each sentence.

1. **estar**

Desde la muerte de su esposa, mi hermano _____ desconso-lado. Sigue hablando de ella como si todavía _____ viva. Me da pena porque él _____ tan desolado. Me alegro de que _____ pensando hablar con el sacerdote esta semana.

2. **venir**

Ayer me llamó mi hermano para decirme que _____ a visi-tarme en julio. Me gustaría más si _____ en junio cuando me hija se casa. La última vez que mi hermano _____ a nuestra casa fue en 1984 para el bautismo de su sobrino. No es seguro, pero es posible que también _____ sus dos hijos.

3. **ser**

Ojalá que yo _____ hombre. Los hombres _____ los dueños de la tierra. Siempre me ha parecido injusto que ellos _____ los que mandan. Me gustaría que yo _____ igual a ellos.

F 4. hayan 5. hubieran, habría 6. has 7. Ha 8. hubiera 9. haya 10. han
G 1. ha estado; estuviera; está; esté 2. vendría; viniera; vino; vengan 3. fuera; son; sean; fuera

4. **satisfacer**

Yo nunca he podido ＿＿＿＿＿＿ a mi mamá. Cuando yo creo que

la he ＿＿＿＿＿＿ , siempre estoy equivocada. Yo creo que no hay nada

que la ＿＿＿＿＿＿ . No tengo la menor idea de lo que la ＿＿＿＿＿＿

en el pasado.

5. **pedir**

Ayer fui a un restaurante chino y ＿＿＿＿＿＿ un plato especial.

Pero cuando me trajeron la comida no era lo que yo ＿＿＿＿＿＿ . Se lo

dije al camarero (*waiter*) y él me preguntó qué ＿＿＿＿＿＿ . La próxima

vez que yo vaya a un restaurante chino ＿＿＿＿＿＿ un plato más fácil

de pronunciar.

H. Translate the following sentences to English.
1. ¿Qué hora será?
2. Ojalá que tengas suerte.
3. Me enojaba de que lo supieras.
4. ¿Dónde estará el ministro?
5. Yo nunca lo habría dicho.
6. Habla como si fuera sacerdote.
7. No había más remedio que llamarla.
8. Yo la haría si tuviera tiempo.

I. Translate the following sentences to Spanish.
1. I wonder who it is.
2. What would you (*tú*) do?
3. I was planning to visit her.
4. I wanted her to know.
5. There was nothing I could do.
6. You (*Ud.*) are probably tired.
7. She hurt (harmed) herself.
8. I'm happy they arrived.

G 4. satisfacer; satisfecho; satisfaga; haya satisfecho 5. pedí; había pedido; había pedido; pediré

H 1. I wonder what time it is. 2. I hope you're lucky. 3. I was angry that you knew it. 4. I wonder where the minister is. 5. I never would have said it. 6. He speaks as if he were a priest. 7. There was no other recourse than to call her. 8. I would do it if I had time.

I 1. ¿Quién será? 2. ¿Qué harías tú? 3. Pensaba visitarla. 4. Quería que ella lo supiera. 5. No había nada que pudiera hacer. 6. Estará (debe estar) cansado/a. 7. Se hizo daño. 8. Me alegro de que hayan llegado.

Combinándolo todo

PRÁCTICA COMUNICATIVA: Consejos espirituales

Conversación parcial

Practique Ud. oralmente la conversación siguiente. Cada raya (/) implica que falta una palabra. Es necesario conjugar cada verbo *en bastardillas.*

El empleado	*La señora Gómez*
1. Ud. / *ver* muy desanimada / que *fallecer* / esposo.	Pues, / *encontrar* muy / desde / velorio.
2. Ud. *tener* / comprender / *ser* natural sentirse / .	Sí, / *saber;* pero *querer* / mejor.
3. / esposa y yo / *dar* nuestro / pésame, señora.	Gracias, muy / . Mi esposo *ser* / santo.
4. ¿ / qué / *morir* su esposo?	/ *morir* / cáncer / estómago.
5. ¡ / pena! *Ser* muy / para Ud.	Sí, / *ser.* A mí / gustaría hablar con / que me *poder* ayudar.
6. ¿Quisiera Ud. / yo *llamar* / sacerdote?	Pues, no *saber.* Es que no / *fiar* / la religión.
7. Antes, Ud. / *fiar* mucho / el catolicismo.	Sí, pero ahora no / *consolar.*
8. No / más remedio / hablar / confianza con / .	Ojalá / *tener* más / en Dios. Eso / *ayudar* antes.

Pregunte Ud.

Ud. se encuentra en el velorio de la esposa de Juan López, uno de sus clientes. Dé Ud. oralmente las preguntas necesarias en la siguiente conversación con él.

1. Sí, fue repentino. Murió en un accidente.

2. Sí, señor/a, ha sido una pérdida tremenda para mí.

3. Sí, he pensado en matarme en tres ocasiones.

4. No, no me fío mucho de la religión.

5. No, no quisiera hablar con el sacerdote.

6. No me consuela ni me satisface la religión católica.

7. Me gustaría hablar con alguien con quien tuviera confianza.

8. Sufro mucho porque sé que la había herido muchas veces.

9. Si estuviera viva, ella me diría que me había perdonado.

10. Ojalá que pudiera verla una vez más para pedirle perdón.

Dígalo

Pregúntele a un/a compañero/a lo que le diga su profesor/a sobre los temas de la fe religiosa, la confianza, el desengaño, y las situaciones hipotéticas.

Escuche bien

A. Ud. oirá a diez clientes que hablan de cosas importantes de la vida. Escriba Ud.:
A—si el/la cliente tiene un problema espiritual
B—si el/la cliente parece tener fe
C—si el/la cliente no se refiere a su fe espiritual

1. _____	4. _____	7. _____
2. _____	5. _____	8. _____
3. _____	6. _____	9. _____

B. Ud. oirá a nueve clientes hablando de situaciones hipotéticas. Escriba Ud.:
A—si existe una posibilidad de *50-50* que se cumpla
B—si sólo existe el *0-5%* de posibilidad de que se cumpla en el presente o en el futoro
C—si se refiere a una situación hipotética del pasado, con el *0%* de posibilidad de cumplirse

1. _____	4. _____	7. _____
2. _____	5. _____	8. _____
3. _____	6. _____	9. _____

Diálogos cortos

I. *Una vecina*   *La esposa del difunto*

(En el velorio)

Ay, _____ Meléndez. Mi   Gracias, señora. ¡Qué pena me da!

más _____ pésame.

También _____ mí. Su   Sí, lo era. Tal vez fuera demasiado bueno.

esposo _____ un hombre
muy bueno.

No entiendo qué quiere   Pues, él siempre pensaba en los otros y
_____ "demasiado   nunca en sí mismo. Por eso murió a una
bueno".   edad tan joven.

Una vecina

La esposa del difunto

_____ , señora. Nadie sabe cuándo es _____ de morir.

Sí, Ud. tiene razón. Tal vez a Dios le hiciera falta un hombre bueno.

Seguramente su _____ está _____ Dios ahora y puede _____ por toda la familia.

Puede ser. Pero, hablando en confianza, yo no sé cómo puedo vivir sin él.

Pues, señora, no _____ más remedio que aprender _____ hacerlo. Yo la ayudaré.

Gracias, señora. Ud. siempre ha sido muy buena con nosotros.

II. *El trabajador social*

Rafael Santiago

Rafael, ¿ _____ estás? Hace mucho que no nos _____ .

Pues, Sr. Ríos, no estoy muy bien.

¿Qué te _____ , Rafi?

Me siento muy desengañado. Hace seis meses que busco empleo y no he encontrado nada.

¿Qué tipo de trabajo _____ buscado?

De todas clases. Pero cuando la gente me ve, yo creo que sólo ve a un trigueño y no a una persona.

Entonces, ¿tú crees que no _____ podido encontrar _____ por el racismo?

Sí, señor. Yo he hablado con muchas personas y todos me miran como si fuera un ser inferior.

Puede _____ tu imaginación.

Tal vez. Sin embargo, yo sé que el prejuicio es bastante fuerte en este país.

Pero, no hay más _____ que seguir luchando (*fighting*).

Sí, es verdad. ¿Ud. me puede ayudar?

Ayude al cliente

You have been Reinaldo Esquival's spiritual counselor for the last six months. He has decided to return to Mexico because his mother is very ill. He would like to continue counseling with his parish priest there, el Padre Rodríguez. Write a letter to Padre Rodríguez, beginning it as usual.

1. Tell him your name and your occupation, and explain your relationship with Reinaldo, mentioning the length of time you've been working with him.

2. Mention that Reinaldo is a very trustworthy person but that right now he is feeling very disillusioned. State that he seems to have lost his faith in God since his wife died last August.

3. State that Reinaldo feels that he has suffered a great deal in the United States because of the color of his skin. Mention that he has told you many times that his life would be better off if he were white. State that in his last visit to your office he said to you, "I wish I had never come to the United States."

4. End the letter by stating that you think that Reinaldo would be happier if he were living in his homeland again. Tell Padre Rodríguez to write you if he has any questions.

5. Close the letter as usual and sign your name.

¿Comprende Ud.?

Escuche bien a las cuatro personas que hablan de sus creencias espirituales. Escriba Ud.:

A—si la persona expresa fe en una religión de la tradición cristiana o judía;
B—si expresa fe en creencias de otro tipo

Después, escriba los factores que hayan influído en su decisión sobre qué creencias tiene cada uno.

	Tipo de creencia	*Factores que influyeron en su decisión*
1.	_____	_____
		_____
2.	_____	_____
		_____
3.	_____	_____
		_____
4.	_____	_____
		_____

Piénselo

Prepárese para poder hablar con el/la profesor/a o con otros estudiantes sobre los siguientes temas, contestando las preguntas que le sugiera el/la profesor/a.

1. Las costumbres del velorio

2. La religión de hoy día

3. El ser "diferente" en los Estados Unidos

4. La vida del más allá

SITUACIONES DE LA VIDA REAL

Imagínese

1. ¿Cómo se llama este señor?
2. ¿Cómo se siente hoy?
3. ¿Por qué se siente así?
4. ¿Qué quisiera Ud. decirle al señor para consolarlo?
5. ¿Cree Ud. que este señor es una persona religiosa? Explique.
6. ¿Tendrá el señor una familia grande?
7. ¿Dónde estará la esposa de él?
8. ¿Cree Ud. que este señor tiene mucha fe? Explique.

**EXAMEN DE CONCIENCIA
ANTES DE LA CONFESIÓN
LOS 7 PECADOS CAPITALES:**
Soberbia, Pereza, Avaricia,
Lujuria, Ira, Gula, y Envidia
**VIRTUDES
BUENAS OBRAS**
Los principales pecados contra los
Mandamientos de la Ley de Dios son:

EL PRIMERO: Negar, dudar alguna verdad de la fe; hablar mal de la religión, sacerdotes, etc.; avergonzarse de practicar la religión; asistir al culto protestante, sesiones espiritistas; creer en supersticiones; recibir mal algún sacramento, como la Confesión, la Comunión.

EL SEGUNDO: Blasfemar, quejarse, maldecir contra Dios y los Santos; jurar sin necesidad, o con mentira; jurar hacer una cosa mala; hacer votos sin cumplirlos.

EL TERCERO: Faltar por su propia culpa a Misa los domingos y días de guardar; llegar tarde; trabajar los domingos sin necesidad.

EL CUARTO: Desobedecer a los padres; faltarles respeto; desearles mal; negarles el sustento. No educar a los hijos cristianamente; darles mal ejemplo; malgastar el sueldo necesario para el sostén de la familia.

EL QUINTO: Maldecir a otros; odiarles; pelearse; vengarse; beber hasta embriagarse; intentar suicidarse. Enseñar, aconsejar el mal a otros.

EL SEXTO Y EL NOVENO: Deleitarse en pensamientos, deseos, conversaciones, miradas, lecturas, espectáculos deshonestos; hacer cosas deshonestas a solas o con otra persona; evitar la prole. Faltas en el comportamiento entre los esposos.

EL SÉPTIMO Y EL DÉCIMO: Robar; dañar a otro en sus bienes; engañar en los negocios; jugar con trampas. Desear robar o negociar mal.

EL OCTAVO: Mentir; juzgar mal de otros; revelar secretos; repetir chismes; murmurar, calumniar; dar falso testimonio.

Los principales pecados contra los Mandamientos de la Santa Madre Iglesia son: Comer carne los viernes y demás días de abstinencia; no guardar los ayunos; no confesarse a lo menos una vez al año; no comulgar durante el tiempo Pascual; no contribuir para los gastos de la Iglesia; casarse a lo civil o a lo protestante.

ACTO DE CONTRICIÓN

¡Oh, Dios mío! Con todo mi corazón me pesa de haberte ofendido; aborrezco todos mis pecados por el miedo de perder el cielo y merecer el infierno; pero más me pesa haberte ofendido porque eres infinitamente bueno y digno de ser amado. Firmemente resuelvo con la ayuda de Tu gracia, confesar mis pecados, hacer penitencia y enmendar mi vida. *Amén.*

1. ¿Cuáles son los siete pecados capitales?
2. ¿Comprende Ud. lo que quiere decir cada uno de ellos?
3. ¿Cuántos mandamientos de la ley de Dios hay?
4. ¿Cree Ud. que asistir a una sesión espiritista es un pecado? Explique.
5. ¿Cómo puede una persona pecar contra el segundo mandamiento?
6. ¿Contra qué mandamiento es pecado trabajar los domingos sin necesidad?
7. ¿Cree Ud. que es pecado engañar en los negocios? ¿Puede Ud. dar un ejemplo?
8. ¿Qué cree Ud. que quiere decir *chismes* en la discusión del octavo mandamiento?
9. ¿Qué quiere decir *deshonesto* en la discusión del sexto y noveno mandamientos?
10. ¿Todavía es pecado en la religión católica comer carne los viernes?
11. ¿Sabía Ud. que en la religión católica es pecado casarse por lo civil?
12. ¿Qué sentimientos se expresan en el acto de contrición?

¿Por qué?

Si no estás contento de ti,
    ¿quién lo estará?

Si no sientes orgullo por lo que haces,
    ¿quién lo sentirá?

Si no tienes respeto por tus acciones,
    ¿quién lo tendrá?

Si no sientes admiración por lo que emprendes,
    ¿quién la sentirá?

Si no das crédito a tus decisiones,
    ¿quién se fiará de ellas?

Si eres capaz de engañarte a ti mismo,
    ¿a quién no engañarás?

Si aún no has aprendido el verbo comprender,
    ¿cómo pretendes conjugar el verbo amar?

Si pones hiel en las más puras emociones,
    ¿por qué te quejas de llevar una vida amarga?

Si destruyes todos los caminos que te traen afecto,
    ¿por qué lamentas la soledad en que vives?

Si oscilas entre el pasado y el futuro,
    ¿cómo puedes disfrutar el presente?

Si no te dispones a perdonar las faltas ajenas,
    ¿con qué derecho esperas perdón para las
    tuyas?

Si nunca te decides a partir,
    ¿por qué ansías tanto llegar?

¿Por qué?

1. ¿Ha entendido bien todas las palabras del poema? ¿Cuáles no ha entendido?
2. ¿Qué quiere decir *orgullo*? ¿Es Ud. una persona orgullosa?
3. ¿Es Ud. capaz de engañarse? Explique.
4. ¿Ud. se cree una persona contenta? Explique.
5. ¿Oscila Ud. entre el pasado y el futuro o vive en el presente? Dé Ud. ejemplos.
6. ¿Ud. se dispone a perdonar las faltas "ajenas"(*de otros*)?
7. ¿Tiene Ud. respeto por sus acciones? Explique.
8. ¿Se queja Ud. de llevar una vida amarga (*bitter*)?
9. ¿Es Ud. una persona sentimental? ¿De qué manera?
10. ¿Cree Ud. que este poema dice la verdad? Explique.

1. ¿Quién murió?
2. ¿Cuántos años tenía?
3. ¿De qué murió?
4. ¿Tenía una familia grande?
5. ¿Tenía muchas amistades el/la difunto/a?
6. ¿Qué tipo de persona era?
7. ¿Qué sentimientos experimenta la familia?
8. En los Estados Unidos, entierran a un difunto de la misma manera que se ve en la foto? ¿Cuáles son las diferencias?
9. ¿Cree Ud. que en la cultura norteamericana se acepta fácilmente la muerte? Explique.
10. Cuándo Ud. se muera, ¿qué tipo de entierro quisiera?

Haciendo el papel

1. Ud. está aconsejando a la señora María Carrera de Rodríguez. Su esposo murió la semana pasada. Consulte Ud. el siguiente obituario de su esposo para saber más de ella. Ya sabe que tiene cuarenta y cinco años y ahora tiene que criar sola a su familia. También tiene que dirigir la pequeña compañía que era de su esposo. Naturalmente, ella se siente afligida y desorientada. ¿Cómo la puede ayudar?

HA FALLECIDO
Fernando Alt. Ureña Rodríguez
(Coronel Retirado P.N.)

Su esposa: María Carrera hoy Vda. Rodríguez; sus hijos: Ramón José, Dra. Irene María, Juliana, Rafael y demás familiares y amigos pasan por la pena de participar su sentido fallecimiento. Al mismo tiempo invitan al acto del sepelio que se llevará a cabo hoy a las 5:00 P. M., en el Cementerio Cristo Redentor. Su cadáver está siendo velado en la Capilla La Altagracia.

"Sólo nos resta desear a aquéllos que mataron a nuestro padre FERNANDO ALTAGRACIA UREÑA RODRÍGUEZ, que algún día puedan vivir una hora de bondad y amor como vivió en vida él".

---

2. Ud. es un médico que ha dado a un nuevo paciente, el señor Simeón Espinosa, un reconocimiento físico. Las pruebas no indican ninguna causa fisiológica que expliquen los síntomas que experimenta. Sin embargo, el señor Espinosa sigue quejándose de cansancio, dolores de cabeza, insomnio y debilidad general. Ud. cree que los síntomas son una reacción a la muerte repentina de su hija en enero. Ayúdelo a hablar de sus sentimientos para que lo pueda referir a un consejero que se especialice en estos asuntos.

3. Su cliente, Alicia Sánchez, tiene mucha confianza en Ud. Mientras Ud. le habla de otra cosa, ella le enseña el siguiente anuncio de una consejera síquica que se llama la Profesora Nirvana. Ella le pide a Ud. su opinión sobre la posibilidad de recibir ayuda de la Profesora Nirvana con sus problemas emocionales. Ud. sabe que Alicia se fía mucho en Dios y que también tiene mucho interés en los fenómenos síquicos. Le ha sido difícil aceptar el suicidio de su hijo Ricardo y ella cree que la Profesora Nirvana le puede dar más información sobre su muerte. ¿Qué le aconseja Ud.?

REFLEJOS DE LA CULTURA: "El norte"

The experience of leaving one's homeland to begin anew in a foreign country with different cultural mores is never easy. Although culture shock may be viewed as an opportunity for growth, the stress it produces in the individual with a foot in each of two different cultures is still painful. The toll it takes on personal integrity is often devastating. Yet immigration continues as long as the promise of a better life beckons to those who seek to survive economic and/or political repression in their native land.

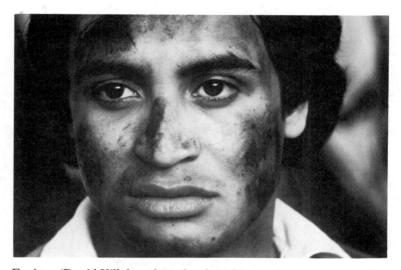

Enrique (David Villalpando), a hard-working and earnest young Guatemalan, is driven by fate to embark on an odyssey to the north, in a scene from *El Norte*. From Cinecom International Films and Island Alive. Copyright © 1983 Cinecom International Films.

The film, *El norte,* was written by Anna Thomas and Gregory Nava (he also directed it). Produced by Island Alive and Independent Productions, it poignantly describes the side effects of immigration that are experienced by a Guatemalan brother and sister, Enrique and Rosa. Seeking to escape from political repression in their homeland, these two young Hispanics journey through Mexico without visas or passports, finding their way to Los Angeles by eluding the vigilant *Migra* (U.S. Department of Immigration) with the help of a *coyote.*

Their eagerness to adapt to their new environment continues throughout the film, despite traumatic living conditions, denunciation to the *Migra,* and a crisis in which Enrique must choose between personal success according to Anglo values and family loyalty so important in Hispanic cultures.

The following excerpts from the script highlight the dreams and fears, and the joys and sorrows of these two young people. Despite setbacks, the eternal optimism common to those who struggle to survive against tremendous odds as strangers in a new land shines through. Common Central American dialectal expressions, including the verb forms using *vos* are italicized. Other regionalisms such as the use of adjectives made more intensive by the prefix *re-* (*rechulo, reduro*) and slang expressions such as *pisto* (*money*) are also indicated. Translation is based on the English subtitles used in the film, and, at times, is not the literal equivalent of the Spanish.

Scene: *Rosa and Enrique in their village in Guatemala after the murders of their parents, as they consider fleeing for their lives.*

Enrique	¡Rosa! ¿Qué estás haciendo?	Rosa! What are you doing?
Rosa	Me voy con *vos*.	I'm going with you.
Enrique	¿Con las cosas tan *rejodidas* como están? Y *vos sos* mujer, hombre!	With things the way they are now? And you're a woman.
Rosa	Y *vos sos* hombre, pues. Acaso no matan a los dos igual por aquí.	And you're a man. They kill them both the same here.
Enrique	Pero es peligrosísimo. Ramón dice que es como la guerra. Pero a lo mejor no paso. Y ahora *con vos* . . . ?	But it's so dangerous. Ramón says it's like war. I probably won't make it. And now with you . . . ?
Rosa	Es que no hay otro modo, Enrique. ¿Acaso *vos creís* que cuando regresen los soldados a mí, no me van a agarrar? Yo tengo miedo, Enrique, mucho miedo.	There's no other way, Enrique. When the soldiers come back they'll take me. I'm afraid, Enrique, I'm so afraid.
Enrique	¿Pero y el *pisto pa'* (para) pasar? ¿Y tu novio?	But the money? We don't have enough. And your sweetheart?
Rosa	Las cosas de antes acabaron, Enrique. . . .	The past is gone forever, Enrique. . . .
Enrique	*Oís*, vamos a vivir. Y en el norte ya no nos seguirán jodiendo. Ya no aguantamos el abuso. Y ganaremos mucho *pisto*. Vamos a tener todo lo que deseamos. Y regresaremos — y algún dia regresaremos. Ya vamos a tener buena suerte. ¡*Estáte* segura!	We're going to live! And in the north we won't be treated this way. We'll make a lot of money. We'll have everything we want. And we'll return one day. We'll have good luck now. I'm sure of it.

Scene: *Settled in Los Angeles, Enrique has been promoted from busboy to waiter's assistant.*

Enrique	¡Rosa, mírame!	Look at me!
Rosa	¿Qué pasó? Pero estás *rechulo*.	What happened? You look wonderful.
Enrique	Me promovieron, que le dicen. Viste tú, Rosa. ¡Me estoy volviendo gente importante. . . .	I've been promoted. See — I'm becoming somebody important. . . .
Rosa	Estoy muy orgullosa de tí, Enrique — muy orgullosa.	I'm so proud of you, Enrique — very proud.

Rosa, (Zaide Silvia Gutierrez) compliments Enrique (David Villalpando), her brother, in a scene from *El Norte*. From Cinecom International Films and Island Alive. Copyright © 1983 Cinecom International Films.

Enrique Rosa, te voy a contar algo que mi papá me dijo antes de que se muriera. Me dijo que para los ricos todos los campesinos son tan sólo un par de brazos. Pero el quería que yo fuera algo más. Quería que todos supieran que era un hombre — todo un hombre con alma y corazón.

Rosa, I'm going to tell you something that my father told me before he died. He told me that for the rich all peasants are just a pair of arms (to do their work). But he wanted me to be something more. He wanted everyone to know that I was a man — a man complete with a soul and a heart.

¡Y mírame ahora! La gente me mirará y me respetará. En este país se trabaja *reduro,* pero también llegas a ser alguien. Te dije, Rosita — las cosas se compondrían para nosotros. Hemos tenido tiempos muy difíciles pero mira *nomás* ahora — ya nada puede regresarnos, ahora. Nada.

Look at me now! People will see me and respect me. In this country you work hard, but you can get to be somebody. I told you, Rosita — things would work out for us. We've had some very hard times but look now — nothing can stop us now. Nothing.

Scene: *Nacha, a friend of Rosa's, frantically searches for Enrique to tell him of his sister's serious illness just as he is about to leave for Chicago and the chance for legal immigration status in a well-paying job. He must leave tonight in order to get the post.*

Enrique ¡Nacha!

Nacha!

Nacha Gracias a Dios que te encontré, Enrique. Tienes que venir conmigo inmediatamente. ¡Ven!

Thank God I found you! You've got to come with me immediately. Come on!

Enrique	¿Qué pasa?	What's going on?
Nacha	¡Rosa está en el hospital!	Rosa's in the hospital!
Enrique	¿Qué tiene?	What's wrong?
Nacha	No sé. Se puso mal ahora en la mañana y el doctor me mandó que te viniera a traer. ¡Tienes que venir conmigo inmediatamente!	I don't know. She got sick in the morning and the doctor sent me to come to get you. You have to come with me right now!
Enrique	Pero, precisamente ahora no puedo.	But, I just can't go right now.
Nacha	¿Por qué?	Why?
Enrique	Tengo que viajar. Me voy a Chicago — tengo que irme hoy en la noche.	I've got to travel. I'm going to Chicago — I have to leave tonight.
Nacha	¿Pero qué estás diciendo? ¿Qué, estás loco? ¡Rosa está en el hospital!	What are you saying? Are you crazy? Rosa is in the hospital!
Enrique	Cuídala tú, Nacha. Se compondrá — sé que se curará. Yo llamo en cuanto llegue. Nacha, debo ir. ¡No tengo trabajo! No tengo mucho tiempo. Debo irme ahorita. Nacha, cuídala, por favor.	You take care of her, Nacha. She'll get better — I know she'll get better. I'll call as soon as I arrive. Nacha, I must go. I don't have a job! I don't have much time. I must go right now. Nacha, take care of her, please.
Nacha	No puedo creerlo, Enrique. El médico me ha dicho que te encuentre. Rosa está grave y puede morirse. ¡Escucha, Enrique! ¡Se puede morir! ¿Qué no me estás oyendo?	I can't believe it. The doctor told me to find you. Rosa could die. Listen to me! She could die!
Enrique	¡Déjame solo! ¡Déjame!	Leave me alone! Leave me!
Nacha	Está bien. Rosa se puede morir pero tú ya estás muerto.	All right. Rosa may be dying — but you — are already dead.

Scene: *Enrique is at Rosa's bedside in the hospital. Rosa awakens briefly from her delirium.*

Rosa	En sueños, sentí mucho miedo, Enrique. Sentí como aquel día en San Pedro cuando creí que nunca volverías. Pero al despertar, tú estabas aquí, conmigo.	In my dreams, I felt afraid. I felt like that day in San Pedro when I thought you would never come back. But when I woke up you were here, with me.
Enrique	Claro que sí. Tú eres la única familia que tengo. Tenemos que estar siempre juntos.	Of course. You're the only family I have. We have to stay together.

Rosa	La vida aquí es muy difícil, Enrique. ¿No somos libres, verdad? ¿Verdad que no somos libres, Enrique?	Life here is very hard, Enrique. We're not free. Isn't it true that we're not free?
Enrique	Sí, es difícil la vida aquí. Es cierto. Hay que trabajar muy duro.	Yes, life is difficult here. You have to work very hard.
Rosa	En nuestra tierra no hay lugar para nosotros. Nos quieren matar. No hay lugar allí para nosotros. En México solo hay pobreza — tampoco hay lugar para nosotros. Y aquí en el norte, no somos aceptados, pues.	In our own land we have no home. They want to kill us. There's no home for us there. In Mexico there is only poverty — we can't make a home there either. And here in the north, we aren't accepted.
	¿Cuándo vamos a encontrar un lugar, Enrique? Tal vez sólo muertos encontramos un lugarcito.	When will we find a home, Enrique? Maybe when we die we'll find a home.
Enrique	No digas eso, Rosita. Es difícil, pero ya vamos a tener mucha suerte. Y ahora sí vamos a tener todo lo que queremos. Y vamos a ganar mucho *pisto*. Y vamos a regresar al pueblo. Y cuando nos pasemos por las calles, la gente nos va a mirar con envidia. Las cosas están cambiando. Sí, ya vamos a tener mucha suerte. Yo de eso estoy seguro. Nomás hay que no perder la fe. Eso es. Lo importante es no perder la fe.	Don't say that, Rosita. It's hard, but we're going to have luck. And we'll get everything we want. And we'll make a lot of money. And we'll return to our village. And when we walk down the streets, people will look at us with envy. Things are changing. Yes, we'll have a lot of luck now. I'm sure of it. The only thing is not to lose faith. That's it — the important thing is not to lose faith.

Evaluación del progreso — Lecciones 11–12

RAISING AWARENESS

A. Give three strategies that can help to build empathy with your Hispanic clients.

B. Name the five levels of consciousness and their corresponding behaviors in the cross-cultural communication process.

C. In what theories of diseases might some of your Hispanic clients believe, and what treatments might they use to cure illnesses?

D. How does the reality of Hispanics in the United States differ from that of other immigrant groups?

E. Give three strategies that can help non-Hispanic health-care providers to serve their Spanish-speaking clients better.

F. Explain the conflicts that can arise when the Hispanic value of anticipating needs meets the Anglo tendency toward frankness and self-assertion.

COMUNICÁNDOSE EN ESPAÑOL

A. **Pronunciación**   Write the following sentences your instructor dictates.

1. _____

2. _____

3. _____

B. **Discriminación auditiva**   Circle the letter of the most appropriate response to each oral question or statement you hear.

1. a	b	c	5. a	b	c	8. a	b	c
2. a	b	c	6. a	b	c	9. a	b	c
3. a	b	c	7. a	b	c	10. a	b	c
4. a	b	c						

COMBINÁNDOLO TODO

A. **Comprensión oral**   Circle **sí** if the client's statement indicates a current physical, emotional, or spiritual problem needing intervention and **no** if it does not. Write the problem briefly in *English* when one is expressed.

Problem?   *State the problem*

1. **sí   no**   _____

2. **sí   no**   _____

      Problem?   *State the problem*

3. **sí no**   _____

4. **sí no**   _____

5. **sí no**   _____

6. **sí no**   _____

7. **sí no**   _____

8. **sí no**   _____

9. **sí no**   _____

10. **sí no**   _____

B. La entrevista Give the questions and/or responses needed in the following dialogue, which takes place in the doctor's office.

La Dra. Williams	*Mirta Vargas*
	Doctora, no sé qué me pasa. Tengo ganas de vomitar todas las mañanas.
1. ¿ _____ síntomas _____ ?	Pues, no tengo mucho apetito; también me encuentro siempre rendida.
2. ¿ _____ Ud. bien?	Sí, pero siempre tengo sueño al levantarme.
3. Mirta, ¿cuándo _____ que le vino la regla (*menstrual period*)?	Pues, hace más de dos meses.
4. ¿Y ha _____ dos meses?	Sí, doctora, con mi esposo.
5. Bueno, me hace falta _____, pero creo que _____ .	¿A mi edad? ¡Voy a cumplir cuarenta años en enero! ¡Ud tiene que estar equivocada!
6. Pues, _____ posible. _____ esperar hasta _____ _____ para estar seguras.	Pues, doctora, vamos a ver. Hay que cumplir con la ley de Dios. Si él me manda uno de sus hijos a criar, yo, con mucho gusto, lo acepto.

C. En acción   Choose one of the following situations and act it out with your instructor or another classmate.

1. Discussing the diagnosis and treatment of a young patient's serious illness with the child's mother

2. Getting the facts regarding an automobile accident in which your client was injured and the driver of the other vehicle died

3. Counseling a young single woman who is a devout Catholic over the guilt she feels after getting an abortion

4. Trying to convince a suicidal client to get help

5. Discussing with a dark-skinned client who has been discriminated against in the job and housing markets his feelings about living in the United States

6. Counseling a young man with a deep religious sense regarding a series of misfortunes he has experienced

Glossary

adj	adjective	**indef art**	indefinite article
adv	adverb	**interrog**	interrogative
ang	anglicism	**io**	indirect object
aug	augmentative	**m**	masculine noun (gender not indicated for masculine nouns ending in -o)
C	Cuban dialect		
colloq	colloquialism	**M**	Mexican dialect
conj	conjunction	**MA**	Mexican American dialect
contr	contraction	**n**	noun
def art	definite article	**O**	other Spanish dialect
dim	diminutive	**pl**	plural
do	direct object	**poss**	possessive
f	feminine noun (gender not indicated for feminine nouns ending in -a)	**PR**	Puerto Rican dialect
		prep	preposition
fam	familiar	**pron**	pronoun
fig	figurative	**reflex**	reflexive
form	formal	**rel**	relative
i	stem-changing verb (e–i)	**s**	singular
ie	stem-changing verb (e–ie)	**ue**	stem-changing verb (o–ue)
imp	imperative	**v**	verb

a (prep) to, at; **a la hora** per hour; **a la moda** fashionable; **a la semana** per week; **a menos que** unless; **a menudo** often; **a pesar de** despite; **a veces** at times

abandonar to abandon, leave, neglect

abanico fan; **abanico giratorio** electric fan

abarrotes (tienda de) (M) grocery store

abogado/a lawyer

abrazar to hug

abril (m) April

abrir to open

abstinencia abstinence

abuelo/a grandfather/grandmother; **abuelito/a** (dim)

491

aburrir to bore

acá (adv) here, over here, this way; **ven (tú)/venga (Ud.) acá** come here

acabar to finish, end; **acabarse** to run out, deplete; **acabar de . . .** to have just . . .

acaso (adv) perhaps, maybe

acceder to accede, consent

accidente (m) accident, mishap, chance

acción (f) action

aceite (m) oil

aceituna olive

acento stress, accent

aceptar to accept, admit, receive

aciago/a (adj) ill-fated, unlucky, ominous

acomodado/a (adj) well to do

acompañar to accompany

acondicionador de aire (m) air conditioner

aconsejar to advise

acordarse (ue) de to remember

acorralado/a (adj) pent up (**acorralar** to corral, shut up)

acostar (ue) to put to bed; **acostarse** to go to bed

acostumbrado/a (adj) accustomed, usual, habitual; (**acostumbrarse a** to become accustomed to)

actitud (f) attitude

actual (adj) present, current; **actualmente** (adv) at the present time

acusado/a (n) defendant, (adj) accused

acusar to accuse, charge (with a crime)

adaptar to adapt

adecuado/a (adj) adequate

adelantado/a (adj) ahead (used with clocks, watches, etc.)

adelante (adv) ahead; **¡Adelante!** Come in!; **más adelante** later on

además (adv) moreover, furthermore

adiestrado/a (adj) trained, skilled

adiestramiento training

adiós goodbye, so long

admiración (f) admiration, wonder

admitir to admit, accept

adonde (adv) where, to what place

adopción (f) adoption

adventista (m/f) Seventh Day Adventist

adverso/a (adj) adverse, contrary, unfavorable

advertir (ie) to notice, advise, warn

afanarse to be eager

afectar to move (emotionally)

aferrar to grasp, seize, take hold of

aficionado/a fan, devotee, amateur

afirmar to affirm, assert, maintain

afligido/a (adj) afflicted, grieving, (**afligir** to grieve)

afortunadamente (adv) fortunately

afuera (adv) out, outside

agarrar to hold, grasp; to catch (an illness)

agencia agency

agosto August

agradecer to appreciate; to thank (someone) for (something)

agregar to add

agresión (f) aggression, battery (legal sense)

agua, el (f) water

aguacate (m) avocado

aguantar to bear, withstand, not give up

aguantón/a (aug) a person who endures much suffering

ahora (adv) now, right now; **ahora mismo** immediately

ahorrar to save (money, time)

aire (m) air, wind; look, appearance

ajeno/a (adj) another's, belonging to someone else

ají (m) hot chile pepper

ajiaco hot pepper soup

ajo garlic

al (a + el) see **a**; **al año** per year; **al cabo de** at the end of; **al día** per day; **al mes** per month

albaricoque (m) apricot

alcance (m) reach

alcapurria (PR) fried snack of plantain and meat

alcoba bedroom

alcohol alcohol

alcohólico/a (adj/n) alcoholic

aleccionador/a (adj) instructive

alegar to allege, assert, state

alegrar to cheer up, make happy; **alegrarse de (que)** to be happy (that)

alegría happiness, joy

alergia allergy

alfabeto alphabet

algo (pron) something; (adv) somewhat, rather (before adj)

alguien (pron) somebody, someone

alguno (adj) some, any (**algún** before masculine, singular noun)

alimentar to feed, nourish

aliviar to relieve, alleviate; **aliviarse (de)** to get better, to get relief from

alivio relief

alma, el (f) soul

almeja clam

almíbar (m) heavy syrup

almorzar (ue) to eat the midday meal

almuerzo midday meal, lunch

aló (PR) hello (in answering the phone)

alquilado/a (adj) rented (**aquilar** to rent)

alquiler (m) rent

alta presión (de la sangre) (f) high blood pressure

alternativa (n) alternative

alto/a (adj) high, tall, loud (voice)

alzar to raise

allá there, over there; **más allá** farther on, beyond

allí there; **allí mero** (MA) right over there

ama de casa housewife

amable (adj) kindly, amiable

amargo/a (adj) bitter

ambiente (m) atmosphere, environment
americano/a (adj/n) American
amigo/a (n) friend
amigdalitis (f) tonsilitis
amistad (f) friendship
amor (m) love; darling, sweetheart; **amores** (m, pl) affairs of the heart
amueblado/a, amoblado/a (adj) furnished (**amueblar** to furnish)
amuleto amulet, charm
ándale (M) go on, you don't say
andaluz/a (adj/n) Andalusian
andar to walk, go on foot
anemia anemia
analfabeto/a (adj/n) illiterate
anfetamina amphetamine
anglo (adj/n) non-Hispanic
animar to cheer up
ánimo state of mind, mood
anís (m) anise
aniversario anniversary
anoche (adv) last night
anón (C) tropical fruit
ansia restlessness, anxiety, strong desire
ansioso/a (adj) anxious, eager, impatient
ante (adv) in front of, before (a person)
anteanoche (adv) night before last
anteayer (adv) day before yesterday
anterior (adj) previous, former, preceding; **anteriormente** (adv) previously, before
antes (adv) before, formerly; **antes de** (prep)/**antes (de) que** (conj) before; **antes dicho** mentioned above
antiguo/a (adj) former, old, ancient
anual (adj) yearly; **anualmente** (adv) yearly
añadir to add
año year; **¿Cuántos años tiene?** How old are you?
apagado/a (adj) turned off (lights, radio) (**apagar** to turn off, extinguish)
aparato apparatus; **aparato eléctrico** small appliance
aparecer to appear (physically)
apariencia appearance, looks
apartamento apartment
apellido surname, family name
apenas (adv) hardly, scarcely
aperitivo appetizer
apetito appetite
apio celery
aplicación (f) application form (ang for **solicitud**)
apodo nickname
apreciar to appreciate, to value
aprender to learn
apropiado/a (adj) appropriate
aquí (adv) here; **por aquí** this way
aquel, aquella (adj) that; **aquellos, aquellas** (adj) those; **aquél, aquélla** (pron) that one; **aquéllos, aquéllas** (pron) those

aquilatar to evaluate the worth of something or someone
aragonés/a (adj/n) Aragonese (Spain)
archivo file
arder to burn
ardor (m) ardor, burning sensation
argentino/a (adj/n) Argentine
argumento discussion, plot
arma, el (f) weapon
armada navy, fleet
armario cupboard, closet
arreglo arrangement (**arreglar** to arrange, fix up, repair)
arrepentido/a (adj) repentant, regretful (**arrepentirse [ie] [de]** to repent)
arrestar to arrest
arriba (adv) on top, upstairs, up, upwards
arroz (m) rice; **arroz con habichuelas** (PR) rice and beans
arrullo cooing, lullaby
artículo article
artista (m/f) artist
asado/a (adj) roasted (**asar** to roast)
asalto assault
ascensor (m) elevator
asegurado/a (adj) assured (**asegurar** to assure)
asesinato murder, homicide
así (adv) thus, like this, in this way
asistir to attend (a function); (ang) to assist, aid
asma, el asthma
asociado/a (adj) associated (**asociar** to associate)
asomarse to begin to appear, to peep out
aspecto aspect
aspiradora (de polvo) vacuum cleaner
astilla splinter
Asunción Assumption (of the Virgin Mary); female name
asunto subject, matter, question
asustar to frighten; **asustarse (de)** to become frightened
atacado/a (adj) attacked (**atacar** to attack)
ataque (m) attack; **ataque al cerebro** stroke; **ataque al corazón** heart attack; **ataque de nervios** nervous attack
atentamente (adv) politely, courteously; Very truly yours (letter ending)
atento/a (adj) polite, courteous, attentive
atole (m) hot nonalcoholic drink used in Mexico and Central America
atormentado/a (adj) tormented, tortured (**atormentar** to torment)
atrás (adv) back, behind; (colloq) ago
atrasado/a (adj) backward, behind (in work, studies, time) (**atrasar** to delay, detain)
atún (m) tuna fish
aturdido/a (adj) rattled, stunned (**aturdir** to rattle, stun)

auditivo/a (adj) auditory
aumento increase (**aumentar** to increase)
aun (adv) even, still more
aunque (conj) though, although
autobús (m) bus
automóvil (m) automobile
autónomo (adj) autonomous
autor/a (n) author
autoridad (f) authority
avaricia greed, avarice
avenida avenue
aventura adventure
averiguar to find out
avisar to advise, warn, inform
¡ay! ouch!, oh!, oh, dear!; **¡ay de mí!** poor me!
ayer (adv) yesterday
ayudante (m/f) aide
ayudar to help
azafrán (m) saffron
azúcar (m) sugar
azul (adj) blue

bacalao codfish; **bacalao salado** (PR) salted codfish
bachiller (m/f) holder of a high school degree
bachillerato high school diploma
bailar to dance
bajo/a (adj) low, short; **bajo** (adv) below, under; **bajo fianza** on bail
banco bank; bench
bandeja tray
bandido/a bandit
bañadera (C) bathtub
bañera bathtub
baño bath, bathroom
barato/a (adj) cheap, inexpensive
barbaridad (f) atrocity; something foolish or preposterous
barbitúrico barbiturate
barrer to sweep
barriga belly, bulge
barrio city district; suburb; **barrio hispano** Spanish-speaking area of a U.S. city
básico/a (adj) basic
bastante (adj) enough, sufficient; (adv.) enough, sufficiently, rather
bata dressing gown; robe
batata (PR, O) sweet potato
bate (m) baseball bat
batida (**batido,** C) blended drink of fruit, milk, ice, and sugar
bautismo Baptism
bautista (m/f) Baptist (religion)
bautizar to baptize
bebé (m/f) baby
beber to drink
bebida drink, beverage
béisbol (m) baseball

bello/a (adj) beautiful
bendecir to bless
bendición (f) blessing, benediction
beneficio favor, benefit, profit
besar to kiss; **beso** kiss
betabel (M, O) (f) beet
bien (m) good; (adv) well, very; **bien educado** well-mannered; **bien preparado** well-educated; **bien vestido** well-dressed
bienestar (m) well-being, comfort
bienestar público (m) Welfare (state assistance)
bijol (C) spice for cooking
bigote (m) moustache; **bigote fifí** thin moustache
bilingüe (adj) bilingual
billete (m) ticket
biología biology
bistec (also **biftec**) (m) steak, beefsteak
bizcocho sponge cake, cookie
blusa blouse
boca mouth; entrance (cave, subway)
bocadillo (C, PR, O) sandwich, stuffed roll
boda wedding
bodega cellar, storehouse; (PR) grocery store
bolillo (M, MA) bread roll
boliviano/a (adj/n) Bolivian
bolsillo pocket
bollo de pan (PR) bread roll
bombilla lightbulb; (PR) "upper" (amphetamine)
bondad kindness, goodness; **Tenga la bondad de** (+ inf) Please . . .
boniato (C) sweet potato
bonito (C) tuna fish
boricua (m/f) (adj/n) name used by some Puerto Ricans for self-identification
Borinquén native name for Puerto Rico
Borinqueña, la Puerto Rican national anthem
borracho/a (adj/n) drunk/drunkard
bota boot, wine bag
botana (M) hors d'oeuvre
botánica (C, PR) neighborhood "pharmacy" dispensing herbal and other medicines
botar to throw out; fire (from a job)
brasileño/a (adj/n) Brazilian
bueno/a (adj) (**buen** before masculine, singular noun) good, appropriate; **buenos días** good morning; **buenas noches** good night; **buenas tardes** good afternoon
burro donkey, ass, jackass
buscar to look for, search
butaca armchair; orchestra seat

caballero gentleman; horseman
caballo horse
cabeza head
cabezal (m) headboard
cabrito goat's meat
cacahuate (MA), **cacahuete** (m) peanut

cacique (m) chief, political boss

cada (adj) each, every

cadáver (m) corpse, cadaver

cadera hip

caer(se) to fall, drop, fall down

café (m) coffee; café; **café con leche** mixture of hot milk and coffee

cafetería cafeteria

calabaza pumpkin, squash; **dar calabazas** to refuse, reject (an amorous proposal)

calamar (m) squid

calambre (m) muscle cramp

calendario calendar

cálculo calculation; gallstone

calefacción (f) heating, heating system; (ang) **el caliente**

calificación (f) qualification, rating

calificar to determine or express the qualities of someone or something

calmar to calm, quiet; **calmarse** to calm down

calor (m) heat, warmth, hotness

callado/a (adj) silent, quiet, reticent (**callar(se)** to be quiet)

calle (f) street

cama bed, couch

camarero/a waiter, waitress

camarón (m) shrimp, prawn

cambiar to change, alter; **cambiar de** (+ n) to change something (jobs, names, etc.)

cambio change, exchange, barter

caminar to walk, travel, move along

camino path, road, way, track

camisa shirt

camote (M, MA) sweet potato

campesino/a (n) peasant, rural dweller

campo field, country, countryside

canalla (m/f) rascal, scoundrel

cáncer (m) cancer

cancha de baloncesto basketball court

candidato/a candidate

cansado/a (adj) tired (**cansar** to tire; **cansarse** to get tired)

cansancio tiredness, fatigue

cantidad (f) amount, quantity

cañón (m) barrel of a gun; cannon

capaz (adj) capable, competent

capital (f) capital (city); (m) capital (financial)

cara face

característica (n) characteristic

caracterizar to characterize

¡carajo! damn! (also **¡carijo!**)

caramelo caramel, candy

cárcel (f) jail, prison

cardiólogo/a cardiologist

caribe (adj/n) Caribbean

cariñoso/a (adj) affectionate, loving, kind

carnaval (m) carnival (feast before Lent)

carne (f) flesh, meat; **carne de res** beef; **carne entomatada** meat cooked in tomato sauce; **carne guisada** stewed meat; **carne molida** ground meat

caro/a (adj) expensive

carpintero/a carpenter

carrera career; course or route

carro car, cart, vehicle

carta letter

cartera pocketbook, wallet

casa house, building, establishment

casado/a (adj) married, (**casar** to marry; **casarse con** to get married to)

casero/a (adj) pertaining to the home; domestic

casi (adv) almost, nearly

caso case, event, happening

castellano (n) Spanish language; **castellano/a** (adj) Castilian

castigo punishment

catalán/a (adj/n) Catalan, Catalonian

categoría category, class, rank

catolicismo Catholicism

católico/a (adj/n) Catholic

catorce fourteen

causa cause, origin, reason

Cayo Hueso original Spanish name for Key West, Florida

cebolla onion

celebrar to celebrate

celos (m, pl) jealousy; **dar celos** to make jealous; **tener celos** to be jealous

celoso/a (adj) jealous, suspicious

cementerio cemetery, graveyard

cena supper

cenar to have supper

ceniza ash, ashes

céntrico/a (adj) central, downtown

centro center, center of a town

cerámica ceramics

cerca (adv) nearly, close; **cerca de** (prep) near

cercano/a (adj) nearby

cerdo swine, pig, hog

cereal (m) cereal

cerebro head, brains; judgement

cereza cherry

cero zero

cerveza beer

cerrado/a (adj) closed, shut (**cerrar** [ie] to close)

ciego/a (adj) blind; (n) a blind person

cielo sky, heaven

cien hundred, a hundred (before a noun)

ciencia science, knowledge, learning

ciencia política political science

ciento hundred; one hundred (when *not* before a noun)

cierto/a (adj) certain, sure, true

cilantro coriander

cinco five

cincuenta fifty

cine (m) movie theater
ciruela plum, prune
cita appointment
ciudad (f) city
ciudadanía citizenship
ciudadano/a (n) citizen
civil (adj) civil; **estado civil** marital status
claramente (adv) clearly
claro/a (adj) clear, transparent, bright; (adv) clearly
clase (f) class, order, type
cláusula clause, sentence
clavado/a (adj) nailed; exact
cliente (m/f) client, customer
clima (m) climate
clínica clinic; private hospital
clóset (m, ang) closet
cobarde (adj) cowardly, timid; (m/f) coward
cobija covering, bed cover
cobrar to charge; to get paid; to cash a check
cocaína cocaine
cocina kitchen; stove
cocinar to cook
codo elbow
coger to take, grab, seize, catch
col (f) cabbage
colcha (C) blanket, bedspread
colectivo/a (adj) collective
colega (m/f) colleague
colegio school, private academy; (PR) college
colgar to hang, suspend
colmado (PR) small grocery store
colmado/a (adj) full; abundant
colmo limit, "last straw"
Colón Christopher Columbus
columna column
colombiano/a (adj/n) Colombian
comadre mother and godmother with respect to each other
combinándolo todo putting it all together (**combinar** to combine)
comedor (m) dining room
comer to eat
comestible (adj) edible, comestible; (m) food, foodstuff
comida food; meal
comino cumin
como (adv) as, like
¿cómo? (interrog) how?; **¿Cómo estás?** How are you?; **¿Cómo le va?** How's it going?; **¿Cómo no?** Why not?; **¿Cómo se dice . . . ?** How do you say?; **¿Cómo se llama?** What's your name?
cómoda (n) chest of drawers
cómodo/a (adj) comfortable
compadrazgo the system of extending the family by naming godparents for religious rites
compañero/a companion, partner
compañía company
compartir to share, divide

compasivo/a (adj) compassionate
compatriota (m/f) compatriot
competente (adj) competent, able
completo/a (adj) complete; **por completo** completely; **completamente** (adv) completely
componer to compose, make up; to prepare; to repair
comportarse to comport oneself, behave
comprar to buy; **comprar al contado** to purchase with cash; **comprar a plazos** to purchase in installments
comprender to comprehend, understand
comprensión (f) comprehension, understanding
comprensivo/a (adj) comprehensive, understanding
comprometer to compromise; to make a commitment
comprometido/a (adj) compromised, committed; engaged
compromiso commitment, pledge
computadora (n) computer
comulgar to receive or administer Holy Communion
común (adj) common, ordinary; **comúnmente** (adv) commonly, usually
comunicación (f) communication
comunicar(se) to communicate, correspond; **comunicándose en español** communicating in Spanish
comunicativo/a (adj) communicative
comunidad (f) community, commonwealth
con (prep) with; **con cuidado** carefully; **con mucho gusto** with pleasure; **con permiso** excuse me; **con tal que** provided that
concepción (f) conception
concertar (ie) to assemble, put in order; **concertarse** to come to an agreement
concubinato state of living together with a partner of the opposite sex without being married
condado county
condena sentence (punishment)
condenado/a (adj) sentenced, condemned
condensado/a (adj) condensed
condición (f) condition; class; nature
conducir to convey; to conduct, guide; to drive
confesar to confess, acknowledge
confesión (f) confession
confiado/a (adj) trusting, confiding (**confiar** to confide; **confiar en** to trust, rely on)
confianza confidence, trust
confidencial (adj) confidential
confirmar to confirm
conflicto conflict
conformar to conform, adapt
congelador (m) freezer
congénito/a (adj) congenital
conmigo (prep + pron) with me
congrí (C, m) mixture of rice and red beans
conjugar to conjugate
conocido/a (adj) known (**conocer** to know, meet; to be acquainted with)
conquistador (m) conquistador, conquerer
conseguir to obtain, get

consejero/a advisor, counselor

consejo advice, counsel

conserje (m/f) concierge, janitor

consecuencia consequence, result

considerar to consider, think over; to believe

consolar (ue) to console, comfort; consolarse to be consoled

constante (adj) constant, firm

constipación (f) cold, chill; head congestion

consuelo consolation, comfort

consultar to consult

consultorio medical office

contacto contact

contado/a (adj) counted, numbered; comprar al contado buy with cash

contador/a (m/f) accountant

contar (ue) to count, number; to tell, narrate

contener (ie) to contain, comprise

contento/a (adj) contented, pleased

contestar to answer, reply

contexto context

contigo (prep + pron) with you (fam)

continuar to continue

continuo/a (adj) continuous

contra (prep) against

Contras (m, pl) anti-Sandinista forces in Nicaragua

contribuido/a (adj) contributed (contribuir to contribute)

contrición (f) contrition

controlar to control

convencer to convince; convencerse to become convinced

convenir (ie) to agree, come together; to be convenient

conversación (f) conversation; conversación parcial partial conversation

¡coño! an obscenity

compadre father and godfather with respect to each other

coquetería coquetry, flirtatiousness

coquito quemao (C) macaroon

corazón (m) heart

corbata necktie, scarf

cordero lamb

cornudo (also cuernudo) horned; cuckolded

coro chorus; choir

correo mail; post office

correr to run

correspondiente (adj) correspondent, respective

corrida run; corrida de toros bullfight

corriente (adj) flowing, running; common, usual

corro circle (of people)

corromper to corrupt, seduce

cortar to cut, slash

corte (f) (legal) court; (m) cut, cutting edge

cortés (adj) courteous, polite

cortesía courtesy, compliment

corta (n) cutting; corto/a (adj) short, brief

cosa thing, matter

costar (ue) to cost

costarricense (adj/n) Costa Rican

costumbre (f) custom, habit

costurera seamstress

coyote (M, n, m/f, colloq) bilingual/bicultural person who earns a living by "brokering" between the two cultures

creativo/a (adj) creative

crecer to grow, increase

crédito credit, credence

creencia belief, religion

creer to believe, think

crema cream, custard

crianza upbringing, education, manners

criar to raise, produce; to bring up

crimen (m) crime, felony

criminal (adj/n) criminal

crisis (f) crisis

cristiano/a (adj/n) Christian

crueldad (f) cruelty

cruz (f) cross; Cruz Azul (f) Blue Cross

cuadra block

cual (rel pron) who, which; ¿cuál? (interrog) which?; what?

cualidad (f) quality; trait

cualquier (indef adj) any (before a noun); de cualquier manera in whichever way; cualquiera (pron) anyone, anybody

cuando (adv) when; aun cuando even when, even though; ¿cuándo? (interrog) when?

cuanto (adv) as much as; cuanto antes as soon as possible

¿cuánto/a? (interrog adj) how much?

¿cuá ̣os/as? (interrog adj) how many?

cuarenta forty

Cuaresma Lent

cuarto (n) quarter; room; cuarto de baño bathroom; cuarto de dormir bedroom; cuarto/a (adj) quarter, fourth part

cuartel (m) headquarters (military, police, etc.)

cuatro four

cubano/a (adj/n) Cuban

cubrecama bedspread

cucaracha cockroach

cuello neck

cuenta bill, account

cuento story

cuerpo body, corpse

cuerpo policíaco police force

cuidar(se) to take care of (oneself)

culpa guilt, fault, blame

culpable (adj) guilty, culpable

cultura (n) culture; cultural (adj) cultural

cumpleaños (m, s) birthday

cumplir to accomplish; to do; to reach (a birthday); cumplir con to fulfill (one's duties)

cuna cradle; place of birth

cuñado/a brother/sister-in-law

cupón (m) coupon; **cupones de alimento** (PR) food stamps

curandero/a folk healer

curanderismo belief in folk medicine

curar to cure, heal; **curarse** to get better, recover

cursar to frequent; to attend

curtido/a (adj) tanned; thick-skinned

custodia custody, care

cuyo/a (poss adj) whose, of which

chabacano (M) apricot

chalupa (M) maize pancake

chamaco/a (M,O) youngster

chamba (M) job

champiñón (M, O, m) mushroom

chaparro/a (adj) short (physically)

chaqueta jacket, coat

cheque (m) check (money)

chequeo check-up

chicano/a (adj/n) self-identification term used by some Mexican Americans

chico/a (n) boy, girl; (adj) small

chícharo (M, MA) pea

chicharrón (m) fried pork rind

chile (m) chile, red pepper; **chile verde** green chile pepper

chileno/a (adj/n) Chilean

chillo (PR) red snapper

china (PR) orange (fruit)

chingar (M, MA) to "screw" (obscenity)

chino/a (adj) Chinese

chisme/s (m, s/pl) gossip

chocolate (m) chocolate; **chocolate caliente** hot chocolate

chofer (m) chauffeur, driver

chuleta meat chop

chupar to suck, draw out

dama lady

danza (f) dance; dancing; (PR) a folkloric dance

daño harm, damage; **hacer daño a** to do harm to (**dañar** to harm, to damage)

dar to give; **dar a luz** to give birth; **dar clases** to give classes, teach; **dar(se) la mano** to shake hands; **darle a uno** to hit; **darle de alta** to release (from a hospital, etc.); **darse cuenta de** to realize, become aware of

dato fact, datum; **datos personales** personal information

de (prep) of; **de nada** you are welcome; **¿De parte de quién?** Who is calling? (when answering the telephone); **de repente** (adv) suddenly, unexpectedly; **de veras** (adv) really; **de vez en cuando** (adv) from time to time

deber to owe; to have to; (m) obligation, duty

debido a (prep) owing to, on account of

débil (adj) weak

debilidad (f) weakness

decidir to decide, settle

décimo/a (adj) tenth

decir to say, tell

decisión (f) decision, issue

declaración (f) declaration

declarar to testify; **declararse** to declare oneself, plead (in a legal sense)

decorativo/a (adj) decorative

defecto defect, fault

defender (ie) to defend, protect

defensor/a defender; **defensor/a público/a** public defender

dejar to leave, to permit; **dejar de** to stop; **dejar ir** to let go

del (de + el) see **de**

delante (de) (prep) in front (of); (adv) before

delgado/a (adj) thin

delito misdemeanor, crime

demanda petition, request

demás (adj/pron) the other, the rest of (used with **lo, la, los, las**)

demasiado (adv) too, excessively; **demasiado/a** (adj) too much, too many

democracia democracy

democrático/a (adj) democratic

demostrar (ue) to demonstrate, show

denominar to indicate, denominate

dentista (m/f) dentist

denunciar to denounce, accuse

departamento department; district; (M) apartment; **departamento de empleo** employment office

depender (de) to depend (on)

depósito deposit

deprimido/a (adj) depressed (**deprimir** to depress)

derecha (n) right; right-hand side; **a la derecha** to the right

derecho (n) right, justice, equity; (adv) straight ahead; **derecho/a** (adj) pertaining to the right-hand side

desanimado/a (adj) discouraged, lacking animation

desarrollo development

desayuno breakfast (**desayunar** to eat breakfast)

descansado/a (adj) relaxed (**descansar** to relax)

desconocer to disregard, ignore

descremado/a (adj) skimmed (without cream)

describir to describe

descripción (f) description

descubrir to discover

desde (prep) since, from

desear to desire, wish

desechar to reject, put aside

desempleo unemployment

desengañado/a (adj) disillusioned (**desengañar** to disillusion, undeceive)

desengaño disillusion, disappointment

desgraciadamente (adv) unfortunately

desgraciado/a (adj) unfortunate; disagreeable

deshonesto/a (adj) immodest, indecent; dishonest

desilusión (f) disillusionment

desmayar to be dismayed, depressed, discouraged; **desmayarse** to faint

desmayo (n) dismay; faint

desolado/a (adj) desolate; disconsolate

desorientado/a (adj) disoriented

despacio (adv) slowly, deliberately

despacho office

despachado/a (adj) sent off (**despachar** to send off)

despedida (n) farewell; leave-taking

despedir (i) to throw, emit; to fire (from a job); **despedirse (de)** to part; say good-bye (to)

despertar (ie) to wake; **despertarse** to wake up

después (adv) after; afterwards; **después de** (prep) after

desterrado/a (adj) exiled (**desterrar [ie]** to banish, exile)

destino destiny; destination

destruir to destroy

desventaja disadvantage

detective (m/f) detective

detalle (m) detail

detener (ie) to stop, detain

detestar to detest

deuda debt

diabetes (f) diabetes

día (m) day; **día de independencia** Independence Day; **día de la raza** Columbus Day (October 12); **día de los difuntos** All Souls' Day (November 2); **día de reyes** Epiphany (January 6); **día del santo** Saint's Day; **día de San Juan** St. John's Day (June 24); **día de todos los santos** All Saints' Day (November 1); **día feriado** national holiday; **día festivo** holy day

diagnóstico/a (adj) diagnostic

diálogo dialogue; **diálogo introductorio** introductory dialogue; **diálogos cortos** short dialogues

diariamente (adv) daily, everyday

diario/a (adj) daily

diarrea diarrhea

diáspora diaspora, dispersal

diciembre (m) December

dictado dictation

dicho (n) saying, proverb; **dicho/a** (adj) said, mentioned

diecinueve nineteen

dieciocho eighteen

dieciséis sixteen

diecisiete seventeen

diente (m) tooth

dieta diet

dietista (m/f) dietitian

diez ten

diferencia difference

difícil (adj) difficult

dificultad (f) difficulty; objection

difunto/a (adj/n) deceased

diga (PR, C, O) used to answer the telephone; **dígalo** "say it" (imp)

digestivo/a (adj) digestive

dignidad (f) dignity

dinero money; currency

Dios (m) God; **Dios te bendiga** God bless you

dirección (f) address, direction

director/a (m/f) director, manager

dirigir to direct

discriminación (f) discrimination; **discriminación auditiva** auditory discrimination

disculpar(se) to exculpate, excuse

disparar to shoot, fire

disimular to conceal, dissimulate

disponer to dispose, arrange; **disponer de** to have at one's disposal; **disponerse (a)** to get ready, prepare

disponible (adj) available

disputa dispute

distinguido/a (adj) distinguished (**distinguir** to distinguish)

distinto/a (adj) different, distinct

divertir (ie) to amuse, entertain; **divertirse** to have a good time

divorciado/a (adj) divorced (**divorciarse [de]** to get a divorce [from])

divorcio divorce

doble (adj) double

doce twelve

doctor/a (m/f) doctor

documento document, paper

dólar (m) dollar

dolencia pain; disease

doler (ue) to hurt, pain

dolor (m) pain; **dolor de cabeza** headache

dominar to know well (a language); to dominate

dominicano/a (adj/n) Dominican

domingo Sunday

dominó dominoes (game)

don/doña title used before a given name to indicate respect

donde (adv) where; **¿dónde?** (interrog) where?; **dondequiera** wherever

dormitorio bedroom; (ang) dormitory

dormir (ue) to sleep

dos two

dosel (m) backdrop

dosis (f) dose

drama (m) play, drama

dramáticamente (adv) dramatically

droga drug

dueño/a owner, landlord

dulce (m) candy; (adj) sweet

dulcero/a (n) confectioner

durante (adv) during

durar to last

durazno (M, MA) peach

duro/a (adj) hard

e and (before word beginning with **i** or **hi**)

echar to throw; to throw out; to pour; **echarse** to lie down; **echarse a perder** to spoil, go bad

económico/a (adj) economical; inexpensive

ecuatoriano/a (adj/n) Ecuadorian
edad (f) age
edificio building, edifice
educación (f) breeding, upbringing; education
educativo/a (adj) educational
efectivo (n) cash; **efectivo/a** (adj) effective
efectuar to carry out, put into effect
egoísta (m/f) egotist; (adj) selfish
ejemplo example
ejercer to handle, hold; to practice
ejercicio exercise
ejote (M/m) stringbean
el (def art) the
él (pron) he
electricidad (f) electricity
eléctrico/a (adj) electric
electricista (m/f) electrician
elevador (m, ang) elevator
eliminar to eliminate
elote (M/m) corn on the cob
ella (pron) she
embarazada (adj) pregnant
emborrachado/a drunk, (**emborracharse** to get drunk)
emergencia emergency
emergente (adj) emerging
emigración (f) emigration
emigrado/a (adj/n) emigree (**emigrar** to emigrate)
empacho (n) childhood affliction causing nausea, vomiting, diarrhea
empanada (C, M) turnover; meat pie
empeñarse to insist
empeorarse to grow worse
empezar (ie) to begin
empleado/a employee
emplear to use, employ
empleo employment
en (prep) in, on; **en acción** in action; **en caso de que** in case of; **en confianza** confidentially; **en contra de** against; **en deuda** indebted; **¿En qué puedo servirle?** How may I help you?; **en seguida** at once
enamorado/a (adj) in love (**enamorarse [de]** to fall in love [with])
encantado/a (adj) charmed, delighted; pleased (to meet you) (**encantar** to charm, delight)
encarcelación (f) imprisonment
encarcelar to imprison
encargado/a (adj) in charge
encargar to entrust; **encargarse (de)** to take charge (of)
enchilada filled soft tortilla; **enchilada de queso** enchilada filled with cheese; **enchilada suiza** cheese enchilada topped with green sauce
encima (adv) above; **encima de** (prep) on top of
encinta (adj) pregnant
encontrar (ue) to find; to meet; **encontrarse (con)** to meet (up with); to come upon
encuentro meeting, encounter
enema enema

energía energy
enero January
enfermedad (f) illness, sickness
enfermera nurse; **enfermera practicante** practical nurse
enfermo/a (n) sick person; (adj) ill, sick
engañar to deceive
engaño (n) deceit
enojar to anger; **enojarse** to get angry
enojo (n) anger
ensalada salad
enseñanza instruction, teaching (**enseñar** to teach)
enseres eléctricos (PR) appliances
entendido/a (adj) understood (**entender [ie]** to understand)
enterrado/a (adj) buried (**enterrar [ie]** to bury)
entonces (adv) so then, then, at the time
entrada entrance; admission; ticket
entrar to enter
entre (prep) between
entrega delivery (**entregar,** to deliver, hand over; **entregarse** to give in, yield)
entremeses hors d'oeuvres
entrenamiento training (**entrenar** to train)
entrevista interview
entrevistar to interview
envase (m) container
envidia envy
época period of time
equivocado/a (adj) mistaken (**equivocar** to mistake; **equivocarse** to make a mistake)
erupción (f) rash
escalera stairway
escarcha frost
escarlatina scarlet fever
escoba broom
escoger to choose, select
escribir to write
escritor/a (m/f) writer
escritorio desk
escrúpulo scruple
escuchar to listen
escuela school; **escuela primaria** elementary school; **escuela superior** high school
ese, esa (adj) that; **esos, esas** those; **ése, ésa** (pron) that one; **ésos, ésas** (pron) those
eso (neuter pron) that
espacio space
espalda back (of the body)
especia spice
especial (adj) special
especialidad (f) specialty
especialista (m/f) specialist
especializarse (en) to specialize (in); to major (in)
especialmente (adv) specially
espejo mirror
esperanza hope

esperar to hope, expect; to wait; **espere un momento** wait a moment (imp)

espina thorn

espinacas (pl) spinach

espiritismo religious belief that evil spirits cause illness, emotional and social problems

espiritista (m/f) spiritualist who contacts spirits

espiritual (adj) spiritual

esposo/a husband, wife

esqueleto skeleton

establecer to establish, set up; **establecerse** to establish oneself

establecimiento establishment

estado state; condition; **en estado** pregnant; **estado civil** marital status; **Estado Libre Asociado** Free Associated State (current status of Puerto Rico with respect to U.S.)

Estados Unidos (EE.UU.) United States (USA)

estampa sketch (drama)

estampilla postage stamp; **estampillas de alimento** food stamps

estar to be; to look; **estar al día** to be up to date; **estar a solas** to be alone; **estar de mal humor** to be in a bad mood; **estar de pie** to be standing; **estar al tanto** to keep informed, to be on the alert

este, esta (adj) this, **estos, estas** these; **éste, ésta** (pron) this one; **éstos, éstas** (pron), these

estereofónico/a (adj) stereophonic

estilista (m/f) stylist

estilo style

estimado/a (adj) dear, esteemed, valued, (**estimar** to value, respect)

estipendio stipend, salary, wage

esto (neutral pron) this

estómago stomach

estoy de lo más bien (PR) I'm feeling great

estreñimiento constipation

estructura structure; **estructuras básicas** basic structures

estudiante (m/f) student

estudiantil (adj) student

estudiar to study

estudio study, library; **estudios** studies, education

estufa stove, heater

estupendo/a (adj) stupendous, wonderful

etiqueta label; etiquette

Europa Europe

evaluación (f) evaluation

evidencia evidence

evidente (adj) evident, obvious

evitar to avoid, elude; to prevent

exactamente (adv) exactly

exacto/a (adj) exact, accurate

exagerar to exaggerate

examen (m) examination; **examen físico** physical exam

excelente (adj) excellent, very good

excepción (f) exception

excepcional (adj) exceptional

exclamar to exclaim, cry out

excusado (MA, n) bathroom; **excusado/a** (adj) exempt; private

exilio exile

existencia existence

éxito success

éxodo exodus

experiencia experience

experimentar to experience; **experimentado/a** (adj) experienced (person)

explicar to explain

exportador/a (m/f) exporter; (adj) exporting

expresar to express

extranjerizante foreignizing

extranjero/a (n) foreigner

extrañar to miss (someone or something emotionally)

extraordinariamente (adv) extraordinarily

extraordinario/a (adj) extraordinary

fábrica factory, mill

fachada front

fácil (adj) easy

fácilmente (adv) easily

factor (m) factor, agent

factoría (ang) factory

facultad (f) faculty, ability

falso/a (adj) false

faltar to lack; to be lacking or needed; **faltar a** to be absent from

fallecer to die, pass away

familia family

familiar (m) relative, member of the family; (adj) familiar

famoso/a (adj) famous

fantástico/a (adj) fantastic, unbelievable

farmacéutico/a (n) pharmacist; (adj) pharmaceutical

farmacia pharmacy

fascinación (f) fascination

fatalismo fatalism

fe (f) faith

febrero February

fecha date

feliz (adj) happy

fenómeno (n) phenomenon; freak

feria country market, fair

ferino/a (adj) ferocious

feroz (adj) ferocious, fierce

feto fetus

fianza bail, bond

fiar to give credit; **fiarse de** to trust, rely on; **ser de fiar** to be trustworthy

fricasé (m) fricassee

fiebre (f) fever; **fiebre reumática** rheumatic fever

fiel (adj) faithful, loyal

fiesta party, celebration

figura figure, build

fijar to fix, make fast; to establish; **fijarse (en)** to notice, pay attention (to)
fin (m) end
financiar to finance
financiero/a (n) financier; (adj) financial
finca farm, country estate
físico/a (adj) physical
fisiológico/a (adj) physiological
flan (m) custard
flema phlegm
florido/a (adj) florid, flowery
forma form, shape; (ang) application form
formación (f) formation, training
formulario (n) form (written)
fortuna fortune, chance
foto (f) (also **fotografía**) photograph
francamente (adv) frankly
frasco bottle, flask
frecuencia frequency; **¿con qué frecuencia?** how often
fregadero kitchen sink
fresa strawberry
fresco/a (adj) cool; fresh
frigorífico (O) refrigerator
frijol (M/m) bean; **frijoles refritos** refried beans
frío/a (adj) cold
frisa (PR) blanket
frito/a (adj) fried (**freír** to fry)
fritura fried food
fruta fruit; **fruta bomba** (C) papaya
fuego fire
fuera (adv) out, outside; **fuera de** (prep) outside of
fuerte (adj) strong
fuerza strength, force
fumar to smoke
función (f) function
funcionar to function, work
furioso/a (adj) furious
fútbol (m) soccer; **fútbol americano** football
futuro (n) future; **futuro/a** (adj) future

gallego/a (adj/n) Galician
galleta (MA, PR) cookie, cracker; **galletica** (C) cookie, cracker; **galletita** (PR) cookie
gallina hen
gallo rooster
gamba shrimp
ganar to gain, earn, win; **ganarse la vida** to earn one's living
gana desire; **tener ganas (de)** to feel like (doing something)
ganchito (dim) small hook
garaje (m) garage
garbanzo chickpea
gas (m) gas (vapor)
gaseosa soda pop
gaseoso/a (adj) gaseous
gasto expense (**gastar** to spend)

gavetero chest of drawers
general (adj/n) general; **por lo general, generalmente** (adv) usually, generally
gente (f) people; **gente acomodada** wealthy class; upper class
gentilmente (adv) kindly, graciously
gerente (m/f) manager
gesto gesture, expression
giratorio/a (adj) revolving
gloria glory, heaven
gobernador/a (m/f) governor
goloso/a (adj) sweet-toothed
golosina delicacy
goma de pegar glue
gordo/a (adj) fat
gozar to enjoy
gracia humor, charm
gracias thanks
grado degree, grade (level in school)
graduarse to graduate
grande (adj) large; great (**gran** before singular noun)
grasa fat, grease
grasoso/a (adj) greasy
grave (adj) serious
griego/a (adj/n) Greek
grifo faucet
gringo/a (colloq) Anglo Saxon
gripe (also **gripa**) (f) grippe, cold
gritar to shout, cry out
grupo group, cluster
guachinango (M) red snapper
guajiro/a (C) farmworker, peasant
guanábana soursop fruit
guardar to save; to keep, to watch over; **guardar cama** to stay in bed
guardarropa (m) wardrobe
guatemalteco/a (adj/n) Guatemalan
guayaba guava; **guayaba con queso** guava (paste) with cheese
guerra war, warfare
guía (m/f) guide, leader; (f) guidebook, directory; **guía telefónica** telephone directory
guineo (C, PR) banana
güiro Caribbean musical instrument
guisado (u) stew; **guisado/a** (adj) cooked, stewed (**guisar** to cook, stew)
guisante (m) pea
guitarra guitar
gula glottony
gustar to please, to taste
gusto taste, flavor; liking; pleasure

¿Ha entendido bien? Have you understood well?
haber to have (auxiliary)
habichuela kidney bean; **habichuelas rosadas** pink beans; **habichuelas tiernas** (MA, PR) green beans
hábil (adj) skillful

habilidad (f) ability
habitación (f) dwelling; room; bedroom
hábito habit, custom
hablar to speak, talk
hacer to make; to have; to do; **hacer falta** to be necessary, needed; **hacer preguntas** to ask questions; **hacerle confidencias (a alguien)** to confide (in someone); **hacerle daño (a alguien)** to hurt, injure someone
hacienda large farm, landed estate
haciendo el papel role-playing
hambre, el (f) hunger
hamburguesa hamburger
harina wheat flour
hartarse to gorge, stuff oneself
hasta (prep) until, till; as far as; **hasta luego** see you later, until later; **hasta mañana** see you tomorrow, until tomorrow; **hasta que** (conj) until
hay there is, there are (from **haber**)
hecho/a (adj) made, done, finished; **hecho/a a mano** (adj) hand-made
helado (n) ice cream; **helado/a** (adj) frozen
hembra female
hembrismo belief in the special spiritual qualities of women
herir (ie) to wound
hermano/a brother/sister
heroína heroine; heroin
hidalgo nobleman, gentleman
hielera (MA) refrigerator
hierba grass; (colloq) marijuana
hierro iron
hígado liver
hijo/a son/daughter
hijo de puta bastard
hinchar to swell
hinchazón (f) swelling, lump
hipoteca mortgage
hispano (adj/n) Hispanic
Hispanoamérica Latin America
hispanoparlante (also **hispanohablante**) (m/f) Spanish-speaker
historia history, story
historial (adj) historical; **historial médico** (m) medical history
hito highlight
hogar (m) home, hearth
¡hola! hello!
hombre (m) man; **hombre de negocios** businessman; **hombre honrado** honorable man
hombro shoulder
hondureño/a (adj/n) Honduran
hongo (PR, O) mushroom
honor (m) honor
honra reputation, honor, respect
honradez (f) honesty, integrity
hora hour; time (of day)

horario schedule, timetable
horizontal (adj) horizontal
hormigueo tingling sensation
hornear to bake bread
horno oven
horrible (adj) horrid, horrible
hospital (m) hospital
hospitalizado/a (adj) hospitalized (**hospitalizar** to hospitalize)
hoy (adv) today; **hoy (en) día** nowadays
hueso bone
huevo egg; (colloq) testicle; **huevos fritos** fried eggs; **huevos revueltos** scrambled eggs
humilde (adj) humble; lowly
hurto theft, pilferage

Iberoamérica Latin America
ictericia jaundice
idealista (m/f) idealist; (adj) idealistic
identidad (f) identity
identificar to identify
idioma (m) language
iglesia church
igual (adj) equal; **igualmente** (adv) equally
ilustrado/a (adj) illustrated, made clear (**ilustrar** to illustrate)
imaginación (f) imagination
imaginar to imagine; **¡imagínese!** just imagine!
implicar to implicate, involve, to imply
importador/a (m/f) importer; (adj) importing
importancia importance
importante (adj) important
importar to be important, to matter; to import
imposible (adj) impossible
impuesto (n) tax, duty; **impuesto/a** (adj) imposed
incidente (m) incident; (adj) incidental
incluir to include; to enclose
incoherente (adj) incoherent, disconnected
incompetente (adj) incompetent
increíble (adj) incredible
indicar to indicate, point out
indicativo (n) indicative mood (grammar); **indicativo/a** (adj) indicative
indiferente (adj) indifferent, unconcerned
indirecto/a (adj) indirect
indispensable (adj) indispensable, necessary
individuo (n); **individuo/a** (adj) individual
inesperado/a (adj) unexpected
inestabilidad (f) instability
infamia infamy; infamous act
infancia infancy, babyhood
infección (f) infection; **infección venérea** venereal infection
inferior (adj) inferior; lower
infierno hell, inferno
influencia influence
influir to influence, act on

información (f) information
informar to inform
ingeniero/a engineer; **ingeniero/a civil** civil engineer
inglés (m) English language; **inglés/a** (adj/n) English
ingreso (n) entrance; **ingresos** earnings, income
inherente inherent
ininterrumpido/a (adj) uninterrupted (**interrumpir** to interrupt)
inmediatamente (adv) immediately
inocente (adj/n) innocent
inodoro toilet
inofensivo/a (adj) inoffensive
inquisición (f) inquisition, investigation
inseguridad (f) insecurity
insignificante (adj) insignificant
insípido/a (adj) insipid, tasteless
insistir to insist
insomnio insomnia
institucional (adj) institutional
instrucción (f) instruction, teaching
instrumento instrument, tool
insular (n) islander; (adj) insular
insulina insulin
insulto insult, affront
inteligencia intelligence
inteligente (adj) intelligent, understanding
intentar to try
interés (m) interest
interesar to interest; **interesarse (en/por)** to be interested (in)
interior (adj/n, m) interior
internar(se) to enter a hospital as an inpatient
intérprete (m/f) interpreter
interrogar to interrogate, question
interrogatorio (n) interrogatory, questioning
intervenir (ie) to intervene, to take part
intestinal (adj) intestinal
intestino (n) intestine; (adj) intestinal
intoxicado/a (adj) poisoned; (ang) intoxicated (**intoxicar** to poison)
intransigencia intransigence
introducir to insert, to introduce
inútil (adj) useless
investigar to investigate
invitado/a (n) invited guest; (adj) invited
inyección (f) injection; **ponerle una inyección a alguien** to give someone an injection
ir to go, proceed, walk; **irse** to leave
ira anger
isla island
izquierda left-hand side; **a la izquierda** to the left
izquierdo (adj) left

jamón (m) ham
jamonada (C) pork sausage
jaqueca migraine headache
jardín (m) garden
jefe/a (m/f) boss, chief

jefito/a (dim/MA) father/mother
Jesucristo Jesus Christ
Jesús/a (m/f) common Hispanic name
jíbaro/a (PR) peasant, country dweller
joder (C, PR, O) to "screw" (obscenity)
joven (m/f) youth, young man/woman; (adj) young
judía (verde) string (green) bean
judío/a (adj/n) Jew(ish)
juego play, playing; game
jueves (m) Thursday
juez (m) judge
jugar (ue) to play; to gamble
jugo juice; **jugo de tomate** tomato juice; **jugo de china** (PR) orange juice
juguete (m) toy, plaything
juicio judgement; wisdom; trial
julio July
junio June
junta (n) board (executive group); military junta
junto (adv) close by, near; **junto a** (prep) next to, beside
junto/a (adj) united, assembled
jurado (n) jury, panel
justicia justice, virtue
justo (adv) justly, rightly; **justo/a** (adj) just, fair
juzgado court of law; **juzgado de paz** Justice of the Peace
juzgar to judge, try

kilo kilogram
kilómetro kilometer

la (def art) the (before nouns); (s do pron) her
labio lip
laboratorio laboratory
lado side; **por un lado** on the one hand; **por otro lado** on the other hand
ladrón thief, robber
lámpara lamp
langostino prawn
largo (adv) largely, extendedly; **largo/a** (adj) long
latino/a (adj/n) Latin, Hispanic
lavabo washstand; washroom
lavadora washing machine
lavamanos (m, s) washstand, lavatory
lavaplatos (m, s) dishwasher
lavar to wash, clean
le (s io pron) him, to or for him; her, to or for her; you, to or for you (form)
lección (f) lesson
leche (f) milk; **leche descremada** skimmed milk
lecho bed, couch
lechón (m) pig, pork; **lechón asado** roasted pork; **lechón/a** (adj) dirty, sluggish
lechosa (PR, O) papaya
lechuga lettuce
leer to read
legal (adj) legal, lawful
legumbre (f) legume, vegetable

lejos (adv) far, far away; **lejos de** (prep) far from
lengua tongue; language
lenguado sole, flounder
les (pl io pron) them, to or for them; you, to or for you
letra letter (of the alphabet); handwriting
leucemia leukemia
levantar to raise, lift; **levantarse** to get up (from bed)
ley (f) law
liberal (n) a politically liberal person; (adj) liberal, generous
libertad (f) liberty, freedom
libre (adj) free, independent
libremente (adv) freely; boldly
licencia license, permission, permit; **licencia de conducir** driver's license
licenciado/a (n) licenciate, graduate; lawyer
licor (m) liquor
ligero (adv) fast, rapidly; **ligero/a** (adj) light; swift
límite (m) limit, bound
limón (m) lemon
lindo/a (adj) beautiful, pretty
línea line
lingüística (n) linguistics; **lingüístico/a** (adj) linguistic; **notas lingüísticas** grammar notes
líquido (n) liquid; **líquido/a** (adj) liquid
lista list; menu
listo/a (adj) ready (with **estar**); intelligent, witty (with **ser**)
lo (neuter pron) it, that which is; (s do pron) him, you (form); **lo que** that which; **lo siento** I'm sorry, I regret it
loco/a (adj) crazy
lograr to get, acquire; to achieve; to succeed at
los (def art) the; (pl do pron) them, you (m, pl)
luchar to fight, struggle
luego (adv) afterward, later, then
lugar (m) place; **lugarcito** (dim)
lujo luxury
luna moon; **luna de miel** honeymoon
lunes (m) Monday
luz (f) light

llamar to call; to telephone; **llamarse** to be called or named
llanta (n) tire
llave (f) key; water faucet
llegar to arrive
llenar to fill
lleno/a (adj) full
llevar to carry, take; (with expressions of time) to have been ¿**Cuánto tiempo lleva aquí?** How long have you been here?; **llevarse** to take with, carry off; to steal; **llevarse bien (con alguien)** to get along well (with someone)

machete (m) machete (knife)
machismo male Hispanic behavior code
machista (adj) pertaining to male-oriented cultures

macho (n) male
madre (f) mother
madrileño/a (adj/n) Madrilenian (from Madrid)
madrina godmother
madrugada dawn, daybreak
madurar to mature, ripen
maduro (C, PR, n) fried ripe plantain; **maduro/a** (adj) mature, ripe
maestría (n) master's degree
maestro/a (n) teacher; (adj) masterful, great; **maestro/a de primaria** elementary school teacher
magia magic
mágico/a (adj) magic
magnífico/a (adj) magnificent
maguey (m) maguey, century plant
maíz (m) corn
mal (m) illness; harm; **mal de ojo** evil eye; (adv) badly; ill (with **estar**)
malicia malice
malnutrición (f) malnutrition
malo/a (adj) (**mal** before masculine, singular noun) bad; **mal humor** bad mood; **mal puesto** sorcery; **mala suerte** bad luck
malta malt, roasted barley
maltratado/a (adj) mistreated (**maltratar** to mistrust, abuse)
maltrato (n) abuse
mamá mama, mother; **mamita** (dim)
mandamiento mandate, order, command, commandment
mandar to command, order; to send
mandato order, command
manejar to manage, handle; to drive
manera way, manner
mango handle; mango (fruit)
maní (C, PR, m) peanut
mano (f) hand; **a mano armada** (adj) armed (with a weapon
manta blanket
manteca lard, fat
mantecado (C, PR, n) ice cream
mantener to support, provide for; to maintain
mantenimiento maintenance; upkeep
mantequilla butter
manual (m) handbook; (adj) manual, physical
manzana apple
manzanilla camomile (herb)
mañana (n) morning, tomorrow; (adv) tomorrow
máquina machine; **máquina de coser** sewing machine
maquinaria machinery
mar (m/f) sea
maravilloso/a (adj) wonderful
marear to bother; **marearse** to get dizzy, seasick
mareos (m, pl) dizzyness
margarina margarine
marianismo female Hispanic behavior code patterned after the Virgin Mary
maricón (m) homosexual (derrogatory term)

marido husband

marielito Cuban refugee who arrived in U.S. via the 1980 Mariel boatlift

marihuana marijuana

marisco shellfish

martes (m) Tuesday; **martes de carnaval** Shrove Tuesday

marzo March

más (adv; adj) more, most; **más bien** (adv) rather; **más o menos** more or less

masa dough; mass (of people)

mate (m) South American tea; (adj) dull, lusterless

matar to kill, murder

matemáticas (f, pl) mathematics

matemático/a (n) mathematician; (adj) mathematical

materia matter, material; subject, class (in school)

matrícula registration; matriculation; **matrícula de vehículo** motor vehicle registration

matrimonial (adj) matrimonial

matrimonio (n) matrimony, marriage; married couple

matriz (f) womb

máximo (n) maximum; **máximo/a** maximum

mayo May

mayor (m/f) major; (adj) larger, largest; older, oldest; **la mayor parte** greater part, majority

mayoría majority

mazorca ear of corn

me (do, io, reflex pron) me, to or for me, myself

mecánico/a (n) mechanic; (adj) mechanical

media stocking, sock

medianoche (f) midnight

medicamento medication

medicina medicine

médico/a (n) physician; (adj) medical

medio (n) middle; means; (adv) half; **medio/a** (adj) half

mediodía (m) noon, midday

medir (i) to measure

mejilla cheek

mejor (adj) better, best

mejorar to improve, recover; **mejorarse** to get better

melocotón (PR, O, m) peach; **melocotones en almíbar** peaches in heavy syrup

melón (m) melon, cantaloupe; **melón de agua** (PR) watermelon

mencionado/a (adj) mentioned (**mencionar** to mention)

menor (m/f) minor; (adj) smaller, smallest; younger, youngest

menos (adv) less, least; (conj) except; but

mensaje (m) message

mensual (adj) monthly

mentira lie, fib

menú (m) menu

menudo (n) change (coins); (PR, C) tripe stew; **menudo/a** (adj) small

mercado market

merecer to deserve

merienda afternoon snack

mermelada marmalade

mes (m) month

mesa table

mestizo/a (adj/n) half-breed (Indian/European)

meter to put (into); **meterse** to meddle, interfere; **meterse la aguja** to "shoot up" drugs

método (n) method

mexicano/a (adj/n) Mexican

mi (poss adj) my

mí (pron used after a prep) me

miedo fear; **tener miedo (de)** to be afraid (of)

miedoso/a (adj) fearful, afraid

miembro member; limb

mientras (adv/conj) while

miércoles (m) Wednesday; **miércoles de ceniza** Ash Wednesday

mierda "shit" (obscenity)

Migra, (La) (colloq) U.S. immigration officers

mil one thousand; **mil gracias** thank you very much; **miles (de)** (pl) thousands (of)

milagro miracle

millón (de) (m) million

ministro minister

minuto (n) minute

mío, mía, míos, mías (adj) mine, of mine; (pron) mine

mirada glance, look

mirar to look at

miserable (adj) miserable

mismo (adv) right; **ahora mismo** right now; **aquí mismo** right here; **mismo/a** (adj) same; very; self; **ella misma** she herself

misterio mystery

moda fashion, style

moderno/a (adj) modern

modoso/a (adj) quiet, well-behaved

mojito (C) alcoholic drink of rum, lemon, mint

mole poblano Mexican sauce of chocolate, chilies and tomatoes

molestar to disturb; annoy; **molestarse** to be annoyed

molestia trouble; discomfort

molesto/a (adj) irritated, bothered

molestoso/a (adj) troublesome

momento moment; **momentito** (dim) a little while

monga (PR) flu

monstruo (n) monster

montado/a (adj) mounted (**montar** to mount)

mordida (M, colloq) bribe

morir(se) (ue) to die

moro/a (n) Moor; (adj) Moorish; **moros y cristianos** (C) black beans and white rice

mortadella (C) type of sausage

mostrar (ue) to show, exhibit

mota (colloq) marijuana

muchacho/a boy, girl

mucho (adv) much, a lot, often; **mucho/a** (adj) much, many **muchas gracias** (many) thanks; **mucho gusto** pleased to meet you; **con mucho gusto** with much pleasure

mucosidad (f) mucosity

mueble (m) a piece of furniture
muerte (f) death
mujer (f) woman
mujeriego (m, colloq) womanizer
mulato/a (adj/n) mulatto
mundial (adj) universal, worldwide
mundo (n) world
muy (adv) very, very much, most

nacer to be born; (fig) to sprout
nacimiento birth
nación (f) nation
nacional (adj) national
nacionalidad (f) nationality
nada (n) nothing, not anything; **de nada** you're welcome (in response to **gracias**); (adv) not at all
nadie (pron) nobody, no one
naranja (n) orange (fruit); **naranja china** (C) orange
nariz (f) nose
nativo/a (adj/n) native
natural (adj) natural, native
náusea nausea
navaja pen knife, clasp knife
Navidad (f) Christmas
necesariamente (adv) necessarily
necesario/a (adj) necessary
necesidad (f) necessity
necesitar to need, necessitate
negocio business, interest
negro/a (n) Negro; also used as a term of endearment; (adj) black
neoyorquino/a (adj/n) Puerto Rican born on the mainland (New York)
nene/a (PR, C; m/f) baby, child
nervio nerve
nerviosidad (f) nervousness
nervioso/a (adj) nervous
nevera (PR, O) refrigerator
ni (conj) neither, nor
nicaragüense (adj; m/f) Nicaraguan
nieto/a grandchild
ninguno (adj) no, not one, not any (**ningún** before masculine, singular noun)
niño/a male/female child; infant
nítido/a (adj) neat; clear; sharp
nivel (m) level
no no, not; **no hay de qué** don't mention it; **no más** only; ¡**No me diga!** You don't say!
nocturno/a (adj) nocturnal, evening
noche (f) night, evening
Nochebuena Christmas Eve
nombrar to name, mention, appoint
nombre (m) name
norsa (PR) nurse
norte (m) north
norteamericano/a (adj/n) North American (from the U.S.)
nos (do, io, reflex pron) us, to or for us

nosotros/as (m/f, pron) we
noticia news item; (pl) news
nota note; grade, mark; fame
novecientos nine hundred
noveno/a (adj) ninth
noventa ninety
noviazgo engagement
noviembre (m) November
novio/a sweetheart, fiancé/e
nuestro/a (poss adj) our; (poss pron) ours
nuevamente (adv) again
nueve nine
nuevo/a (adj) new
nuez (f) walnut; nut
numérico/a (adj) numerical
número (n) number
nunca (adv) never
nutrición (f) nutrition, nourishment
nutritivo/a (adj) nutritious

o (conj) or, either; **o . . . o** either . . . or
objetivo (n) objective; **objetivo/a** (adj) objective
obituario obituary
obligación (f) obligation, duty
obligado/a (adj) obliged (**obligar** to oblige)
obra work, piece of work; act; labor
obscuro/a (adj) dark
obscuridad (f) darkness, obscurity
obtener (ie) to obtain; to attain
ocasión (f) occasion, opportunity
octavo/a (adj) eighth
octubre (m) October
ocupado/a (adj) busy (**ocupar** to occupy; **ocuparse en** to be engaged in)
ocurrir to occur
ochenta eighty
ocho eight
oda ode
odio hatred
ofender to offend; to displease
ofensa offense
oficial (m) official, officer; (adj) official
oficina office, shop
oficinista (m/f) office worker
oficio office, position, trade
ofrecer to offer; to promise
oído hearing; inner ear
oigo (C) hello (used to answer the telephone)
oír to hear, listen
ojalá may God grant that . . . ; I hope that . . .
ojo (n) eye
ola (n) (sea)wave
olvidar to forget; **olvidarse de** to forget (about)
once eleven
opción (f) option, choice
operación (f) operation
operar to operate; to take effect
opinión (f) opinion

oración (f) oration; prayer; sentence
oral (adj) oral; oralmente (adv) orally
orar to pray
orden (m) order, sequence; (f) command; a la orden, a sus órdenes at your service
oreja ear
órgano organ; instrument
orgullo pride; arrogance
orgulloso/a (adj) proud, arrogant
origen (m) origin, source
originalmente (adv) originally
orinar to urinate
oro gold
otro/a (adj/pron) other, another
ovario ovary

paciente (m/f) (medical) patient; (adj) patient
padecer to suffer
padre (m) father; priest; padres parents; ancestors
padrino godfather
pagar to pay (for)
pago payment; prize
país (m) country
paisaje (m) landscape
palabra word; promise; palabra de honor word of honor
pan (m) bread; pan tostado toast
panal (m) honeycomb; sweetmeat
panameño/a (adj/n) Panamanian
páncreas (m) pancreas
panecito (C, PR, O) roll, bun
pánico (n) panic
panqué (m) small cake, cupcake; (C) muffin
pantalon/es (m, s/p) trousers, pants
panzón (m/aug) (also panza) belly; (adj/aug) big-bellied belly
papa (f) potato; Papa (m) (the) Pope
papá (m) daddy, father; papito (dim)
papaya papaya
papel (m) paper; document
par (adj) even; (m) pair, couple
para (prep) for, to, toward
parado/a (adj) stopped; standing (parar to stop; pararse to stand up)
paraguayo/a (adj/n) Paraguayan
paraíso paradise, heaven
paramédico paramedic
parcial (adj) partial; parcialmente (adv) partially
parecer to seem, appear; parecerse a to resemble
parentesco kinship, relationship
pariente (m/f) relative, relation
parte (f) part; share
participar to participate, share
partida (n) departure
partido (n) (political) party, faction; game; partido/a (adj) broken
Partido Revolucionario Institucional (PRI) Institutional Revolutionary Party, principal political party of Mexico
partir to divide, share; to depart
parranda spree, revel
pasado (n) past; pasado/a (adj) past
pasar to pass; to spend (time); to go by; to happen; ¿Qué le pasa? What is wrong?
pasatiempo pastime, hobby
Pascua Easter; Pascua Florida Easter Sunday; Las Pascuas Christmas
pasillo aisle; hallway
pastel (m) pie, pastry; (C, M, O) cake; pastelillos (PR) fried pastry with meat filling
pastilla tablet, pill
pasto pasture; (colloq) marijuana
pata foot, leg (of animal or furniture); pata de cerdo pig's foot; patica rebozada (C) breaded pig's foot
patio patio, courtyard
patria fatherland, native country
patriótico/a (adj) patriotic
patrón/a patron saint; boss; proprietor
pavo turkey
payaso clown
pecado sin, imperfection; pecado capital deadly sin
pecador/a (m/f) sinner; (adj) sinning, sinful
pecho chest; breast
pedazo piece, portion
pedido order, request (pedir [i] to request; to ask for)
pega (n) act of sticking together; (C/colloq) a job
pegadura (n) glue
pegar to glue, cement, paste; to hit
peinado (n) hairdo; peinado/a (adj) combed
pelea fight, battle, combat; pelea de gallo cockfight
pelear to fight; to quarrel
peligroso/a (adj) dangerous; peligrosísimo/a (adj) very dangerous
peor (adj/adv) worse; worst
pena (n) penalty, punishment; bother; heartache; pena de muerte death penalty; dar pena to arouse pity
pendejo (n) "asshole" (obscenity)
pensar (ie) to think, think over; to intend; pensar en to think about someone or something; pensar de to think of, have an opinion about; piénselo (imp) think about it
pensión (f) pension
pequeño/a (adj) small
perder (ie) to lose; to miss; to ruin; perderse to get lost
pérdida (n) loss; waste
perdón (m) pardon, forgiveness; ¡Perdón! Excuse me! (said before interrupting someone)
perdonar to pardon, forgive
pereza laziness
perezoso/a (adj) lazy
perfecto/a (adj) perfect
pérfido/a (adj) perfidious, treacherous
perfume (m) perfume, fragrance
permanecer to remain, last, endure

permiso permission, license
permitir to permit; to grant
pero (conj) but, except, yet
perro dog
persona person; personage
personal (m) personnel; (adj) personal
personalismo belief in the person rather than in the system
personalmente (adv) personally
peruano/a (adj/n) Peruvian
perverso/a (adj) perverse, wicked
pesadilla nightmare
pesado/a (adj) heavy; tiresome, boring
pesadumbre (f) grief, sorrow
pésame (m) condolence, expression of sympathy
pesar to weigh; to consider; to have weight or value; to cause grief
pescado (n) fish (as food); **pescado frito** fried fish
pescar to fish; to catch
petate (m) bundle; straw mat
pez (m) fish (while alive)
pez vela (m) sailfish
picadillo (C) meat and vegetable hash; mincemeat
picante (adj) pricking; spicy
picar to prick; to pierce; to bite; to itch
picazón (f) itch, itching
pichón (m) pigeon; dupe, novice; **pichón/a** (adj/ang) timid, shy
pie (m) foot; stem; base
piedad (f) piety; pity; mercy
piel (f) skin; hide, leather; fur
pierna leg
pieza piece; part; room; play; (M) bedroom
pila basin; electric battery; (C) faucet
pimienta (n) ground black pepper
pimiento green or red pepper
pintura painting; paint, pigment
piña pineapple
piñata hanging container filled with candy, fruit, etc.
piropo flattery, compliment
pirulí (C) lollipop
piso floor, story; pavement; apartment
pisto (O/colloq) money
pistola pistol
placa badge; plaque; license plate; (PR) X-ray
placer to please; (m) pleasure
plácido/a (adj) placid
plan (m) plan; design; project
planear to plan; to glide
planta baja ground floor
plata silver; money; wage; **ganar buena plata** (colloq) to earn a good wage
plátano plantain; plantain tree
plato plate; dinner course
playa beach, shore
plazo (n) term, time; seat; **a plazos** on credit
plegaria supplication, prayer

pleno/a (adj) full; **en plena calle** in the middle of the street
plomero/a plumber
pluma de agua (PR) faucet
población (f) population; town
pobre (adj) poor; unfortunate (before a noun)
pobreza poverty; need
poco (n), **poquito** (dim) a little bit; **poco/a** (adj), **poquito/a** (dim) little, scanty; small
poder (ue) to be able; (m) power
poema (m) poem
policía (f) police force; policewoman; (m) policeman
policíaco/a (adj) pertaining to the police
póliza policy, written contract
pollo chicken; **pollo al horno** baked chicken
poner to put, place; to set; **ponerse** to place oneself; to put on (clothes); to become (+ adj); **ponerse celoso** to become jealous
popular (adj) popular
por (prep) by; for; for the sake of; because of; through; in exchange for; in place of; during; about; around; **por el estilo** along those lines; **por favor** please; **por fin** at last, finally; **por fortuna** fortunately; **por medio de** by means of; **¿por qué?** why?; **por si acaso** in case; **por su propia cuenta** on one's own
porque (m) reason; (conj) because, for, as
porquería dirty trick; filth
posada (n) inn
posesión (f) possession; property
posibilidad (f) possibility
postal (f) postcard; (adj) postal, mail
postre (m) dessert
práctica practice, exercise; **práctica preliminar** preliminary practice
practicante (m/f) doctor's assistant, hospital intern; (adj) practicing; **enfermera practicante** practical nurse
practicar to practice; to put into practice
precisamente (adv) precisely, exactly
predicador/a (m/f) preacher; (adj) preaching
predicar to preach
preferible (adj) preferable
preferir (ie) to prefer
pregunta question
preguntar to ask (a question); **pregunte Ud.** (imp) ask (the question)
prejuicio prejudice
preliminar (adj) preliminary
preocupar to preoccupy; to worry; **preocuparse (de, por)** to be preoccupied (with), to worry (about); **¡No se preocupe!** (imp) Don't worry!
preocupación (f) preoccupation, worry
preparación (f) preparation
preparar to prepare; **prepararse** to get ready, be prepared
presentar to present, introduce; **presentarse** to appear; to introduce oneself

presente (adj/n, m) present
presión (f) pressure; **alta presión (de la sangre)** high (blood) pressure
prestar to loan; **prestar atención** to pay attention
previo/a (adj) previous
primario/a (adj) primary, principal
primero (adv) first; foremost; **primero/a** (adj) (**primer** before masculine, singular noun) first, former; leading; principal
primo/a cousin
principio (n) principal; beginning
prisa speed, haste
privado/a (adj) private; personal
probatoria probation
problema (m) problem
procedimiento procedure; method, process; conduct
procesar to prosecute; to accuse; to indict; to sue
proceso process; lawsuit; lapse of time; trial
procurar to procure, obtain; to try
producir to produce; to bring about
producto product
profesión (f) profession, calling; professing
profesor/a (n) professor, teacher
programa (m) program
progreso progress
prometido/a (adj) promised; betrothed; (m/f) fiancé(e) (**prometer** to promise)
promover (ue) to promote, further, start
pronto (adv) soon; **pronto/a** (adj) prompt, quick
pronunciación (f) pronunciation
propina (n) tip, fee, gratuity
propio/a (adj) one's own; proper, peculiar, appropriate
proponer to propose; to nominate
proporcionar to give, provide
prostituta prostitute
protestante (adj/n) Protestant; (adj) protesting
provecho advantage, benefit, **buen provecho** enjoy your food (said to someone who is eating)
próximo/a (adj) near; neighboring; next
prueba proof, demonstration, evidence; test
(p)sicólogo/a (n) psychologist
(p)siquiatra (m/f) psychiatrist
(p)siquiátrico/a (adj) psychiatric
(p)síquico/a (adj/n) psychic
público (m) public; audience; **público/a** (adj) public
pudor (m) modesty, chastity
pueblo town; people; nation
puerco (m) pig, hog; **puerco/a** (adj) dirty; piggish
puerta door, doorway, entrance
puerto port, harbor, haven
puertorriqueño/a (adj/n) Puerto Rican
pues (conj) because, for, since
puesto (n) place; stand; office, job; **puesto/a** (adj) placed, put, set
pulcro/a (adj) neat
pulgada inch
pulmón (m) lung
pulmonía pneumonia

pulpo octopus
pulque (M, m) pulque, fermented "home brew"
puta harlot, whore

que (rel pron) that; which; who; whom; (conj) that; for, because
qué (interrog adj/pron) what?; (interrog adv) how?; **¡Qué barbaridad!** What an atrocity!; (interrog adj/pron) **¡Qué bueno!** How wonderful!; **¿Qué hay?** What's up?, What's new?; **¿Qué importa?** What does it matter?; **¿Qué le pasa?** What's wrong (with you)?; What's happening?; **¡Qué más da!** What does it matter!; **¡Qué pena!** What a shame!; **¿Qué tal?** How's it going?; **¿Qué tiene?** What's wrong?; **¡Qué va!** Nonsense!; Go on! (expresses disbelief)
quedar to stay, remain; to be left; **quedarse** to remain
quejarse (de) to complain (about); to grumble
queque (MA) cake
querer (ie) to want, wish, desire; to will; to love
querido/a (n) lover; **querido/a** (adj) beloved, dear
queso cheese; **queso del país** local cheese
quien (rel pron) who, whom; he who, she who; **¿quién?** (interrog pron) who?, whom?
quieto/a (adj) quiet, still, calm
químico/a (n) chemist; (adj) chemical
quince fifteen
quinceañero celebration of a girl's fifteenth birthday
quinto/a (adj) fifth
quitar to remove; to take away; **quitarse** to take off (clothing); to remove oneself
quizá/s (adv) perhaps, maybe

rabino rabbi
racionado/a (adj) rationed
racismo racism
racista (adj; m/f) racist
radiografía radiography, x-ray photography
rancho hut; cattle ranch
rato short while
raya dash, line; ray
rayo-X (m) X-ray
raza race (anthropological)
Raza, la term used by Hispanics, especially Mexicans, to refer to their unique mixed heritage (also **Raza de Oro**)
razón (f) reason; sanity; explanation; **tener razón** to be right
reaccionar to react
real (adj) real, actual
realidad (f) reality
rebajar to reduce, lower; to lose weight
rebozado/a (adj) covered up (**rebozar** to wrap oneself in a **rebozo**, cloak)
rebuenísimo (adj, colloq) *very* good
recado message, errand
recámara (M) bedroom
recepción (f) reception, formal gathering
recepcionista (m/f) receptionist

receta prescription; recipe
recetar to order, prescribe
recibir to receive
recién (adv) recently, lately; **recién llegado** newcomer
reciente (adj) recent, new; **recientemente** (adv) recently, lately
recoger to collect, gather up, pick up
recomendación (f) recommendation
recomendar (ie) to recommend
reconocer to inspect, examine; to recognize
reconocimiento inspection, examination; recognition; **reconocimiento médico** medical examination
reconquista (n) reconquest
récord (ang, m) record, mark (in sports, etc.)
recordar (ue) to remember; to remind
recto (n) rectum; **recto/a** (adj) straight; just, fair
recuperado/a (adj) recovered (**recuperar** to recover, regain; **recuperarse** to recuperate)
rechazar to reject, repel
rechazo rejection, rebound, recoil, repercussion
rechulo (adj, colloq) wonderful
reduro (adj/adv, colloq) *very* hard
referencia (n) reference
referir (ie) to relate, narrate; to refer; **referirse (a)** to refer (to)
reflejo (n) reflection; **reflejos de la cultura** cultural reflections; **reflejo/a** (adj) reflected (**reflejar** to reflect)
reflexivo/a (adj) reflexive (grammar)
refrán (m) adage, proverb
refresco refreshment, cold drink, soft drink
refrigerador (m) refrigerator
refritos (n, m, pl) refried beans; **refrito/a** (adj) fried again
refugio shelter, refuge, asylum
regatear to bargain
regla rule, regulation; ruler (for drawing lines)
regresar to return
regular (adj) regular, usual, moderate; (v) to regulate
rejodido/a (adj, colloq) messed up
relación (f) relation; story; **relaciones sexuales** sexual relations
relacionado/a (adj) related, connected (**relacionar** to relate; **relacionarse [con]** to have dealings [with])
relevante (adj) excellent, eminent; (ang) relevant
reloj (m) timepiece, clock, watch
relleno/a (adj) filled up, stuffed (**rellenar** to fill, stuff)
remedio remedy; **remedio casero** home remedy; **no hay más remedio que . . .** there's nothing else to do but . . .
remolacha (PR, C) beet
remordimiento remorse
rendido/a (adj) fatigued, exhausted
renta rent; interest, profit
reo/a (n) offender, culprit; (adj) guilty
reojo (mirar de) to look at out of the corner of one's eye
repentino/a (adj) sudden
repetir (i) to repeat

repollo (PR, C) cabbage
reporte (m) news, information, report
representación (f) representation
representante (m/f) representative; (adj) representative, representing
representar to represent, to show
reproductivo/a (adj) reproductive
requerir (ie) to require, request, order
requerido/a (adj) required
requisito prerequisite; requirement
res (f) head of cattle; **carne de res** beef
reservación (f) reservation
reservado/a (adj) reserved; discreet (**reservar** to hold in reserve, to keep back)
resfriado cold, catarrh
resfrío (MA) head cold
residencia residence; **residencia estudiantil** student dormitory
residente (m/f) resident, dweller; (adj) resident, residing
residir to reside
resignado/a (adj) resigned, committed (**resignar** to hand over one's power; **resignarse [a]** to be resigned [to])
resistir to resist, withstand
resolver (ue) to resolve; to solve
respetado/a (adj) respected (**respetar** to respect, honor)
respeto respect
respirar to breathe
responder to answer, respond to
responsabilidad (f) responsibility; liability
responsable (adj) responsible; liable
respuesta answer
restaurante (m) restaurant
resto remainder, balance, rest
resultado (n) result
resultar to result, follow, to come out
retener (ie) to retain
reumático/a (adj) rheumatic
reunión (f) reunion; gathering, meeting
reunir to reunite, gather together; **reunirse** to assemble
revolución (f) revolution
revolucionario/a (adj/n) revolutionary
revolver (ue) to stir, shake; disarrange
revólver (m) revolver
rezar to pray
rico/a (adj) rich; abundant; delicious
rigor (m) rigor, severity
riñón (m) kidney
robar to rob, plunder; to steal
robo robbery, theft
rodilla knee
romper to break; to shatter; to tear
ron (m) rum
ropa clothing
ropero closet, wardrobe
rosado/a (adj) rosy, rose-colored

rosario rosary
rótulo label, sign, poster
rubio/a (adj) blond; fair-skinned
rueda wheel
ruido noise; quarrel
rutina routine

sábado Saturday; **sábado de gloria** Holy Saturday (day before Easter)
saber to know; to know how to; **¿Sabe Ud.?** Do you know?
sabiamente wisely, prudently
sabio/a (n) learned person; (adj) wise, learned
saborear to savor; to season
sabroso/a (adj) savory, tasty; pleasant
sacar to draw, pull or take out; to put (something out); **sacar copias** to make copies; **sacar fotografías** to take photos
sacerdote (m) priest
sal (f) salt; **tener sal** to be lively
sala room; living room; **sala de espera** waiting room
salado/a (adj) salted, salty; cute; vivacious
salario salary
salchichón (m) pepperoni
saldina (PR, colloq) sardine
salida exit; departure
salir (de) to go out (of); to leave; to result
salsa sauce; gravy; (PR) lively Latin music popular among Puerto Ricans
saltar to jump; to bounce
salud (f) health; welfare
saludo salute, nod, greeting (**saludar** to greet)
salvadoreño/a (adj/n) Salvadoran
salvar to save, rescue; to exclude; **salvarse** to be saved, to escape
sancocho (PR, C) stew of meat, chicken and root vegetables
sandía watermelon
sangrar to bleed
sangre (f) blood
santería belief in the power of saints to speak and cure through living persons
santero/a (n) medium through whom a saint speaks or cures
Santiago Saint James (war cry of medieval Spaniards; patron saint of Spaniards during the Reconquest of Spain)
santo/a (n) saint; (adj) holy; **santón/a** (aug) very saintly
santo oficio Holy See office (Vatican)
sapo toad
sarampión (m) measles
sardina sardine
satisfacer to satisfy; to appease; **satisfacerse** to be satisfied
sazón (f) Caribbean mixture of spices
se (refl pron) oneself, himself, herself, yourself (form), themselves, yourselves; (io pron) to or for him, her, you (s/p form), them

secadora (clothes) dryer
secretario/a secretary
secuestrar to seize; to kidnap
secundaria (n) high school; **secundario/a** (adj) secondary
seda silk
sede (f) seat, see
seguido (adv) without interruption; **seguido/a** (adj) continuous, straight
seguir (i) to follow; to continue; to pursue
según (prep) according to; as
segundo (n) second; **segundo/a** (adj) second
seguro (n) insurance; **seguro/a** (adj) sure; secure, safe
seguro social social security
seis six
sello seal; stamp
semana week; **la semana pasada** last week
semanal (adj) weekly
seno breast, bosom; womb
sensatez (f) prudence, common sense
sentado/a seated (**sentar** to seat; **sentarse** to sit down)
sentido (n) sense; meaning; direction; **sentido/a** (adj) sincere; moving
sentimental (adj) sentimental
sentimiento sentiment, feeling
sentir (ie) to feel, sense; to regret; to be sorry; **sentirse** to feel
señal (f) mark; signal
señalar to mark; to point out; to set
señor (m) Mr.; sir; man
señora Mrs., madam; woman, lady
señorita Miss; young lady
separación (f) separation
separado/a (adj) separate (**separar** to separate; **separarse (de)** to cease living with one's spouse)
sepelio burial
se(p)tiembre (m) September
sé(p)timo/a (adj) seventh
ser (m) being; existence; **ser humano** human being; (v) to be; **ser de fiar** to be trustworthy
serie (f) series
serio/a (adj) serious, dignified
servicio service, duty; restroom
servidor/a (m/f) servant; **su seguro/a servidor/a** yours truly
servir (i) to serve; **servirse** to help oneself
sesenta sixty
sesión (f) session, meeting
seta (C, PR) mushroom
setenta seventy
sexo sex, gender
sexto/a (adj) sixth
sexual (adj) sexual
sí (adv) yes
si (conj) if, whether; **si Dios quiere** if God wills it, grants it; **si no** otherwise, else
sicólogo see **(p)sicólogo**
siempre (adv) always

siesta afternoon nap
siete seven
siglo century; period, epoch
signo sign; mark; signal
siguiente (adj) following
silla chair; saddle; **sillón** (m) large chair; easy chair
simpatía congeniality; harmony
simpático/a (adj) empathetic, pleasant, nice
simplemente (adv) simply
sin (prep) without; besides, not counting; **sin embargo** nevertheless, still, yet, however; **sin fuerzas** without energy
singular (adj) unique; **singularísimo** very unique
sino (conj) but
síntoma (m) symptom
sistema (m) system
situación (f) site, location; situation; predicament; **situaciones de la vida real** situations from real life
soberbia arrogance
sobornar to bribe
soborno bribery; bribe
sobre (m) envelope; (prep) over; on; upon; about, concerning
sobrecama bedspread
sobrepasar to exceed
sobrino/a nephew/niece
social (adj) social; sociable
sociedad (f) society; partnership; company
sofá (m) sofa
sofrito (PR, C) mixture of cooking spices
sol (m) sun; sunshine
solamente (adv) only
solar (m) plot of ground; site occupied by a building
soldado soldier
soledad (f) solitude; loneliness; sorrow
soler (ue) to have the custom of, to be in the habit of
solicitar to solicit; to apply for; to beg, ask for
solicitud (f) care, concern; application form
solo/a (adj) alone; lonely
sólo (adv) only
soltar (ue) to loosen; to let out; to drop, let go
soltero/a (n) unmarried person; (adj) single, not married
sombrero hat
sonreír (i) to smile
sonrisa smile
sopa soup
sorprender to surprise; to catch
sorpresa surprise
sospecha suspicion (**sospechar** to suspect)
sostén (m) support; sustenance; brassiere
sostener (ie) to hold; to maintain; to support
su, sus (poss adj) your (form, s/p), his, her, its, their
subir to go up; to lift up; to raise; to increase
subjuntivo (n) subjunctive mood (grammar)
subordinado/a (adj) subordinate; subservient
subrayado/a (adj) underlined (**subrayar** to underline)
suceder to happen

suceso event
sucio/a (adj) dirty
suegro/a father-/mother-in-law
sueldo salary
sueño sleep; dream; sleepyness; **tener sueño** to be sleepy
suerte (f) fate; fortune; chance; kind
suficiente (adj) sufficient
sufrido/a (adj) suffering, patient (**sufrir** to suffer; to endure; to allow; to undergo)
sufrimiento suffering; patience
sugerencia suggestion
sugerir (ie) to suggest
suicidarse to commit suicide
suicidio suicide
suizo (adj/n) Swiss
superintendente (m/f) superintendent; supervisor
supermercado supermarket
supervisor/a (n) supervisor
supervivencia survival
suponer to suppose
supremo/a (adj) supreme; final
surtido (n) assortment, supply; **surtido/a** (adj) assorted
susidio anxiety
sustancia substance
susto (n) scare
suyo (adj) his, of his; hers, of hers; your, of yours (form, s/p); their, of theirs; (pron) his, her, yours (form, s/p), theirs

tacaño/a (adj) stingy
taco (M, MA) fried tortilla filled with meat or beans
tacón (m) heel of a shoe
tal such, such as; **tal vez** perhaps; **tal y tal** such and such
tamal (M, MA; m) tamale (steamed corn meal patty)
también (adv) also; likewise
tampoco (adv) neither, not either, either
tan (adv) so, as, such a; **tan pronto como** as soon as; **tan pronto posible** as soon as possible
tanto (pron, adv) so much, so (**tan** before an adjective); **tanto/a . . . como** (adj) as much . . . as; **tantos/as . . . como** (adj) as many . . . as
tardar to delay, be long; to take (time)
tarde (f) afternoon, early evening; (adv) late; **más tardecito** a little later
tarjeta card; visiting card; filing card; **tarjeta blanca** "white" card (permits border resident to work in U.S.); **tarjeta de crédito** credit card; **tarjeta verde** "green" card (grants residence status in U.S. to those born elsewhere)
té (m) tea; **té de manzanilla** camomile tea; **té helado** iced tea
te (do, io, reflex pron) you, to you; yourself, to yourself (fam)
teatro theater; stage; scene
techo roof; ceiling
telefónico/a (adj) telephonic, telephone

teléfono telephone
telegrama (m) telegram
televisor (m) television set
tema (m) theme, subject
temer to fear; to suspect
temeroso/a (adj) fearful
temperatura temperature
temprano (adv) early; **temprano/a** (adj) early; premature
tender (ie) to stretch, spread out; to hang; to extend; to build
tener (ie) to have, hold; to have to; to desire, feel like; to be; **tener calor** to be hot; **tener confianza con** to be on intimate terms with; **tener confianza en** to trust; **tener éxito** to be successful; **tener frío** to be cold; **tener ganas de** to feel like; **tener hambre** to be hungry; **tener la culpa** to be guilty; **tener miedo** to be afraid; **tener prisa** to be in a hurry; **tener que . . .** to have to . . . ; **tener razón** to be right; **tener sal** to be feisty; **tener sed** to be thirsty; **tener vergüenza** to be ashamed
tercero (n) third; **tercer/a** (adj) (**tercer** before masculine, singular noun)
terminado/a (adj) terminated (**terminar** to terminate, end; to finish)
termómetro thermometer
ternera veal; female calf
testigo (n) witness
tiempo time; weather; tense (of verbs)
tienda store; tent; **tienda de abarrotes** grocery store
tierno/a (adj) tender; young
tierra earth; land; ground; native land
tina (M) bathtub
tío (n, colloq) guy; **tío/a** uncle/aunt
típico/a (adj) typical
tipo type, class; model; standard
tiroides (m) thyroid
título title, heading; degree
tobillo ankle
tocacasete (m) cassette player
tocar to touch; to play (an instrument); to toll, ring; to knock, rap
tocineta (PR) bacon
tocino bacon; salt pork; lard
todavía (adv) still; yet; even
todo/a (adj) all, whole; every, each; **todo el mundo** everybody; the whole world; **todito** (dim) the whole, all over (emphatic)
tolerar to tolerate; to allow; to overlook
tomar to take; to catch; to drink
tomate (m) tomato
toro bull
torta torte, round cake
tortilla (M) tortilla, pancake; **tortilla española** omelet made with potatoes; **tortilla con ají** tortilla with hot sauce
tortura torture

tos (f) cough; **tos ferina** whooping cough
toser to cough
tostado/a (adj) toasted; roasted; tanned
tostón (PR, m) fried green plantain
trabajador/a (n) worker, laborer; (adj) industrious; **trabajador/a social** social worker
trabajar to work; to strive
trabajo work, job; difficulty, trouble
tradición (f) tradition
traducción (f) translation
trágico/a (adj) tragic
trago swallow, gulp; (colloq) a drink
trámite (m) step (in a project)
tranquilamente (adv) tranquilly
tranquilizar(se) to calm down
tranquilizante tranquilizer
tranquilo/a (adj) tranquil
transmitido/a (adj) transmitted
transporte (m) transportation
trasiego (n) upset, disorder, displacement
trasplante (m) transplant, transplantation
trastorno (n) upset, disarrangement; disturbance
tratamiento treatment, usage
tratar to treat; **tratar de** to try to
traer to bring; to wear; to carry; to have
trece thirteen
treinta thirty
tremendo/a (adj) tremendous; terrible
tres three
trigueño/a (adj) swarthy; brunette; dark-complected
Trinidad (f) Holy Trinity
triste (adj) sad; (colloq) depressed
tristeza sadness
tú (pron) you (fam s)
tu (poss adj) your (fam s)
tubería tubing, plumbing
tumba tomb, grave
tuyo (poss adj) your, of yours (fam s); (poss pron) yours

u (conj) or (before words beginning with **o-** or **ho-**)
ubicado/a located (**ubicar**, to locate)
úlcera ulcer, sore
último/a (adj) last; ultimate
único/a (adj) only; unique, singular
unidad (f) unity; (monetary) unit
universidad (f) university
uno one (**un** before a masculine, singular noun, **una** before a feminine, singular noun); (indef art) a, an
unos/as (adj, pl) some, a few
urbano/a (adj) urban; courteous
uruguayo/a (adj/n) Uruguayan
urgente (adj) urgent
urólogo/a urologist
usar to use; to wear
uso (n) use
usted you (form); **Ud.** (abbreviation); **usté** dialectal variation

útil useful
utilidad (f) usefulness, utility
uva grape

vaca cow
vacaciones (f, pl) vacation
vacío (n) empty space; vacío/a (adj) void, empty
valenciano/a (adj/n) Valencian
valentía courage
valer to cost, be worth; valer la pena to be worthwhile
válido/a (adj) valid
valiente (adj) brave
valle (m) valley
valor (m) value, price; courage
variación (f) variation, change
variar to vary; to change
variedad (f) variety; change
varios (adj, pl) various; several
varón (m) male (refers to humans)
vasco/a (adj/n) Basque
vaso (m) drinking glass
vecindario neighborhood
vecino/a (n) neighbor; resident; citizen
vegetal (adj/m) vegetable
vehículo vehicle
veinte twenty
vejiga bladder
vela vigil, watch; candle; sail
velar to stay up; to keep watch
velorio wake
velocidad (f) velocity
vender to sell
veneno poison, venom
venéreo (n) venereal disease; venéreo/a (adj) venereal
venezolano/a (adj/n) Venezuelan
venir (ie) to come
venta sale, selling
ventaja advantage
ventana window; window shutter
ver to see; to look at
veracruzano/a (adj/n) someone from Veracruz, Mexico
verbo word; verb
verdad (f) truth
verdadero/a (adj) real, true; sincere
verde (adj) green; unripe, young
verdura verdure; green vegetable
vergüenza shame; shyness
verificar to verify, test
vertical (adj) vertical
vesícula gall bladder
vestido clothing; dress
vestir (i) to dress; to wear; vestirse to dress oneself

vestuario wardrobe, clothes
vez (f) time, occasion; turn; a la vez at the same time; a veces at times; alguna vez sometime; de vez en cuando from time to time
vía way; road; vía digestiva digestive tract
viceversa (adv) vice versa
vicisitud (f) viscissitude; vicisitudes (f, pl) ups and downs
víctima (m/f) victim
vida life; living; ganarse la vida to earn one's living
viejo/a (adj) old, ancient
viernes Friday; viernes santo Good Friday
vigencia state of being in force (law)
vínculo bond, chain, tie
vino wine (also *he came*, preterite of venir)
violado/a (adj) violated, raped (violar to violate, rape)
violencia violence
virar to turn
virgen (adj/f) virgin; Virgen de Guadalupe (n, f) Virgin of Guadalupe, patron saint of Mexico
virtud (f) virtue; efficacy
visitante (m) visitor; (adj) visiting
visitar to visit; to inspect
vista eyesight; view
viudo/a widower/widow
vivienda dwelling; apartment
vivir to live; vivir en concubinato cohabit in a common law marriage
vocal (f) vowel; (adj) vocal; oral
voltear to turn; to revolve; voltearse to turn over
volver (ue) to return; volverse (+ adj) to turn, become; volverse loco to go crazy
vomitar to vomit
vómito vomit; vomiting
vos you (fam, colloq)
voz (f) voice

y (conj) and (e before words beginning with i- or hi-)
ya (adv) already; now; finally; at once; ya no no longer; ya que since
yerba herb, grass; marijuana (colloq)
yerno son-in-law
yo (pron) I
yuca yucca; cassava

Zacatecas state in northern Mexico
zanahoria carrot
zapato shoe
zapote (C, m) marmalade fruit
zodiacal (adj) referring to the zodiac, zodiacal
zona district, zone

Selected bibliography

CROSS-CULTURAL COMMUNICATION

Batchelder, Donald, and Elizabeth G. Warner, eds. 1977. *Beyond Experience: The Experiential Approach to Cross-Cultural Communication*. Brattleboro, Vt.: The Experiment Press.

Birdwhistell, Ray L. 1970. *Kinesics and Context: Essays on Body Motion Communication*. Philadelphia: University of Pennsylvania Press.

Casse, Pierre. 1980. *Training for the Cross-Cultural Mind*. Washington, D.C.: Society for International Education, Training and Research.

Fantini, Alvino, ed. 1984. *Cross-Cultural Orientation: A Guide for Leaders and Educators*. Brattleboro, Vt.: The Experiment in International Living.

———, ed. 1984. *Getting the Whole Picture: Students' Field Guide to Language Acquisition and Culture Exploration*. Brattleboro, Vt.: The Experiment in International Living.

Frymier, Jack R., ed. 1971. *The Challenge of Nonverbal Awareness*. Theory into Practice, Vol. 10 (4). Columbus: The Ohio State University Press.

Hall, Edward T. 1959. *The Silent Language*. New York: Fawcett.

———. 1976. *Beyond Culture*. Garden City, N.Y.: Anchor Press/Doubleday.

———. 1966. *The Hidden Dimension*. Garden City, N.Y.: Doubleday.

Hoggart, Richard. 1972. *On Culture and Communication*. New York: Oxford University Press.

Kaplan, Bert, ed. 1961. *Studying Personality Cross-Culturally*. Evanston, Ill.: Row, Peterson.

Kohls, L. Robert. 1979. *Survival Kit for Overseas Living*. Chicago: Intercultural Press.

Morain, Genelle G. 1978. *Kinesics and Cross-Cultural Understanding*. Language in Education: Theory and Practice (7). Washington, D.C.: Center for Applied Linguistics.

Smith, Elise C., and Louise F. Luce, eds. 1979. *Toward Internationalism: Readings in Cross-Cultural Communication.* Rowley, Mass.: Newbury House Publishers.

UNDERSTANDING HISPANIC CULTURES

California State Department of Education. 1970. *TV Study Guide: Unconscious Cultural Clashes.* (Accompanies six 30-minute 16mm films). Santa Clara, Calif.: KTEH/Channel 54.

Guicciardini, Francesco. 1961. Vittorio de Caprariis, ed. *Relazione di Spagna.* Milano: Opere.

Miller, J. Dale, John Drayton, and Ted Lyon. 1979. *USA–Hispanic South America Culture Capsules.* Rowley, Mass.: Newbury House Publishers.

Miller, J. Dale, and Russell H. Bishop. 1979. *USA–Mexico Culture Capsules.* Rowley, Mass.: Newbury House Publishers.

Narganes, Joseph, and Dr. Richard I. Javert. 1976. *Hispanic Culture Capsules.* New York: Gessler Publishing Company.

Nine Curt, Carmen. 1976. *Teacher Training Pack for a Course on Cultural Awareness.* Cambridge, Mass.: National Assessment and Dissemination Center.

———. 1978. *Nonverbal Communication.* Cambridge, Mass.: National Assessment and Dissemination Center.

Poyatos, Fernando. 1970. "Kinésica del español actual." *Hispania* 53 (September): 444–452.

Scott, Joseph Reid. 1976. *Understanding Spanish-Speaking Cultures.* Hayward, Calif.: Alameda County School Department.

Zambrana, Ruth E., ed. 1982. *Work, Family, and Health: Latina Women in Transition.* Monograph Series, Monograph No. 7. New York: Hispanic Research Center, Fordham University.

Zanger, Virginia V. 1984. *Exploración intercultural: Una guía para el estudiante.* Rowley, Mass.: Newbury House Publishers.

CULTURE OF CUBANS IN THE UNITED STATES

Álvarez, Orlando. 1976. *Estudio social y económico de la comunidad latina del condado Dade.* Miami, Fla.: Editorial AIP.

Childs, George. 1978. *¡Esto es Miami Chaguito! Las mejores columnas de George Childs.* Miami, Fla.: Miami Herald Publishing Company.

Sánchez-Boudy, José. 1977. *El picúo, el fisto, el barrio y otras estampas cubanas.* Miami, Fla.: Ediciones Universal.

———. 1978. *Lilayando pal tu (Mojito y picardía cubana).* Miami, Fla.: Ediciones Universal.

Zalamea, Luis. 1978. *España omnipresente en la Florida (ensayo histórico-literario).* Miami, Fla.: Ediciones Universal.

CULTURE OF MEXICAN AMERICANS

Barrios, Ernie, ed. 1971. *Bibliografía de Aztlán: An Annotated Chicano Bibliography.* San Diego: Centro de Estudios Chicanos Publications.

Casas, J. Manuel, and Susan E. Keefe, eds. 1978. *Family and Mental Health in the Mexican American Community.* Los Angeles: Spanish Speaking Mental Health Research Center, University of California at Los Angeles.

Elsasser, Nan, Kyle MacKenzie, and Yvonne Tixier y Vigil. 1980. *Las mujeres: Conversations from a Hispanic Community.* New York: The Feminist Press and The McGraw-Hill Book Company.

Hernández, Carrol A., Marsha J. Haug, and Nathaniel N. Wagner. 1976. *Chicanos: Social and Psychological Perspectives.* Saint Louis: The C. V. Mosby Company.

Madsen, William, 1966. *The Mexican-Americans of South Texas.* New York: Holt, Rinehart and Winston.

Manuel, Herschel T. 1965. *Spanish-Speaking Children of the Southwest: Their Education and the Public Welfare.* Austin: University of Texas Press.

Mirandé, Alfredo, and Evangelina Enríquez. 1979. *La Chicana: The Mexican-American Woman.* Chicago: The University of Chicago Press.

Stoddard, Ellwyn R. 1973. *Mexican Americans.* New York: Random House.

U.S. Commission on Civil Rights. 1972. *The Excluded Student: Educational Practices Affecting Mexican Americans in the Southwest,* Mexican American Education Study, Report No. III. Washington, D.C.: U.S. Government Printing Office.

CULTURE OF PUERTO RICANS IN THE UNITED STATES

Belaval, Emilio S. 1977. *Los problemas de la cultura puertorriqueña.* Río Piedras, Puerto Rico: Editorial Cultural.

Fitzpatrick, Joseph P. 1971. *Puerto Rican Americans: The Meaning of Migration to the Mainland.* Englewood Cliffs, N.J.: Prentice-Hall.

Galíndez, Jesús de. 1969. *Puerto Rico en Nueva York: Sociología de una inmigración.* Buenos Aires, Argentina: Editorial Tiempo Contemporáneo.

González, José Luis. 1982. *El país de cuatro pisos.* Río Piedras, Puerto Rico: Ediciones Huracán.

Iglesias, César Andreu, ed. 1980. *Memorias de Bernardo Vega.* Río Piedras, Puerto Rico: Ediciones Huracán.

Morales, Julio. 1986. *Puerto Rican Poverty and Migration.* New York: Praeger.

Méndez, José Luis. 1980. *La agresión cultural norteamericana en Puerto Rico.* México, D.F.: Editorial Grijalbo, S.A.

Nieves Falcón, Luis. 1975. *El emigrante puertorriqeño.* Río Piedras, Puerto Rico: Editorial Edil.

Palma, Marigloria. 1981. *Muestras del folklore puertorriqueño.* San Juan, Puerto Rico: Editorial Edil.

Seda Bonilla, Eduardo. 1974. *Requiem para una cultura.* Río Piedras, Puerto Rico: Ediciones Bayoan.

Varo, Carlos. 1973. *Puerto Rico: Radiografía de un pueblo asediado.* Río Piedras, Puerto Rico: Ediciones Puerto.

SPANISH LINGUISTICS

Bull, William E. 1965. *Spanish for Teachers: Applied Linguistics.* New York: The Ronald Press.

Nash, Rose. 1977. *Comparing English and Spanish: Patterns in Phonology and Orthography.* New York: Regents Publishing Company.

————. 1978. *Readings in Spanish–English Contrastive Linguistics.* San Juan, Puerto Rico: Inter American University Press.

Nash, Rose, and Domitila Belaval, eds. 1980. *Readings in Spanish–English Contrastive Linguistics,* Vol. II. San Juan, Puerto Rico: Inter American University Press.

————, eds. 1982. *Readings in Spanish–English Contrastive Linguistics,* Vol. III. San Juan, Puerto Rico: Inter American University Press.

Peñalosa, Fernando. 1980. *Chicano Sociolinguistics: A Brief Introduction.* Rowley, Mass.: Newbury House Publishers.

Stockwell, Robert P., and Donald J. Bowen. 1965. *The Sounds of English and Spanish.* Chicago: University of Chicago Press.

DIALECTICAL VARIATIONS

del Rosario, Rubén. 1965. *Vocabulario puertorriqueño.* Puerto Rico: Realidad y Anhelo, número 1. Sharon, Conn.: Troutman Press.

————. 1969. *La lengua de Puerto Rico: Ensayos.* Río Piedras, Puerto Rico: Editorial Cultural, Inc.

————. 1970. *El español de América.* Sharon, Conn.: Troutman Press.

Gallo, Cristino. 1980. *Language of the Puerto Rican Street: A Slang Dictionary.* Santurce, Puerto Rico: Book Service of Puerto Rico.

Galván, Roberto A., and Richard V. Teschner. 1975. *El diccionario del español chicano: The Dictionary of Chicano Spanish.* Silver Spring, Md.: Institute of Modern Languages.

Hernández-Chávez, Eduardo, Andrew D. Cohen, and Anthony Beltramo. 1975. *El lenguaje de los chicanos: Regional and Social Characteristics Used by Mexican Americans.* Arlington, Va.: Center for Applied Linguistics.

Navarro, Tomás. 1974. *El español en Puerto Rico,* 3rd ed. Río Pedras, Puerto Rico: Editorial Universitaria.

Vanson, George N., and Marilyn R. Frankenthaler. 1982. *Spanish–English Legal Terminology.* Cincinnati: South-Western Publishing Company.

Werner, David. 1975. *Donde no hay doctor: Una guía para los campesinos que viven lejos de los centros médicos.* México, D.F.: Editorial Pax-México.

BILINGUAL EDUCATION

Center for Applied Linguistics. 1977. *Bilingual Education: Current Perspectives,* Vol. 2: *Linguistics.* Arlington, Va.: Center for Applied Linguistics.

Mackey, William F., and Von Nieda Beebe. 1977. *Bilingual Schools for a Bicultural Community: Miami's Adaption to the Cuban Refugees.* Rowley, Mass.: Newbury House Publishers.

Mackey, William F., and Jacob Ornstein. 1977. *The Bilingual Education Movement: Essays on Its Progress,* Studies in Language and Linguistics, 1977–1978. El Paso: Texas Western Press.

Manning, William A. 1975. *A Mosaic of Readings in Bilingual Education: English–Spanish.* San José, Calif.: Spartan Bookstore, San José State University.

Turner, Paul R., ed. 1973. *Bilingualism in the Southwest.* Tucson: The University of Arizona Press.

Valencia, Atilano A. 1972. Bilingual–Bicultural Education for the *Spanish–English Bilingual.* Las Vegas, N.M.: New Mexico Highlands University.

Verb forms

			INDICATIVE					SUBJUNCTIVE	
Infinitive	Present/Past Participles	Subject Pronouns	Present	Imperfect	Preterite	Future	Conditional	Present	Past
REGULAR VERBS									
hablar *to speak* model for regular -ar verbs	hablando hablado	yo tú Ud., él, ella nosotros/as Uds., ellos/as	hablo hablas habla hablamos hablan	hablaba hablabas hablaba hablábamos hablaban	hablé hablaste habló hablamos hablaron	hablaré hablarás hablará hablaremos hablarán	hablaría hablarías hablaría hablaríamos hablarían	hable hables hable hablemos hablen	hablara hablaras hablara habláramos hablaran
comer *to eat* model for regular -er verbs	comiendo comido	yo tú Ud., él, ella nosotros/as Uds., ellos/as	como comes come comemos comen	comía comías comía comíamos comían	comí comiste comió comimos comieron	comeré comerás comerá comeremos comerán	comería comerías comería comeríamos comerían	coma comas coma comamos coman	comiera comieras comiera comiéramos comieran
vivir *to live* model for regular -ir verbs	viviendo vivido	yo tú Ud., él, ella nosotros/as Uds., ellos/as	vivo vives vive vivimos viven	vivía vivías vivía vivíamos vivían	viví viviste vivió vivimos vivieron	viviré vivirás vivirá viviremos vivirán	viviría vivirías viviría viviríamos vivirían	viva vivas viva vivamos vivan	viviera vivieras viviera viviéramos vivieran
STEM-CHANGING VERBS									
pensar[1] *to think* model for (e→ie) stem-changing -ar, -er verbs	pensando pensado	yo tú Ud., él, ella nosotros/as Uds., ellos/as	pienso piensas piensa pensamos piensan	pensaba pensabas pensaba pensábamos pensaban	pensé pensaste pensó pensamos pensaron	pensaré pensarás pensará pensaremos pensarán	pensaría pensarías pensaría pensaríamos pensarían	piense pienses piense pensemos piensen	pensara pensaras pensara pensáramos pensaran
contar[2] *to count; to tell* model for (o→ue) stem-changing -ar, -er verbs	contando contado	yo tú Ud., él, ella nosotros/as Uds., ellos/as	cuento cuentas cuenta contamos cuentan	contaba contabas contaba contábamos contaban	conté contaste contó contamos contaron	contaré contarás contará contaremos contarán	contaría contarías contaría contaríamos contarían	cuente cuentes cuente contemos cuenten	contara contaras contara contáramos contaran
sentir[3] *to feel, regret* model for (e→ie) stem-changing -ir verbs	sintiendo sentido	yo tú Ud., él, ella nosotros/as Uds., ellos/as	siento sientes siente sentimos sienten	sentía sentías sentía sentíamos sentían	sentí sentiste sintió sentimos sintieron	sentiré sentirás sentirá sentiremos sentirán	sentiría sentirías sentiría sentiríamos sentirían	sienta sientas sienta sintamos sientan	sintiera sintieras sintiera sintiéramos sintieran
dormir[4] *to sleep* model for (o→ue) stem-changing -ir verbs	durmiendo dormido	yo tú Ud., él, ella nosotros/as Uds., ellos/as	duermo duermes duerme dormimos duermen	dormía dormías dormía dormíamos dormían	dormí dormiste durmió dormimos durmieron	dormiré dormirás dormirá dormiremos dormirán	dormiría dormirías dormiría dormiríamos dormirían	duerma duermas duerma durmamos duerman	durmiera durmieras durmiera durmiéramos durmieran

[1]Like *pensar*: (-ar verbs) comenzar, despertar(se), empezar, enterrar, negar, sentar(se); (-er verbs) entender, perder, querer (tener, querer also have other irregularities).
[2]Like **contar**: (-ar verbs) acordarse, acostar(se) almorzar, encontrar probar, rogar; (jugar changes u→ue); (-er verbs) devolver, doler, poder (poder also has other irregularities), volver, resolver (vuelto, resuelto = past participles).
[3]Like **sentir: convertir(se), divertir(se), invertir, preferir.**
[4]Like **dormir: morir.**

				INDICATIVE					SUBJUNCTIVE	
	Infinitive	Present/Past Participles	Subject Pronouns	Present	Imperfect	Preterite	Future	Conditional	Present	Past
STEM-CHANGING VERBS	**pedir**[5] *to ask for* model for (e→i) stem-changing -ir verbs	pidiendo pedido	yo tú Ud., él, ella nosotros/as Uds., ellos/as	pido pides pide pedimos piden	pedía pedías pedía pedíamos pedían	pedí pediste pidió pedimos pidieron	pediré pedirás pedirá pediremos pedirán	pediría pedirías pediría pediríamos pedirían	pida pidas pida pidamos pidan	pidiera pidieras pidiera pidiéramos pidieran
	pagar[6] *to pay (for)* model for (g→gu) orthographic changing verbs	pagando pagado	yo tú Ud., él, ella nosotros/as Uds., ellos/as	pago pagas paga pagamos pagan	pagaba pagabas pagaba pagábamos pagaban	pagué pagaste pagó pagamos pagaron	pagaré pagarás pagará pagaremos pagarán	pagaría pagarías pagaría pagaríamos pagarían	pague pagues pague paguemos paguen	pagara pagaras pagara pagáramos pagaran
	buscar[7] *to look (for)* model for (c→qu) orthographic changing verbs	buscando buscado	yo tú Ud., él, ella nosotros/as Uds., ellos/as	busco buscas busca buscamos buscan	buscaba buscabas buscaba buscábamos buscaban	busqué buscaste buscó buscamos buscaron	buscaré buscarás buscará buscaremos buscarán	buscaría buscarías buscaría buscaríamos buscarían	busque busques busque busquemos busquen	buscara buscaras buscara buscáramos buscaran
ORTHO-GRAPHIC CHANGING VERBS	**rezar**[8] *to pray* model for (z→c) orthographic changing verbs	rezando rezado	yo tú Ud., él, ella nosotros/as Uds., ellos/as	rezo rezas reza rezamos rezan	rezaba rezabas rezaba rezábamos rezaban	recé rezaste rezó rezamos rezaron	rezaré rezarás rezará rezaremos rezarán	rezaría rezarías rezaría rezaríamos rezarían	rece reces rece recemos recen	rezara rezaras rezara rezáramos rezaran
	escoger[9] *to choose* model for (g→j) orthographic changing verbs	escogiendo escogido	yo tú Ud., él, ella nosotros/as Uds., ellos/as	escojo escoges escoge escogimos escogen	escogía escogías escogía escogíamos escogían	escogí escogiste escogió escogimos escogieron	escogeré escogerás escogerá escogeremos escogerán	escogería escogerías escogería escogeríamos escogerían	escoja escojas escoja escojamos escojan	escogiera escogieras escogiera escogiéramos escogieran
	conocer[10] *to know* model for (c→zc) orthographic changing verbs	conociendo conocido	yo tú Ud., él, ella nosotros/as Uds., ellos/as	conozco conoces conoce conocemos conocen	conocía conocías conocía conocíamos conocían	conocí conociste conoció conocimos conocieron	conoceré conocerás conocerá conoceremos conocerán	conocería conocerías conocería conoceríamos conocerían	conozca conozcas conozca conozcamos conozcan	conociera conocieras conociera conociéramos conocieran
	creer[11] *to believe* model for (i→y) orthographic changing verbs	creyendo creído	yo tú Ud., él, ella nosotros/as Uds., ellos/as	creo crees cree creemos creen	creía creías creía creíamos creían	creí creíste creyó creímos creyeron	creeré creerás creerá creeremos creerán	creería creerías creería creeríamos creerían	crea creas crea creamos crean	creyera creyeras creyera creyéramos creyeran

[5] Like pedir: conseguir, decir (decir also has other irregularities), impedir, reír, repetir, seguir (gu→g before o or a) servir, vestir(se).
[6] Like pagar: apagar, castigar, entregar, jugar (ue), juzgar, llegar, negar, rogar (ue).
[7] Like buscar: acercarse, dedicar(se), practicar, sacar, tocar.
[8] Like rezar: almorzar (ue), comenzar (ie), cruzar, empezar (ie), organizar, realizar.
[9] Like escoger: coger, exigir, recoger, proteger.
[10] Like conocer: nacer, producir (produj- = stem for preterite and past subjunctive, follows decir in these tenses); reconocer.
[11] Like creer: caer, leer, oír, (caer, oír, also have other irregularities).

IRREGULAR VERBS

Infinitive	Present/Past Participles	Subject Pronouns	INDICATIVE					SUBJUNCTIVE	
			Present	Imperfect	Preterite	Future	Conditional	Present	Past
dar *to give*	dando dado	yo	doy	daba	di	daré	daría	dé	diera
		tú	das	dabas	diste	darás	darías	des	dieras
		Ud., él, ella	da	daba	dio	dará	daría	dé	diera
		nosotros/as	damos	dábamos	dimos	daremos	daríamos	demos	diéramos
		Uds., ellos/as	dan	daban	dieron	darán	darían	den	dieran
decir *to say, tell*	diciendo dicho	yo	digo	decía	dije	diré	diría	diga	dijera
		tú	dices	decías	dijiste	dirás	dirías	digas	dijeras
		Ud., él, ella	dice	decía	dijo	dirá	diría	diga	dijera
		nosotros/as	decimos	decíamos	dijimos	diremos	diríamos	digamos	dijéramos
		Uds., ellos/as	dicen	decían	dijeron	dirán	dirían	digan	dijeran
estar *to be*	estando estado	yo	estoy	estaba	estuve	estaré	estaría	esté	estuviera
		tú	estás	estabas	estuviste	estarás	estarías	estés	estuvieras
		Ud., él, ella	está	estaba	estuvo	estará	estaría	esté	estuviera
		nosotros/as	estamos	estábamos	estuvimos	estaremos	estaríamos	estemos	estuviéramos
		Uds., ellos/as	están	estaban	estuvieron	estarán	estarían	estén	estuvieran
haber *to have* (auxiliary verb used with past participle)	habiendo habido	yo	he	había	hube	habré	habría	haya	hubiera
		tú	has	habías	hubiste	habrás	habrías	hayas	hubieras
		Ud., él, ella	ha	había	hubo	habrá	habría	haya	hubiera
		nosotros/as	hemos	habíamos	hubimos	habremos	habríamos	hayamos	hubiéramos
		Uds., ellos/as	han	habían	hubieron	habrán	habrían	hayan	hubieran
hacer *to do, make* satisfacer has same irregularities	haciendo hecho	yo	hago	hacía	hice	haré	haría	haga	hiciera
		tú	haces	hacías	hiciste	harás	harías	hagas	hicieras
		Ud., él, ella	hace	hacía	hizo	hará	haría	haga	hiciera
		nosotros/as	hacemos	hacíamos	hicimos	haremos	haríamos	hagamos	hiciéramos
		Uds., ellos/as	hacen	hacían	hicieron	harán	harían	hagan	hicieran
ir *to go*	yendo ido	yo	voy	iba	fui	iré	iría	vaya	fuera
		tú	vas	ibas	fuiste	irás	irías	vayas	fueras
		Ud., él, ella	va	iba	fue	irá	iría	vaya	fuera
		nosotros/as	vamos	íbamos	fuimos	iremos	iríamos	vayamos	fuéramos
		Uds., ellos/as	van	iban	fueron	irán	irían	vayan	fueran
oír *to hear*	oyendo oído	yo	oigo	oía	oí	oiré	oiría	oiga	oyera
		tú	oyes	oías	oíste	oirás	oirías	oigas	oyeras
		Ud., él, ella	oye	oía	oyó	oirá	oiría	oiga	oyera
		nosotros/as	oímos	oíamos	oímos	oiremos	oiríamos	oigamos	oyéramos
		Uds., ellos/as	oyen	oían	oyeron	oirán	oirían	oigan	oyeran
poder *to be able to* stem change o→ue	pudiendo podido	yo	puedo	podía	pude	podré	podría	pueda	pudiera
		tú	puedes	podías	pudiste	podrás	podrías	puedas	pudieras
		Ud., él, ella	puede	podía	pudo	podrá	podría	pueda	pudiera
		nosotros/as	podemos	podíamos	pudimos	podremos	podríamos	podamos	pudiéramos
		Uds., ellos/as	pueden	podían	pudieron	podrán	podrían	puedan	pudieran

			INDICATIVE					SUBJUNCTIVE	
Infinitive	Present/Past Participles	Subject Pronouns	Present	Imperfect	Preterite	Future	Conditional	Present	Past
poner *to put, place*	poniendo puesto	*yo*	pongo	ponía	puse	pondré	pondría	ponga	pusiera
		tú	pones	ponías	pusiste	pondrás	pondrías	pongas	pusieras
		Ud., él, ella	pone	ponía	puso	pondrá	pondría	ponga	pusiera
		nosotros/as	ponemos	poníamos	pusimos	pndremos	pondríamos	pongamos	pusiéramos
		Uds., ellos/as	ponen	ponían	pusieron	pondrán	pondrían	pongan	pusieran
querer *to want, wish* stem change e→ie	queriendo querido	*yo*	quiero	quería	quise	querré	querría	quiera	quisiera
		tú	quieres	querías	quisiste	querrás	querrías	quieras	quisieras
		Ud., él, ella	quiere	quería	quiso	querrá	querría	quiera	quisiera
		nosotros/as	queremos	queríamos	quisimos	querremos	querríamos	queramos	quisiéramos
		Uds., ellos/as	quieren	querían	quisieron	querrán	querrían	quieran	quisieran
saber *to know* (intellectually)	sabiendo sabido	*yo*	sé	sabía	supe	sabré	sabría	sepa	supiera
		tú	sabes	sabías	supiste	sabrás	sabrias	sepas	supieras
		Ud., él, ella	sabe	sabía	supo	sabrá	sabría	sepa	supiera
		nosotros/as	sabemos	sabíamos	supimos	sabremos	sabríamos	sepamos	supiéramos
		Uds., ellos/as	saben	sabían	supieron	sabrán	sabrían	sepan	supieran
salir *to leave, go out (of)*	saliendo salido	*yo*	salgo	salía	salí	saldré	saldría	salga	saliera
		tú	sales	salías	saliste	saldrás	saldrías	salgas	salieras
		Ud., él, ella	sale	salía	salió	saldrá	saldría	salga	saliera
		nosotros/as	salimos	salíamos	salimos	saldremos	saldríamos	salgamos	saliéramos
		Uds., ellos/as	salen	salían	salieron	saldrán	saldrían	salgan	salieran
tener *to have* **mantener** has same irregularities; stem change e→ie	teniendo tenido	*yo*	tengo	tenía	tuve	tendré	tendría	tenga	tuviera
		tú	tienes	tenías	tuviste	tendrás	tendrías	tengas	tuvieras
		Ud., él, ella	tiene	tenía	tuvo	tendrá	tendría	tenga	tuviera
		nosotros/as	tenemos	teníamos	tuvimos	tendremos	tendríamos	tengamos	tuviéramos
		Uds., ellos/as	tienen	tenían	tuvieron	tendrán	tendrían	tengan	tuvieran
traer *to bring*	trayendo traído	*yo*	traigo	traía	traje	traeré	traería	traiga	trajera
		tú	traes	traías	trajiste	traerás	traerías	traigas	trajeras
		Ud., él, ella	trae	traía	trajo	traerá	traería	traiga	trajera
		nosotros/as	traemos	traíamos	trajimos	traeremos	traeríamos	traigamos	trajéramos
		Uds., ellos/as	traen	traían	trajeron	traerán	traerían	traigan	trajeran
venir *to come* **convenir** has same irregularities; stem change e→ie	viniendo venido	*yo*	vengo	venía	vine	vendré	vendría	venga	viniera
		tú	vienes	venías	viniste	vendrás	vendrías	vengas	vinieras
		Ud., él, ella	viene	venía	vino	vendrá	vendría	venga	viniera
		nosotros/as	venimos	veníamos	vinimos	vendremos	vendríamos	vengamos	viniéramos
		Uds., ellos/as	vienen	venían	vinieron	vendrán	vendrían	vengan	vinieran
ver *to see*	viendo visto	*yo*	veo	veía	vi	veré	vería	vea	viera
		tú	ves	veías	viste	verás	verías	veas	vieras
		Ud., él, ella	ve	veía	vio	verá	vería	vea	viera
		nosotros/as	vemos	veíamos	vimos	veremos	veríamos	veamos	viéramos
		Uds., ellos/as	ven	veían	vieron	verán	verían	vean	vieran

IRREGULAR VERBS

527

Index

Art credits

ILLUSTRATIONS AND REALIA

Kathie Kelleher: cartoons, pages 10, 46, 82, 112, 150, 194, 236, 280, 330, 374, 418, 458.

Elizabeth M. Clark: line drawings, pages 2, 5, 6, 30, 31, 72, 73, 103 (bottom), 105, 108, 132, 139, 145, 177, 216 (bottom), 265, 316, 358, 365, 407, 444.

Donna Janus: illustrations of hand gestures, pages 40–43, 68–69.

Lisa Kokin: "Portrait of Farabundo Marti," page 38. Batik © 1982 by Lisa Kokin. For more information on Lisa Kokin, please write 4992 N.W. 6th Street, Delray Beach, Florida 33445.

Taller de Gráfica Popular (México, D.F.): etchings, pages 67, 98.

Comisión para los asuntos de la mujer (Puerto Rico): "La mejor alternativa," page 214 (top); "Maltrato de la mujer," page 395.

Reinaldo Changsut: handwritten letters, pages 303, 352.

Sheraton Hotel: dance advertisement, page 351 (bottom).

Colegio de Farmacéuticos de Puerto Rico: "El uso de las medicinas," page 437.

¿Qué pasa? (Hartford, Connecticut): "Botánica Orula," page 438 (top).

The Christophers: "Experiencia de la enfermedad," page 438 (bottom).

Language Research Press (Miami, Florida): "¿Por qué?," page 480.

Diseños: "PAZ," page 487.

PHOTOGRAPHS

© Jack Delano: pages 29 (all photos), 35 (all photos), 64 (top), 71 (left), 74, 137 (both photos), 142 (both photos), 184 (right), 187, 218, 254 (bottom right), 255 (top right), 263 (both photos), 269 (top right), 270, 271, 301, 322 (left), 357 (left), 367.

El mundo (San Juan, Puerto Rico): pages 96 (top), 169 (bottom), 300, 302, 405 (right), 436.

Pedro Espinoza and Juan Brito, *¿Qué pasa?* (Hartford, Connecticut): pages 1 (both photos), 7 (left), 26 (top and bottom left), 71 (right), 79, 133, 172, 175 (right), 183, 215 (top), 274, 308, 405 (left), 412, 414, 443 (left), 450, 454.

© Juan Fuentes: pages 66, 101 (right), 129, 171, 182 (both photos), 188, 229, 370, 440.

Barbara Lotito: pages 7 (right), 26 (top right), 28, 77, 101 (left), 107, 184 (left), 175 (left), 214 (bottom), 223 (both photos), 254 (top and bottom left, top right), 255 (top and bottom left, bottom right), 269 (bottom left), 323, 394, 398, 481 (top).

The San Juan Star (San Juan, Puerto Rico): pages 26 (bottom right), 64 (bottom), 96 (bottom), 168, 169 (top), 216 (top), 275, 315 (right), 321, 351 (top), 353, 357 (right), 396 (top), 443 (right), 478.

Betty Schober: pages 37, 315 (left), 322 (right), 355.

© Cinecom International Films and Island Alive Productions: pages 483, 485.